DICTIONARY OF LEGAL
ABBREVIATIONS USED IN
AMERICAN LAW BOOKS

DICTIONARY OF LEGAL ABBREVIATIONS USED IN AMERICAN LAW BOOKS

Compiled by
Doris M. Bieber
Law Librarian
Vanderbilt Legal Information
Center/Law Library
Nashville, Tennessee

William S. Hein & Co., 1979

First Printing

Library of Congress Card Number 78-60173

ISBN 0-930342-96 - 8

Printed in the United States of America

This Dictionary is Dedicated

To

My Parents and Mrs. Julia Raftery

Foreword

Legal literature is replete with obscure and infrequently used abbreviations. Identifying and deciphering them can be extremely irksome; and at times, when confronted with a familiar-looking acronym which defeats instant recollection, the situation can become downright embarrassing. At times like these one craves for a handy reference book which would list all or at least most of the abbreviations, acronyms, and symbols customarily used by legal writers. So far there has not been a work of this kind for American legal abbreviations. It is true that various abbreviation lists may be found scattered through such publications as **Black's Law Dictionary**, the "Blue Book" (**A Uniform System of Citation**), Jacobstein and Mersky's **Fundamentals of Legal Research,** etc., but these lists are either selective or very short; their purpose is to instruct rather than to inform. A more ambitious work is Marion D. Powers' **Legal Citation Directory** (1971). However, this work is not a handbook nor a dictionary either, as it does precisely what its title states: identify accepted and recognized citation forms for federal and state law reports.

The compiler of the present work has had a long and extensive professional experience in some of the leading law libraries of the United States. She has spent many years wrestling with the problem of identifying obscure or difficult abbreviations, and she is well aware of the frustration it involves and time it consumes. Several years ago, in order to shorten repetitive reference searches, she began to compile her own list of legal abbreviations which eventually grew into a sizable manuscript of some 17,000 entries. She has converted this manuscript into a publication of impeccable professional quality.

The purpose of the **Dictionary of Legal Abbreviations used in American Law Books** is to shorten the process of searching for the precise meaning of various letter symbols used in American law books. In this respect, the work succeeds admirably. It includes an extensive--and literally comprehensive--range of acronyms and symbols for domestic and foreign names or titles appearing in American legal literature and government publications. It does not refer to abbreviations or symbols used in legal publications of countries other than the United States (for these several excellent sources of abbreviations may be consulted, including Sprudzs, **Benelux Abbreviations and Symbols** 1971; Sprudzs, **Italian Abbreviations and Symbols; Law and Related Subjects** 1969; Sprudzs, **Foreign Law Abbreviations: French** 1967; and Kirchner, **Abkürzungsverzeichnis der Rechtssprache** 1968), but it does give abbreviations for many foreign agencies, organizations, periodicals, and other publications as they are used in American law books.

Persons who frequently use legal literature will find this book an indispensable reference tool. It will save them a lot of time and many irritations.

Igor I. Kavass
August, 1978

GUIDE FOR THE USE OF THIS VOLUME

The abbreviations included in this volume are arranged alphabetically according to the first symbol of each entry. For purposes of this volume, a symbol is composed of either a capital letter standing by itself, a lower case letter standing by itself, or a capital letter followed immediately by either a single or several lower case letter(s) to form a group (e.g. Aav. or Cai.). In those cases in which the first symbol of several entries are identical, the arrangement of such entries follows the alphabetical sequence of second symbols. Similarly, when the first two symbols of several entries are identical, the third symobls are alphabetized, and so on. Abbreviations containing an ampersant (&) symbol are arranged at the end of each group of entries under which they would fall alphabetically. For example, the following entries are arranged accordingly:

C	Dav. Pat. Cas.	E.A.L.R.
C &	Dav. Prec. Conv.	E.African L.J.
Ca	Dav. Rep.	EBT
Ca &	Dou. El. Ca.	EEO
Cu		E & A
Cu &		Eag.
		Eccl. Stat.
		Eccl. & Ad.
		Ed. Bro.
		Ed. C.R.
		Edw. Pr. Cas.
		Edw. Pr. Ct. Cas.
		Ex. C.R.

Abbreviations having multiple meanings are distinguished by black dots. In some descriptions of the meanings, the names of countries and states are abbreviated. For example, (Eng.) is used in place of England or English; (Sc.) is used for Scotland or Scotch; (Aus.) is used for Australia or Australian; (S.Africa) is used for South Africa; (Pa.) used in place of Pennsylvania; etc.

The scope of this work extends to abbreviations that are used or listed in such categories of books as legal encyclopedias, law dictionaries, law reporters, loose-leaf services, law reviews, legal treatises, government documents, legal reference books, citators, and some other popular materials that would be found in a medium-size law library. More specifically, the abbreviations included in this volume are used or listed in the following sources: C.J.S. (West), Am. Jur. 2d (Lawyer's Co-op.), U.S. Code (GPO), U.S.C.A. (West), U.S.C.S. (Lawyer's Co-op.), U.S. Code Cong. & Adm. News (West), National reporter System (West), A.L.R. series (Lawyer's Co-op.), **Index to Legal Periodicals** (AALL/Wilson), **English Reprints, United Nations Treaty series, U.S. Treaties and Other International Agreements, Black's Law Dictionary, Ballentine's Law Dictionary, Words and Phrases, Who is Who, U.S. Government Organization Manual** and many other sources.

This work, however, is not intended to be used as a guide for sample legal citation forms. In determining proper citation form, one should always consult the **Uniform System of Citation** or some other authoritative source.

In addition to this work, the following books may be consulted as authoritative sources for English and American legal abbreviations:

Price and Bitner, **Effective Legal Research.** New York, Prentice-Hall, Inc., 1953. pp. 511-620.

Jacobstein and Mersky, **Fundamentals of Legal Research,** Mineola, N.Y., The Foundation Press, Inc., 1977. pp. 538-583 (legal citation form) and pp. 584-649.

Black's Law Dictionary. Revised 4th ed. St. Paul, Minn., West Publishing Co., 1968. pp. 1797-1882.

Hicks, **Materials and Methods of Legal Research.** 3rd revised ed. Rochester, N.Y., The Lawyers Co-operative Publishing Company, 1942. pp. 571-651.

James, **Stroud's Judicial Dictionary of Words and Phrases.** 4th ed. London, Sweet & Maxwell Limited, 1971. Vol. 1, pp. xiii-xxiv.

Sweet & Maxwell's Guide to Law Reports and Statutes. 4th ed. London, Sweet & Maxwell, 1962. pp. 67-122.

Ballentine's Law Dictionary. 3rd ed. (Edited by William S. Anderson). Rochester, N.Y., The Lawyers Co-operative Publishing Company, 1969. pp. 1389-1429.

Those who use this work are invited to write to D.M. Bieber at the Vanderbilt Law Library to offer both their criticisms of this volume and their suggestions as to how it may be improved and made more useful.

The compilation of this volume was inspired and encouraged by Professor Igor I. Kavass, Professor of Law and Director of the Vanderbilt Legal Information Center/Law Library. Without his unfailing patience and guidance, this work would not have been successfully compiled and completed. I am, therefore, indebted to him. I also wish to express my thanks to a number of student assistants in the Vanderbilt Law Library for their assistance in alphabetizing. I am especially thankful to Patrick W. Youngblood and Linda S. Campbell for their editorial assistance.

Doris M. Bieber

A

A • Abbott
- Acquiescence
- Adam's Justiciary Reports (1893-1916) (Sc.)
- Affirmed
- Alabama
- Amended
- American
- Anonymous
- Arabic
- Arkansas
- Association(s)
- Atlantic Reporter
- Indian Reports, Allahabad Series
- Louisiana Annuals

A. Atlantic Reporter

A.2d Atlantic Reporter, Second Series

AA • Able and Available
- Ars Aequi, Juridisch Studentenblad (Holland)

AAA • Agricultural Adjustment Act
- American Arbitration Association

A.A.B.D. Aid to the Aged, Blind, or Disabled

A.A.C. Anno ante Christum, the year before Christ

A.A.C.N. Anno ante christum natum, the year before the birth of Christ

AAJE American Academy of Judicial Education

AALL American Association of Law Libraries

AALS Association of American Law Schools

AALS Proc. Association of American Law Schools Proceedings

AAPSO Afro-Asian People's Solidarity Organization

AASM Associated African States and Madagascar

A.A.U.P. American Association of University Professors

A.Ae. Are Aequi (Netherlands)

A.B. Assembly Bill (state legislatures)

AB Alberta

A.B. • Able Seaman
- Aid to the Blind
- Anonymous Reports at end of Benloe, or Bendloe (1661) (Eng.)

ABA American Bar Association

A.B.A. • American Bankers' Association
- American Bar Association

ABA Antitrust L.J. American Bar Association Antitrust Law Journal

ABACPD American Bar Association Center for Professional Discipline

A.B.A.J. American Bar Association Journal

A.B.A.Jo American Bar Association Journal

A.B.A.Jour. American Bar Association Journal

ABA Rep. • American Bar Association Reporter
- American Bar Association Reports

ABA Sec Lab Rel L American Bar Association Section of Labor Relations Law

ABA Sect Ins N&CL American Bar Association Section of Insurance, Negligence & Compensation Law

A.B.C. Australian Bankruptcy Cases

A.B.C. Newsl. International Association of Accident Boards and Commissions Newsletter

ABF American Bar Foundation

A.B.F. American Bar Foundation

ABM Anti-ballistic missiles

ABMC American Battle Monuments Commission

A.B.R. American Bankruptcy Reports

A'B.R.J.N.S.W. A'Beckett Reserved Judgements (Eq.), New South Wales (Aus.)

A'B.R.J.P.P. A'Beckett Reserved Judgements, Port Philip, New South Wales (Aus.)

A.B.R.N.S. American Bankruptcy Reports, New Series

A.B.Rep. American Bankruptcy Reports

A.B.Rev. American Bankruptcy Review

A.C.
- Advance California Reports
- Appeal Cases
- Appeal Cases (Can.)
- Appeal Cases (Ceylon)
- Appellate Court
- Buchanan, Cape Colony Court of Appeal Rep.
- Case on Appeal
- Law Reports Appeal Cases (Eng.)
- Law Reports Appeal Cases (Eng.) Third Series

A/C Account

ACA
- Administrator of Civil Aeronautics
- Advance California Appellate Reports
- Americans for Constitutional Action

ACAA Agricultural Conservation & Adjustment Administration

ACABQ Advisory Committee on Administrative and Budgetary Questions

ACC
- Agricultural Credit Corporation
- Administrative Committee on Coordination

A.C.C.
- Allahabad Criminal Cases, India
- American Corporation Cases, by Withrow

ACDA Arms Control and Disarmament Agency

ACE Active Corps of Executives

A.C.J.A. American Criminal Justice Association

A.C.L.J. American Civil Law Journal, New York

A.C.L.U. American Civil Liberties Union

ACLUF American Civil Liberties Union Foundation

A.C.L.U.Leg. Action Bull. American Civil Liberties Union Legislative Action Bulletin.

ACM Arab Common Market

A.C.M. Court-Martial Reports, Air Force Cases

A.C.M.S. Special Court-Martial, U.S. Air Force

ACP African, Caribbean, and Pacific States

A.C.P. Agriculture Conservation Program

A.C.R. American Criminal Reports, edit. by Hawley; Appeal Court Reports, Ceylon

ACUS Administration Conference of the United States

A.Cr.C. Allahabad Criminal Cases (India)

A.D.
- Agriculture Decisions
- American Decisions
- New York Supreme Court Appellate Division Reports
- S. African Law Reports, Appellate Division

AD2d. New York Appellate Division Reports, Second Series

ADA Americans for Democratic Action

ADAMHA Alcohol, Drug Abuse, and Mental Health Administration

ADB Asian Development Bank

ADC Acta Dominorum Concilii 3 vols. (1839-1943) (Sc.)

A.D.C. Appeal Cases, District of Columbia Reports

A.D.I.L. Annual Digest of International Law

ADP Automatic Data Processing

ADPSO Association of Data Process Service Organizations

ADTC American District Telegraph Company

ADTS Automated Data and Telecommunications Service

A.E. Atomic Energy

A/E Registration Board of Architects and Professional Engineers

AEC Atomic Energy Commission (U.S.)

A.E.C.
- American Electrical Cases
- Atomic Energy Commission U.S.
- Atomic Energy Commission Reports

A.E.L.R. All England Law Reports

A.E.R. All England Law Reports

A.F. Air Force

AFDB African Development Bank

AFDE Aid to Families with Dependent Children

A.F.JAG L. Rev. Air Force JAG Law Review

A.F.L. American Federation of Labor

A.F.L.-C.I.O. American Federation of Labor and Congress of Industrial Organizations

A.F.L.R. Air Force Law Review

A.F.Rep. Alaska Federal Reports

AFTR American Federal Tax Reports (P-H)

AG Attorney General's Opinions

A.G.Dec. Attorney General's Decisions

A.G.O. Attorney General, Opinions

AHA American Hospital Association

AICLE Alabama Institute for Continuing Legal Education

AID • Agency for International Development
       • Accident/Injury/Damages

AIM • American Indian Movement
       • American Institute of Management

AIOEC Association of Iron Ore Exporting Countries

AIP American Independent Party

A.I.R. All India Law Reporter (Usually followed by a province abbreviation, (as A.I.R. All., for Allahabad), Bom. for Bombay, Dacca for Dacca, H.P. for Himachal Pradesh, Hyd. for Hyderabad, etc.)

A.Ins.R. American Insolvency Reports

A.J. • American Jurist
     • Associate Judge
     • British Guiana Supreme Court, Appellate Jurisdiction

A.J.C.L. American Journal of Comparative Law

A.J.I.L. American Journal of International Law

A.J.R. Australian Jurist Reports

AJS American Judicature Society

A.Jur.Rep. Australian Jurist Reports

a.k.a. also known as

A.K.Marsh. A.K. Marshall's Kentucky Supreme Court Reports (1817-1821)

ALA • Alliance for Labor Action
      • American Library Association

A.L.A.A. American Labor Arbitration Awards (P-H)

A.L.C.(or ALC) American Labor Cases (P-H)

ALEHU Advanced Legal Education, Hamline University School of Law

A.L.I. American Law Institute

ALIABA American Law Institute-American Bar Association Committee on Continuing Professional Education

A.L.J. • Albany Law Journal
      • Allahabad Law Journal (India)
      • Australian Law Journal

A.L.J.N.S. American Law Journal, New Series, Philadelphia

A.L.M. American Law Magazine, Philadelphia

A.L.R. • Aden Law Reports
      • Alberta Law Reports (Canada)
      • American Labor Cases(P-H)
      • American Law Reports
      • American Law Reports, Annotated
      • Argus Law Reports (Victoria)

A.L.R.(C.N.) Argus Law Reports Current Notes

A.L.R.2d American Law Reports Annotated, Second Series

A.L.R.3d American Law Reports Annotated, Third Series

A.L.R.Fed. American Law Reports Annotated, Federal

A.L.Rec. American Law Record, Cincinnati

A.L.Reg. American Law Register, Philadelphia.

A.L.Reg.(N.S.) American Law Register, New Series

A.L.Reg. (O.S.) American Law Register, Old Series

A.L.Rep. American Law Reporter, Davenport, Iowa

A.L.Rev. American Law Review, Boston

A.L.T.
- American Law Times
- Australian Law Times

A.L.T. Bankr. American Law Times, Bankruptcy Reports

A.L.T.R. American Law Times Reports

AMA American Management Associations

A.M.A.
- Agricultural Marketing
- Agricultural Marketing Administration. (U.S.)
- American Medical Association

AMAS African and Malagasy Associated States

A.M.C. American Maritime Cases

A.M.L.J. Ajmer-Merwara Law Journal (India)

AMR Advanced Management Research

AMS Agricultural Marketing Services

A.M.S., P.&S. Agricultural Marketing Service, P.&S. Docket (U.S.)

A.M.&O. Armstrong, Macartney & Ogle Nisi Prius (1840-42) (Ir.)

A.Moo. A. Moor's Reports, in 1 Bosanquet & Puller (Eng.)

A.N.
- Abbott's New Cases (N.Y.)
- Appeals Notes

A.N.C.
- Abbott's New Cases N.Y.
- American Negligence Cases

ANF Agriculture, Nutrition, and Forrestry

A.N.R. American Negligence Reports, Current Series

ANRPC Association of Natural Rubber Producing Countries

ANZUS ANZUS Council; treaty signed by Austrailia, New Zealand, and the United States

A.O. Administrative orders or directives

AOA Administration of Aging

A.O.C.Newsl. Administrative Office of the Courts Newsletter

A.P. Annual Practice (Eng.)

APA Assistance Payments Administration

A.P.B. Ashurst's Paper Books, in Lincoln's Inn Library

APC
- African Peanut (Groundnut) Council
- Alien Property Custodian (U.S.)

A.P.C.N. Anno post Christum natum, the year after the birth of Christ

A.P.D. Alien Property Division (Justice Dept.) (U.S.)

APHIS Animal and Plant Health Inspection Service

A.P.R.C. Anno post Roman conditam, year after the foundation of Rome

A.P.S. The Acts of the Parliaments of Scotland (1124-1707, 1814-1875)

A.P.S.C. Alabama Public Service Commission Decisions

A.P.S.R. American Political Science Review

A.P.T.D. Aid to the Permanently and Totally Disabled

A.R.
- American Reports
- Anno Regni. In the Year of the reign
- Army Regulations
- Argus Reports (Aus.)
- Atlantic Reporter
- Industrial Arbitration Reports (New South Wales)
- Ontario Appeal Reports

ARA
- Agricultural Research Administration (U.S.)
- Area Redevelopment Administration

A.R.A.M.C.O. Arabian American Oil Company

A.R. (Austrl.) Industrial Arbitration Reports (New South Wales)

A.R.B. Labor Arbitration Awards (CCH)

ARBA
- American Revolution Bicentenial Administration
- Arkansas Bar Association

A.R.C.
- American Railway Cases
- American Red Cross
- American Ruling Cases

ARD Application for Review Decisions

ARKCLE Arkansas Institute for Continuing Legal Education

A.R.M. Internal Revenue Bureau Committee on Appeals & Review, Memorandum (U.S.)

A.R.(N.S.W.) Industrial Arbitration Reports (New South Wales)

A.R.(Ont.) Ontario Appeal Reports

A.R.R.
- American Railway Reports
- Internal Revenue Bureau Committee on Appeals & Review, Recommendation (U.S.)

A.R.S.
- Agricultural Research Service
- Advanced Record System
- Arizona Revised Statutes

A.R.V.R.22. Anno Regni Victoriae Regina Vicesimo Secundo

A.Rep.
- American Reports
- Atlantic Reporter (Commonly cited Atl. or A.)

A.S.
- Act of Sederunt, Scotland
- American Samoa
- Armed Services

AS or A/S or A/s. Account sales; also after sight, at sight

ASAL Annual Survey of American Law

A.S.A.Newsl. Association for the Study of Abortion Newsletter

ASB Air Safty Board (U.S.)

A.S.C.A.P.Copyright L.Symp. Copyright Law Symposium (American Society of Composers, Authors and Publishers)

ASCS Agricultural Stabilization and Conservation Service

A.S.Code American Samoa Code

ASEAN Association of Southeast Asian Nations

ASHA American Society of Hospital Attorneys

ASIL American Society of International Law

ASIL Proc. Proceedings of the American Society of International Law

ASPAC Asian and Pacific Council

ASPR Armed Services Procurement Regulation

A.S.R. American State Reports

ASRB Armed Services Renegotiation Board (U.S.)

ASSIMER International Mercury Producers Association

AT Appeal Tribunal

A.T. Alcohol & Tobacco Tax. Div., Internal Revenue Bureau (U.S.)

A.T.C. Annotated Tax Cases (Eng.)

A.T.D. Australian Tax Decisions

ATLA Association of Trial Lawyers of America

A.T.L.A.J. American Trial Lawyers Association Journal

A.T. & T. Co. Com.L. American Telephone and Telegraph Co. Commission Leaflets

A.T. & T. Co. T.C. American Telephone and Telegraph Co. Commission Telephone Cases

AULR American University Review

A/V Adult and Vocational Education

A.W. Articles of War

AWD Aussenwirtschaftsdienst des Betriebsberaters (Ger.)

A.W.N. Allahabad Weekly Notes (India)

A.W.O.L. Absent Without Leave (military term)

AZO Allgemeine Zollordnung (German General Customs Regulations)

A. & A.Corp. Angell & Ames on Corporations

A. & C. Cir. Accounts and Collection Unit Circulars

A. & E.
- Admiralty and Ecclesiastical
- Adolphus & Ellis Queen's Bench Reports (1834-40) (Eng.)

A. & E.A.C. American and English Annotated Cases

A. & E. Ann Cas. American & English Annotated Cases

A. & E. Anno. American & English Annotated Cases

A. & E. Cas. American & English Annotated Cases

A. & E. Corp.Cas. American & English Corporation Cases

A. & E. Corp.Cas.N.S. American and English Corporation Cases, New Series

A. & E. Enc. American & English Encyclopedia of Law and Practice

A. & E. Ency. American & English Encyclopedia of Law

A. & E. Ency. Law American & English Encyclopedia of Law and Practice

A. & E. (n.s.) Adolphus and Ellis's Queen's Bench, New Series (1841-52)

A. & E.N.S. Adolphus & Ellis, English Queen's Bench Reports. New Series

A. & E.P. & P. American & English Pleading and Practice

A. & E. Pat.Cas. American & English Patent Cas.

A. & E.R. Cas. American & English Railroad Cases

A. & E.R. Cas., N.S. American & English Railroad Cases, New Series

A. & E. R.R.C. American & English Railroad Cases

A. & E.R.R.Cas. American & English Railroad Cases

A. & E.R.R.Cas. (N.S.) American & English Railroad Cases, New Series

A. & F. Fix. Amos & Ferard on Fixtures

A. & H. Arnold & Hodges' English Queen's Bench Reports (1840-41)

A. & N. Alcock & Napier's Irish King's Bench Reports. (1831-33)

Ab
- Abridgment
- Abstracts
- Abstracts of Treasury Decisions (U.S.)

Ab.Eq.Cas. Equity Cases Abridged

Ab.N. Abstracts, Treasury Decisions, New Series

Aband.Prop. Abandoned Property

Abb. Abbott, United States Circuit and District Court Reports

Abb.Adm. Abbott, Admiralty Reports (U.S.)

Abb.App.Dec. Abbott's Appeals Decisions, N.Y.

Abb.Beech.Tr. Abbott's Reports of the Beecher Trial

Abb.C.C. Abbott's Circuit Court Reports (U.S.)

Abb.Cl.Ass. Abbott's Clerks and Conveyancers' Assistant

Abb.Ct.App. Abbott Court of Appeals Decisions

Abb.Dec. Abbott's Decisions

Abb.Dig. Abbott's New York Digest

Abb.Dig.Corp. Abbott's Digest of the Law of Corporations

Abb.F. Abbott's Forms of Pleading

Abb.F.Sup. Abbott's Forms of Pleading, Supplement

Abb.Int. Abbott's Introduction to Practice under the Codes

Abb. Law Dict. Abbott's Law Dictionary (1879)

Abb.Leg. Rem. Abbott, Legal Remembrancer

Abb.Mo.Ind. Abbott's Monthly Index

Abb.N.C. Abbott's New Cases, New York

Abb.N.Cas. Abbott's New Cases, New York

Abb.N.S. Abbott's Practice Reports, New Series

Abb.N.Y.App. Abbott Court of Appeals Decisions (N.Y.)

Abb.N.Y.Dig. Abbott's New York Digest

Abb.NY Dig 2d Abbott's New York Digest 2d

Abb. Nat.Dig. Abbott's National Digest

Abb. Pl. Abbott's Pleadings under the Code

Abb.Pr. Abbott's New York Practice Reports (1854-1875)

Abb.Pr.N.S. Abbott's New York Practice Reports, New Series

Abb.R.P.S. Abbott's Real Property Statutes (Wn.)

Abb. Sh. Abbott on Shipping

Abb.Ship. Abbot (Lord Tenterden) on Shipping

Abb.Tr.Ev. Abbott's Trial Evidence

Abb.U.S. Abbott, Circuit Ct. Reports (U.S.)

Abb.Y.Bk. Abbott's Year Book of Jurisprudence

Abbott • Abbott's Dictionary
 • Abbott on Merchant Ships and Seaman (1802-1901)

Abbott, Civ Jury Trials Abbott on Civil Jury Trials

Abbott, Crim.Tr.Pr. Abbott on Criminal Trial Practice

Abbrev. Plac. Placitorum Abbreviatis, Record Commissioner (Eng.)

Abdy R. Pr. Abdy's Roman Civil Procedure

Abdy & W. Gai. Abdy & Walker's Gaius & Ulpian

Abdy & W. Just. Abdy & Walker's Justinian

A'Beck.Judg.Vict. A'Beckett, Reserved Judgments (Victoria)

A'Beck.R.J.N.S.W. A'Becketts Reserved (Equity) Judgments (New South Wales)

A'Beck.R.J.P.P. A'Beckett's Reserved Judgments. (Port Phillip)

A'Beck.Res.Judgm. A'Beckett's Reserved Judgments (Victoria)

A'Beckett Judgements of the Supreme Court of New South Wales for the District of Port Philip. 1846-51

Abr. • Abridged
 • Abridgement

Abr. Ca. Eq. Abridgment of Cases in Equity. (1667-1744)

Abr. Cas. Crawford & Dix, Abridged Cases (1937-38) (Ir.)

Abr.Cas.Eq. Equity Cases Abridged (1667-1744) (Eng.)

Abs. • Absent or Abstain
 • Abstracts, Treasury Decisions
 • Ohio Law Abstract

Abs(NS) Abstracts, New Series Treasury Decisions)

Acad. Academy

Acad.Pol.Sci.Proc. Academy of Political Science Proceedings (U.S.)

acct. account

Acct.L.Rep. Accountant Law Reports (Eng.)

Accy Accountancy Board

acq. • Acquitted
 • Acquittal

acq. in result Acquitted in result

Act. • Action
 • Action Prize Cases (1809-10) Privy Council (Eng.)

Act.Ass. Acts of the General Assembly, Church of Scotland (1638-1842)

Act.Can. Acta Cancellariae, by Monroe (Eng.)

Act.Cur.Ad.Sc. Acta Curiae Admiralatus Scotiae (Wade)

Act.Lawt.Ct. Acts of Lawting Court (Sc.)

Act.Ld.Aud.C. Acts of Lords Auditors of Causes (Sc.)

Act.Ld.Co.C.C. Acts of Lords of Council in Civil Causes (1478-1501) (Sc.)

Act.Ld.Co.Pub.Aff. Acts of the Lords of Council in Public Affairs (Sc.)

Act of Sed. Act of Sederunt

Act.P.C. Acts of the Privy Council (Dasent) (Eng.)

Act.P.C.N.S. Same as above, New Series (Eng.)

Act.Pr.C. Acton's reports, Prize Cases (Eng.)

Act.Pr.C.Col.S. Acts of the Privy Council, Colonial Series (Eng.)

Act. Reg. Acta Regia, an Abstract of Rymer's Foedera

Act. Sed. Act of Sederunt (Sc.)

Acta Crim. Acta Criminologica

Acta Jur. Acta Juridica

Acta Juridica. Acta Juridica Academiae Scientiarum Hungaricae

Acta Oeconomica. Acta Oeconomica Academiae Scientiarum Hungaricae

Acton Acton Prize Cases Privy Council (Eng.) (12 Eng. Reprint)

Acts Austl.P. Acts of the Australian Parliament

Acts S.Austl. Acts of South Australia

Acts Tasm. Acts of Tasmania (Aus.)

Acts Van Diem.L. Acts of Van Dieman's Land (Aus.)

Acts. Vict. Acts of the Parliament of Victoria (Aus.)

Acts & Ords.Interregnum. Acts and Ordinances of the Interregnum (1642-1660) (United Kingdom)

Ad.
- Addams' Ecclesiastical Reports (1822-26) (Eng.)
- Administrator
- Administration,
- -tive

Ad. Con. Addison's Contracts

Ad. Eq. Adam's Equity.

Ad. & E. Adolphus & Ellis' English King's Bench Reports (1834-40)

Ad. & El. Adolphus & Ellis. English King's Bench Reports.

Ad. & El.(Eng) Adolphus & Ellis (King's Bench) Reports (110-113 Eng. Reprint)

Ad.& Ell.N.S. Adolphus & Ellis' Reports, New Series; English Queen's Bench (commonly cited Q.B.)

Ad.Jus. Adam's Justiciary Reports (Sc.)

Ad.L. Administrative Law

Ad.L.2D Pike and Fischer. Administrative Law Reporter, Second Series

Ad.L.Rev. Administrative Law Review

Adam. Justiciary Reports (1893-1916) (Sc.)

Adams
- Adam's Reports (41, 42 Maine)
- Adams' Reports (1 New Hampshire)

Adams, Eq. Adams' Equity

Adams L.J. Adams County Legal Journal (Pa.)

Adams Leg.J. (Pa) Adams Legal Journal

Adams, Rom. Ant. Adams' Roman Antiquities.

Add.
- Addams' Ecclesastical Reports (Eng.)
- Addison's Reports (Pa. Supreme Court)
- Additional

Add.C. Addison on Contracts

Add.Ch. Addison Charges (see Addison's Pennsylvania Reports p. 49)

Add. Con. Addison on Contracts

Add.Cont. Addison on Contracts

Add.E.R. Addams' Ecclesiastical Reports. (1822-26)

Add Ecc. Addams' Ecclesiastical Reports

Add.Eccl. Addams' Ecclesiastical Reports

Add.Eccl.Rep. Addams' Ecclesiastical Reports (Eng.)

Add.Pa. Addison's County Court Reports

Add.Rep. Addison's County Court Reports (Pa.)

Add. T. Addison on Torts

Add. Tor. Addison on Torts

Add.Torts. Addison on Torts

Addams Addams' Ecclesiastical Reports (162 Eng. Reprint)

Addams Eccl.(Eng.) Addams, Ecclesiastical (162 Eng. Reprint)

Addis Addison's County Court Reports (Pa.)

Addison (Pa) Addison's County Court Reports (Pa.)

addit. additional

Adel. Adelaide

Adelaide L.Rev. Adelaide Law Review

Adj. Adjust; Adjustment

Adj.Sess. Adjourned Session

Adjournal, Books of. The Records of the Court of Justiciary. (Sc.)

Adm.
- Administrative
- Administrator
- Admiralty
- Admitted
- High Court of Admiralty (Eng.)

Adm. & Ecc. English Law Reports, Admiralty and Ecclesiastical

Adm. & Eccl. English Law Reports, Admiralty and Ecclesiastical

Adm.Interp. Administrative Interpretations

Admin. Administration

Admin.Cd. Administrative Code

Admin. Dec. Administrative Decisions

adminstr. administrator

administrn. administration

Adminstrv. administrative

Admir. Admiralty Division

Admr. (also Adm.) Administrator

Admty. Admiralty

Admx. Administratix

Adol.&El.N.S. Adolphus & Ellis'
Reports, New Series, English Queen's
Bench

Adolph & E. Adolphus & Ellis'
English King's Bench Reports

adv. • advocate
  • advisory

Adv. Chron. The Advocates' Chronicle (India)

Adv. O. Advance Opinions in Lawyers' Edition of United States Reports

Adv.Ops. Advance Opinions

Adv.Rep.N.J. New Jersey Advance
Reports & Weekly Review

advt. advertising

Adv.Sh. Advance Sheet

Adye C. M. Adye on Courts-Martial

Aelf. C. Canons of Aelfric

Aer State Aeronautics Commission

Af Afghan

Aff. • Affairs
  • affirmed in, or affirming

Aff'd Affirmed

Aff'g Affirming

aff reh affirmed on rehearing, or
affirming on rehearing

Afr. • Africa
  • African
  • Afrikaans

Ag. Agency

Ag State Department of Agriculture

Agcy. Agency

Agn. Fr. Agnew on the Statute of
Frauds

Agn. Pat. Agnew on Patents

Agr. • Agreement
  • Agriculture

Agra H.C. Agra High Court Reports
(India)

AgriDec. Agriculture Decisions

Agric. Agriculture

Agric.C. Agricultural Code

Agric.Conserv.&Adj. Agricultural
Conservation and Adjustment

Agric.Dec. Agricultural Decisions

Agric.&Mkts. Agriculture & Markets

agt. agent

agy. agency

Aik. Aikens' Vermont Supreme Court
Reports (1825-1828)

Aik. Dig. Aiken's Digest of Alabama
Statutes

Aik. Stat. Aiken's Digest of Alabama
Statutes

Ainsw. Ainsworth's Lexicon

Ainsworth, Lex. Ainsworth's Latin-
English Dictionary (1837)

Air L.R. Air Law Review

Aird Civ. Law. Aird's Civil Laws of
France

Aiyar Aiyar's Company Cases (India)

Aiyar C.C. Aiyar's Company Cases
(India)

Aiyar L.P.C. Aiyar's Leading Privy
Council Cases (India)

Aiyar Unrep.D. Aiyar's Unreported
Decisions (India)

Ajmer-Merwara L.J. Ajmer-Merwara
Law Journal (India)

Ak • Arkansas Reports
  • Alaska

Akron L.Rev. Akron Law Review

Al. • Alabama
  • Alevn. King's Bench Reports
    (1846-49) (Eng.)
  • Albanian

Alcock & N Alcock & Napier King's
Bench (Ir.) 1 vol

Al.Kada Native Tribunals' Reports
(Egypt)

Al.Ser. Indian Law Reports,
Allahabad Series

Al.Tel.Ca. Allen's Telegraph Cases

Al. & N. Alcock & Napier. Irish King's
Bench Reports (1831-33)

Al. & Nap. Alcock & Napier's Irish
King's Bench Reports

Ala. • Alabama
  • Alabama Reports
  • Alabama Supreme Court
  • Alabama Supreme Court
    Reports

Ala.A. Alabama Appellate Court

Ala.Acts. Acts of Alabama

Ala.App. • Alabama Appellate
    Court Reports
  • Alabama Court of
    Appeals

Ala. Code Code of Alabama

Ala. L.J. Alabama Law Journal

Ala.L.Rev. Alabama Law Review

Ala Law Alabama Lawyer

Ala.N.S. Alabama Reports. New Series

Ala.P.S.C. Alabama Public Service Commission

Ala.R.C. Alabama Railroad Commission

Ala. S.B.A. Alabama State Bar Association

Ala.Sel.Cas. Alabama Select Cases (Sup. Ct) by Shepherd. vols. 37, 38 & 39

Ala.St.B.Found.Bull. Alabama State Bar Foundation Bulletin

Ala.St.Bar Assn. Alabama State Bar Association

Alas. Alaska

Alaska Alaska Reports

Alaska B.J. Alaska Bar Journal

Alaska Co. Alaska Codes, Carter

Alaska Fed. Alaska Federal Reports

Alaska Fed.Rep. Alaska Federal Reports

Alaska L.J. Alaska Law Journal

Alaska Sess.Laws. Alaska Session Laws

Alaska Stat. Alaska Statutes

Alb. Albany

Alb.Arb. Albert Arbitration (Lord Cairns' Decisions)

Alb.L.J. Albany Law Journal

Alb.L.Q. Alberta Law Quarterly

Alb.L.R. Alberta Law Reports

Alb.L.Rev. Albany Law Review

Alb.L.S.Jour. Albany Law School Journal

Alb.Law J. Albany Law Journal

Albany L.Rev. Albany Law Review

Alberta L.(Can) Alberta Law Reports

Alberta L.Q. Alberta Law Quarterly

Alberta L.Rev. Alberta Law Review

Alc.Reg.C. Alcock's Registry Cases (1832-41) (Ir.)

Ale. & N. Alcock & Napier, Irish King's Bench Reports and Exchequer

Alc. & Nap. Alcock & Napier's Irish King's Bench Reports

Alco.Bev. Alcoholic Beverage

Alco.Bev.Cont. Alcoholic Beverage Control

Ald. Alden's Condensed Reports (Pa.)

Alex.Br.Stat. Alexander's British Statutes in Force in Maryland

Alex.Cas. Report of the "Alexandra" Case by Dudley

Alex.Ins. Alexander on Life Insurance in New York

Alexander. Alexander's Reports, vols. 66-72 Mississippi

Aleyn Aleyn's Select Cases, English King's Bench. (82 Eng. Bench)

Aleyn (Eng.) Aleyn, Select Cases (82 Eng. Reprint)

Alg.Med. Algemene Mededelingen (Netherlands)

Alger's Law Promoters & Prom. Corp. Alger's Law in Relation to Promoters and Promotion of Corporations

Alis.Princ.Scotch Law. Alison's Principles of the Criminal Law of Scotland

Alk ● Alaska
    ● Alaska Reports

All. ● Indian Law Reports, Allahabad Series (India)
    ● Allen's Massachusetts Reports

All.Cr.Cas. Allahabad Criminal Cases

All.E.R. All England Law Reports (formerly All England Law Reports Annotated)

All Eng All England Law Reports

All I. R. All India Reports

All Ind.Cr.R. All Indian Criminal Reports

All Ind.Cr.T. All India Criminal Times

All Ind.Rep. All India Reporter

All Ind.Rep.N.S. All India Reporter, New Series

All India Crim.Dec. All India Criminal Decisions

All India Rptr. All India Reporter

All.L.J. & Rep. Allahabad Law Journal and Reports. (India)

All.L.T. Allahabad Law Times (India)

All.N.B. Allen's New Brunswick Reports (1848-66) (Canada)

All Pak.Leg.Dec. All Pakistan Legal Decisions

All.Ser. Allahabad Series, Indian Law Reports

All.Tel.Cas. Allen, Telegraph Cases (American and English)

All.W.N. Allahabad Weekly Notes (and Supplement) (India)

All.W.R. Allahabad Weekly Reporter (India)

Allen ● Allen's Massachusetts Supreme Judicial Court Reports (1861-1867)
● Allen's Reports, New Brunswick (Canada)
● Allen's Reports (Washington Territory, 1854-1885)
● Aleyn's English King's Bench Reports

Allen Tel.Cas. Allen's Telegraph Cases

Allin. Allinson's Penn. Superior and Dist. Court Reports

Allinson Allinson, Pennsylvania Superior and District Court Reports

Allison's Am.Dict. Allison's American Dictionary

allowing app. allowing appeal

allowing reh. allowing rehearing

Allwood Allwood's Appeal Cases under the Weights & Measures Act (Eng.)

Alsager. Alsager's Dictionary of Business Terms

Alt. Alternative

Alt.County Gov't. Alternative County Government

Alta. ● Alberta
● Alberta Law Reports (1907-1932) (Canada)

Alta.L. Alberta Law

Alta.L.Q. Alberta Law Quarterly (1908-32) (Canada)

Alta.L.R. Alberta Law Reports. (Canada)

Alta.L.Rev. Alberta Law Review

Alta.Rev.Stat. Alberta Revised Statutes (Canada)

Alta.Stat. Alberta Statutes (Canada)

Alves Dampier & Maxwell's British Guiana Reports

Am. ● American
● Amended
● Amendment
● Amharic

Am.Acad.Matri.Law.J. American Academy of Matrimonial Lawyers Journal

Am.Ann.Cas. American Annotated Cases (1904-1912)

Am.B.A. American Bar Association

Am.B.(N.S.) American Bankruptcy, New Series

Am.B.R. American Bankruptcy Reports

Am.B.R. (N.S.) American Bankruptcy Reports, New Series

Am.Bank.Rev. American Bankruptcy Review

Am.Bankr. American Bankruptcy

Am.Bankr.L.J. American Bankruptcy Law Journal

Am.Bankr.N.S. American Bankruptcy, New Series

Am.Bankr.R. American Bankruptcy Reports

Am.Bankr.R. (N.S.) American Bankruptcy Reports, New Series

Am.Bankr.Reg. American Bankruptcy Register (U.S.)

Am.Bankr.Rep. American Bankruptcy Reports

Am.Bankr.Rep.N.S. American Bankruptcy Reports, New Series

Am.Bankr.Rev. American Bankruptcy Review

Am.Bar Ass.J. American Bar Assn. Journal

Am.Bar Asso.Jour. American Bar Association Journal

Am Bar Asso Rep American Bar Association Reports

Am. B'Kc'y. Rep. American Bankruptcy Reports

Am.Bus.L.J. American Business Law Journal

Am.C.L.J. American Civil Law Journal, New York

Am Cent Dig American Digest (Century Edition)

Am.Ch.Dig. American Chancery Digest

Am.Civ.L.J. American Civil Law Journal

Am.Consul.Bul. American Consular Bulletin

Am.Corp.Cas. American Corporation Cases (Withrow)

Am.Cr. American Criminal Reports

Am.Cr.Rep. American Criminal Reports, edited by Hawley

Am.Cr.Tr. American Criminal Trials, Chandler's

Am.Crim.L.Q. American Criminal Law Quarterly

Am.Crim.L.Rev. American Criminal Law Review

Am.Dec. American Decisions (Select Cases), San Francisco

Am.Dig. American Digest

Am.Dig.Cent.Ed. American Digest (Century Edition)

Am.Dig.Dec.Ed.(or Decen.Ed.). American Digest (Decennial Edition)

Am.Dig.Eighth Dec.Ed. American Digest (Eighth Decennial Edition)

Am.Dig.Fifth Dec.Ed. American Digest (Fifth Decennial Edition)

Am.Dig.Fourth Dec.Ed. American Digest (Fourth Decennial Edition)

Am.Dig. Key No.Ser. American Digest (Key Number Series)

Am.Dig.Secd.Dec.Ed. American Digest (Second Decennial Edition)

Am.Dig.Seventh Dec.Ed. American Digest (Seventh Decennial Edition)

Am.Dig.Sixth Dec.Ed. American Digest (Sixth Decennial Edition)

Am.Dig.Third Dec.Ed. American Digest (Third Decennial Edition)

Am.Econ.Rev. American Economic Review

Am.Ed. American Edition

Am.El.Ca. American Electrical Cases

Am.Elec.Ca. American Electrical Cases

Am.Elect.Cas. American Electrical Cases

Am.Electl.Cas. American Electrical Cases

Am.Electr.Cas. American Electrical Cases

Am.Enc.Dict. American Encyclopedic Dictionary

Am.Fed.Tax R. American Federal Tax Reports

Am.Fed.TaxR.2d American Federal Tax Reports, Second Series (P-H)

Am.Hist.Rev. American Historical Review

Am.Ins. Arnold on Marine Insurance

Am.Ins.Rep. American Insolvency Reports

Am.Insolv.Rep. American Insolvency Reports

Am.J.2d American Jurisprudence (Second Edition)

Am.J.Comp.Law American Journal of Comparative Law

Am.J.Crim.L. American Journal of Criminal Law

Am.J.Int.L. American Journal of International Law

Am.J.Int.Law Proc. American Journal of International Law, Proceedings

Am.J.Jurisprud. American Journal of Jurisprudence

Am.J.Leg.Forms Anno. American Jurisprudence Legal Forms Annotated

Am.J.Legal Hist. American Journal of Legal History

Am.J.Pl. & Pr.Forms Anno. American Jurisprudence Pleading & Practice Forms Annotated

Am.J.Proof of Facts American Jurisprudence Proof of Facts

Am.J.Trials American Jurisprudence Trials

Am.Jour.Pol. American Journal of Politics

Am.Jud.Soc. American Judicature Society (Bulletins or Journal)

Am.Jur. • American Jurisprudence
            • American Jurist

Am.Jur.2d American Jurisprudence, Second Series

Am.Jur.Leg.Forms Anno. American Jurisprudence Legal Forms Annotated

Am.Jur.Legal Forms American Jurisprudence Legal Forms

Am.Jur.Legal Forms 2d. American Jurisprudence Legal Forms, Second Edition

Am.Jur.Pl. & Pr.Forms American Jurisprudence Pleading and Practice Forms Annotated

Am.Jur.Pl. & Pr.Forms (Rev.ed.) American Jurisprudence Pleading and Practice Forms, Revised Editions

Am.Jur.Proof of Facts American Jurisprudence Proof of Facts

Am.Jur.Proof of Facts Anno. American Jurisprudence Proof of Facts Annotated

Am.Jur.Trials American Jurisprudence Trials

Am.Jurist American Jurist

Am.L.C.R.P. Sharswood and Budd's Leading Cases on Real Property

Am.L.Cas. American Leading Cases

Am.L.Ins. ● American Law Institute
● American Law Institute, Restatement of the Law

Am.L.Inst. American Law Institute, Restatement of the Law

Am.L.J. ● American Law Journal (Hall's) (Philadelphia)
● American Law Journal (Ohio)

Am.L.J.N.S. American Law Journal, New Series, Philadelphia

Am.L.J. (N.S.) American Law Journal (Clark's)

Am.L.J. (O) American Law Journal (Ohio)

Am.L.J. (O.S.) American Law Journal (Hall's)

Am.L.M. American Law Magazine, Philadelphia

Am.L.Rec. American Law Record (Ohio)

Am.L.Reg. American Law Register, Philadelphia

Am.L.Reg.(N.S.) American Law Register, New Series

Am.L.Reg., (O.S.) American Law Register, Old Series

Am.L.Reg. & Rev. American Law Register and Review

Am.L.Rep. American Law Reporter, Davenport (Iowa)

Am.L.Rev. American Law Review

Am.L.S.Rev. American Law School Review

Am.L.T. American Law Times, Washington, D.C. and New York

Am.L.T.Bankr. American Law Times Bankruptcy Reports

Am.L.T.Bankr.Rep. American Law Times Bankruptcy Reports

Am.L.T.R. American Law Times Reports

Am.L.T.R.N.S. American Law Times Reports, New Series

Am.L.T.Rep. American Law Times Reports

Am.Lab.Arb. Awards (P-H) American Labor Arbitration Awards (P-H)

Am.Lab.Arb.Cas. American Labor Arbitration Cases (P-H)

Am.Lab.Cas. American Labor Cases (P-H)

Am.Lab.Cas.(P-H) American Labor Cases (P-H)

Am.Lab.Leg.Rev. American Labor Legislation Review

Am.Labor Legis.Rev. American Labor Legislation Review

Am.Law Inst. American Law Institute, Restatement of the Law

Am.Law J. American Law Journal

Am.Law J.N.S. American Law Journal, New Series

Am.Law Mag. American Law Magazine

Am.Law Rec. American Law Record (Cincinnati)

Am.Law Reg. American Law Register

Am.Law Reg.N.S. American Law Register, New Series

Am.Law Reg.O.S. American Law Register, Old Series

Am.Law Rev. American Law Review

Am.Law S.Rev. American Law School Review

Am.Law T.Rep. American Law Times Reports

Am.Lawy. American Lawyer

Am.Lead.Cas. American Leading Cases (Hare & Wallace's)

Am.Lead.Cas.(H & W) American Leading Cases (Hare & Wallace)

Am.Leg.N. American Legal News

Am.Mar.Cas. American Maritime Cases

Am.Neg.Ca. American Negligence Cases

Am.Neg.Cas. American Negligence Cases

Am.Neg.Dig. American Negligence Digest

Am.Neg.Rep. American Negligence Reports

Am.Negl.Cas. American Negligence Cases

Am.Negl.R. American Negligence Reports

Am.Negl.Rep. American Negligence Reports

Am.Pol.Sci.Rev. American Political Science Review

Am.Pol.Science Rev. American Political Science Review

Am.Pr. American Practice

Am.Pr.Rep. American Practice Reports (D.C.)

Am.Pr.Rep.NS American Practice Reports, New Series

Am.Prob. American Probate Reports

Am.Prob.N.S. American Probate, New Series

Am.Prob.Rep. American Probate Reports

Am.Property American Law of Property

Am.R. American Reports

Am.R.Ca. American Railway Cases

Am.R.R.Cas. American Railway Cases (Smith & Bates')

Am.R.R. & C.Rep. American Railroad & Corporation Reports

Am.R.Rep. American Railway Reports

Am.R. & Corp. American Railroad Corporation

Am.Rail.Cas. American Railway Cases

Am.Rail.R. American Railway Reports

Am.Railw.Cas. American Railway Cases (Smith & Bates)

Am.Rep. American Reports

Am.Ry.Ca. American Railway Cases

Am.Ry.Rep. American Railway Reports

Am.S.R. American State Reports

Am.Soc.Int.L.Proc. American Society of International Law Proceedings

Am.St.P. American State Papers

Am.St.R. American State Reports (1886-1911)

Am.St.R.D. American Street Railway Decisions

Am.St.Rep. American State Reports

Am.St.Ry.Dec. American Street Railway Decisions

Am.St.Ry.Rep. American Street Railway Reports

Am.Stock Ex.Guide. American Stock Exchange Guide (CCH)

Am.Taxp.Q. American Taxpayers' Quarterly

Am.Them. American Themis

Am.Tr.M.Cas. Cox's American Trade Mark Cases

Am.Trade Mark Cas. American Trade Mark Cases (Cox)

Am.Trial Law.L.J. American Trial Lawyers Law Journal

Am.U.Int.L.Rev. American University, Intramural Law Review

Am.U.Intra.L.Rev. American University Intramural Law Review

Am.U.L.Rev. American University Law Review

Am.Vets. American Law of Veterans

Am. & E.Corp.Cas. American & English Corporation Cases

Am. & E.Corp.Cas.N.S. American & English Corporation Cases New Series

Am. & E.Eq.D. American & English Decisions in Equity

Am. & E.R.Cas. American & English Railroad Cases

Am. & E.R.Cas.N.S. American & English Railroad Cases New Series

Am. & Eng.Ann.Cas. American & English Annotated Cases

Am. & Eng.Corp.Cas. American & English Corporation Cases

Am. & Eng.Corp.Cas.N.S. American & English Corporation cases, New Series

Am. & Eng.Dec.Eq. American and English Decisions in Equity

Am. & Eng.Dec. in Eq. American and English Decisions in Equity

Am. & Eng.Enc.Law American and English Encyclopedia of Law

Am. & Eng.Enc.Law Sup. American and English Encyclopedia of Law, Supplement

Am. & Eng.Enc.Law & Pr. American & English Encyclopedia of Law & Practice

Am. & Eng.Ency.Law American and English Encyclopedia of Law

Am. & Eng.Eq.D. American & English Decisions in Equity

Am. & Eng.Pat.Ca. American and English Patent Cases

Am. & Eng.Pat.Cas. American and English Patent Cases

Am. & Eng. R.Cas. American and English Railroad Cases

Am. & Eng.R.Cas.N.S. American and English Railroad Cases, New Series

Am. & Eng.R.R.Ca. American and English Railroad Cases

Am. & Eng.R.R.Cas. American and English Railroad Cases

Am. & Eng.Ry.Cas. American and English Railway Cases

Am. & Eng.Ry.Cas.N.S. American & English Railroad Cases, New Series

Am. & Engl.R.C. American and English Railway Cases

Amb. Ambler's Reports, Chancery. (27 Eng. Reprint) (Eng.)

Ambl. Ambler's Reports, Chancery. (27 Eng. Reprint) (Eng.)

Amend. Amendment

amend. amended; amending; amendment; amendments

amends. amendments

Amer. ● America; American
● Amerman's Reports (Vols. 111-115 Pennsylvania Reports)

Amer.Econ.Rev. American Economic Review

Amer.Fed.Tax Rep. American Federal Tax Rep. (P-H)

Amer.J.Comp.L. American Journal of Comparative Law

Amer.J.Econ. & Soc. American Journal of Economics and Sociology

Amer.J.Int'l.L. American Journal of International Law

Amer.Jur. American Jurist

Amer.Law. American Lawyer, New York

Amer.Law Reg. (N.S.) American Law Register, New Series

Amer.Law Reg. (O.S.) American Law Register, Old Series

Amer.Law Rev. American Law Review.

Amer.Lawy. American Lawyer

Amer.Rev.E.-W.Tr. American Review of East-West Trade

Amer. & Eng.Enc.Law. American & English Encyclopedia of Law

Ames ● Ames' Reports (1 Minnesota)
● Ames' Reports (4-7 Rhode Island)

Ames Cas.B. & N. Ames' Cases on Bills and Notes

Ames Cas.Par. Ames' Cases on Partnership

Ames Cas.Pl. Ames' Cases on Pleading

Ames Cas.Sur. Ames' Cases on Suretyship

Ames Cas.Trusts. Ames' Cases on Trusts

Ames, K. & B. Ames, Knowles & Bradley's Reports (8 Rhode Island)

Amos & F.Fixt. Amos & Ferrard on Fixtures

Amtrak National Railroad Passenger Corporation

An. Anonymous, at end of Benloe Reports 1661

An.B. Anonymous Reports at end of Benloe, or Bendloe (1661) (Eng.)

Anal. Analysis

Anc.Charters Ancient Charters, 1692

And. ● Anderson's Agriculture Cases (Eng.)
● Anderson's English Common Pleas Reports (1534-1605)
● Andrew's English King's Bench Reports (1737-38)
● Andrews' Reports (63-73 Conn.)

And.Agr.Dec. Anderson's Agricultural Decisions (Sc.)

And.Cr.Law. Andrews on Criminal Law

And.Dig. Andrews, Digest of the Opinions of the Attorneys-General

And.Law Dict. Anderson's Law Dictionary

And. & Ston.J.A. Andrews & Stoney's Supreme Court of Judicature Acts.

Ander.(Eng.) Anderson's Reports, English Court of Common Pleas

Anders. Anderson's Reports, English Court of Common Pleas

Anderson Anderson's Reports, English Court of Common Pleas

Anderson UCC Anderson's Uniform Commercial Code

Andr. Andrews, English King's Bench Reports (95 Eng. Reprint)

Andrews (Eng.) Andrews, English King's Bench Reports. (95 Eng. Reprint)

Ang. ● Angell's Rhode Island Reports
    ● Angell & Durfee Reports (1 Rhode Island)

Ang.Car. Angell on Carriers

Ang.Highw. Angell & Durfee on Highways

Ang.Ins. Angell on Insurance

Ang.Lim. Angell on Limitation of Actions

Ang.Tide Waters Angell on Tide Waters

Ang.Water Courses Angell on Water Courses

Ang. & A.Corp. Angell & Ames on Corporations

Ang. & Dur. Angell & Durfee's Reports (1 Rhode Island)

Ann. ● Annaly's Hardwicke, 7-10 Geo. II, King's Bench, tempore (1733-38)
    ● annotated
    ● Annual
    ● Cases in King's Bench, 7-10 Geo.. II. tempore
    ● Cunningham's Reports, King's Bench, 7-10 Geo. II. tempore
    ● Queen Anne, as 8 Ann. c. 19

Ann.Am.Acad. Annals of the American Academy of Political and Social Science

Ann.Cal.Codes West's Annotated California Codes

Ann.Cas. ● American & English Annotated Cases
    ● American Annotated Cases
    ● New York Annotated Cases

Ann.Code. Annotated Code

Ann.Codes & St. Bellinger and Cotton's Annotated Codes and Statutes, Or.

Ann.Cong. Annals of Congress

Ann.Dig. Annual Digest and Reports of International Law Cases

Ann.L.Rep. Annotated Law Reporter (1932-35) (India)

Ann.Law Reg. Annual Law Register of the U.S.

Ann.Leg.Forms Mag. Annotated Legal Forms Magazine

Ann.Pr. Annual Practice

Ann.Proc.Nat.Asso.R.Comr.s Annual Proceedings of the National Association of Railway Commissions

Ann.Reg. Annual Register, London

Ann.Reg.N.S. Annual Register, New Series

Ann.Rep. Annual Report

Ann.St. Annotated Statutes

Ann.St.Ind.T. Annotated Statutes of Indian Territory

Ann.Tax Cas. Annotated Tax Cases (Eng.)

Annals. Annals of the American Academy of Political and Social Science

Annaly Lee's K.B. Report temp. Hardwicke. Annaly edition (1733-38) (Eng.)

Anne. Queen Anne (thus "1 Anne," denotes the first year of the reign of Queen Anne)

Anno. Annotated

anon. anonymous

Ans.Con. Anson on Contracts

Anson, Cont. Anson on Contracts

Anst. Anstruther's English Exchequer Reports (145 Eng. Reprint)

Anstr. Anstruther's English Exchequer Reports (145 Eng. Reprint)

Anstr. (Eng) Anstruther's English Exchequer Reports (145 Eng. Reprint)

Anth. Anthon's New York Nisi Prius Reports

Anth.Shep. Anthony's edition of Shephard's Touchstone

Anthon NP (N.Y.) Anthon's New York Nisi Prius Reports

Antitrust Bull. Antitrust Bulletin

Antitrust L.J. Antitrust Law Journal

Antitrust L.Sym. Antitrust Law Symposium

Antitrust L. & Econ.Rev. Antitrust Law and Economics Review

Antitrust & Trade Reg.Rep. Antitrust & Trade Regulation Report (BNA)

Ap. New York-Supreme Court Appellate Division Reports

Ap.2d New York Appellate Division Reports, Second Series

Ap.Bre. Appendix to Breese's Reports (Illinois)

Ap.Just. Apud Justinianum (or Justinian's Institutes)

Ap.Justin. Apud Justinianum; In Justinian's Institutes

App. ● Appeal Cases (D.C.)
    ● appendix
    ● Appleton's Reports (19, 20 Maine) Ohio Appellate Reports
    ● Cour d'Appel, Hof van Beroep (District Court of Appeal)

app.allowed appeal allowed

App.Bd.O.C.S. Office of Contract Settlement, Appeal Board Decisions

App.Ca. Buchanan, Reports of Courts of Appeal, Cape Colony (S. Africa)

App.Cas. ● Appeal Cases, English Law Reports (1875-90)
    ● Appeal cases in the United States
    ● Appeal cases, District of Columbia
    ● Appeal cases of the different states
    ● Law Reports, Appeal Cases (Eng.)

App.Cas.Beng. Sevestre & Marshall's Bengal Reports

App.Ct.Rep. ● Appeal Court Reports, New Zealand
    ● Bradwell's Illinois Appeal Court Reports

App.D. South Africa Law Reports, Appellate Division

App.D.C. Appeals Cases, District of Columbia (1893-1941)

app.den. appeal denied

App.Dep't Appellate Department

app.dism. appeal dismissed

App.Div. ● Appellate Division
    ● New York Supreme Court, Appellate Division Reports
    ● Supreme Court, Appellate Division

App.Div. (NY) New York Supreme Court, Appellate Division Reports

App.Div. 2d New York Supreme Court, Appellate Division Reports, Second Series

App.Exam. Appeal (s) Examiner

App.Fish.Com. Appeals from Fisheries Commission (1861-93) (Ir.)

App.Jur.Act 1876. Appellate Jurisdiction Act, 1876, 39 & 40 Vict., c.59

App.N.Z. Appeal Reports, New Zealand

App.R.N.Z. Appeal Reports, New Zealand

App.Ref. Appeal (s) Referee

App.Rep. Ontario Appeal Reports (1876-1900) (Canada)

App.Rep.Ont. Ontario Appeal Reports

App.T. Supreme Court Appellate Term

App.Tax Serv. Appeals Relating to Tax on Servants 1781 (Eng.)

App.Trib. (also AT) Appeal Tribunal

Appd. Approved

Append. Appendix

Appleton. Appleton's Reports (vols. 19, 20 Maine)

appr. approved in, or approving

Approp. Appropriation (s)

apps. appendixes

Appx.Bre. Appendix to Breese's Reports, Illinois

Apr. April

Ar.J. Arbitration Journal (new series)

Ar.Rep. Argus Reports, Victoria

Arabin. Decision of SergeantArabin

Arb. ● Arbitrator
    ● Arbitration
    ● Labor Arbitration Awards (CCH)

Arb G. Arbeitsgericht--Labour Tribunal (Ger.)

Arb.J. Arbitration Journal

Arb.J. (N.S.) Arbitration Journal, New Series

Arb.J.(O.S.) Arbitration Journal, Old Series

Arb.J. of the Inst. of Arbitrators Arbitration Journal of the Institute of Arbitrators

Arb.L.Dig. Arbitration Law; A Digest of Court Decisions

Arbitr. Arbitration

Arbuth. Arbuthnot's Select Criminal Cases, (Madras)

Arch. Court of Arches (Eng.)

Arch.Bank. Archbold on Bankruptcy (1825-56)

Arch.C.L.Pr. Archbold's New Common Law Practice

Arch.C.P. Archbold's Practice in the Common Pleas

Arch.Civ.Pl. Archbold's Civil Pleading and Evidence

Arch.Cr. Archbold's Pleading and Evidence in Criminal Cases (1822-1959)

Arch.Cr.L. Archbold's Criminal Law

Arch.Cr.Pl. Archbold's Criminal Pleading

Arch.Cr.Pl. (or Archb.Crim.Pl.). Archbold's Criminal Pleading

Arch.Cr.Prac. Archbold's Criminal Practice

Arch.J.C.Pr. Archibald on Practice of Judges Chambers

Arch.K.B.Forms Archbold's Forms in King's Bench and Common Pleas

Arch.K.B.Pr. Archbold's King's Bench Practice

Arch.L.R. Architects Law Reports (1904-09) (Eng.)

Arch.N.P. Archbold's Law of Nisi Prius

Arch.P.C. Archbold's Pleas of the Crown

Arch.P.Ch. Archbold's Practice by Chitty

Arch.P.K.B. Archbold's Practice in the King's Bench

Arch.P.L. Archbold's Poor Law (1840-1930)

Arch.P.L.Cas. Archbold's Abridgment of Poor Law Cases (1842-58)

Arch.Part. Archbold's Law of Partnership

Arch.Pl.Cas. Archbold's Abridgment of Poor Law Cases

Arch.Pr.Q.S. Archbold's Practice in Quarter Sessions

Arch.Sum. Archbold's Summary of Laws of England

Archb.Civil Pl. Archbold's Civil Pleading

Archb.Cr.Law Archbold's Pleading and Evidence in Criminal Cases

Archb.Cr.Prac. & Pl. Archbold's Pleading and Evidence in Criminal Cases

Archb.Crim.Pl. Archbold's Criminal Pleading

Archb.Landl. & Ten. Archbold's Landlord and Tenant

Archb.N.P. Archbold's Nisi Prius Law

Archb.N.Prac. Archbold's New Practice

Archb.New Pr. Archbold's New Practice

Archb.Pr. Archbold's Practice

Archb.Pr.K.B. Archbold's Practice King's Bench

Archer Archer's Reports (2 Florida)

Archer & H. Archer & Hogue Reports (vol.2 Florida)

Archer & Hogue Archer & Hogue's Reports (vol. 2 Florida)

Architects' L.R. Architects' Law Reports, 4 vols. 1904-09

Arg.Bills Ex. Argles' French Law of Bills of Exchange

Arg.Fr.Merc.Law. Argles (Napoleon), Treatise Upon French Mercantile Law, etc.

Arg.Inst. Institution au Droit Francais, par M. Argon

Arg.L.R. Argus Law Reports (Aus.)

Arg.Mo. Moore's King's Bench Reports (Arguments of Moore) (Eng.)

Arg.Rep. Reports printed in Melbourne Argus, Australia

Argen. Argentina

Argus L.R. Argus Law Reports

Ariz. ● Arizona
 ● Arizona Supreme Court Reports

Ariz.App. Arizona Appeals Reports

Ariz.B.J. Arizona Bar Journal

Ariz.C.C. Arizona Corporation Commission

Ariz.L.Rev. Arizona Law Review

Ariz.Legis.Serv. Arizona Legislative Service (West)

Ariz.R.C. Arizona Railway Commission

Ariz.Rev.State Arizona Revised Statutes

Ariz.Rev.Stat.Ann. Arizona Revised Statutes Annotated

Ariz.Sess.Laws Arizona Session Laws

Ark. • Arkansas
  • Arkansas Supreme Court Reports
  • Arkley's Justiciary Reports (1846-48) (Sc.)

Ark.Acts General Acts of Arkansas

Ark.B.A. Arkansas Bar Association

Ark.C.C. Arkansas Corporation Commission Report

Ark.Just. Arkley's Justiciary Reports (Sc.)

Ark.L.J. Arkansas Law Journal

Ark.L.Rev. Arkansas Law Review

Ark.P.U. Arkansas Department of Public Utilities Report

Ark.R.C. Arkansas Railroad Commission

Ark.Stat.Ann. Arkansas Statutes Annotated

Arkl. Arkley's Justiciary Reports, (Sc.)

Arkley Arkley's Justiciary Reports (Sc.)

Arm.M. & O. Armstrong, Macartney and Ogle's Reports

Armour Manitoba Queen's Bench tempore Wood, by Armour

Arms.Br.P.Cas. Armstrong's Breach of Privilege Cases, New York

Arms.Con.El. Armstrong Contested Election Cases (N.Y.)

Arms.Con.Elec. Armstrong's New York Contested Elections

Arms.Elect.Cas. Armstrong's Cases of Contested Elections, New York

Arms.M. & O. Armstrong, Macartney & Ogle's Irish Nisi Prius Reports

Arms.Mac. & Og. Armstrong, Macartney, & Ogle's Irish Nisi Prius Reports

Arms.Tr. Armstrong's Limerick Trials, (Ir.)

Armstrong M & O (Ir) Armstrong, Macartney, & Ogle's Irish Nisi Prius Reports

Arn. • Arnold's English Common Pleas Reports (1838-39)
  • Arnot's Criminal Trials (1536-1784) (Sc.)
  • Arnould on Marine Insurance

Arn.El.Cas. Arnold's Election Cases (Eng.)

Arn.Ins. Arnould on Marine Insurance

Arn.Mun.Cor. Arnold's Municipal Corporations

Arn. & H. Arnold & Hodges Queen's Bench Reports (1840-41) (Eng.)

Arn. & H.B.C. Arnold & Hodges' Bail Court Reports (Eng.)

Arn. & Hod. Arnold and Hodges' English Queen's Bench Reports

Arn. & Hod.B.C. Arnold & Hodges' English Bail Court Reports

Arn. & Hod.P.C. Arnold & Hodges' Practice Cases (Eng.)

Arn. & Hod.Pr.Cas. Arnold & Hodges' Practice Cases, English

Arnold Arnold's Common Pleas Reports (Eng.)

Arnold & H Arnold & Hodges Queen's Report (Eng.)

Arnot Cr.C. Arnot's Criminal Cases, Scotland. (1536-1784)

Arrang. Arrangement

Art. Article

Artic.Cleri Articuli Cleri (Articles of the Clergy)

Artic.sup.Chart. Articuli super Chartas (Articles upon the charters)

arts. articles

Arun.Mines Arundell on the law of Mines

Ash. Ashmead Pennsylvania Reports, 1808-1841

Ashe Ashe's Tables to the Year Books, Coke's Reports, or Dyer's Reports

Ashm. Ashmead Pennsylvania Reports, 1808-1841

Ashm. (Pa.) Ashmead Pennsylvania Reports, 1808-1841

Ashton. Ashton's Reports, vols. 9-12 Opinions of the United States Attorneys General

Ashurst • Ashurst's Paper Books, Lincoln's Inn Library
• Ashurst's manuscript Reports, printed in vol. 2, Chitty

Ashurst MS. • Ashurst's Paper Books, Lincoln's Inn Library
• Ashurst's Manuscript Reports, printed in vol. 2, Chitty

Asp. Aspinall's Maritime Cases (1871-1940) (Eng.)

Asp.Cas. Aspinall's Maritime Cases (1871-1940) (Eng.)

Asp.M.C. Aspinall's Maritime Cases (1871-1940) (Eng.)

Asp.M.L.C. Aspinall's Maritime Law Cases (1871-1940) (Eng.)

Asp.Mar.L.Cas.(Eng.) Aspinall's Maritime Law Cases (1871-1940) (Eng.)

Asp.Mar.Law Cas. Aspinall's Maritime Law Cases (1871-1940) (Eng.)

Aspin. Aspinall's Maritime Cases (1871-1940) (Eng.)

Ass. Liber Assissarum or Pleas of the Crown (Book of Assizes), Pt. 5 of Year Books (1327-77)

Ass.Tax. Assessed Taxes (Decisions of Judges)

Assd. Assigned

Assem. Assembly, State Legislature

Assn. Association

Asso & Man. Asso & Manuel's Institutes of Spanish Civil Law

assoc. associate

asst. assistant

Ast.Ent. Aston's Entries, 1673

At. Atlantic Reporter

Atch. Atchison, English Navigation and Trade Reports

Atch.E.C. Atcheson's Election Cases. (Eng.)

Ath. State Athletic Commission

Ath.Mar.Set. Atherley on Marriage Settlements

Atk. • Atkinson's Quarter Sessions Records, Yorkshire (Eng.)
• Atkyns' English Chancery Reports (1736-55)

Atk.P.T. Atkyn's Parliamentary Tracts

Atk.Sher. Atkinson on Sheriffs

Atkinson Atkinson's Law of Solicitors' Liens. 1905

Atl. Atlantic

Atl.2d Atlantic Reporter, Second Series (West)

Atl.Mo. Atlantic Monthly

Atl.R. Atlantic Reporter

Atl.Rep. Atlantic Reporter

Atom. Atomic

Atom.En.L.Rep.CCH. Atomic Energy Law Reporter (CCH)

Atomic Energy L.J. Atomic Energy Law Journal

Att.Gen.A.G. Attorney-General

atty. attorney

Atty.Gen. Attorney General

Atty.Gen.Op. Attorney General's Opinions

Atty.Gen.Op.N.Y. Attorney-Generals' Opinions, New York

Att'y.Gen.Rep. United States Attorneys General's Reports

Atw. Atwater's Reports (vol. 1 Minnesota)

Atwater. Atwater's Reports, vol. 1 Minnesota

Auch. Auchinleck's Manuscript Cases, Scotch Court of Session

Auck.U.L.Rev. Auckland University Law Review

Auct.Reg. & L.Chron. Auction Register & Law Chronicle

Aud. Audit; Auditor

Aug. August

Aul.Gell.Noct.Att. Auli Gellii Noctes Atticae

Ault. Court Rolls of Ramsey Abbey (1928) (Eng.)

Aus. Austria

Aust. • Austin's English County Court Cases (1867-69)
• Australia
• Austria

Aust.Bankr.Cas. Australian Bankruptcy Cases

Aust.Jur. ● Austin's Lectures on Jurisprudence
    ● Australian Jurist

Aust.Jur.Abr. Austin's Lectures on Jurisprudence, abridged

Aust.K.A. Austin's Kandran Appeals (Ceylon)

Aust.L.J. Australian Law Journal

Aust.L.T. Australian Law Times

Aust.Yearbook Int.L. Austrailian Yearbook of International Law

Austin Austin's Reports (Ceylon)

Austin C.C. Austin's English County Court Reports

Austin (Ceylon). Austin's Ceylon Reports

Austl. Australia

Austl.Argus L.R. Austrialian Argus Law Reports

Austl.Bankr.Cas. Australian Bankruptcy Cases

Austl.Com.J. Austrialian Commercial Journal

Austl.J.For.Sci. Australian Journal of Forensic Sciences

Austl.Jur.R. Australian Jurist Reports (1870-1874)

Austl.L.J. Australian Law Journal

Austl.L.J.Rep. Australian Law Journal Reports

Austl.Stat.R.Consol. Statutory Rules, Consolidation, Australian Parliament

Austl.Tax Australian Tax Decisions

Austl.Y.B.Int'l L. Australian Yearbook of International Law

Austr.B.C. Australian Bankrupts' Cases

Austr.C.L.R. Austrialia, Commonwealth Law Rep.

Austr.Jur. Australian Jurist

Austr.L.J. Australian Law Journal

Austr.L.T. Australian Law Times

Austr.Tax D. Australian Tax Decisions

Auth. Authorities; Authority

Auto. Automobile

Auto.Cas. Automobile Cases (CCH)

Auto.Cas.2d Automobile Cases, Second Series (CCH)

Auto.Ins.Cas. Automobile Insurance Cases (CCH)

Auto.L.Rep. Automobile Law Reporter (CCH)

Av. Aviation

Av.Cas. Aviation Cases (CCH)

Av.L.Rep. Aviation Law Reporter (CCH)

Ave. Avenue

Averbach Acci.Cas. Averbach on Handling Accident Cases

Aviation Q. United States Aviation Quarterly

Ayl.Pan. Ayliffe's Pandect of the Roman Civil Law

Ayl.Pand. Ayliffe's Pandect of the Roman Civil Law

Ayl.Par. Ayliffe's Parergon Juris Canonici Anglicani (1726-1734)

Ayliffe. Ayliffe's Pandects; Ayliffe's Parergon Juris Canonici Angelicani

Ayliffe Pererg. See Ayliffe

Ayr Ary's Registration Cases (Sc.)

Ayr & Wig. Ayr & Wigton's Registration Cases (Sc.)

Az. ● Arizona
    ● Arizona Reports

Az.A. Arizona Court of Appeals Reports

Az.L. Arizona Law Review

Az.L.R. Arizona Law Review

Az.Mar.Law. Azuni's Maritime Law

Azuni Mar.Law Azuni on Maritime Law

B

B.
- Bar
- Barber's Gold Law (S. Africa)
- Barbour's N.Y. Reports
- Baron
- Beavan's Rolls Court Reports (1838-66) (Eng.)
- Boston
- Budget
- Bulgarian
- Common Bench
- Indian Law Reports, Bombay Series Weekly Law Bulletin (Ohio)

B.A.Bull.L.A. Bar Assn. Bulletin, Los Angeles

BAE Bureau of Agricultural Economics

BAG Bundesarbeitsgericht--Federal Supreme Labour Court (Ger)

B.A.I. Bureau of Animal Industry Docket

B.A.I.M.R. U.S. Bureau of Animal Industry. Monthly Record

BAJI. California Jury Instructions, Civil

BASF The Bar Association of San Francisco

B.Bar Bench & Bar

B.C.
- Bail Court
- Bankruptcy Cases
- British Columbia Law Reports (Canada)

B.C.A. Board of Contract Appeals Decisions

B.C. Branch Lectures British Columbia Branch Lectures

B.C.C.
- Bail Court Reports, Sanders & Cole (Eng.)
- Bail Court Cases Lowndes & Maxwell (1852-54) (Eng.)
- Brown's Chancery Cases (Eng.)
- British Columbia Reports

B.C.Ind.Com'l.'L.Rev. Boston College Industrial and Commercial Law Review

B.C.Ind. & Com.L.Rev. Boston College Industrial and Commercial Law Review

B.C.L.
- Bachelor of Civil Law
- Bachelor of Cannon Law

BCLB Bituminous Coal Labor Board

B.C.(N.S.W.) New South Wales Bankruptcy Cases (1890-99)

B.C.R.
- Bail Court Reports, Sanders & Cole (1846-47) (Eng.)
- Bail Court Cases, Lowndes & Maxwell (1852-54) (Eng.)
- Brown's Chancery Cases (1778-94) (Eng.)
- British Columbia Reports

B.C.Rep.
- Bail Court Reports, Sanders & Cole (Eng.)
- Bail Court Cases, Lowndes & Maxwell (Eng.)
- Brown's Chancery Cases (Eng.)
- British Columbia Reports

B.C.Rev.Stat. British Columbia Revised Statutes (Canada)

B.C.Stat. British Columbia Statutes (Canada)

B.Ch. Barbour's Chancery Reports, New York

BDC Bureau of Domestic Commerce

B.D. & O. Blackham, Dundas, & Osborne's Nisi Prius Reports (1846-48) (Ir.)

B.E. "Baron of the Court of Exchequer"

BEC Bureau of Employees' Compensation

BENELUX Belgium, Netherlands, Luxembourg Economic Union

BEPQ Bureau of Entomology and Plant Quarantine

BES Bureau of Employment Security

BEW Board of Economic Welfare

BEWT Bureau of East-West Trade

B.F. bonum factum, a good or proper act, deed, or decree; signifies "approved"

BFH Bundesfinanzhof--Federal Supreme Fiscal Court (Ger)

BFHE Entscheidungen des Bundesfinanzhofs (Germany)

b.f.p. bona fide purchaser

B.F.U.A. Banking, Finance and Urban Affairs

BG Bundesgericht--Federal Supreme Court

B.G. British Guiana Law Reports

BGB Burgerliches Gesetzbuch (German Civil Code)

BGE Entscheidungen des Schweizerischen Bundesgerichtes (Switzerland)

BGH Bundesgerichtshof--Federal Supreme Court (Ger)

B.G.L. Bachelor of General Laws

B.G.L.R. British Guiana Law Reports (Old and New Series)

B.H.C. Bombay High Court Reports (India)

BHUA Banking, Housing and Urban Affairs

BIA Bureau of Indian Affairs

BIB Board of International Broadcasting

BIC Bureau of International Commerce

BIEPR Bureau of International Economic Policy and Research

BIS Bank for International Settlements

BIT Business insurance trust

B.J.A.L. British Journal of Administrative Law

B.Jur. Baccalaureus Juris

BKA Bundeskartellamt--Federal Cartel Office (Germany quasijudicial administrative)

b/l bill of lading

BL Business Lawyer

BLEU Belgium-Luxembourg Economic Union

B.L.J. Burma Law Journal (India)

BLM Bureau of Land Management

B.L.P.,L. & M.Cas. Brainard's Legal Precedents in Land and Mining Cases, Washington

B.L.R.
- Bahamas Law Reports
- Barbados Law Reports
- Baylor Law Review
- Bengal Law Reports, High Court (India)
- Bermuda Law Reports

B.L.R.A.C. Bengal Law Reports, Appeal Cases

B.L.R.P.C. Bengal Law Rep. Privy Council

B.L.R.Suppl.Vol. Bengal Law Reports, Supplemental Volume, Full Bench Rulings

BLS
- Bureau of Labor Statistics
- Business Lawyer, Special Issue

B.L.T.
- Baltimore Law Transcript
- Burma Law Times

B.M.
- Burrow's Reports tempore Mansfield (1756-72) (Eng.)
- Ben Monroe's Reports, Kentucky
- Moore's Reports (Eng.)

B.Mon. Ben Monroe's Kentucky Supreme Court Reports (1840-1857)

B.Mon.(Ky.) Ben Monroe's Reports, Kentucky (vols. 40-57)

B.Monr.
- Burrow's Reports tempore Mansfield (Eng.)
- Ben Monroe's Reports, Kentucky
- Moore's Reports (Eng.)

B.Moore. Bayly Moore, English Common Pleas Reports

B.N.A. Bureau of National Affairs, Inc. Washington, D.C.

B.N.A.Act. British North America Act

BNA Sec.Reg. Securities Regulation & Law Report

B.N.B. Bracton's Note Book. (Temp. Henry III)

B.N.C.
- Bingham, New Cases, English Common Pleas (1834-40)
- Brooke, New Cases, English King's Bench (1515-58)
- Busbee, North Carolina Law Reports (vols. 44,45 North Carolina)

BNDD Bureau of Narcotics and Dangerous Drugs

B.N.P. Buller's Nisi Prius

BOM Bureau of Mines

BP Benefit Principles

BPA Bonneville Power Administration

B.P.B. Buller's Paper Book, Lincoln's Inn Library

B.P.C. Brown's Cases in Parliament (1701-1800)

B.P.L. Bott's Poor Law Cases (1560-1833) (Eng.)

B.P.L.Cas. Bott's Poor Law Cases (1560-1833)

B.P.N.R. Bosanquet & Puller's New Reports, English Common Pleas (1804-07)

B.P.R. Brown's Parliamentary Reports (Eng.)

B.Proc. Baccalaureus Procurationis

BPS Bureau of Product Safety

BR Board of Review

B.R.
- Baltimore City Reports
- Bancus Regis, or King's Bench
- Bancus Reginae, or Queen's Bench
- Bankruptcy Reports
- Bankruptcy Register
- Board of Review, U.S. Army (1929-1949)
- Brooklyn Law Review (N.Y.)

B.R.A. Butterworth's Rating Appeals (1913-31) (Eng.)

B.R.(Army) Board of Review (Army)

B.R.C. British Ruling Cases

B.R.H. Cases in King's Bench tempore Hardwicke (1733-38) (Eng.)

B.R.-J.C.(Army) Board of Review and Judicial Council of the Army

BRTA Bureau of Resources and Trade Assistance

B.Reg. Bankrupt Register

B/S Bill of sale

B.S.
- Bancus Superior, that is, upper bench
- Brown's Suppt. to Morison's Dictionary of Decisions, Court of Sessions (1622-1780) (Sc.)

B.S.E.I.U. Building Service Employees' International Union

BSSUI Benefit Series Service, Unemployment Insurance (U.S. Dept. of Labor)

BSozG Bundessozialgericht--Federal Supreme Social Security Court (Ger)

B.T.A. United States Board of Tax Appeals Reports

B.T.A.C.C.H. Board of Tax Appeals Decisions (CCH)

B.T.A.P.H. Board of Tax Appeals Decisions (P-H)

B.T.R.
- Brewing Trade Review Licensing Law Reports (Eng.)
- British Tax Review

B.T.R.L.R. Brewing Trade Review Law Reports

B.Tr. Bishop's Trial

B.U.L.Rev. Boston University Law Review

BUSL Boston University School of Law

B/V Book value

BVerfG Bundesverfassungsgericht--Federal Constitutional Court (Ger.)

BVerwG Bundesverwaltungsgericht--Federal Supreme Administrative Court (Ger.)

B.W.C.C. Butterworth's Workmen's Compensation Cases (1908-49) (Eng.)

B.W.C.C. (Eng.) Butterworth's Workmen's Compensation Cases (1908-49)

B.Y. Brigham Young

B. & A.
- Barnewell & Adolphus' English King's Bench Reports
- Barnewell & Alderson's English King's Bench Reports (1817-22)
- Barron & Arnold's English Election Cases (1843-46)
- Barron & Austin's English Election Cases (1842)
- Banning & Arden's Patent Reports (U.S.)

B. & Ad. Barnewall & Adolphus' English King's Bench Reports (1830-34)

B. & Ald. Barnewall & Alderson's English King's Bench Reports

B. & Arn. Barron & Arnold's English Election Cases (1843-46)

B. & Aust. Barron & Austin's English Election Cases (1842)

B. & B.
- Ball & Beatty Chancery Reports (1807-14) (Ir.)

- Bench & Bar (periodical)
- Bowler & Bowers, vols. 2, 3 U.S. Comptroller's Decisions
- Broderip & Bingham's Common Pleas Reports (1819-22) (Eng.)

B. & Bar Bench & Bar

B. & C. Barnewall & Cresswell's English King's Bench Reports (1822-30)

B. & C.Comp. Bellinger and Cotton's Annotated Codes and Statutes (Or.)

B. & C.Pr.Cas. British & Colonial Prize Cases (1914-22) (Eng.)

B. & C.R. Reports of Bankruptcy & Companies Winding up Cases (1918-41) (Eng.)

B. & D. Benloe & Dalison Common Pleas Reports (Eng.)

B. & F. Brodrick & Fremantle, English Ecclesiastical Reports (1840-64)

B. & G. Brownlow and Goldesborough (N.P. Reports) (1569-1624) (Eng.)

B. & H. Blatchford & Howland's United States District Court Reports

B. & H.Cr.Cas. Bennett & Heard Leading Criminal Cases (Eng.)

B. & H.Dig. Bennett & Heard's Massachusetts Digest

B. & H. Lead. Ca. Bennett & Heard's Leading Criminal Cases (Eng.)

B. & H.Lead.Cas. Bennett & Heard Leading Criminal Cases (Eng.)

B. & I. Bankruptcy and Insolvency Cases (1853-55) (Eng.)

B. & L. Browning & Lushington's Admiralty Reports (1864-65) (Eng.)

B. & L.Pr. Bullen & Leake's Precedents of Pleading

B. & M. Brown & Macnamara Railway Cases (Eng.)

B. & Mac. Browne and Macnamara Railway Cases (Eng.)

B. & O.Bd. of Rev. Selected Decisions of the Board of Revenue, Bihar and Orissa

B. & P. Bosanquet & Puller, English Common Pleas, Exchequer and House of Lords Reports (1796-1804)

B. & P.N.R. Bosanquet & Puller's New Reports (1804-07) (Eng.)

B. & S.
- Best & Smith, English Queen's Bench Reports (1861-70)
- Beven and Siebel's Reports (Ceylon)

B. & T. Bank and Trust

BUC Bureau of Unemployment Compensation

B. & V. Beling & Vanderstraaten's Reports, Ceylon

Ba.L.R. University of Baltimore Law Review

Ba. & Be. Ball & Beatty's Irish Chancery Reports

Bab. Auc. Babington's Law of Auctions

Bab. Set-off. Babington's Law of Set-off

Bac.Ab. Bacon's Abridgment (1736-1832)

Bac.Abr. Bacon's Abridgment (1736-1832) (Eng.)

Bac.Aph. Bacon's (Sir Francis) Aphorisms

Bac.Aphorisms Bacon's (Sir Francis) Aphorisms

Bac.Ben.Soc. Bacon on Benefit Societies and Life Insurance

Bac.Ca. Bacon's Case of Treason, 1641

Bac.Chanc. Bacon's Chancery Cases (Eng.)

Bac.Comp.Arb. Bacon's Complete Arbitration

Bac.Dig. Bacon's Georgia Digest

Bac.Gov. Bacon on Government

Bac.Ins. Bacon on Benefit Societies and Life Insurance

Bac. Law Tr. Bacon's Law Tracts

Bac.Law Tracts Bacon's Law Tracts

Bac. Lease. Bacon on Leases and Terms of Years

Bac.Lib.Reg. (or T.E.) Bacon's Liber Regis, vel Thesaurus Rerum Ecclesiasticarum

Bac. Max. Bacon's Maxims of the Law

Bac.Read.Uses. Bacon (Sir Francis), Reading upon the Statute of Uses

Bac.Rep. Bacon's Decisions (Ritchie) (Eng.)

Bac.St.Uses. Bacon (Sir Francis), Reading upon the Statute of Uses

Bac.Tr. Bacon's (Sir Francis) Law Tracts

Bac.Uses. Bacon's Essay on Uses

Bac.Works. Bacon's (Sir Francis), Works

Bach. Bach's Reports (vols. 19-21 Montana Reports)

Bacon
- Bacon's Abridgment
- Bacon's Aphorisms
- Bacon's Complete Arbitrator
- Bacon's Elements of the Common Law
- Bacon on Government
- Bacon's Law Tracts
- Bacon on Leases and Terms of Years
- Bacon's Maxims
- Bacon on Uses

Bag. & Har. Bagley & Harman (Cal.)

Bagl. (Cal.) Bagley's Reports (Vols. 16-19 California)

Bagl. & H. Bagley & Harman's Reports (Vols. 17-19 California)

Bagl. & Har. Bagley & Harman's Reports (Vols. 17-19 California)

Bagl. & Har. (Cal.) Bagley & Harman's Reports (Vols. 17-19 California)

Bah.L.R. Bahamas Law Reports (1900-06)

Bai. Bailey's Law Reports, South Carolina

Bai.Eq. Bailey's Equity Reports, South Carolina

Bail. Bailey's Law Reports, South Carolina (1828-1832)

Bail C.C. Lowndes & Maxwell, English Bail Court Cases (1852-54)

Bail Cr.Rep. Lowndes & Maxwell, English Bail Court Cases

Bail Ct.Cas. Lowndes & Maxwell English Bail Court Cases (1852-54)

Bail Ct.R. Bail Court Reports, Saunders and Cole. (1846-48)

Bail Ct.Rep.
- Saunders & Cole, English Bail Court Reports (1846-48)

- Lowndes & Maxwell, English Bail Court Cases (1852-54)

Bail.Dig. Bailey's North Carolina Digest

Bail.Eq. Bailey's Equity Reports (South Carolina 1830-1831)

Bail.Eq. (S.C.) Bailey's Equity Reports, South Carolina (1830-1831)

Bail.L. Bailey's Law Reports, South Carolina

Bail.L.(S.C.) Bailey's Law Reports, South Carolina

Baild. Baildon's Select Cases in Chancery (Selden Society Publication, Vol. 10)

Bailey Bailey's Equity or Law Reports, South Carolina

Bailey, Ch. Bailey's Chancery Reports South Carolina

Bailey, Dict. Nathan Bailey's English Dictionary

Bailey Eq. Bailey's Equity Reports, South Carolina Court of Appeals

Bailey, Mast.Liab. Bailey's Law of Master's Liability for Injuries to Servant

Baill.Dig. Baillie's Digest of Mohammedan Law

Bainb.Mines Bainbridge on Mines and Minerals

Baker, Quar. Baker's Law of Quarantine

Bal.
- Balance
- Balasingham's Reports, Ceylon

Bal.Ann.Codes Ballinger's Annotated Codes & Statutes (Wash.)

Bal.R.D. Baldeva Ram Dave, Privy Council Judgment (India)

Balas. Balasingham's Supreme Court Reports (Ceylon)

Balas.N.C. Balasingham's Notes of Cases (Ceylon)

Bald.
- Baldwin's United States Circuit Court Reports
- Baldus (Commentator on the Code)
- Baldasseroni (on Maritime Law)

Bald.App. Appendix to 11 Peters, U.S. Reports

Bald.C.C. ● Baldwin's United States Circuit Court Reports
● Baldus (Commentator on the Code)
● Baldasseroni (on Maritime Law)

Bald.Const. (or Op.) Baldwin, View of the United States Constitution with Opinions

Bald.Pat.Cas. Baldwin's Patent, Copyright, Trade-Mark Cases (U.S.)

Bald.Pat.Etc.Cas. Baldwin Patent, Copyright, Trade-mark Cases (1930) 10 vols.

Bald.U.S.Sup.Ct.Rep. United States Supreme Court Reports, Photo reproduction set by Baldwin

Baldw. ● Baldwin's United States Circuit Court Reports
● Baldus (Commentator on the Code)
● Baldasseroni (on Maritime Law)

Baldw.Dig. Baldwin's Connecticut Digest

Baldwin Baldwin on Bankruptcy

Balf. Balfour's Practice, Laws of Scotland (1754)

Balf.Pr. Balfour's Practice, Laws of Scotland

Ball. Ballard's Somerton Court Rolls (Oxford Arch. Soc. No. 50) (Eng.)

Ball.Lim. Ballantine on Limitations

Ball & B. Ball & Beatty's Irish Chancery Reports (1807-14)

Ball & B. (Ir.) Ball & Beatty's Irish Chancery Reports (1807-14)

Ball & Beatty Ball & Beatty's Irish Chancery Reports (1807-14)

Ballentine's Law Dict.
● Ballentine's Law Dictionary
● Ballentine's Self Pronouncing Law Dictionary

Ballinger's Ann.Codes & St. Ballinger's Annotated Codes and Statues, Washington

Balt. Baltimore

Balt.C.Rep. Baltimore City Reports

Balt.L.T. Baltimore Law Transcript

Balt.L.Tr. Baltimore Law Transcript

Bamber. Report of mining cases decided by the Railway and Canal Commission

Ban. & A. Banning & Arden's Patent Cases, U.S.

Banc.Sup. Upper Bench

Bang.L.R. Bangala Law Reporter (India)

Bank. ● Bankruptcy
● Bankruptcy Court
● International Bank for Reconstruction and Development

Bank.C. Banking Code

Bank.Cas. Banking Cases

Bank.Ct.Rep. ● Bankrupt Court Reporter (New York)
● The American Law Times Bankruptcy Reports

Bank.Gaz. Bankruptcy Gazette

Bank.I. Bankter's Institutes of Scottish Law

Bank.Inst. Bankter's Institutes of Scottish Law

Bank.L.J. Banking Law Journal

Bank.Mag. Banker's Magazine

Bank.Reg. Bankruptcy Register

Bank.Rep. American Law Times Bankruptcy Rep.

Bank. & Ins. Bankruptcy and Insolvency Reports (1853-55) (Eng.)

Bank. & Ins.R. Bankruptcy and Insolvency Reports (1853-55) (Eng.)

Banker's L.J. Banker's Law Journal

Bankr. Bankruptcy

Bankr.Act. Bankruptcy Act

Bankr.Form Bankruptcy Forms

Bankr.L.Rep. Bankruptcy Law Reporter (CCH)

Bankr.Reg. National Bankruptcy Register (N.Y.)

Banks. Banks' Reports (vols. 1-5 Kansas)

Bankt. MacDouall's (Lord Bankton) Institute of Laws of Scotland. 3 vols. (1751-53)

Bann. Bannister's Reports, English Common Pleas

Bann.Br. Bannister's edition of O. Bridgman's English Common Pleas Reports

Bann. & A. Banning & Arden's Patent Cases (U.S.)

Bann. & A.Pat.Cas. Banning & Arden's Patent Cases (U.S.)

Bann. & Ard. Banning & Arden, Patent Cases (U.S.)

Bar. ● Barnardiston's English King's Bench Reports
- ● Barnardiston's Chancery
- ● Bar Reports in all the Courts (Eng.)
- ● Barbour's Supreme Court Reports (New York)
- ● Barrows' Reports (vol. 18 Rhode Island)

Bar Bull.(N.Y.County L.A.) Bar Bulletin, New York County Lawyers' Association

Bar.Ch. Barnardiston's English Chancery Reports

Bar.Chy. Barnardiston's English Chancery Reports

Bar.Eq. Barton's Suit in Equity

Bar Ex.Jour. Bar Examination Journal (London)

Bar Exam. Bar Examiner

Bar Int.Pr.R. Bar, Das Internationale Privat-und-Strafrecht

Bar.Mag. Barrington's Magna Charta

Bar.N. Barnes' Notes, English Common Pleas Reports

Bar.Obs.St. Barrington's Observations upon the Statutes from Magna Charta to 21 James I

Bar Re. Bar Reports in all Courts (1865-71) (Eng.)

Bar Rep. Bar Reports (see Law Times Reports, v. 1-12) (1865-71)

Bar. & Al. Barnewall & Alderson's English King's Bench Reports

Bar. & Arn. Barron & Arnold, Election Cases (1843-46) (Eng.)

Bar. & Au. Barron & Austin's English Election Cases (1842)

Bar. & Aust. Barron & Austin's English Election Cases (1842)

Bar. & Cr. Barnewall & Cresswell's English King's Bench Reports

Bar & Leg.W. Bar & Legal World (Eng.)

Barb. ● Barber's Gold Law (S. Africa)
- ● Barber's Reports (vols. 14-24 Arkansas)
- ● Barbour's Supreme Court Reports (N.Y.)

Barb.Abs. Barbour's Abstracts of Chancellor's Decisions (N.Y.)

Barb.App.Dig. Barber's Digest (N.Y.)

Barb.Ark. Barber's Reports (vols. 14-24 Arkansas)

Barb.Ch. Barbour's Chancery Reports (N.Y.)

Barb.Ch.(N.Y.) Barbour's Chancery Reports (N.Y.)

Barb.Ch.Pr. Barbour's Chancery Practice (N.Y.)

Barb.Cr.Law Barbour's Criminal Law

Barb.Cr.P. Barbour's Criminal Pleadings

Barb.Dig. Barber's Digest of Kentucky

Barb.L.R. Barbados Law Reports

Barb.S.C. Barbour's Supreme Court Reports (N.Y.)

Barb. & C.Ky.St. Barbour and Carroll's Kentucky Statutes

Barbe. Barber's Reports, Arkansas

Barber ● Barber's Gold Law (S. Africa)
- ● Barber's Reports (vols. 14-42 Arkansas)

Barc.Dig. Barclay's Missouri Digest

Barc.Dig.Law Sc. Barclay's Digest of the Law of Scotland

Barn. ● Barnardiston's English King's Bench Reports
- ● Barnes' English Common Pleas Reports
- ● Barnfield's Reports (vols. 19-20 Rhode Island)

Barn.C. Barnardiston's Reports, Chancery (1740-41)

Barn.Ch. Barnardiston's English Chancery Reports (1740-41)

Barn.K.B. Barnardiston, King's Bench Reports (1726-34) (Eng.)

Barn.No. Barnes' Note of Cases, English Common Pleas

Barn.Pr.M. Barnstaple, Printed Minutes and Proceedings

Barn. & Ad. Barnewall & Adolphus, King's Bench (vols. 109, 110 Eng. Reprint)

Barn & Ad.(Eng.) Barnewall & Adolphus, King's Bench (vols. 109, 110 Eng. Reprint)

Barn. & Adol. Barnewall and Adolphus' English King's Bench Reports (1830-34)

Barn. & Ald. Barnewall & Alderson, English King's Bench Reports (vol. 106 Eng. Reprint)

Barn. & Ald.(Eng.) Barnewall & Alderson, English King's Bench Reports (vol. 106 Eng. Reprint)

Barn. & C. Barnewall & Cresswell's English King's Bench Reports (vols. 107-109 Eng. Reprint)

Barn. & C.(Eng.) Barnewall & Cresswell's English King's Bench Reports (vols. 107-109 Eng. Reprint)

Barn. & Cr. Barnewall & Cresswell's English King's Bench Reports (vols. 107-109 Eng. Reprint)

Barn. & Cress. Barnewall & Cresswell's English King's Bench Reports (vols. 107-109 Eng. Reprint)

Barnard. Barnardiston, K.B. (1726-34)

Barnard. Barnardiston, King's Bench Reports (1726-34) (Eng.)

Barnard.Ch. Barnardiston's English Chancery Reports (27 Eng. Reprint)

Barnard.Ch.(Eng.) Barnardiston's English Chancery Reports (27 Eng. Reprint)

Barnard.Ch.Rep. Barnardiston's Reports, Chancery (1740-41)

Barnard.K.B. Barnardiston's King's Bench Reports (94 Eng. Reprint)

Barnardiston C.C. Barnardiston's Chancery Cases (1740-1741)

Barnes Barnes' Notes of Cases of Practice in Common Pleas (94 Eng. Reprint)

Barnes, N.C. Barnes' Notes of Cases of Practice in Common Pleas (94 Eng. Reprint)

Barnes Notes Barnes' Notes of Cases of Practice in Common Pleas (94 Eng. Reprint)

Barnes Notes (Eng.) Barnes' Notes of Cases of Practice in Common Pleas (94 Eng. Reprint)

Barnes's Fed.Code. Barnes's Federal Code

Barnet. Barnet, English Central Criminal Courts Reports (vols. 27-92)

Barnf. & S. Barnfield and Stiness' Reports (vol. 20 Rhode Island)

Barnw.Dig. Barnwall's Digest of the Year Books

Baroda L.R. Baroda Law Reports (India)

Barr. ● Barr's Reports (vols. 1-10, Pennsylvania)
   ● The Barrister
   ● Barrows' Reports (vol. 18, Rhode Island)

Barr.Ch.Pr. Barroll Chancery Practice (Md.)

Barr.MSS. Barradall Manuscript Reports (Va.)

Barr.Obs.St. Barrington's Observations on the Statutes.

Barr.(Pa.) Barr's Reports (vols. 1-10, Pennsylvania)

Barr.St. Barrington's Observations upon the Statutes from Magna Charta to 21 James I

Barr. & Arn. Barron & Arnold's English Election Cases

Barr. & Aus. Barron & Austin's English Election Cases

Barring.Obs.St. Barrington's Observations upon the Statutes from Magna Charta to 21 James I

Barring.St. Barrington's Observations upon the Statutes from Magna Charta to 21 James I

Barron Barony of Urie Court Records (1604-1747) (Sc.)

Barron Mir. Barron's Mirror of Parliament

Barron & H.Fed.Pr. & Proc. Barron & Holtzoff's Federal Practice & Procedure

Barrows Barrows' Reports (vol. 18, Rhode Island)

Barrows(R.I.) Barrows' Reports (vol. 18 Rhode Island)

Bart.El.Cas. Bartlett's Congressional Election Cases

Bart.Eq. Barton's Suit in Equity

Bart.L.Pr. Barton's Law Practice

Bartholoman Bartholoman's Reports, Yorkshire Lent Assize, March 9, 1911 (Eng.)

Bat.Dig. Battle's Digest, North Carolina

Bat.Stat. Battle's Revised Statutes of North Carolina, 1873

Bates' Ann.St. Bates' Annotated Revised Statutes, Ohio

Bates' Dig. Bates' Digest, Ohio

Bates, Part. Bates' Law of Partnership

Bateson Leicester Records (Municipal Courts 1103-1603) (Eng.)

Batt. Batty's Irish King's Bench Reports (1825-26)

Batts' Ann.St. Batts' Annotated Revised Civil Statutes, Texas

Batts' Rev.St. Batts' Annotated Revised Civil Statutes, Tex.

Batty (Ir.) Batty's Irish King's Bench Reports

Bax. Baxter's Reports (vols. 60-68 Tennessee)

Baxt.(Tenn.) Baxter's Reports (vols. 60-68 Tennessee)

Baxter Baxter's Reports (vols. 60-68 Tennessee)

Bay Bay's Reports (1-3, 5-8 Missouri) Bay's South Carolina Reports (1783-1804)

Bayley, Bills Bayley on Bills

Baylles, Sur. Baylles on Sureties and Guarantors

Baylor L.Rev. Baylor Law Review

Bd. Board

Bd. of Rev. Board of Review

Bd.Cont.App.Dec. Board of Contract Appeals Decisions

Bea. Beavan (1838-66)

Bea C.E. Beames' Costs in Equity

Bea.Costs (or C.E.) Beames' Costs in Equity

Bea.Eq.Pl. Beames' Equity Pleading

Bea. Ne Ex. Beames on the Writ of Ne Exeat Regno

Bea.Ord. Beames' Orders in Chancery (Eng.)

Bea.Pl.Eq. Beames' Pleas in Equity

Beach, Contrib.Neg. Beach on Contributory Negligence

Beach, Eq.Prac. Beach's Modern Practice in Equity

Beach,Inj. Beach on Injunctions

Beach,Mod.Eq.Jur. Beach's Commentaries on Modern Equity Jurisprudence

Beach,Priv.Corp. Beach on Private Corporations

Beach,Pub.Corp. Beach on Public Corporations

Beach,Rec. Beach on the Law of Receivers

Beames,Glanv. Beames' Glanville

Beas. ● Beasley's New Jersey Chancery Reports

      ● Beasley's New Jersey Equity Reports (vols. 12-13)

Beasl. Beasley, New Jersey Equity Reports

Beat. Beatty's Irish Chancery Reports (1814-36)

Beatt. Beatty's Irish Chancery Reports (1814-36)

Beatty Beatty's Irish Chancery Reports (1814-36)

Beatty Ir.Ch. Beatty's Irish Chancery Reports (1814-36)

Beav. Beavan's English Rolls Court Reports (vols. 48-55 Eng. Reprint)

Beav.(Eng.) Beavan's English Rolls Court Reports (vols. 48-55 Eng. Reprint)

Beav.O.C. Beavan's Ordines Cancellariae

Beav.R. & C. Beavan, Railway & Canal Cases (Eng.)

Beav.R. & C.Cas. English Railway and Canal Cases, by Beavan and others

Beav. & W. Beavan and Walford's Railway Cases (1846)

Beav. & W.Ry.Cas. Beavan & Walford's Railway & Canal Cases (Eng.)

Beav. & Wal.Ry.Cas. Beavan & Walford's Railway and Canal Cases (Eng.)

Beavan, Ch. Beavan's English Rolls Court Reports

Beaver Beaver County Legal Journal (Pa.)

Beaver Co.L.J.(Pa.) Beaver County Legal Journal (Pennsylvania)

Beaw. Beawes' Lex Mercatoria (Eng.)

Beaw.Lex Mer. Beawes Lex Mercatoria (Eng.)

Beaw.Lex Merc. Beawes' Lex Mercatoria

Beawes' Lex Merc. Meawes' Lex Mercatoria (Eng.)

Bec.Cr. Beccaria on Crimes and Punishments

Beck Beck's Colorado Reports: vols. 12-16 Colorado, and vol. 1 Colorado Court of Appeals

Beck (Colo.) Beck's Colorado Reports: vols. 12-16 Colorado, and vol. 1 Colorado Court of Appeals

Beck, Med.Jur. Beck's Medical Jurisprudence

Bedell Bedell's Reports (163-191 N.Y.)

Bee Bee's United States District Court Reports

Bee Adm. Bee's Admiralty. An Appendix to Bee's District Court Reports

Bee Adm. Bee's Admiralty. An Appendix to Bee's District Court Reports

Bee C.C.R. Bee's Crown Cases Reserved (Eng.)

Beebe Cit. Beebe's Ohio Citations

Behari Revenue Reports of Upper Provinces (India)

Bel. ● Bellewe's English King's Bench Reports (1378-1400)
    ● Belasis' Bombay Reports
    ● Beling's Ceylon Reports
    ● Bellinger's Reports (vols. 4-8 Oregon)

Bel.Ca.t.H.VIII Bellewe's Cases tempore. Henry VIII, Brooke's New Cases (Eng.)

Bel.Prob. Belknap's Probate Law of California

Belg. Belgium

Beling Beling's Ceylon Reports

Beling & Van. Beling & Vanderstraaten's Ceylon Reports

Bell. ● Bell, English Crown Cases Reserved
    ● Bell, Scotch Appeal Cases (1842-50)
    ● Bell, Scotch Session Cases
    ● Bell, Calcutta Reports
    ● Bellewe, English King's Bench Reports
    ● Brooke, New Cases, by Bellewe

● Bellinger, Reports (vols. 4-8 Oregon)

● Bellasis Bombay Reports

Bell (In.) Bell's Reports (India)

Bell.(Or.) Bellinger's Reports (Oregon)

Bell Ap.Ca. Bell's Scotch Appeals

Bell App.Bell (Sc.) House of Lords (1842-50)

Bell App.Cas. Bell's House of Lords Appeal Cases (Sc.)

Bell Arb. Bell's Law of Arbitration in Scotland

Bell C. Bell (Sc.) Court of Session (1790-95)

Bell C.C. ● Bell, English Crown Cases Reserved (vol. 169 Eng. Reprint)
    ● Bellasis, Civil Cases (Bombay)
    ● Bellasis, Criminal Cases (Bombay)

Bell C.C.(Eng.) ● Bell, English Crown Cases Reserved (vol. 169 Eng. Reprint)
    ● Bellasis, Civil Cases (Bombay)
    ● Bellasis, Criminal Cases (Bombay)

Bell C.H.C. Bell's Reports, Calcutta High Court (India)

Bell Cas. Bell's Cases, Scotch Court of Session

Bell.Cas.t.H.VIII Brooke's New Cases (collected by Bellewe)

Bell.Cas.t.Hen.VIII Brooke's New Cases (1515-58)

Bell.Cas.t.R.II Bellewe's King's Bench Reports (1378-1400)

Bell.Cas.t.Rich.II Bellewe's English King's Bench Reports (time of Richard II)

Bell Comm. Bell's Commentaries on the Law of Scotland

Bell Cr.C. ● Bell's English Crown Cases
    ● Beller's Criminal Cases (Bombay)

Bell Cr.Ca.
- Bell's English Crown Cases
- Beller's Criminal Cases (Bombay)

Bell Cr.Cas.
- Bell's English Crown Cases
- Beller's Criminal Cases (Bombay)

Bell Ct.of Sess. R. Bell's Decisions, Court of Session (Sc.)

Bell.Del. Beller's Delineations of Universal Law

Bell Dict. Bell's Dictionary and Digest of the Laws of Scotland

Bell Dict.Dec. Bell, Dictionary of Decisions, Court of Session (Sc.)

Bell fol. Bell's folio Reports, Scotch Court of Session (1794-95)

Bell H.C. Bell's Reports, High Court of Calcutta (India)

Bell H.L. Bell's House of Lords Cases, Scotch Appeal (1842-50) (Eng.)

Bell H.L.Sc. Bell's House of Lords Cases, Scotch Appeals

Bell Med.L.J. Bell's Medico Legal Journal

Bell Oct.(or 8vo.) Bell's octavo Reports Scotch Court of Session (1790-92)

Bell P.C. Bell's Cases in Parliament: Scotch Appeals

Bell Prin. Bell's Principles of the Law of Scotland. 10 editions (1829-99)

Bell Put.Mar. Bell's Putative Marriage Case (Sc.)

Bell Sc.App. Bell's Appeals to House of Lords from Scotland

Bell Sc.App.Cas.(Sc.) Bell, Scotch Appeal Cases

Bell Sc.Cas. Bell's Scotch Court of Sessions Cases

Bell Sc.Dig. Bell's Scottish Digest

Bell Ses.Cas. Bell's Cases in the Scotch Court of Session

Bellas. Bellasis Criminal (or Civil) cases (Bombay)

Bellasis Bombay Sudder Dewanny Adawlut Reports

Bellewe Bellewe's English King's Bench Reports

Bellewe (Eng.) Bellewe's English King's Bench Reports

Bellewe t.H.VIII Brooke's New Cases (collected by Bellewe)

Bellewe's Ca.temp.Hen.VIII Brooke's New Cases (1515-58)

Bellewe's Ca.temp.R.II Bellewe's Richard II (1378-1400)

Bellinger. Bellinger's Reports (vols. 4-8 Oregon)

Bellingh.Tr. Report of Bellingham's Trial

Belli's Mod.Trials Belli's Modern Trials

Bell's Comm.Bell's Commentaries on Laws of Scotland. 7 editions (1800-70)

Bell's Dict. Bell's Dictionary of Decisions (Sc.), Court of Session (1808-32)

Belt Bro. Belt's edition of Brown's Chancery Reports (1778-94)

Belt.Sup. Belt's Supplement to Vesey Senior's English Chancery Reports (1746-56)

Belt.Sup.Ves. Belt's Supplement to Vesey Senior's English Chancery Reports (1746-56)

Belt Supp. Belt's Supplement to Vesey, Sen. (1746-56)

Belt Ves.Sen. Belt's edition of Vesey Senior's English Chancery Reports

Belt's Supp.(Eng.) Belt's Supplement to Vesey Senior's English Chancery Reports (1746-56)

Ben.
- Benedict United States District Reports
- Bengal Law Reports
- Benloe's English Reports, King's Bench and Common Pleas

Ben.Adm. Benedict's American Admiralty Practice

Ben.Adm.Prac. Benedict's Admiralty Practice

Ben.F.B. Full Bench Rulings, High Court, Fort William (Bengal)

Ben.F.I.Cas. Bennett's Fire Insurance Cases

Ben.Ins.Cas. Bennett's Insurance Cases

Ben.Monroe Ben Monroe's Kentucky Reports, vols. 40-57

Ben.Ord. Benevolent Orders

Ben. & D. Benloe and Dalison (1486-1580)

Ben. & Dal. Benloe & Dalison's English Common Pleas Reports

Ben. & H.L.C. Bennett & Heard Leading Criminal Cases (Eng.)

Ben. & S.Dig. Benjamin & Slidell's Louisiana Digest

Bench & B. Bench and Bar (periodical)

Bendl. Bendloe's English Common Pleas (1531-1628)

Bendloe Bendloe's or New Benloe's Reports, English Common Pleas, Edition of 1661

Bened. Benedict, United States District Court Reports

Benedict Benedict's United States District Court Reports

Benedict, Admiralty Benedict on Admiralty

Benef. Beneficiary

Benefit Series,U.C.I.S. U.S. Social Security Board Unemployment Compensation Interpretation Service. Benelit Series

Benet Ct.-M Benet on Military Law and Courts-Martial

Beng.L.R. Bengal Law Reports (India)

Beng.L.R.App.Cas. Bengal Law Reports, Appeal Cases (India)

Beng.L.R.P.C. Bengal Law Reports, Privy Council (India)

Beng.L.R.Supp. Bengal Law Reports, Supp. (India)

Beng.S.D.A. Bengal Sadr Diwani Adalat Cases (India)

Beng.Zillah Decisions of the Zillah Courts, Lower Provinces (India)

Benj.   ● Benjamin on Sales of Personal Property (1868-1955)
       ● Benjamin. New York Annotated Cases

Benj.Chalm.Bills & N. Benjamin's Chalmer's Bills and Notes

Benj.Sa. Benjamin on Sales (1868-1955)

Benj.Sales Benjamin on Sales (1868-1955)

Benl. Benloe's or Bendloe's English King's Bench Reports (73 Eng. Reprint)

Benl.(Eng.) Benloe's or Bendloe's English King's Bench Reports (73 Eng. Reprint)

Benl.in Ashe. Benloe at the end of Ashe's Tables

Benl.in Keil. Benloe or Bendloe in Keilway's Reports

Benl.K.B. Benloe's King's Bench (1531-1628) (Eng.)

Benl.New. Benloe, Reports, English King's Bench, Common Pleas, Ed. of 1661

Benl.Old. Benloe & Dalison, English Common Pleas Reports, Edition of 1689

Benl. & D. Benloe & Dalison Common Pleas (123 Eng. Reprint)

Benl. & D.(Eng.) Benlow & Dalison Common Pleas (123 Eng. Reprint)

Benl. & Dal. Benloe & Dalison's English Common Pleas Reports (123 Eng. Reprint)

Benloe Benloe's or New Benloe's Reports. English King's Bench. Edition of 1661

Benn. Bennett's Reports (1 California) Bennett's Reports (1 Dakota) Bennett's Reports (16-21 Missouri)

Benn.Cal. Bennett's Reports, vol. 1 California

Benn.(Dak.) Bennett's Dakota Cases

Benn.F.I.Cas. Bennett's Fire Insurance Cases

Benn.(Mo.) Bennett's Missouri Cases

Benn. & H.Cr.Cas. Bennett & Heard's Leading Criminal Cases

Benn. & H.Dig. Bennett & Herard Massachusetts Digest

Benne. Reporter of vol. 7, Modern Reports (Eng.)

Bennett   ● Bennett, Reports (1 California)
       ● Bennett, Reports, (1 Dakota)
       ● Bennett, Reports (16-21 Missouri)

Bent. Bentley's Reports, Irish Chancery

Bent.Cod. Bentham's Codification

Bent.Const.Code Bentham's Constitutional Code for all Nations

Bent.Ev.(or Jud.Ev.) Bentham's Judicial Evidence

Bent.Mor. & Leg. Bentham's Principles of Morals and Legislation

Bent.Pun. Bentham's Rationale of Punishment

Bent.The.Leg. Bentham's Theory of Legislation

Benth.Ev. Bentham on Rationale of Judicial Evidence

Benth.Jud.Ev. Bentham on Rationale of Judicial Evidence

Bentl.Atty.-Gen. Bentley's Reports, vols. 13-19 Attorneys-General's Opinions

Beor. Queensland Law Reports (1876-78) (Aus.)

Ber. Berton. New Brunswick Reports (2 New Brunswick Reports) (1835-39)

Berar Berar Law Journal (India)

Berk Co.L.J. Berk's County Law Journal (Pa.)

Berks Berks County Law Journal (Pa.)

Berks Co LJ(Pa) Berk's County Law Journal (Pa.)

Bern. Bernard's Church Cases (Ir.)

Bern.Ch.Cas. Bernard's Church Cases (1870-75) (Ir.)

Berry Berry's Reports (1-28 Missouri Appeals)

Bert. Berton's New Brunswick Reports, vol. 2

Best Beg. & Rep. Best on the Right to Begin and Reply

Best Ev. Best on Evidence

Best Jur.Tr. Best on Trial by Jury

Best, Pres. Best on Presumptions of Law and Fact

Best, Presumptions Best on Presumptions of Law and Fact

Best & S. Best and Smith's English Queen's Bench Reports (1861-69)

Best & S.(Eng.) Best and Smith's English Queen's Bench Reports (1861-69)

Best & Sm. Best and Smith's English Queen's Bench Reports (121, 122 Eng. Reprint)

Betts' Adm.Pr. Betts' Admiralty Practice

Betts' Dec. ● Blatchford & Howland's United States District Court Reports

● Olcott's United States District Court Reports

Be.(Ceylon) Beven's Ceylon Reports

Bev.Emp.L. Bevin on Employer's Liability for Negligence of Servants

Bev.Pat. Bevill's Patent Cases (Eng.)

Bev. & M. Bevin & Mill's Reports (Ceylon)

Bev. & Sieb. Beven & Sievel's Reports (Ceylon)

Beven ● Beven on Negligence in Law (1889-1928)

● Beven's Ceylon Reports

Bew. & N.Pr. Bewley & Naish on Common Law Procedure

BezG. Bezirksgericht--District Court

Bez.Ger. Bezirksgericht (District Court)

Bgt. Bought

Bhd. Brotherhood

Bi-Mo.L.Rev. Bi-Monthly Law Review, University of Detroit

Bibb. Bibb's Kentucky Reports (1808-17) (vol. 4-7 Kentucky)

Bibb.(Ky.) Bibb's Kentucky Reports (1808-17) (vol. 4-7 Kentucky)

Bich.Crim.Proc. Bishop on Criminal Procedure

Bick. Bicknell & Hawley's Reports (vols. 10-20 Nevada)

Bick.(In.) Bicknell's Reports (India)

Bick. & H. Bicknell & Hawley's Reports (vols. 10-20 Nevada)

Bick. & Hawl. Bicknell & Hawley's Reports (vols. 10-20 Nevada)

Bid. ● Bidder's Court of Referees Reports (Eng.)

● Bidder's Locus Standi Reports (Eng.)

Bid.Ins. Biddle on Insurance

Bid.War.Sale Chat. Biddle on Warranties in Sale of Chattels

Bidd. Bidder's Locus Standi Reports, I. (1920-36)

Big. Bignell, Reports, India

Big.Cas. Bigelow, Cases, William I. to Richard I

Big.Cas.B. & N. Bigelow's Cases on Bills & Notes

Big.Cas.Torts Bigelow's Leading Cases in Torts

Big.Eng.Proc. Bigelow's English Procedure

Big.Eq. Bigelow on Equity

Big.Est. Bigelow on Estoppel

Big.Fr. Bigelow on Frauds

Big.Jarm.Wills Bigelow's edition of Jarman on Wills

Big.L. & A.Ins.Cas. Bigelow's Life and Accident Insurance Cases

Big.Lead.Cas. Bigelow's Leading Cases in Bills and Notes; Torts; or Wills

Big.Ov.Cas. Bigelow's Overruled Cases (U.S., Eng., Ir.)

Big.Plac. Bigelow's Placita Anglo-Normanica (1066-1195) (Eng.)

Big.Proc. Bigelow's English Procedure

Big.Torts Bigelow on Torts

Bigelow, Estop. Bigelow on Estoppel

Bigelow, Lead.Cas. Bigelow's Leading Cases on Bills and Notes, Torts, or Wills

Bigg.L.I.Cas. Bigelow's Life and Accident Insurance Cases

Bign. Bignell's Reports (Bengal) India

Bih.Rep. Bihar Reports (India)

Bilb.Ord. Ordinances of Bilboa

Bill of Rights J. Bill of Rights Journal

Billot Extrad. Billot, Traité de l'Extradition

Bin. Binney's Reports (Pa. 1799-1814)

Bin.Dig. Binmore's Digest, Michigan

Bing. Bingham's English Common Pleas Reports (vols. 130, 131 Eng. Reprint)

Bing.(Eng.) Bingham's English Common Pleas Reports (vols. 130, 131 Eng. Reprint)

Bing.Act. & Def. Bingham's Actions and Defences in Real Property

Bing.N.C. Bingham, New Cases, English Common Pleas (131-133 Eng. Reprint)

Bing.N.C.(Eng.) Bingham, New Cases, English Common Pleas (131-133 Eng. Reprint)

Bing.N.Cas. Bingham, New Cases, English Common Pleas (131-133 Eng. Reprint)

Bing.R.P. Bingham on the Law of Real Property

Binm.Ind. Binmore's Index-Digest of Michigan Reports

Binn. Binney's Pennsylvania Supreme Court Reports (1799-1814)

Binn.(Pa.) Binney's Pennsylvania Reports (1799-1814)

Binns' Just. Binns' Justice (Pa.)

Bird. Supp. Bird's Supplement to Barton's Conveyancing

Birds.St. Birdseye's Statutes (N.Y.)

Birdw. Birdwood's Printed Judgments (India)

Biret, Vocab. Biret Vocabularie des Cinq Codes, ou definitions simp lifées des termes de droit et de jurisprudence exprimés dan ces codes (1862)

Birk.J. Birkenhead's Judgments, House of Lords (1919-22) (Eng.)

Bis. Bissell's United States Circuit Court Reports

Bish.Burr. Bishop's edition of Burrill on Assignments

Bish.Con. Bishop on Contracts

Bish.Cont. Bishop on Contracts

Bish.Cr.Law Bishop on Criminal Law

Bish.Cr.Proc. Bishop on Criminal Procedure

Bish.Mar.,Div. & Sep. Bishop on Marriage, Divorce, and Separation

Bish.Mar.Wom. Bishop on Married Women

Bish.Mar. & Div. Bishop on Marriage and Divorce

Bish.New Cr.Law Bishop's New Criminal Law

Bish.New Cr.Proc. Bishop's New Criminal Procedure

Bish.Noll.Pros. Bishop's Law of Nolle Prosequi

Bish.Non-Cont.Law Bishop on Non-Contract Law, Rights and Torts

Bish.St.Crimes Bishop on Statutory Crimes

Bish.Stat.Cr. Bishop on Statutory Crimes

Bishop Dig. Bishop's Digest, Montana

Bisp.Eq. Bispham's Principles of Equity

Bisph.Eq. Bispham's Principles of Equity

Biss. Bissell's United States Circuit Court Reports

Biss.Stat. Bissell's Minnesota Statutes

Biss. & Sm. Bissett & Smith's Digest (S. Africa)

Bissett, Est. Bissett on Estates for Life

Bit. & Wise Bittleston and Wise, New Magistrate Cases (Eng.)

Bitt. Bittleston's Reports in Chambers, Queen's Bench Division (Eng.)

Bitt.Ch. Bittleston's Reports in Chambers, Queen's Bench Division (Eng.)

Bitt.Cha.Cas. Bittleston's Chambers Cases (1883-84)

Bitt.Chamb.Rep. Bittleston's Reports in Chambers, Queen's Bench Division (Eng.)

Bitt.P.C. Bittleston's Practice Cases under Judicature Acts (Eng.)

Bitt.Pr.Cas. Bittleston's Practice Cases (1844-48)

Bitt.Pr.Case Bittleston's Practice Cases, under Judicature Act (Eng.)

Bitt.Prac.Cas. Bittleston's Practice Cases, under Judicature Act (Eng.)

Bitt.Rep.in Ch. Bittleston's Reports in Chambers, Queen's Bench Division (Eng.)

Bitt.W. & P. Bittleson, Wise & Parnell's Reports (2, 3 New Practice Cases) (Eng.)

Bk. ● Black. United States Supreme Court Reports, vols. 66-67
   ● book

Bk.Judg. Book of Judgments by Townshend

Bk.L.J. Banking Law Journal

Bkg. Banking Deparment

bks. Books

Bl. ● Black's United States Supreme Court Reports
   ● Blatchford's United States Circuit Court Reports
   ● Blackford's Indiana Reports (1817-47)
   ● Blount's Law Dictionary
   ● Henry Blackstone's English Common Pleas Reports
   ● William Blackstone's English King's Bench Reports
   ● Blackstone's Commentaries

Bl.C.C. Blatchford's United States Circuit Court Reports

Bl.Comm. Blackstone's Commentaries on the Law of England

Bl.D. & O. Blackham, Dundas & Osborne's Irish Nisi Pruis Reports (1846-48)

Bl.D. & Osb. Blackham, Dundas and Osborne's Reports, N.P. Ireland (1846-48)

Bl.Dict. Black's Law Dictionary

Bl.H. Henry Blackstone's English Common Pleas Reports (1788-96)

Bl.Judgm. Black on Judgments

Bl.L.T. Blackstone's Law Tracts

Bl.Law Tracts Blackstone's Law Tracts

Bl.N.S. Bligh, House of Lords Reports, New Series

Bl.Pr.Cas. Blatchford. Prize Cases, United States

Bl.Prize Blatchford's Prize Cases

Bl.R. Sir William Blackstone's English King's Bench Reports (1746-80)

Bl. & H. ● Blatchford & Howland's United States District Court Reports
   ● Blake & Hedges' Reports (vols. 2-3 Montana)

Bl. & How. Blatchford & Howland's United States District Court Reports

Bl. & W.Mines Blanchard & Weeks' Leading Cases on Mines

Bla. ● Black (see also Bl.)
   ● Blackstone, W. 1746-80

Bla.Ch. Bland's Maryland Chancery Reports

Bla.Com. Blackstone's Commentaries on the Law of England

Bl.Comm. Blackstone's Commentaries on the Laws of England

Bla.H. Henry Blackstone's English Common Pleas Reports

Bla.W. Sir William Blackstone's Reports English King's Bench

Black ● Black's Reports (vols. 30-53 Indiana)
   ● Black's Supreme Court Reports (vols. 66, 67 U.S. Reports)
   ● Blackerby's Magistrates Reports (1327-1716) (Eng.)

● Blackford's Reports (Indiana 1817-1847, vols. 30-53 Indiana)

● H. Blackstone's Common Pleas Reports (1788-96) (Eng.)

● W. Blackstone's King's Bench Reports (1746-80) (Eng.)

● Blackstone's Reports, King's Bench, tempore George II & III; Common Pleas, George III (Eng.)

Black.Anal. Blackstone's Analysis of the Laws of England

Black.Com. Blackstone's Commentaries on the Laws of England

Black.Cond. Blackwell's Condensed Illinois Reports

Black.Cond.Rep. Blackwell's Condensed Illinois Reports

Black, Const.Law Black on Constitutional Law

Black, Const.Prohib. Black's Constitutional Prohibitions

Black.D. & O. Blackham, Dundas, & Osborne's Irish Nisi Prius Reports

Black.Dict. Black's Law Dictionary

Black.H. Henry Blackstone's English Common Pleas Reports (1788-96)

Black, Interp.Laws Black on the Construction and Interpretation of Laws

Black, Intox.Liq. Black on the Laws Regulating the Manufacture and Sale of Intoxicating Liquors

Black, Judg. Black on Judgments

Black, Judgm. Black on Judgments

Black.Jus. Blackerby's Justices' Cases (Eng.)

Black L.J. Black Law Journal

Black, Law Dict. Black's Law Dictionary

Black.Mag.Ch. Blackstone on Magna Charta

Black R. ● Black's United States Supreme Court Reports

● W. Blackstone's English King's Bench Reports (1746-80)

Black Ship.Ca. Black's Decisions in Shipping Cases

Black St.Const. Black on Construction and Interpretation of Laws

Black Tax Titles Black on Tax Titles

Black.W. William Blackstone's English King's Bench Reports (1746-80)

Blackb. Blackburn on Sales. 3 editions (1845-1910)

Blackb.Sales Blackburn on Sales

Blackf. Blackford's Reports (Indiana 1817-47)

Blackf.(Ind.) Blackford's Reports (Indiana 1817-47)

Black's Law Dict. Black's Law Dictionary

Blackst. Blackstone's Reports in King's Bench. temp. George II & III; and Common Pleas, George III (1746-80)

Blackst.R. William Blackstone's King's Bench (1746-80) (Eng.)

Blackstone's Commen. Blackstone's Commentaries on the Laws of England

Blackw.Cond. Blackwell's Condensed Reports (Ill.)

Blackw.Sc.Atc. Blackwell's Scotch Acts

Blackw.Tax Titles Blackwell's Tax Titles

Blair Co. Blair County Law Reports, Pennsylvania

Blair Co.L.R. Blair County Law Reports, Pennsylvania

Blair Co.L.R.(Pa.) Blair County Law Reports, Pennsylvania

Blake Blake's Reports (vols. 1-3 Montana)

Blake Ch.Pa. Blake's Chancery Practice, New York

Blake & H. Blake and Hedges' Reports (vols. 2-3 Montana)

Blan.Lim. Blanshard on Statute of Limitations

Blan. & W.Lead.Cas. Blanchard & Weeks' Leading Cases, Mines

Blanc. & W.L.C. Blanchard & Weeks' Leading Cases on Mines, etc.

Bland Bland's Maryland Chancery Reports (1811-32)

Bland Ch.(Md.) Bland's Maryland Chancery Reports

Bland's Ch. Bland's Maryland Chancery Reports

Blash.Juries Blashfield, Instructions to Juries

Blatchf. Blatchford's United States Circuit Court Reports

Blatchf.C.C. Blatchford's United States Circuit Court Reports

Blatchf.Pr.Cas. Blatchford, Prize Cases

Blatchf.Prize Cas. Blatchford's Prize Cases (U.S.)

Blatchf. & H. Blatchford & Howland's United States District Court Reports

Blax.Eng.Co. Blaxland's Codex Legum Angelicanum

Bldg. Building

Bleck. Bleckley's Reports (vols. 34, 35 Georgia)

Bleckley Bleckley's Reports (vols. 34, 35 Georgia)

Bli. Bligh's English House of Lords Reports

Bli.N.S. Bligh's English House of Lords Reports, New Series (1827-37)

Bli.(N.S.) Bligh's English House of Lords Reports, New Series (1827-37)

Bli.(O.S.) Bligh's English House of Lords Reports, Old Series (1819-21)

Bligh Bligh's English House of Lords Reports (1819-21)

Bligh (Eng.) Bligh's English House of Lords Reports (1819-21)

Bligh N.S.(Eng.) Bligh's English House of Lords Reports, New Series (1827-37) (vols. 4-6 Eng. Reprint)

Bliss. Delaware County Reports, Pennsylvania

Bliss Co.Pl. Bliss on Code Pleading

Bliss Ins. Bliss on Life Insurance

Bliss N.Y.Co. Bliss's New York Code

Blk. Block

Bloom.Man. Bloomfield's Manumission (or Negro) Cases, New Jersey

Bloom.Man.Neg.Cas. Bloomfield's Manumission (or Negro) Cases, New Jersey

Blount Blount's Law Dictionary

Blount Tr. Blount's Impeachment Trial

Blue Sky L.Rep. Blue Sky Law Reporter (CCH)

Bluett Bluett's Isle of Man Cases

Blunt.Mod.Volk. Bluntschli, Das Moderne Völkerrecht

Bogert, Trusts Bogert on Trusts & Trustees

Boh.Dec. Bohun's Declarations and Pleadings

Bohun Bohun's Election Cases (Eng.)

Bohun.Curs.Canc. Bohun's Cursus Cancellariae

Bohun, Inst.Leg. Bohun's Institutio Legalis

Bol. Bolivia

Bol.Min.Justica Boletim do Ministéro de Justica (Portugal)

Bolland Select Bills in Eyre (Selden Society Pub. v. 30) (Eng.)

Bom. Bombay High Court Reports (India)

Bom.A.C. Bombay Reports, Appellate Juris (India)

Bom.Cr.Cas. Bombay Reports, Crown Cases (India)

Bom.L.J. Bombay Law Journal (India)

Bom.O.C. ● Bombay Reports, Original Civil Jurisdiction (India)

              ● Bombay Reports, Oudh Cases (India)

Bomb. Indian Law Reports, Bombay Series (India)

Bomb.Cr.Rul. Bombay High Ct., Criminal Rulings (India)

Bomb.H.C. Bombay High Ct. Reports (India)

Bomb.H.Ct. Bombay High Court Reports

Bomb.L.R. Bombay Law Reporter

Bomb.Sel.Cas. Bombay Select Cases, Sadr Diwani Adalat (India)

Bomb.Ser. Indian Law Reports, Bombay Series (India)

Bond Bond's United States Circuit Reports

Bond Md.App. Proceedings of Court of Appeal of Maryland (in American Legal Records, v. 1)

Bonnetti, Ital.Dict. Bonnetti's Italian Dictionary

Bonnier, E.des Preuves Bonnier's E. Traite des Preuves (1852)

Book of Judg. Book of Judgments (Eng.)

Boor. Booraem's Reports (vols. 6-8 California)

Booraem Booraem's Reports (vols. 6-8 California)

Boote Boote's Suit at Law

Boote, Suit at Law Boote's Suit at Law

Booth Chester Palatine Courts 1811 (Eng.)

Booth, Real Act. Booth on Real Action

Bos. Bostworth's Superior Court Reports (N.Y.)

Bos.Pl. Bosanquet's Rules of Pleading

Bos.Pol.Rep. Boston Police Reports

Bos. & D. Lim. Bosanquet & Darby's Limitations

Bos. & P. Bosanquet and Puller's English Common Pleas Reports

Bos. & P.(Eng.) Bosanquet & Puller's English Common Pleas Reports (vols. 126, 127 Eng. Reprint)

Bos. & P.N.R. Bosanquet & Puller's New Reports, English Common Pleas (127 Eng. Reprint)

Bos. & P.N.R.(Eng.) Bosanquet & Puller's New Reports, English Common Pleas (127 Eng. Reprint)

Bos. & Pu. Bosanquet and Puller's English Common Pleas Reports (126, 127 Eng. Reprint)

Bos. & Pul. Bosanquet & Puller's English Common Pleas Reports (vols. 126, 127 Eng. Reprint)

Box. & Pul.N.R. Bosanquet & Puller's New Reports, English Common Pleas

Bosc.Con. Boscawen on Convictions

Bost.L.R. Boston Law Reporter

Bost.Law Rep. Boston Law Reporter

Bost.Pol.Rep. Boston Police Court Reports

Bost.U.L.Rev. Boston University Law Review

Boston B.J. Boston Bar Journal

Boston U.L.Rev. Boston University Law Review

Bosw. • Boswell's Reports (Scotch Court of Sessions)
- Bosworth, New York Superior Court Reports, vols. 14-23

Bott P.L. Bott's Poor Laws

Bott P.L.Cas. Bott's Poor Law Cases (1560-1833) (Eng.)

Bott P.L.Const. Const's Edition of Bott's Poor Law Cases

Bott Poor Law Cas. Bott's Poor Laws Settlement Cases (Eng.)

Bott Set.Cas. Bott's Poor Law (Settlement) Cases

Bou.Inst. Bouvier's Institutes of American Law

Bouch.Inst. Boucher's Institutes au Droit Maritime

Boul.P.Dr.Com. Boulay-Paty Droit Common

Bould. Bouldin's Reports (vol. 119 Alabama)

Bouln. Boulnois' Reports, Bengal

Boulnois Boulnois' Reports, Bengal

Bourke Bourke's Reports, Calcutta High Court (India)

Bourke P.P. Bourke's Parliamentary Precedents (1842-56) (Eng.)

Bousq.Dict.de Dr. Bousquet, Dictionnaire de Droit

Bouv. Bouvier Law Dictionary

Bouv.Inst. Bouvier's Institutes of American Law

Bouv.L.Dict. Bouvier Law Dictionary

Bouv.Law Dict. Bouvier's Law Dictionary

Bouvier Bouvier's Law Dictionary

Bov.Pat.Ca. Bovill's Patent Cases

Bow. • Bowler & Bowers (U.S. Comptroller's Dec., v. 2, 3)
- Bowler's London Session Records (1605-85)

Bowen, Pol.Econ. Bowen's Political Economy

Bowstead Bowstead on Agency (1896-1951)

Bowyer, Mod.Civil Law Bowyer's Modern Civil Law

Boyce Boyce's Delaware Supreme Court Reports (1909-19)

Boyd.Adm. Boyd's Admiralty Law, Ireland

Boyle Act. Boyle's Précis of an Action at Common Law

Br. • Bracton
- Bradford

- Bradwell
- Brayton
- Breese
- Brevard
- Brewster
- Bridgman
- Brightly
- British
- Britton
- Brockenbrough
- Brooke
- Broom
- Brown
- Brownlow
- Bruce, Reports, Court of Session (1714-15) (Sc.)

Br.Abr. Brooke's Abridgment (Eng.)

Br.Brev.Jud. Brownlow's Brevia Judicialia, etc.(1662)

Br.Bro. Brooke, Browne, Brownlow

Br.Bur. British Burmah

Br.C.C.
- British (or English) Crown Cases (American reprint)
- Brown's Chancery Cases, (Eng.)

Br.Col. British Columbia

Br.Cr.Ca. British (or English) Crown Cases (American Reprint)

Br.Fed.Dig. Brightly's Federal Digest

Br.L.R. Brooklyn Law Review

Br.Leg.Max. Broom's Legal Maxims

Br.N.B. Braeton's Note Book (1217-40)

Br.N.C. Brooke's New Cases, English King's Bench (1515-58)

Br.N.Cas. Brooks New Cases, King's Bench (Eng.)

Br.Not. Brooke's Office of a Notary

Br.P.C. Brown's Chancery Cases (Eng.)

Br.R. Browne's Reports (Ceylon)

Br.Reg. Braithwaite's Register

Br.Rul.Cas. British Ruling Cases

Br.Sup. Brown's Supplement to Morrison's Dictionary, Sessions Cases (1622-1780) (Sc.)

Br.Syn. Brown, Synopsis of Decisions, Scotch Court of Session (1540-1827)

Br. & B. Broderip & Bingham, Common Pleas (Eng.)

Br. & Col. British & Colonial Prize Cases

Br. & Col.Pr.Cas. British and Colonial Prize Cases (1914-19)

Br. & F.Ecc. Broderick & Fremantle's Ecclesiastical Cases (1840-64) (Eng.)

Br. & Fr. Broderick & Fremantle's Ecclesiastical Cases (1840-64) (Eng.)

Br. & G. Brownlow and Goldesborough's Reports, Common Pleas (1569-1624)

Br. & Gold. Brownlow & Goldesborough, English Common Pleas Reports

Br. & L. Browning & Lushington, English Admiralty Reports (1863-65)

Br. & Lush Browning & Lushington, English Admiralty Reports (1863-65)

Br. & R. Brown & Rader's Reports (vol. 137 Missouri)

Bra.
- Bracton de Legibus Angliae
- Brady's English History (1684)

Brac.
- Bracton de Legibus et Consuetudinibus Angliae (Eng.)
- Bracton's Note Book, King's Bench (1217-40)

Bract. Bracton de Legibus et Consuetudinibus Angliae (Eng.)

Bracton Bracton de Legibus et Consuetudinibus Angliae (Eng.)

Brad.
- Bradford's Reports (Iowa (1838-41)
- Bradford's New York Surrogate Reports
- Bradford's Somerset Star Chamber
- Bradwell's Reports (1-20 Ill. App.) Cases (Somerset Record Society No. 27 (Eng.)

Bradb. Bradbury's Pleading and Practice Reports (N.Y.)

Bradf.
- Bradford's Proceedings in the Court of Star Chamber (Somerset Record Society Publications, vol. 27)
- Bradford's New York Surrogate Reports
- Bradford's Reports (Iowa)

Bradf.Sur. Bradford's New York Surrogate Court Reports

Bradf.Surr. Bradford's New York Surrogate Court Reports

Bradford Bradford's Iowa Supreme Court Reports (1839-41)

Bradl. Bradley's Rhode Island Reports

Bradl.(R.I.) Bradley's Rhode Island Reports

Bradw. Bradwell's Appellate Reports (Illinois)

Brady Ind. Brady's Index, Arkansas Reports

Brain.L.P. Brainard's Legal Precedents in Land & Mining Cases (U.S.)

Braith. Jamaica Law Reports (Braithwaite)

Brame. Brame's Reports (vols. 66-72 Mississippi)

Branch. Branch's Reports (vol. 1 Florida)

Branch, Max. Branch's Maxims

Branch Pr. Branch's Principia Legis et Equitatis (Maxims)

Branch, Princ. Branch's Principia Legis et Equitatis

Brand. Brandenburg's Reports, vol. 21, Opinions Attorneys-General

Brand.F.Attachm. (Or Brand.For Attachm.) Brandon on Foreign Attachment

Brande. Brande's Dictionary of Science, etc.

Brandenburg Bankr. Brandenburg's Bankruptcy

Brandenburg Dig. Brandenburg's Bankruptcy Digest

Brandt, Sur. Brandt on Suretyship and Guaranty

Brans.Dig. Branson's Digest (Bombay)

Brant. Brantly's Reports, (vols. 80-90 Maryland)

Brantly Brantly's Reports (vols. 80-90 Maryland)

Brayt. Brayton's Reports (1815-19)

Brayton (Vt.) Brayton's Reports (Vermont)

Braz. Brazil

Breese Breese's Reports (vol. 1 Illinois)

Brett Ca.Eq. Brett's Cases in Modern Equity

Brev. Brevard's South Carolina Reports (1793-1816)

Brev.Dig. Brevard's Digest of the Public Statute Law, South Carolina

Brev.Ju. Brevia Judicialia (Judicial Writs)

Brev.Sel. Brevia Selecta, or Choice Writs

Brew. Brewer's Reports (vols. 19-26 Maryland)

Brew.(Md.) Brewer's Reports (vols. 19-26 Maryland)

Brewer Brewer, Reports (19-26 Maryland)

Brewst. Brewster (Pennsylvania Reports, 4 vols.)

Brice Ult.V. Brice's Ultra Vires

Brick.Dig. Brickell's Digest (Alabama)

Bridg. J. Bridgman's Reports, Common Pleas (1614-21)

Bridg.Dig.Ind. Bridgman's Digested Index

Bridg.Eq.Ind. Bridgman. Index to Equity Cases

Bridg.J. Sir J. Bridgman, English Common Pleas Reports

Bridg.O. Sir Orlando Bridgman, English Common Pleas Reports (1660-67)

Brief. Brief of the Phi Delta Phi (Menasha, Wisconsin)

Brief Case Brief Case, National Legal Aid Association

Bright. Brightly, Pennsylvania Nisi Prius Reports

Bright.Dig.
- Brightly's Digest (New York)
- Brightly's Digest (Pennsylvania)
- Brightly's Analytical Digest of the Laws of the United States

Bright.E.C. Brightly's Leading Election Cases (Pa.)

Bright.Elec.Cas. Brightly's Leading Election Cases (Pa.)

Bright.N.P. Brightly's Pennsylvania Nisi Prius Reports

Bright.Pur.Dig. Brightly's Edition of Purdon's Digest of Pennsylvania Laws

Bright.Purd. Brightly's Edition of Purdon's Digest of Pennsylvania Laws

Brightly Brightly, Pennsylvania Nisi Prius Reports

Brightly Dig. ● Brightly's Digest (New York)
● Brightly's Digest (Pennsylvania
● Brightly's Analytical Digest of the Laws of the United States

Brightly, Elect.Cas. Brightly's Leading Election Cases (Pa.)

Brightly Election Cas.(Pa.) Brightly's Leading Election Cases (Pa.)

Brightly, N.P. Brightly's Nisi Prius Reports (Pa.)

Brisb.Minn. Brisbin's Reports (vol.1 Minnesota)

Brisbin Brisbin's Reports (vol. 1 Minnesota)

Brissonius. Brissonius de Verborum Significatione

Brit. ● British
● Britton's Ancient Pleas of the Crown

Brit.Burm British Burmah

Brit.Col.(Can.) British Columbia

Brit.Cr.Cas. British (or English) Crown Cases

Brit.Gui. British Guiana

Brit.Hond. British Hounduras

Brit.J.Criminol. British Journal of Criminology

Brit.Quar.Rev. British Quarterly Review

Brit.Rul.Cas. British Ruling Cases

Brit.Tax Rev. British Tax Review

Brit.Y.B.Int'l. British Yearbook of International Law

Brit.Y.B.Int'l.L. British Yearbook of International Law

Brit. & Col.Pr.Cas. British & Colonial Prize Cases

Britt. Britton's Ancient Pleas of the Crown

Brn. Brownlow and Goldesborough (1569-1625)

Bro. ● Brown's English Chancery Reports
● Brown's Parliamentary Cases (Eng.)
● Brown's Michigan Nisi Prius Reports

● Brown's Reports (53-65 Missouri)
● Brown's Reports (80-136 Missouri)
● Browne's Reports (Pa. 1801-14)
● Browne's Reports (1872-1902) (Ceylon)

Bro.A. & R. Brown, United States District Court Reports (Admiralty and Revenue Cases)

Bro.Ab. Brooke's Abridgment (1573, 1576, 1586 Editions) (Eng.)

Bro.Abr. Brooke's Abridgment (1573, 1576, 1586 Editions) (Eng.)

Bro.Abr.In Eq. Browne's New Abridgment of Cases in Equity

Bro.Adm. Brown's United States Admiralty Reports

Bro.C.C. Brown's English Chancery Cases, or Reports (1778-94)

Bro.Ch. Brown's English Chancery Reports (28, 29 Eng. Reprint)

Bro.Ch.Cas. Brown's English Chancery Reports (28, 29 Eng. Reprint)

Bro.Ch.Pr. Browne's Practice of the High Court of Chancery

Bro.Ch.R. Brown's English Chancery Reports (28, 29 Eng. Reprint)

Bro.Civ.Law. Browne's Civil and Admiralty Law

Bro.Div.Pr. Browne's Divorce Court Practice

Bro.Ecc. Brooke, Six Judgments in Ecclesiastical Cases (1850-72) (Eng.)

Bro.Ent. ● Brown's Entries
● Brownlow's Latine Redivivus; or Entries

Bro.Fr. Browne on the Statute of Frauds

Bro.Just. Broun's Justiciary, Scotland

Bro.Leg.Max. Brooms' Legal Maxims

Bro.Max. Brooms' Legal Maxims

Bro.N.B.Cas. Browne, National Bank Cases

Bro.N.C. Brooke, New Cases, English King's Bench (1515-58)

Bro.N.P. ● Brown's Michigan Nisi Prius Reports
● Brown's Nisi Prius Cases (Eng.)

Bro.P.C. Brown, English Parliamentary Cases (1-3 Eng. Reprint)

Bro.Pa. Browne's Pennsylvania Rep. (1801-14)

Bro.(Pa.). Browne's Pennsylvania Reports

Bro.Parl.Cas. Brown's Cases in Parliament

Bro.Prac. Brown's Practice (Praxis), or Precedents in Chancery

Bro.Prob.Pr. Browne's Probate Practice

Bro.St.Fr. Browne on the Statute of Frauds

Bro.Sup. to Mor. Brown's Supplement to Morrison's Dictionary of Decisions (1622-1780) (Sc.)

Bro.Supp. Brown, Supplement to Morrison's Dictionary, Court of Session (1622-1780, 5 vols.) (Sc.)

Bro.Syn. Brown's Synopsis of Decisions, Scotch Court of Sessions (1540-1827)

Bro.Synop. Brown's Synopsis of Decisions, Scotch Court of Sessions (1540-1827)

Bro.Tr.M. Browne on Trade Marks

Bro.Us. & Cus. Browne's Law of Usages and Customs

Bro.V.M. Brown's Vade Mecum

Bro. & F. Broderick & Freemantle's Ecclesiastical (Eng.)

Bro. & Fr. Broderick & Freemantle's Ecclesiastical Cases (Eng.)

Bro. & G. Brownlow & Goldesborough's English Common Pleas Reports

Bro. & H. Brown & Hemingway's Reports (53-65 Mississippi) ▪

Bro. & L. Browning & Lushington's English Admiralty Reports (1863-65)

Bro. & Lush. Browning & Lushington's English Admiralty Reports (1863-65)

Bro. & M. ● Brown & Macnamara, Railway Cases (1855)

● Brown & McCall's Yorkshire Star Chamber (Yorkshire Arch. Society Record, Series 44, 45, 51, 70)

Bro. & Mac. Browne and Macnamara's Ry. Cases (1855)

Brock. Brockenbrough's Marshall's Decisions, United States Circuit Court

Brock.C.C. Brockenbrough's Marshall's Decisions, United States Circuit Court

Brock.Cas. Brockenbrough, Virginia Cases

Brock.Marsh. Brockenbrough's Marshall's Decisions, United States Circuit Court

Brock. & H. Brockenbrough & Holmes (Va.)

Brock. & Ho. Brockenbrough & Holmes, "Virginia Cases," v. 1

Brod. Brodrick & Freemantle Ecclesiastical Cases

Brod.Stair. Brodie's Notes to Stair's Institutes (Sc.)

Brod. & B. Broderip & Bingham's English Common Pleas Reports (129 Eng. Reprint)

Brod. & Bing. Broderip & Bingham's English Common Pleas Reports (129 Eng. Reprint)

Brod. & F. Broderick & Freemantle's Ecclesiastical Cases (1840-64)

Brod. & F.(Eng.) Broderick & Freemantle's Ecclesiastical Cases (1840-64)

Brod. & Fr. Broderick & Freemantle's Ecclesiastical Cases (1840-64)

Brod. & Frem. Brodrick and Freemantle's Ecclesiastical Cases (1840-64)

Brodix Am. & E.Pat.Cas. Brodix's American & English Patent Cases

Brodix Am. & Eng.Pat.Cas. Brodix's American and English Patent Cases

Brook Abr. Brook's Abridgments (Eng.)

Brook N.Cas. Brook's New Cases, King's Bench (Eng.)

Brooke ● Brooke's Ecclesiastical Cases (1850-72) (Eng.)

● Brooke's New Cases, King's Bench (Eng.)

Brooke (Petit). Brooke, New Cases

Brooke, Abr. Brooke's Abridgment (73 Eng. Reprint)

Brooke Eccl. Brooke's Six Ecclesiastical Judgments

Brooke Eccl.Judg. Brooke's Ecclesiastical Judgments

Brooke N.C. Brooke, New Cases, English King's Bench Reports

Brooke Not. Brooke on the Office and Practice of a Notary

Brooke Six Judg. Brooke's Six Ecclesiastical Judgments (or Reports)

Brookl.Bar. Brooklyn Barrister Brooklyn Bar Association

Brookl.L.Rev. Brooklyn Law Review

Brookl.Rec. Brooklyn Daily Record, Brooklyn, New York

Brooklyn Daily Rec. Brooklyn Daily Record

Brooklyn L.Rev. Brooklyn Law Review

Brooks. Brooks' Reports (vols. 106-119 Michigan)

Broom, Com.Law. Broom's Commentaries on the Common Law

Broom, Leg.Max. (or Broom, Max.). Broom's Legal Maxims

Broom & H.Comm. Broom & Hadley's Commentaries on the Law of England

Bros. Brothers

Brough.Civ.Pro. Broughton's Indian Civil Procedure

Broun. Broun's Justiciary Reports, Scotland (1842-45)

Broun.Just. Broun's Reports, Scotch Justiciary Court (1842-45)

Brown ● Brownlow (& Goldesborough's English Common Pleas Reports
- Brown's Reports (vols. 53-65 Mississippi)
- Brown's English Parliamentary Cases
- Brown's English Chancery Reports
- Brown's Law Dictionary
- Brown's Law Dictionary and Institute (1874)
- Brown's Scotch Reports
- Brown's United States District Court Reports
- Brown's United States Admiralty Reports
- Brown's Michigan Nisi Prius Reports
- Brown's Reports (vols. 4-25 Nebraska)

- Brown's Reports (vols. 80-137 Missouri)

Brown A. & R. Brown's United States District Court Reports (Admiralty and Revenue Cases)

Brown Adm. Brown's Admiralty (U.S.)

Brown C. Brown's English Chancery Cases or Reports (Eng.)

Brown,C.C. Brown's English Chancery Cases or Reports

Brown Ch. Brown's Chancery Cases (Eng.), tempore Lord Thurlow

Brown Ch.C. Brown's Chancery Cases (Eng.), tempore Lord Thurlow

Brown,Civ. & Adm.Law. Brown's Civil and Admiralty Law

Brown Dict. Brown's Law Dictionary

Brown Ecc. Brown's Ecclesiastical (Eng.)

Brown,Ga.Pl. & Pr.Anno. Brown, Georgia Pleading & Practice & Legal Forms Annotated

Brown N.P. Brown's Michigan Nisi Prius Reports

Brown N.P.Cas. Brown's Nisi Prius Cases (Eng.)

Brown P.C. Brown's House of Lords Cases (Eng.)

Brown Parl. Brown's House of Lords Cases (Eng.)

Brown Sup. or Brown Sup.Dec. Brown's Supplement to Morrison's Dictionary, Session Cases (Sc.)

Brown Syn. Brown's Synopsis of Decisions of the Scotch Court of Session

Brown. & G.(Eng.) Brownlow & Goldesborough. English Common Pleas Reports, 2 Parts, tempore Eliz. & Jac, 1675. (123 Eng. Reprint)

Brown. & Gold. Brownlow & Goldesborough English Common Pleas Reports

Brown & H. Brown & Hemingway's Reports (53-58 Mississippi)

Brown & Hemingway. Brown & Hemingway's Reports (53-58 Mississippi)

Brown. & L. Browning & Lushington's English Admiralty Reports (167 Eng. Reprint)

Brown. & L.(Eng.) Browning & Lushington's English Admiralty Reports (167 Eng. Reprint)

Brown. & Lush. Browning & Lushington's English Admiralty Reports (167 Eng. Reprint)

Brown & Lush.M. & D. Browning & Lushington on Marriage and Divorce

Brown & MacN. Brown & MacNamara, Railway Cases (Eng.)

Brown & R. Brown & Rader (Mo.)

Browne ● Browne's Reports (Ceylon)

● Browne's Reports (97-109 Massachusetts)

● Browne's Civil Procedure Reports (N.Y.)

● Browne's Reports (Pennsylvania 1801-1814)

Browne Bank.Cas. Browne's National Bank Case

Browne, Civ.Law Browne's Civil and Admiralty Law

Browne, Div. Browne's Divorce Court Practice

Browne, Jud.Interp. Browne's Judical Interpretation of Common Words and Phrases

Browne N.B.C. Browne's National Bank Cases

Browne, Prob.Pr. Browne's Probate Practice

Browne, St.Frauds Browne on Statute of Frauds

Browne Us. Browne on Usages and Customs

Browne & G. Browne & Gray's Reports (vols. 110-111 Massachusetts)

Browne & Gray. Browne & Gray's Reports (110-114 Massachusetts)

Browne & H. Browne & Hemingway (Miss.)

Browne & Macn. Browne & MacNamara's English Railway and Canal Cases

Brownl. Brownlow & Goldesborough. English Common Pleas Reports. 2 Parts, tempore Eliz. & Jac, 1675 (123 Eng. Reprint)

Brownl.Redv. Brownlow's Latine Redivivus

Brownl. & G. Brownlow & Goldesborough. English Common Pleas Reports. 2 Parts, tempore Eliz. & Jac, 1675 (123 Eng. Reprint)

Brownl. & Gold. Brownlow & Goldesborough. English Common Pleas Reports, 2 Parts, tempore Eliz. & Jac, 1675. (123 Eng. Reprint)

Brown's Roman Law Brown's Epitome and Analysis of Savigny's Treatise on Obligations in Roman Law

Bru. Bruce's Scotch Court of Session Reports (1714-15)

Bruce Bruce's Scotch Court of Session Reports (1714-15)

Brunk.Ir.Dig. Brunker's Irish Common Law Digest

Brunn.Coll.Cas. Brunner's Collected Cases (U.S.)

Brunner Col.Cas.(F) Brunner's Collected Cases (U.S.)

Brunner Sel.Cas. Brunner's Selected Cases United States Circuit Courts

Bruns.L.C. Brunskill's Land Cases (Ir.)

Bryce Civ.L. Bryce's Study of the Civil Law

Bs/L Bills of Lading

Bt. Benedict's United States District Court Reports

Bu.L.R. Buffalo Law Review

Buch. ● Buchanan (Eben J. or James) Reports (Cape of Good Hope)

● Buchanan, Supreme Court Reports (Cape Colony)

● Buchanan's New Jersey Equity Reports (vols. 71-85)

● Buchanan (Sc.), Court of Session (1800-13.)

Buch.A.C. Buchanan's Reports of Appeal Court (Cape of Good Hope)

Buch.Cas. (or Tr.) Buchanan's Remarkable Criminal Cases (Sc.)

Buch.Ct.Ap.Cape G.H. Buchanan's Court of Appeals Reports (Cape of Good Hope)

Buch.E.Cape G.H. E. Buchanan's Reports (Cape of Good Hope)

Buch.E.D. Cape G.H. Buchanan's Eastern District Reports (Cape of Good Hope)

Buch.Eq.(N.J.) Buchanan's New Jersey Equity Reports

Buch.J.Cape G.H. J. Buchanan's Reports (Cape of Good Hope)

Buch.Rep. Buchanan's (Eben J. or James) Reports (Cape of Good Hope)

Buchanan. Buchanan's Reports, Court of Session and Justiciary (Sc.)

Buck ● Buck, English Cases in Bankruptcy (1816-20)
● Buck's Reports (vols. 7-8 Montana)

Buck Bankr.(Eng.) Buck, English Cases in Bankruptcy (1816-20)

Buck Cas. Buck's Bankruptcy Cases (Eng.)

Buck.Cooke Bucknill's Cooke's Cases of Practice, Common Pleas (Eng.)

Buck.Dec. Buckner's Decisions (in Freeman's Mississippi Chancery Reports 1839-43)

Buckl. Buckley on the Companies Acts (1873-1949)

Bucks Bucks County Law Reporter, Pa.

Bucks Co.L.R.(Pa) Bucks County Law Reporter (Pa.)

Bucks Co.L.Rep. Bucks County (Pennsylvania) Law Reporter

Buff.L.Rev. Buffalo Law Review

Buff.Super.Ct. Sheldon's Superior Court Reports (Buffalo, New York)

Buff.Super.Ct.(N.Y.) Sheldon's Superior Court Reports (Buffalo, New York)

Buffalo L.Rev. Buffalo Law Review

Bull. ● Bulletin
● Bulletin Weekly Law Bulletin (Ohio)

Bull.Can.Welfare L. Bulletin of Canadian Welfare Law

Bull. Copyright Soc'y. Bulletin of the Copyright Society of the U.S.A.

Bull.Cr.Soc. Bulletin of the Copyright Society of the U.S.A.

Bull.C'right Soc'y. Bulletin of the Copyright Society of the U.S.A.

Bull.Czech.L. Bulletin of Czechoslovak Law

Bull.JAG Bulletin of Judge Advocate General of Army (U.S.)

Bull.N.P. Buller's Law of Nisi Prius (Eng.)

Bull. NP (Eng.) Buller's Law of Nisi Prius (Eng.)

Bull.Nat.Tax Assoc. Bulletin of the National Tax Association

Bull.O. Weekly Law Bulletin (Ohio)

Bull. (Ohio) Weekly Law Bulletin (Ohio)

Bull. & C.Dig. Bullard & Curry's Louisiana Digest.

Bull. & L. Bullen and Leake's Pleadings on Actions in King's Bench Decisions, 11 editions (1860-1959)

Buller MSS. J. Buller's Paper Books, Lincoln's Inn Library

Buller N.P. Buller's Nisi Prius (Eng.)

Bulletin Comp.L. Bulletin, Comparative Law Bureau

Bulst. Bulstrode's English King's Bench Reports (1610-25)

Bulstr. Bulstrode (London), English King's Bench Reports (80, 81 Eng. Reprint)

Bump Const.Dec. Bump, Notes of Constitutional Decisions

Bump Fr.Conv. Bump on Fraudulent Conveyances

Bump.Fraud.Conv. Bump on Fraudulent Conveyances

Bump N.C. Bump's Notes on Constitutional Decisions

Bump's Int.Rev.Law Bump's Internal Revenue Laws

Bunb. Bunbury, English Exchequer Reports (145 Eng. Reprint)

Bunbury (Eng.) Bunbury, English Exchequer Reports (145 Eng. Reprint)

Bur. : ● Bureau
● Burnett's Wisconsin Supreme Court Reports (1841-43)
● Burrow, English King's Bench Reports

Bur.L.R. Burma Law Reports (India)

Bur.L.T. Burma Law Times (India)

Bur.M. Burrow's Reports tempore Mansfield (Eng.)

Bur.S.C. Burrow's Settlement Cases

Bur. & Gres.Eq.Pl. Burroughs & Gresson's Irish Equity Pleader

Burdick, Crime Burdick's Law of Crime

Burdick, Roman Law Burdick's Principles of Roman Law

Burf. Burford's Reports (6-18 Oklahoma)

Burg.Dig. Burgwyn's Digest Maryland Reports

Burg, Col.& For.Law Burge on Colonial and Foreign Law

Burge, Confl.Law. Burge on the Conflict of Laws

Burge, Sur. Burge on Suretyship

Burgess Burgess' Reports (vols. 16-49 Ohio State)

Burke Cel.Tr. Burke's Celebrated Trials

Burke Tr. Burke's Celebrated Trials

Burks Burks' Reports (91-98 Virginia)

Burl.Nat. Burlamaqui's Natural and Politic Law

Burl.Natural & Pol.Law Burlamaqui's Natural and Politic Law

Burlamaqui. Burlamaqui's Natural and Political Law

Burlesque Reps. Skillman's New York Police Reports

Burm.L.R. Burma Law Reports (India)

Burm.L.T. Burma Law Times (India)

Burma L.R. Burma Law Reports (1948)

Burn. ● High Commission Court 1865 (Eng.)
     ● Star Chamber Proceedings (Eng.)
     ● Burnett's Reports (Wisconsin)

Burn, Dict. Burn's Law Dictionary

Burn, Ecc.Law. Burn's Ecclesiastical Law

Burn Eccl. Burn's Ecclesiastical Law

Burn, J.P. Burn's Justice of the Peace

Burnet Burnet, Manuscript Decisions, Scotch Court of Session

Burnett ● Burnett's Wisconsin Reports
       ● Burnett's Reports (vols. 20-22 Oregon)

Burnett (Wis.) Burnett's Wisconsin Reports

Burns' Ann.St. Burns' Annotated Statutes (Ind.)

Burns-Begg Southern Rhodesia Reports

Burns' Ecc.Law Burns' Ecclesiastical Law

Burn's JP (Eng.) Burn's Justice of Peace

Burns' Rev.St. Burns' Annotated Statutes (Ind.)

Burr. Burrow, English King's Bench Reports tempore Lord Mansfield (97, 98 Eng. Reprint)

Burr.Adm. Burrell's Admiralty Cases. (1584-1839)

Burr.Dict. Burrill's Law Dictionary

Burr.(Eng.) Burrow, English King's Bench Reports tempore Lord Mansfield (97, 98 Eng. Reprint)

Burr.Law Dict. Burrill's Law Dictionary

Burr.Pr. Burrill's New York Practice

Burr.S.C. Burrows' English Settlement Cases (1732-76)

Burr.S.Cas. Burrows' English Settlement Cases (1732-76)

Burr.Sett.Cas. Burrows' English Settlement Cases (1732-76)

Burr.Sett.Cas.(Eng.) Burrows' English Settlement Cases (1732-76)

Burr.t.M. Burrow's Reports, tempore Mansfield (Eng.)

Burr.Tr. Burr's Trial, reported by Robertson

Burr.Tr.Rob. Burr's Trial, reported by Robertson

Burr.& Gr.Eq.Pl. Burroughs & Gresson, Irish Equity Pleader

Burrell Burrell's Reports, Admiralty, ed. by Marsden. (167 Eng. Reprint)

Burrell (Eng.) Burrell's Reports, Admiralty, ed. by Marsden. (167 Eng. Reprint)

Burrill Burrill's Law Dictionary

Burrill, Assignm. Burrill on Assignments

Burrill, Circ.Ev. Burrill on Circumstantial Evidence

Burrill, Pr. Burrill's Practice

Burrnett. Burrnett's Oregon Reports (vols. 20-22)

Burrow. Burrow's Reports, English King's Bench

Burrow, Sett.Cas. Burrow's English Settlement Cases

Burt.Cas. Burton's Collection of Cases and Opinions (Eng.)

Burt.Parl. Burton's Parliamentary Diary

Burt.Real Prop. Burton on Real Property

Burt.Sc.Tr. Burton's Scotch Trials

Bus. Business

Bus.Corp. Business Corporation

Bus.L. The Business Lawyer

Bus.L.J. Business Law Journal

Bus.Law Business Lawyer

Bus.Reg. Business Regulation

Bus. & Com. Business and Commerce

Bus. & Prof. Business and Professions

Bus. & Prof.C. Business and Professions Code

Busb. Busbee's Law Reports (vol. 44 North Carolina) (1852-53)

Busb.Cr.Dig. Busbee's Criminal Digest (North Carolina)

Busb.Eq. Busbee, Equity Reports (1852-53) (vol. 45, North Carolina)

Busb.L. Busbee Law (N.C.)

Busbee Eq.(N.C.) Busbee, Equity Reports (North Carolina, vol. 45)

Bush Bush's Kentucky Reports (vols. 64-77 Kentucky)

Bush (Ky.) Bush's Kentucky Report, (vols. 64-77 Kentucky)

Bush Dig. Bush's Digest of Florida Laws

Business L.J. Business Law Journal

Business L.R. Business Law Review

Business Q. Business Quarterly

Butler, Co.Litt. Butler's Notes to Coke on Littleton

Butler, Hor.Jur. Butler's Horae Juridicae

Butt.Rat.App. Butterworth's Rating Appeals (Eng.)

Butts Sh. Butts' edition of Shower's English King's Bench Reports

Buxton Buxton's Reports (vols. 123-129 North Carolina)

Buxton (N.C.) Buxton's Reports (vols. 123-129 North Carolina)

By.L.R. Baylor Law Review

Byl.Bills. Byles on Bills of Exchange

Byl.Exch. Byles' Law of Exchange

Byl.Us.L. Byles on the Usury Laws

Byles Byles on Bills of Exchange. 20 editions (1829-1939)

Byles, Bills Byles on Bills

Byn.War. Bynkershoek's Law of War

Bynk. Bynkershoek's Quaestionum Juris Publici

Bynk.Obs.Jur.Rom. Bynkershoeks Observationüm Juris Roman Libri

C

c.   ● cases
      ● chapter
      ● civil
      ● condemnation
      ● criticised; soundness of decision or reasoning in cited case criticised for reasons given. (Used in Shephard's Citations)

C   ● California
      ● California Reports
      ● Canada (Province)
      ● Chancellor
      ● Chapter
      ● Chinese
      ● Circuit
      ● College
      ● Colorado
      ● Connecticut
      ● Conservative Party
      ● Cowen (New York)
      ● Indian Law Reports, Calcutta Series

C.2d California Appellate Reports, Second Series

C.3d California Supreme Court Reports, Third Series

C.A.   ● California Appellate Reports
      ● Court of Appeal
      ● Court of Appeals
      ● Court of Appeals Reports (New Zealand)
      ● Court of Customs Appeals Reports
      ● Court of Customs and Patent Appeals Reports (Customs)
      ● Customs Appeals Reports (U.S.)
      ● United States Court of Appeals

C.A.2d California Appellate Reports, Second Series

C.A.3d California Appellate Reports, Third Series

C.A.A.   ● Civil Aeronautics Administration
      ● Civil Aeronautics Authority
      ● Civil Aeronautics Authority Reports

C.A.A.J. Civil Aeronautics Journal

C.A.A.Op. Civil Aeronautics Authority Opinions

CAB Contract Adjustment Board

C.A.B.   ● Civil Aeronautics Board
      ● Civil Aeronautics Board Reports

CACM Central American Common Market

C.A.D. Canadian Annual Digest

C.A.D.C. District of Columbia Circuit Court or District of Columbia Court of Appeals

C.A.F. cost and freight

CAJR New York State Commission on Administration of Justice, Report

C.A.L.Bull. Association of the Bar, City of New York, Committee on Amendment of the Law, Bulletin

CALE Conference of American Legal Executives

CALT Center for Advanced Legal Training

CAM   ● Church Assembly Measure
      ● Civil Aeronautics Manual

CAP Civil Air Patrol

C.A.P.A. Comision Aeronautica Permanente Americana

CAPDA California Public Defenders Association

C.A.R.   ● Civil Air Regulations ("Safety Regulations") (U.S.)
      ● Commonwealth Arbitration Reports (Australia)
      ● Criminal Appeal Reports (Eng.)

CARICOM Caribbean Common Market

CARIFTA Caribbean Free Trade Association

C.A.S. Codifying Act of Sederunt

C.A.3S. California Appellate Reports, Third Series Supplement

C.A.Supp. California Appellate Reports Supplement

C.A.2d Supp. California Appellate Reports, Second Series Supplement

CATx. Civil Appeals Texas

C.A.V. Curia advisari vult (court will be advised)

C.App.R. Criminal Appeal Reports (Eng.)

CB
- Chief Baron
- The Conference Board, Inc.

C.B.
- Cumulative Bulletin, Internal Revenue Bureau (U.S.)
- Customs Bulletin
- English Common Bench Reports (1840-56)

CBA Connecticut Bar Association

C.B.Dig. U.S. Customs Bureau, Digest of Customs and Related Laws

C.B.(Eng.) English Common Bench Reports, Manning, Granger, & Scott (vols. 135-139 Eng. Reprint)

C.B.J. Connecticut Bar Journal

C.B.(N.S.) English Common Bench Reports, Manning, Granger, & Scott, New Series (vols. 140-144 Eng. Reprint)

C.B.N.S.(Eng.) English Common Bench Reports, Manning, Granger, & Scott, New Series (vols. 140-144 Eng. Reprint)

CBO Congressional Budget Office

C.B.R.
- Canadian Bankruptcy Reports (Anno.)
- Cour du Banc de la Reine (Quebec)

cc Connected case: different case from case cited but arising out of same subject matter or intimately connected therewith (used in Shepard's Citations)

C.C.
- California Compensation Cases
- Cases in Chancery (Eng.)
- Causes Celebres
- Cepi Corpus
- Circuit Court
- City Court
- Civil Code
- Code Civil Francais, or Code Napoleon
- Coleman's New York Cases

- County Council
- County Court
- Crown Cases
- Federal Carriers Reporter, Federal Carriers Cases (Commerce Clearing House)
- Ohio Circuit Court Reports

C.C.A.
- Circuit Court of Appeals, prior to Sept. 1, 1948 (U.S.)
- County Court Appeals
- Court of Criminal Appeal (Eng.)

C.C.A.(U.S.) Circuit Court of Appeals (United States)

C.C.B. Code de Commerce Belge

C.C.C.
- Canadian Criminal Cases
- Central Criminal Court (Old Bailey)
- Choyce Cases in Chancery (1557-1606)
- Civilian Conservation Corps (U.S.)
- Commodity Credit Corporation (U.S.)
- Cox's English Criminal Cases (1844-1941)

C.C..C.Bull. Bulletin, Committee on Criminal Courts' Law & Procedure, Assn. of the Bar, City of New York

C.C.C.Sess.Pap. Central Criminal Court Session Paper (1834-1913) (Eng.)

C.C.Chr. Chancery Cases Chronicle (Ontario)

C.C.Chron.
- Chancery Cases Chronicle (Ontario)
- County Courts Chronicle (1848-59) (Eng.)

C.C.Ct.Cas. Central Criminal Court Cases (1834-1913) (Eng.)

CCE Center for Continuing Education

C.C.E.
- Caines' Cases in Error, New York
- Cases of Contested Elections

CCEB Continuing Legal Education of the Bar, University of California Extension

C.C.F. Contract Cases Federal (CCH)

CCH Commerce Clearing House, Inc.

CCH Atom.En.L.Rep. Atomic Energy Law Reporter (CCH)

CCH Comm.Mkt.Rep. Common Market Reporter (CCH)

CCH Fed. Banking l.rep. Federal Banking Law Reporter (CCH)

CCH Fed.Sec.L.Rep. Federal Securities Law Reporter (CCH)

CCH Inh.Est. & Gift Tax Rep. Inheritance, Estate, and Gift Tax Reporter (CCH)

CCH Lab.Arb. Awards Labor Arbitration Awards (CCH)

CCH Lab.Cas. Labor Cases (CCH)

CCH Lab.L.Rep. Labor Law Reporter (CCH)

CCH Stand.Fed.Tax Rep. Standard Federal Tax Reporter (CCH)

CCH State Tax Cas.Rep. State Tax Cases Reporter (CCH)

CCH State Tax Rev. State Tax Review (CCH)

CCH Tax Ct.Mem. Tax Court Memorandum Decisions (CCH)

CCH Tax Ct.Rep. Tax Court Reporter (CCH)

C.C.L.C. Civil Code (Quebec)

CCLE Continuing Legal Education in Colorado, Inc.

C.C.N.S. Ohio Circuit Court Reports, New Series

C.C.(N.S.) Ohio Circuit Court Reports, New Series

C.C.P. • Code of Civil Procedure
• Court of Common Pleas

C.C.P.A. • Court of Customs & Patent Appeals (U.S.)
• Court of Customs & Patent Appeals Reports

C.C.R. • Circuit Court Reports
• City Courts Reports
• County Courts Reports
• Court of Crown Cases Reserved (Eng.)
• Crown Cases Reserved (1865-75)

C.C.Rep. County Courts Reporter (in Law Journal, London)

C.C.Supp. City Court Reports, Supplement (N.Y.)

C.C.U.S. Circuit of the United States

C.Civ. Code Civile

C.Cl. Court of Claims Reports (U.S.)

C.Cost. Corte Costituzionale (Italian Constitutional Court)

C.Cr.Pr. Code of Criminal Procedure

C/D Certificate of deposit

C.D. • Application for certiorari denied
• Century Digest, in American Digest System
• Chancery Division, English Law Reports
• Circuit Decisions
• Commissioner's Decisions, U.S. Patent Office
• Complaint Docket
• Customs Court Decisions
• Customs Decisions (U.S.) Treasury Dept.)
• Ohio Circuit Decisions

CDC • Center for Disease Control
• Civil Defense Committee

C.D.E. Cahiers de Droit Europeen (Belg.)

C.E. Conseil d'Etat--Supreme Administrative Court (France III & Belguim III)

CEA • Commodity Exchange Authority
• Council of Economic Advisers

CEAO West African Economic Community

CEB California Continuing Education of the Bar (CEB Legal Services Gazette)

C.E.D. Canadian Encyclopedic Digest

C.E.Gr. C.E.Greene, New Jersey Equity Reports, (vols. 16-27)

C.E.Greene C.E.Greene, New Jersey Equity Reports (vols. 16-27)

CEMA Council for Economic Mutual Assistance

CENTO • Central Tready Organization

- Colombo Plan
- Council of Europe

CLP Concentrated Employment Program

CEQ Council on Environmental Quality

C.E.S. Court of Exchequer (Sc.)

CET Common External Tariff

CETA Comprehensive Employment and Training Act

C.F. Code Forestier Francais

CFA Consumer Federation of America

C.F.R. Code of Federal Regulations (U.S.)

CFTC Commodity Futures Trading Commission

C.F. & I. Cost, freight and insurance

CG Coast Guard

CGCM Court Martial Reports, Coast Guard Cases (N.Y.)

CGCMM Coast Guard Court-Martial Manual (1949) (U.S.)

CGCMS Special Court-Martial, Coast Guard (U.S.)

C.G.O. Comptroller General's Opinion (U.S. Treasury Department)

CGR Coast Guard Regulations (U.S.)

C.G.S.A. Connecticut General Statutes Annotated

CGSMCM Coast Guard Supplement to Manual for Courts-Martial (U.S.)

CHOB Cannon House Office Building

C.H.Rec. City Hall Recorder (Rogers), New York City

C.H.Rep. City Hall Reporter (Lomas), New York City

C.H. & A. Carro, Hamerton & Allen's New Session Cases (1844-51) (Eng.)

C.Home Clerk Home Court of Session. (1735-44) (Sc.)

C.I. Cumulative Index

CIA
- Central Intelligence Agency (U.S.)
- Coopers' International Union of North America

C.I.C. Current Indian Cases, Old Series (India)

CIEP Council on International Economic Policy

C.I.F. Cost, insurance, and freight

CILS Center for International Legal Studies

CIM International Convention for the Carriage of Goods by Rail (1961)

CIO
- Committee for Industrial Organization
- Congress of Industrial Organizations

CIPEC Intergovernmental Council of Copper Exporting Countries

C.I.R. Commissioner of Internal Revenue

CITEJA International Technical Committee of Aerial Legal Experts

C.Instr.Cr. Code d'Instruction Criminelle

C.J.
- Chief Justice
- Circuit Judge
- Corpus Juris
- Journal of the House of Commons
- Lord Chief Justice (Eng.)

C.J.Ann. Corpus Juris Annotations

C.J.C.
- Corpus Juris Civilis
- Couper's Judiciary Cases (1868-85) (Sc.)

C.J.Can. Corpus Juris Canonici

C.J.Civ. Corpus Juris Civilis

CJL Columbia Journal of Law and Social Problems

C.J.S. Corpus Juris Secundum

C.K. Chicago-Kent Law Review (Ill.)

C.K.L.R. Chicago-Kent Law Review

C.L.
- Civil Law
- English Common Law Reports, American Reprint
- Current Law Yearbooks (1947)
- Commission Leaflets, American Telephone and Telegraph Cases
- Compiled Laws
- Irish Common Law Reports, (17 vols.)

CLA Computer Law Association

C.L.A. University of California at Los Angeles Law Review

C.L.A.S. Criminal Law Audio Series

C.L.C. Current Law Consolidation (Eng.)

C.L.Ch. Common Law Chamber Reports (Ontario)

C.L.Chamb.
- Chamber's Common Law, (Upper Canada)

- Common Law Chamber Reports, Ontario

C.L.Chamb.Rep. Common Law Chamber Reports, Ontario

C.L.Chambers Chambers' Common Law (Upper Can.)

CLEM Continuing Legal Education, University of Montana

CLEW Continuing Legal Education for Wisconsin

C.L.F. Current Legal Forms with Tax Analysis

C.L.J.
- Calcutta Law Journal
- California Law Journal
- Cambridge Law Journal
- Canada Law Journal
- Cape Law Journal
- Central Law Journal
- Chicago Law Journal
- Colonial Law Journal Reports
- Criminal Law Journal (India)

C.L.J.N.S. Canada Law Journal, New Series

C.L.J.O.S. Canada Law Journal, Old Series

C.L.J. & Lit.Rev. California Law Journal and Literary Review

C.L.L.C. Canadian Labour Law Cases

C.L.L.R. Crown Lands Law Reports (Queensland)

C.L.N. Chicago Legal News

C.L.P.
- Common law procedure (Eng.)
- Current Legal Problems

C.L.P.Act. English Common Law Procedure Act

C.L.Q.
- Cornell Law Quarterly (New York)
- Crown Land Reports, Queensland

C.L.R.
- Calcutta Law Reporter
- Canada Law Reports
- Cape Law Reports (S. Africa)
- Ceylon Law Reports
- Cleveland Law Record
- Columbia Law Review
- Common Law Reports (1853-55) (Eng.)

- Commonwealth Law Reports (Aus.)
- Crown Lands Reports, Queensland
- Current Law Reports (Palestine)
- Cyprus Law Reports (1883)

C.L.R.(Can.)
- Common Law Reports (Canada), (1835-55)
- Canada Law Reports, Exchequer Court and Supreme Court: series began 1923 and is properly cited by year as 1923 Ex.C.R. and 1923 S.C.R. etc.

C.L.Rec. Cleveland Law Record

C.L.Reg. Cleveland Law Register

C.L.Rep. Cleveland Law Reporter

CLS Cornell Law School

C.L.T. Canadian Law Times (1881-1922)

C.L.T.Occ.N. Canadian Law Times Occasional Notes

CLU Chartered Life Underwriter

CLUU The College of Law, University of Utah

C.L.Y.B. Current Law Year Book (Eng.)

C.Leg.Rec. California Legal Record

C/M Chattel mortgage

C.M.
- Cleveland State Law Review
- Cleveland-Marshall Law Review (Ohio)
- Court Martial Report Army Cases (U.S.)

C.M.A.
- Court of Military Appeals
- Court of Military Appeals Reports

CMC Collective Measures Commission (UN)

C.M-E.T.O. Court-Martial, European Theater of Operations (U.S.)

C.M.J. Canadian Municipal Journal

C.M.L.R.
- Cleveland-Marshall Law Review

- Common Market Law Reports (Eng.)
- Common Market Law Review

C.M.O. U.S. Judge-Advocate-General (Navy) Compilation of Court-Martial Orders

CMP Reg. Controlled Materials Plan Regulation (National Production)

CMR Convention on the Contract for the International Carriage of Goods by Road (Geneva, 19 May 1956)

CMR, Cit. & Ind. Court Martial Reports, Citators & Indexes

CMR JAG AF. Court Martial Reports of the Judge Advocate General of the Air Force

CMR JAG & US Ct.of Mil.App. Court Martial Reports of the Judge Advocate General of the Armed Forces and the U.S. Court of Military Appeals

C.M.R.
- Common Market Reporter (CCH)
- Court-Martial Reports, judge Advocates General of the Armed Forces and the United States Court of Military Appeals
- Court of Military Review

C.M.R.(Air Force) Court-Martial Reports of the Judge Advocate General of the Air Force

C.M. & H. Cox, Macrae and Hertslet, County Courts (1847-58) (Eng.)

C.M. & R. Compton, Meeson, & Roscoe's English Exchequer Reports 1834-36)

C.N. Code Napoleon (or Civil Code)

C.N.Conf. Cameron & Norwood's North Carolina Conference Reports

C.N.J.F.D.C. Food and Drug Administration. Notices of Judgment: Cosmetics

CNO Chief of Naval Operations

C.N.P. Cases at Nisi Prius

C.N.P.C. Campbell's Nisi Prius Cases (Eng.)

C.N.R. Canadian National Railways

C.O. Common Orders

C.O.M.S.A.T. Communications Satellite Corporation

CONUS Continental United States

COPE Committee on Political Education

C.of C.E. Cases of Contested Elections (U.S.)

C. of S.Ca. Court of Session Cases (Sc.)

C. of S.Ca. 1st Series Court of Session Cases, First Series. By Shaw, Dunlop, & Bell (Sc.)

C. of S.Ca. 2d Series. Court of Session Cases, Second Series. By Dunlop, Bell & Murray (Sc.)

C. of S.Ca. 3rd Series. Court of Session Cases, Third Series. By Maepherson, Lee & Bell (Sc.)

C. of S.Ca. 4th Series. Court of Session Cases, Fourth Series. By Rettie, Crawford & Melville (Sc.)

C. of S.Ca. 5th Series. Court of Session Cases, Fifth Series (Sc.)

C.P.
- Civil Procedure Reports (New York)
- Common Pleas
- Upper Canada Common Pleas
- Law Reports, Common Pleas (Eng.)

C.P.A.
- Certified Public Accountant
- Civil Practice Act, New York

C.P.A.M. Caisse Primaire d'Assurance Maladie

CPC Committee for Programme and Co-ordination

C.P.C.
- C.P. Cooper's English Chancery Practice Cases (1837-38)
- Code de Procedure Civile
- Code of Civil Procedure, Quebec

C.P.C.t.Br. C.P. Cooper's English Chancery Reports tempore Brougham

C.P.C.t.Cott. C.P. Cooper's English Chancery Reports tempore Cottenham

C.P.C.U. Chartered Property and Casualty Underwriter

C.P.Cooper Cooper's English Chancery (1837-38)

C.P.D.
- Cape Provincial Division Report (S. Africa)
- Commissioner of the Public Debt
- Law Reports, Common Pleas Division (1875-80) (Eng.)
- South African Law Reports, Cape Provincial Division (S. Africa)

C.P.Div. Common Pleas Division, English Law Reports (1875-80)

C.P.Div.(Eng.) Common Pleas Division, English Law Reports (1875-80)

CPEPBA Committee on Professional Education of The Philadelphia Bar Association

C.P.(Eng.) Common Pleas Division, English Law Reports (1875-80)

CPI
- Consumer Price Index
- Court Practice Institute

C.P.L.
- Conveyancer and Property Lawyer (New Series) (Eng.)
- Current Property Lawyer (1852-53) (Eng.)

C.P.L.R.
- Central Provinces Law Reports (India)
- Civil Practice Law and Rules

C.P.Moore (Eng.) See J.B. Moore

C.P.Q. Code of Civil Procedure, Quebec (1897)

C.P.R.
- Canadian Pacific Railway Company
- Canadian Patent Reporter
- Ceiling Price Regulation

C.P.Rep. Common Pleas Reporter, Scranton, Pennsylvania

C.P.Rept. Common Pleas Reporter, Scranton, Pa.

CPS Act Consumer Product Safety Act

CPSC Consumer Product Safety Commission

CPS Commission Consumer Product Safety Commission

C.P.U.C. Common Pleas Reports, Upper Canada

C.Pr.
- Code of Procedure
- Code de Procedure Civile

C.R.
- Canadian Reports, Appeal Cases

- Chancery Reports tempore Car. I to Queen Anne
- Central Reporter
- Code Reporter
- Columbia Law Review
- Criminal Reports (Canada)
- Curia regis (King's Court)

C.R. [date] A.C. Canadian Appeal Cases

C.R.C.
- California Railroad Commission Decisions
- Canadian Railway Cases

C.R.-C.L. Civil Rights - Civil Liberties

CRD Customs Rules Decisions

C.R.N.S.
- Code Reports, New Series, New York
- Criminal Reports (Canada) New Series

C.R.R. Chief Registrar's Reports (Fr. Soc.) (Eng.)

C.R.S.
- Congressional Research Service
- Community Relations Service

C.R.T.C. Canadian Railway & Transport Cases

C.Rob. Christopher Robinson's English Admiralty Reports (165 Eng. Reprint)

C.Rob.Adm. Christopher Robinson's English Admiralty Reports

C.Rob.(Eng.) Christopher Robinson's English Admiralty Reports (165 Eng. Reprint)

C.S.
- Compiled Statutes
- Connecticut Supplement
- Consolidated Statutes
- Court of Session, Scotland
- Quebec Reports, Supreme Court
- Camden Society

CSA Community Services Administration

C.S.A.B.
- Civil Service Arbitration Awards
- Contract Settlement Appeal Board (U.S.)

C.S.B.C. Consolidated Statutes, British Columbia

C.S.C.
- Canada Supreme Court
- Consolidated Statutes of Canada

- Court of Sessions Cases (Scotland)
- Civil Service Commission (United States)

C.S.C.R. Cincinnati Superior Court Reporter

CSJAG Opinion of Judge Advocate General, U.S. Army

CSJAGA Military Affairs Division, Judge Advocate of U.S. Army

CSJAGE Assistant Judge Advocate General for Procurement (Army); Contract Division Office of Judge Advocate General of Army

C.S.L.C. Consolidated Statutes of Lower Canada

C.S.L.R. Cleveland State Law Review

C.S.M. Consolidated Statutes of Manitoba

C.S.N.B. Consolidated Statutes of New Brunswick

CSRS Cooperative State Research Service

CSS Commodity Stabilization Service

C.S.Supp. Supplement to the Compiled Statutes

C.S.T.
- Capital Stock Tax Ruling, Internal Revenue Bureau (U.S.)
- Commerce, Science, and Transportation

C.S.U.C. Consolidated Statutes, Upper Canada

CSULA California State University, Los Angeles

C.S. & J. Cushing, Storey & Joselyn's Election Cases (Mass.)

C.S. & P. Craigie, Stewart & Paton's Scotch Appeal Cases (1726-1821)

C.t.K. Cases tempore King (Macnaghten's Select English Chancery Cases)

C.t.N. Cases tempore Northington (Eden's English Chancery Reports).

C.t.T. Cases tempore Talbot, English Chancery.

C.T.
- Cape Times
- Carrier's Tax
- Carriers Taxing Ruling (I.R. Bull)
- Constitutiones Tiberii

- Court Trust (includes executor, administrator, guardian)

C.T.A. Cum testamento annexo (with will annexed)

C.T.C. Canada Tax Cases

C.T.C.L.R. Cape Times Common Law Reports (S. Africa)

C.T.R. Cape Times Supreme Court Reports, Cape of Good Hope (S. Africa)

C.Tax C. Canadian Tax Cases

C.Theod. Codex Theodosiani

C.Tr. Corporate trust

C.U. California Unreported Cases

C.U.A.L.R. Catholic University of America Law Review

CUALS Catholic University of America Law School

CUR Curia (court)

C.U.R. University of Colorado Law Review

C.Vict. Dominion of Canada Statutes in the Reign of Victoria

CWA Communications Workers of America

C.W.Dud. C.W. Dudley's Law or Equity Reports, South Carolina

C.W.Dudl.Eq. C.W. Dudley's Equity (S.C.)

C.W.L. Case Western Reserve Law Review (Ohio)

C.W.N. Calcutta Weekly Notes (India)

CWU Congress of World Unity

C.Y.C. Cyclopedia of Law and Procedure, New York

C.Z. Canal Zone

C.Z. Code Canal Zone Code

C.Z.Rep. Canal Zone Reports, Supreme and District Courts

C. & A. Cook & Alcock's Irish King's Bench Reports (1833-34)

C. & C.
- Case and Comment
- Colemand & Caines Cases (N.Y.)

C. & D.
- Corbett and Daniell's English Election Cases (1819)
- Crawford & Dix's Irish Circuit Cases

C. & D.A.C. Crawford & Dix's Irish Abridged Cases (1839-46)

C. & D.C.C. Crawford & Dix's Irish Circuit Cases (1841-42)

C. & E. Cababe & Ellis Queen's Bench (1882-85) (Eng.)

C. & F. ● Clark & Finnelley's English House of Lords Reports
● Cost and freight (1831-46)

C. & H.Dig. Coventry & Hughes' Digest

C. & H.Elec.Cas. Clarke & Hall, Cases of Contested Elections in Congress (1789-1834) (U.S.)

C. & J. Crompton & Jervis' English Exchequer Reports (1830-32)

C. & K. Carrington & Kirwan's English Nisi Prius Reports (1843-50)

C. & L. Conner & Lawson's Irish Chancery Reports (1841-43)

C. & L.C.C. Caines & Leigh Crown Cases (Eng.)

C. & L.Dig. Cohen & Lee's Maryland Digest

C. & M. ● Crompton & Meeson's English Exchequer Reports (1832-34)
● Carrington & Marshman's English Nisi Prius Reports (1840-42)

C. & Mar. Carrington and Marshman's Reports, Nisi Prius (1841-42)

C. & Marsh. Carrington & Marshman's English Nisi Prius Reports

C. & N. Cameron & Norwood's North Carolina Conference Reports

C. & O.R.Cas. Carrow & Oliver's English Railway & Canal Cases

C. & P. ● Carrington & Payne's English Nisi Prius Reports (1823-41)
● Craig & Phillips' Chancery Reports (1840-41)

C. & R. ● Clifford and Richards, Locus Standi (1873-84) (Eng.)
● Cockburn and Rowe's Election Cases. (1833) (Eng.)

C. & S. ● Clarke & Scully's Drainage Cases (Ontario)

● Clifford & Stephen, English Locus Standi Reports (1867-72)

C. & S.Dig. Connor & Simonton's South Carolina Digest

Ca. ● California
● Cambodian
● Case or Placitum
● Cases

Ca.2d California Supreme Court Reports, Second Series

Ca.A. California Appellate Reports

Ca.A.2d California Appellate Reports, Second Series

Ca.A.3d California Appellate Reports, Third Series

Ca.Celeb. Causes Celebres (Quebec Provincial Reports)

Ca.L.R. California Law Review

Ca. P. Cases in Parliament (Eng.)

Ca.Prac.C.P. Cooke's Practice Cases. (1706-47) (Eng.)

Ca.R. California Reporter

Ca.sa. Capias ad satisfaciendum (writ of execution)

Ca. Sett. Cases of Settlements and Removals. (1710-42) (Eng.)

Ca.t.Hard. Cases tempore Hardwicke, King's Bench. (1733-38) (Eng.)

Ca.t.K. ● Cases tempore King
● Cases tempore King, Chancery (1724-33)

Ca.t.King Cases temp. King, Chancery. (1724-33)

Ca.t.Lee Cases temp. Lee. (1752-58)

Ca.t.Talb. Cases tempore Talbot, Chancery (1734-38)

Ca.temp.F. Cases tempore Finch, Chancery (1673-81)

Ca.temp.H. Cases tempore, Hardwicke, King's Bench (1733-38)

Ca.temp.Hard. Cases tempore Hardwicke, King's Bench (1733-38)

Ca.temp.Holt. Cases tempore Holt, King's Bench

Ca.temp.K. Cases in Chancery tempore King, King's Bench (1724-33) (Eng.)

Ca.temp.Talb. Cases in Chancery tempore Talbot, King's Bench (1734-38) (Eng.)

Ca.temp.Talbot Cases tempore Talbot (1734-38)

Ca.U. California Unreported Cases

Ca.W.I.R. California Western Law Review

Cab.Lawy. Cabinet Lawyer by John Wade (Eng.)

Cab. & E. Cababe and Ellis' Queen's Bench Reports (1882-85) (Eng.)

Cab. & El. Cababe and Ellis' Queen's Bench Reports (1882-85) (Eng.)

Cab. & El. (Eng.) Cababe and Ellis' Queen's Bench Reports (1882-85) (Eng.)

Cab.& Ell. Cababe and Ellis' Queen's Bench Reports (1882-85)

Cadw.Dig. Cadwalader's Digest of Attorney-General's Opinions

Cadwalader. Cadwalader's Cases, U.S. District Court, Eastern District of Pennsylvania

Cahill's Ill.St. Cahill's Illinois Statutes

Cai. ● Caines' New York Cases in Error (1796-1805)
 ● Caines' Reports, New York Supreme Court
 ● Caines' Term Reports, New York Supreme Court

Cai.Cas. ● Caines' New York Cases in Error
 ● Caines' Reports, New York Supreme Court (1803-1805)
 ● Caines' Term Reports, New York Supreme Court

Cai.Cas.Err. Caines' New York Cases in Error

Cai.Pr. Caines' Practice

Cai.R. ● Caines' New York Cases in Error
 ● Caines' Reports, New York Supreme Court
 ● Caines' Term Reports, New York Supreme Court

Cai.T.R. Caines' Term Reports, New York Supreme Court

Cain. ● Caines' New York Cases in Error
 ● Caines' Reports, New York Supreme Court

 ● Caines' Term Reports, New York Supreme Court

Caines ● Caines' New York Cases in Error
 ● Caines' Reports, New York Supreme Court
 ● Caines' Term Reports, New York Supreme Court

Caines Cas. ● Caines' New York Cases in Error
 ● Caines' Reports, New York Supreme Court
 ● Caines' Term Reports, New York Supreme Court

Caines (N.Y.) ● Caines' New York Cases in Error
 ● Caines' Reports, New York Supreme Court
 ● Caines' Term Reports, New York Supreme Court

Caines Term.Rep. (N.Y.) Caines' Term Reports, New York Supreme Court

Cairns Dec. Cairns, Decisions in the Albert Arbitration (Reilly) (1871-75) (Eng.)

Cal. ● California
 ● California Reports
 ● Calcutta (Indian Law Reports, Calcutta Series)
 ● Calthrop English King's Bench Reports (1609-18)
 ● Caldecott, English Settlement Cases (1776-85)
 ● Calendars of the Proceedings in Chancery, Record Commission

Cal.2d California Reports, Second Series

Cal.Adm.Code. California Administrative Code

Cal.Adv.Legis.Serv. California Advance Legislative Service (Deering)

Cal.Agric.Code California Agriculture Code

Cal.App. California Appellate Reports

Cal.App.2d California Appellate Reports, Second Series

Cal.App.2d (Adv—) California Appellate Reports, 2d Series (Advance Parts)

Cal.App.Dec. California Appellate Decisions

Cal.App.Supp. · California Appellate Reports Supplement

Cal.App.2d Supp. California Appellate Reports, Second Series Supplement

Cal.App.3d Supp. California Appellate Reports, Third Series, Supplement

Cal.Bd.R.Co. California Board of Railroad Commissioners

Cal.Ch. Calendar of Proceedings in Chancery, tempore Elizabeth (1827-32)

Cal. [subject] Code (Deering) Deering's Annotated California Code

Cal. [subject] Code (West) West's Annotated California Code

Cal.Comp.Cases. California Compensation Cases

Cal.Dec. California Decisions

Cal.Gen.Laws Ann. Deering's California General Laws Annotated

Cal.Gen.Laws Ann. (Deering) Deering's California General Laws Annotated

Cal.I.A.C.C.C. California Industrial Accident Commission, Compensation Cases

Cal.I.A.C.Dec. California Industrial Accident Decisions

Cal.Ind.Acci.Dec. California Industrial Accidents Decisions

Cal.J.I.C. California Jury Instructions, Criminal

Cal.Jur. California Jurisprudence

Cal.Jur.2d California Jurisprudence, Second Edition

Cal.L.J. ● Calcutta Law Journal Reports (India)
● California Law Journal

Cal.L.R. Calcutta Law Reporter (India)

Cal.L.Rev. California Law Review

Cal.Leg.Adv. Calcutta Legal Adviser (India)

Cal.Leg.Obs. Calcutta Legal Observer (India)

Cal.Leg.Rec. California Legal Record, San Francisco

Cal.Legis.Serv. California Legislative Service (West)

Cal.P.Ch. Calendar of Proceedings in Chancery, tempore Elizabeth (1827-32)

Cal.P.U.C. Decisions of the California Public Utilities Commission

Cal.Penal Code California Penal Code

Cal.Prac. California Practice

Cal.R.C.Dec. California Railroad Commission Decisions

Cal.R.C.Dec.Dig. California Railroad Commission Digest of Decisions

Cal.R.Com. Opinions and Orders of the Railroad Commission of California

Cal.Rep. ● California Reports
● Calthrop, English King's Bench Reports

Cal.Rptr. California Reporter (West)

Cal.S.B.J. California State Bar Journal

Cal.S.D.A. Calcutta Sadr Diwani Adalat Reports (India)

Cal.Ser. Calcutta Series, Indian Law Reports

Cal.Stats. Statutes of California

Cal.Sup. California Superior Court, Reports of Cases in Appellate Departments

Cal.Sup.(Cal.) California Superior Court, Reports of Cases in Appellate Departments

Cal.Supp. California Superior Court, Reports of Cases in Appellate Departments

Cal.Unrep. California Unreported Cases (1855-1910)

Cal.Unrep.Cas. California Unreported Cases (1855-1910)

Cal.W.R. Calcutta Weekly Reporter (India)

Calc.L.J. Calcutta Law Journal (India)

Calc.Ser. Calcutta Series, Indian Law Reports

Calc.W.N. Calcutta Weekly Notes, (India)

Calcutta L.J. Calcutta Law Journal

Calcutta W.N. Calcutta Weekly Notes

Cald. • Caldecott's Magistrates' and Settlement Cases (1776-85) (Eng.)
• Caldwell's Reports (vols. 25-36 West Virginia)

Cald.(Eng.) Caldecott's Magistrates' and Settlement Cases (Eng.)

Cald.J.P. Caldecott's Magistrates' and Settlement Cases (Eng.)

Cald.M.Cas. Caldecott's Magistrates' and Settlement Cases (Eng.)

Cald.Mag.Cas. Caldecott's Magistrates' and Settlement Cases (Eng.)

Cald.Set.Cas. Caldecott's Magistrates' and Settlement Cases (Eng.)

Calif.L.Rev. California Law Review

Calif.Management Rev. California Management Review

Calif.S.B.J. California State Bar Journal

Calif.W.Int'l L.J. California Western International Law Journal

Calif.W.L.Rev. California Western Law Review

Calif.West.Int'l L.J. California Western International Law Journal

Calif.Western Int.L.J. California Western International Law Journal

Calif.Western L.Rev. California Western Law Review

Call Call's Virginia Reports (1797-1825) (vols. 5-10 Virginia)

Call.Sew. Callis on Sewers

Call.(Va.) Call, Virginia Reports (1797-1825) (vols. 5-10 Virginia)

Callis The Reading of Robert Callis on the Statute of Sewers. 23 Hen. 8. c. 5. delivered by him at Gray's Inn August 1622

Callis, Sew. Callis on Sewers

Callman, Unfair Comp. Callman on Unfair Competition & Trade Marks

Calth. • Calthrop's City of London Cases, King's Bench (Eng.)
• Calthrop's King's Bench Reports (vol. 80 Eng. Reprint)

Calth.(Eng.) • Calthrop's City of London Cases, King's Bench (Eng.)

• Calthrop's King's Bench Reports (vol. 80 Eng. Reprint)

Calthr. • Calthrop's City of London Cases, King's Bench (Eng.)
• Calthrop's King's Bench Reports (vol. 80 Eng. Reprint)

Calv.Lex. Calvini Lexicon Juridicum

Calv.Parties Calvert's Parties to Suits in Equity

Calvin. Calvinus Lexicon Juridicum

Calvin, Lex. Calvin's Lexicon Juridicum

Calvin.Lex.Jurid. Calvinus Lexicon Juridicum

Cam. Cameron, Reports, Upper Canada, Queen's Bench

Cam.Cas. Cameron's Supreme Court Cases, Canada

Cam.Duc. Camera Ducata (Duchy Chamber)

Cam.Op. Cameron's Legal Opinions, Toronto

Cam.Prac. Cameron's Supreme Ct. Practice (Canada)

Cam.S.C. Cameron's Supreme Court Cases (Canada)

Cam.Scacc. Camera Scaccarii (Exchequer Chamber) (Eng.)

Cam.Stell. Camera Stellate (Star Chamber) (Eng.)

Cam. & N. Cameron & Norwood's North Carolina Conference Reports

Cam. & Nor. Cameron & Norwood's North Carolina Conference Reports (1800-04)

Camb.L.J. Cambridge Law Journal

Cambria Cambria County Legal Journal (Pa.)

Cambria Co.L.J. Cambria County Legal Journal (Pa.)

Cambria Co.(Pa.) Cambria County Legal Journal (Pa.)

Cambridge L.J. Cambridge Law Journal

Camd.Brit. Camden's Britannia

Camden Camden's Britannia

Cameron Cameron's Supreme Court Cases

Cameron (Can.) Cameron's Supreme Court Cases (Canada)

Cameron Cas.(Can.) Cameron's Supreme Court Cases (Canada)

Cameron Pr. Cameron's Practice (Canada)

Cameron Pr.(Can.) Cameron's Practice (Canada)

Camp.
- Campbell's English Nisi Prius Reports
- Campbell's Reports of Taney's United States Circuit Court Decisions
- Campbell's Legal Gazette Reports (Pa.)
- Campbell's Reports (vols. 27-58 Nebraska)
- Campbell's Compendium of Roman Law
- Camp's Reports (vol. 1 North Dakota)

Camp.Ch.Jus. Campbell's Lives of the Chief Justices

Camp.Dec. Campbell's Reports of Taney's Decisions, U.S. Circuit Court

Camp.Ld.Ch. Campbell's Lives of the Lord Chancellors

Camp.Lives Ld.Ch. Campbell's Lives of the Lord Chancellors

Camp.N.P. Campbell's English Nisi Prius Reports (1807-16)

Camp.Rom.L. Campbell's Compendium of Roman Law

Camp.Rom.L.Comp. Campbell's Compendium of Roman Law

Campb.
- Campbell's English Nisi Prius Reports
- Campbell's Reports of Taney's United States Circuit Court Decisions
- Campbell's Legal Gazette Reports, Pennsylvania
- Campbell's Reports (vols. 27-58 Nebraska)
- Campbell's Compendium of Roman Law

Campb.Dec. Campbell's Reports of Taney's Decisions, U.S. Circuit Court

Campb.(Eng.) Campbell's English Nisi Prius Reports (170, 171 Eng. Reprint)

Campb.(Pa.) Campbell's Legal Gazette Reports (Pa.)

Campbell
- Campbell's English Nisi Prius Reports
- Campbell's Reports of Taney's United States Circuit Court Decisions
- Campbell's Legal Gazette Reports (Pa.)
- Campbell's Reports (vols. 27-58 Nebraska)
- Campbell's Compendium of Roman Law

Can. Canada

Can.Abr. Canadian Abridgment

Can.App. Canadian Reports, Appellate Cases

Can.App.Cas. Canadian Appeal Cases

Can.B.A.J. Canadian Bar Association Journal

Can.B.J. Canadian Bar Journal

Can.B.R. Canadian Bar Review

Can.B.Rev. Canadian Bar Review

Can.B.Year Book. Canadian Bar Association Year Book

Can.Bank. Canadian Banker and ICB Review

Can.Bank.R. Canadian Bankruptcy Reports

Can.Bankr. Canadian Bankruptcy Reports

Can.Bankr. Canadian Bankrupty Reports Annotated

Can.Bankr.Ann.(N.S.) Canadian Bankruptcy Reports Annotated, New Series

Can.Bar.Rev. Canadian Bar Review

Can.C.C. Canada Criminal Cases Annotated

Can.Chart.Acc. Canadian Chartered Accountant

Can.Com.Cas. Canadian Commercial Law Reports (1901-05)

Can.Com.L.R. Canadian Commercial Law Reports (1901-05)

Can.Com.R. Canadian Commercial Law Reports (1901-05)

Can.Cr.Acts. Canada Criminal Acts, Taschereau's edition

Can.Cr.Cas. Canadian Criminal Cases

Can.Crim. Criminal Reports (Canada)

Can.Crim.Cas. Canadian Criminal Cases Annotated

Can.Crim.Cas.Ann. Canadian Criminal Cases Annotated

Can.Crim.Cas.(N.S.) Canadian Criminal Cases, New Series

Can.Ex.R. Canadian Exchequer Reports

Can.Exch.
- Canada Law Reports, Exchequer
- Canada Exchequer Court Reports

Can.Gaz. Canada Gazette (regulations)

Can.J.Correction Canadian Journal of Correction

Can.J.Pol.Sc. Canadian Journal of Political Science

Can.L.J.
- Canada Law Journal, Montreal
- Canada Law Journal, Toronto

Can.L.J.N.S. Canada Law Journal, New Series

Can.L.R. Canada Law Reports, Exchequer & Supreme Court, in two series

Can.L.Rev. Canadian Law Review

Can.L.T. Canadian Law Times

Can.L.T.Occ.N. Canadian Law Times, Occasional Notes

Can.Lab. Canadian Labour

Can.Leg.N. Canada Legal News

Can.Mun.J. Canadian Municipal Journal

Can.P.R. Canadian Patent Reporter

Can.Persp. Canadian Perspectives on International Law and Organization

Can.Pub.Admin. Canadian Public Administration

Can.R.A.C. Canadian Reports, Appeal Cases

Can.R.App.Cas. Canadian Reports, Appeal Cases

Can.R.C. Railway Commission of Canada

Can.R.Cas. Canadian Railway Cases

Can.Rev.Stat. Revised Statutes of Canada

Can.Ry.Cas. Canada Railway Cases

Can.Ry. & T.Cas. Canadian Railway and Transport Cases

Can.S.C.
- Canada Supreme Court
- Canada Supreme Court Reports

Can.S.C.Rep. Canada Supreme Court Reports

Can.S.Ct.
- Canada Law Reports, Supreme Court
- Canada Supreme Court Reports

Can.Stat. Statutes of Canada

Can.Sup.Ct. Canada Supreme Court Reports

Can.T.S. Canada Treaty Series

Can.Tax App.Bd. Canada Tax Appeal Board Cases

Can.Tax Cas.Ann. Canada Tax Cases Annotated

Can.Tax J. Canadian Tax Journal

Can.Tax News. Canadian Tax News

Can.Terr. Territories Law Reports (1885-1907) (Canada)

Can.Wel. Canadian Welfare

Can.Y.B.Int'l L. Canadian Yearbook of International Law

Can.Yearbook Int.L. Canadian Yearbook of International Law

Canada Commerce. Canadian Department of Industry, Trade and Commerce

Canada L.T. Canadian Law Times

Canal Zone Canal Zone Supreme Court

Canal Zone Sup.Ct. Canal Zone Supreme Court Reports

Candy. Printed Judgments of Sind by Candy and Birdwood (India)

Cane & L. Cane & Leigh Crown Cases Reserved (Eng.)

Cantor, Med. & Surg. Cantor's Traumatic Medicine & Surgery for the Attorney

Cantwell Cantwell's Cases on Tolls & Customs (Ir.)

Cap.
- Capital
- Chapter

Cape L.J. Cape Law Journal (S. Africa)

Cape Law J. Cape Law Journal, Grahamstown (Cape of Good Hope)

Cape P.Div. Cape Provincial Division Reports (S. Africa)

Cape T.Div. Cape Provincial Division Reports (S. Africa)

Cape T.R. Cape Times Reports, Supreme Court, Cape of Good Hope (S. Africa)

Capital U.L.Rev. Capital University Law Review

Car. ● Carolus (as 4 Car.II)
     ● Carolina

Car.H. & A. Carrow, Hamerton & Allen's New Sessions Cases (1844-51) (Eng.)

Car.L.J. Carolina Law Journal

Car.L.Rep. Carolina Law Repository, North Carolina Reports, vol. 4 (1813-16)

Car.Laws. Caruther's History of a Lawsuit. Cases in Chancery

Car.Law Repos. Carolina Law Repository (N.C.)

Car. O. & B. English Railway & Canal Cases, by Carrow, Oliver, Bevan et al (1835-55)

Car. & K. Carrington & Kirwan's English Nisi Prius Reports (vols. 174, 175 Eng. Reprint)

Car. & K.(Eng.) Carrington & Kirwan's English Nisi Prius Reports (vols. 174, 175 Eng. Reprint)

Car. & Kir. Carrington & Kirwan's English Nisi Prius Reports (vols. 174, 175 Eng. Reprint)

Car. & M. Carrington & Marshman's English Nisi Prius Reports (1840-42)

Car. & M.(Eng.) Carrington & Marshman's English Nisi Prius Reports (1840-42)

Car. & Mar. Carrington & Marshman's English Nisi Prius Reports (1840-42)

Car. & O. English Railway & Canal Cases, by Carrow, Oliver et al (1835-55)

Car. & Ol. English Railway & Canal Cases, by Carrow, Oliver et al (1835-55)

Car. & P. Carrington's & Payne's English Nisi Prius Reports (1823-41)

Car. & P.(Eng.) Carrington's & Payne's English Nisi Prius Reports (1823-41)

Carey.M.R. Manitoba Reports (1875)

Carl. Carleton, New Brunswick Reports

Carmody-Wait, N.Y.Prac. Carmody-Witt Cyclopedia of New York Practice

Carp. ● Carpenter's Reports (vols. 52-53 California)
     ● Carpmael's Patent Cases (1602-1842)

Carp.P.C. Carpmael's Patent Cases (1602-1842) (Eng.)

Carpenter Carpenter's Reports (vols. 52-53 California)

Carr. Carriers

Carr.Cas. Carran's Summary Cases, India

Carr.,Ham.& Al. Carrow, Hamerton & Allen's New Sessions Cases (Eng.)

Carr. & K. Carrington & Kirwan

Carr. & M. Carrington and Marshman's English Nisi Prius Reports

Carrau. Carrau's edition of "Summary Cases," Bengal

Carsh. Carshaltown's Court Rolls (Eng.)

Cart. ● Carter's English Common Pleas Reports, 1664-76
     ● Carter's Reports (1, 2 Indiana)
     ● Carthew's English King's Bench Reports (1686-1701)
     ● Cartwright's Cases on British North America Act (Canada)

Cart.B.N.A. Cartwright's Constitutional Cases (1868-96) (Can.)

Cart.Cas.(Can.) Cartwright's Cases

Cart.de For. Carta de Foresta (the Charter of the Forest)

Carter ● Carter's English Common Pleas Reports, same as Orlando Bridgman
     ● Carter's Reports (vols. 1, 2 Indiana)

Carter (Eng.) Carter (124 Eng. Reprint)

Carth. Carthew's English King's Bench Reports (1686-1701)

Carth.(Eng.) Carthew (King's Bench) (90 Eng. Reprint)

Cartm. Cartmell's Trade Mark Cases (1876-92) (Eng.)

Cartw.C.C. Cartwright's Constitutional Cases (Canada)

Cartwr.Cas. Cartwright's Cases (Canada)

Carv.Carr. Carver's Treatise on the Law Relating to the Carriage of Goods by Sea

Carver. Carver on Carriage of Goods by Sea (1885-1957)

Cary. Cary's English Chancery Reports (1537-1604)

Cary(Eng.) Cary (21 Eng. Reprint)

Cary Lit. Cary's Commentary on Littleton's Tenures

Cas. ● Casey's Reports (vols. 25-36 Pennsylvania State)
     ● Casualty

Cas.App. Cases of Appeal to the House of Lords

Cas.Arg. & Dec. Cases Argued and Decreed in Chancery, English

Cas.B.R. Cases Banco Regis tempore William III (12 Modern Reports)

Cas.B.R. (T.W. III) 12 Modern Reports (1690-1702) (Eng.)

Cas.B.R.Holt. Cases and Resolutions (of settlements; not Holt's King's Bench Reports) (Eng.)

Cas.C.L. Cases in Crown Law (Eng.)

Cas.C.R. Cases tempore Wm.III (vol. 12 Modern Reports) (Eng.)

Cas.Ch. ● Cases in Chancery (Eng.)
     ● Select Cases in Chancery (1724-33) (Eng.)
     ● Cases in Chancery (vol. 9 Modern Reports)

Cas.Ch. 1, 2, 3 Cases in Chancery tempore Car. II

Cas.Eq. ● Cases in Equity, Gilbert's Reports
     ● Cases and Opinions in Law Equity, and Conveyancing

Cas.Eq.Abr. Cases in Equity Abridged (1667-1744) (Eng.)

Cas.F.T. Cases tempore Talbot, by Forrester, English Chancery

Cas.H.L. Cases in the House of Lords (Eng.)

Cas. in C. ● Cases in Chancery (Eng.)
     ● Select Cases in Chancery (Eng.)

Cas.in.Ch. Cases in Chancery, 3 Parts. (1660-88) (Eng.)

Cas.K.B. Cases in King's Bench (8 Modern Reports) (Eng.)

Cas.K.B.t.H. Cases tempore Hardwicke (W. Kelynge, English King's Bench Reports)

Cas.K.B. & Hard. Kelynge (W.) (1730-32)

Cas.L.Eq. Cases in Law and Equity (10 Mod.) (1720-73)

Cas.L. & Eq. ● Cases in Law and Equity (vol. 10 Modern Reports) (Eng.)
     ● (Gilbert's) Cases in Law and Equity (Eng.)

Cas.Op. Burton. Cases and Opinions

Cas.P. (or Parl.) Cases in Parliament

Cas.Pr. Cases of Practice, English King's Bench

Cas.Pr.C.P. Cases of Practice. English Common Pleas (Cooke's Reports) (1702-27)

Cas.Pr.K.B. Cases of Practice in the King's Bench (1702-27) (Eng.)

Cas.Pra.C.P. Cases of Practice, Common Pleas (1702-27) (Eng.)

Cas.Pra.K.B. Cases of Practice in King's Bench (1702-27) (Eng.)

Cas.Prac.C.P. Cases of Practice, Common Pleas (1702-27) (Eng.)

Cas.R. Casey's Reports (25-36, Pennsylvania State)

Cas.S.C. (Cape G.H.) Cases in the Supreme Court, Cape of Good Hope

Cas.S.M. Cases of Settlement, King's Bench (1713-15) (Eng.)

Cas.Self Def. Horrigan & Thompson's Cases on Self-Defense

Cas.Sett. Cases of Settlement and Removals (1710-42) (Eng.)

Cas.Six Cir. Cases on the Six Circuits, (1841-43) (Ireland)

Cas.t.ch.II. Cases tempore Charles II., in vol. 3 of Reports in Chancery (Eng.)

Cas.t.F. Cases tempore Finch, English Chancery (23 Eng. Reprint)

Cas.t.Finch (Eng.) Cases tempore Finch, English Chancery (23 Eng. Reprint)

Cas.t.Geo.I. Cases tempore George I., English Chancery (8, 9 Modern Reports)

Cas.t.H.
- Cases tempore Hardwicke, English King's Bench (Ridgway, Lee, or Annaly) (1733-38)
- Cases tempore Holt, English King's Bench (Holt's Reports)
- West, Chancery Reports, tempore Hardwicke

Cas.t.Hard.(by Lee) Cases tempore Hardwicke, Lee's English King's Bench Reports (1733-38)

Cas.t.Hardw.
- Cases tempore Hardwicke, English King's Bench (Ridgway, Lee or Annaly) (1733-38)
- West, Chancery Reports, tempore Hardwicke (Eng.)

Cas.t.Holt. Cases tempore Holt, English King's Bench (Holt's Reports)

Cas.t.K.
- Select Cases tempore King, English Chancery (edited by MacNaghten) (1724-33)
- Moseley, Chancery Reports, tempore King

Cas.t.King
- Select Cases tempore King, English Chancery (edited by Macnaghten) (1724-33)
- Moseley, Chancery Reports, tempore King (Eng.)

Cas.t.Lee. (Phillimore) Cases tempore Lee, English Ecclesiastical

Cas.t.Mac. Cases tempore Macelesfield (10 Modern Reports) (1710-25) (Eng.)

Cas.t.Maccl. Cases tempore Macelesfield (10 Modern Reports) (1710-25) (Eng.)

Cas.t.Q.A. Cases tempore Queen Anne (11 Modern Reports) (1702-30) (Eng.)

Cas.t.Q.Anne Cases tempore Queen Anne (11 Modern Reports) (1702-30) (Eng.)

Cas.t.Sugd. Cases tempore Sugden, Irish Chancery

Cas.t.Tal. Cases tempore Talbot, English Chancery (1734-38)

Cas.t.Talb. Cases tempore Talbot (1734-38) (Eng.)

Cas.t.Wm.III. Cases tempore William III. (12 Modern Reports)

Cas.temp.Hardw. Cases tempore Hardwicke

Cas.temp.Lee. Cases tempore Lee (Eng. Ecc.)

Cas.temp.Talb. Cases tempore Talbot

Cas.Tak. & Adj. Cases Taken and Adjudged (first edition of Reports in Chancery; see n. 5, p. 76) (Eng.)

Cas.Tax Canada Tax Cases Annotated

Cas.w.Op. Cases with opinions, by Eminent Counsel (1700-75)

Cas.Wm.I. Bigelow, Cases, William I. to Richard I.

Cas. & Op. Cases with Opinions, by Eminent Counsel (1700-75) (Eng.)

Case W.Res.J.Int.L. Case Western Reserve Journal of International Law

Case W.Res.L.Rev. Case Western Reserve Law Review

Case & Com. Case and Comment

Cases in Ch. Select Cases in Chancery (Eng.)

Casey. Casey's Reports (25-36 Pennsylvania State)

Cass. Cour de Cassation, Corte di Cassazione (Supreme Court of Appeal)

Cass.Dig. Cassel's Digest (Canada)

Cass.L.G.B. Casson's Local Government Board Decisions (1902-16) (Eng.)

Cass.Prac. Cassels' Practice Cases (Can.)

Cass.S.C. Cassels' Supreme Court Decisions

Cass.Sup.C.Prac. Cassel's Supreme Court Practice, 2d edition by Masters

Cassiod.Var. Cassiodori Variarum

Cates. Cates' Reports (vols. 109-127 Tennessee Reports)

Cath. Catholic

Catholic Law. The Catholic Lawyer

Catholic U.L.R. Catholic University Law Review

Catholic Univ.L.Rev. Catholic University Law Review

Cawl. Cawley's Laws concerning Jesuits, etc. 1680

Cay Abr. Cay's Abridgment or the English Statutes

Cb.L.R. Columbia Law Review

Cel.Tr. Burke's Celebrated Trials

Census Bureau of the Census

Cent. ● Central
      ● Central Reporter (Pa.)

Cent.Crim.C.Cas. Central Criminal Court Cases, Sessions Papers (Eng.)

Cent.Crim.C.R. Central Criminal Court Reports (Eng.)

Cent.Dict. Century Dictionary

Cent.Dict.and Cyc. Century Dictionary and Cyclopedia

Cent.Dict. & Ency. Century Dictionary and Encyclopedia

Cent.Dig. Century Edition of the American Digest System (West)

Cent.L.J. Central Law Journal (St. Louis, Mo.)

Cent.L.Mo. Central Law Monthly

Cent.Law J. Central Law Journal (St. Louis, Mo.)

Cent.Prov.L.R. Central Provinces Law Reports (India)

Cent.R.(Pa.) Central Reporter (Pa.)

Cent.Rep. Central Reporter

Centr.Cr.Ct.R. Central Criminal Court, Sessions Papers, London

cert. ● certified from, or certified to
      ● Certiorari

cert.den. Certiorari denied

cert.dis. Certiorari dismissed

cert.dismissed certiorari dismissed

Cert.granted Petition to U.S. Supreme Court for writ of certiorari granted

Ceyl.Cr.App.R. Ceylon Criminal Appeal Reports

Ceyl.L.J. Ceylon Law Journal

Ceyl.L.R. Ceylon Law Recorder

Ceyl.L.Rec. Ceylon Law Recorder

Ceyl.L.Rev. Ceylon Law Review

Ceyl.Leg.Misc. Ceylon Legal Miscellany

Ceylon L.R. Ceylon Law Review and Reports

cf. conferre (compare)

Ch. ● Chalmers' Colonial Opinions
      ● Chancellor's Court (Eng.)
      ● Chancery Court or Division
      ● Chapter
      ● Court of Chancery, New Jersey
      ● English Law Reports, Chancery Division
      ● English Law Reports, (1891 onwards) Chancery Appeals

Ch.App. ● Chambre d'Appel
      ● Court of Appeal in Chancery (Eng.)
      ● Law Reports, Chancery Appeals (1865-75) (Eng.)

Ch.App.Cas. Chancery Appeal Cases, English Law Reports

Ch.Bills. Chitty on Bills

Ch.Black. ● Chitty's Blackstone
      ● Chase's Blackstone

Ch.Cal. Calendar of Proceedings in Chancery (Eng.)

Ch.Cas. ● Cases in Chancery (1660-97) (Eng.)
      ● Cases in Chancery tempore King's Bench (Eng.)

Ch.Cas.(Eng.) Cases in Chancery (1660-97) (Eng.)

Ch.Ca.Ch.(or C.L.) Choyce Cases in Chancery (1557-1606) (Eng.) or Common Law

Ch.Cas.in Ch. Choyce Cases in Chancery (1557-1606) (Eng.)

Ch.Ch. Upper Canada Chancery Chambers Reports

Ch.Cham. Upper Canada Chancery Chambers Reports

Ch.Chamb. Chancery Chambers (Upper Canada)

Ch.Chamb.(Can.) Chancery Chambers (Upper Canada)

Ch.Col.Op.   Chalmers' Colonial Opinions (Eng.)

Ch.Cr.L.   Chitty's Criminal Law

Ch.ct.   Chancery Court

Ch.D.   English Law Reports, Chancery Division

Ch.D.2d   English Law Reports, Chancery Division, Second Series

Ch.Dig.   Chaney's Digest, Michigan Reports

Ch.Div.   English Law Reports, Chancery Division

Ch.Div.(Eng.)   English Law Reports, Chancery Division

Ch.Div'l Ct.   Chancery Divisional Court (Eng.)

Ch.(Eng.)   ● Chalmers' Colonial Opinions
● English Law Reports, Chancery Division
● English Law Reports, Chancery Appeals

Ch.Is.Rolls.   Rolls of the Assizes in Channel Islands

Ch.J.   Chief Justice

Ch.K.   Charter K, Home Loan Bank Board (U.S.)

Ch.L.   University of Chicago Law Review

Ch.L.R.   University of Chicago Law Review

Ch.Pl.   Chitty on Pleading

Ch.Pre.   Precedents in Chancery (1689-1723) (Eng.)

Ch.R.   ● Chitty's King's Bench Reports (Eng.)
● Irish Chancery Reports
● Reports in Chancery (1615-1712) (Eng.)
● Upper Canada Chancery Chambers Reports

Ch.R.M.   Charlton's Reports (Georgia Reports, 1811-37)

Ch.Rep.   ● Reports in Chancery
● Irish Chancery Reports

Ch.Rep.Ir.   Irish Chancery Reports

Ch.Repts.   ● Reports in Chancery
● Irish Chancery Reports

Ch.Rob.   Robinson's Admiralty Reports (1799-1808) (Eng.)

Ch.Sent.   Chancery Sentinel, Saratoga, New York

Ch.Sent(NY)   Chancery Sentinel, Saratoga, New York

Ch.T.U.P.   T.U.P. Charlton's Georgia Reports

Ch.& Cl.Cas.   Cripp's Church and Clergy Cases

Ch.& P.   Chambers and Pretty, Cases on Finance Act (1909-10) (Eng.)

Cha.App.   Chancery Appeal Cases English Law Reports

Chaffee & Admin.Law   Chaffe & Nathanson's Administrative Law, Cases & Materials

Chal.Op.   Chalmers' Opinions, Constitutional Law (1669-1809) (Eng.)

Challis   Challis on Real Property (1885-1911)

Chalmers   Chalmers on Bills of Exchange (1878-1952)

Cham.   Chambers' Upper Canada Reports

Cham.Rep.   Chambers Reports, Upper Canada (1849-82)

Chamb.   Chambers' Upper Canada Reports

Chamb.Dig.P.H.C.   Chambers' Digest of Public Health Cases

Chamb.Rep.   Chancery Chambers' Reports, Ontario

Chamber.   Chamber Reports, Upper Canada

Chambers' Cyclopedia.   Ephraim Chambers English Cyclopedia

Champ.   Champions's Cases, Wine & Beer-Houses Act (Eng.)

Chan.   ● Chaney's Reports (vols. 37-58 Michigan)
● Chancellor
● Chancery

Chan.Cas.   Cases in Chancery (1660-97)

Chan.Chamb.   Chancery Chambers Reports, Upper Canada (1857-72)

Chan.Ct.   Chancery Court

Chan.Rep.C.   Reports in Chancery (1615-1712)

Chan Toon.   Leading Cases on Buddhist Law

Chand.   ● Chandler's Reports (vols. 20, 38-44 New Hampshire)

- Chandler's Reports (Wisconsin (1849-52)

Chand.Cr.T. Chandler's American Criminal Trials

Chand.Crim.Tr. Chandler's American Criminal Trials

Chand.(NH) Chandler's Reports (vols. 20, 38-44 New Hampshire)

Chand.(Wis.) Chandler's Reports (Wisconsin 1849-52)

Chandl.
- Chandler's Reports (Wisconsin) (1849-52)
- Chandler's Reports (vols. 20, 38-44 New Hampshire)

Chaney Chaney's Reports (vols. 37-58 Michigan)

Chaney (Mich.) Chaney's Reports (vols. 37-58 Michigan)

Char.Cham.Cas. Charley's Chamber Cases (Eng.)

Char.Merc. Charta Mercatoria

Char.Pr.Cas. Charley's Practice Cases (1875-81) (Eng.)

Charl.Chas.Ca. Charley's Chamber Cases (1875-76) (Eng.)

Charl.Pr.Cas. Charley's Practice Cases (1875-81) (Eng.)

Charl.R.M. R.M. Charlton's Georgia Reports

Charlet.(Ga.) R.M. Charlton's Georgia Reports

Charley Pr.Cas. Charley's Practice Cases (Eng.)

Charlt.
- R.M. Charlton's Georgia Reports
- T.U.P. Charlton's Georgia Reports

Charlt.R.M. R.M. Charlton's Georgia Reports

Charlt.T.U.P. T.U.P. Charlton's Georgia Reports

Chart. Rotulus Chartarum (The Charter Roll)

Chart.Foresta. Charta de Foresta

Chase. Chase's United States Circuit Court Decisions

Chase Dec. Chase, U.S. Circuit Court Decisions

Chase, Steph.Dig.Ev. Chase on Stephens' Digest of Evidence

Chase Tr. Chase's Trial (Impeachment) by the United States Senate

Chem. Chemical

Ches.Ca. Report of the Chesapeake Case, New Brunswick

Chest. Chester County (Pa.)

Chest.Co.Rep. Chester County Reports (Pa.)

Chester Co.(Pa.) Chester County Reports (Pa.)

Chester Co.Rep. Chester County Reports (Pa.)

Chetty Sudder Dewanny Adawlut Cases, Madras (India)

Chev. Cheves' South Carolina Law Reports (1839-1940)

Chev.Ch. Cheves' South Carolina Equity Reports (1839-1940)

Chev.Eq. Cheves' South Carolina Equity Reports (1839-1940)

Cheves. Cheves' South Carolina Law Reports (1839-1940)

Cheves Eq.(SC) Cheves' South Carolina Equity Reports

Cheves L.(SC) Cheves' South Carolina Equity Reports (1839-1940)

Chi. Chicago

Chi.B.Rec. Chicago Bar Record

Chi.-Kent Chicago-Kent

Chi-Kent L.Rev. Chicago-Kent Law Review

Chi-Kent Rev. Chicago-Kent Law Review

Chi.L.B. Chicago Law Bulletin

Chi.L.J. Chicago Law Journal

Chi.L.R. Chicago Law Record

Chi.Leg.N. Chicago Legal News (Ill.)

Chic.L.R. Chicago Law Bulletin, Illinois

Chic.L.J. Chicago Law Journal

Chic.L.R. Chicago Law Record

Chic.L.T. Chicago Law Times

Chic.Leg.N. Chicago Legal News, Illinois

Chicago L.B. Chicago Law Bulletin, Ill.

Chicago L.J. Chicago Law Journal

Chicago L.Rec. Chicago Law Record

Chicago L.Record (Ill.) Chicago Law Record

Chicago L.T. Chicago Law Times

Chicago Leg.News (Ill.) Chicago Legal News

Child.Ct. Children's Court

China (PR) People's Republic of China

China (Rep.) Republic of China

China Law Rev. China Law Review, Shanghai, China

Chip. ● Chipman's Reports, New Brunswick (1825-35)
● Chipman's Reports (Vermont 1789-1824)

Chip.D. D.Chipman, Vermont Reports, 2 vols.

Chip.Ms. Chipman's Manuscript Reports, New Brunswick

Chip.N. N. Chipman's Vermont Reports

Chip (Vt.) Chipman's Reports (Vermont 1789-1824)

Chip.W. Chipman's New Brunswick Reports

Chir. Wisconsin Board of Examiners in Chiropractic

Chit. ● Chitty's English Bail Court Reports
● Chitty's English King's Bench Practice Reports (1819-20)

Chit.Arch.Pr. Chitty's Edition of Archbold's Practice

Chit.Archb.Pr. Chitty's Archbold's Practice

Chit.B.C. Chitty's English Bail Court Reports (1770-1822) (Eng.)

Chit.Bills Chitty on Bills

Chit.Bl. Chitty's edition of Blackstone's Commentaries

Chit.Bl.Comm. Chitty's Edition of Blackstone's Commentaries

Chit.Burn's J. Chitty's edition of Burn's Justice

Chit.Com.Law. Chitty on Commercial Law

Chit.Con. Chitty on Contracts

Chit.Cont. Chitty on Contracts

Chit.Cr.L. Chitty's Criminal Law

Chit.Cr.Law Chitty's Criminal Law

Chit.Crim.Law Chitty's Criminal Law

Chit.Des. Chitty on the Law of Descents

Chit.F. Chitty's King's Bench Forms (Eng.)

Chit.Gen.Pr. Chitty's General Practice

Chit.Med.Jur. Chitty on Medical Jurisprudence

Chit.Pl. Chitty on Pleading

Chit.Pr. Chitty's General Practice

Chit.Prec. Chitty's Precedents in Pleading

Chit.Prer. Chitty's Prerogatives of the Crown

Chit.R. Chitty's English Bail Court Reports

Chit.St. Chitty's Statutes of Practical Utility (1235-1948) (Eng.)

Chit.Stat. Chitty's Statutes of Practical Utility (1235-1948) (Eng.)

Chit.& H.Bills. Chitty & Hulme on Bills of Exchange

Chitt. Chitty's English Bail Court Reports

Chitt.& Pat. Chitty & Patell's Supreme Court Appeals (India)

Chitty. Chitty on Bills

Chitty BC (Eng.) Chitty Bail Court Reports

Chitty, Bl.Comm. Chitty's Edition of Blackstone's Commentaries

Chitty, Com.Law. Chitty on Commercial Law

Chitty, Contracts Chitty on Contracts

Chitty Eq.Ind. Chitty's Equity Index

Chitty's L.J. Chitty's Law Journal

Cho.Ca.Ch. Choyce Cases in Chancery (1557-1606) (Eng.)

Choyce Cas.Ch. Choyce's Cases in Chancery (Eng.)

Choyce Cas.(Eng.) Choyce's Cases in Chancery (Eng.)

Chr.Rep. Chamber Reports (Upper Canada)

Chr.Rob.. Christopher Robinson's English Admiralty Reports

Chron.Div.Cts. Chronicles of the Divorce Courts

Chron.Jur. Chronica Juridicalia

chs. chapters

Chute, Eq. Chute's Equity under the Judicature Act

Chy.Ch. Upper Canada Chancery Chambers Reports

Chy.Chrs. Upper Canada Chancery Chambers Reports

Ci.L.R. Cincinnati Law Review

Cie. Compagnie (French term for "company")

Cin.   Cincinnati

Cin.L.Rev.   University of Cincinnati Law Review

Cin.Law Bul.   Cincinnati Law Bulletin

Cin.Law Rev.   University of Cincinnati Law Review

Cin.Mun.Dec.   Cincinnati Municipal Decisions

Cin.R.   Cincinnati Superior Court Reports (Ohio)

Cin.Rep.   Cincinnati Superior Court Reports (Ohio)

Cin.S.C.R.   Cincinnati Superior Court Reports (Ohio)

Cin.S.C.Rep.   Cincinnati Superior Court Reports (Ohio)

Cin.Sup.Ct.Rep.   Cincinnati Superior Court Reports (Ohio)

Cin.Super.Ct.Rep'r.   Cincinnati Superior Court Reports (Ohio)

Cin.Super.(Ohio)   Cincinnati Superior Court Reports (Ohio)

Cinc.L.Bul.   ● Cincinnati Law Bulletin
         ● Weekly Law Bulletin (Ohio)

Cir.   ● Circuit Court of Appeals
     ● Connecticut Circuit Court Reports

Cir.Ct.   Circuit Court

Cir.Ct.App.   Circuit Court of Appeal

Cir.Ct.Dec.   Circuit Court Decisions

Cir.Ct.Dec.(Ohio)   Circuit Court Decisions (Ohio)

Cir.Ct.R.   Circuit Court Reports (Ohio)

Cir.Ct.Rule   Circuit Court Rule

Cir.Ord.N.W.P.   Circular Orders, Northwestern Provinces (India)

cit.   ● The Citator
     ● cited in
     ● citing

City Civ.Ct.Act.   New York City Civil Court Act

City Crim.Ct.Act.   New York City Criminal Court Act

City Ct.   City Court

City Ct.R.   City Court Reports (New York)

City Ct.R.Supp.   City Court Reports, Supplement (New York)

City Ct.Rep.   City Court Reports (New York)

City Ct.Rep.Supp.   City Court Reports, Supplement (New York)

City Ct.Supp.(NY)   City Court Reports, Supplement (New York)

City H.Rec.   New York, City Hall Recorder

City H.Rep.   City Hall Reporter (Lomas, N.Y.)

City Hall Rec.   City Hall Recorder (New York)

City Hall Rec.(NY)   City Hall Recorder (New York)

City Hall Rep.   City Hall Reporter, Lomas (New York)

City Hall Rep.(NY)   City Hall Reporter, Lomas (New York)

City Rec.   New York, City Record

City Rec.(NY)   New York, City Record

Civ.   ● Civil
     ● civile (for civil cases)
     ● Texas Civil Appeals Reports

Civ.App.   Court of Civil Appeals

Civ.Code   Civil Code

Civ.Code Practice   Civil Code of Practice

Civ.Ct.   Civil Court

Civ.Ct.Rec.   Civil Court of Record

Civ.Lib.Dock.   Civil Liberties Docket

Civ.Lib.Rptr.   Civil Liberties Reporter

Civ.Pr.   Civil Procedure Reports, New York

Civ.Pr.Rep.   Civil Procedure Reports, New York

Civ.Prac.   Civil Practice Law and Rules

Civ.Prac.Act   Civil Practice Act

Civ.Prac.(NY)   New York Civil Practice

Civ.Pro.   Civil Procedure Reports (New York)

Civ.Pro.R.   Civil Procedure Reports (New York)

Civ.Proc.   Civil Procedure

Civ.Proc.(NY)   New York Civil Procedure

Civ.Proc.R.   Civil Procedure Reports (New York)

Civ.Proc.Rep.   Civil Procedure Reports (New York)

Civ.Rights   Civil Rights

Civ.Serv.   Civil Service

Civ. & Cr.L.S.   Civil & Criminal Law Series (India)

Cl.
- Rotulus Clausarum (Close Roll) (Eng.)
- Clark
- Clarke
- clause

Cl.App. Clark's Appeal Cases, House of Lords (Eng.)

Cl.Can.Ins. Clarke's Canada Insolvent Acts

Cl.Ch. Clarke's New York Chancery Reports (1839-41)

Cl.Home. Clerk Home, Scotch Session Cases

Cl.R. Clarke's New York Chancery Reports

Cl. & F. Clark & Finnelly's House of Lords Cases (1831-46) (Eng.)

Cl. & Fin. Clark & Finnelly's House of Lords Cases (1831-46) (Eng.)

Cl. & H. Clarke's & Hall's Contested Elections in Congress

Cl. & Sc.Dr.Cas. Clarke & Scully's Drainage Cases (Canada)

Clancy, Husb. & W. Clancy's Treatise of the Rights, Duties, and Liabilities of Husband and Wife

Clancy Rights Clancy's Treatise of the Rights, Duties, and Liabilities of Husband and Wife

Clar.Parl.Chr. Clarendon's Parliamentary Chronicle

Clark
- English House of Lords Cases, by Clark
- Pennsylvania Law Journal Reports, edited by Clark
- Clark's Reports (vol. 58 Alabama)

Clark(Ala). Clark's Reports (vol. 58 Alabama)

Clark App. Clark Appeal Cases House of Lords (Eng.)

Clark Col.Law Clark Colonial House

Clark Dig. Clark's Digest, House of Lords Reports

Clark(Jam.) Judgments, Jamaica Supreme Court of Judicature

Clark(Pa.) Clark's Pennsylvania Law Journal Reports

Clark, Receivers Clark on Receivers

Clark & F. Clark and Finnelly's House of Lords Reports (6-8 Eng. Reprint)

Clark & F.(Eng.) Clark and Finnelly's House of Lords Reports (6-8 Eng. Reprint)

Clark & F.(N.S.) Clark and Finnelly's House of Lords Reports (New Series)

Clark & F.(N.S.), Eng. Clark and Finnelly's House of Lords Cases New Series (Eng.)

Clark & Fin. Clark and Finnelly's House of Lords Cases (Eng.)

Clarke
- Clarke, New York Chancery Reports
- Clarke, edition of 1-8 Iowa
- Clarke, Reports (19-22 Michigan)
- Clarke, Notes of Cases, Bengal
- Clarke's Pennsylvania Reports, 5 vols.

Clarke Ch. Clarke's New York Chancery Reports

Clarke Ch.(NY) Clarke's New York Chancery Reports

Clarke(Ia.) Clarke, edition of 1-8 Iowa

Clarke(Mich.) Clarke, Reports (19-22 Michigan)

Clarke Not. Clarke's Notes of Cases, in his "Rules and Orders," Bengal

Clarke(Pa.) Clarke's Pennsylvania, 5 vols.

Clarke R. & O. Clarke's Notes of Cases, in his "Rules and Orders," Bengal

Clarke & H.Elec.Cas. Clarke & Hall's Contested Elections in Congress (U.S.)

Clarke & S.Dr.Cas. Clarke & Scully's Drainage Cases (Canada)

Clark's Code. Clark's Annotated Code of Civil Procedure (N.C.)

Clark's Summary Clark's Summary of American Law

Clay. Clayton's Reports & Pleas of Assizes at York (1631-50) (Eng.)

Clay's Dig. Clay's Digest of Laws of Alabama

Clayt. Clayton's English Reports, York Assizes

Clayton Clayton's English Reports, York Assizes

Clayton(Eng.) Clayton's English Reports, York Assizes

Clearinghouse Rev. Clearinghouse Review

Cleary R.C. Cleary's Registration Cases (Eng.)

Clem. Clemens Reports (57-59 Kansas)

Clerk Home. Clerk Home's Decisions, Scotch Court of Session (1735-44)

Clerke Pr. Clerke's (or Clarke's) Praxis Admiralitatis

Clerke, Prax. Clerke's Praxis Curiae Admiralitatis

Clev. Cleveland

Clev.B.J. Journal of the Cleveland Bar Association

Clev.Bar Ass'n.J. Cleveland Bar Association Journal

Clev.Insan. Clevenger's Medical Jurisprudence of Insanity

Clev.L.Rec. Cleveland Law Record (Ohio)

Clev.L.Reg. Cleveland Law Register (Ohio)

Clev.L.Rep. Cleveland Law Reporter (Ohio)

Clev.-Mar. Cleveland-Marshall

Clev.-Mar.L.Rev. Cleveland-Marshall Law Review

Cleve.I.R.(Ohio) Cleveland Law Reporter (Ohio)

Cleve.L.Rec. Cleveland Law Record (Ohio)

Cleve.L.Rec.(Ohio) Cleveland Law Record (Ohio)

Cleve.L.Reg. Cleveland Law Register (Ohio)

Cleve.L.Reg.(Ohio) Cleveland Law Register (Ohio)

Cleve.L.Rep. Cleveland Law Reporter (Ohio)

Cleve.Law R. Cleveland Law Reporter (Ohio)

Cleve.Law Rec. Cleveland Law Record (Ohio)

Cleve.Law Reg. Cleveland Law Register (Ohio)

Cleve.Law Rep. Cleveland Law Reporter (Ohio)

Clif. Clifford, United States Circuit Court Reports, 1st Circuit

Clif.El. Clifford's English Southwick Election Cases (1796-97)

Clif.El.Cas. Clifford's English Southwick Election Cases (1796-97)

Clif.South.El. Clifford's English Southwick Election Cases (1796-97)

Clif. & R. Clifford & Rickard's English Locus Standi Reports

Clif. & Rick. Clifford & Rickard's English Locus Standi Reports (1873-84)

Clif. & St. Clifford & Stephens' English Locus Standi Reports (1867-72)

Cliff. Clifford, United States Circuit Court Reports, 1st Circuit

Cliff.El.Cas. Clifford's Southwick Election Cases (Eng.)

Cliff.& Steph. Clifford and Stephens, Locus Standi Reports (1867-72)

Clift Clift's Entries (1719) (Eng.)

clin. clinical

Clin.Dig. Clinton's Digest, New York

Clk. Clerk

Clk's.Mag. ● Clerk's Magazine (London)
● Clerk's Magazine (R.I.)
● Clerk's Magazine (Upper Canada)

Clms. Claims

Clow L.C. on Torts. Clow's Leading Cases on Torts

Cls. ● Claims
● clauses

Co. ● Colorado
● Colorado Reports
● Coke's English King's Bench Reports (1572-1616)
● Company
● County

Co.A. ● Cook's Lower Canada Admiralty Court Cases
● Colorado Court of Appeals Reports

Co.Cop. Coke's Compleat Copyholder 5 editions (1630-73) (Eng.)

Co.Ct. County Court

Co.Ct.Cas. County Court Cases (Eng.)

Co.Ct.Ch. County Court Chronicle (Eng.)

Co.Ct.Chr. County Courts Chronicles (1847-1920) (Eng.)

Co.Ct.I.L.T. Irish Law Times, County Courts

Co.Ct.Rep. ● County Courts Reports (1860-1920) (Eng.)
● Pennsylvania County Court Reports

Co.Ct.Rep.(Pa.) County Court Reports (Pa.)

Co.Cts. Coke's Courts (4th Institute) (Eng.)

Code of Civ.Proc. Code of Civil Procedure

Co.Ent. Coke's Book of Entries (1614) (Eng.)

Co.G. Reports and Cases of Practice in Common Pleas tempore Anne, Geo. I., and Geo II., by Sir G. Coke. (Same as Cooke's Practice Reports) (1706-47) (Eng.)

Co.Inst. Coke's Institutes (Eng.)

Co.Inst.(Eng.) Coke's Institutes (Eng.)

Co.L.J. Cochin Law Journal Colonial Law Journal (New Zealand)

Co.Lit. Coke on Littleton (1 Inst.)

Co.Litt. Coke on Littleton (Eng.)

Co.Litt.(Eng.) Coke on Littleton (Eng.)

Co.M.C. Coke's Magna Charta (2d Institute)

Co.Mass.Pr. Colby Mass. Practice

Co.on Courts Coke's 4th Institute (Eng.)

Co.P.C. Coke's Pleas of the Crown (3d Institute)

Co.Pl. Coke's Pleadings (sometimes published separately)

Co.R. Code Reporter (New York)

Co.R.N.S. Code Reporter, New Series (New York)

Co.R.(N.Y.) Code Reporter (New York)

Co.Rep. ● Coke, Reports, King's Bench (1572-1616) (Eng.)
● Code Reporter (New York)

Co-T/Agt. Co-transfer agent

Co-Tr. Co-trustee

Co. & Al. Cooke & Alcocks's Great Britain Reports (Ir.)

Cob.St.Tr. Cobbett's (Howell's) State Trials (1163-1820) (Eng.)

Cobb. ● Cobb's New Digest, Laws of Georgia (1851)
● Cobb's Reports (vols. 4-20 Georgia)
● Cobb's Reports (vol. 121 Alabama)

Cobb, Dig. Cobb's Digest of Statute Laws (Ga.)

Cobb.Parl.Hist. Cobbett's Parliamentary History

Cobb.St.Tr. Cobbett's (afterwards Howell's) State Trials

Cobbey, Repl. Cobbey's Practical Treatise on the Law of Replevin

Cobbey's Ann.St. Cobbey's Annotated Statutes (Neb.)

Coch. Cochran's Nova Scotia Reports (1859)

Coch.Ch.Ct. Chief Court of Cochin, Select Decisions

Cochin Cochin Law Reports

Cochin L.J. Cochin Law Journal

Cochr. Cochran's Nova Scotia Reports Cochran's Reports (3-10 North Dakota)

Cochran. Cochran's Reports (vols. 3-10 North Dakota Reports)

Cock.Tich.Ca. Cockburn's Charge in the Tichborne Case

Cock.& R. Cockburn and Rowe's English Election Cases (1833)

Cock.& Rowe Cockburn & Rowe's English Election Cases (1833)

Cockb.& R. Cockburn & Rowe's Election Cases (Eng.)

Cocke ● Cocke, Reports (vols. 16-18 Alabama)
● Cocke, Reports (vols. 14, 15 Florida)

Cod. ● Codex Justinianus
● Gibson's Codex Ecclesiastia, (1715)

Cod.Jur. Gibson's Codex Ecclesiastia (1715)

Cod.Jur.Civ. ● Codex Juris Civilis
● Justinian's Code

Cod.St. Codified Statutes

Cod.Theodos. Codex Theodorianus

Code. • Code of Justinian (Roman Law)
  • Codex Justiniani
Code Am. Code Amendments
Code.Civ. Code Civile Francaise (or Code Napoleon)
Code.Civ.Pro.(or Proc.) Code of Civil Procedure
Code Civ.Proc. Code of Civil Procedure
Code Civil. Code Civil or Civil Code of France
Code Com.B. Code de Commerce, Belge
Code Com.I. Code de Commerce, Italien
Code Cr.Pro.(or Proc.) Code of Criminal Procedure
Code Cr.Proc., Code of Criminal Procedure
Code Crim.Proc. Code of Criminal Procedure
Code de Com. Code de Commerce
Code d'Instr.Crim. Code d'Instruction Criminelle
Code Fed.Reg. Code of Federal Regulations
Code For. Code Forestier Francais
Code Gen.Laws Code of General Laws
Code I. Code d'Instruction Criminelle
Code La. Civil Code of Louisiana
Code M. Code Municipal, Quebec
Code N.(or Nap.) Code Napoleon (or Code Civil)
Code P. Code Penal
Code P.C. Code de Procedure Civile
Code Prac. Code of Practice
Code Pro. Code of Procedure
Code Pub.Gen.Laws Code of Public General Laws
Code Pub.Loc.Laws Code of Public Local Laws
Code R.N.S. Code Reports, New Series, New York
Code R.N.S.(NY) Code Reports, New Series, New York
Code R.(NY) Code Reports, New York
Code Rep. Code Reporter (N.Y.)
Code Rep.N.S. New York Code Reports, New Series
Code Supp. Supplement to the Code

Code Theod. Code of Theodosius (Roman Law)
Code Theodos. Codex Theodosianus
Codes Fr. Les Codes Francaises
Cof. Coffey's California Probate. Decisions
Cof.Dig. Cofer's Kentucky Digest
Cof.Prob.Dec.(Cal.) Coffey's California Probate Decisions
Coff.Prob. Coffey's California Probate Decisions
Coffey's Prob.Dec. Coffey's California Decisions
Cogh.Epit. Coghlan's Epitome of Hindu Law Cases
Cohen, Adm.Law Cohen's Admiralty Jurisdiction, Law, and Practice
Coke Coke, English King's Bench Reports (76, 77 Eng. Reprint)
Coke (Eng.) Coke, English King's Bench Reports (76, 77 Eng. Reprint)
Coke Ent. Coke's Book of Entries
Coke Inst. Coke's Institutes
Coke Lit. Coke on Littleton
Col. • Coldwell's Reports (vols. 41-47 Tennessee)
  • Colonial
  • Colorado Reports
  • Coleman's Reports, (vols. 99, 101, 106, 110-129 Alabama)
  • Columbia
  • column
Col.App. Colorado Appeals Reports
Col.C.C. Collyer's English Chancery Cases (1845-47)
Col.Cas. Coleman, Cases (of Practice) (New York)
Col.Cas.(NY) Coleman Cases (of Practice) (New York)
Col.L.J. Colonial Law Journal (New Zealand)
Col.L.Rep. Colorado Law Reporter
Col.L.Rev. Columbia Law Review
Col.Law Review Columbia Law Review
Col.N.P. Colorado Nisi Prius Decisions
Col.& C.Cas. Coleman & Caines' Cases (N.Y.)
Col.& Cai. Coleman and Caines' Cases, New York

Col.& Cai.Cas. Coleman and Caines, New York Cases

Col. & Caines Cas.(N.Y.) Coleman & Caines' Cases (Common Law)

Cold. Coldwell's Tennessee Supreme Court Reports (1860-70)

Colds.Pr. Coldstream's Scotch Court of Session Procedure

Coldw. Coldwell's Reports (vols. 41-47 Tennessee)

Coldw.(Tenn.) Coldwell's Reports (vols. 41-47 Tennessee)

Cole. ● Cole's edition of Iowa Reports
● Coleman's Reports (vols. 99, 101-106, 110-129 Alabama)

Cole.Cas. Coleman's Cases, New York (1791-1800)

Cole.Cas.Pr. Coleman's Cases, New York

Cole.& Cai.Cas. Coleman & Caines' Cases (New York 1794-1805)

Colem.Cas. Coleman, New York Cases

Colem.& C.Cas. Coleman & Caines, New York Cases

Coll. ● Collector
● Colles, Parliamentary Cases (1697-1714)
● Collyer, English Chancery Cases (1845-47)

Coll.Bank. Collier's Law of Bankruptcy

Coll.C.R. Collyer's Chancery Reports (Eng.)

Coll.Caus.Cel. Collection des Causes Célèbres, Paris

Coll.Jurid. Collectanea Juridica (Eng.)

Coll.L.D.et O. Collection des Lois, Decrets et Ordonnances

Coll.P.C. Colles' English Parliamentary (House of Lords) Cases (1697-1714)

Coll.Tr. Collateral trust

Coll.& E.Bank. Collier's & Eaton's American Bankruptcy Reports

Colles Colles Cases in Parliament (1697-1714) (Eng.)

Colles (Eng.) Colles Cases in Parliament (1697-1714) (Eng.)

Colles,P.C. Colles's Cases in Parliament (1697-1714) (Eng.)

Collier,Bankr. Collier's Bankruptcy

Collier & E.Am.Bankr. Collier & Eaton's American Bankruptcy

Colly. Collyer's English vice Chancellors' Reports (1845-47)

Colly Ch.Cas.(Eng.) Collyer, Chancery Cases (63 Eng. Reprint)

Colly.Part. Collyer on Partnership

Colly.Partn. Collyer on Partnership

Colo. ● Colorado
● Colorado Reports

Colo.App. Colorado Court of Appeals Reports

Colo.B.A. Colorado Bar Association

Colo.Dec. Colorado Decisions

Colo.Dec.Fed. Colorado Decisions, Federal

Colo.Dec.Supp. Colorado Decisions Supplement

Colo.I.C. Colorado Industrial Commission Report

Colo.I.R. Colorado Law Reporter

Colo.Law Rep. Colorado Law Reporter

ColoN.P.Dec. Colorado Nisi Prius Decisions (1900-02)

Colo.P.U.C. Colorado Public Utilities Commission Decisions

Colo.P.U.C.Rep. Colorado Public Utilities Commission Report

Colo.Rev.Stat. Colorado Revised Statutes

Colo.S.R.C. Colorado State Railroad Commission

Colo.Sess.Laws. Session Laws of Colorado

Colom. Colombia

Colq. Colquit's Reports (1 Modern) (Eng.)

Colq.Civ.Law. Colquhoun on Roman Civil Law

Colquit. Modern Reports, pt. 1

cols. columns

Colt. Coltman Registration Appeal Cases (1879-85) (Eng.)

Colt.(Reg.Ca.) Coltman's Registration Cases (1879-85)

Colt.Reg.Cas. Coltman Registration Appeal Cases (1879-85) (Eng.)

Coltm. Coltman Registration Appeal Cases (1879-85) (Eng.)

Colum. Columbia

Colum.Human Rights L.Rev. Columbia Human Rights Law Review

Colum.J.L.& Soc.Prob. Columbia Journal of Law & Social Problems

Colum.J.Transnat'l.Law Columbia Journal of Transnational Law

Colum.J.World Bus. Columbia Journal of World Business

Colum.Jur. Columbia Jurist

Colum.L.Rev. Columbia Law Review

Colum.L.T. Columbia Law Times

Colum.Soc'y.Int'l.L.Bull. Columbia Society of International Law Bulletin

Colum.Survey Human Rights L. Columbia Survey of Human Rights Law

Colvil. Colvil's Manuscript Decisions, Scotch Court of Session

Coly.Guar.(De) Colyar on Guarantees

Com. ● Comberbach, English King's Bench Reports (1685-99)
- ● Comment
- ● Commerce(ial)
- ● Commission
- ● committee
- ● Common
- ● Commonwealth
- ● Communication(s)
- ● Comstock, Reports (vols. 1-4 New York Court of Appeals)
- ● Comyn, Reports, English King's Bench, 2 vols. (1695-1741)
- ● U.S. Commerce Court Opinions

Com.Affrs. Community Affairs

Com.B. Common Bench Reports (Manning, Granger, and Scott) (1846-65) (Eng.)

Com.B.N.S. English Common Bench Reports, New Series

Com.Cas. ● Commercial Cases (1896-1941) (Eng.)
- ● Company Cases (India)

Com.Dec. Commissioners' Decisions (Patent)

Comm.Del.Order Commissioner's Delegation Order

Com.Dig. Comyn, Digest of the Laws of England (1762-1882)

Com.Jour. Journals of the House of Commons

Com.L. Commercial Law (Canada)

Com.L.J. Commercial Law Journal

Com.L.League J. Commercial Law League Journal

Com.L.R. ● English Common Law Reports (1853-55)
- ● Common Law Reports, published by Spottiswoode

Com.Law Commercial Law

Com.Law R. ● English Common Law Reports (1853-55)
- ● Common Law Reports, published by Spottiswoode

Com.Law Rep. ● English Common Law Reports
- ● Common Law Reports, published by Spottiswoode

Com.on Con. Comyn's Law of Contracts

Com.P.Div. Common Pleas Division, English law Reports

Com.P.Reptr. Common Pleas Reporter (Scranton)

Com.Pl. Common Pleas, English Law Reports

Com.Pl.Div. Common Pleas Division, English Law Reports

Com.Pl.R.(Pa.) Common Pleas Reporter, Scranton, Pennsylvania

Com.Pl.Reptr. Common Pleas Reporter, Scranton, Pennsylvania

Com.Rep. Comyns, English King's Bench Reports (1695-1741)

Com.& Leg.Rep. Commercial & Legal Reporter

Com.& Mun.L.Rep. Commercial & Municipal Law Reporter

Comb. Comberbach English King's Bench Reports (1685-99)

Comb.B.(N.S.) Common Bench (Manning, Granger & Scott) (Eng.)

comd. commanded
com'l. commercial
comm. commission
Comm. ● Blackstone's Commentaries
● Commentaries
● Commerce, Tribunal de Commerce, Rechtbank van Koophandel (Commercial Court)
● Committee
Comm.A.R. Commonwealth Arbitration Reports (Aus.)
Comm.Fut.L.Rep. Commodity Futures Law Reporter (CCH)
Comm.Journ. House of Commons Journal (Eng.)
Comm.L.R. ● Commercial Law Reports (Canada)
● Commonwealth Law Reports (Aus.)
Comm.Mkt.L.R. Common Market Law Reports
Comm.Mkt.L.Rev. Common Market Law Review
Comm.Mkt.Rep. Common Market Reporter (CCH)
Comm.Tel.Cas. Commission Telephone Cases Leaflets (New York)
commd. commissioned
Commiss. Commission
comml. commercial
commr. commissioner
Commrs. Commissioners
Commw.Arb. Commonwealth Arbitration Reports (Aus.)
Commw.Art. Commonwealth Arbitration Reports (Aus.)
Commw.Ct. Commonwealth Court
Commw.L.R. Commonwealth Law Reports (Aus.)
Comp. ● Comparative
● Compensation
● compilation
● Compiled
Comp.Armed Forces Compendium of Laws of Armed Forces
Comp.Dec. Decisions of the Comptroller of the Treasury (U.S.)
Comp.Gen. ● Comptroller General

● Decisions of the Comptroller General
Comp.Gen.Op. Comptroller General Opinion
Comp.Jurid.Rev. Comparative Juridical Review
Comp.Laws. Compiled Laws
Comp.Rev. Compensation Review (India)
Comp.St. Compiled Statutes
Comp.Stat. Compiled Statutes
Comp. & Int'l.L.J.S.Afr. Comparative and International Law Journal of South Africa
Comptr.Treas.Dec. Comptroller Treasury Decisions
Com'r. Commissioner
Comr.of Bkg.and Ins. Commissioner of Banking and Insurance
Comst.(or Coms.) Comstock's Reports (vols. 1-4 New York Court of Appeals)
Com'w'th. Commonwealth
Comyn, Usury. Comyn on Usury
Comyns. Comyns' English King's Bench Reports
Comyns' Dig. Comyns' Digest (Eng.)
Con. ● Conover's Reports (Wisconsin)
● Continuation of Rolle's Reports (2 Rolle)
● Connoly, New York Criminal
Con.B.J. Connecticut Bar Journal
Con.Cus. Conroy's Custodian Reports (Eng., Ir.)
Con.St. Consolidated Statutes
Con.Sur. Connolly's Surrogate (N.Y.)
Con.& L. Connor & Lawson's Irish Chancery Reports (1841-43)
Con.& Law. Connor & Lawson's Irish Chancery Reports (1841-43)
Con.& Sim. Connor and Simonton's South Carolina Equity Digest
Cond.Ch.R. Condensed English Chancery Reports
Cond.Ecc.R. Condensed Ecclesiastical Reports
Cond.Eccl. Condensed Ecclesiastical Reports

Cond.Eng.Ch. Condensed English Chancery Reports

Cond.Ex.R. Condensed Exchequer Reports

Cond.Exch.R. Condensed Exchequer Reports

CondH.C. Conders Highway Cases

Cond.Rep.U.S. Peters, Condensed United States Reports

Condem. Condemnation

Condit.Sale--Chat.Mort.Rep. Conditional Sale--Chattel Mortgage Reporter (CCH)

Conf.
- Conference
- Conference Reports (by Cameron and Norwood (North Carolina)
- Confirming

Conf.Chart. Confirmatio Chartarum

Conf.Comm.Uniformity Legis. Conference of Commissioners on Uniformity of Legislation in Canada

Conf.Pers.Fin.L.Q.R. Conference on Personal Finance Law, Quarterly Report

Conf.Rept. Conference Report

Conference (NC) Conference Reports (N.C.)

Cong.
- Congress
- Congressional

Cong.Deb. Congressional Debates (U.S.)

Cong.Dig. Congdon's Digest (Canada)

Cong.El.Cas. Congressional Election Cases (U.S.)

Cong.Gl. Congressional Globe

Cong.Q.W.Repts. Congressional Quarterly Weekly Reports

Cong.Rec. Congressional Record (U.S.)

Congl.
- Congregational
- Congressional

Conk.Adm. Conkling's Admiralty

Conn.
- Connecticut
- Connecticut Reports

Conn.App.Proc. Maltbie's Appellate Procedure

Conn.B.J. Connecticut Bar Journal

Conn.Cir. Connecticut Circuit Court Reports

Conn.Cir.Ct. Connecticut Circuit Court Reports

Conn.Comp.Com. Connecticut Compensation Commissioners, Compendium of Awards

Conn.Comp.Dec. Connecticut Workmen's Compensation Decisions

Conn.Dec. Connecticut Decisions

Conn.Gen.Stat. General Statutes of Connecticut

Conn.Gen.Stat.Ann. Connecticut General Statutes Annotated

Conn.L.Rev. Connecticut Law Review

Conn.Legis.Serv. Connecticut Legislative Service (West)

Conn.P.U.C. Connecticut Public Utilities Commission

Conn.Pub.Acts. Connecticut Public Acts

Conn.R.C. Connecticut Railroad Commissioners

Conn.S. Connecticut Supplement

Conn.Supp. Connecticut Supplement

Conn.Surr. Connolly's New York Surrogate Reports

Connoly. Connoly's New York Surrogate Reports

Connor.& L. Connor and Lawson Chancery Reports (Ir.)

Conover Conover Reports (vols. 16-153 Wisconsin Reports)

Conr. Conroy, Custodian Reports (1652-1788) (Ir.)

Cons.
- Conservator
- Consolidated
- Consulting, consultant

Cons.Cred.Guide. Consumer Credit Guide (CCH)

Cons.del M. Consolato del Marc

Cons.Ord.in Ch. Consolidated General Orders in Chancery

Consist. English Consistorial Reports, by Haggard (1788-1821)

Consist.Rep. English Consistorial Reports, by Haggard

consol. consolidated

Consol.del Mare. Consolato del Mare

Consolid.Ord. Consolidated General Orders in Chancery

Const.
- Bott's Poor Laws, by Const. (1560-1833)
- Constitution(al)
- Constitutional Reports, South Carolina, by Mills

- Constitutional Reports, South Carolina, by Treadway
- Constitutional Reports, vol. 1, South Carolina, by Harper
- Construction

Const.Amend. Amendment to Constitution

Const.Hist. Hallam's Consitutional History of England

Const.N.S. Constitutional Reports, (Mill), South Carolina, New Series

Const.Oth. Constitutiones Othoni (found at the end of Lyndewood's Provinciale)

Const.R.S.C. Constitutional Reports, South Carolina, printed by Treadway

Const.Rep. Constitutional Reports (S.C.)

Const.Rev. Constitutional Review

Const.S.C. Constitutional Reports (South Carolina, printed by Treadway)

Const.S.C.N.S. S.C. Constitutional Reports, New Series, Printed by Mills

Const.U.S. Constitution of the United States

Const.U.S.Amend. Amendment to the Constitution of the United States

constl. constitutional

constn. constitution

Constr. Construction

Consuet.Feud. Consuetudiness Feudorum; or, the Book of Feuds

Consumerism Consumerism (CCH)

Consv. Conservatorship

Cont. ● Contracts
      ● Control(s)

Cont.Cas.Fed. Contract Cases, Federal

Cont.El. Controverted Elections Judgts (Eng.)

Cont.Elect.Case. Contested Election Cases (U.S.)

Cont.L.Rev. Contemporary Law Review (India)

Contemp. Contemporary

conv. ● convention
      ● convertible
      ● Conveyancer & Property Lawyer

Conv.Est. Convention of the Estates of Scotland

Conv.(N.S.) Conveyancer and Property Lawyer (New 1936, current Series)

Convey. Conveyancer

Convey.N.S. Conveyancer & Property Lawyer, New Series

Coo.& Al. Cooke & Alcock, Irish King's Bench Reports (1833-34)

Coo.& H.Tr. Cooke & Harwood's Charitable Trusts Acts

Cook, Corp. Cook on Corporations

Cook, Stock, Stockh.& Corp.Law. Cook on Stock, Stockholders, and General Corporation Law

Cook V.Adm. Cook's Vice-Admiralty Reports (Nova Scotia)

Cook Vice-Adm. Cook's Vice-Admiralty Reports (Nova Scotia)

Cooke. ● Cooke, Act Book of the Ecclesiastical Court of Whalley
      ● Cooke's Cases of Practice, English Common Pleas
      ● Cases under Sugden's Act (1838) (Eng.)
      ● Cooke's Reports (vol. 3 Tennessee) (1811-14)

Cooke B.L. Cooke's Bankrupt Laws

Cooke C.P. Cooke's Common Pleas Reports (1706-47) (Eng.)

Cooke(Eng.) Cooke, Cases of Practice (125 Eng. Reprint)

Cooke, Incl.Acts. Cooke's Inclosure Acts

Cooke,Ins. Cooke on Life Insurance

Cooke Pr.Cas. Cooke's Practice Reports, English Common Pleas

Cooke Pr.Reg. Cooke's Practical Register of the Common Pleas

Cooke(Tenn.) Cooke's Tennessee Reports (vol. 3 Tennessee)

Cooke & A. Cooke & Alcock's Reports (Ir.)

Cooke & Al. Cooke & Alcock's Reports (Ir.)

Cooke & Al.(Ir.) Cooke & Alcock Reparts, Irish Kings Bench

Cooke & Alc. Cooke & Alcock's Reports (Ir.)

Cooke & H.Ch.Tr. Cooke & Harwood's Charitable Trust Acts

Cook's Pen.Code. Cook's Penal Code (N.Y.)

Cool.Black. Cooley's edition of Blackstone

Cool.Con.Law. Cooley's Constitutional Law

Cool.Con.Lim. Cooley's Constitutional Limitations

Cooley. Cooley's Reports (vols. 5-12 Michigan)

Cooley, Bl.Comm. Cooley's Edition of Blackstone's Commentaries

Cooley,Const.Law. Cooley's Constitutional Law

Cooley,Const.Lim. Cooley on Constitutional Limitations

Cooley, Const.Limit. Cooley on Constitutional Limitations

Cooley, Tax'n.(or Cooley, Tax) Cooley on Taxation

Cooley, Torts. Cooley on Torts

Co-op. Co-operative

Coop.
- Cooper, Tennessee Chancery Reports, 3 vols.
- Cooper, English Chancery Reports tempore Eldon
- Cooper, English Chancery tempore Cottenham
- Cooper, English Chancery Reports tempore Brougham
- Cooper, English Practice Cases, Chancery
- Cooperative
- Cooper's Reports, Florida Reports, (vols. 21-24)

Coop.C.C. Cooper's Chancery Cases tempore Cottenham (Eng.)

Coop.C.& P.R. Cooper's Chancery & Practice Reporter, Upper Canada

Coop.Ch. Cooper's Tennessee Chancery Reports

Coop.Ch.(Eng.) Cooper's Chancery (35 Eng. Reprint)

Coop.Ch.Pr. Cooper's Chancery Practice Reports (Eng.)

Coop.Corp. Cooperative Corporations

Co-op.Dig. Co-operative Digest, United States Reports

Coop.Eq.Pl. Cooper's Equity Pleading

Coop.G. G.Cooper's Chancery Reports (Eng.)

Coop.Inst. Cooper's Institutes of Justinian

Coop.Pr.C. Cooper's Practice Cases (1837-89)

Coop.Pr.Cas. Cooper's Practice Cases, English Chancery

Coop.Rec. Cooper's Public Records of Great Britain

Coop.Sel.Ca. Cooper's Select Cases tempore Eldon, English Chancery

Coop.Sel.E.C. Cooper's Select Early Cases (Sc.)

Coop.t.Br. Cooper's Cases tempore Brougham, English Chancery

Coop.t.Brough. Cooper's Cases tempore Brougham Chancery (1833-34) (Eng.)

Coop.t.Brougham (Eng.) Cooper, Cases tempore Brougham (47 Eng. Reprint)

Coop.t.Cott. Cooper's Reports tempore Cottenham (1846-48)

Coop.t.Cott.(Eng.) Cooper, Cases tempore Cottenham (47 Eng. Reprint)

Coop.t.Eld. Cooper's Reports tempore Eldon (1815) (Eng.)

Coop.t.Eld.(Eng.) Cooper Reports tempore Eldon (1815) (Eng.)

Coop.temp. Cooper, Cases tempore

Coop.temp.Brougham Cooper C.P. tempore Brougham (1832-34)

Coop.temp.Cottenham Cooper C.P. tempore Cottenham (1846-48)

Coop.Ten.Chy. Cooper's Tennessee Chancery Reports

Coop.Tenn.Ch. Cooper's Tennessee Chancery Reports

Cooper. Cooper's Tennessee Chancery Reports (1837-39)

Cooper, C.P. Cooper, Charles Purton (1837-38)

Cooper, G. Cooper, George (1815, with a few earlier cases in and from 1792)

Cooper, Just.Inst. Cooper's Justinian's Institutes

Cooper Pr.Cas.(Eng.) Cooper's Practice Cases (47 Eng. Reprint)

Coopert.Brougham Cooper, Charles Purton, tempore Brougham (1833-34)

Cooper t.Cott. Cooper, Charles Purton, tempore Cottenham (1846-48)

Coord. Coordinator

Coote. Coote on Mortgages

Cope. Cope's Reports (vols. 63-72 California Reports)

Copp.L.L. Copp's Public Land Laws

Copp Land. Copp's Land Office Decisions

Copp. Min.Dec. Copp's United States Mining Decisions

Copp Pub.Land Laws. Copp's United States Public Land Laws

Copy.Dec. Copyright Decisions

Copyright L.Sym.(ASCAP) Copyright Law Symposium (ASCAP)

Cor. ● Cornell Law Review
      ● Coryton's Reports (Bengal)

Cor.Cas. American & English Corporation Cases

Cor.Jud. Correspondances Judiciaires (Canada)

Cor.L.Q. Cornell Law Quarterly

Cor.Soc.Cas. Coroner's Society Cases (Eng.)

Corb.& D[an.] Corbett & Daniell's Election Cases (1819) (Eng.)

Corn.Deeds. Cornish on Purchase Deeds

Cornell Int'l.L.J. Cornell International Law Journal

Cornell L.Q. Cornell Law Quarterly

Cornell L.Rev. Cornell Law Reveiw

Cornish, Purch.Deeds. Cornish on Purchase Deeds

Corp. ● Corporate
      ● Corporation
      ● Pennsylvania Corporation Reporter

Corp.C. Corporations Code

Corp.Dep. Corporate depositary

Corp.Guide. Corporation Guide (P-H)

Corp.J. Corporation Journal

Corp.Jur. Corpus Juris

Corp.Jur.Can. Corpus Juris Canonici

Corp.Jus.Canon. Corpus Juris Canonique

Corp.Jur.Civ. Corpus Juris Civilis

Corp.Jur.Germ. Corpus Juris Germaniel

Corp.L.Guide. Corporation Law Guide (CCH)

Corp.Prac.Rev. Corporate Practice Reveiw

Corp.Pract.Comment. Corporate Practice Commentator

Corp.Reorg. Corporate Reorganizations

Corp.Reorg.& Am.Bank.Rev. Corporate Reorganization & American Bankrupty Review

Corp.Rep.(Pa.) Pennsylvania Corporation Reporter

Corp.Tr. Corporate trustee

Corp.& Ass'ns. Corporations and Associations

corr. correspondent; corresponding; correspondence

Correc. Correction

Correspondences Jud. Correspondences Judiciaires (Canada)

Corvin.Et. Corvinus Elementa Juris Civilis

Cory. Coryton's Reports (Calcutta)

Coryton. Coryton's Reports, Calcutta High Court

Cosm. Cosmetic

Cost Acc'g.Stand.Guide. Cost Accounting Standards Guide (CCH)

Cot.Abr. Cotton's Abridgment of the Records

Cou. Couper's Justiciary Reports (Sc.)

couns. counsel

Couns.Mag. Counsellors' Magazine (1796-98)

Counsellor. The Counsellor (New York City)

Count.Cts.Ch. County Courts Chronicle (1847-1920) (London)

Count.Cts.Chron. County Courts Chronicle (1847-1920) (London)

County Co.Cas. County Council Cases (Sc.)

County Ct. County Court

County Cts.Chron. County Courts Chronicle (1847-1920)

County Cts.Rep. County Courts Reports (1860-1919)

County Cts.& Bankr.Cas. County Courts & Bankruptcy Cases

County J.Ct. County Judge's Court

County R. County Reports

Coup. Couper's Justiciary Reports (1868-85) (Sc.)

Coup.Just. Couper's Justiciary Reports (Sc.)

Couper Couper's Justiciary Reports (Sc.)

Cour.& Macl. Courtenay & Maclean's Scotch Appeals (6 & 7 Wilson & Shaw)

Court Cl. United States Court of Claims Reports

Court J.& Dist.Ct.Rec. Court Journal and District Court Record

Court Sess.Ca. Court of Sessions Cases (Sc.)

Court.& Macl. Courtnay & Maclean's Scotch Appeals (6 and 7 Wilson and Shaw)

Cout. Coutlee's Unreported Cases (Canada)

Cout.de N. Coutumes de Normandie

Cout.de P. Coutumes de Paris

Cout.Dig. Coutlee's Digest, Canada Supreme Court

Cout.S.C. Notes of Unreported Cases, Supreme Court of Canada (Coutlee)

Coutlea Coutlea's Supreme Court Cases

Coutlee Unrep.(Can.) Coutlee's Unreported Cases

Cow. ● Cowen's New York Reports
      ● Cowper's English King's Bench Reports

Cow.Cr. Cowen's Criminal Reports, New York

Cow.Cr.Dig. Cowen's Criminal Digest

Cow.Cr.R. Cowen's Criminal Reports, New York

Cow.Cr.Rep. Cowen's Criminal Reports, New York

Cow.Crim.(NY) Cowen's Criminal Reports

Cow.Dic.(or Dict.) Cowell's Law Dictionary

Cow.Dig. Cowell's East India Digest

Cow.Int. Cowell's Interpreter

Cow.N.Y. Cowen's New York Reports

Cowell. ● Cowell's Law Dictionary
      ● Cowell's Interpreter

Cowp. Cowper's English King's Bench Reports (1774-78)

Cowp.Cas. Cowper's Cases (in the third volume of Reports in Chancery)

Cowp.(Eng.) Cowper's English King's Bench Reports (1774-78)

Cox ● Cox's English Chancery Reports (1783-96)
      ● Cox's English Criminal Cases
      ● Cox's Reports (vols. 25-27 Arkansas)

Cox Am.T.Cas. Cox's American Trademark Cases

Cox Am.T.M.Cas. Cox's American Trade-Mark Cases

Cox C.C. ● Cox's English Criminal Cases (1843-1948)
      ● Cox's Crown Cases
      ● Cox's County Court Cases

Cox C.L.Pr. Cox, Common Law Practice

Cox Ch. Cox's English Chancery Cases

Cox ch.Cas.(Eng.) Cox, Chancery Cases (29, 30 Eng. Reprint)

Cox, Ch.Pr. Cox, Chancery Practice

Cox, Cr.Ca. Cox, English Criminal Cases

Cox Cr.Cas. Cox's English Criminal Cases

Cox Cr.Dig. Cox's Criminal Law Digest

Cox Crim.Cas. Cox's Criminal Cases

Cox Cty.Ct.Ca. Cox's County Court Cases (1860-1919) (Eng.)

Cox Eq. Cox's Equity Cases (Eng.)

Cox Eq.Cas. Cox's Equity Cases (Eng.)

Cox Inst. Cox's Institutions of the English Government

Cox J.S.Cas. Cox's Joint Stock Cases

Cox Jt.Stk. Cox's Joint Stock Co. Cases (1864-72) (Eng.)

Cox M.C. Cox's Magistrates' Cases (1859-1919) (Eng.)

Cox, M.& H. Cox, McCrae & Hertslet's English County Court Reports

Cox Mag.Ca. Cox's Magistrate Cases

Cox Man.Tr.M. Cox's Manual of Trade-Mark Cases

Cox, Mc.& H. Cox, McCrae & Hertslet's English County Court Reports (1847-58)

Cox, McC.& H. Cox, McCrae & Hertslet's English County Court Reports

Cox P.W. Cox's ed. of Peere Williams' Reports (Eng.)

Cox Tr.M. Cox's Manual of Trade-Mark Cases

Cox Tr.M.Cas. Cox's American Trade-Mark Cases

Cox & Atk. Cox & Atkinson's Registration Appeal Cases (1843-46) (Eng.)

Coxe Coxe's Reports (1 New Jersey Law)

Coxe Bract. Coxe's translation of Güterbach's Bracton

Cp. Compare

Cr. ● Craig (Sir T.), Jus Feudale. 5 editions (1655-1934)
    ● Cranch's Reports, United States Supreme Court
    ● Cranch's United States Circuit Court Reports
    ● Credit
    ● Texas Court of Appeals Reports
    ● Texas Criminal Reports

Cr.Act. Criminal Act

Cr.App. Criminal Appeals (Eng.)

Cr.App.R. Criminal Appeal Reports (1908)

Cr.C.C. Cranch's United States Circuit Court Cases (Reports)

Cr.Cas.Res. Crown Cases Reserved

Cr.Cir.Comp. Crown Circuit Companion, Irish

Cr.Code. Criminal Code

Cr.Code Prac. Criminal Code of Practice

Cr.L. The Criminal Lawyer (India)

Cr.L.J. Criminal Law Journal (India)

Cr.L.Mag. Criminal Law Magazine

Cr.L.R. Criminal Law Reporter (India)

Cr.Law Mag. Criminal Law Magazine (N.J.)

Cr.Law Rec. Criminal Law Recorder

Cr.Law Rep. Criminal Law Reporter

Cr.M.& R. Crompton, Meeson & Roscoe's English Exchequer Reports (1834-36)

Cr.Pat.Dec. Cranch's Decisions on Patent Appeals

Cr.Prac.Act. Criminal Practice Act

Cr.Proc.Act. Ciminal Procedure Act

Cr.R. The Criminal Reports (India)

Cr.Rg. Criminal Rulings, Bombay (India)

Cr.S.& P. Craigie, Stewart and Paton's Scottish Appeal Cases (1726-1821)

Cr.St. Criminal Statutes

Cr.& Dix. Crowford & Dix's Irish Circuit Court Cases (1839-46)

Cr.& Dix Ab.Ca. Crawford and Dix's Abridged Cases (1837-38)

Cr.& Dix Ab.Cas. Crawford & Dix's Irish Abridged Cases (1837-38)

Cr.& Dix C.C. Crawford & Dix's Irish Circuit Court Cases

Cr.& J. Crompton & Jervis (1830-32)

Cr.& M. Crompton & Meeson's English Exchequer Reports (1832-34)

Cr.& Ph. Craig & Phillps' English Chancery Reports (1840-41)

Cr.& St. Craigie, Stewart, & Paton's Scotch Appeal Cases

Cra. Cranch's United States Circuit Court Reports

Cra.C.C. Cranch's United States Circuit Court Reports

Crab. Crabbe's United States District Court Reports

Crabb, Com.Law. Crabb on the Common Law

Crabb Conv. Crabb's Treatise on Conveyancing

Crabb, Eng. Crabb's English Synonyms

Crabb Eng.L. Crabb's History of the English Law

Crabb, Eng.Law. Crabb's History of the English Law

Crabb, Hist.Eng.Law. Crabb's History of the English Law

Crabb R.P. Crabb on Real Property

Crabb, Real Prop. Crabb on the Law of Real Property

Crabb, Technol.Dict. Crabb's Technological Dictionary

Crabbe Crabbe's United States District Court Reports

Craig, Dict. Craig's Etymological, Technological, and Pronouncing Dictionary

Craig.S.& P. Craigie, Stewart & Paton's Appeal Cases (Sc.)

Craig.St.& Pat. Craigie, Stewart, and Paton, Scotch Appeals Cases

Craig & P. Craig and Phillips' English Chancery Reports

Craig & Ph. Craig & Phillips Chancery (1840-41) (Eng.)

Craig & Ph.(Eng.) Craig & Phillips, Chancery (41 Eng. Reprint)

Craig.& St. Craigie, Stewart & Paton's Appeal Cases (1726-1821) (Sc.)

Craigius, Jus Feud. Craigius Jus Feudale

Craik C.C. Craik's English Causes Celebres

Cranch Cranch's United States Supreme Court Reports (vols. 5-13 United States) (1801-40)

Cranch C.C. ● Cranch's Circuit Court Reports, United States
● District of Columbia Appeals Cases (vols. 1-5 United States Reports)

Cranch D.C. Cranch's United States Circuit Court Reports, District of Columbia

Cranch Pat.Dec. Cranch's Patent Decisions (U.S.)

Cranch(US) Cranch's United States Supreme Court Reports (vols. 5-13 United States Reports)

Crane Crane's Reports (vols. 22-29 Montana)

Crane.C.C. Cranenburgh's Criminal Cases (India)

Craw. Crawford's Reports (vols. 53-69, 72-101 Arkansas Reports)

Craw(Ark) Crawford's Reports (vols. 53-69, 72-101 Arkansas Reports)

Craw Co.Leg.J.(Pa.) Crawford County Legal Journal (Pa.)

Craw.& D. Crawford & Dix, Circuit Court Cases (Ir.)

Craw.& D. Ab.Cas. Crawford & Dix's Abridged Cases (Ir.)

Craw.& D.Abr.Cas. Crawford & Dix's Abridged Cases (Ir.)

Craw.& D.C.C.(Ir.) Crawford & Dix Circuit Cases (Ir.)

Craw.&D.(Ir.) Crawford & Dix (Abridged Cases) (Ir.)

Craw.& Dix Crawford & Dix's Circuit Cases (Ir.)

Crawf.& D. Crawford & Dix's Circuit Court Cases (Ir.)

Crawf.& D.Abr.Cas. Crawford & Dix's Abridged Cases (Ir.)

Creas.Col.Const. Creasy's Colonial Constitutions

Creas.Eng.Cons. Creasy's Rise and Progress of the English Constitution

Creas.Int.L. Creasy on International Law

Creasy. Creasy's Ceylon Reports

Creighton L.Rev. Creighton Law Review

Cress. Cresswell's Insolvency Cases (1827-29) (Eng.)

Cress.Ins.Ca. Cresswell's Insolvency Cases (1827-29) (Eng.)

Cress.Ins.Cas. Cresswell's Insolvency Cases (1827-29) (Eng.)

Cress.Insolv.Cas. Cresswell's Insolvency Cases (1827-29) (Eng.)

Crim. Criminal

Crim.App. ● Court of Criminal Appeals
● Criminal Appeal Reports (Eng.)

Crim.App.(Eng.) Criminal Appeal Reports (Eng.)

Crim.App.Rep. Cohen's Criminal Appeals Reports (Eng.)

Crim.L.Bull. Criminal Law Bulletin

Crim.L.J.I. Criminal Law Journal of India

Crim.L.Mag. Criminal Law Magazine (Jersey City, N.J.)

Crim.L.Q. Criminal Law Quarterly

Crim.L.R. Criminal Law Review

Crim.L.Rec. Criminal Law Recorder (1804-09, 1815)

Crim.L.Rep. ● Criminal Law Reporter (BNA)
● Criminal Law Reporter (CCH)

Crim.L.Rev. Criminal Law Review

Crim.L.Rptr. Criminal Law Reporter

Crim.Law Criminal Law

Crim.Pro. Criminal Procedure

Crim.Proc. Criminal Procedure

Crim.R.(Can.) Criminal Reports

Crim.Rec.
- Criminal Recorder, Philadelphia
- Criminal Recorder, London (1804-09) (1815)
- Criminal Recorder (1 Wheeler's New York Criminal Reports)

Crim.Rep.(N.S.) Criminal Reports, New Series

Crime & Delin. Crime & Delinquency

Crime & Delin'cy. Crime & Delinquency

Criminal L.Q. Criminal Law Quarterly

Cripp Ch.Cas. Cripp's Church and Clergy Cases

Cripps Cripps' Church & Clergy Cases (1847-50) (Eng.)

Cripps Cas. Cripps' Church and Clergy Cases (1847-50)

Cripp's Ch.Cas. Cripp's Church and Clergy Cases (1847-50)

Crit. criticized in or criticizing

Critch. Critchfield's Reports (vols. 5-21 Ohio State)

Critch(Ohio St.) Critchfield's Reports (vols. 5-21 Ohio State)

Cro.
- Croke, English King's Bench Reports (1582-1641)
- Keilway, English King's Bench Reports (1496-1531)

Cro.Car. Croke's English King's Bench Reports tempore Charles I, 3 Cro. (79 Eng. Reprint)

Cro.Car.(Eng.) Croke's English King's Bench Reports tempore Charles I, 3 Cro. (79 Eng. Reprint)

Cro.Cas. Croke's English King's Bench Reports tempore Charles I, 3 Cro. (79 Eng. Reprint)

Cro.Eliz. Croke's English King's Bench Reports tempore Elizabeth, 1 Cro. (78 Eng. Reprint)

Cro.Eliz.(Eng.) Croke's English King's Bench Reports tempore Elizabeth, 1 Cro. (78 Eng. Reprint)

Cro.Jac. Croke's Reports tempore James (Jacobus), English (79 Eng. Reprint)

Cro.Jac.(Eng.) Croke's Reports tempore James (Jacobus), English (79 Eng. Reprint)

Crockford. English Maritime Law Reports, published by Crockford (1860-71)

Croke Croke's King's Bench Reports (1582-1641) (Eng.)

Crom. Crompton's Office of a Justice of the Peace (1637)

Cromp. Star Chamber Cases by Crompton

Cromp.Exch.R. Crompton's Exchequer Reports (Eng.)

Cromp.J.C. Crompton's Jurisdiction of Courts

Cromp.Jur. Crompton's Jurisdiction of Courts

Cromp.Just. Crompton's Office of Justice of the Peace

Cromp.M.& R. Crompton, Meeson & Roscoe, Exchequer, (149, 150 Eng. Reprint)

Cromp.M.& R.(Eng.) Crompton, Meeson & Roscoe, Exchequer, England (149, 150 Eng. Reprint)

Cromp.R.& C.Pr. Crompton's Rules and Cases of Practice

Cromp.& F. Fitzherbert's Justice, enlarged by Crompton

Cromp.& J. Crompton & Jervis English Exchequer Reports (148, 149 Eng. Reprint)

Cromp.& J.(Eng.) Crompton & Jervis English Exchequer Reports (148, 149 Eng. Reprint)

Cromp.& Jer. Crompton and Jervis's Exchequer Reports (1830-32)

Cromp.& Jerv. Crompton & Jervis, English Exchequer Reports (1830-32)

Cromp.& M. Crompton & Meeson's English Exchequer Reports (149 Eng. Reprint)

Cromp.& M.(Eng.) Crompton & Meeson's English Exchequer Reports (149 Eng. Reprint)

Cromp.& Mees. Crompton & Meeson's English Exchequer Reports (1832-34) (149 Eng. Reprint)

Crompt. Star Chamber Cases by Crompton

Crosw.Pat.Ca. Croswell's Collection of Patent Cases, United States

Crosw.Pat.Cas. Croswell's Collection of Patent Cases, United States

Crounse. Crounse's Reports (vol. 3 Nebraska Reports)

Crow. Crowther's Reports (Ceylon)

Crown L.C. Crown Land Cases (Aus.)

Crowth. Crowther's Ceylon Reports

Crowther. Crowther's Ceylon Reports

Cru. Cruise's Digest (1804-35) (Eng.)

Cru.Dig. Cruise, Digest of Law of Real Property

Cru.Dign. Cruise on Dignities

Cru.Fin. Cruise's Fines and Recoveries

Cru.Us. Cruise on Uses

Cruise Dig. Cruise's Digest of the Law of Real Property

Cruise's Dig. Cruise's Digest of the Law of Real Property

Crump Ins. Crump on Marine Insurance

Crumrine ● Crumrine's Reports (vols. 116-146 Pennsylvania)
 ● Pittsburgh Reports, edited by Crumrine

Ct. ● Connecticut
 ● Connecticut Reports
 ● Court

Ct.App. Court of Appeals

Ct.App.N.Z. Court of Appeals Reports (New Zealand)

Ct.Cl. United States Court of Claims Reports

Ct.Cl.Act. Court of Claims Act

Ct.Cl.N.Y. Court of Claims Reports (N.Y.)

Ct.Cls. U.S. Court of Claims

Ct.Com.Pl. Court of Common Pleas

Ct.Com.Pleas. Court of Common Pleas

Ct.Crim.App. Court of Criminal Appeal (Eng.)

Ct.Cust.App. Court of Customs Appeals Reports (1919-29)

Ct.Cust.& Pat.App. Court of Customs & Patent Appeals

Ct.D. Court Decisions Relating to the National Labor Relations Act

Ct.Err.& App. Court of Errors and Appeals

Ct.Errors and App. Court of Errors and Appeals (New Jersey)

Ct.Gen.Sess. Court of General Sessions

Ct.Just. Court of Justiciary

Ct/O. Court Order

Ct.of App. Court of Appeals

Ct.of Cls. U.S. Court of Claims

Ct.of Com.Pleas. Court of Common Pleas

Ct.of Er.and Appeals. Court of Errors and Appeals, New Jersey

Ct.of Sp.App. Court of Special Appeals

Ct.Rep.N.Z. Court of Appeals Reports (New Zealand)

Ct.Rev. Court Review

Ct.[Gen.,Spec.] Sess. Court of [General, Special] Sessions

Ct.Sess.Cas. Court of Session Cases (Sc.)

Ct.Sess.Ist Ser. Scotch Court of Sessions Cases, 1st Series

Ctf. Certificate

Cts.& Jud.Proc. Courts and Judicial Proceedings

Cty. ● County
 ● Counties

Cty.Ct. County Court

Cu.Ct. Customs Court Reports

Cujacius Cujacius, Opera, quae de Jure feeit, etc.

Cum. ● Cumberland
 ● Cumulative

Cum.Bull. Cumulative Bulletin, Internal Revenue Bureau, Treasury Department

Cum.L.Rev. Cumberland Law Review

Cum.P.P. Cumulative Pocket Parts

Cum.Supp. Cumulative Supplement

Cum.& Dun.Rem.Tr. Cummins & Dunphy's Remarkable Trials

Cumb. Cumberland Law Journal (Pa.)

Cumberland L.J.(Pa.) Cumberland Law Journal

Cummins Cummins' Reports (Idaho 1866-67)

Cun. Cunningham's English King's Bench Reports

Cun.Bill.Exch. Cunningham's Law of Notes and Bills of Exchange

Cun.Dict. Cunningham's Dictionary

Cunn. Cunningham King's Bench (1734-36) (Eng.)

Cunningham Cunningham's Reports, English King's Bench

Cunningham(Eng.) Cunningham's Reports, English King's Bench

Cur. ● Curtis' United States Circuit Court Reports
     ● Curia

Cur.Com. Current Comment & Legal Miscellany

Cur.Dec. Curtis' Decisions, United States Supreme Court

Cur.L.R. Current Law Reports (Ceylon)

Cur.Leg.Thought Current Legal Thought

Cur.Ov.Ca. Curwen, Overruled Cases (Ohio)

Cur.Reg.R. Curia Regis Rolls (Eng.)

Current Ct.Dec. Current Court Decisions

Current L. Current Law

Current L.Y.B. Current Law Yearbook

Current Legal Prob. Current Legal Problems

Current Med. Current Medicine for Attorneys

Curry. Curry's Reports (6-19 Louisiana

Curt. ● Curtis' Circuit Court Reports, United States
     ● Curtis' Edition, U.S. Supreme Court Reports
     ● Curteis' Ecclesiastical Reports (1834-44) (Eng.)

Curt.Adm.Dig. Curtis' Admiralty Digest

Curt.C.C. Curtis' United States Circuit Court Decisions

Curt.Cond. Curtis' Edition, U.S. Supreme Court Reports

Curt.Dec. Curtis' United States Supreme Court Decisions

Curt.Dig. Curtis' Digest, United States

Curt.Ecc. Curteis' English Ecclesiastical Reports (163 Eng. Reprint)

Curt.Eccl. Curteis' English Ecclesiastical Reports (163 Eng. Reprint)

Curt.Eccl.(Eng.) Curteis' English Ecclesiastical Reports (163 Eng. Reprint)

Curt.Pat. Curtis on Patents

Curtis ● Curtis' Circuit Court Reports (U.S.)
     ● Curtis' Edition, U.S. Supreme Court Reports

Curw. ● Curwen's Overruled Cases
     ● Curwen's Statutes of Ohio

Curw.L.O. Curwen's Laws of Ohio 1854, 1 vol.

Curw.Ov.Cas. Curwen's Overruled Ohio Cases

Curw.R.S. Curwen's Revised Statutes of Ohio

Cush. ● Cushing's Massachusetts Supreme Judicial Court Reports (1848-53) (vols. 55-66 Massachusetts Reports)
     ● Cushman, Mississippi Reports (vols. 23-29 Mississippi)

Cush.Elec.Cas. Cushing's Election Cases in Massachusetts

Cush.Law & Prac.Leg.Assem. Cushing's Law and Practice of Legislative Assemblies

Cush.Man. Cushing's Manual of Parliamentary Law

Cush.(Mass.) Cushing's Reports (vols. 55-66 Massachusetts)

Cush.Parl.Law. Cushing's Law and Practice of Legislative Assemblies

Cushing. Cushing's Reports (55-66 Massachusetts)

Cushm. Cushman's Reports (vols. 23-29 Mississippi)

Cust. Custody

Cust.A. United States Customs Appeals

Cust.App. United States Customs Appeals

Cust.B.& Dec. Customs Bulletin and Decisions

Cust.Ct. Custom Court Reports (U.S.)

Cust.Rep. Custer's Ecclesiastical Reports

Cust.&Pat.App.(Cust.)(F) Customs And Patent Appeals Reports (Customs)

Cust.&Pat.App.(Pat.)(F) Customs and Patent Appeals Reports (Patents)

Customs United States Customs Service

Cut.Pat.Cas. Cutler's Trademark & Patent Cases

Cutler Reports of Patent Cases (1884)

Cy. Connoly's Surrogate's Court Reports (N.Y.)

Cyc. Cyclopedia of Law & Procedure

Cyc.Ann. Cyclopedia of Law & Procedure Annotations

Cyc.Corp. Fletcher's Cyclopedia of Corporations

Cyc.Dict. Cyclopedic Law Dictionary

Cyc.Law & Proc. Cyclopedia of Law and Procedure

Cyclop.Dict. Shumaker & Longsdorf's Cyclopedic Dictionary

Cyprus L.R. Cyprus Law Reports

Cz. Czech

Czech. Czechoslovakia

D

d distinguished: case at bar different either in law or fact from case cited for reasons given (used in Shepard's Citations)

D.
- Application for writ of error dismissed for want of jurisdiction
- Court of Divorce and Matrimonial Causes (Eng.)
- Dallas' U.S. & Pennsylvania Reports
- Davis
- Delaware Reports
- Democrat
- Denio's Reports (New York)
- Denison's Crown Cases (1844-52) (Eng.)
- Dictionary (particularly Morison's Dictionary of Scotch Session Cases)
- Digest (Justinian's)
- Dismissed: appeal from the same case dismissed
- Disney's Ohio Superior Court Reports
- District Court (federal)
- Dunlop, Bell, & Murray, Reports, Scotch Session Cases, Second Series (1838-62)
- Dutch
- Duxbury
- Duxbury's Reports of the High Court of the South African Republic
- Dyer, ed. Valiant. King's Bench Reports (1513-82) (Eng.)

D.A.   District Attorney

DAC   Development Assistance Committee (OECD)

DALBA   Dallas Bar Association

DAP   Application for writ of error dismissed by agreement of parties

DARPA   Defense Advanced Research Projects Agency

DATA   Defense Air Transportation Administration (U.S.)

D.Abr.   D'Anvers' Abridgment

D'Agu.Env.   D'Aguesseau, Ceuvres

D'An.   d'Anvers' Abridgment of Common Law. 2 editions (1705-37, 1725-37)

D'Anv.Abr.   D'Anver's Abridgment, (Eng.)

DB   Der Betrieb (Ger.)

D.B.   Domesday Book

d.b.a.
- de bonis asportatis (trespass to personalty)
- Doing business as

D.B.E.   De bene esse, (q.v.) (conditionally)

D.B.J.   Duke Bar Journal

D.B.N.   De bonis non (of the goods not administered)

D.B. & M.   Dunlop, Bell & Murray's Court of Session Cares (Sc.) (1838-62)

D.C.
- Disarmament Commission (UN)
- District Court
- District of Columbia
- District of Columbia Reports
- Divisional Court
- Treasury Department Circular (U.S.)
- United States District Court

D.C.2d   Pennsylvania District and County Reports, Second Series

D.C.A.   Dorion's Queen's Bench Reports (Canada)

DCAA   Defense Contract Audit Agency

D.C.App.   District of Columbia Appeals Reports

DCBA   The Bar Association of the District of Columbia

D.C.B.J.   District of Columbia Bar Journal

DCCA   District of Columbia Compensation Act

D.C.C.E.   District of Columbia Code Encyclopedia

D.C.Cir.   District of Columbia Court of Appeals Cases

D.C.Code   District of Columbia Code

D.C.Code Encycl.   (West) District of Columbia Code Encyclopedia

D.C.Code Legis & Admin.Serv. District of Columbia Code Legislative and Administrative Service (West)

D.C.Dist.Col. United States District Court for the District of Columbia

D.C.H. Reports of the United States District Court of Hawaii

D.C.L.
- Doctor of Civil Law
- Doctor of Comparative Law

D.C.Lab.S. Dominion of Canada Labour Service (CCH)

DCMA District of Columbia Manpower Administration

D.C.Mun.App. Municipal Court of Appeals, D.C.

DCPA Defense Civil Preparedness Agency

D.Ch. Delaware Chancery Reports

D.Chip. D. Chipman's Vermont Supreme Court Repforts (1789-1824)

D.Chip.(Vt.) D. Chipman's Reports (1789-1824) (Vermont)

D.Chipm. D. Chipman's Reports (1789-1824) (Vermont)

D.Ct. District Court (usually U.S.)

DDA Dividend Disbursing Agent

D.D.C. District Court, District of Columbia

D.D.N.J.,F.D.C. Food and Drug Administration. Notices of Judgment

D.Dec. Dix, School Law Decisions, New York

D.E. Department of Employment Division of Employment

DEA Drug Enforcement Administration

DEPA Defense Electric Power Administration

DES
- Division of Employment Security
- Department of Economic Security
- Department of Employment Security

D.E.R.I.C. De ea re ita censuere (concerning that matter have so decreed)

DFA Defense Fisheries Administration (U.S.)

DFL Democrat-Farmer-Labor party

DFO Defense Food Order (Production & Marketing Adm.) (U.S.)

DFO,SO Defense Food Order, Sub-Order (U.S.)

D.F.& J. DeGex, Fisher & Jones' Chancery Reports (1860-62) (Eng.)

D.F. & J.B. De Gex, Fisher & Jones, English Bankruptcy Reports (1860)

D.G. De Gex, English Bankruptcy Reports (1845-50)

D.G.F. & J. De Gex, Fisher, & Jones' English Chancery Reports

D.G.F. & J.B. De Gex, Fisher, & Jones' English Bankruptcy Reports

D.G.J. & S. De Gex, Jones, & Smith's English Chancery Reports

D.G.J. & S.B. De Gex, Jones, & Smith's English Bankruptcy Reports

D.G.M. & G. De Gex, Macnaghten, & Gordon's English Chancery Reports

D.G.M. & G.B. De Gex, Macnaghten, & Gordon's English Bankruptcy Reports

D.H.L. House of Lords Appeals, in Dunlop's Court of Session Cases from vol. 13 (1851-62)

D.I. Disability Insurance, Trust Fund

DIA Defense Intelligence Agency

DIBA Domestic and International Business Administration

DIR Department of Industrial Relations

DIS Defense Investigative Service

D.J.
- Denver Law Journal (Colo.)
- District Judge

DJC Application for writ of error dismissed, judgment correct

D.J. & S. De Gex, Jones & Smith, English Chancery Reports (1862-66)

D.J. & S.B. De Gex, Jones & Smith English Bankruptcy Reports (1862-65)

DLC
- Disaster Loan Corporation (U.S.)
- Donation Land Claim

DLI Department of Labor and Industry

D.L.J. University of Detroit Law Journal (Mich.)

D.L.N. Daily Legal News

D.L.R.
- Dickinson Law Review (Pennsylvania)
- Dominion Law Reports (Canada)

- Dominion Law Reporter (India), usually with a Province abbreviation, as D.L.M. (A.M.), Ajmer-Merwara

D.L.R.2d. Dominion Law Reports, 2d Series (Canada)

D.L.R.3d. Dominion Law Reports, 3d Series (Canada)

D.L.R.(Can.) Dominion Law Reports (Canada)

D.L.R.2d.(Can.) Dominion Law Reports, Second Series (Canada)

D.M. & G. De Gex, Macnaghten & Gordon, English Chancery Reports (1851-57)

D.M. & G.B. De Gex, Macnaghten & Gordon, English Bankruptcy Reports

DMA Defense Manpower Administration (U.S.)

DMB Defense Mobilization Board (U.S.)

DMEA Defense Materials Exploration Agency (U.S.)

DMO Defense Mobilization Order (U.S.)

DMP Defense Materials Procurement Agency (U.S.)

DNA Defense Nuclear Agency

D.N.S.
- Dow, New Series (Dow & Clark, English House of Lords Cases)
- Dowling's Reports, New Series, English Bail Court

DO Delegation Order

DOA Dead on arrival at hospital

DOB Date of Birth

DOC Department of Commerce

DOD Department of Defense

DOE Department of Energy

DOI Department of the Interior

DOJ Department of Justice

DOT Department of Transportation

D.P.
- Data processing
- Domus Procerum (the House of Lords)

DPA Defense Production Adm. (U.S.)

D.P.B. Dampier Paper Book, in Lincoln's Inn Library

D.P.C. Dowling, English Practice Cases (1830-40)

D.P.L.R. De Paul Law Review

D.P.P. Director of Public Prosecutions

D.P.R. Porto Rico Reports (Spanish ed.)

D.P.U.C. Division on Placement and Unemployment Compensation

D.P.U.I. Division on Placement and Unemployment Insurance

DR
- Dacca Reports (India)
- De-rating and Rating Appeals, England and Scotland
- Distribution Regulation (Office of Price Stabilization, U.S.)
- Drake Law Review (Iowa)

D.R.A. De-rating Appeals (Eng.)

DRC Defense Relocation Corporation (U.S.)

D.R.S. Dominion Report Service (Canada)

D.Rep. Ohio Decisions Reprint

D.Repr. Ohio Decisions Reprint

DS Deputy Sheriff

DSA Defense Supply Agency

DSAA Defense Security Assistance Agency

DSARC Defense Systems Acquisition Review Council

DSB Drug Supervisory Body (UN)

D.S.B. Debitum sine brevi, debit sans breve (debt without writ)

DSFA Defense Solid Fuels Administration (U.S.)

DSM Designation of Scarce Materials (U.S.)

DSOB Dirksen Senate Office Building (also known as NSOB)

DTA Defense Transport Administration (U.S.)

D.T.C. Dominion Tax Cases

DUC Division of Unemployment Compensation

D.U.L.R.
- Dublin University Law Review
- Duquesne University Law Review

d.v.n. devisavit vel non (issue of fact as to whether a will in question was made by the testator)

DWB Dismissed for want of bond

D.W.I.
- Descriptive Word Index
- Died without issue
- Driving while intoxicated

DWP Dismissed for want of prosecution

D.& A. Deas and Anderson, Session Cases (1829-32) (Sc.)

D. & B.
- Dearsly & Bell, English Crown Cases (1856-58)
- Devereux & Battle, North Carolina Law Reports (vols. 18-20)

D. & B.C.C. Dearsley & Bell, English Crown Cases

D. & C.
- Deacon & Chitty's English Bankruptcy Reports
- District and County Reports, Pennsylvania
- Dow & Clark, English House of Lords (Parliamentary) Cases (1827-32)

D. & C.2d District and County, Second Series, Pa.

D. & Ch. Deacon & Chitty's English Bankruptcy Reports (1832-35)

D. & Chit. Deacon & Chitty's English Bankruptcy Reports (1832-35)

D. & Cl. Dow and Clark's Reports

D. & D. Drunk and Disorderly

D. & E. Durnford & East (Term) Reports, English King's Bench (1785-1800)

D. & F. Judgments of Divisional and Full Courts, Gold Coast

D. & G. Diprose & Gammon's Reports of Law Affecting Friendly Societies (1801-97) (Eng.)

D. & J. De Gex & Jones' English Chancery Reports (1857-60)

D. & J.B. De Gex & Jones' English Bankruptcy Reports (1857-59)

D. & L. Dowling & Lowndes' English Bail Court Reports (1843-49)

D. & M. Davison & Merivale's English Queen's Bench Reports

D. & Mer. Davison and Merivale's Queen's Bench Reports (1843-44) (Eng.)

D. & P. Denison & Pearce's Crown Cases (Eng.)

D. & R. Dowling & Ryland's English King's Bench Reports (1821-27)

D. & R.M.C. Dowling & Ryland's English Magistrates' Cases (1822-27)

D. & R.Mag.Cas. Dowling & Ryland's Magistrate Cases (Eng.)

D. & R.N.P. Dowling & Ryland's English Nisi Prius Cases (1822-23)

D. & R.N.P.C. Dowling & Ryland's English Nisi Prius Cases

D. & S.
- Deane & Swabey, English Ecclesiastical Reports
- Doctor and Student
- Drewry & Smale's Chancery Reports (1860-65) (Eng.)

D. & Sm. Drewry & Smale's Chancery (Eng.)

D. & Sw. Deane & Swabey Ecclesiastical (Eng.)

D. & W.
- Drury & Walsh's Irish Chancery Reports (1837-40)
- Drury & Warren's Irish Chancery Reports (1841-43)

D. & War. Drewry & Warren's Chancery (Ir.)

Da.
- Dakota
- Dakota Territory Reports
- Danish

Dady. Dadyburjar, Small Court Appeals (India)

Dai.Reg. New York Daily Register

Daily L.N. Daily Legal News (Pa.)

Daily L.R. Daily Legal Record (Pa.)

Daily Leg.News (Pa.) Daily Legal News

Daily Leg.(Pa.) Daily Legal Record

Daily Trans. New York Daily Transcript, Old and New Series

Dak.
- Dakota
- Dakota Territory Reports

Dak.L.Rev. Dakota Law Review

Dak.Law Rev. Dakota Law Review

Dal.
- Benloe and Dalison's Common Pleas Reports (1486-1580) (Eng.)
- Dalison's Common Pleas Reports (Eng.)
- Dallas' United States Reports (vols. 1-4 U.S.)
- Dallas' Pennsylvania Reports (1754-1806)
- Dalrymple's Session Cases (Sc.)
- Daly's Reports (New York)

Dal.C.P. Dalison's Common Pleas (Eng.)

Dal.Coop. Dallas' Report of Cooper's Opinion on the Sentence of a Foreign Court of Admiralty

Dal.in Keil. Dalison's Reports in Keilway (1533-64) (Eng.)

Dale ● Dale's Judgments (1868-71) (Eng.)
      ● Dale's Reports (2-4 Oklahoma)

Dale Ecc. Dale's Ecclesiastical Reports (Eng.)

Dale Eccl. Dale's Ecclesiastical Reports (Eng.)

Dale Leg.Rit. Dale's Legal Ritual (Ecclesiastical) Reports (1868-71) (Eng.)

Dalhousie L.J. Dalhousie Law Journal

Dalison Dalison's English Common Pleas Reports, bound with Benloe (123 Eng. Reprint)

Dalison (Eng.) Dalison's English Common Pleas Reports, bound with Benloe (123 Eng. Reprint)

Dall. ● Dallam's Texas Supreme Court Decisions
      ● Dallas' Pennsylvania and United States Reports (1754-1809)
      ● Dallas' Styles, Scotland
      ● Dallas, Laws of Pennsylvania

Dall.Coop. Dallas, Report of Cooper's Opinion on the Sentence of a Foreign Court of Admiralty

Dall.Dec. Dallam's Texas Decisions, from Dallam's Digest

Dall.Dig. Dallam's Digest and Opinions (Tex.)

Dall. in Kell. Dallison in Keilway's Reports, English King's Bench

Dall.Laws Dallas' Laws (Pa.)

Dall.S.C. Dallas' United States Supreme Court Reports

Dall.(Tex.) Dallam's Texas Supreme Court Decisions

Dallam Dig.(Tex.) Dallam's Digest

Dallas Dallas' Pennsylvania and United States Reports

Dalloz Recueil Dalloz Sirey (France)

Dalr. ● Dalrymple's Decisions, Scotch Court of Session (1698-1718)
      ● (Dalrymple of) Stair's Decisions, Scotch Court of Session
      ● (Dalrymple of) Hailes' Scotch Session Cases

Dalr.Dec. Dalrymple's Decisions (Sc.)

Dalr.Feud.Prop. Dalrymple on Feudal Property

Dalrymple ● (Sir Hew) Dalrymple's Scotch Session Cases
      ● (Sir David Dalrymple of) Hailes' Scotch Session Cases
      ● (Sir James Dalrymple of) Stair's Scotch Session Cases

Dalt. Dalton's Justices of the Peace. Many editions (1618-1746)

Daly Daly's New York Common Pleas Reports

Daly (NY) Daly's New York Common Pleas Reports

Dampier MSS. Dampier's Paper Book, Lincoln's Inn Library

Dan. ● Dana's Reports (31-39 Ky.)
      ● Daniels' Compendium Compensation Cases (Eng.)
      ● Daniell's Excheq. in Equity Reports (Sc.)
      ● Danner's Reports (42 Alabama)

Dan.Ch. Daniell's Chancery Practice, 8 editions (1837-1914)

Dan.Ch.Pr. Daniell's Chancery Practice, 8 editions (1837-1914)

Dan.Exch.(Eng.) Daniell's Exchequer & Equity (159 Eng. Reprint)

Dan.Neg.Ins. Daniel's Negotiable Instruments

Dan.Ord. Danish Ordinances

Dan.& L. Danson and Lloyd's Mercantile Cases

Dan.& Ll. Danson and Lloyd's Mercantile Cases (Eng.)

Dana Dana's Kentucky Supreme Court Reports (1833-40)

Dana (Ky.) Dana's Reports (vols. 31-39 Kentucky)

Dana Wh. Dana's edition of Wheaton's International Law

Dane Abr. Dane's Abridgment of American Law

Dane's Abr. Dane's Abridgment of American Law

Daniel, Neg.Inst. Daniel's Negotiable Instruments

Daniell, Ch.Pl.& Prac. Daniell's Chancery Pleading and Practice

Daniell, Ch.Pr. Daniell's Chancery Pleading and Practice

Daniell, Ch.Prac. Daniell's Chancery Pleading and Practice

Dann. • Dann's Reports (1 Arizona)
• Dann's Reports (in 22 California) 2d ed. 1871
• Danner's Reports (42 Alabama)

Danner Danner's Reports (42 Alabama)

Danquah Cases in Gold Coast Law

Dans.& L. Danson & Lloyd's English Mercantile Cases

Dans.& Ll. Danson & Lloyd's Mercantile Cases (Eng.)

Dans.& Lld. Danson & Lloyd's English Mercantile Cases

Danv. Danvers' Abridgment (Eng.)

Danv.Abr. D'Anvers' Abridgment of Law

Darl.Pr.Ct.Sess. Darling, Practice of the Court of Session (Sc.)

Dart Dart on Vendors and Purchasers 8 editions (1851-1929)

Dart.Col.Ca. Dartmouth College Case

Dart, Vend. Dart on Vendors and Purchasers

Das. • Common Law Reports, v. 3 (Eng.)
• Dasent's Bankruptcy & Insolvency Reports (1853-55) (Eng.)

Dasent • Acts of Privy Council, ed. Dasent (Eng.)
• Dasent's Bankruptcy & Insolvency Rep. (Eng.)

Dass.Dig. Dassler's Kansas Digest

Dass.Ed. Dassler's Edition, Kansas Reports

Dass.Ed.(Kan.) Dassler's Edition, Kansas Reports

Dass.Stat. Dassler's Kansas Statutes

Dauph. Dauphin County Reporter (Pa.)

Dauph.Co. Dauphin County (Pa.)

Dauph.Co.(Pa.) Dauphin County (Pa.)

Dauph.Co.Rep. Dauphin County Reporter (Pa.)

Dav. • Davies' English Patent Cases
• Davies' King's Bench & Exchequer Reports (1604-12) (Ir.)
• Davies' United States District Court Reports (now republished as 2 Ware)
• Davis' Reports (Abridgment of Sir Edward Coke's Reports)
• Davis' Reports (vol. 2 Hawaii)
• Davis' United States Supreme Court Reports

Dav.Coke. Davis' Abridgment of Coke's Reports

Dav.Conv. Davidson's Conveyancing

Dav.Dig. Davis' Indiana Digest

Dav.Ir. Davys' or Davies' Reports, Irish King's Bench

Dav.Ir.K.B. Davys' or Davies' Reports, Irish King's Bench

Dav.P.C. Davies' English Patent Cases (1785-1816)

Dav.Pat.Cas. Davies' English Patent Cases (1785-1816)

Dav.Prec.Conv. Davidson's Precedents in Conveyancing

Dav.Rep. Davies' (Sir John) Reports, King's Bench (Ir.)

Dav.(U.S.) Davies District Court Reports (v. 2 of Ware) (U.S.)

Dav.& M. Davison & Merivale Queen's Bench (Eng.)

Dav.& M.(Eng.) Davison & Merivale Queen's Bench (Eng.)

Dav.& Mer. Davison & Merivale Queen's Bench (1843-44) (Eng.)

Davidson Davidson's Reports (vols. 92-111 North Carolina)

Davies   ●   Davies, United States District Court Reports Ware, vol. 2)

      ●   Davies (or Davis, or Davys), Irish King's Bench Reports

Davies (Eng.)   Davies' English Patent Cases

Davies (Ir.)   Davies' King's Bench Reports

Davies (U.S.)   Davies' District Court Reports, v. 2 of Ware (U.S.)

Davis   ●   Davis' Hawaiian Reports

     ●   Davies' (or Davys') Irish King's Bench Reports

     ●   Davis' Reports, vols. 108-176, United States Supreme Court

Davis, Admin.Law   Davis' Administrative Law Treatise

Davis, Bldg.Soc.   Davis' Law of Building Societies

Davis, Cr.Law   Davis Criminal Law

Davis (J.C.B.)   Davis' United States Supreme Court Reports

Davis Land Ct.Dec.(Mass.)   Davis Land Court Decisions

Davis, Mass.Convey.Hdbk.   Davis' Massachusetts Conveyancer's Handbook

Davis Rep.   Davis' Hawaiian Reports (Sandwich Islands)

Davys   Davys King's Bench Reports (Eng.)

Davys (Eng.)   Davys King's Bench Reports (Eng.)

Dawson's Code   Dawson's Code of Civil Procedure, Colo.

Day   ●   Day's Eelction Cases (1892-93) (Eng.)

    ●   Day's Connecticut Reports (1802-13)

Day (Conn.)   Connecticut Reports, by Day (1802-13)

Dayt.Term Rep.   Dayton Term Reports (Dayton, Ohio)

Dayton   ●   Dayton (Laning) Reports (Ohio)

     ●   Dayton Superior & Common Pleas Reports (Ohio)

Dayton (Ohio)   Dayton Ohio Reports

Dayton Term.Rep.   Dayton Term Report (Iddings)

De.   Delaware

De B.Mar.Int.L.   De Burgh's Maritime International Laws

De.CH.   Delaware Chancery Reports

De Col.   De Colyar's English County Court Cases (1867-82)

De G.Bankr.(Eng.)   De Gex, Bankruptcy Reports

De G.F.& J.   De Gex, Fisher, & Jones' English Chancery Reports (45 Eng. Reprint)

De G.J.& J.By.   DeGex, Fisher & Jones Bankruptcy Appeals (1860) (Eng.)

De G.J.& S.   De Gex, Jones & Smith Chancery Reports, England (46 Eng. Reprint)

De G.J.& S.By.   De Gex, Jones & Smith's English Bankruptcy Appeals (1862-65)

De G.J.& S.(Eng.)   De Gex, Jones & Smith Chancery Reports, England (46 Eng. Reprint)

De G.M.& G.   ●   De Gex, Macnaghten, & Gordon's English Bankruptcy Reports

     ●   De Gex, Macnaghten, & Gordon's English Chancery Reports (42-44 Eng. Reprint)

DeG.M.& G.By.   DeGex, Macnaghten, & Gordon Bankruptcy Appeals (1837-55) (Eng.)

De G.& J.   De Gex & Jones' English Chancery Reports (44, 45 Eng. Reprint)

De G.& J.By.   De Gex & Jones' English Bankruptcy Appeals (1857-59)

De G.& J.(Eng.)   De Gex & Jones' English Chancery Reports (44, 45 Eng. Reprint)

De G.& S.(Eng.)   De Gex & Smale's English Chancery Reports (63, 64 Eng. Reprint)

De G.& Sm.   De Gex & Smale's English Chancery Reports (63, 64 Eng. Reprint)

De Gex   De Gex's English Bankruptcy Reports (1844-50)

De Gex, F.& J. De Gex, Fisher & Jones' English Chancery Reports

De Gex, J.& S. De Gex, Jones, and Smith's English Chancery Reports

De Gex, M.& G. De Gex, Macnaghten & Gordon's Reports (Eng.)

De Hart, Mil.Law De Hart on Military Law

De Jure Mar. Hale's De Jure Maris, Appendix to Hall on the Sea Shore

De Krets. DeKretser's Matara Appeals (Ceylon)

De Lolme, Eng.Const. De Lolme on the English Constitution

De Orat. Cicero, De Oratore

DeP. DePaul Law Review (Ill.)

DePaul L.Rev. DePaul Law Review

DeWitt DeWitt's Reports (24-42 Ohio State)

Dea. Deady, United States Circuit and District Court Reports

Dea.& Ch. Deacon & Chitty, Bankruptcy Reports

Dea.& Chit. Deacon & Chitty's English Bankruptcy Reports

Dea.& Sw. Deane & Swabey, English Ecclesiastical Reports (1855-57)

Deac. Deacon, English Bankruptcy Reports (1835-40)

Deac.Cr.Law Deacon on Criminal Law of England

Deac.Dig. Deacon's Digest of the Criminal Law

Deac.& C. Deacon & Chitty's English Bankruptcy Reports

Deac.& Chit. Deacon and Chitty's Bankruptcy Reports (1832-35)

Deacon, Bankr.Cas. Deacon, Bankruptcy (Eng.)

Deacon Bankr.(Eng.) Deacon, Bankruptcy (Eng.)

Deacon & C.Bankr.Cas.(Eng.) Deacon & Chitty, Bankruptcy Cases (Eng.)

Dead.Or.Laws Deady & Lane's Oregon General Laws

Deady Deady's Circuit & District Court Reports (U.S.)

Deane • Deane's Reports (24-26 Vermont)

   • Deane & Swabey's Ecc. Reports (Eng.)

   • Deane & Swabey's Probate & Divorce Reports (Eng.)

   • Deane's Blockade Cases (Eng.)

Deane Ecc.Rep. Deane & Swabey's Ecclesiastical Reports (Eng.)

Deane Ecc.Rep.B. Deane and Swabey's Ecclesiastical Reports (1855-57)

Deane & S.Eccl.(Eng.) Deane & Swabey, Ecclesiastical (164 Eng. Reprint)

Deane & S.Eccl.Rep. Deane & Swabey's Ecclesiastical Reports (Eng.)

Deane & Sw. Deane & Swabey's Ecclesiastical Reports (Eng.)

Dears.C.C. Dearsly's Crown Cases (1852-56) (Eng.)

Dears.& B. Dearsley and Bell's English Crown Cases (1856-58)

Dears.& B.C.C. Dearsley and Bell's English Crown Cases (1856-58)

Dears.& B.Crown Cas. Dearsley and Bell's English Crown Cases (1856-58)

Deas & A. Deas & Anderson's Decisions (1829-32)

Deb. Debenture

Debt.& Cred. Debtor and Creditor

Dec. Decision

Dec.Ch. Decisions from the Chair (Parliamentary) (Eng.)

Dec.Col. Coleccion de los Decretos

Dec.Com.Pat. Decisions of the Commissioner of Patents

Dec.Dig. American Digest System, Decennial Digests

Dec.Fed.Mar.Comm'n. Decisions of the Federal Maritime Commission

Dec.Fern. Decretos del Fernando, Mexico

Dec.O. Ohio Decisions

Dec.Rep. Ohio Decisons, Reprint

Dec.S.D.A. Bengal Sadr Diwani Adalat Decisions

Dec.t.H.& M. Admiralty Decisions tempore Hay & Marriott (Eng.)

Dec.U.S.Compt.Gen. Decisions of U.S. Comptroller General

Dec.U.S.Mar.Comm'n. Decisions of the United States Maritime Commission

Decalogue J. Decalogue Journal

Dec'd. Deceased

Decen.Dig. American Digest, Decennial Edition

Decret.Childeb.ad L.Salic. Decreta Childeberti ad Legem Salicam

Decretal. The Decretalia of the Canon Law

Decs. Decisions

Def. Defense

Defense L.J. Defense Law Journal

Del.
- Delane's English Revision Cases (1832-35)
- Delaware
- Delaware County Reports, Pennsylvania
- Delaware Supreme Court Reports

De.C.Ann. Delaware Code Annotated

Del.Cas. Delaware Cases (1792-1830)

Del.Ch. Delaware Chancery Reports

Del.Civ.Dec. Delhi Civil Decisions (India)

Del.Co.L.J.(Pa.) Delaware County Law Journal (Pa.)

Del.Co.(Pa.) Delaware County Reports (Pa.)

Del.Co.R. Delaware County Reports (Pa.)

Del.Code Delaware Code

Del.Code Ann. Delawre Code Annotated

Del.County Delaware County Reports

Del.Cr.Cas. Delaware Criminal Cases

Del.El.Cas. Delane's Election Revision Cases (Eng.)

Del.Laws Laws of Delaware

Del.Order Delegation Order

Del.Term R. Delaware Term Reports

Delane Delane's Revision Courts Decisions (Eng.)

Delehanty New York Miscellaneous Reports

Dell. Dellam's Texas Opinions (1840-44)

Dem. Demarest's Surrogate's Court Reports (New York)

Dem.Cond.Etran. Demangeat's Condition Civile, Etrangers en France

Dem.(NY) Demarest's Surrogate's Court Reports (New York)

Dem.Sur. Demarest's Surrogate (New York)

Dem.Surr. Demarest's Surrogate (New York)

Demol. Demolombe's Code Napoleon

Demol.C.N. Demolombe's Code Napoleon

Den.
- Denied
- Denio's New York Reports
- Denis' Reports (vols. 32-46 Louisiana)
- Denmark
- Denver

den.app. denying appeal

Den.C.C. Denison's Crown Cases (1844-52) (Eng.)

Den.L.J. Denver Law Journal

Den.L.N. Denver Legal News

den.rearg. denying reargument

den.reh. denying rehearing

den.writ of error denying writ of error

Den.& P. Denison & Pearce's Crown Cases (1844-52) (Eng.)

Den.& P.C.C. Denison and Pearce's Crown Cases (1844-52) (Eng.)

Den.& Sc.Pr. Denison & Scott's House of Lords Appeal Practice

Denio Denio's New York Supreme Court Reports (1845-48)

Denis Denis' Reports (vols. 32-46 Louisiana)

Denison, Cr.Cas. Denison's English Crown Cases

Denom. Denomination

Dens. Denslow's Notes to second edition (vols. 1-3 Michigan Reports)

Denver L.J. Denver Law Journal

Denver L.N. Denver Legal News

Dep.
- Deposit; Depositary
- Deputy

Dept. Department

Dept.Dec. Departmental Decisions (Eng.)

Dept.R. Department Reports, State Dept. (N.Y.)

Dept.R.Un. New York State Department Reports, Unofficial

Dept.State Bull. Department of State Bulletin

Des. Desaussure, South Carolina Equity Reports (1784-1816)

Desai. Handbook of Criminal Cases (India)

Desaus Desaussure, South Carolina Equity Reports

Desaus.Eq. Desaussure, South Carolina Equity Reports

Descr. Description

Dest.Cal.Dig. Desty's California Digest

Dest.Sh. & Adm. Desty on Shipping and Admiralty

Desty, Tax'n. Desty on Taxation

Det. ● Detachable
● Detroit

Det.L.Rev. Detroit Law Review

Det.Law Detroit Lawyer (Detroit Bar Association)

Det.Leg.N. Detroit Legal News

Detroit L.Rev. Detroit Law Review

Dev. ● Development
● Devereux's North Carolina Law Reports (1826-34)
● Devereux's Reports, United States Court of Claims

Dev.C.C. Devereux's Reports, United States Court of Claims

Dev.Ct.Cl. Devereux's Reports, United States Court of Claims

Dev.Deeds. Devlin, Deeds and Real Estate

Dev.Eq. Devereux's North Carolina Equity (1826-34)

Dev.L. Devereux's North Carolina Law Reports

Dev.& B. Devereux & Battle's Reports (vols. 21, 22 North Carolina Equity)

Dev.& B.Eq. Devereux & Battle's Reports (vols. 21, 22 North Carolina Equity) (1834-39)

Dev.& BL.(NC) Devereux & Battle's Reports (vols. 17-20 North Carolina Law Reports)

Dev.& Bat. Devereux & Battle's Reports (vols. 17-20 North Carolina Law Reports)

Dev.& Bat.Eq. Devereux & Battle's Reports (vols. 21, 22 North Carolina Equity) (1834-39)

Devl.Deeds Devlin on Deeds

Dew. ● Dewey's Reports (60-70 Kansas)
● Dewey's Kansas Court of Appeals Reports

Dial.de Scacc. Dialogus de Scaccario

Dial.Sc. Dialogue de Scaccario

Dic. Dicta

Dic.Dom. Dicey on Domicil

Dic.Par. Dicey on Parties to Actions

Dice Dice's Reports (vols. 79-91 Indiana)

Dicey, Confl.Laws Dicey on Conflict of Laws

Dicey, Const. Dicey, Lectures Introductory to the Study of the Law of the English Constitution

Dicey, Dom. Dicey's Law of Domicil

Dicey, Domicil Dicey's Law of Domicil

Dick. ● Dickens' English Chancery Reports (1559-1798)
● Dickens, Scotland
● Dickinson, New Jersey
● Dickenson's Reports (vols. 46-58 New Jersey Equity)

Dick.Ch.(Eng.) Dicken's Chancery Reports (21 Eng. Reprint)

Dick.L.R. Dickinson Law Review

Dick.L.Rev. Dickinson Law Review

Dick.(NJ) Dickinson's New Jersey Equity

Dickens Dickens' English Chancery Reports

Dickinson L.Rev. Dickinson Law Review

Dict. Dictionary

Dict.C.F. Dictionnaire des Codes Francais

Dict.de Jur. Dictionnaire de Jurisprudence

Dict.Dr.Com. Dictionnaire Droit Commercial

Dict.Droit Civil Dictionnaire Droit Civil

Dict.Nat. Dictionnaire du Notariat

Dicta Dicta of Denver Bar Association

Dig. ● Digest
● Digest of Writs
● Digesta
● Digesta of Justinian
● Digestum

Dig.Fla. Thompson's Digest of Laws (Fla.)

Dig.Ops.J.A.G. Digest of Opinions of Judge Advocate General, United States

Dig.Proem. Digest of Justinian, Proem

Dig.R.Pr. Digby's Introduction to the History of Real Property

Dig.St. English's Digest of the Statutes (Ark.)

Digby, R.P. Digby's History of the Law of Real Property

Digest Digest of Justinina (Roman Law)

Dil. Dillon's United States Circuit Court Reports

Dill. Dillon's United States Circuit Court Reports

Dill.Laws Eng.& Am. Dillon's Laws and Jurisprudence of England and America

Dill.Mun.Bonds Dillon on Municipal Bonds

Dill.Mun.Corp. Dillon on Municipal Corporations

Dill.Rem.Caus. Dillon on the Removal of Causes

Dillon Dillon's United States Circuit Court Reports

Dillon, Mun.Corp. Dillon on Municipal Corporation

Dir. Director

Dir.Aut. Diritto di Autore (Italy)

Dir.e Giur. Diritto e Giurisprudenza (Italy)

Dir.Mar. Diritto Marittimo (Italy)

Dir.Sc.Int. Diritto negli Scambi Internazionali (Il) (Italy)

Dirl. Dirleton's Decisions, Court of Sessions (1665-77) (Sc.)

Dirl.Dec. Dirleton's Decisions, Court of Sessions (Sc.)

Dis. Disney's Ohio Superior Court Reports

dis.op. dissenting opinion

disappr. disapproved in or disapproving

Disc. Discount

dism.app. dismissing appeal

Dism'd. Dismissed

Dism'g. Dismissing

Disn. Disney's Ohio Superior Court Reports

Disn.(Ohio) Disney's Ohio Superior Court Reports

Disney Disney's Ohio Superior Court Reports

Diss. ad Flet. Selden's Dissertatio ad Fletam

Dist. ● distinguished

- distinguishing
- district

Dist.Col. District of Columbia

Dist.Col.App. District of Columbia Court of Appeals

Dist.Col.P.U. District of Columbia Public Utilities Commission

Dist.Ct. District Court (state)

Dist.Ct.App. District Court of Appeal

Dist.Rep. District Reports

Distr. Distribution; Distributive

Distrib. Distribute or Distributing

Div. ● Dividend
- division
- divinity
- divorce proceedings

Div.Ct. Divisional Court Selected Judgments, Divisional Courts of the Gold Coast Colony

Dix.Dec. Dix's School Decisions, New York

Dix.Dec.(NY) Dix's School Decisions (New York)

Dk.L.R. Dickinson Law Review

Dkt. Docket

Dn.L.J. Denver Law Journal

Doc. Document

Docket The Docket

Doct.and Stud. Doctor and Student

Doct.Plac. Doctrina Placitandi

Doct.& St. Doctor & Student (Eng.)

Doct.& Stud. Doctor and Student

Dod. Dodson's English Admiralty Reports (165 Eng. Reprint)

Dod.Adm. Dodson's Reports, English Admiralty Courts

Dods. Dodson's English Admiralty Reports (165 Eng. Reprint)

Dodson Adm.(Eng.) Dodson's English Admiralty Reports (165 Eng. Reprint)

Dom.Boc. Domesday Book

Dom.Book Domesday Book

Dom.Civ.Law Domat's Civil Law

Dom.L.R. Dominion Law Reports (Canada)

Dom.Proc. Domus Procerum; In the House of Lords

Dom.Rel. Domestic Relations

Dom.Rel.Ct. Domestic Relations Court

Dom.Rep. Dominican Republic

Domat, Civ.Law Domat's Civil Law

Domat, Dr.Pub. Domat's Droit Publique

Domat, Liv.Prel. Domat's Livres du Droit Public

Domes. Domesday Book

Domesday Domesday Book

Donaker Donaker's Reports (154 Indiana)

Donn. ● Donnelly's Reports, English Chancery (1836-37)
● Donnell's Irish Land Cases (1871-76)

Donnelly Donnelly's Chancery Reports (47 Eng. Reprint)

Donnelly (Eng.) Donnelly's Chancery Reports (47 Eng. Reprint)

Dor. Dorion's Reports (Quebec)

Dor.Md.Laws Dorsey's Maryland Laws

Dor.Q.B. Dorion's Quebec Queen's Bench Reports

Dorion Dorion's Quebec Queen's Bench Reports

Dorion (Can.) Dorion's Quebec Queen's Bench Reports

Dorion Q.B. Dorion's Quebec Queen's Bench Reports

Dos Passos, Stock-Brok. Dos Passos on Stock-Brokers and Stock Exchanges

Doug. ● Douglas' English King's Bench Reports (1778-85)
● Douglas' English Election Cases (1774-76)
● Douglas' Michigan Supreme Court Reports
● Douglass' Reports

Doug.El.Ca. Douglas' English Election Cases

Doug.K.B. Douglas' English King's Bench Reports (1778-85)

Doug.(Mich.) Douglas Michigan Supreme Court Reports

Dougl.El.Cas. Douglas English Election Cases (1774-76)

Dougl.K.B. Douglas, King's Bench Reports (99 Eng. Reprint)

Dougl.K.B.(Eng.) Douglas, King's Bench Reports (99 Eng. Reprint)

Dougl.(Mich.) Douglas' Michigan Supreme Court Reports

Dow ● Dow's House of Lords (Parliamentary) Cases, same as Dow's Reports (3 Eng. Reprint)
● Dowling's English Practice Cases (1812-18)

Dow N.S. Dow & Clark's English House of Lords Cases (1827-32) (1841-42)

Dow P.C. ● Dow's House of Lords (Parliamentary) Cases, same as Dow's Reports (3 Eng. Reprint)
● Dowling's English Practice Cases (1812-18) (1830-41)

Dow.PC(Eng.) ● Dow's House of Lords (Parliamentary) cases, same as Dow's Reports (3 Eng. Reprint)
● Dowling's English Practice Cases (1812-18) (1830-40)

Dow.P.R. Dowling's Practice Cases (1830-41)

Dow & C. Dow & Clark's English House of Lords Cases (6 Eng. Reprint)

Dow & C.(Eng.) Dow & Clark's English House of Lords Cases (6 Eng. Reprint)

Dow & Cl. Dow & Clark's English House of Lords Cases (6 Eng. Reprint)

Dow.& L. Dowling & Lowndes' English Bail Court Reports (1841-49)

Dow.& Ry. ● Dowling & Ryland's English King's Bench Reports (1821-27)
● Dowling & Ryland's English Nisi Prius Cases

Dow.& Ry.K.B. ● Dowling & Ryland's English King's Bench Reports

● Dowling & Ryland's English Nisi Prius Cases

Dow.& Ry.M.C. Dowling & Ryland's English Magistrates' Cases (1822-27)

Dow.& Ry.N.P. Dowling & Ryland's English Nisi Prius Cases

Dowl. Dowling's English Bail Court (Practice) Cases (1830-41)

Dowl.(Eng.) Dowling's English Bail Court (Practice) Cases

Dowl.N.S. Dowling's English Bail Court Reports, New Series (1841-43)

Dowl.NS(Eng.) Dowling's English Bail Court Reports, New Series (1841-43)

Dowl.P.C. Dowling's English Bail Court (Practice) Cases

Dowl.PC(Eng.) Dowling's English Bail Court (Practice) Cases

Dowl.P.C.(N.S.) Dowling Practice Cases, New Series (Eng.)

Dowl.P.C.N.S. Dowling's Practice Cases, New Series (Eng.)

Dowl.P.R. Dowling Practice Reports

Dowl.Pr. Dowling's Common Law Practice

Dowl.Pr.C.N.S. Dowling's Reports, New Series, English Practice Cases

Dowl.Pr.Cas. Dowling Practice Cases (Eng.)

Dowl.& L. Dowling & Lowndes' English Bail Court Reports

Dowl.& Lownd. Dowling & Lowndes' English Bail Court Reports

Dowl.& R. Dowling and Ryland's English King's Bench Reports

Dowl.& R.(Eng.) Dowling and Ryland's English King's Bench Reports

Dowl.& R.Mag.Cas.(Eng.) Dowling & Ryland's Magistrates' Cases

Dowl.& R.NP(Eng.) Dowling & Ryland's Nisi Prius Cases (171 Eng. Reprint)

Dowl.& Ryl. Dowling and Ryland's English King's Bench Reports

Dowl.& Ryl.M.C. Dowling & Ryland's English Magistrates' Cases

Dowl.& Ryl.N.P. Dowling & Ryland's English Nisi Prius Cases

Down.& Lud. Downton & Luder's English Election Cases

Dr. ● Drewry's English Vice Chancellor's Reports (1852-59)

● Drury's Irish Chancery Reports tempore Sugden (1843-44)

● Drury's Irish Chancery Reports tempore Napier (1858-59)

Dr.L.R. Drake Law Review

Dr.R.t.Nap. Drury's Irish Chancery Reports tempore Napier

Dr.R.t.Sug. Drury's Irish Chancery Reports tempore Sugden

Dr.t.Nap. Drury's Irish Chancery Report tempore Napier

Dr.& Sm. Drewry & Smale's English Vice Chancellors' Reports (1860-65)

Dr.& Wal. Drury & Walsh, Irish Chancery Reports (1837-40)

Dr.& War. Drury & Warren's Irish Chancery Reports (1841-43)

Dra. Draper's Upper Canada King's Bench Reports

Drake Att. Drake on Attachment

Drake L.Rev. Drake Law Review

Draper Draper's Upper Canada King's Bench Reports (1828-31)

Draper (Can.) Draper's Upper Canada King's Bench Reports

Draper (Ont.) Draper's Upper Canada King's Bench Reports

Drew. ● Drewry's English Vice Chancellors' Reports (61, 62 Eng. Reprint)

● Drew's Reports (13 Florida)

Drew.(Eng.) Drewry's English Chancery Reports (Eng.)

Drew.Eq.Pl. Drewry's Equity Pleading

Drew.& S. Drewry & Smale's Chancery (Eng.)

Drew.& S.(Eng.) Drewry & Smale's Chancery Reports (Eng.)

Drew.& Sm. Drewry & Smale's Chancery Reports (Eng.)

Drink. Drinkwater's English Common Pleas Reports (1840-41)

Drinkw. Drinkwater Common Pleas (Eng.)

Drinkw.(Eng.) Drinkwater Common Pleas

Drone Cop. Drone on Copyrights

Dru. Drury's Irish Chancery Reports tempore Sugden

Dru.t.Nap. Drury's Irish Chancery Reports tempore Napier

Dru.t.Sug. Drury's Reports tempore Sugden Chancery (Ir.)

Dru.& Wal. Drury & Walsh's Irish Chancery Reports (1837-40)

Dru.& War. Drury & Warren's Irish Chancery Reports (1841-43)

Drug Abuse L.Rev. Drug Abuse Law Review

Drury Drury's Chancery Irish Reports

Drury (Ir.) Drury's Chancery Irish Reports

Drury t.Sug. Drury's Irish Chancery Reports tempore Sugden

Drury & Wal.(Ir.) Drury & Walsh's Irish Chancery Reports

Drury & War.(Ir.) Drury & Warren's Irish Chancery Reports

Du Cange. Du Cange's Glossarium

Du.L.J. Duke Law Journal

Dublin U.L.Rev. Dublin University Law Review

Dud. ● Dudley's Georgia Reports
● Dudley's South Carolina Law Reports (1837-38)

Dud.Eq. Dudley's South Carolina Equity Reports (1837-38)

Dud.Eq.(S.C.) Dudley's Equity Reports (South Carolina)

Dud.(Ga.) Dudley's Georgia Reports (1830-35)

Dud.L. Dudley's South Carolina Law Reports (1837-38)

Dud.L.S.C. Dudley's South Carolina Law Reports (1837-38)

Dud.Law Dudley's South Carolina Law Reports (1837-38)

Dud.S.C. Dudley's South Carolina Law Reports (1837-38)

Dud.(S.C.) Dudley's Law Reports (South Carolina)

Dudl. ● Dudley's Georgia Reports (1830-35)
● Dudley's South Carolina Equity Reports

● Dudley's South Carolina Law Reports (1837-38)

Dudley (Ga.) Dudley's Georgia Reports (1830-35)

Duer. Duer's New York Superior Court Reports

Duer, Ins. Duer on Insurance

Duer (NY) Duer's New York Superior Court Reports

Dufresne Dufresne's Glossary

Dug.Orig. Dugdale's Origines Juridiciales

Dugd. Dugdale's Origines Juridiciales

Dugd.Orig.Jur. Dugdale's Origines Juridiciales

Duke Duke's Law of Charitable Uses

Duke B.A.J. Duke Bar Association Journal

Duke B.A.Jo. Duke University Bar Association Journal

Duke B.J. Duke University Bar Association Journal

Duke Ch.Us. Duke on Charitable Uses (1676)

Duke L.J. Duke Law Journal

Dulck. Dulcken's Eastern District Reports, Cape Colony (S. Africa)

Dun. ● Duncan
● Dunlap

Dun.& Cum. Dunphy & Cummins' Remarkable Trials

Dunc.Eccl.L. Duncan's Scotch Parochial Ecclesiastical Law

Dunc.Ent.Cas. Duncan's Scotch Entail Cases

Dunc.Merc.Cas. Duncan's Mercantile Cases (1885-86) (Sc.)

Dunc.N.P. Duncombe's Nisi Prius

Dund.L.C. Dundee Law Chronicle (1853-58)

Dungl.Med.Dict. Dunglison, Dictionary of Medical Science and Literature

Dunl. Dunlop, Bell & Murray's Reports, Second Series, Scotch Session Cases (1838-62)

Dunl.Abr. Dunlap's Abridgment of Coke's Reports

Dunl.Adm.Pr. Dunlop's Admiralty Practice

Dunl.B.& M. Dunlop, Bell & Murray's Reports, Second Series, Scotch Session Cases

Dunlop Dunlop, Bell & Murray's Reports, Second Series, Scotch Session Cases (1838-62)

Dunn. Dunning's English King's Bench Reports (1753-54)

Dunning Dunning's Reports (King's Bench) (1753-54)

Dup.Jur. Duponceau on Jurisiction of United States Courts

Duponceau, U.S.Cts. Duponceau on Jurisdiction of United States Courts

Duq. Duquesne Law Review (Pa.)

Duquesne U.L.Rev. Duquesne Univeristy Law Review

Durand.Spec.Jur. Durandi Speculum Juris

Durf. Durfee's Reports (2 Rhode Island)

Durie Durie's Court of Session Decisions (1621-42) (Sc.)

Durn.& E. Durnford & East's (Term) Reports (1785-1800) (Eng.)

Dutch. Dutcher's Reports (25-29 N.J. Law Reports)

Duv. ● Duvall's Reports (62, 63 Kentucky)
  ● Duvall's Supreme Court Reports (Canada)

Duv.(Can.) Duval's Reports, Canada Supreme Court

Duval Duval's Reports, Canada Supreme Court

Dw.Stat. Dwarris on Statutes

Dwar. Dwarris on Statutes (1830-48)

Dwar.St. Dwarris on Statutes

Dwight Dwight's Charity Cases (Eng.)

Dy. Dyer's English King's Bench Reports (73 Eng. Reprint)

Dyche & P.Dict. Dyche and Pardon's Dictionary

Dyer Dyer's English King's Bench Reports (73 Eng. Reprint)

Dyer (Eng.) Dyer's English King's Bench Reports (73 Eng. Reprint)

E

e Explained; Statement of import of decision in cited case. Not merely a restatement of the facts.

E. Exchequer; English; Edward; Equity; East; Eastern; Easter; Ecclesiastical; East's English King's Bench Reports (1801-12)

E.A. Europe Archiv

EAC East African Community

E.A.C.A. Law Reports of the Court of Appeals of Eastern Africa

EAGGF European Agricultural Guidance and Guarantee Fund

E.A.L.R. East Africa Law Reports

EAMA African States associated with the EEC

E.A.Prot.L.R. East Africa Protectorate Law Reports .

E.A.S. Executive Agreement Series. United States

E.Afr.L.R. East Africa Law Reports

E.African L.J. East African Law Journal

EST Employee benefit trust

E.B.& E. Ellis, Blackburn & Ellis' English Queen's Bench Reports (1858)

E.B.& S. (Ellis) Best & Smith's English Queen's Bench Reports

E.C.
- Election Cases
- Employment Commission
- English Chancery
- English Chancery Reports (American reprint)
- European Communities

ECA
- Economic Commission for Africa
- Economic Corporation Administration (U.S.)
- United Nations Economic Commission for Africa

ECAFE Economic Commission for Asia & the Far East (UN)

ECE Economic Commission for Europe (UN)

ECITO European Inland Transport Organization

E.C.J. Court of Justice of the European Communities

ECLA Economic Commission for Latin America (UN)

E.C.L.(Eng.) English Common Law Reports, American Reprint

ECMT European Conference of Ministers of Transport

ECOSOC United Nations Economic and Social Council

ECOWAS Economic Community of West African States

ECPA Energy Conservation and Production Act

E.C.R. European Court Reports (European Communities)

ECS European Company Statute

ECSC European Coal and Steel Community

ECWA Economic Commission for Western Asia (UN)

E.D. Exchequer Division, Law Reports (Eng.)

EDA Economic Development Administration

E.D.C. Eastern District Court Reports, Cape of Good Hope (S. Africa)

EDE European Defense Community

EDF European Development Fund

E.D.L. South African Law Reports, Eastern Districts Local Division (S. Africa)

EDP Electronic data processing

E.D.R. Roscoe, Eastern District Reports (Cape of Good Hope)

E.D.S. E.D. Smith's New York Common Pleas Reports

E.D.Smith E.D. Smith's New York Common Pleas Reports

E.D.Smith (N.Y.) E.D. Smith's New York Common Pleas Reports

E.E. English Exchequer Reports (American reprint) Equity Exchequer

EEC European Economic Community (Common Market)

EEI Executive Enterprises, Inc.

EEO Equal Employment Opportunity

EEOC Equal Employment Opportunity Commission

EEOC Compl.Man. Equal Employment Opportunity Commission Compliance Manual (CCH)

E.E.R.
- English Ecclesiastical Reports (American Reprint)
- European Economic Review

EFG Entscheidungen der Finanzgerichte (Germany)

EFT Electronic Fund Transfers

EFTA European Free Trade Association

e.g. exempli gratia (for example)

E.G.D.C. Estates Gazette Digest of Cases

E.G.L. Encyclopedia of Georgia Law

EHS Environmental Health Services

EIA Energy Information Administration

EIB European Investment Bank

EIC Energy Information Council

E.I.R.R. European Industrial Relations Review

E.I.S. Environmental Impact Statement

E.L. Education and Labor

E.L.C.Acts Expiring Laws Continuance Acts

ELDO European Space Vehicle Launcher Development Organization

ELI Environmental Law Institute

E.L.R. Eastern Law Reporter (Canada)

E.L.Rev. European Law Review

E.L.& Eq. English Law and Equity, American Reprint

EMA European Monetary Agreement

EMCF European Monetary and Co-operation Fund

EMS Export Marketing Service

EMU Economic and Monetary Union

ENDC Eighteen-Nation Disarmament Committee

ENR Energy and Natural Resources

ENTENTE Political-Economic Association of Ivory Coast, Dahomey, Niger, Upper Volta, and Togo

E.O. Presidential Executive Order (U.S.)

E.P. Estate Planning

E.P.A. Environmental Protection Agency

E.P.C.
- East's Pleas of the Crown (Eng.)
- Excess Profits Tax Council Ruling or Memorandum, Internal Revenue Bureau (U.S.)
- Roscoe's Prize Cases (Eng.)

E.P.C.A. Energy Policy and Conservation Act

EPGA Emergency Petroleum and Gas Administration

EPU European Payments Union

EPW Environment and Public Works

E.R.
- East's King's Bench Reports (Eng.)
- Election Reports (Ontario)
- English Reports, Full Reprint (1220-1865)
- Economic Regulations (CAB)

E.R.A. English Reports Annotated

ERB Employment Relations Board

ERC Energy Resources Council

E.R.C.
- English Ruling Cases
- Environmental Reporter Cases (BNA)

E.R.C.(Eng.) English Ruling Cases

ERDA Energy Research and Development Administration

E.R.L.R. Eastern Region of Nigeria Law Reports

EROS Earth Resources Observation Systems

ERP European Recovery Program

ERS Economic Research Service

ESA
- Economic Stabilization Agency
- Employment Security Agency
- Employment Standard Administration
- European Space Agency

ESARS Employment Service Automated Reporting System

ESB
- Economisch Statistische Berichten
- Employment Security Board
- Employment Services Bureau

ESC
- Economic and Social Committee

- Employment Security Commission
- Employment Stabilization Commission

ESCAP Economic and Social Commission for Asia and the Pacific (UN)

ESD ● Employment Security Division
- Employment Security Department
- Employment Service Division

ESRO European Space Research Organization

ESV Experimental Safety Vehicle

E.School L.Rev. Eastern School Law Review

E.T. Estate and gift tax ruling

ETA Employment and Training Administration

EURATOM European Atomic Energy Community

EVSt. Einfuhr-und Vorratsstelle für Getreide und Futtermittel

E.W.T. Eastern War Time

EXIMBANK Export-Import Bank of the United States

E.& A. ● Ecclesiastical and Admiralty Report (1853-55)
- Error and Appeal
- Spink's Ecclesiastical and Admiralty Reports
- Upper Canada Error and Appeal Reports

E.& A.R. Error and Appeal Reports, Ontario (1846-66)

E.& A.W.C. Grant's Error and Appeal Reports (Ontario)

E.& B. Ellis & Blackburn's English Queen's Bench Reports (1852-58)

E.& E. Ellis & Ellis' English Queen's Bench Reports (1858-61)

E.& E.Dig. English and Empire Digest

E.& I. English and Irish Appeals, House of Lords

E.& I.App. Law Reports, House of Lords, English and Irish Appeals

E.& Y. Eagle & Younge, English Tithe Cases (1204-1825)

Ea. East's English King's Bench Reports (1801-12)

Eag.& Y. Eagle & Younge's English Tithe Cases

Eag.& Yo. Eagle & Younge's English Tithe Cases

Earw. Earwalker's Manchester Court Leet Records (Eng.)

East ● East's King's Bench Reports (102-104 Eng. Reprint)
- East's Notes of Cases in Morley's East Indian Digest

East Af. East Africa Court of Appeals Reports

East.D.C. Eastern District Court Reports (S. Africa)

East.D.L. Eastern Districts, Local Division, South African Law Reports

East (Eng.) ● East's King's Bench Reports (102-104 Eng. Reprint)
- East's Notes of Cases in Morley's East Indian Digest

East Europe International Market Letter: East Europe

East.L.R. Eastern Law Reporter (Canada)

East.L.R.(Can.) Eastern Law Reporter (Canada)

East N.of C. East's Notes of Cases (in Morley's East Indian Digest)

East P.C. East's Pleas of the Crown (1803)

East PC(Eng.) East's Pleas of the Crown

East Pl.Cr. East's Pleas of the Crown

East.Rep. Eastern Reporter

East.T. Eastern Term (Eng.)

Eastern J.Int'l.L. Eastern Journal of International Law

Ebersole Ebersole's Reports (59-80 Iowa)

Ebersole (Ia.) Ebersole's Reports (59-80 Iowa)

Ec.& Mar. Notes of Cases, Ecclesiastical & Maritime Courts (1844-50) (Eng.)

Ecc.& Ad. Spink's Ecclesiastical and Admiralty Reports (1853-55)

Eccl.R. English Ecclesiastical Reports

Eccl.Stat. Ecclesiastical Statutes

Eccl.& Ad. ● Ecclesiastical and Admiralty

- Spink's Ecclesiastical and Admiralty Reports

Eccl.& Adm. Spink's Ecclesiastical & Admiralty (Upper Can.)

Ecology L.Q. Ecology Law Quarterly

Econ. Economic(s); Economy

Econ.Bull.for Europe Economic Bulletin for Europe

Econ.Cont. Economic Controls (CCH)

Ed.
- Edition
- Editor
- Eden's English Chancery Reports (1757-66)

Ed.Bro. Eden's Edition of English Chancery Reports (1757-66)

Ed.C.R. Edwards' New York Chancery Reports

Ed.Ch. Edward's New York Chancery Reports

Ed.Comment Editorial Comment

Ed.Cr. Edwards' New York Chancery Reports

Ed.et Ord. Edits et Ordonnances (Lower Canada)

Ed.L.J. Edinburgh Law Journal (1831-37)

Ed.O. Education Order

Eden. Eden, English Chancery Reports (28 Eng. Reprint)

Eden.Bankr. Eden's Bankrupt Law

Eden (Eng.) Eden, English Chancery Reports (28 Eng. Reprint)

Eden, Pen.Law Eden's Principles of Penal Law

Eden's Prin.P.L. Eden's Principles of Penal Law

Edg. Edgar's Reports. Court of Session, Scotland (1724-25)

Edg.C. Cannons enacted under King Edgar

Edict Edicts of Justinian

Edicta Edicts of Justinian

Edinb.L.J. Edinburgh Law Journal

Edm.Sel.Ca. Edmonds' New York Select Cases

Edm.Sel.Cas. Edmonds' New York Select Cases

Edm.Sel.Cas.(NY) Edmonds' New York Select Cases

Edmonds' St.at Large Edmonds' Statutes at Large (N.Y.)

Educ. Education; Educational

Edw.
- Edwards' Chester Palatine Courts (Eng.)
- Edwards' English Admiralty Reports
- Edwards' New York Chancery Reports
- Edwards' Reports (vols. 2, 3 Missouri)

Edw.Abr.
- Edward's Abridgment Privy Council
- Edward's Abridgment Prerogative Court Cases (1846)

Edw.Adm. Edward's Admiralty (Eng.) (165 Eng. Reprint)

Edw.Adm.(Eng.) Edward's Admiralty (Eng.) (165 Eng. Reprint)

Edw.Bailm. Edwards on the Law of Bailments

Edw.Bills & N. Edwards on Bills and Notes

Edw.Brok.& F. Edwards on Factors and Brokers

Edw.Ch. Edwards' New York Chancery Reports (1831-50)

Edw.Ch.(NY) Edwards' New York Chancery Reports

Edw.Lead.Dec. Edwards' Leading Decisions in Admiralty (Edwards' Admiralty Reports)

Edw.Mo. Edward's Reports (vols. 2-3 Missouri)

Edw.P.C. Edwards' Prize Cases (Eng.)

Edw.Pr.Cas. Edwards' Prize Cases (English Admiralty Reports)

Edw.Pr.Ct.Cas. Edwards' Abridgment of Prerogative Court Cases

Edw.Rec. Edwards on Receivers in Equity

Edw.(Tho.) Edwards' English Admiralty Reports

Eff. Effective

Efird Efird's Reports (vols. 45-56 South Carolina)

Eir. Lambards Eirenarcha

El. Elchies' Decisions, Scotch Court of Session

El.B.& E. Ellis, Blackburn, & Ellis' English Queen's Bench Reports

El.B.& El. Ellis, Blackburn, & Ellis' English Queen's Bench Reports

El.B.& S.(Eng.) Ellis, Best, & Smith, English Queen's Bench Reports

El.,Bl.& El. Ellis, Blackburn, and Ellis' English Queen's Bench Reports (120 Eng. Reprint)

El.Bl.& El.(Eng.) Ellis, Blackburn, and Ellis' English Queen's Bench Reports (120 Eng. Reprint)

El.Cas. ● Election Cases (Ontario)
● New York Election Cases (Armstrong's)

El.Cas.(NY) New York Election Cases (Armstrong's)

El.Dict. Elchies' Dictionary of Decisions, Court of Session (Sc.)

El.Sal. El Salvador

El.& B. Ellis & Blackburn's English Queen's Bench Reports (118-120 Eng. Reprint)

El.& Bl. Ellis & Blackburn's English Queen's Bench Reports (118-120 Eng. Reprint)

El.& Bl.(Eng.) Ellis & Blackburn's English Queen's Bench Reports (118-120 Eng. Reprint)

El.& El. Ellis & Ellis' English Queen's Bench Reports (120, 121 Eng. Reprint)

El.& El.(Eng.) Ellis & Ellis' English Queen's Bench Reports (120, 121 Eng. Reprint)

Elch. Elchies, Court of Session Cases (Sc.)

Elchies Elchies' Court of Session Decisions (Sc.)

Elchies' Dict. Elchies' (Dictionary of) Decisions, Scotch Court of Session

Elec. ● Election
● Electric[ity]
● Electronic

Elec.C. Elections Code

Elect.Cas.N.Y. New York Election Cases (Armstrong's)

Elect.Rep. Election Reports (Ontario)

Eliz. Queen Elizabeth, as 13 Eliz.

Ell.B.& S. Ellis, Best and Smith Queen's Bench Reports

Ell.Bl.& Ell. Ellis, Blackburn, & Ellis' English Queen's Bench Reports

El.Dig. Eller's Minnesota Digest

Ell.& Bl. Ellis & Blackburn's English Queen's Bench Reports

Ell.& Ell. Ellis & Ellis' English Queen's Bench Reports

Elliot, Deb.Fed.Const. Elliot's Debates on the Federal Constitution

Elliott, App.Proc. Elliott's Appellate Procedure

Elliott, Roads & S. Elliott on Roads and Streets

Elliott, Supp. Elliott Supplement to the Indiana Revised Statutes

Ellis & Vl. Ellis and Blackburn's English Queen's Bench Reports

Elm.Dig. Elmer's Digest of Laws (N.J.)

Elm.Dilap. Elmes on Ecclesiastical Civil Dilapidation

Elmer, Lun. Elmer's Practice in Lunacy

Elph. Elphinstone, Norton and Clark, Interpretation of Deeds (1885)

Elph.Conv. Elphinstone's Introduction to Conveyancing

Elph.Interp.Deeds Elphinstone's Rules for Interpretation of Deeds

Els.W.Bl. Elsley's edition of Wm. Blackstone's English King's Bench Reports

Elton, Com. Elton on Commons and Waste Lands

Elton, Copyh. Elton on Copyholds

Elw.Mal. Elwell on Malpractice and Medical Jurisprudence

Elw.Med.Jur. Elwell on Malpractice and Medical Jurisprudence

Em.App. Emergency Court of Appeals (U.S.)

Em.Ct.App. Emergency Court of Appeals (U.S.)

Em.T. ● Employment Tax Ruling (U.S.)
● Employment Taxes, Social Security Act rulings (U.S. Internal Revenue Service)

Emer.Ct.App. Emergency Court of Appeals (U.S.)

Emer.Ins. Emerigon on Insurance

Emer.Mar.Lo. Emerigon on Maritime Loans

Emerig.Assur. Emerigon, Traité des Assurances et des Contrats à la Grosse

Emerig.Ins. Emerigon on Insurance

Emerig.Mar.Loans Emerigon on Maritime Loans

Emerig.Tr.des Ass. Emerigon, Traite des Assurances

Emerig.Tr.des Assur. Emerigon Traite des Assurances

Emerig.Traite des Assur. Emerigon, Traite des Assurances

Emerson & Haber, Pol.& Civ.Rts. Emerson & Haber's Political & Civil Rights in the United States

Empl.Com. Employment Commission

Empl.Comp.App.Bd. Decisions of the Employees' Compensation Appeals Board

Empl.Prac.Dec. Employment Practices Decisions (CCH)

Empl.Prac.Guide Employment Practices Guide (CCH)

Empl'rs.Liab. Employers' Liability

EnUsers Rep. Energy Users Report (CCH)

Enc.Amer. Encyclopedia Americana

Enc.Arch. Gwilt's Encyclopedia of Architecture

Enc.Brit. Encyclopedia Britannica

Enc.Dict. Encyclopedia Dictionary, Edited by Robert Hunter (1879-88)

Enc.Forms Encyclopedia of Forms

Enc.Ins.U.S. Insurance Year-Book

Enc.Law American and English Encyclopedia of Law

Enc.Pl.& Pr. Encyclopedia of Pleading and Practice

Enc.Pl.& Prac. Encyclopedia of Pleading and Practice

Enc.U.S.Sup.Ct.Rep. Encyclopedia of United States Supreme Court Reports

Ency.L.& P. American & English Encyclopedia of Law & Practice

Ency.Law American and English Encyclopedia of Law

Ency.of Ev. Encyclopedia of Evidence

Ency.of Forms Encyclopedia of Forms & Precedents

Ency.of L.& Pr. Encyclopedia of Law and Practice

Ency.of Pl.& Pr. Encyclopedia of Pleading and Practice

Ency.P.& P. Encyclopedia of Pleading & Practice

Ency.U.S.Sup.Ct.Rep. Encyclopedia of Pleading and Practice Supplement

Ency.U.S.Sup.Ct. Encyclopedia of United States Supreme Court Reports

Encyc. Encyclopedia of the Laws of England, 2 editions (1897-1919)

End.Bdg.Ass. Endlich on Building Associations

Endl.Bldg.Ass'ns. Endlich on Building Associations

End.Interp.St. Endlich's Commentaries on the Interpretation of Statutes

Enf'd. Enforced

Eng. • England
   • English
   • English's Reports (vols. 6-13 Arkansas)
   • English Reports by N.C. Moak

Eng.Ad. • English Admiralty
   • English Admiralty Reports

Eng.Adm.R. English Admiralty Reports

Eng.C.C. English Crown Cases (American Reprint)

Eng.C.L. English Common Law Reports (American Reprint)

Eng.Ch. • English Chancery
   • English Chancery Reports (American Reprint)

Eng.Com.L.R. English Common Law Reports

Eng.Cr.Cas. English Crown Cases (American Reprint)

Eng.Ecc.R. English Ecclesiastical Reports

Eng.Eccl. English Ecclesiastical Reports

Eng.Exch. English Exchequer Reports

Eng.Hist.Rev. English Historical Review

Eng.Ir.App. Law Reports, English and Irish Appeal Cases

Eng.Judg. Scotch Court of Session Cases, decided by the English Judges (1655-61)

Eng.L.& Eq. English Law and Equity Reports (American Reprint)

Eng.L.& Eq.R. English Law and Equity Reports (American Reprint)

Eng.Law & Eq. English Law and Equity Reports (American Reprint)

Eng.Pr.Cas. Roscoe's English Prize Cases

Eng.R.R.Ca. English Railway & Canal Cases

Eng.R.& C.Cas. English Railway and Canal Cases

Eng.Re. English Reports (Full Reprint)

Eng.Rep.
- English Reports, Full Reprint (1378-1865)
- English Reports (Moaks Amer. Reprint)
- English's Reports (6-13 Arkansas)

Eng.Rep.Anno. English Reports Annotated

Eng.Rep.R. English Reports (Full Reprint)

Eng.Rep.Re. English Reports (Full Reprint)

Eng.Reprint English Reprint

Eng.Ru.Ca. English Ruling Cases

Eng.Rul.Cas. English Ruling Cases

Eng.Ry.& C.Cas. English Railway and Canal Cases

Eng.Sc.Ecc. English & Scotch Ecclesiastical Reports

Eng.& Ir.App. Law Reports, English & Irish Appeal Cases

Engl. England

English English's Reports (6-13 Arkansas)

Eng'r. Engineer; Engineering

Ent.
- Coke's Entries
- Rastell's Entries

Entries, Antient. Rastell's Entries (so cited in Rolle Abr.)

Env.L. Environmental Law

Env.L.Rev. Environmental Law Review

Env.L.Rptr. Environmental Law Reporter

Envir.Conserv. Environmental Conservation

Envir.L.Rep. Environmental Law Reporter

Envir.Rep. Environment Reporter (BNA)

Envt'l. Environmental

Eq.
- Equity Court or Division
- Equity Reports (1835-55)

Eq.Ab. Abridgment of Cases in Equity

Eq.Cas.
- Equity Cases, Modern Reports (vols. 9, 10)
- Gilbert, Equity Cases

Eq.Cas.Abr. Equity Cases Abridged (English), 2 vols. (21, 22 Eng. Reprint)

Eq.Cas.Abr.(Eng.) Equity Cases abridged (English), 2 vols. (21, 22 Eng. Reprint)

Eq.Draft. Equity Draftsman (Van Heythuysen's, edited by Hughes)

Eq.Judg. Equity Judgments (by A'Beckett) New South Wales

Eq.R.(Eng.) Equity Reports

Eq.Rep.
- Equity Reports (1853-55)
- Equity Reports, published by Spottiswoode
- Gilbert's Equity Reports (1705-27)
- Harper's South Carolina Equity Reports

Equip. Equipment

Equity Rep.
- Equity Reports (Gilbert) (Eng.)
- Harper's Equity (S.C.)
- English Chancery Appeals

Ex.Or. Executive Orders

Erck Erck's Ecclesiastical Register (1608-1825) (Eng.)

Erie Co.L.J.(Pa.) Erie County Law Journal (Pa.)

Erie Co.Leg.J. Erie County Legal Journal

Err.& App. Error and Appeals Reports (Upper Canada)

Ersk.
- Erskine's Institutes of the Law of Scotland
- Erskine's Principles of the Law of Scotland

Ersk.Dec. Erskine's United States Circuit Court, etc., Decisions (vol. 35 Georgia)

Ersk.Inst. Erskine's Institutes of the Law of Scotland

Ersk.Prin. Erskine's Principles of the Law of Scotland

Ersk.Speeches Erskine's Speeches

Erskine I. Erskine's Institutes. 8 editions (1773-1871)

Erskine, Inst. Erskine's Institutes of the Law of Scotland. 8 editions (1773-1871)

Esc. Escrow

Escriche Escriche, Diccionario Razonado de Legislacion y Jurisprudencia

Escriche, Dic.Leg. Escriche, Diccionario Razonado de Legislacion y Jurisprudencia

Escriche, Dict. Escriche's Dictionary of Jurisprudence

Esp. Espinasse's English Nisi Prius Reports (1793-1810)

Esp.Dig. Espinasse's Digest of the Law of Actions and Trials

Esp.(Eng.) Espinasse (170 Eng. Reprint)

Esp.N.P. Espinasse's English Nisi Prius Reports (1793-1810)

Esprit des Lois Montesquleu, Esprit des Lois

Esq. Esquire

Est. Estate(s)

Est.Prac. Estee's Code Pleading, Practice and Forms

Est.Prac.Pl. Estee's Code Pleading Practice and Forms

Est.& Trusts Estates and Trusts

Estab. Establishment

Estates Q. Estates and Trusts Quarterly

Estee Estee's District Court of Hawaii

Estee (Hawaii) Estee's District Court of Hawaii

Estm. Estimated

et al. et alii (and others)

et seq. ● et sequens (and the following)
● et sequitur (and as follows)

et ux. et uxor (and wife)

et vir. And husband

etc. et cetera (and the others, and so forth)

Eth.Nic. Aristotle, Nicomachean Ethics

EuR. Europarecht (Germany)

Euer Euer Doctrina Placitandi (Eng.)

Eun. Wynne's Eunomus

Eur.Ass.Arb. European Assurance Arbitration (1872-75)

Eur.C.J. European Court of Justice

Eur.Comm.on Human Rights European Community on Human Rights

Eur.Parl.Deb. European Parliamentary Assembly Debates

Eur.Parl.Doc. European Parliament Working Documents

Eur.T.L. European Transport Law (Belgium)

Euratom European Atomic Energy Community

Europ.T.S. European Treaty Series

Ev. Evidence

Ev.Tr. Evans' Trial

Evans ● Evans' Reports, Washington Territory (announced, but never published)
● Lord Mansfield's Decisions (1799-1814) (Eng.)

Everybody's L.M. Everybody's Law Magazine

Evid. Evidence

Ewell Bl. Ewell's edition of Blackstone

Ewell Cas.Inf.(or L.C.) Ewell's Leading Cases on Infancy, etc.

Ewell Fix. Ewell on the Law of Fixtures

Ewell L.C. Ewell's Leading Cases on Infancy, etc.

Ex. ● Citation in Examiner's decision
● Court of Exchequer (Eng.)
● English Exchequer Reports (1848-56)
● Examiner's decision

Ex.C.R. ● Canada Exchequer Court Reports
● Canada Law Reports (Ex. Court)

Ex.D. Law Reports Exchequer Division (1875-80) (Eng.)

ex rel. ex relatione (on the relation of)

Ex.Sess. Extra Session

Exam. The Examiner

Exch. ● Exchange
● Exchequer
● Exchequer Reports (Welsby, Hurlstone, & Gordon)
● English Law Reports, Exchequer
● English Exchequer Reports

Exch.C. Canada Law Reports, Exchequer Court

Exch.C.R. Exchequer Court Reports (Canada)

Exch.Can. Exchequer Reports (Canada)

Exch.Cas. Exchequer Cases (Legacy Duties, etc. (Sc.)

Exch.Ct.(Can.) Canada Law Reports, Exchequer Court

Exch.Div. Exchequer Division, English Law Reports

Exch.Div.(Eng.) Exchequer Division, English Law Reports

Exch.Rep.
- Exchequer Reports (Welsby, Hurlstone & Gordon), 11 vols.
- English Exchequer Reports (American Reprint)

Exec.
- Executive
- Executor

Exec.Order Presidential Executive Order (U.S.)

Eximbank Export-Import Bank

Exp. Expenses

exr. executor

Ex'r[x]. Executor[trix]

Ext. Extended; extension

Extd. Extended

Exter.Ca. Lobingier's Extra-territorial Cases, U.S. Court for China

Extl. External

Extn. Extension

Extra.Ca. Lobingier's Extra-territorial Cases, U.S. Court for China

Extra.Sess. Extraordinary Session

Eyre Eyre's King's Bench Reports tempore William III (Eng.)

Eyre, MS Eyre, Manuscript Notes of Cases, King's Bench (in Library of the New York Law Institute)

F

f • followed
  • Cited as controlling (used in Shepard's Citations)
  • footnote
F. • Faculty Collection, Court of Sessions Decisions, Scotland
  • Federal Reporter (US)
  • Finance
  • Foord's Cape of Good Hope Reports (S. Africa)
  • Foord, Supreme Court Reports, Cape Colony
  • Fraser, Scotch Sessions Cases, 5th Series (1898-1905)
  • Forum
  • French
F.2d   Federal Reporter, Second Series
FAA   Federal Aviation Administration
F.A.A.   Free of all average
F.A.D.   Federal Anti-Trust Decisions
FAIR   Fair Access to Insurance Requirements
FAO   Food and Agriculture Organization of the United Nations
F.A.S. • Foreign Agricultural Service
  • Free alongside ship
FASB   Financial Accounting Standards Board
F.Abr.   Fitzherbert's Abridgment
FBA   Federal Bar Association
F.B.C.   Fonblanque, Bankruptcy Cases
FBI   Federal Bureau of Investigation
F.B.I.   Full Bench Decisions (India)
FBILEB   FBI Law Enforcement Bulletin
F/B/O   For benefit of
F.B.R.   Full Bench Rulings Bengal (India)
F.B.R.N.W.P.   Full Bench Rulings, Northwest Provinces (India)
F.C. • Faculty Collection of Decisions, Scotch Court of Session (1738-1841)
  • Federal Cases, (United States), 31 vols.
  • Selected Judgments of the Full Court, Accra and Gold Coast

FCA   Farm Credit Administration
F.C.A.   Federal Code Annotated
FCC   Federal Communications Commission
F.C.C.   Federal Communications Commission Reports
FCDA   Federal Civil Defense Administration
FCIA   Foreign Credit Insurance Association
FCIC   Federal Crop Insurance Corporation
F.C.L.   Femme Couleur Libre
FCLI   Fordham University School of Law, Corporate Law Institute
F.C.R. • Federal Court Reports (India)
  • Fearne on Contingent Remainders
FCS   Farmer Cooperative Service
FC(Scott)   Faculty Collection of Decisions
FCU   Federal Credit Union (U.S.)
F.Carr.Cas.   Federal Carriers Cases (CCH)
F.Carrier Cas.   Federal Carrier Cases (CCH)
F.Cas.   Federal Cases (1789-1880)
F.Cas.No.   Federal Cases Number
F.Ct.Sess.   Fraser's Court of Sessions Cases (Sc.)
F.D.   Family Division
FDA   Food and Drug Administration
FDAA   Federal Disaster Assistance Administration
FDC   Food, Drug and Cosmetic Docket
F.D.C.Act   Federal Food, Drug, and Cosmetic Act
F.D.Cosm.L.Rep.   Food, Drug, Cosmetic Law Reporter (CCH)
FDIC   Federal Deposit Insurance Corporation
FDPC   Federal Data Processing Centers
F.Dict.   Kames & Woodhouselee, (folio) Dictionary, Scotch Court of Session Cases

FEA ● Federal Energy Administration
● Foreign Economic Administration

FEB Fair Employment Board

FEBs Federal Executive Boards

FEC Far Eastern Commission

FEP Fair Employment Practice Cases (BNA)

FERA Federal Emergency Relief Administration

FES Final Environmental Statement

FET Federal estate tax

FFC Fiscal and Financial Committee

FFMC Federal Farm Mortgage Corp.

FG Finanzgericht--Fiscal Court (Ger.)

F.G.A. Free from general average; foreign general average

FGT Federal gift tax

FHA Federal Housing Administration

F.H.L. Fraser, House of Lords Reports (Sc.)

FHLBB Federal Home Loan Bank Board

FHLMC Federal Home Loan Mortgage Corporation

FHWA Federal Highway Administration

FIA Federal Insurance Administration

FIC Federal Information Centers

FICA Federal Insurance Contribution Act

FICB Federal Intermediate Credit Banks

FICEI Federal Inter-Agency Council on Energy Information

FIN.E.F.T.A. Finland-European Free Trade Association Treaty

FIP Forestry Incentive Program

FIT Federal insurance tax

FIU Florida International University

F.J. First Judge

F.J.C. ● The Federal Judicial Center
● Fraser, Reports, Justiciary Court (Sc.)

FLB The Florida Bar

FLETC Federal Law Enforcement Training Center

F.L.J. ● Canada Fortnightly Law Journal
● Federal Law Journal (India)

F.L.P. Florida Law and Practice

F.L.R. ● Federal Law Reports (India)
● Fiji Law Reports
● University of Florida Law Review

F.L.Rev. Federal Law Review

FLSA Fair Labor Standards Act U.S.

FM Field Manual, U.S. Army

FMC Federal Maritime Commission

FMCS Federal Mediation and Conciliation Service

F.M.S.L.R. Federated Malay States Reports

F.M.S.R. Federated Malay States Reports

F.Moore English King's Bench Reports (72 Eng. Reprint)

F.N.B. Fitzherbert's Natura Brevium (Eng.)

F.N.D. Finnemore's Notes and Digest of Natal Cases

F.N.J.,F.D.C. U.S. Food and Drug Administration. Notices of Judgment: Foods

FNMA Federal National Mortgage Association

FNS Food and Nutrition Service

F.P.A. ● Federal Preparedness Agency
● Free from particular average

FPC ● Federal Power Commission
● Federal Power Commission Reports

F.P.C. U.S. Federal Power Commission Opinions and Decisions

FPI Federal Publications Inc.

F.P.R. Federal Procurement Regulations

F.R. ● Federal Register
● Federal Reporter
● Fordham Law Review (N.Y.)
● Foreign Relations

FRA ● Federal Railroad Administration
● Federal Reports Act

FRB Federal Reserve Board, Board of Governors of the Federal Reserve System

F.R.B. Federal Reserve Bulletin

FRC Federal Radio Commission

F.R.C.P. Federal Rules of Civil Procedure

FRCs Federal Regional Councils

F.R.D. Federal Rules Decisions

F.R.S. Federal Reserve System (U.S.)

F.S. Federal Supplement

FSA ● Farm Security Administration

● Federal Security Agency (U.S.)

F.S.A. ● Federal Statutes Annotated

● Florida Statutes Annotated

F.S.L.I.C. Federal Savings and Loan Insurance Corp.

F.S.O. Foreign Service Officer

F.S.R. Fleet Street Reports of Patent Cases (Eng.)

FSS Federal Supply Service

F.Supp. Federal Supplement

FTC Federal Trade Commission

F.T.C. Federal Trade Commission Decisions

FTS Federal Telecommunications System

FURA Federal Utility Regulation Annotated

FUTA Federal Unemployment Tax Act

FWPCA Federal Water Pollution Control Act

FWS Fish and Wildlife Service

FY Fiscal Year

F.& C.C. Fire & Casualty Cases (CCH)

F.& F. Foster & Finlason's English Nisi Prius Reports (1856-67)

F.& Fitz. Falconer & Fitzherbert's English Election Cases (1835-39)

F.& J.Bank.De Gex Fisher & Jones' English Bankruptcy Reports

F.& S. Fox and Smith's Irish King's Bench Reports (1822-24)

Fa. Firma

Fac. Faculty of Advocate, Collection of Decisions

Fac.Coll. Faculty Collection of Decisions, Court of Sessions (Sc.) First and Second Series, 38 vols.

Fac.Coll.N.S. Faculty of Advocates Collection of Decisions, Court of Session (Sc.)

Fac.Dec. Faculty Collection of Decisions, Court of Sessions (Sc.) First and Second Series, 38 vols.

Fac.L.Rev. Faculty of Law Review (Toronto)

Fair Empl.Prac.Cas. Fair Employment Practices Cases

Fairchild Fairchild's Reports (10-12 Maine)

Fairf. Fairfield's Reports (10-12 Maine)

Fairf.(Me.) Fairfield's Reports (10-12 Maine)

Fairfield Fairfield's Reports (10-12 Maine)

Falc. Falconer's Scotch Court of Session Cases (1744-51)

Falc.Co.Cts. Falconer, County Court Cases (Eng.)

Falc.Marine Dict. Falconer's Marine Dictionary

Falc.& F. Falconer & Fitzherbert's Election Cases (Eng.)

Falc.& Fitz. Falconer & Fitzherbert's Election Cases (1835-39) (Eng.)

Fam. Family

Fam.Cas.Cir.Ev. Famous Cases of Circumstantial Evidence, by Phillips

Fam.Ct. Family Court

Fam.Ct.Act. Family Court Act

Fam.L.Rep. Family Law Reporter (BNA)

Fam.Law Family Law

Family L.Q. Family Law Quarterly

Far. ● Farresley's Reports, vol. 7 Modern Reports

● Farresley's Cases in Holt's King's Bench Reports

Far Eastern Econ.Rev. Far Eastern Economic Review

Farwell Farwell on Powers 3 editions (1874-1916)

fasc. fascicle (installment)

Faust Faust's Compiled Laws, (S.C.)

Fawc. Fawcett's Court of Referees Report (Eng.)

Fawc.Ref. Fawcett, Court of Referees (1866)

Fawcett Fawcett on Landlord and Tenant 3 editions (1870-1905)

Fay.L.J. ● Fayette Law Journal (Pa.)
         ● Fayette Legal Journal (Pa.)

Fayette Leg.J.(Pa.) Fayette Legal Journal (Pa.)

Fdn. Foundation

Fear.Rem. Fearne on Contingent Remainders (1772-1844)

Fed. ● Federal
     ● Federal Reporter (US)
     ● The Federalist, by Hamilton

Fed.2d Federal Reporter, Second Series

Fed.Alc.Adm. Federal Alcohol Administration

Fed.Anti-Tr.Dec. Federal Anti-Trust Decisions

Fed.B.A.J. Federal Bar Association Journal

Fed.B.A.Jo. Federal Bar Association Journal

Fed.B.J. Federal Bar Journal

Fed.Banking L.Rep. Federal Banking Law Reporter (CCH)

Fed.Ca. Federal Cases

Fed.Carr.Cas. Federal Carrier Cases (CCH)

Fed.Carr.Rep. Federal Carriers Reporter (CCH)

Fed.Cas. Federal Cases

Fed.Cas.No. Federal Case Number

Fed.Comm.B.J. Federal Communications Bar Journal

Fed.Est.& Gift Tax Rep. Federal Estate and Gift Tax Reporter (CCH)

Fed.Ex.Tax Rep. Federal Excise Tax Reporter (CCH)

Fed.Juror Federal Juror

Fed.L.J.Ind. Federal Law Journal of India

Fed.L.Q. Federal Law Quarterly

Fed.L.Rep. Federal Law Reports

Fed.L.Rev. Federal Law Review

Fed.Prob. Federal Probate, Washington, D.C.

Fed.R. Federal Reporter

Fed.R.Civ.P. Federal Rules of Civil Procedure

Fed.R.D. Federal Rules Decisions

Fed.R.Evid. Federal Rules of Evidence

Fed.Reg. Federal Register

Fed.Rep. Federal Reporter

Fed.Res.Bull. Federal Reserve Bulletin

Fed.Rules Civ.Proc. Federal Rules of Civil Procedure

Fed.Rules Cr.Proc. Federal Rules of Criminal Procedure

Fed.Rules Serv. Federal Rules Service

Fed.Rules Serv.2d Federal Rules Service, Second Series

Fed.Sec.L.Rep. Federal Securities Law Reporter (CCH)

Fed.Stat.Ann. Federal Statutes Annotated

Fed.Sup. Federal Supplement

Fed.Supp. Federal Supplement

Fed.Taxes Federal Taxes (P-H)

Fed.Taxes Est.& Gift Federal Taxes: Estate and Gift Taxes (P-H)

Fed.Taxes Excise Federal Taxes: Excise Taxes (P-H)

Fed.Tr.Rep. Federal Trade Reporter

Fed'n. Federation

Fed'n.Ins.Counsel Q. Federation of Insurance Counsel Quarterly

Fent. ● Fenton's Important Judgments (New Zealand)
     ● Fenton's Reports (New Zealand)

Fent.Imp.Judg. Fenton's Important Judgements (New Zealand)

Fent.N.Z. Fenton's New Zealand Reports

Fent.(New Zealand) Fenton's New Zealand Reports

Ferard, Fixt. Amos & Ferard on Fixtures

Ferg. ● James Fergusson's Consistorial Decisions, Scotland
     ● Consistorial Decisions, Scotland, by George Ferguson, Lord Hermand

Ferg.Cons. Fergusson's (Sc.) Consistorial Reports

Ferg.M.& D. Fergusson, Divorce Decisions by Consistorial Courts (Sc.)

Ferg.Ry.Cas. Fergusson's Five Years' Railway Cases

Fergusson ● Fergusson's Consistorial Decisions (Scotland)
     ● Fergusson's Scotch Session Cases (1738-52)

Fern.Dec. Decretos del Fernando (Mexico)

Fernald, Eng.Synonyms Fernald's English Synonyms

Ferriere Ferriere's Dictionnaire de Droit et de Pratique

Ferriere, Dict.de Jur. Ferriere's Dictionary of Jurisprudence

Fessen.Pat. Fessenden on Patents

Fett.Carr. Fetter's Treatise on Carriers of Passengers

Feud.Lib. The Book of Feuds. See this dictionary, 8. v. "Liber Feudorum"

Fi. Finnish

fi.fa. fieri facias (Writ of execution of property)

Fid.L.Chron. Fiduciary Law Chronicle

Fiduciary Fiduciary Reporter (Pa.)

Fiduciary R.(Pa.) Fiduciary Reporter (Pa.)

Field Corp. Field on Corporations

Fiji L.R. Fiji Law Reports

Fin. ● Finance
     ● Financial
     ● Finch's English Chancery Reports (1673-81)
     ● Finland
     ● Finlay's Irish Digest

Fin.C. Financial Code

Fin.H. H. Finch's Chancery Reports (1673-81) (Eng.)

Fin.Pr. T. Finch's Precedents in Chancery (1689-1722) (Eng.)

Fin.T. T. Finch's Precedents in Chancery (1689-1722) (Eng.)

Fin.& Dul. Finnemore & Dulcken's Natal Law Reports

Finch. ● English Chancery Reports tempore Finch
     ● Finch's Precedents in Chancery (Eng.)

Finch (Eng.) ● English Chancery Reports tempore Finch

● Finch's Precedents in Chancery (Eng.)

Finch Ins.Dig. Finch's Insurance Digest

Finch L.C. Finch's Land Cases

Finch, Law Finch, Sir Henry; a Discourse of Law (1759)

Finch Nomot. Finch's Nomotechnia

Finch Prec. Precedents in Chancery, edited by Finch

Finkel, Medical Cyc. Finkel, et al., Lawyers' Medical Cyclopedia

Finl.Dig. Finlay's Irish Digest

Finl.L.C. Finlason's Leading Cases on Pleading

Finl.Rep. Finlason's Report of the Gurney Case

Fire & Casualty Cas. Fire and Casualty Cases (CCH)

First Bk.Judg. First Book of Judgments (1655) (Eng.)

First pt.Edw.III. Part II. of the Year Books

First Pt.H.VI. Part VII. of the Year Books

Fish. ● Fisher's U.S. Patent Cases
     ● Fisher's U.S. Prize Cases

Fish.C.L.Dig. Fisher's Digest of English Common Law Reports

Fish.Cas. Fisher's Cases, United States District Courts

Fish.Crim.Dig. Fisher's Digest of English Criminal Law

Fish.Dig. Fisher's English Common Law Digest

Fish.Mortg. Fisher on Mortgages

Fish.Pat. Fisher's United States Patent Cases

Fish.Pat.Cas. Fisher's United States Patent Cases

Fish.Pat.Rep. Fisher's United States Patent Reports

Fish.Pr.Cas. Fisher's United States Prize Cases

Fish.Prize Fisher's United States Prize Cases

Fish.Prize Cas. Fisher's Prize Cases, U.S.

Fish & G.C. Fish and Game Code

Fisher ● Fisher on Mortgages 7 editions (1856-1947)
     ● Fisher's Prize Cases, U.S.

Fisher Pat.Cas.(F.) Fisher, US Patent Cases

Fisher Pr.Cas.(F.) Fisher, US Prize Cases

Fisher Pr.Cas.(Pa.) Fisher Pennsylvania Prize Cases

Fits.Nat.Brev. Fitzherbert's Natura Brevium

Fitz.Abridg. Fitzherbert's Abridgment (1516)

Fitz.L.G.Dec. Fitzgibbon, Irish Local Government Decisions

Fitzg.   ● Fitzgibbon's King's Bench Reports (1728-33) (Eng.)
     ● Fitzgibbon's Land Reports (Ir.)
     ● Fitzgibbon's Registration Appeals (Ir.)

Fitzg.Land R. Fitzgibbon's Irish Land Reports

Fitzg.Reg.Ca. Fitzgibbon's Irish Registration Appeals (1894)

Fitzh.Abr. Fitzherbert's Abridgment (1516)

Fitzh.N.B. Fitzherbert, New Natura Brevium (1534)

Fitzh.N.Br. Fitzherbert's Natura Brevium (Eng.)

Fitzh.Nat.Brev. Fitzherbert's Natura Brevium

Fixt. Fixtures

Fl.   ● Fleta, seu Commentarius Juris Anglici (1647) (Eng.)
   ● Florida

Fl.L.R. University of Florida Law Review

Fl.S. Florida Supplement

Fl.& K. Flanagan & Kelly's Rolls Court Reports (Ireland) (1840-42)

Fla.   ● **Florida**
     ● **Florida Reports**

Fla.B.J. Florida Bar Journal

Fla.Dig. Thompson's Digest of Laws (Florida)

Fla.Jur. Florida Jurisprudence

Fla.L.J. Florida Law Journal

Fla.L.Rev. Florida Law Review

Fla.Laws Laws of Florida

Fla.R.C. Railroad Commission for the State of Florida

Fla.S.B.A.Jo. Florida State Bar Association Journal

Fla.Sess.Law Serv. Florida Session Law Service (West)

Fla.St.Univ.Slavic Papers Florida State University Slavic Papers

Fla.Stat. Florida Statutes

Fla.Stat.Ann. Florida Statutes Annotated

Fla.Stat.Anno. Annotations to Official Florida Statutes

Fla.Supp. Florida Supplement

Fla.& K. Flanagan & Kelly, Rolls (Ir.)

Flan.& Kel. Flanagan & Kelly, Rolls (Ir.)

Fland.Ch.J. Flanders' Lives of the Chief Justices of the United States

Fleta Fleta, seu Commentarius Juris Anglici

Fletcher, Corporations Fletcher's Cyclopedia Corporations

Fletcher Cyc.Corp. Fletcher, Cyclopedia Corporations

Fleury, Hist. Fleury's History of the Origin of French Laws (1724)

Flip. Flippin's Circuit Court Reports (U.S.)

Flipp.(F.) Flippin's Circuit Court Reports (U.S.)

Flor.   ● Florida
     ● Florida Reports

Florida Florida Reports

Fm.H.A. Farmers Home Administration

Fo.L.R. Fordham Law Review

Foelix, Droit Int.Princ. Foelix, Droit International Prive

Fogg Fogg's Reports (32-35 New Hampshire)

Fol.   ● Foley's Poor Law Cases (Eng.)
     ● folio

Fol.Dict. Kames & Woodhouselee's Dictionary, Court of Session (Sc.)

Fol.P.L.Cas. Foley's English Poor Law Cases (1556-1730)

foll. followed in, or following

fols. folios

Fon.B.C. Fonblanque, Bankruptcy Cases (1849-1852)

Fonb.Eq. Fonblanque's Equity (Eng.)

Fonbl.   ● Fonblanque's Equity

- Fonblanque on Medical Jurisprudence
- Fonblanque's New Reports, English Bankruptcy

Fonbl.Eq. Fonblanque's Equity (Eng.)

Fonbl.Eq.(Eng.) Fonblanque's Equity (Eng.)

Fonbl.N.R.
- Fonblanque's Cases in Chancery (Eng.)
- Fonblanque's Equity
- Fonblanque on Medical Jurisprudence
- Fonblanque's New ports, English Bankruptcy (1849-52)

Fonbl.R. Fonblanque's English Cases (or New Reports) in Bankruptcy (1849-52)

Food Drug Cos.L.Rep. Food Drug Cosmetic Law Reporter (CCH)

Food Drug Cosm.L.J. Food Drug Cosmetic Law Journal

Food & Agric. Food and Agricultural

Foord Foord, Supreme Court Reports, Cape Colony (S. Africa)

Foote & E.Incorp.Co. Foote and Everett's Law of Incorporated Companies Operating under Municipal Franchises

For.
- Foreign
- Forensic
- Forrest's Exchequer Reports
- Forrester's Chancery Reports (cases tempore Talbot)
- Fortescue de Laudibus Legum Angliae

For.Aff. Foreign Affairs

For.Cas.& Op. Forsyth's Cases and Opinions on Constitutional Law

For.de Laud. Fortescue de Laudibus Legum Angliae

For.Pla. Brown's Formulae bene Placitandi

For.Tax L.W.Bull. Foreign Tax Law Weekly Bulletin

Forb.
- Forbes' Court of Session Dec. (Sc.)
- Forbes' Cases in St.

Andrews Bishop's Court
- Forbes' Journal of the Session (1705-13) (Sc.)

Forb.Inst. Forbes' Institutes of the Law of Scotland

Forbes. Forbes' Journal of the Session (1705-13).(Sc.)

Ford.L.Rev. Fordham Law Review

Ford.Urban L.J. Fordham Urban Law Journal

Fordham L.Rev. Fordham Law Review

Forester Chancery Cases tempore Talbot (Eng.)

Form. Forman's Reports (1 Scammon, 2 Illinois)

Forman Forman's Reports (1 Scammon, 2 Illinois)

Forman (Ill.) Forman's Reports (1 Scammon, 2 Illinois)

Formul.Solen. Formulae Solemnes

Foro It. Foro Italiano (Il.) (Italy)

Forr.
- Forrest's English Exchequer Reports
- Forrester's English Chancery Cases (commonly cited, Cases tempore Talbot) (1734-38)

Forrest Forrest's Reports, English Exchequer (1800-01)

Forrester Forrester's Chancery Cases tempore Talbot (Eng.)

Fors.Cas.& Op. Forsyth's Cases and Opinions on Constitutional Law (1869)

Fort. Fortescue's King's Bench Reports (1695-1738) (Eng.)

Fort.de Laud. Fortescue de Laudibus Legum Angliae (1616)

Fort.L.J. Fortnightly Law Journal

Fortes. Fortescue's Reports, English courts

Fortes.de Laud. Fortescue, De Laudibus Legum Angliae

Fortes.Rep. Fortescue's King's Bench Reports (Eng.)

Fortesc. Fortescue's English King's Bench Reports (92 Eng. Reprint)

Fortesc.de L.L.Angl. Fortescue de Laudibus Legum Angliae

Fortescue (Eng.) Fortescue's English King's Bench Reports (92 Eng. Reprint)

Fortn.L.J.   Fortnightly Law Journal

Fortnightly L.J. Fortnightly Law Journal

Forum   ● The Forum
- Forum: Bench & Bar Review
- Forum Law Review
- Forum, Dickinson School of Law

Foss Judg.   Foss' Judges of England

Fost.   ● Foster's English Crown Law or Crown Cases (1743-61)
- Foster's New Hampshire Reports
- Foster's Legal Chronicle Reports, Pennsylvania
- Foster's Reports (vols. 5, 6, and 8 Hawaii)

Fost.C.L.(Eng.) Foster's English Crown Law or Crown Cases (168 Eng. Reprint)

Fost.Cr.Law Foster's English Crown Law or Crown Cases (168 Eng. Reprint)

Fost.Crown Law Foster's English Crown Law or Crown Cases (168 Eng. Reprint)

Fost.Fed.Prac. Foster's Treatise on Pleading and Practice in Equity in Courts of United States

Fost.(Haw.) Foster's Hawaiian Reports (vols 5, 6 and 8)

Fost.(N.H.) Foster's Reports (New Hampshire, vols. 21-31)

Fost.on Sci.Fa. Foster on the Writ of Scire Facias

Fost.& F. Foster and Finlason's English Nisi Prius Reports (175, 176 Eng. Reprint)

Fost.& F.(Eng.) Foster and Finlason's English Nisi Prius Reports (175, 176 Eng. Reprint)

Fost.& Fin. Foster and Finlason's English Nisi Prius Reports (175, 176 Eng. Reprint)

Foster   ● Foster's English Crown Law
- Legal Chronicle Reports (Pennsylvania), edited by Foster
- Foster's New Hampshire Reports

Foster Fed.Pr. Foster on Federal Practice

Foster (Pa.) Foster Legal Chronicle Reports

Fount. Fountainhall's Decisions, Scotch Court of Session (1678-1712)

Fount.Dec. Fountainhall's Decisions (Sc.)

Fowl.L.Cas. Fowler's Leading Cases on Collieries

Fox   ● Fox's Patent, Trade Mark, Design & Copyright Cases (Canada)
- Fox's Circuit & District Court Decisions (U.S.)
- Fox's Registration Cases (Eng.)

Fox Pat.C. Fox's Patent, Trade Mark, Design & Copyright Cases (Canada)

Fox Pat.Cas. Fox's Patent, Trade Mark, Design & Copyright Cases (Canada)

Fox Reg.Ca. Fox's Registration Cases

Fox & S. Fox & Smith's Irish King's Bench Reports

Fox & S.Ir. Fox & Smith's Irish King's Bench Reports

Fox & S.(Ir.) Fox & Smith's Irish King's Bench Reports

Fox & S.Reg. Fox and Smith's Registration Cases (Eng.)

Fox & Sm.   ● Fox & Smith, Irish King's Bench Reports (1822-24)
- Fox & Smith, Registration Cases (1886-95)

Fr.   ● Fragment or Excerpt, or Laws in titles of Pandects
- France
- Freeman, English King's Bench and Chancery Reports
- French

Fr.Ch.   ● Freeman's English Chancery Reports (1660-1706)
- Freeman's Mississippi Chancery Reports

Fr.Chy.   ● Freeman, English Chancery Reports (1660-1706)
- Freeman, Mississippi Chancery Reports

Fr.E.C. Fraser's Election Cases (1776-1777)

Fra. Francis' Maxims of Equity; 4 editions (1722-1746)

Frac. Fractional

Fran.Max. Francis' Maxims of Equity

Franc.Judg. Francillon's County Court Judgments (Eng.)

France France's Reports (vols. 3-11 Colorado)

France (Colo.) France's Reports (vols. 3-11 Colorado)

Francis, Max. Francis' Maxims

Fras. Fraser's Election Cases (Eng.)

Fras.Dom.Rel. Fraser on Personal and Domestic Relations (Sc.)

Fras.Elec.Cas. Fraser's English Election Cases

Fraser ● Fraser, English Cases of Controverted Elections (1776-77)
● Fraser's Husband and Wife (1876-1878) (Sc.)
● Scotch Court of Session Cases, 5th Series, by Fraser

Fraser (Scot.) ● Fraser, English Cases of Controverted Elections (1776-77)
● Scotch Court of Session Cases, 5th Series, by Fraser

Fraz. Frazer's Admiralty Cases, etc. (Sc.)

Fraz.Adm. Frazer's Admiralty Cases, etc. (Sc.)

Fred.Code Frederician Code, Prussia

Free. ● Freeman's Chancery Reports (1660-1706) (Eng.)
● Freeman's King's Bench Reports (1670-1704) (Eng.)
● Freeman's Reports (31-96 Illinois)

Free.Ch. ● Freeman's English Chancery Reports (1660-1706)
● Freeman's Mississippi Chancery Reports (1839-43)

Freem.C.C. Freeman's English Chancery Cases

Freem.Ch. Freeman's English Chancery Reports (22 Eng. Reprint)

Freem.Ch.(Eng.) Freeman's English Chancery Reports (22 Eng. Reprint)

Freem.Ch.(Miss.) Freeman's Mississippi Chancery Reports

Freem.Compar.Politics Freeman, Comparative Politics

Freem.(Ill.) Freeman's Reports (31-96 Illinois)

Freem.Judgm. Freeman on Judgments

Freem.K.B. Freeman's English King's Bench & Common Pleas Reports (89 Eng. Reprint)

Freem.(Miss.) Freeman's Chancery Reports (Mississippi)

French French's Reports (6 New Hampshire)

French(N.H.) French's Reports (6 New Hampshire)

Fries Tr. Trial of John Fries (Treason)

Frith. United States Opinions Attorneys-General (pt. 2, vol. 21)

Fry Fry on Specific Performance of Contracts

Fry Lun. Fry on Lunacy

Fry Sp.Per. Fry on Specific Performance of Contracts

Full B.R. Bengal Full Bench Rulings (North-Western Provinces) (India)

Fuller Fuller's Reports (59-105 Mich.)

Fuller (Mich.) Fuller's Reports (59-105 Mich.)

Fulton Fulton, Supreme Court Reports Bengal (India)

Fund International Monetary Fund

G

G. • Gale, English Exchequer Reports
• King George, as 15 Geo. II
• Georgia
• German
• Gift tax
• Application for writ of error granted
• Gregorowski's Reports of the High Court of the Orange Free State, South Africa

GA General Assembly (UN)

G.A. • Decisions of General Appraisers (U.S.)
• General Assembly (United Nations)
• Governmental Affairs

GAO General Accounting Office

GAOR General Assembly Official Record (United Nations)

GATT General Agreement on Tariffs and Trade

GATT/CP General Agreement Tariffs & Trade, Contracting Parties (U.S.)

G.A.W. Guranteed Annual Wage

G.B.J. Georgia Bar Journal

G.C. General Code

G.C.D.C. Gold Coast Divisional Court Reports

G.C.Div.Ct. Gold Coast Selected Judgments of the Divisional Courts

G.C.F.C. Gold Coast Full Court Selected Judgments

GCM General Counsel's, Assistant General Counsel's, or Chief Counsel's memorandum (U.S. Internal Revenue Service)

GCP Government Contracts Program, George Washington University Law Center

G.C.P.R. General Ceiling Price Regulation

G.Coop. G.Cooper's English Chancery (35 Eng. Reprint)

G. Cooper (Eng.) G. Cooper's English Chancery (35 Eng. Reprint)

GDN. Guardian

G.E.R.R. Government Employee Relations Report (BNA)

GFR General Flight Rules (CAB) U.S.

GGUALE Golden Gate University Advanced Legal Education Program

G.Gr. G. Green's Reports (Iowa 1847-1854)

G.Greene (Iowa) G. Green's Reports (Iowa 1847-1854)

GIA General International Agreement

GICLE Institute of Continuing Legal Education in Georgia, University of Georgia School of Law

GII Government Institutes, Inc.

G.J. Gill and Johnson's Reports (Maryland)

G.L. General Laws

GLO General Land Office (Interior Dept.) (U.S.)

G.L.R. Gazette Law Reports (New Zealand)

G.M.Dud. Dudley's Reports (Georgia 1830-1833)

G.M.Dudl. Dudley's Reports (Georgia 1830-1833)

GNMA Government National Mortgage Association

GNP Gross national product

G.O. General Orders, Court of Chancery (Ontario)

GODPT General Order Defense Transport Administration (U.S.)

GOR General Overruling Regulation (Office of Price Stabilization) (U.S.)

GPO Government Printing Office

GRASR General Railroad and Airline Stabilization Regulations (U.S.)

GSA General Services Administration (U.S.)

G.S.B. Georgia State Bar Journal

GSO General Salary Order (U.S.)

G.S.R. Gongwer's State Reports (Ohio)

GSSR General Salary Stabilization Regulations (U.S.)

GT Gift Tax Ruling

G.W. George Washington Law Review

GWB Gesetz gegen Wettbewerbsbeschrankungen (German Law against Restraint of Competition)

G.W.D. South African Law Reports, Griqualand West Local Division

G.W.L. Reports of Cases decided in the Supreme Court of South Africa (Griqualand West Local Division) by Kitchin

G.W.L.D. South Africa Law Reports, Griqualand West Local Division

G.W.L.R. George Washington Law Review

G.W.R. Griqualand High Court Reports

GWSR General Wage Stabilization Regulations (U.S.)

G. & D. Gale & Davidson's English Queen's Bench Reports (1841-43)

G. & G. Goldsmith & Guthrie's Reports (36-67 Missouri Appeals)

G. & G.(Mo.) Goldsmith & Guthrie's Reports (36-67 Missouri Appeals)

G. & H. Gavin & Hord's Indiana Statutes

G. & J. ● Gill and Johnson's Maryland Court of Appeals Reports (1829-42)
- Glyn & Jameson's English Bankruptcy Reports (1821-28)

G. & R. Geldert & Russell's Nova Scotia Reports

G. & T. Gould & Tucker's Notes on Revised Statutes of United States

Ga. ● General Appraisers' Decisions (U.S.)
- Georgia
- Georgia Supreme Court Reports

Ga.App. Georgia Appeals Reports (1807-date)

Ga.B.A. Georgia Bar Association

Ga.B.J. Georgia Bar Journal

Ga.Bus.Law. Georgia Business Lawyer

Ga.Code Code of Georgia

Ga.Code Ann. Code of Georgia Annotated

Ga.Dec. Georgia Decisions

Ga.J.Int'l.& Comp.L. Georgia Journal of International & Comparative Law

Ga.L. ● Georgia Law Review
- Georgia Lawyer

● Georgia Session Laws

Ga.L.J. Georgia Law Journal

Ga.L.Rep. Georgia Law Reporter

Ga.L.Rev. Georgia Law Review

Ga.Laws Georgia Laws

Ga.Lawyer Georgia Lawyer

Ga.P.S.C. Georgia Public Service Commission Reports

Ga.Prac. Stand, Georgia Practice

Ga.R.C. Georgia Railroad Commission

Ga.St.B.J. Georgia State Bar Journal

Ga.Supp. Lester's Supplement to 33 Georgia

Gabb.Cr.Law. Gabbett's Criminal Law

Gaii. Gaius' Institutes (Gaii Institutionum Commentarii)

Gaius Gaius' Institutes (Gaii Institutionum Commentarii)

Gaius, Inst. Gaius' Institutes

Gal. Gallison's Reports, United States Circuit Courts

Gal. & Dav. Gale & Davison's Queen's Bench Reports (Eng.)

Galb.& M. Galbraith & Meek's Reports (9-12 Florida)

Galb.& M. (Fla.) Galbraith & Meek's Reports (9-12 Florida)

Galbraith Galbraith's Reports (9-12 Florida)

Gale ● Gale's Exchequer Reports (1835-36) (Eng.) Gale's New Forest Decisions (Eng.)
- Gale on Easements, 12 editions (1839-1950)

Gale & D. Gale & Davison's Queen's Bench Reports (18421-43) (Eng.)

Gale & D.(Eng.) Gale & Davison's Queen's Bench Reports (1841-43) (Eng.)

Gale & Dav. Gale & Davison's Queen's Bench Reports (1841-43) (Eng.)

Gale & Whatley Easem. Gale and Whatley, afterwards Gale, on Easements

Gale's St. Gale's Statutes (Ill.)

Gall. Gallison's Reports, United States Circuit Courts

Gall.Cr.Cas. Gallick's Reports (French Criminal Cases)

Gallison Gallison's United States Circuit Court Reports.

Gamb. & Barl. Gamble & Barlow's Digest (Ir.)

Gamboa. Gamboa's Introduction to Philippine Law

Gamboa, Philippine Law. Gamboa's Introduction to Philippine Law

Ganatra Ganatra's Criminal Cases (India)

Gane Eastern District Court Reports, Cape Colony (S. Africa)

Gantt Dig. Gantt's Digest Statutes, Arkansas

Gard.N.Y.Rep. Gardenier's New York Reporter

Gard.N.Y.Rept. Gardenier, New York Reporter

Gard.N.Y.Reptr. Gardenier's New York Reporter

Garden. Gardenhire (Mo.)

Gardenhire. Gardenhire's Reports (vols. 14, 15 Missouri)

Gardn.P.C. Gardner Peerage Case, reported by Le Marchant

Gaspar. Gaspar's Small Cause Court Reports (Bengal)

Gav.& H.Rev.St. Gavin and Hord's Revised Statutes (Ind.)

Gay.(La.) Gayarre's Reports (25-28 Louisiana Annual)

Gayarre Gayarre's Reports (25-28 Louisiana Annual)

Gaz. Weekly Law Gazette, Cincinnati

Gaz.Bank. Gazette of Bankruptcy, London (1862-63)

Gaz.Bank.Dig. Gazzam, Digest of Bankruptcy Decisions

Gaz.L.R. Gazette Law Reports

Gaz.L.R.(N.Z.) New Zealand Gazette Law Reports

Gaz. & B.C.Rep. Gazette & Bankrupt Court Reporter, New York

Gazette. The Law Society Gazette

Gear,Landl. & T. Gear on Landlord and Tenant

Geld. & M. Geldart & Maddock's English Chancery Reports, vol. 6 Maddock's Reports

Geld.& O. Nova Scotia Decisions by Geldert & Oxley

Geld.& Ox. Nova Scotia Decisions by Geldert & Oxley

Geld.& R. Geldert & Russel Reports (28-39, 41-60 Novia Scotia Reports)

Geldart. Geldart & Maddock's English Chancery Reports (vol. 6 Maddock's Reports)

Gen. General

Gen.Abr.Cas.Eq. General Abridgment of Cases in Equity (Equity Cases Abridged (1677-1744))

Gen.Assem. General Assembly

Gen.Ass'ns. General Associations

Gen.Bus. General Business

Gen.City General City

Gen.Constr. General Construction

Gen.Dig. General Digest

Gen.Dig.N.S. General Digest, New Series

Gen.Dig.U.S. General Digest of the United States.

Gen.Laws General Laws

Gen.Mtg. General mortgage

Gen.Mun. General Municipal

Gen.Oblig. General Obligations

Gen.Ord. General Orders, Ontario Court of Chancery

Gen.Ord.Ch. General Orders of the English High Court of Chancery

Gen.Prov. General Provisions

Gen.R.R.Act General Railroad Act

Gen.St. General Statutes

Gen.Stat.Ann. general statute annotated

Geo.
  • King George, as 15 Geo. II
  • Georgetown
  • Georgetown Law Journal (D.C.)
  • Georgia

Geo.Coop. George Cooper's English Chancery Cases, time of Eldon

Geo.Dec. Georgia Decisions

Geo.Dig. George's Digest (Mississippi)

Geo.L.J.´ Georgetown Law Journal

Geo.Wash.L.Rev. George Washington Law Review

George. George's Reports (30-39 Mississippi)

George.Partn. George on Partnership

Georget.L.J. Georgetown Law Journal

Georgia L.Rev. Georgia Law Review

Ger.(E. & W.) Germany (East and West)

Germany (DR) German Democrat Republic

Germany (FR) Federal Republic of Germany

Gib. Gibbons' Surrogate's Court Reports (N.Y.)

Gib.Cod. Gibson's Codex Juris Ecclesiastical Anglicani

Gib.Dec. Gibson's Scottish Decisions

Gibb.Rom.Emp. Gibbon's Decline and Fall of the Roman Empire

Gibb.Sur. Gibbon's Surrogate (N.Y.)

Gibb.Surr. Gibbon's Surrogate (N.Y.)

Gibbon Gibbon on Nuisances

Gibbon,Rom.Emp. Gibbon, History of the Decline and Fall of the Roman Empire

Gibbons Gibbons' Reports, New York Surrogate Court

Gibbons (N.Y.) Gibbons' Reports, New York Surrogate Court

Gibbs Gibbs' Reports (2-4 Michigan)

Gibbs' Jud.Chr. Gibbs' Judicial Chronicle

Gibs.Camd. Gibson's [edition of] Camden's Britannia

Gibs.Code. Gibson's Codex

Gibson. (Gibson of) Durie's Decisions, Scotch Court of Session (1621-42)

Gif. Giffard's English Chancery Reports (65-66 Eng. Reprint)

Giff. Giffard's English Vice-Chancellor's Reports (65-66 Eng. Reprint)

Giff.(Eng.) Giffard's English Vice-Chancellor's Reports (65-66 Eng. Reprint)

Giff.& H. Giffard and Hemming's Reports, English Chancery

Giffard. Giffard (Eng.)

Gil. ● Gilbert's Chancery Reports (1705-1727)
   ● Gilbert's Cases in Law and Equity
   ● Gilfillan's Reports (1-20 Minnesota)
   ● Gilman's Reports (6-10 Illinois)
   ● Gilmer's Reports (21 Virginia)

Gil.(Minn.) Gilfillan's Edition (vols. 1-20 Minnesota)

Gil. & Fal. Gilmour & Falconer's Scotch Session Cases (1661-86)

Gilb. ● Gilbert's Chancery Reports (1705-1727)
   ● Gilbert's Cases in Law and Equity

Gilb.C.P. Gilbert's Common Pleas (93 Eng. Reprint)

Gilb.Cas. Gilbert's Cases, Law & Equity (1713-15) (Eng.)

Gilb.Cas.L.& Eq.(Eng.) Gilbert's Common Pleas, (93 Eng. Reprint)

Gilb.Ch. Giltert, English Chancery Reports (1705-27)

Gilb.Com.Pl. Gilbert's Common Pleas (93 Eng. Reprint)

Gilb.Eq.(Eng.) Gilbert's English Equity or Chancery Reports (25 Eng. Reprint)

Gilb.Eq.Rep. Gilbert, English Equity or Chancery Reports

Gilb.Exch. Gilbert's Exchequer Reports (Eng.)

Gilb.For.Rom. Gilbert's Forum Romanum

Gilb.Forum Rom. Gilbert's Forum Romanum.

Gilb.K.B. Gilbert's Cases in Law and Equity (Eng.)

Gilb.Rents. Gilbert's Treatise on Rents

Gilb.Rep. Gilbert, English Chancery Reports

Gilb.Repl. Gilbert on Replevin

Gilb.Ten. Gilbert on Tenure

Gilb.Uses. Gilbert on Uses and Trusts

Gilbert,Ev. Gilbert's Law of Evidence

Gilbert,Tenures. Gilbert on tenures

Gilbert,Uses,by Sugd. Gilbert's Uses and Trusts by Sugden

Gilchr. Gilchrist's Local Government Cases

Gild. Gildersleeve's Reports (vols. 1-8 New Mexico)

Gildersleeve Gildersleeve's Reports (1-10 New Mexico)

Gildersleeve (N.Mex.) Gildersleeve's Reports (1-10 New Mexico)

Gildr. Gildersleeve (N.Mex.)

Gilfillan. Gilfillan's Reports (1-20 Minnesota)

Gill Gill's Maryland Court of Appeals Reports (1843-1851)

Gill (Md.) Gill's Maryland Reports

Gill Pol.Rep. Gill's Police Court Reports (Boston, Mass.)

Gill.& J. Gill & Johnson's Reports (Maryland)

Gill.& J.(Md.) Gill & Johnson's Reports (Maryland)

Gill & Johns. Gill & Johnson's Reports (Maryland)

Gillett,Cr.Law Gillett's Treatise on Criminal Law and Procedure in Criminal Cases

Gilm.   • Gilman's Reports (vols. 6-10 Illinois)

       • Gilmer's Reports (21 Virginia)

       • Gilmour's Reports, Scotch Court of Session (1661-66)

Gilm.Dig. Gilman's Digest (Illinois and Indiana)

Gilm.(Ill.) Gilman's Reports (vols. 6-10 Illinois)

Gilm.& Falc. Gilmour & Falconer's Reports, Scotch Court of Session

Gilman Gilman's Reports (6-10 Illinois)

Gilmer Gilmer's Reports (1820-1821) (21 Virginia)

Gilmer (Va.) Gilmer's Reports (21 Virginia)

Gilp. Gilpin, United States District Court Reports

Gilp.Opin. Gilpin, Opinions of the United States Attorneys-General

Giur.Cost. Giurisprudenza Constituzionale (Italy)

Gl.& J. Glyn & Jameson's Bankruptcy Reports (1821-28) (Eng.)

Glan.llb. Glanville, De Legibus et Consuetudinibus Angliae

Glanv. Glanville, De Legibus et Consuetudinibus Angliae (1554)

Glanv.El.Cas. Glanville, English Election Cases (1624)

Glanvil. Glanville, De Legibus et Consuetudinibus Angliae

Glas. Glascock's Reports in all the Courts of Ireland (1831-32)

Glasc. Glascock's Reports in all the Courts of Ireland

Glascock Glascock's Reports in all the Courts of Ireland

Glenn Glenn's Reports (16-18 La. Annual)

Glov.Mun.Cor. Glover's Municipal Corporations

Glov.Mun.Corp. Glover on Municipal Corporations

Glyn.& J. Glyn & Jameson English Reports, English Bankruptcy

Glyn.& J.(Eng.) Glyn & Jameson English Reports, English Bankruptcy

Glyn & Jam. Glyn & Jameson English Reports, English Bankruptcy (1821-28)

Go. Goebel's Probate Court Cases (Ohio)

Godb.(Eng.) Godbolt's English King's Bench Reports (78 Eng. Reprint)

Godd.Easem. Goddard on Easements

Goddard. Goddard on Easements, 8 editions (1871-1921)

Godefroi Godefroi on Trusts and Trustees, 5 editions (1879-1927)

Godo.   • Godolphin on Admiralty Jurisdiction

       • Godolphin's Abridgment of Ecclesiastical Law

       • Godolphin's Orphan's Legacy

       • Godolphin's Repertorium Canonicum

Godol. Godolphin's Orphan's Legacy

Godolph.Ecc.Law. Godolphin's Ecclesiastical Law

Godolph.Orph.Leg. Godolphin's Orphan's Legacy

Godson Godson's Mining Commissioner's Cases (Ontario)

Goeb. Goebel's Probate Court Cases (Ohio)

Goebel (Ohio) Goebel's Probate Court Cases (Ohio)

Gold. Goldesborough's or Gouldsbourough's English King's Bench Reports (1586-1602)

Gold Coast Judgments (Full Court, Privy Council, Divisional Courts)

Gold.& G. Goldsmith & Guthrie's Reports (36, 37 Missouri Appeals)

Goldb. Goldbolt's King's Bench, Common Pleas, and Exchequer Reports (Eng.)

Golden Gate L.Rev. Golden Gate Law Review

Goldes. Goldesborough's or Gouldsborough's English King's Bench Reports

Gonz. Gonzaga

Gonzaga L.Rev. Gonzaga Law Review

Good.Pat. Goodeve's Abstract of Patent Cases (1785-1883) (Eng.)

Good.& Wood. Full Bench Rulings, Bengal (edited by Goodeve & Woodman)

Goodeve Goodeve on Real Property. (1883-1906)

Goodrich-Amram Goodrich-Amram Procedural Rules Service

Gord.Tr. Gordon's Treason Trials

Gordon Gordon's Reports (vols. 24-26 Colorado and vols. 10-13 Colorado Appeals)

GORMAC Government Research Management Consultants

Gosf. Gosford's Manuscript Reports, Scotch Court of Session

Gottschall Gottschall's Dayton (Ohio) Superior Court Reports

Gould. Gouldsborough's English King's Bench Reports (1586-1602)

Gould,Pl. Gould on the Principles of Pleading in Civil Actions

Gould Sten.Rep. Gould's Stenographic Reporter (Monographic Series Albany, N.Y.)

Gould, Wat. Gould on Waters

Gould & T. Gould & Tucker's Notes on Revised Statutes of United States

Gould's Dig. Gould's Digest of Laws (Ark.)

Gouldsb. Gouldsborough's English King's Bench Reports (75 Eng. Reprint)

Gouldsb.(Eng.) Gouldsborough's English King's Bench Reports (75 Eng. Reprint)

Gour. Gourick's Patent Digest (1889-91)

Gov. Governor

Govt. Government

Gov't.Cont.Rep. Government Contracts Reporter (CCH)

Gov't.Empl.Rel.Rep. Government Employee Relations Report (BNA)

govtl. governmental

Gow. Gow's English Nisi Prius Cases (171 Eng. Reprint)

Gow N.P. Gow's English Nisi Prius Cases (171 Eng. Reprint)

Gow.N.P. (Eng.) Gow's Nisi Prius Cases (171 Eng. Reprint)

Gow Part. Gow on Partnership

Gr. ● Grant's Upper Canada Chancery Reports
     ● Grant's Pennsylvania Cases (1814-63)
     ● Green's Reports (N.J. Law & Equity)
     ● Greenleaf's Reports (1-9 Maine)
     ● Greek

Gr.Brice. Green's edition of Brice on Ultra Vires

Gr.Brit. Great Britain

Gr.Brit.T.S. Great Britain Treaty Series

Gr.Ca. Grant's Cases

Gr.Eq. ● H.W. Green's New Jersey Equity Reports
     ● Gresley's Equity Evidence

Gr.Ev. Greenleaf on Evidence

Gr.S. GroBer Senat (in banc)

Gra. ● Graham's Reports (vols. 98-107 Georgia)
     ● Grant

Grah.& W.New Trials Graham and Waterman on New Trials

Grah.& W.New Trials. Graham and Waterman on New Trials

Grand Cou. Grand Coutumier de Normandie

Grand Coust.Norm. Grand Coustumier of Normandy

Grand Cout. Grand Coutumier de Normandie

Granger. Granger's Reports (vols. 22-23 Ohio State.)

Grant ● Grant of Elchies' Scotch Session Cases
     ● Grant's Jamaica Reports
     ● Grant's Pennsylvania Cases (3 vols.)
     ● Grant's Upper Canada (Ontario) Chancery Reports (1849-82)

Grant,Bank. Grant on Banking.

Grant Cas. Grant's Pennsylvania Cases

Grant Cas.(Pa.) Grant's Pennsylvania Cases

Grant Ch. Grant's Upper Canada Chancery Reports

Grant Ch.(Can.) Grant's Upper Canada Chancery Reports

Grant,Corp. Grant on Corporations

Grant E.& A. Grant's Error and Appeal Reports, (1846-66) (Ontario)

Grant Err.& App. Grant's Error & Appeal, Upper Canada

Grant,Jamaica Grant's Jamaica Reports

Grant Pa. Grant's Pennsylvania Cases

Grant (Pa) Grant, Pennsylvania Cases

Grant U.C. Grant's Upper Canada Chancery Reports

Grant U.S. Grant's Upper Canada Chancery Reports

Grat. Grattan's Virginia Reports

Gratt. Grattan's Virginia Supreme Court Reports (1844-1880)

Gratt.(Va.) Grattan's Virginia Reports

Grav.de Jur.Nat.Gent. Gravina, De Jure Naturale Gentium, etc.

Graves Proceedings in King's Council (1392-93) (Eng.)

Gravin. Gravina, Originum Juris Civilis.

Gray ● Gray's Massachusetts Supreme Judicial Court Reports (1854-1860) (67-82 Massachusetts)

    ● Gray's Reports (112-22 North Carolina)

Gray (Mass.) Gray's Massachusetts Reports (vols. 67-82)

Gray,Perpetuities Gray's Rule Against Perpetuities

Graya Graya (a periodical)

Green ● Green's Reports (N.J. Law & Equity)

    ● Green's Reports (1-9 Maine)

    ● Green's Reports (1 Oklahoma)

    ● Green's Reports (11-17 Rhode Island)

Green Bag Green Bag, A Legal Journal (Boston)

Green Bri. Green's edition of Brice's Ultra Vires

Green C.E. Green's Reports (16-27 N.J. Equity)

Green (C.E.) C.E. Green's Chancery Reports (New Jersey)

Green.C.E. C.E. Greene's Chancery Reports (New Jersey)

Green Ch. H.W. Green's New Jersey Chancery Reports (vols. 2-4 New Jersey Equity)

Green Cr. Green's Criminal Law, (Eng.)

Green Cr.L.Rep. Green's Criminal Law Reports

Green, Cr.Law R. Green's Criminal Law Reports (N.Y.)

Green L. J.S. Green's Law Reports (13-15 New Jersey)

Green (NJ) Green's New Jersey Law or Equity

Green.Ov.Cas. Greenleaf's Overruled Cases

Green R.I. Green's Reports (11-17 R.I.)

Green (R.I.). Green's Reports (Rhode Island. vol. 11.)

Green Cr.Cas. Green's Criminal Cases

Green Sc.Tr. Green's Scottish Trials for Treason

Greene Greene's Iowa Reports 1847-54 Greene's Reports (7 N.Y. Ann. Cases)

Greene G.(Iowa) G. Greene's Iowa Reports

Greenh.Pub.Pol. Greenhood's Doctrine of Public Policy in the Law of Contracts

Greenl. Greenleaf's Reports (1-9 Maine)

Greenl.Cruise Greenleaf's Edition of Cruise's Digest of Real Property

Greenl.Cruise Real Prop. Greenleaf's Edition of Cruise's Digest of Real Property

Greenl.Ev. Greenleaf on Evidence

Greenl.Ov.Cas. Greenleaf's Overruled Cases

Green's Brice, Ultra Vires. Green's Edition of Brice's Ultra Vires

Greer. Greer, Irish Land Acts. Leading Cases. (1872-1903)

Greg. Gregorowski's High Court Reports

Greg.Turon. Gregory of Tours.

Gregorowski High Court Reports, Orange Free State

Grein.Pr.   Greiner Louisiana Practice

Gren.   Grenier's Ceylon Reports

Grenier   Grenier, Ceylon Reports

Cres.Eq.Ev.   Gresley's Equity Evidence

Gretton   Oxford Quarter Sessions Records (Oxford Record Soc. 16)

Grif.L.Reg.   Griffith's Law Register Burlington, New Jersey)

Grif.P.L.Cas.   Griffith's London Poor Law Cases (1821-31)

Grif.P.R.Cas.   Griffith's English Poor Rate Cases

Griffin P.C.   Griffin's Abstract of Patent Cases (Eng.)

Griffin Pat.Cas.   Griffin's Patent Cases (England) (1866-87)

Griffith   Griffith's Reports (vols. 1-5 Indiana Appeals and vols. 117-132 Indiana)

Grisw.   Griswold's Reports (14-19 Ohio)

Griswold   Griswold's Reports (14-19 Ohio)

Gro.   ●   Gross' Select Cases Concerning the Law Merchant (Selden Society)

      ●   Grotius' Rights of War and Peace; many editions (1625-1901)

Gro.B.P.   Grotius, De Jure Belli ac P'acis

Gro.de J.B.   Grotius, De Jure Belli et P'acis

Gro.Dr.   Grotius, Le Droit de la Guerre

Gro.Ges. & Verord.   Grotofend's Gesetze und Verordnungen

Gross,St.   Gross Illinois Compiled Laws, or Statutes

Grot.de Aequit.   Grotius de Aequitate

Grot.de Jr.B.   Grotius, De Jure Belli et P'acis

Grotius.   Grotins' Latin Law

Grotius de Jure Belli.   Grotius de Jure Belli ac Pacis

Gt.L.J.   Georgetown Law Journal

Gtd.   Guaranteed

Gty.   Guaranty

Gu.   Guam

Guam Civ.Code   Guam Civil Code

Guam Code Civ.Pro.   Guam Code of Civil Procedure

Guam Gov't.Code   Guam Government Code

Guam Prob.Code   Guam Probate Code

Guar.   Guaranty

Guat.   Guatemala

Guild Law.   Guild Lawyer, National Lawyers' Guild, N.Y. Chapter

Guild Prac.   Guild Practitioner

Guild Q.   National Lawyers' Guild Quarterly

Guizot,Hist.Civilization.   Guizot, General History of Civilization in Europe

Guizot,Rep.Govt.   Guizot, History of Representative Government

Gunby   Gunby's District Court Reports (La.1885)

Gunby(La.)   Gunby's District Court Reports (La. 1885)

Gundry.   Gundry Manuscripts in Lincoln's Inn Library

Gut.Brac.   Guterbock's Bracton

Guth.Sh.Cas.   Guthrie's Sheriff Court Cases (1861-92) (Sc.)

Guthrie   ●   Guthrie's Reports (33-83 Mo. Appeals)

      ●   Guthrie's Sheriff Court Cases (Sc.)

Guy,Med.Jur.   Guy, Medical Jurisprudence

Guyot,Inst.Feod.   Guyot, Institutes Feodales.

Gwil.   Gwillim's Tithe Cases (1224-1824)

Gwil.Ti.Cas.   Gwillim's Tithe Cases, (Eng.)

Gwill   Gwillim's Tithe Cases (Eng.)

Gwill.Bac.Abr.   Gwillim's edition of Bacon's Abridgment

Gwill.T.Cas.   Gwillim's Tithe Cases (Eng.)

Gwill.Ti.Cas.   Gwillim's Tithe Cases (Eng.)

H

h. harmonized: apparent inconsistency explained and shown not to exist (used in Shepard's Citations)

H.
- Handy's Reports
- Hare's Chancery Reports (Eng.)
- Hawaii Reports
- Hebrew
- Hertzog's High Court Reports (S.Af.)
- Hill New York Reports (1841-44)
- House Bill
- House Bill (State Legislatures)
- Howard Supreme Court Reports (42-65 U.S.)

H.A.
- Hoc anno (this year)
- House Administration

H.A.S.C. House Armed Services Committee

H.B.
- House Bill
- House Bill (state Legislatures)

H.B.M. His (or Her) Britannic Majesty

H.B.R. Hansell's Bankruptcy Reports (1915-17)

H.Bl. H. Blackstone's Common Pleas Reports (1788-96)

H.Bl.(Eng.) Henry Blackstone's Common Pleas (Eng.) (126 Eng. Reprint)

H.C.
- Habeas corpus
- Reports of the High Court of Griqualand West, South Africa
- House of Commons
- High Court--High Court (Eire I)

H.C.A. High Court of Australia

H.C.G. Griqualand High Court Reports (S. Africa)

H.C.J. High Court of Justiciary (Sc.)

H.C.Jour. House of Commons Journals (United Kingdom)

H.C.R. High Court Reports (India)

H.C.R.N.W.F. High Court Reports, North West Frontier

H.C.R.N.W.P. High Court Reports, Northwest Provinces (India)

H.C.Res. House of Representatives Concurrent Resolution

H.Con.Res. House of Representatives Concurrent Resolution

H.Cr. Houston's Criminal Reports (Del.)

HCTAA Hastings Center for Trial and Appellate Advocacy

H.Doc. House of Representatives Document

H.E.C. Hodgin's Election Cases (Ontario)

HEW Department of Health, Education, and Welfare

HGB Handelsgesetzbuch (German Commercial Code)

H.H. Hayward and Hazelton's Reports

HHFA Housing & Home Finance Agency (U.S.)

H.H.L. Court of Session Cases. House of Lords (Sc.)

H.(Ha.) Hare tempore Wigram, etc. (1841-53)

H.(Hil.) Hilary Term

HICOG High Commissioner for Germany (U.S.)

H.I.H. His (or Her) Imperial Highness

H.I.Rep. Hawaiian Islands Reports

H.J.Res. U.S. House of Representatives Joint Resolution

H.K.L.R. Hong Kong Law Reports

H.L. House of Lords Clark's House of Lords Cases (Eng.)

HLBB Home Loan Bank Board (U.S.)

H.L.C. Clark's House of Lords Cases (Eng.)

H.L.Cas. House of Lords' Cases (Clark) (1847-66)

H.L.Cas.(Eng.) House of Lords Cases (9-11 Eng. Reprint)

H.L.J.
- Hastings Law Journal
- Hindu Law Journal

H.L.Jour. House of Lords Journals (Eng.)

H.L.R.   Harvard Law Review

H.L.Rep.   English House of Lords Reports

H.L.S   Harvard Law School

H.L.Sc.App.Cas.   English Law Reports, House of Lords, Scotch and Divorce Appeal Cases (1866-1875)

HOLC   Home Owners' Loan Corporation (U.S.)

H.P.C.
- Hale's Pleas of the Crown 7 editions (1716-1824)
- Hawkins' Pleas of the Crown

H.Pr.   Howard's Practice Reports, New Series (N.Y.)

H.R.
- Designates file number of a bill as introduced in the U.S. House of Representatives
- Hoge Raad (Dutch Supreme Court)
- House Roll
- Human Resources
- Højesteret--Supreme Court (Denmark)

HRA   Health Resources Administration

H.R.Rep.   House of Representatives Report

H.Rept.   House of Representatives Report

H.Res.   House of Representatives Resolution

HSA   Health Services Administration

H.T.   Hoc titulo (this title)

HUD   Department of Housing and Development

H.U.L.   Houston Law Review (Tex.)

H.V.   Hoc verbo or hac voce (this word, under this word)

H.W.Gr.   H.W. Green's Reports (2-4 N.J. Eq.)

HZA   Hauptzollamt (Chief Customs Office)

H.& B.   Hudson & Brooke's Irish King's Bench Reports (1827-31)

H.& C.   Hurlstone & Coltman, English Exchequer Reports (1862-66)

H.& D.   Lalor's Supplement to Hill & Deniò's New York Reports

H.& G.
- Harris & Gill's Maryland Court of Appeals Reports (1826-29)
- Hurlstone's & Gordon's Reports (Eng.)

H.& H.
- Harrison & Hodgin's Municipal Reports (Upper Canada)
- Horn & Hurlstone's English Exchequer Reports (1838-39)

H.& J.
- Harris and Johnson's Maryland Court of Appeals Reports (1800-26)
- Hayes & Jones' Exchequer Reports (1832-34) (Ir.)

H.& J.Ir.   Hayes & Jones' Exchequer Reports (1832-34) (Ir.)

H.& M.
- Hemming & Miller's Vice-Chancellor's Reports (1862-65) (Eng.)
- Hening & Munford's Reports (11-14 Virginia)

H.& M.Ch.   Hemming & Miller's English Vice-Chancellors' Reports

H.& McH.   Harris and McHenry's Maryland Court of Appeals Reports (1785-99)

H.& N.   Hurlstone & Norman's Exchequer (1856-62) (Eng.)

H.& P.   Hopwood & Philbrick's English Election Cases (1863-67)

H.& R.   Harrison & Rutherfurd's English Common Pleas Reports (1865-66)

H.& R.Bank.   Hazlitt & Roche's Bankruptcy Reports

H.& S.   Harris & Simrall's Reports (49-52 Miss.)

H.& T.   Hall & Twell's Chancery Reports (1849-50) (Eng.)

H.& T.Self-Def.   Harrigan & Thompson's Cases on the Law of Self-Defense

H.& Tw.   Hall & Twells, English Chancery Reports (1849-50)

H.& W.
- Harrison & Wollaston's K.B. Reports (1835-36)
- Hazzard & Warburton's Prince Edward Island Reports
- Hurlstone & Walmsley's Exchequer Reports (1840-41) (Eng.)

Ha. ● Haggard
    ● Hall
    ● Hare, English Vice-Chancellors' Reports (1841-53)

Ha.App. Appendix to volume 10 of Hare's Vice-Chancellor's Reports (Eng.)

Ha.& Tw. Hall & Twell, English Chancery Reports (1849-50)

Had. ● Haddington, Reports, Scotch Court of Session (1592-1624)
    ● Hadley's Reports (45-48 New Hampshire)

Hadd. Haddington, Manuscript Reports, Scotch Court of Session

Haddington Haddington, Manuscript Reports, Scotch Court of Session

Hadl. Hadley's Reports (vols. 45-48 New Hampshire)

Hadl.Rom.Law Hadley's Introduction to the Roman Law

Hadley Hadley's Reports (45-48 New Hampshire)

Hag. ● Hagans' Reports (1-5 West Virginia)
    ● Haggard's Admiralty Reports (Eng.)

Hag.Adm. Haggard, English Admiralty Reports, 3 vols. (1822-38)

Hag.Con. Haggard's Consistory Reports (1789-1821) (Eng.)

Hag.Ecc. Haggard's English Ecclesiastical Reports (1827-33)

Hagan Hagan's Reports (1, 2 Utah)

Hagans Hagans' Reports (1-5 West Virginia)

Hagg.Adm. Haggard's English Admiralty Reports (166 Eng. Reprint)

Hagg.Adm.(Eng.) Haggard's English Admiralty Reports (166 Eng. Reprint)

Hagg.Con. Haggard's English Consistory Reports (161 Eng. Reprint)

Hagg.Cons. Haggard's English Consistory Reports (161 Eng. Reprint)

Hagg.Consist. Haggard's English Consistory Reports (161 Eng. Reprint)

Hagg.Consist.(Eng.) Haggard's English Consistory Reports (161 Eng. Reprint)

Hagg.Ecc. Haggard's English Ecclesiastical Reports (162 Eng. Reprint)

Hagg.Eccl.(Eng.) Haggard's Ecclesiastical Reports (162 Eng. Reprint)

Hagn.& M. Hagner & Miller's Reports (2 Maryland Chancery)

Hagn.& Mill. Hagner & Miller's Reports (2 Maryland Chancery)

Hague Ct.Rep. Hague Court Reports

Hailes Dalrymple (Lord Hailes) Decisions of the Court of Session (1776-91((Sc.)

Hailes Dec. Hailes' Decisions, Scotch Court of Sessions

Haiti Haiti

Hal.Int.Law Halleck's International Law

Hal.Law Halsted's Reports (6-12 N.J. Law)

Halc. Halcomb's Mining Cases (Eng.)

Halc.Min.Cas. Halcomb's Mining Cases (London, 1826)

Hale ● Hale's Reports (vols. 33-37 California)
    ● Hale's Common Law (Eng.)

Hale, Anal. Hale's Analysis of the Law

Hale C.L. Hale's History of the Common Law

Hale Com.Law Hale's History of the Common Law

Hale Cr.Prec. Hale's Precedents in Criminal Cases (1475-1640) (Eng.)

Hale, De Jure Mar. Hale's De Jure Maris, Appendix to Hall on the Sea Shore

Hale Ecc. Hale's Ecclesiastical Reports (1583-1736) (Eng.)

Hale, Hist.Eng.Law Hale's History of the English Law

Hale P.C. Hale's Pleas of the Crown (Eng.)

Hale P.C.(Eng.) Hale's Pleas of the Crown (Eng.)

Hale Prec. Hale's Precedents in (Ecclesiastical) Criminal Cases

Hale, Torts Hale on Torts

Halifax, Anal. Halifax' Analysis of the Roman Civil Law

Halk. ● Halkerston's Compendium of Scotch Faculty Decisions
    ● Halkerston's Digest of the Scotch Marriage Law

- Halkerston's Latin Maxims

Halk.Comp. Halkerston's Compendium of Scotch Faculty Decisions

Halk.Lat.Max. Halkerston's Latin Maxims

Halk.Tech.Terms Halkerston's Technical Terms of the Law

Hall.
- Hall's New York Superior Court Reports
- Hall's Reports (56, 57 New Hampshire)
- Hallett's Reports (1, 2 Colorado)

Hall A.L.J. Hall's American Law Journal

Hall Am.L.J. Hall's American Law Journal

Hall.(Col.) Hallett's Colorado Reports

Hall.Const.Hist. Hallam's Constitutional History of England

Hall, Emerig.Mar.Loans Hall, Essay on Maritime Loans from the French of Emerigon

Hall Int.Law
- Hall on International Law
- Halleck's International Law

Hall, J.Criminal Law Hall, Jerome on General Principles of Criminal Law

Hall Jour.Jur. Journal of Jurisprudence (Hall's)

Hall L.J. Hall's American Law Journal

Hall. Law of W. Halleck's Law of War

Hall, Marit.Loans Hall, Essay on Maritime Loans from the French of Emerigon

Hall, Mex.Law Hall, Laws of Mexico Relating to Real Property, etc.

Hall N.H. Hall's Reports (56, 57 New Hamp.)

Hall (N.Y.) Hall's New York Superior Court Reports

Hall, Profits à Prendre Hall, Treatise on the Law Relating to Profits à Prendre, etc.

Hall & T. Hall & Twell, Reports, English Chancery (47 Eng. Reprint)

Hall & Tw. Hall & Twell, Reports, English Chancery (47 Eng. Reprint)

Hall & Tw.(Eng.) Hall & Twell, Reports, English Chancery (47 Eng. Reprint)

Hallam. Hallam's Constitutional History of England

Halleck, Int.Law Halleck's International Law

Hallet Hallett's Reports (1, 2 Colorado)

Hallifax, Anal.(or Civil Law) Hallifax's Analysis of the Civil Law

Hall's Am.L.J. Hall's American Law Journal

Hals. Halsted's Reports (6-12 N.J. Law Reports)

Hals.Ch. Halsted's Reports (5-8 N.J. Equity Reports)

Hals.Eq. Halsted's New Jersey Equity Reports

Halsbury Halsbury's Laws of England

Halsbury L.Eng. Halsbury's Law of England

Halst.
- Halsted's Equity (N.J.)
- Halsted's Law (N.J.)

Halst.Ch. Halsted's Chancery (New Jersey)

Halsted (N.J.) Halsted's Chancery (New Jersey)

Ham.
- Hamilton's Court of Session Reports (Sc.)
- Hammond's India & Burma Election Cases
- Hammond's Reports (1-9 Ohio State Reports)

Ham.A. & O. Hammerton, Allen & Otter, English Magistrates' Cases (vol. 3 New Sessions Cases)

Ham.Cont. Hammon on Contracts

Ham.N.P. Hammond's Nisi Prius

Ham.Parties Hammond on Parties to Action

Ham.& J. Hammond & Jackson's Reports (45 Georgia)

Hamel, Cust. Hamel's Laws of the Customs

Hamilton
- Haddington's Manuscript Cases, Court of Session (Sc.)
- Hamilton's American Negligence Cases
- Hamilton on Company Law, 3 editions (1891-1910)

Hamlin Hamlin's Reports (vols. 81-93 Maine)

Hammond ● Hammond's Reports (36-45 Georgia)
     ● Hammond's Reports (1-9 Ohio)

Hammond & Jackson Hammond & Jackson's Reports (45 Georgia)

Hamps.Co.Cas. Hampshire County Court Reports (Eng.)

Han. ● Handy's Ohio Reports (12 Ohio Dec.)
     ● Hannay's Reports (12, 13 New Brunswick)
     ● Hansard's Book of Entries (1685)
     ● Hanson's Bankruptcy Reports (1915-17)

Han.(N.B.) Hannay's Reports (New Brunswick)

Hand. ● Hand's Reports (40-45 New York)
     ● Handy's Ohio Reports (12 Ohio Decisions)

Handb.Mag. Handbook for Magistrates (1853-55)

Handelsgericht Commercial Court (Switz.)

Handy Handy's Ohio Reports (12 Ohio Decisions)

Handy (Ohio) Handy's Ohio Reports (12 Ohio Decisions)

Hanes Hanes' English Chancery

Hanf. Hanford's Entries (1685)

Hanmer Lord Kenyon's Notes (English King's Bench Reports), edited by Hanmer

Hann. Hannay's Reports (12, 13 New Brunswick) (1867-71)

Hans.Deb. Hansard's Parliamentary Debates (Eng.)

Hansb. Hansbrough's Reports (76-90 Virginia)

Har. ● Harrington (Delaware)
     ● Harrington's Chancery (Michigan)
     ● Harrison (Louisiana)
     ● Harrison's Chancery (Michigan)

Har.App. Hare's Ch.Reports, Appendix to v. X (Eng.)

Har.Del. Harrington's Reports (1-5 Delaware)

Har.L.R. Harvard Law Review

Har.St.Tr. Hargrave's State Trials

Har. & Gil. Harris & Gill's Maryland Reports, 2 vols.

Har. & Gill Harris & Gill's Maryland Reports

Har. & J. Harris & Johnson's Maryland Reports

Har. & J.(Md.) Harris & Johnson's Maryland Reports

Har. & McH. Harris & McHenry's Maryland Reports

Har. & Nav. Harbors & Navigation

Har. & Ruth. Harrison & Rutherfurd's English Common Pleas Reports (1865-66)

Har. & Woll. Harrison & Wollaston's English King's Bench Reports, 2 vols. (1835-36)

Harb. & Nav.C. Harbors and Navigation Code

Harc. Harcarse's Decisions, Scotch Court of Session (1681-91)

Hard. ● Hardin's Reports (3 Kentucky) (1805-08)
     ● Hardres' English Exchequer Reports (145 Eng. Reprint)
     ● Kelyngs (W.), Chancery Reports (Eng.)

Hardin Hardin's Kentucky Reports

Hardin (Ky.) Hardin's Kentucky Reports

Hardr.(Eng.) Hardres' English Exchequer Reports (145 Eng. Reprint)

Hardres Hardres' English Exchequer Reports (145 Eng. Reprint)

Hardw. ● Cases tempore Hardwicke, by Lee
     ● Cases tempore Hardwicke, by Ridgeway

Hardw.Cas.Temp. Cases tempore Hardwicke, by Lee and Hardwicke

Hardw.(Eng.) ● Cases tempore Hardwicke, by Lee
     ● Cases tempore Hardwicke, by Ridgeway

Hardw.N.B. Hardwicke, Note Books

Hare Hare's English Vice-Chancellors' Reports (1841-53) (66-68 Eng. Reprint)

Hare App. Hare's Reports (Appendix to vol. X)

Hare, Const.Law Hare's American Constitutional Law

Hare (Eng.) Hare's English Vice-Chancellors' Reports (1841-53) (66-68 Eng. Reprint)

Hare & W. Hare & Wallace's American Leading Cases

Hare & Wal.L.C. American Leading Cases, edited by Hare & Wallace

Harg. Hargrave's State Trials (Eng.) Hargrove's Reports (68-75 North Carolina)

Harg.Co.Litt. Hargrave's Notes to Coke on Littleton

Harg.Law Tracts Hargrave's Law Tracts

Harg.St.Tr. Hargrave's State Trials (1407-1776)

Harg.State Tr. Hargrave's State Trials

Hargr.Co.Litt. Hargrave's Notes to Coke on Littleton

Hargrave & Butlers Notes on Co.Litt. Hargrave and Butler's Notes on Coke on Littleton

Hargrove Hargrove's Reports (68-75 North Carolina)

Hari Rao Indian Income Tax Decisions

Harland Manchester Court Leet Records

Harm. ● Harmon's Reports (13-15 California)
● Harmon's Upper Canada Common Pleas Reports (1850-81)

Harp. ● Harper's Equity Reports (South Carolina)
● Harper's South Carolina Law Reports (1823-30)

Harp.Con.Cas. Harper's Conspiracy Cases (Maryland)

Harp.Eq. Harper's Equity Reports (South Carolina)

Harp.Eq.(S.C.) Harper's Reports (1824 South Carolina Equity)

Harp.L. Harper's Reports (1823-30 South Carolina Law)

Harp.L.(S.C.) Harper's Reports (1823-30 South Carolina Law)

Harper Harper's Conspiracy Cases (Md.)

Harper & James, Torts Harper & James on Torts

Harr. ● Harrington's Reports (1-5 Delaware)
● Harrington's Chancery Rep. (Mich. 1836-42)
● Harris' Reports (13-24 Pa. State)
● Harrison's Reports (15-17, 23-29 Indiana)
● Harrison's Reports (16-19 N.J. Law Reports)

Harr.Ch. Harrington's Chancery Reports (Michigan)

Harr.Ch.(Mich.) Harrington's Chancery Reports (Michigan)

Harr.Con.La.R. Harrison's Condensed Louisiana Reports

Harr.(Del.) Harrington Reports, Delaware

Harr.Dig. Harrison's Digest (Eng.)

Harr.(Mich.) Harrington's Michigan Chancery Reports

Harr.N.J. Harrison's Reports (16-19 N.J. Law Reports)

Harr.& G. Harris & Gill's Maryland Reports

Harr.& H. Harrison & Hodgin's Upper Canada Municipal Reports (1845-51)

Harr.& Hodg. Harrison & Hodgin's Upper Canada Municipal Reports (1845-51)

Harr.& J. Harris & Johnson's Maryland Reports

Harr.& J.(Md.) Harris & Johnson's Maryland Reports

Harr.& M'H. Harris & M'Henry's Maryland Reports

Harr.& McH. Harris & McHenry's Maryland Reports

Harr.& McH.(Md.) Harris & McHenry's Maryland Reports

Harr.& R. Harrison & Rutherford's English Common Pleas Reports

Harr.& Ruth. Harrison & Rutherford's English Common Pleas Reports (1865-66)

Harr.& Sim. Harris & Simrall's Reports (49-52 Mississippi)

Harr.& W. Harrison & Wollaston's English King's Bench Reports

Harr.& W.(Eng.) Harrison & Wollaston's English King's Bench Reports

Harr.& Woll. Harrison & Wollaston's English King's Bench Reports (1835-36)

Harring. ● Harrington's Reports (1-5 Delaware)
● Harrington's Michigan Chancery

Harrington Harrington's Delaware Supreme Court Reports (1832-55)

Harris Harris' Reports

Harris Dig. Harris' Digest (Georgia)

Harris & G. Harris & Gill's Reports (Maryland)

Harris & S. Harris & Simrall's Reports (49-52 Mississippi)

Harris & Sim. Harris & Simrall's Reports (49-52 Mississippi)

Harris & Simrall Harris & Simrall's Reports (49-52 Mississippi)

Harrison ● Harrison's Reports (15-17, 23-29 Indiana)
● Harrison's Reports (16-19 N.J. Law Reports)

Harrison, Ch. Harrison's Chancery Practice

Hart. ● Hartley's Reports (4-10 Texas)
● Hartley's Digest of Texas Laws

Hart.Dig. Hartley's Digest of Laws (Texas)

Hart.& H. Hartley & Hartley, Reports (11-21 Texas)

Hartley Hartley's Reports (4-10 Texas)

Hartley & Hartley Hartley & Hartley, Reports (11-21 Texas)

Harv. Harvard

Harv.Bus.Rev. Harvard Business Review

Harv.Civ.Rights-Civ.Lib.L.Rev. Harvard Civil Rights—Civil Liberties Law Review

Harv.Int'l.L.J. Harvard International Law Journal

Harv.J.Legis. Harvard Journal on Legislation

Harv.L.Rev. Harvard Law Review

Harv.L.S.Bull. Harvard Law School Bulletin

Hasb. Hasbrouck's Reports (Idaho)

Hask. Haskell's Reports for U.S. Courts in Maine (Fox's Decisions)

Hast. Hastings' Reports (69, 70 Maine)

Hast.L.J. Hastings Law Journal

Hast.Tr. Trial of Warren Hastings

Hatcher's Kan.Dig. Hatcher's Kansas Digest

Hats. Hatsell's Parliamentary Precedents (1290-1818)

Hats.Pr. Hatsell's Parliamentary Precedents

Hav.Ch.Rep. Haviland's Ch. Reports, Prince Edward Island (1850-72)

Hav.P.E.I. Haviland's Reports, Prince Edward Island

Havil. Haviland's Reports, Prince Edward Island

Haw. ● Hawaii Supreme Court Reports
● Hawkins' Pleas of the Crown (Eng.)
● Hawkins Reports (19-24 La. Annual)
● Hawley's Reports (10-20 Nevada)

Haw.Cr.Rep. Hawley's American Criminal Reports

Haw.Fed. Hawaii Federal

Haw.Rev.Stat. Hawaii Revised Statutes

Haw.Sess.Laws Session Laws of Hawaii

Haw.W.C. Hawes' Will Case

Hawaii Hawaii (Sandwich Islands) Reports

Hawaii B.J. Hawaii Bar Journal

Hawaii Dist. U.S. District Courts of Hawaii

Hawaii.Fed. Hawaiian Federal

Hawaii P.U.C.Dec. Hawaii Public Utilities Commission Decisions

Hawaii Rep. Hawaii Reports

Hawaii Rev.Stat. Hawaii Revised Statutes

Hawaiian Rep. Hawaii (Sandwich Islands) Reports

Hawarde Hawarde's Star Chamber Cases (1894) (Eng.)

Hawarde St.Ch. Hawarde, Star Chamber Cases

Hawes, Jur. Hawes on Jurisdiction of Courts

Hawk. Hawkins' Pleas of the Crown (Eng.)

Hawk.Co.Litt. Hawkins' Coke upon Littleton

Hawk.P.C. Hawkins' Pleas of the Crown (Eng.)

Hawk.Pl.Cr. Hawkins' Pleas of the Crown (Eng.)

Hawk.Wills Hawkins' Construction of Wills

Hawkins Hawkins' Reports (19-24 Louisiana Annual)

Hawks Hawks' North Carolina Reports (1820-26)

Hawks (N.C.) Hawks' Reports (8-11 North Carolina)

Hawl. Hawley's Reports (10-20 Nevada)

Hawl.Cr.R. Hawley's American Criminal Reports

Hawley ● Hawley's American Criminal Reports
● Hawley's Reports (10-20 Nevada)

Hay. ● Hayes' Irish Exchequer Reports, (1830-32)
● Hayes' Reports, Calcutta
● Hay's Scotch Decisions
● Haywood's North Carolina Reports
● Haywood's Tennessee Reports (Haywood's Reports are sometimes referred to as though numbered consecutively from North Carolina through Tennessee)

Hay Acc. Hay's Decisions on Accidents and Negligence (1860) (Sc.)

Hay Dec. Hay's Decisions on Accidents and Negligence (1860) (Sc.)

Hay (Calc.) Hay's Reports (Calcutta)

Hay.Exch. Hayes' Irish Exchequer Reports

Hay P.L. Hay's Poor Law Decisions (1711-1859) (Sc.)

Hay.& Haz. Hayward & Hazelton, Circuit Court, District of Columbia Reports (1840-63)

Hay & J. Hayes & Jones' Reports (Irish Exchequer)

Hay & M. Hay & Marriott's Admiralty Reports (usually cited, Marriott's Reports) (165 Eng. Reprint)

Hay & M.(Eng.) Hay & Marriott's Admiralty Reports (usually cited, Marriott's Reports) (165 Eng. Reprint)

Hay & Marr. Hay & Marriott's Admiralty Reports (usually cited, Marriott's Reports) (165 Eng. Reprint)

Hayes Hayes' Irish Exchequer Reports (1830-32)

Hayes, Conv. Hayes on Conveyancing

Hayes Exch. Hayes' Irish Exchequer Reports (1830-32)

Hayes Exch.(Ir.) Hayes' Irish Exchequer Reports

Hayes & J. Hayes & Jones' Irish Exchequer Reports (1832-34)

Hayes & J.(Ir.) Hayes & Jones' Irish Exchequer Reports (1832-34)

Hayes & Jo. Hayes & Jones' Irish Exchequer Reports (1832-34)

Hayes & Jon. Hayes & Jones' Irish Exchequer Reports (1832-34)

Hayford Gold Coast Native Institutions

Hayn.Lead.Cas. Haynes' Students' Leading Cases

Haynes, Eq. Haynes' Outlines of Equity

Hayw. ● Haywood's North Carolina Reports (1789-1806)
● Haywood's Reports (4-6 Tennessee)

Hayw.L.R. Hayward's Law Register, Boston

Hayw.N.C. Haywood's Reports (2-3 North Carolina)

Hayw.(N.C.) Haywood's Reports (2-3 North Carolina)

Hayw.Tenn. Haywood's Reports (4-6 Tennessee)

Hayw.(Tenn.) Haywood's Tennessee Reports

Hayw.& H. ● Hayward & Hazelton's District of Columbia Reports (1840-63)

● Hayward & Hazelton's United States Circuit Court Reports

Haz.P.Reg. Hazard's Pennsylvania Register

Haz.Pa.Reg. Hazard's Pennsylvania Register (16 vols.)

Haz.Pa.Reg.(Pa.) Hazard's Pennsylvania Register (16 vols.)

Haz.Reg. Hazard's Register (Pennsylvania)

Haz.U.S.Reg. Hazard's United States Register

Hdqrs. Headquarters

Head Head's Tennessee Supreme Court Reports (1858-59)

Head (Tenn.) Head's Reports (38-40 Tennessee)

Health & S.C. Health and Safety Code

Hear.Exam. Hearing Examiner

Heard's Shortt, Extr.Rem. Heard's Edition of Shortt on Extraordinary Legal Remedies

Hearnshaw Southampton Court Leet Records

Heath Heath's Reports (36-40 Maine)

Heath, Max. Heath's Maxims

Heck.Cas. Hecker's Cases on Warranty

Hedges Hedges' Reports (vols. 2-6 Montana)

Hein. Heineccius, Elementa Juris Naturae et Gentium

Heinec.Elem.Jur.Camb. Heineccii Elementa Juris Cambialis

Heinec.Elem.Jur.Civ. Heineccii Elementa Juris Civilis

Heinecc.Ant.Rom. Heineccius (J.G.) Antiquitatum Romanarum (Roman Antiquities)

Heinecc.de.Camb. Heineccius (J.G.) Elementa Juris Cambialis

Heinecc.Elem. Heineccius (J.G.) Elementa Juris Civilis (Elements of the Civil Law)

Heisk. Heiskell's Tennessee Supreme Court Reports (1870-74)

Heisk.(Tenn.) Heiskell's Reports (48-59 Tennessee)

Helm Helm's Reports (2-9 Nevada)

Hem. Hempstead

Hem.& M. Hemming & Miller's English Vice-Chancellors' Reports (71 Eng. Reprint)

Hem.& M.(Eng.) Hemming & Miller's English Vice-Chancellors' Reports (71 Eng. Reprint)

Hem.& Mill. Hemming & Miller's English Vice-Chancellors' Reports

Heming. Hemingway's Reports (53-65 Mississippi)

Heming.(Miss.) Hemingway's Mississippi Reports

Hemmant Hemmant's Select Cases in Exchequer Chamber (Selden Society Publ v. 51) (1377-1460)

Hemp. Hempstead's United States Circuit Court Reports

Hempst. Hempstead's United States Circuit Court Reports

Hen. King Henry, as 8 Hen. VI

Hen.Bl. Henry Blackstone's English Common Pleas Reports

Hen.Man.Cas. Henry's Manumission Cases

Hen.St. Hening's Statutes (Va.)

Hen.& M. Hening & Munford's Virginia Supreme Court Reports (1806-10)

Hen.& Mun. Hening & Munford's Reports (11-14 Virginia)

Hennepin Law Hennepin Lawyer

Henry Judg. Henry, Judgment in Ordwin v. Forbes

Hepb. ● Hepburn's Reports (3, 4 California)
● Hepburn's Reports (13 Pennsylvania)

Her. Herne's Law of Charitable Uses (2 editions, 1660, 1663)

Her.Char.U. Herne on Charitable Uses

Her.Est. Herman's Law of Estoppel

Herm. Hermand Consistorial Decisions (1684-1777) (Sc.)

Herm.Chat.Mortg. Herman on Chattel Mortgages

Herm.Estop. Herman's Law of Estoppel

Herm.Ex'ns. Herman's Law of Executions

Hermand Hermand's Consistorial Decisions (Sc.)

Hertzog Hertzog's Reports of Transvaal High Court

Hess. Hessen

Het. Hetley's English Common Pleas Reports (124 Eng. Reprint)

Het.(Eng.) Hetley's English Common Pleas Reports (124 Eng. Reprint)

Heyw.Ca. Heywood's Table of Cases (Georgia)

Hi.
- Hawaii
- Hawaii Reports
- Hindi

Hibb.
- Hibbard's Reports, vol. 20 Opinions Attorneys-General
- Hibbard's Reports (vol. 67 New Hampshire)

Hicks, Ethics Hicks' Organization and Ethics of Bench and Bar

Hicks, Leg.Research Hicks on Materials and Methods of Legal Research

Hicks, Men & Books Hicks on Men and Books Famous in the Law

Hig.Pat.Dig. Higgins' Digest of Patent Cases (1890)

Higgins Higgin's Tennessee Civil Appeals Reports

High. Highway

High Ct. High Court Reports (Northwest Provinces of India)

High Ex.Rem. High on Extraordinary Legal Remedies

High, Extr.Leg.Rem. High on Extraordinary Legal Remedies

High Inj. High on Injunctions

High Rec. High on the Law of Receivers

Hight Hight's Reports (vols. 57-58 Iowa)

Hil.Abr. Hilliard's American Law

Hil.Elem.Law Hilliard's Elements of Law

Hil.T. Hilary Term (Eng.)

Hil.Term 4, Will.IV Hilary Term 4, William IV

Hil.Torts Hilliard on the Law of Torts

Hill
- Hill's New York Supreme Court Reports (1841-44)
- Hill's South Carolina Law Reports (1833-37)

Hill.Am.Law Hilliard's American Law

Hill Ch. Hill's Equity South Carolina Reports (1833-37)

Hill.Cont. Hilliard on Contracts

Hill.Elem.Law Hilliard's Elements of Law

Hill Eq. Hill's Equity South Carolina Reports (1833-37)

Hill Eq.(S.C.) Hill's Equity South Carolina Reports (1833-37)

Hill, Law Hill's Law (S.C.)

Hill.Mortg. Hilliard's Law of Mortgages

Hill N.Y. Hill's New York Reports

Hill.New Trials Hilliard on New Trials

Hill.Real Prop. Hilliard on Real Property

Hill S.C. Hill's South Carolina Reports (Law or Equity)

Hill & D. Lalor's Supplement to Hill & Denio's Reports, New York (1842-44)

Hill & D.Supp. Hill & Denio, Lalor's Supplement (N.Y.)

Hill & Den. Lalor's Supplement to Hill & Denio's Reports, New York (1842-44)

Hill & Den.Supp. Lalor's Supplement to Hill & Denio's Reports, New York (1842-44)

Hilliard, R.P. Hilliard on Real Property

Hill's Ann.Codes & Laws Hill's Annotated Codes and General Laws (Or.)

Hill's Ann.St.& Codes Hill's Annotated General Statutes and Codes (Wash.)

Hill's Code
- Hill's Annotated Codes and General Laws (Oregon)
- Hill's Annotated General Statutes and Codes (Washington)

Hillyer Hillyer's Reports (20-22 California)

Hilt. Hilton's New York Common Pleas Reports

Hilt.(NY) Hilton's New York Common Pleas Reports

Hincmar.Epist. Hincmari Epistolae

Hind.L.J. Hindu Law Journal

Hind.L.Q. Hindu Law Quarterly

Hinde Ch.Pr. Hinde, Modern Practice of the High Court of Chancery

Hines Hines' Reports (83-96 Kentucky)

Hist. ● Historical
● History

Hitch, Pr.&Proc. Hitch's Practice & Procedure in the Probate Court of Massachusetts

Hittell's Laws Hittell's General Laws (Cal.)

Ho.L.Cas. Clark's House of Lords Cases (1847-66) (Eng.)

Ho.Lords Cas. Clark's House of Lords Cases (1847-66) (Eng.)

Ho. of Dels. House of Delegates

Ho.of Reps. House of Representatives

Hob. Hobart's King's Bench Reports (1603-25) (Eng.)

Hobart Hobart's English King's Bench Reports (80 Eng. Reprint)

Hobart (Eng.) Hobart's English King's Bench Reports (80 Eng. Reprint)

Hod. Hodges' English Common Pleas Reports (1835-37)

Hodg. ● Hodges' English Common Pleas Reports (1835-37)
● Hodgins' Election Cases, Ontario (1871-79)

Hodg.Can.Elec.Cas. Hodgin's Canada Election Cases

Hodg.El. Hodgins' Election, Upper Canada

Hodg.El.Cas. Hodgins' Election Cases (Ontario)

Hodg.El.Cas.(Ont.) Hodgins' Election Cases (Ontario)

Hodg.Ont.Elect. Hodgins' Election Cases (Ontario)

Hodge, Presb.Law Hodge on Presbyterian Law

Hodges Hodges' English Common Pleas Reports (1835-37)

Hodges (Eng.) Hodges' English Common Pleas Reports (1835-37)

Hof Gerechtshof--District Court of Appeal (Holland)

Hoff. ● Hoffman's Land Cases. United States District Court
● Hoffman's New York Chancery Reports

Hoff.Ch. Hoffman's New York Chancery Reports (1838-40)

Hoff.Dec. Hoffman's Decisions

Hoff.L.Cas. Hoffman's Land Cases, United States District Court

Hoff.Land Hoffman's Land Cases, United States District Court

Hoff.Lead.Cas. Hoffman's Leading Cases

Hoff.Mast. Hoffman's Master in Chancery

Hoff.N.Y. Hoffman's New York Chancery Reports

Hoff.Op. Hoffman's Opinions

Hoffm. ● Hoffman's Chancery (N.Y.)
● Hoffman's Land Cases (U.S.)

Hoffm.Ch. ● Hoffman's Chancery (N.Y.)
● Hoffman's Land Cases (U.S.)

Hoffm.Ch.(N.Y.) Hoffman's Chancery Reports (New York)

Hoffm.Dec.(F.) Hoffman's Decisions, U.S. District Court

Hoffm.Land Cas.(F.) Hoffman's Land Cases, U.S. District Court

Hoffm.Ops.(F.) Hoffman's Opinions, U.S. District Court

Hofstra L.Rev. Hofstra Law Review

Hog. ● Hogan's Irish Rolls Court Reports (1816-34)
● Hog of Harcarse, Scotch Session Cases

Hog.St.Tr. Hogan's State Trials (Pennsylvania)

Hogan ● Hogan's Irish Rolls Court Reports (2 vols.)
● Hog of Harcarse, Scotch Session Cases

Hogan (Ir.) Hogan's Irish Rolls Court Reports (2 vols.)

Hogue Hogue's Reports (1-4 Florida)

Holc.L.Cas. Holcombe's Leading Cases of Commercial Law

Holdsw.Hist.E.L. Holdsworth History of English Law

Holl. ● Hollinshead's Reports (1 Minn.)
● Holland

Holl.Jur. Holland's Elements of Jurisprudence

Hollinshead Hollinshead's Reports (vol. 1 Minnesota)

Holm. ● Holmes' United States Circuit Court Reports
● Holmes' Reports (vols. 15-17 Oregon)

Holm.Com.Law Holmes on the Common Law

Holt ● Holt's English King's Bench
● Holt's English Nisi Prius Reports
● Holt's English Equity Reports (1845)

Holt Adm. Holt's English Admiralty Cases (Rule of the Road) (1863-67)

Holt Adm.Ca. Holt's Admiralty Cases (1863-67)

Holt Adm.Cas. Holt's English Admiralty Cases (Rule of the Road) (1863-67)

Holt Eq. Holt's English Equity Reports (1845)

Holt K.B. Holt's English King's Bench Reports (1688-1710)

Holt N.P. Holt's English Nisi Prius Reports (1815-17)

Holt R.of R. Holt's Rule of the Road Cases

Holt, Shipp. Holt on Shipping

Holthouse (or Holthouse, Law Dict.) Holthouse's Law Dictionary

Holtz.Enc. Holtzendorff Encyclopädie der Rechtswissenschaft (Encyclopedia of Jurisprudence)

Home Home's Manuscript Decisions, Scotch Court of Session

Home (Cl.) Clerk Home, Decisions of Court of Session (1735-44) (Sc.)

Home Ct.of Sess. Home's Manuscript Decisions, Scotch Court of Session

Home H.Dec. Home's Manuscript Decisions, Scotch Court of Session

Hond. Honduras

Hong Kong L.R. Hong Kong Law Reports

Hong Kong U.L.Jo. Hong Kong University Law Journal

Hooker Hooker's Reports (25-62 Connecticut)

Hoon. Hoonahan's Sind Reports (India)

Hoonahan Hoonahan's Sind Reports (India)

Hop. Hopkins

Hop.Maj.Pr. Hope (Sir T.), Major Practicks, (Sc.)

Hop.Min.Pr. Hope (Sir T.), Major Practicks (Sc.)

Hop.& C. Hopwood & Coltman's Registration Cases (1868-78) (Eng.)

Hop.& Ch. Hopwood & Philbrick's Registration Cases

Hop.& Colt. Hopwood & Coltman's Registration Cases (Eng.)

Hop.& Ph. Hopwood & Philbrick, English Registration Cases (1863-67)

Hope Hope (of Kerse) Manuscript Decisions, Scotch Court of Session

Hope Dec. Hope Manuscript Decisions, Scotch Court of Sessions

Hopk.Adm.Dec. Admiralty Decisions of Hopkinson in Gilpin's Reports

Hokp.Adm. Hopkinson's Pennsylvania Admiralty Judgments

Hopk.Ch. Hopkins' New York Chancery Reports (1823-26)

Hopk.Dec. Hopkins' Decisions (Pa.)

Hopk.Wks. Hopkinson's Works (Pennsylvania)

Hopk.Works (Pa.) Hopkinson's Works (Pa.)

Hopw.& C. Hopwood & Coltman's English Registration Appeal Cases

Hopw.& Colt. Hopwood & Coltman's English Registration Appeal Cases

Hopw.& P. Hopwood & Philbrick's English Registration Appeal Cases

Hopw.& Phil. Hopwood & Philbrick's English Registration Appeal Cases

Hor.& Th.Cas. Horrigan & Thompson's Cases on Self-Defense

Horn & H. Horn & Hurlstone's English Exchequer Reports (1838-39)

Horne, M.J. Horne's Mirror of Justice

Horne Mir. Horne's Mirror of Justice

Horner Horner's Reports (vols. 11-23 South Dakota)

Horner's Ann.St. Horner's Annotated Revised Statutes (Ind.)

Horner's Rev.St. Horner's Annotated Revised Statutes (Ind.)

Horr & B.Mun.Ord. Horr and Bemis' Treatise on Municipal Police Ordinances

Horr.& T.Cas.Self-Def. Horrigan and Thompson's Cases on Self-Defense

Horr.& Th. Horrigan and Thompson's Cases on Self-Defense

Horw.Y.B. Horwood's Year Books of Edward I

Hosea Hosea's Reports (Ohio)

Hoskins Hoskins' Reports (2 North Dakota)

Hosp. Hospital

Hotom.in Verb.Feud. Hotomannus de Verbis Feudalibus

Hou. Houston's Reports (Del.)

Hou.L.R. Houston Law Review

Houard, Ang.Sax.Laws Houard's Anglo-Saxon Laws

Hough C.-M.Cas. Hough's Court-Martial Case Book (London, 1821)

Hough V.-Adm. Reports of Cases in Vice-Admiralty of Province of New York, 1715-88 (1925 Reprint)

Houghton Houghton's Reports (97 Alabama)

Hous. ● Housing
      ● Houston's Delaware Reports

Hous.& Dev.Rep. Housing & Development Reporter (BNA)

House of L. House of Lords Cases

Houst. Houston's Reports (6-14 Delaware)

Houst.Cr. Houston's Criminal Cases (Del.)

Houst.Cr.Cas. Houston's Delaware Criminal Cases (1856-79)

Houst.Crim.(Del.) Houston's Delaware Criminal Cases (1856-79)

Houst.L.Rev. Houston Law Review

Houston Houston's Delaware Supreme Court Reports (1855-1893)

Houston, Tex.P.S.C. Houston, Texas Public Service Commission

Hov. ● Hovenden on Frauds
      ● Hovenden's Supplement to Vesey, Jr's English Chancery Reports

Hov.Ann. Hoveden's Annals

Hov.Sup. Hovenden's Supplement to Vesey, Jr's English Chancery Reports (1789-1817)

Hov.Supp. Hovenden's Supplement to Vesey, Jr., Reports, (1789-1817)

Hoved. Hoveden, Chronica

How. ● Howard's Reports (2-8 Mississippi)
      ● Howard's New York Practice Reports
      ● Howard's Reports (42-65 U.S.)
      ● Howell Reports (22-26 Nevada)

How.A.Cas. Howard's Appeal Cases (New York)

How.Ann.St. Howell's Annotated Statutes (Mich.)

How.App. Howard's Appeal Cases (N.Y.)

How.Cas. ● Howard's New York Court of Appeals Cases
       ● Howard's Property Cases

How.Ch. Howard's Chancery Practice (1760-62) (Ir.)

How.Ch.P. Howard's Chancery Practice (1760-62) (Ir.)

How.Cr.Tr. Howison's Criminal Trials (Virginia)

How.E.E. Howard's Equity Exchequer Reports (Ir.)

How.Eq.Exch. Howard's Equity Exchequer (Ir.)

How.L.J. Howard Law Journal

How.L.Rev. Howard Law Review

How.N.P.(Mich.) Howell, Nisi Prius

How.N.S. Howard's New York Practice Reports, New Series

How.Po.Ca. Howard's Property Cases (1720-73) (Ir.)

How.Po.Cas. Howard Property Cases (1720-73) (Ir)

How.Pr. Howard's New York Practice Reports (1844-86)

How.Pr.N.S. Howard's Practice, New Series (New York)

How.Prac.,N.S. Howard's Practice Reports New Series (New York)

How.Prac.(N.Y.) Howard's Practice Reports (New York)

How.S.C. Howard's United States Supreme Court Reports

How.St. Howell's Annotated Statutes (Michigan)

How.St.Tr. Howell's English State Trials (1163-1820)

How.State Tr. Howell's English State Trials (1163-1820)

How.U.S. Howard's United States Supreme Court Reports

How. & Beat. Howell & Beatty's Reports (vol. 22 Nevada)

How.& H.St. Howard and Hutchinson's Statutes (Mississippi)

How.& Nor. Howell & Norcross' Reports (vols. 23, 24 Nevada)

Howard Howard's Mississippi Supreme Court Reports (1834-1843)

Howard S.C. United States Reports, vols. 42-65

Howell N.P. Howell's Nisi Prius Reports, Michigan

Howell, St.Tr. Howell's English State Trials

Hu.
- Hughes' Kentucky Reports
- Hughes' United States Circuit Court Reports
- Hungarian

Hub.Leg.Direc. Hubbell's Legal Directory

Hub.Prael.J.C. Huber, Praelectiones Juris Civilis

Hubb. Hubbard's Reports 45-51 Maine)

Hubb.Succ. Hubback's Evidence of Succession

Hubbard. Hubbard's Reports (45-51 Maine)

Hud.& B. Hudson & Brooke's Irish King's Bench Reports (1827-31)

Hud.& Br. Hudson & Brooke's Irish King's Bench Reports (1827-31)

Hud.& Bro. Hudson & Brooke's Irish King's Bench Reports (1827-31)

Hudson Hudson on Building Contracts

Hughes'
- Circuit Court Reports (U.S.)
- Hughes' Reports (1 Kentucky)

Hugh.Abr. Hughes' Abridgment (1663-65) (Eng.)

Hugh.Ent. Hughes' Entries (1659)

Hughes
- Hughes' Kentucky Supreme Court Reports (1785-1801)
- Hughes' United States Circuit Court Reports

Hughes Fed.Prac. Hughes Federal Practice

Hugo, Hist.Dr.Rom. Hugo's History Druit Romain.

Hugo,Hist.du Droit Rom. Hugo, Histoire due Droit Romain

Hum. Humphreys' Tennessee Supreme Court Reports (1839-51)

Hume Hume's Court of Session Decisions (1781-1822) (Sc.)

Hume,Hist.Eng. Hume's History of England

Humph. Humphrey's Reports (20-30 Tennessee)

Hun
- New York Supreme Court Reports
- Hun's New York Appellate Division Reports

Hung. Hungary

Hung.L.Rev. Hungarian Law Review

Hunt.
- Hunts' Annuity Cases (Eng.)
- Hunter's Torrens Cases (Canada)

Hunt Ann.Cas. Hunt's Annuity Cases (Eng.)

Hunt, Bound. Hunt's Law of Boundaries and Fences

Hunt Cas. Hunt's Annuity Cases

Hunt,Eq. Hunt's Suit in Equity

Hunt.Torrens Hunter's Torrens Cases

Hunter,Rom.Law. Hunter on Roman Law

Hunter, Suit Eq. Hunter's Proceeding in a Suit in Equity

Hunt's A.C. Hunt's Annuity Cases (1776-96)

Hurd's Rev.St. Hurd's Revised Statutes (Ill.)

Hurd St. Hurd's Illinois Statutes

Hurl.Bonds. Hurlstone on Bonds

Hurl.Colt. Hurlstone & Coltman's English Exchequer Reports (158, 159 Eng. Reprint)

Hurl.& C. Hurlstone & Coltman's English Exchequer Reports (158, 159 Eng. Reprint)

Hurl.& G. Hurlstone and Gordon's Reports, 10, 11, English Exchequer Reports (1847-56)

Hurl.& Gord. Hurlstone and Gordon's Reports (10, 11 Exchequer Reports), (1847-1856)

Hurl.& N. Hurlstone & Norman's English Exchequer Reports (156, 158 Eng. Reprint)

Hurl.& Nor. Hurlstone & Norman's English Exchequer Reports (156, 158 Eng. Reprint)

Hurl. & W. Hurlstone & Walmsley's English Exchequer Reports (1840-41)

Hurl.& Walm. Hurlstone & Walmsley's English Exchequer Reports (1840-41)

Hurlst.& C.(Eng.) Hurlstone & Coltman's English Exchequer Reports (158, 159 Eng. Reprint)

Hurlst.& N.(Eng.) Hurlstone & Norman's English Exchequer Reports (156, 158 Eng. Reprint)

Hurlst.& W.(Eng.) Hurlstone & Walmsley's English Exchequer Reports

Hust. Hustings Court (as in Virginia)

Hut. Hutton's English Common Pleas Reports (1612-39)

Hut.Ct.Req. Hutton's Courts of Requests, 4 editions (1787-1840)

Hutch. Hutcheson's Reports (vols. 81-84 Alabama)

Hutch.Car. Hutchinson on Carriers

Hutch.Carr. Hutchinson on Carriers

Hutch.Code. Hutchinson's Code (Miss.)

Hutch.Dig.St. Hutchinson's Code (Miss.)

Hutt. Hutton's English Common Please Reports (1612-39)

Hutt.Ct.Req. Hutton's Courts of Requests

Hutton (Eng.) Hutton's English Common Pleas Reports (123 Eng. Reprint)

Hux.Judg. Huxley's Second Book of Judgments (1675) (Eng.)

Hy.Bl. Henry Blackstone's Com. Pleas Reports (1788-96) (Eng.)

Hyde Hyde's Bengal Reports (India)

I

I.
- Idaho
- Illinois
- Income tax
- Independent
- Indiana ˙
- Institutes of Justinian
- Iowa
- Irish; Ireland
- Italian

I.A.
- Indian Affairs
- Law Reports, Privy Council, Indian Appeals (1875-1950) (India)

IABD Inter-American Defense Board

IAC Industrial Accident Commission Decisions

IACAC Inter-American Commercial Arbitration Commission

IAD Immediate Action Directive

IADB
- Inter-American Defense Board
- Inter-American Development Bank

IAEA International Atomic Energy Agency (U.N.)

IAIC International Association of Insurance Counsel

IALL International Association of Law Libraries

IALS Institute of Advanced Law Study

IARA Inter-Allied Reparation Agency

I.A.Sup.Vol. English Law Reports, Indian Appeals, Supplementary Volume

I.B.E.W. International Brotherhood of Electrical Workers

I.B.J. Illinois Bar Journal

I.B.R.D. International Bank for Reconstruction and Development (World Bank)

I.C.
- Indian Cases
- Industrial Arbitration Cases (West Australia)
- Interstate Commerce Reports

I.C.A.
- Iowa Code Annotated
- Indian Council of Arbitration

I.C.A.Arb.Q. Indian Council Arbitration Quarterly

ICAC International Cotton Advisory Committee

ICAF Industrial College of the Armed Forces

ICAN International Commission for Air Navigation (UN)

ICAO International Civil Aviation Organization (UN)

ICC
- Indian Claims Commission (U.S.)
- International Chamber of Commerce
- Interstate Commerce Commission (U.S.)

ICCO International Cocoa Council

I.C.C.Pract.J. Interstate Commerce Commission Practitioners' Journal

ICC Valuation Rep. Interstate Commerce Commission, Valuation Reports

ICEF International Children's Emergency Fund (UN)

ICEM Intergovernmental Committee on European Migration

ICFTU International Confederation of Free Trade Unions

ICITO Interim Commission for International Trade Organization (UN)

ICJ International Court of Justice Reports (UN)

ICLEF Indiana Continuing Legal Education Forum

ICJR Institute for Criminal Justice, University of Richmond

I.C.J.Y.B. International Court of Justice Yearbooks

I.C.L.Q. International and Comparative Law Quarterly

I.C.L.R. Irish Common Law Reports (1850-66)

ICM Institute for Court Management

ICNAF International Commission for Northwest Atlantic Fisheries

ICO
- International Coffee Organization
- International Lead and Zinc Study Group

I.C.R.
- Irish Chancery Reports
- Irish Circuit Reports (1841-43)

I.C.Rep. Interstate Commerce Commission Reports (U.S.)

ICSAB International Civil Service Advisory Board

I.C.S.I.D. International Centre for Settlement of Investment Disputes

I-CTUS. Jurisconsultus (one learned in the law)

I.Ch.R. Irish Chancery Reports

I.D. Interior Department Decisions (U.S.)

IDA International Development Association (IBRD Affiliate)

IDB Inter-American Development Bank

IDLF Idaho Law Foundation

IDO International Disarmament Organization

i.e. id est (that is)

IEA International Energy Agency

IEFC International Emergency Food Council

I.E.R. Irish Equity Reports

I.Eq.R. Irish Equity Reports (1838-50)

IFA International Franchise Association

IFAD International Fund for Agricultural Development

IFC ● International Finance Corporation (IBRD Affiliate)
      ● Interstate and Foreign Commerce

IFTU International Federation of Trade Unions

IGC Inter-Governmental Committee on Refugees

IHO International Hydrographic Organization

IIA ● Interior and Insular Affairs
      ● International Institute of Agriculture

IIC International Review of Industrial Property and Copyright Law (Ger.)

IICLE Illinois Institute of Continuing Legal Education

IILS Institute for Improved Legal Services

I/Ins. Inactive Insurance

I.J. ● Indian Jurist, Old Series
      ● Irish Jurist (Dublin)

IJA Indiana Judges Association

IJC Indiana Judicial Center

I.J.C. Irvine, Justiciary Cases (Sc.)

I.J.Cas. Irvine's Justiciary Cases (Sc.)

IJLL International Journal of Law Libraries

I.J.N.S. Irish Jurist, New Series

I.L. The Irish Land Reports (Fitzgibbon)

ILA International Longshoremen's Association (AFL-CIO)

ILC International Law Commission (United Nations)

I.L.E. Indiana Law Encyclopedia

ILGWU International Ladies' Garment Workers' Union (AFL-CIO)

ILIR Institute of Labor and Industrial Relations (University of Illinois)

I.L.J. Indiana Law Journal

I.L.M. International Legal Materials (periodical)

ILO International Labor Organization (UN)

I.L.P. Illinois Law and Practice

I.L.Q. ● Indian Law Quarterly
        ● International Law Quarterly

Í.L.R. ● Indian Law Reports
        ● Insurance Law Reporter (Canada)
        ● International Law Reports
        ● Iowa Law Review
        ● Irish Law Reports

I.L.R.All. Indian Law Reports, Allahabad Series

I.L.R.Bom. Indian Law Reports, Bombay Series

I.L.R.Calc. Indian Law Rep., Calcutta Series

I.L.R.Kar. Indian Law Reports, Karachi Series

I.L.R.Lah. Indian Law Reports, Lahore Series

I.L.R.Luck. Indian Law Reports, Lucknow Series

I.L.R.Mad. Indian Law Reports, Madras Series

I.L.R.Nag. Indian Law Reports, Nagpur Series

I.L.R.Pat. Indian Law Reports, Patna Series

I.L.R.R. Industrial and Labor Relations Review

I.L.R.Ran. Indian Law Reports, Rangoon Series

ILSCLE   Iowa Law School Continuing Legal Education

I.L.T.   Irish Law Times (Dublin)

I.L.T.Jo.   Irish Law Times Journal

I.L.T.R.   Irish Law Times Reports (Eire)

I.L.T.& S.J.   Irish Law Times and Solicitors' Journal

ILWU   International Longshoremen's and Warehousemen's Union

IMAW   International Molders' and Allied Workers' Union of North America (AFL-CIO)

IMC   International Materials Conference

IMCO   Inter-Governmental Maritime Consultative Organization (UN)

IMF   International Monetary Fund (UN)

IMF (FUND)   International Monetary Fund

IMF Staff Papers   International Monetary Fund Staff Papers

IMO   International Meteorological Organization (UN)

IMU   International Mailers' Union

INGO   International Non-Governmental Organization

INS   Immigration and Naturalization Service

INTELSAT   International Telecommunications Satellite Consortium

INTERPOL   International Criminal Police Organization

I.O.   Law Opinions

I.O.C.C.Bull.   Interstate Oil Compact Commission Bulletin

IOOC   International Olive Oil Council

I.P.P.   In Propria Persona (in person)

IPPC   International Penal & Penitentiary Commission (UN)

IPT   The Institute for Paralegal Training

IPU   Inter-Parliamentary Union

I.R.
- Indian Rulings
- Industrial Relations
- Information Release
- Internal Revenue Decisions (U.S. Treasury Department)
- International Relations
- Irish Law Reports

I.R.All.   Indian Rulings, Allahabad Series

I.R.B.   Internal Revenue Bulletin (U.S.)

I.R.Bom.   Indian Rulings, Bombay Series

IRC   International Red Cross

I.R.C.   Internal Revenue Code (U.S.)

I.R.C.L.   Irish Reports, Common Law Series

I.R.Cal.   Indian Rulings, Calcutta Series

I.R.Comrs.   Inland Revenue Commissioners (Eng.)

I.R.Eq.   Irish Reports, Equity Series

I.R.Fed.Ct.   Indian Rulings, Federal Court

I.R.Jour.   Indian Rulings, Journal Section

I.R.Lah.   Indian Rulings, Lahore Series

I.R.-M.I.M.   Published Internal Revenue Mimeograph

I.R.Mad.   Indian Rulings, Madras Series

I.R.Nag.   Indian Rulings, Nagpur Series

IRO   International Refugee Organization (UN)

I.R.Oudh   Indian Rulings, Oudh Series

I.R.Pat.   Indian Rulings, Patna Series

I.R.Pesh.   Indian Rulings, Peshawar Series

I.R.Pr.C.   Indian Rulings, Privy Council

I.R.R.   International Revenue Record (New York City)

I.R.R.& L.   Irish Reports, Registry Appeals in Court of Exhequer Chamber, and Appeals in Court for Land Cases Reserved

I.R.Ran.   Indian Rulings, Rangoon Series

I.R.Rep.   Reports of Inland Revenue Commissioners

IRS   Internal Revenue Service

I.R.Sind.   Indian Rulings, Sind Series

ISBA   Indiana State Bar Association

ISE   Institute for Shipboard Education

I.S.L.R.   International Survey of Legal Decisions on Labour Law

I.S.M.A.C.   Israel-Syrian Mixed Armistice Commission

ISO International Sugar Organization

I.T. ● Income Tax Division Ruling (U.S. Internal Revenue Bureau)

● Income Tax Unit Ruling

ITC International Tin Council

I.T.C. Spinivasan's Reports of Income Tax Cases (India)

I.T.D.A. Income Tax Decisions of Australasia

ITII International Tax Institute, Inc.

I.T.Info. Income Tax Information Release (U.S.)

I.T.L.J. Income Tax Law Journal (India)

ITO International Trade Organization (UN)

I.T.R. ● Income Tax Reports (India)

● Irish Term Reports (Ridgeway, Lapp & Schoales)

ITS International Trading Service

ITU ● International Telecommunication Union (UN)

● Income Tax Unit Order

IT& T International Telephone & Telegraph Co.

IUE International Union of Electrical, Radio and Machine Workers

IUOTO International Union of Official Travel Organizations

IWC ● International Whaling Commission

● International Wheat Council

IWTO International Wool Textile Organization

I.& C.L.Q. International and Comparative Law Quarterly

I.& N. Immigration & Nationality Laws Administrative Decisions (Justice Dept.)

I.& N.Dec. Immigration and Nationality Decisions

I.& N.S. Immigration & Naturalization Service (U.S.)

Ia Iowa Reports

Ia.L.Rev. Iowa Law Review

Ia.R.C. Iowa Board of Railroad Commission

ibid. ibidem (in the same place)

Ic. Icelandic

Id. ● Idaho Reports

● idem (the same)

Id.L.J. Idaho Law Journal

Id.L.R. Idaho Law Review

Ida. Idaho Reports

Ida.I.A.B. Idaho Industrial Accident Board Reports

Ida.P.U.C. Idaho Public Utilities Commission

Idaho Idaho Supreme Court Reports

Idaho Code Idaho Code

Idaho L.J. Idaho Law Journal

Idaho L.Rev. Idaho Law Review

Idaho Sess.Laws Session Laws, Idaho

IDD.T.R. Idding's Term Reports (Dayton, Ohio)

Iddings D.R.D. Iddings Dayton Term Reports

Iddings T.R.D. Iddings' Dayton (Ohio) Term Reports

Idea. Patent, Trademark and Copyright Journal of Research and Education

Il. Illinois Supreme Court Reports

Il.2d. Illinois Supreme Court Reports, Second Series

Il.A. Illinois Appellate Court Reports

IlA.2d. Illinois Appellate Court Reports, Second Series

Il.A.3d. Illinois Appellate Court Reports, Third Series

IlC.Cl. Illinois Court of Claims Reports

Il Cons.Mar. Il Consolato del Mare

Il.L.F. Illinois Law Forum

Ill. Illinois Reports

Ill.2d. Illinois Reports, Second Series

Ill.A. Illinois Appellate Court Reports

Ill.Ann.Stat. Smith-Hurd Illinois Annotated Statutes

Ill.App. Illinois Appellate Court Reports

Ill.App.2d Illinois Appellate Court Reports, 2d Edition

Ill.App.3d Illinois Appellate Court Reports, 3d Edition

Ill.B.J. Illinois Bar Journal

Ill.C.C. Illinois Commerce Commission Opinions & Orders

Ill.Cir.Ct. Illinois Circuit Court Reports

Ill.Cont.Legal Ed. Illinois Continuing Legal Education

Ill.Ct.Cl. Illinois Court of Claims

Ill.L.B. Illinois Law Bulletin

Ill.L.Q. Illinois Law Quarterly

Ill.L.Rec. Illinois Law Record

Ill.L.Rev. Illinois Law Review

Ill.Laws Laws of Illinois

Ill.Leg.N. Illustrated Legal News (India)

Ill.Legis.Serv. Illinois Legislative Service (West)

Ill.P.U.C.Ops. Illinois Public Utilities Commission Opinions & Orders

Ill.R.& W.C. Illinois Railroad & Warehouse Commission Reports

Ill.R.& W.C.D. Illinois Railroad & Warehouse Commission Decisions

Ill.Rev.Stat. Illinois Revised Statutes

Ill.S.B.A. Illinois State Bar Association Reports

Ill.W.C.C. Illinois Workmen's Compensation Cases

Immig.B.Bull. Immigration Bar Bulletin

Imp. Imperial: United Kingdom Statute

Imp.Dict. Imperial Dictionary

Imp.Fed. Imperial Federation (London)

Impt. Improvement

In. Indian Reports

In Indonesian

In.A. ● Indiana Appellate Court Reports
      ● Indiana Court of Appeals Reports

In.L.F. Indiana Legal Forum

In.L.J. Indiana Law Journal

In.L.R. Indiana Law Review

In re In reference to

Inc. ● Income
      ● Incorporated

Inc.Tax Cas. Reports of Cases on Income Tax

Inc.Tax L.J. Income Tax Law Journal (India)

Inc.Tax R. Income Tax Reports (India)

Incl. Including

Ind. ● India
      ● Indiana

      ● Indiana Supreme Court Reports (1848-date)

Ind.A.Dig. U.S. Indian Affairs Office, Digest of Decisions

Ind.Acts Acts, Indiana

Ind.and Labor Rels.Rev. Industrial and Labor Relations Review

Ind.App. ● Indiana Appellate Court Reports
      ● Law Reports, Indian Appeals

Ind.App.Supp. Supplemental Indian Appeals, Law Reports

Ind.Awards Industrial Awards Recommendations (New Zealand)

Ind.C.Aw. Industrial Court Awards

Ind.Cas. Indian Cases (India)

Ind.Code Indiana Code

Ind.Code Ann. Burns Indiana Statutes Annotated Code Edition

Ind.Comm. Industrial Commission

Ind.Court Aw. Industrial Court Awards (Eng.)

Ind.Ct.Awards Industrial Court Awards (Eng.)

Ind.Jur. Indian Jurist (Calcutta or Madras)

Ind.Jur.N.S. Indian Jurist, New Series

Ind.L.C.Eq. Indermaur's Leading Cases in Conveyancing and Equity

Ind.L.J. Indiana Law Journal

Ind.L.Mag. Indian Law Magazine

Ind.L.R. Indian Law Reports (East)

Ind.L.R.All. Indian Law Reports, Allahabad Series

Ind.L.R.Alla. Indian Law Reports, Allahabad Series

Ind.L.R.Bomb. Indian Law Reports, Bombay Series

Ind.L.R.Calc. Indian Law Reports, Calcutta Series

Ind.L.R.Kar. Indian Law Reports, Karachi Series

Ind.L.R.Lah. Indian Law Reports, Lahore Series

Ind.L.R.Luck. Indian Law Reports, Lucknow Series

Ind.L.R.Mad. Indian Law Reports, Madras Series

Ind.L.R.Nag. Indian Law Reports, Nagpur Series

Ind.L.R.Pat. Indian Law Reports, Patna Series

Ind.L.R.Ran. Indian Law Reports, Rangoon Series

Ind.L.Reg. Indiana Legal Register

Ind.L.Rep. Indian Law Reporter

Ind.L.Rev. Indian Law Review

Ind.L.T. Indian Law Times

Ind.Leg.Per. Index to Legal Periodicals

Ind.Legal F. Indiana Legal Forum

Ind.P.S.C. Indiana Public Service Commission

Ind.Prop. Industrial Property

Ind.R.C. Indiana Railroad Commission

Ind.Rel. Industrial Relations (P-H)

Ind.Rel.J.Econ.& Soc. Industrial Relations: Journal of Economy and Society

Ind.Relations Industrial Relations

Ind.Rep. Indiana Reports

Ind.S.B.A. Indiana State Bar Association Reports

Ind.Super. Wilson's Indiana Superior Court Reports

Ind.T. Indian Territory

Ind.T.Ann.St. Indian Territory Annotated Statutes

Ind.Terr. Indian Territory

Ind.U.C.D. Indiana Unemployment Compensation Division, Selected Appeal Tribunal Decisions

Ind.&L.Rel.Rev. Industrial & Labor Relations Review

Ind.& Lab.Rel.Rev. Industrial and Labor Relations Review

Ind.and Labor Rels.Rev. Industrial and Labor Relations Review

Indebt. Indebtedness

Indem. Indemnity

India A.I.R.Manual A.I.R.Manual: Unrepealed Central Acts, 2d edition (India)

India Cen.Acts Central Acts (India)

India Code Civ.P. Code of Civil Procedure (India)

India Code Crim.P. Code of Criminal Procedure (India)

India Crim.L.J.R. Criminal Law Journal Reports

India Gen.R.& O. General Rules and Orders (India)

India Pen.Code Indian Penal Code

India S.Ct. India Supreme Court Reports

India Subs.Leg. Subsidiary Legislation (India)

Indian Indian

Indian App. Law Reports, Privy Council, Indian Appeals (1873-75) (India)

Indian Cas. Indian Cases

Indian J.Int'l.L. Indian Journal of International Law

Indian L.J. Indian Law Journal

Indian L.R. Indian Law Reports

Indian L.R.Calc. Indian Law Reports, Calcutta Series

Indian L.R. Mad. Indian Law Reports, Madras Series

Indian L.Rev. Indian Law Review

Indian Rul. Indian Rulings

Indian Terr. Indian Territory Reports

Indty. Indemnity

Indus. • Industry
 • Industrial

Indus.L.Rev. Industrial Law Review

Indust.Ct.Aw. Industrial Court Awards (Eng.)

Indust.L.Rev.Q. Industrial Law Review Quarterly

Inher. Inheritance

Ins. Insurance

Ins.C. Insurance Code

Ins.Counsel J. Insurance Counsel Journal

Ins.L.J. Insurance Law Journal

Ins.L.R. Insurance Law Reporter

Ins.L.Rep. Insurance Law Reporter (CCH)

Ins.L.Mon. Insurance Monitor

Ins.Law J. Insurance Law Journal

Ins.Mon. Insurance Monitor

Ins.Rep. Insurance Reporter

Inst. • Coke's Institutes (Eng.)
 • Institute; Institution
 • Justinian's Institutes

Inst., 1, 2, 3. Justinian's Inst. lib 1, tit.2, § 3.

Inst., 1, 2, 31. Justinian's Institutes, lib. 1, tit. 2, § 31 (The Institutes of Justinian are divided into four books: each book is divided into titles, and each title into paragraphs, of which the first, described by the letters pr., or princip., is not numbered)

Inst.Cler.   Instructor Clericalis

Inst.Com.Com.   Interstate Commerce Commission Reports (U.S.)

Inst.Epil.   Epilogue to (a designated part or volume of) Coke's Institutes

Inst.Estate Plan   Institute on Estate Planning

Inst.Fed.Tax   Institute of Federal Taxation

Inst.Min.L.   Institute on Mineral Law (La-S-U.)

Inst.Proem.   Proeme (introduction) to (a designated part or volume of) Coke's Institutes

Inst.Securitites Reg.   Institute on Securities Regulation (PLI)

Institutes   Institutes of Justinian (Roman Law)

Instn.   Institution

Instr.Cler.   Instructor Clericalis

Insur.L.Rep.   Insurance Law Reporter (CCH)

Int.   ●   Intelligence
      ●   Interest

Int.Arb.J.   International Arbitration Journal

Int.Cas.   Rowe's Interesting Cases (Eng., Ir.)

Int.Case   Rowe's Interesting Cases (Eng., Ir.)

Int.Com.Commn.   Interstate Commerce Commission

Int.Com.Rep.   Interstate Commerce Commission Reports

Int.Dig.   International Digest

Int.Jurid.Assn.Bull.   International Juridical Association Bulletin

Int.L.N.   International Law Notes

Int.L.Notes   International Law Notes (Eng.)

Int.L.Q.   International Law Quarterly

Int.Law   The International Lawyer

Int.Org.   International Organization

Int.Persp.   International Perspectives

Int.Private Law   Westlake's Private International Law

Int.Rev.Bull.   Internal Revenue Bulletin

Int.Rev.Code   Internal Revenue Code

Int.Rev.Code of 1954   Internal Revenue Code of 1954

Int.Rev.Manual   Internal Revenue Manual

Int.Rev.Rec.   Internal Revenue Record

Int.& Comp.L.Q.   International & Comparative Law Quarterly

Inter.Am.   Inter-American Quarterly

Inter-Am.L.Rev.   Inter-American Law Review

Interior Dec.   Decisons of the Department of the Interior

intern.   international

Interna.L.N.   International Law Notes (London)

Internat.Dict.   Webster's International Dictionary

Internat.L.N.   International Law Notes

Interp.   Interpretation

Interp.No.   Interpretation Number

Interp.Op.   Interpretative Opinion

Inters.Com.   Interstate Commerce

Inters.Com.Com.   Interstate Commerce Commission

Interst.Com.R.   Interstate Commerce Commission Reports

Interstate Com.R.   Interstate Commerce Reports

Intl.   International

Int'l.Aff.   International Affairs

Int'l Affairs   International Affairs

Int'l. Affairs (Moscow)   International Affairs

Int'l.Arb.J.   International Arbitration Journal

Int'l Bull.Research E.Eur.   International Bulletin for Research on Law in Eastern Europe

Int'l.J.   International Journal

Int'l.J.Pol.   International Journal of Politics

Int'l L.Ass'n.   Reports of the International Law Association

Int'l L.Q.   International Law Quarterly

Int'l L.Rep.   International Law Reports

Int'l.Lab.Rev.   International Labour Review

Int'l Law   The International Lawyer

Int'l.Lawyer   International Lawyer

Int'l.Legal Materials   International Legal Materials

Int'l.Rev.Ind.Prop.& C'right L.   International Review of Industrial Property and Copyright Law

Int'l.& Comp.L.Q.   International and Comparative Law Quarterly

Intra.   Intramural

Intra.L.Rev.(N.Y.U.) Intramural Law Review, New York University

Intra.L.Rev.(St.L.U.) Intramural Law Review, St. Louis University

Intra.L.Rev.(U.C.L.A.) Intramural Law Review, University of California at Los Angeles

Intramural L.Rev. Intramural Law Review

Inv. Investment

Inv.Reg.Cas. Notes of Decisions of Appeal Court of Registration at Inverness (1835-53) (Sc.)

Iowa Iowa Supreme Court Reports

Iowa Acts Acts and Joint Resolutions of the State of Iowa

Iowa Code Code of Iowa

Iowa Code Ann. Iowa Code Annotated

Iowa L.B. Iowa Law Bulletin

Iowa L.Bull. Iowa Law Bulletin

Iowa L.Rev. Iowa Law Review

Iowa Legis.Serv. Iowa Legislative Service (West)

Iowa R.C. Iowa Railroad Commissioners Reports

Iowa St.B.A.Q. Iowa State Bar Assn. Quarterly

Iowa Univ.L.Bull Iowa University Law Bull

Iowa W.C.S. Iowa Workmen's Compensation Comm. Reports

Ir.   ● Iredell's North Carolina Law or Equity Reports
     ● Ireland
     ● Irish

Ir.C.L. Irish Common Law Reports (1866-78)

Ir.Ch. Irish Chancery Reports (1850-66)

Ir.Ch.Rep. Irish Chancery Reports

Ir.Cir.Rep. Reports of Irish Circuit Cases

Ir.Circ.Cas. Irish Circuit Cases

Ir.Com.L.Rep. Irish Common Law Reports

Ir.Eccl. Irish Ecclesiastical Reports, by Milward. (1819-43)

Ir.Eq. Irish Equity Reports

Ir.Eq.Rep. Irish Equity Reports

Ir.Jur. Irish Jurist Reports (1849-66)

Ir.Jur.Rep. Irish Jurist Reports (1849-66)

Ir.L. Irish Law Reports. (1839-52)

Ir.L.J. Irish Law Journal (1895-1902)

Ir.L.N.S. Irish Common Law Reports

Ir.L.R. Irish Law Reports (1838-50)

Ir.L.T. Irish Law Times (1867)

Ir.L.T.J. Irish Law Times Journal

Ir.L.T.Jour. Irish Law Times Journal

Ir.L.T.R. Irish Law Times Reports

IR.L.Rec.1st ser. Law Recorder 1st Series, 4 vols (Ir.)

Ir.L.Rec.N.S. Law Recorder (New Series, 6 vols.) (Ir.)

Ir.L.T.Rep. Irish Law Times Reports

Ir.L.& Eq. Irish Law & Equity (1838-50)

Ir.Law Rec. Irish Law Recorder (1827-38)

Ir.Law Rep. Irish Law Reports (1838-50)

Ir.Law Rep.N.S. Irish Common Law Reports

Ir.Law T. Irish Law Times

Ir.Law & Ch. Irish Common Law and Chancery Reports (New Series) (1850-53)

Ir.Law & Eq. Irish Law and Equity Reports (1838-50)

Ir.Pat.Off. Irish Patent Office

Ir.Pet.S.J. Irish Petty Sessions Journal

Ir.R. Irish Law Reports

Ir.R.C.L. Irish Reports, Common Law Series (1867-78)

Ir.R.Ch. Irish Reports, Chancery

Ir.R.Eq. Irish Reports, Equity Series (1866-78)

Ir.R.Reg.App. Irish Reports, Registration Appeals (1868-76)

Ir.R.Reg.& L. Irish Reports, Registry & Land Cases (1868-76)

Ir.Rep.C.L. Irish Reports. Common Law

Ir.Rep.Ch. Irish Reports, Chancery

Ir.Rep.Eq. Irish Reports, Equity

Ir.Rep.N.S. Irish Common Law Reports

Ir.Rep.V.R. Irish Reports, Verbatim Reprint

Ir.St.Tr. Irish State Trials (Ridgeway's)

Ir.Stat. Irish Statutes

Ir.T.R. Irish Term Reports (by Ridgeway, Lapp & Schoales (1793-95)

Ir.Term Rep.   Irish Term Reports (by Ridgeway, Lapp & Schoales)

Ir.W.C.C.   Irish Workmen's Compensation Cases

Ir.W.L.R.   Irish Weekly Law Reports (1895-1902)

Ire.   Ireland

Ired.   Iredell's Reports (36-43 North Carolina Equity)

Ired.Eq.   Iredell's Reports (36-43 N.C. Equity)

Ired.Eq.(N.C.)   Iredell's Reports (36-43 North Carolina Equity)

Ired.L.   Iredell's Reports (36-43 North Carolina Equity)

Ired.L.(NC)   Iredell's Law Reports

Irish Jur.   The Irish Jurist

Irish L.T.   Irish Law Times

Irv.   Irvine's Scotch Justiciary Reports (1851-68)

Irv.Just.   Irvine's Justiciary Cases (Eng.)

Irvine Just.Cas.   Irvine's Justiciary Cases

Irving,Civ.Law.   Irving's Civil Law

Irwin's Code'   Clark, Cobb and Irwin's Code (Ga.)

Israel L.Rev.   Israel Law Review

Iss.   Issue

J

j   dissenting opinion citation in dissenting opinion (used in Shepard's Citations)

J.
- Japanese
- Johnson's New York Reports
- Journal
- Judge
- Justice
- Judiciary
- Justiciary Cases (Scotland)
- Institutes of Justinian
- Juta's South African Reports
- Scottish Jurist (1829-73)

J.A.   Judge Advocate

JAC   Jacobus (James) (Eng. statutes)

JAEC   Headquarters, United States Air Force

JAG   Judge Advocate General

JAGA   Military Affairs Division, Office of Judge Advocate General, U.S. Army

JAG Bull.   JAG Bulletin (USAF)

JAG C.M.R.(A.F.)   Judge Advocate General Court-Martial Reports

JAG Comp.C.M.O.(Navy)   Judge Advocate General Compilation of Court Martial Orders

JAG (Def.Dept.)
- Judge Advocate General (Defense Department) Court Martial Reports
- Holdings & Decisions of Judge Advocate General Boards of Review & United States Court of Military Appeals

JAG Dig.Op.   Judge Advocate General Digest of Opinions

JAG J.   JAG Journal

JAG L.Rev.   United States Air Force Judge Advocate General Law Review

JAGS   Judge Advocate General's School

JAGT.   Procurement Division, Judge Advocate General, U.S. Army

J.A.J.   Judge Advocate Journal

J.A.M.A.   Journal of the American Medical Association

J.Account.   Journal of Accountancy

J.Air.L.   Journal of Air Law

J.Air L. & Com.   Journal of Air Law and Commerce

J.Am.Bankers' Assn.   Journal of American Bankers Association

J.Am.Jud.Soc.   Journal of American Judicature Society

J.Am.Soc.C.L.U.   Journal of American Society of Chartered Life Underwriters

J.Am.Soc'y.C.L.U.   Journal of American Society of Chartered Life Underwriters

J.Ass'n.L.Teachers   Journal of the Association of Law Teachers

J.B.A.D.C.   Journal of Bar Assn. of the District of Columbia

J.B.A.Dist.Colum.   Journal of the Bar Association of the District of Columbia.

J.B.A.Kan.   Journal of Bar Association of Kansas

J.B.Ass'n.St.Kan.   Journal of the Bar Association of the State of Kansas

J.B.C.   Journal of the State Bar of California

J.B.K.   Journal of the Bar Association of the State of Kansas.

J.B.L.   The Journal of Business Law

J.B.Moore (Eng.)   J.B. Moore's English Common Pleas Reports

J.Beverly Hills B.A.   Journal of the Beverly Hills Bar Association

JBl.   Juristische Blatter (Austria)

J.Bridg.   Sir John Bridgman's Reports, Common Pleas, English (123 Eng. Reprint)

J.Bridg.(Eng.)   Sir John Bridgman's Reports, Common Pleas (123 Eng. Reprint)

J.Bridgm.   Sir John Bridgman's Reports, Common Pleas, English (123 Eng. Reprint)

J.Bus.L.   Journal of Business Law
J.C. ● Johnson's Cases or Reports (N.Y.)
   ● Justiciary Cases (Sc.)
JCAE Joint Committee on Atomic Energy
J.C.B. ● Kansas Judicial Council Bulletin
   ● Juris Canonici Bachelor
J.C.L. ● Journal of Criminal Law
   ● Juris Canonici Lector
J.C.L.& I.L. Journal of Comparative Legislation & International Law
J.C.M.S. Juris-Classeur Periodique (La Semaine Juridique)
J.C.P. ● Jurisclasseur Periodique (La Semaine Juridique) (France)
   ● Justice of the Common Pleas
   ● Semaine Juridique (La) (France)
J.C.R. ● Johnson's Chancery (New York)
   ● Judicial Council Reports
JCS Joint Chiefs of Staff (U.S.) (U.S.)
J.Can.B.A. Journal of the Canadian Bar Association
J.Can.B.Ass'n. Journal of the Canadian Bar Association
J.Ch. Johnson's New York Chancery Reports
J.Commerce. Journal of Commerce
J.Common Market Studies. Journal of Common Market Studies
J.Comp.Leg. Journal of Society of Comparative Legislation (London)
J.Comp.Leg.& Int.Law Journal of Comparative Legislation & International Law
J.Comp.Leg.& Int'l.L.3d Journal of Comparative Legislation and International Law, Third Series
J.Conat.Law. Journal of Conational Law
J.Crim.L.,C.& P.S. Journal of Criminal Law, Criminology and Police Science
J.Crim.L.(Eng.) Journal of Criminal Law (Eng.)

J.Crim.L.& Criminology Journal of Criminal Law and Criminology
J.Crim.Law Journal of American Institute of Criminal Law & Criminology (Chicago)
J.D. ● Juris Doctor
   ● Doctor of Jurisprudence
J.d'Ol. Les Jugemens d'Oleron
J.D.R. Juta's Daily Reporter, Cape Provincial Division (South Africa)
JFMIP Joint Financial Management Improvement Program
J.Fam.L. Journal of Family Law
J.For.Med. Journal of Forensic Medicine
J.For.Sci. Journal of Forensic Sciences
J.For.Sci.Soc'y. Journal of the Forensic Science Society
J.H. Journal, House of Representatives (U.S.)
J.I.L. Japan Institute of Labour
J.I.T. Job Instruction Training
J.Int'l.L.& Econ. Journal of International Law and Economics
J.Int'l.L.& Pol. Journal of International Law and Politics
J.J. ● Judges
   ● Junior Judge
   ● Justices
J.J.Mar. Marshall's Reports (24-30 Kentucky)
J.J.Marsh. J.J. Marshall's Kentucky Supreme Court Reports (1829-1832)
J.J.Marsh.(Ky.) Marshall's Reports (24-30 Kentucky)
J.Jur. Journal of Jurisprudence
J.K.B. Justice of the King's Bench
J.Kan.B.A. Journal of the Kansas Bar Association
J.Kel. Sir John Kelyng's English Crown Cases (84 Eng. Reprint)
J.Kelyng (Eng.) Sir John Kelyng's English Crown Cases (84 Eng. Reprint)
J.L.R. ● Jamaica Law Reports (1953-55)
   ● Johore Law Reports (India)
J.L.Soc'y. Journal of the Law Society of Scotland
J.L.& Econ. Journal of Law & Economics
J.L.& Econ.Dev. Journal of Law and Economic Development

J.L.& Econ.Develop. The Journal of Law & Economic Development

J.L.& Educ. Journal of Law & Education

J.Land & P.U.Econ. Journal of Land and Public Utility Economics

J.Land & Pub.Util.Econ. Journal of Land & Public Utility Economics

J.Law Reform Journal of Law Reform

J.Law & Econ. Journal of Law and Economics

J.Law & Econ.Dev. Journal of Law and Economic Development

J.Legal Ed. Journal of Legal Education

J.Legal Educ. Journal of Legal Education

J.Legal Studies Journal of Legal Studies

J.M. Master of Jurisprudence

J.M.J. John Marshall Journal of Practice & Procedure

JMLS John Marshall Law School

J.Mar. John Marshall

J.Mar.Law & Com. Journal of Maritime Law and Commerce

J.Mo.B. Journal of the Missouri Bar

J.Mo.Bar Journal of the Missouri Bar

J.N.A.Referees Bank. Journal of the National Association of Referees in Bankruptcy

J.O.B.S. Job Opportunities in the Business Sector

J.of Account. Journal of Accountancy

J.of Air L.& Commerce Journal of Air Law and Commerce

J.of Business Journal of Business

J.of the B.A.of Kansas The Journal of the Bar Association of the State of Kansas

J.P. ● Juge de Paiz
- ● Journal of Politics
- ● Justice of the Peace & Local Government Review
- ● Justice of the Peace (Weekly Notes of Cases) (Eng.)

J.P.Ct. Justice of the Peace's Court

J.P.(Eng.) ● Justice of the Peace & Local Government Review

- ● Justice of the Peace (Weekly Notes of Cases) (Eng.)

J.P.J. ● Justice of the Peace & Local Government Review
- ● Justice of the Peace (Weekly Notes of Cases)

J.P.Jo. Justice of the Peace (Weekly Notes of Cases) (Eng.)

J.P.L. Journal of Planning Law Journal of Public Law

J.P.N.S.W. Justice of the Peace (New South Wales)

J.P.P.L. Journal of Planning and Property Law

J.P.Sm. J.P. Smith's English King's Bench Reports (1803-06)

J.P.Smith J.P. Smith's English King's Bench Reports

J.P.Smith (Eng.) J.P. Smith's English King's Bench Reports

J.Pat.Off.Soc'y. Journal of the Patent Office Society

J.Pl.L. Journal of Planning Law

J.Plan.& Prop.L. Journal of Planning and Property Law

J.Pol.Econ. Journal of Political Economy

J.Psychological Medicine Journal of Psychological Medicine & Medical Jurisprudence

J.Pub.L. Journal of Public Law

J.Q.B. Justice of the Queen's Bench

J.R. ● Johnson's Reports (N.Y.)
- ● Jurist Reports (1873-78) (New Zealand)

J.R.N.S. Jurist Reports, New Series (New Zealand)

J.R.N.S.C.A. Jurist Reports, New Series, Court of Appeal (New Zealand)

J.R.N.S.M.L. Jurist Reports, New Series, Mining Law Cases (New Zealand)

J.R.N.S.S.C. Jurist Reports, New Series, Supreme Court (New Zealand)

J.Radio L. Journal of Radio Law

J.S. ● Jones and Spencer's Superior Court Reports, New York
- ● Jury Sittings (Faculty Cases, Sc.)

J.S.D. ● Doctor of Juridical Science
      ● Doctor of Juristic Science

J.S.Gr. J.S.Green's Reports (13-15 New Jersey Law Reports)

J.S.Gr.(N.J.) J.S.Green's Reports (13-15 New Jersey Law Reports)

J.S.M. Master of the Science of Law

J.S.T. Job Safety Training

J.Scott Reporter English Common Bench Reports

J.Scott, N.S. English Common Bench Reports, New Series, by John Scott

J.Shaw John Shaw, Justiciary Reports, Scotland (1848-52)

J.Soc.Pub.T.L. Journal of the Society of Public Teachers of Law

J.Soc.Pub.Teach.Law Journal of the Society of Public Teachers of Law

J.Soc.Pub.Teach.Law N.S. Journal of the Society of Public Teachers of Law (New Series)

J.St.Bar Calif. Journal of the State Bar of California

J.T. Journal des Tribunaux (Belgium)

J.T.R.S. Joint tenant with right of survivorship

J.Tax. Journal of Taxation

J.Taxation Journal of Taxation

J.U.B. Justice of the Upper Bench

J.U.D. Juris Utriusque Doctor: Doctor of Both (Canon and Civil) Laws

J.U.L. Journal of Urban Law (Mich.)

J.Urban Journal of Urban Law

J.Voet,Com.ad Pand. Voet (Jan), Commentarius and Pandectas

J.W.T.L. Journal of World Trade Law

J.World Tr.L. Journal of World Trade Law

J.World Trade L. Journal of World Trade Law (Germany)

JZ Juristenzeitung (Germany)

J. & C. Jones & Cary's Irish Exchequer Reports (1838-39)

J.& H. Johnson & Hemming's English Vice-Chancellors' Reports

J.& L. Jones & La Touche's Irish Chancery Reports

J.& La T. Jones & La Touche's Irish Chancery Reports

J.& S. ● Jebb and Syms (1838-40) (Ir.)

● Jones & Spencer's Reports (33-61 New York Superior)

● Judah and Swan Reports, Jamaica (1839)

J.& S.Jam. Judah & Swan's Jamaica Reports

J.& W. Jacob & Walker's English Chancery Reports (1819-21)

Jac. ● Jacobus (King James), as 21 Jac. I

● Jacob's English Chancery Reports (1821-22)

● Jacob's Law Dictionary

Jac.Fish.Dig. Jacob's American edition of Fisher's English Digest

Jac.L.Dict. Jacob's Law Dictionary

Jac.Law Dict. Jacob's Law Dictionary

Jac.Sea Laws. Jacobsen's Law of the Sea

Jac.& W. Jacob & Walker's English Chancery Reports (37 Eng. Reprint)

Jac.& W.(Eng.) Jacob & Walker's English Chancery Reports (37 Eng. Reprint)

Jac.& Walk. Jacob & Walker's English Chancery Reports (37 Eng. Reprint)

Jack.Tex.App. Jackson's Reports (1-29 Court of Appeals Reports)

Jack.& G.Landl.& Ten. Jackson & Gross, Treatise on the Law of Landlord and Tenant in Pennsylvania

Jackson ● Jackson's Reports (46-58 Georgia)

● Jackson's Reports (1-29 Texas Appeals)

Jackson & Lumpkin Jackson & Lumpkin's Reports (59-64 Georgia)

Jacob. Jacob's Law Dictionary. 16 editions (1729-1835.)

Jacob (Eng.) Jacob (37 Eng. Reprint)

Jaeger, Labor Law. Jaeger's Cases and Statutes on Labor Law

Jagg.Torts. Jaggard on Torts

James James' Reports (2 Nova Scotia)

James (N.Sc.) James' Reports (2 Nova Scotia)

James Op. James, Opinions, Charges, etc.

James Sel.Cases. James' Select Cases, Nova Scotia (1835-55)

James.& Mont. Jameson & Montagu's English Bankruptcy Reports (in vol. 2 Glyn & Jameson) (1821-28)

Jan.Angl. Jani Anglorum facies Nova (1680)

Japan Japan

Jar.Chy.Pr. Jarman's Chancery Practice

Jar.Cr.Tr. Jardine's Criminal Trials

Jar.Wills. Jarman on Wills 8 editions, (1841-51)

Jay W. Jaywardine's Appeal Cases (Ceylon)

Jebb. Jebb's Irish Crown Cases (1822-40)

Jebb.C.C. Jebb's Irish Crown Cases (1822-40)

Jebb.C.C.(Ir.) Jebb's Irish Crown Cases (1822-40)

Jebb Cr.& Pr.Cas. Jebb's Irish Crown and Presentment Cases

Jebb.& B. Jebb & Bourke's Irish Queen's Bench Reports (1841-42)

Jebb.& B.(Ir.) Jebb & Bourke's Irish Queen's Bench Reports (1841-42)

Jebb.& S. Jebb & Symes' Irish Queen's Bench Reports (1838-41)

Jebb & S.(Ir.) Jebb & Symes' Irish Queen's Bench Reports

Jebb & Sym. Jebb & Symes' Irish Queen's Bench Reports

Jeff. Jefferson's Reports (Virginia General Court)

Jeff.(Va.) Jefferson's Reports (Virginia General Court)

Jeff.Man. Jefferson's Manual of Parliamentary Law

Jenk. Jenkins, Eight Centuries of Reports, English Exchequer, 1220-1623 (145 Eng. Reprint)

Jenk.Cent. Jenkins' Exchequer Reports (1220-1623)

Jenk.& Formoy Jenkinson & Formoy's Select Cases in the Exchequer of Pleas. (Selden Society Publication, v. 48)

Jenkins (Eng.) Jenkins, Eight Centuries of Reports, English Exchequer, 1220-1623 (145 Eng. Reprint)

Jenks Jenks' Reports (58 New Hampshire)

Jenn. Jennison's Reports (14-18 Michigan).

Jenn.Sug.A. Jennett's Sugden Acts

Jer.Dig. Jeremy's Digest (1817-49)

Jeremy,Eq. Jeremy's Equity Jurisdiction

Jeremy,Eq.Jur. Jeremy's Equity Jurisdiction

Jes. Analysis and Digest of the Decisions of Sir George Jessel (England)

Jo. Jones' Exchequer Reports (1834-1838) (Ir.)

Jo.Ex.Ir. Jones' Exchequer Reports (Ir.)

Jo.Ex.Pro.W. Jones' Exchequer Proceedings Concerning Wales (1939)

Jo.Jur. Journal of Jurisprudence

Jo.Radio Law Journal of Radio Law

Jo.T. T. Jones' King's Bench Reports (Eng.)

Jo.& Car. Jones and Carey's Reports, Exchequer, Ireland (1838-39)

Jo.& La.T. Jones & La Touche, Irish Chancery Reports, 3 vols. (1844-46)

John.
- Johnson's English Vice-Chancellors' Reports (1858-60)
- Johnson's New York Reports
- Johnson's Reports, Chancery, Maryland
- Johnson's Reports of Chase's Decisions

John.Am.Not. John's American Notaries

John.Dict. Johnson's English Dictionary

John.Eng.Ch. Johnson's English Vice-Chancellors' Reports

John Mar.J.Prac.& Proc. John Marshall Journal of Practice and Procedure

John Marsh.L.J. John Marshall Law Journal

John Marsh.L.Q. John Marshall Law Quarterly

John Marsh.L.Rev. John Marshall Law Review

John Marshall J. The John Marshall Journal of Practice and Procedure

John Marshall L.Q. The John Marshall Law Quarterly

John.& H. Johnson and Hemming's English Chancery Reports

John[s].   ● Johnson's Reports (Md. Chancery)
  ● Johnson's Reports (New York Supreme or Chancery)
  ● Chase's Circuit Court Decisions, edited by Johnson (U.S.)
  ● Johnson's Vice-Chancery Reports (Eng.)

Johns.Cas. Johnson's Cases (New York 1799-1803)

Johns.Cas.(N.Y.) Johnson's Cases (New York 1799-1803)

Johns.Ch.   ● Johnson's Maryland Chancery Decisions
  ● Johnson's Chancery Reports (N.Y. 1814-23)
  ● Johnson's Vice-Chancery Reports (Eng.)

Johns.Ch.Cas. Johnson's Chancery Reports (New York)

Johns.Ch.(N.Y.) Johnson's Chancery Reports (New York)

Johns.Ct.Err. Johnson's Reports, New York Court of Errors

Johns.Dec. Johnson's Maryland Chancery Decisions

Johns.Eng.Ch. Johnson's English Chancery Reports

Johns.(N.Y.) Johnson's New York Reports

Johns.N.Z. Johnson's New Zealand Reports

Johns.Pat.Man. Johnson's Patent Manual

Johns.Rep. Johnson's Reports, New York Supreme Court

Johns.Tr. Johnson's Impeachment Trial

Johns.U.S. Johnson's Reports of Chase's United States Circuit Court Decisions

Johns.V.C. Johnson's English Vice-Chancellors' Reports (70 Eng. Reprint)

Johns.V.C.(Eng.) Johnson's English Vice-Chancellor's Reports (70 Eng. Reprint)

Johns.& H. Johnson & Hemming's English Chancery Reports (70 Eng. Reprint)

Johns.& H.(Eng.) Johnson & Hemming's English Chancery Reports (70 Eng. Reprint)

Johns.& Hem. Johnson & Hemming's English Chancery Reports (70 Eng. Reprint)

Johnson.   ● Johnson's English Vice-Chancellors' Reports
  ● Johnson's Maryland Chancery Decisions
  ● Johnson's Reports, New York

Johnson's Quarto Dict. Johnson's Quarto Dictionary

Johnst.(N.Z.) Johnston's Reports, New Zealand

Jon.   ● Jones' Irish Exchequer Reports (Ir.)
  ● T. Jones' King's Bench & Common Pleas Reports (Eng.)
  ● W. Jones' King's Bench & Common Pleas Reports (Eng.)

Jon.Ex. Jones' Exchequer Reports (1934-1938) (Ir.)

Jon.Exch. Jones' Irish Exchequer Reports

Jon.Ir.Exch. Jones' Irish Exchequer Reports

Jon.& Car. Jones & Cary's Irish Exchequer Reports (1838-39)

Jon.& L. Jones & La Touche's Irish Chancery Reports

Jon.& La.T. Jones & La Touche's Irish Chancery Reports

Jones   ● Jones' Reports (43-48, 52-57, 61, 62 Alabama)
  ● Jones' Reports (22-30 Missouri)
  ● Jones' Reports (11, 12 Pennsylvania)
  ● Jones' Reports (N.C. Law or Equity) (1853-1862)
  ● Jones' Irish Exchequer Reports (1834-38)
  ● Jones' Upper Canada Common Pleas Reports (1850-82)

Jones 1. Sir William Jones' English King's Bench Reports (1620-41)

Jones 2. Sir Thomas Jones English King's Bench Reports (1667-85)

Jones B. Jones' Law of Bailments

Jones,B.& W.(Mo.) Jones, Barclay & Whittelsey's Reports (31 Missouri)

Jones, Bailm. Jones' Law of Bailments

Jones, Barclay & Whittelsey. Jones, Barclay, & Whittelsey's Reports (vol. 31 Missouri)

Jones Ch.Mort. Jones on Chattel Mortgages

Jones,Easem. Jones' Treatise on Easements

Jones Eq. Jones, North Carolina Equity Reports (vols. 54-59) (1853-1863)

Jones Eq.(N.C.) Jones, North Carolina Equity Reports (vols. 54-59)

Jones Exch. T. Jones' Irish Exchequer Reports

Jones, French Bar. Jones' History of the French Bar

Jones Ir. Jones' Irish Exchequer Reports

Jones L. Jones, Law Reports

Jones Law. Jones' North Carolina Law Reports

Jones, Liens. Jones on Liens

Jones Mort. Jones on Mortgages

Jones N.C. Jones' North Carolina Law Reports (46-53 N.C. Law)

Jones (Pa.) Jones' Reports (11, 12 Pennsylvania State)

Jones Pa. Jones' Reports (11, 12 Pennsylvania State)

Jones, Pledges. Jones on Pledges and Collateral Securities

Jones, Securities Jones on Railroad Securities

Jones T. Sir Thomas Jones' English King's Bench Reports (1667-85)

Jones U.C. Jones, Reports, Upper Canada

Jones W. Sir William Jones, English King's Bench Reports (1620-44)

Jones & C. Jones & Cary's Irish Exchequer Reports (1838-39)

Jones & L. Jones & La Touche's Irish Chancery Reports

Jones & L.(Ir.) Jones & La Touche's Irish Chancery Reports

Jones & La T. Jones & La Touche's Irish Chancery Reports

Jones & McM. Jones & McMurtrie's Pennsylvania Supreme Court Reports

Jones & McM.(Pa.) Jones & McMurtries Pennsylvania Supreme Court Reports

Jones & S. Jones & Spencer's Reports (33-61 New York Superior)

Jones & Sp. Jones & Spencer's Reports (33-61 New York Superior)

Jones & Spen. Jones & Spencer's Reports (33-61 New York Superior)

Jones & V.Laws. Jones and Varick's Laws (N.Y.)

Jornand.de Reb.Get. Jornandes de Rebus Geticis

Jos. Joseph's Reports (21 Nevada)

Jos.& Bev. Joseph and Beven's Digest of Decisions (Ceylon)

Jour.Am.Jud.Soc. Journal of the American Judicature Society

Jour.Comp.Leg. Journal of the Society of Comparative Legislation

Jour.Conat.Law. Journal of Conational Law

Jour.Crim.L. Journal of Criminal Law and Criminology

Jour.Jur. Journal of Jurisprudence (1857-91) (Sc.)

Jour.Jur.Sc. Journal of Jurisprudence & Scottish Law Magazine

Jour.Juris. Hall's Journal of Jurisprudence

Jour.Law Journal of Law

Jour.Ps.Med. Journal of Psychological Medicine & Medical Jurisprudence

Journ.Jur. Journal of Jurisprudence

Joyce,Ins. Joyce on Insurance

Jt. Joint

Jt.Com. Joint Committee

Ju.D. Doctor of Law

Jud. ● Book of Judgments
● Judicature
● judicial
● judiciary

Jud.Chr. Judicial Chronicle

Jud.Coun.N.Y. Judicial Council, New York, Annual Reports

Jud.G.C.C. Judgments, Gold Coast Colony

Jud.Pan.Mult.Lit. Rulings of the Judicial Panel on Multidistrict Litigation

Jud.Rep. New York Judicial Repository

Jud.Repos. Judicial Repository (N.Y.)

Jud.& Sw. Judah & Swan's Reports, Jamaica (1839)

Judd Judd's Reports (4 Hawaii)

Judg.U.B. Judgments of Upper Bench (Eng.)

Judge Advo.J. The Judge Advocate Journal

Judge's J. Judge's Journal

Judicature Journal of the American Judicature Society

Jug.et Delib. Jugements et Deliberations du Conseil Souverain de la Nouvelle France

Jul.Frontin. Julius Frontinus

Jur. ● Juridical
   ● Jurisprudence
   ● Jurist
   ● The Jurist, or Quarterly Journal of Jurisprudence (1827)
   ● The Jurist, London (1854)
   ● Jurist (New York)
   ● The Jurist (Washington, D.C.)
   ● Jurist Reports (English, 18 vols.)

Jur.(Eng.) The Jurist (London)

Jur.Ex. Hargrave, Francis-Jurisconsult Exercitations

Jur.N.S. The Jurist, New Series Jurist Reports, New Series (Eng.)

Jur.(N.S.) The Jurist (New Series) Reports in all the Courts (London)

Jur.N.S.(Eng.) Jurist (New Series) Exchequer

Jur.(N.S.)Ex. Jurist (New Series) Exchequer

Jur.N.Y. The Jurist, or Law and Equity Reporter (New York)

Jur.Rev. Juridical Review (1889) (Sc.)

Jur.Ros. Roscoe, Jurist (London)

Jur.(Sc.) The Scottish Jurist (Edinburgh)

Jur.Soc.P. Juridical Society Papers (1858-74) (Sc.)

Jurid.Rev. Juridical Review (Edinburgh)

Jurimetrics Jurimetrics Journal

Jurimetrics J. Jurimetrics Journal

Juris. Jurisprudence

Jurispr. The Jurisprudent

Just. ● Justice
   ● Justices' Law Reporter (Pennsylvania)

Just.Cas. Justiciary Cases

Just.Ct. Justice Court

Just.Ct.Act Justice Court Act

Just.Dig. Digest of Justinian, 50 books (Never translated into English)

Just.Inst. Justinian's Institutes

Just.L.R. Justices' Law Reporter (Pa. 1902-18)

Just.P. Justice of the Peace and Local Government Review

Just.Peace Justice of the Peace and Local Government Review

Justice's L.R.(Pa.) Justices' Law Reporter (Pennsylvania)

Juta. ● Juta's Reports, Supreme Court, Cape of Good Hope (1880-1910)
   ● Juta's Daily Reporter (S. Africa)
   ● Juta's Prize Cases (S. Africa)

Juv. Juvenile

Juv.Ct. Juvenile Court

Juv.Ct.J. Juvenile Court Journal

Juv.Justice Juvenile Justice

Juv.& Dom.Rel.Ct. Juvenile and Domestic Relations Court

K

K.   ● Kenyon's King's Bench Reports (England)
         ● Keyes' Court of Appeals Reports (40-43 New York)
         ● Korean
         ● Kotze's Reports, Transvaal High Court (South Africa)

K.B. English Law Reports, King's Bench (1901-52)

K.B.(Eng.) English Law Reports, King's Bench (1901-52)

K.B.(U.C.) King's Bench Reports (Upper Canada)

KBA Joint Committee of CLE of the Kansas Bar Association and the University of Kansas and Washburn University of Topeka Schools of Law

K.B.Div'l.Ct. King's Bench Divisional Court (Eng.)

K.B.J. Kentucky State Bar Journal or Kentucky Bar Journal

K.B.U.C. Upper Canada King's Bench Reports

K.C. King's Counsel

KCLE Continuing Legal Education, University of Kentucky College of Law

KCMOBA Kansas City, Missouri, Bar Association

K.C.Mo.P.U.C. Kansas City, Missouri, Public Utilities Commission Reports

K.C.R.   ● Reports in the time of Chancellor King
            ● The University of Kansas City Law Review
            ● The University of Missouri at Kansas City Law Review

KG   ● Kammergericht--District Court Berlin (Germany)
         ● Kommanditgesellschaft (Limited partnership)

K.I.R. Knight's Industrial Reports

K.K.K. Ku Klux Klan

K.L.J. Kentucky Law Journal

K.L.R. Kathiawar Law Reports (India)

K.L.T. Kerala Law Times (India)

KstG Korperschaftsteuergesetz (German Corporation Taxation Act)

K.& B. Kotze & Barber Transvaal Reports (Supreme or High Court) (1885-88)

K.& F.N.S.W. Knox & Fitzhardinge's New South Wales Reports

K.& G. Keane & Grant, English Registration Appeal Cases (1854-62)

K.& G.R.C. Keane & Grant, English Registration Appeal Cases (1854-62)

K.& Gr. Keane & Grant, English Registration Appeal Cases

K.& J. Kay & Johnson's English Vice-Chancellors' Reports (1854-58)

K.& O. Knapp & Ombler, English Election Cases (1834-35)

K.& R. Kent and Radcliff's Law of New York, Revision of 1801

K.& W.Dic. Kames and Woodhouselee's folio Dictionary (1540-1796) (Sc.)

Ka.A. Kansas Appeals Reports

Kam.   ● Kames' Dictionary of Decisions, Court of Session (Sc.)
           ● Kames, Remarkable Decisions, Scotch Court of Session, 2 vols. (1716-52)

Kam.Rem. Kames, Remarkable Decisions, Scotch Court of Session, 2 vols. (1716-52)

Kam.Sel. Kames' Select Decisions (1752-68) (Sc.)

Kames   ● Kames' Dictionary of Decisions, Court of Session (Sc.)
            ● Kames, Remarkable Decisions, Scotch Court of Session, 2 vols.

Kames Dec. Kames, Dictionary of Decisions, Court of Session (Sc.)

Kames Dict.Dec. Kames' Dictionary of Decisions, Court of Session (Sc.)

Kames Elucid. Kames' Elucidation (Sc.)

Kames, Eq. Kames' Principles of Equity

Kames Sel.Dec. Kames' Select Decisions (Sc.)

Kan. ● Kansas
● Kansas Supreme Court Reports

Kan.App. Kansas Appeals Reports

Kan.B.Ass'n.J. Kansas Bar Association Journal

Kan.C.L.Rep. Kansas City Law Reporter

Kan.C.L.& I.W.C. Kansas Commission of Labor & Industry Workmen's Compensation Dept. Reports

Kan.City L.Rev. Kansas City Law Review

Kan.Civ.Pro.Stat.Ann. Code of Civil Procedure

Kan.Civ.Pro.Stat.Ann.(Vernon) Vernon's Kansas Statutes Annotated, Code of Civil Procedure

Kan.Crim.Code & Code of Crim.Proc. Criminal Code and Code of Criminal Procedure

Kan.Crim.Code & Code of Crim.Proc. (Vernon) Vernon's Kansas Statutes Annotated Criminal Code and Code of Criminal Procedure

Kan.Dig. Hatcher's Kansas Digest

Kan.Jud.Council Bul. Kansas Judicial Council Bulletin

Kan.L.Rev. University of Kansas Law Review

Kan.Law. Kansas Lawyer

Kan.P.S.C. Kansas Public Service Commission

Kan.P.U.C. Kansas Public Utilities Commission

Kan.R.C. Kansas Railroad Commission

Kan.S.C.C. Kansas State Corporation Commission Reports

Kan.Sess.Laws Session Laws of Kansas

Kan.St.L.J. Kansas State Law Journal

Kan.Stat. Kansas Statutes

Kan.Stat.Ann. Kansas Statutes Annotated

Kan.U.C.C.Ann.(Vernon) Vernon's Kansas Statutes Annotated, Uniform Commercial Code

Kan.U.Lawy. Kansas University Lawyer

Kan.Univ.Lawy. Kansas University Lawyer

Kans. Kansas Reports

Kans.App. Kansas Appeals Reports

Kans.S.B.A. Kansas State Bar Association

Kansas L.J. Kansas Law Journal

Kaufm.Mackeld.Civ.Law Kaufmann's Edition of Mackeldey's Civil Law

Kay Kay's English Vice-Chancellors' Reports (69 Eng. Reprint)

Kay (Eng.) Kay's English Vice-Chancellors' Reports (69 Eng. Reprint)

Kay & J. Kay and Johnson's English vice-Chancellors' Reports (69, 70 Eng. Reprint)

Kay & J.(Eng.) Kay and Johnson's English Vice-Chancellors' Reports (69, 70 Eng. Reprint)

Kay & John. Kay and Johnson's English Vice-Chancellors' Reports (69, 70 Eng. Reprint)

Kay & Johns. Kay and Johnson's English Vice-Chancellors' Reports (69, 70 Eng. Reprint)

Ke. Keen's English Rolls Court Reports (1836-38)

Keane & G.R.C. Keane & Grant's Registration Appeal Cases (Eng.)

Keane & Gr. Keane & Grant's English Registration Appeal Cases (1854-62)

Keb. Keble's English King's Bench Reports (83, 84 Eng. Reprint)

Kebl. Keble's English King's Bench Reports (83, 84 Eng. Reprint)

Keble (Eng.) Keble's English King's Bench Reports (83, 84 Eng. Reprint)

Keen Keen's English Rolls Court Reports (48 Eng. Reprint)

Keen Ch. Keen's English Rolls Court Reports (48 Eng. Reprint)

Keen (Eng.) Keen's English Rolls Court Reports (48 Eng. Reprint)

Keener, Quasi Contr. Keener's Cases on Quasi Contracts

Keil. Keilway, English King's Bench Reports (72 Eng. Reprint)

Keilw. Keilway, English King's Bench Reports (72 Eng. Reprint)

Keilw.(Eng.) Keilway, English King's Bench Reports (72 Eng. Reprint)

Keilway Keilway's English King's Bench Reports

Keith Ch.Pa. Registrar's Book, Keith's Court of Chancery (Pa.)

Kel. Sir John Kelyng's English Crown Cases

Kel.1. Sir John Kelyng's English Crown Cases (1662-69)

Kel.2. Wm. Kelynge's English Chancery Reports (1730-36)

Kel.C.C. Sir John Kelyng's English Crown Cases

Kel.Ga. Kelly's Reports (1-3 Georgia)

Kel.J. Sir John Kelyng's English Crown Cases (1662-69)

Kel.W. Wm. Kelynge's English Chancery Reports (1730-36)

Kelham Kelham's Norman Dictionary

Kellen Kellen's Reports (146-55 Mass.)

Kelly Kelly's Reports (1-3 Georgia)

Kelly & Cobb. Kelly & Cobb's Reports (4, 5 Georgia)

Kelyng.J. Kelyng's English Crown Cases

Kelyng.J.(Eng.) Kelyng's English Crown Cases

Kelynge, W. Kelynge's English Chancery Reports

Kelynge W.(Eng.) Kelynge's English Chancery Reports

Kemble, Sax. Kemble, The Saxons in England

Ken. Kenyon's King's Bench Reports (Eng.)

Ken.Dec. Kentucky Decisions, Sneed (2 Ky.)

Ken.L.Re. Kentucky Law Reporter

Ken.Opin. Kentucky Opinions (1864-86)

Kenan Kenan's Reports (76-91 North Carolina)

Kenn.Par.Antiq. Kennett, Parochial Antiquities

Kennett ● Kennett's Glossary
       ● Kennett upon Impropriations

Kennett, Gloss. Kennett's Glossary

Kennett, Par.Ant. Kennett's Parochial Antiquities

Kent Kent's Commentaries on American Law

Kent, Com. Kent's Commentaries on American Law

Kent, Comm. Kent's Commentaries on American Law

Kent & R.St. Kent and Radcliff's Law of New York, Revision of 1801

Kent's Commen. Kent's Commentaries

Keny. ● Kenyon's King's Bench Reports (1753-59) (Eng.)
       ● Kenyon's Notes of King's Bench Reports (Eng.)

Keny.Ch. Chancery Cases (v.2 of Notes of King's Bench Cases) (Eng.)

Keny.Chy.(3 Keny.) Chancery Reports, at end of 2 Kenyon (Eng.)

Kenya L.R. Kenya Law Reports

Kern. ● Kern's Reports (100-116 Indiana)
       ● Kernan's Reports (11-14 New York)

Kerr ● Kerr's Reports (3-5 New Brunswick)
       ● Kerr's Reports (18-22 Indiana)
       ● Kerr's Reports (27-29 N.Y. Civil Procedure Reports)

Kerr, Inj. Kerr on Injunctions

Kerr (N.B.) Kerr's New Brunswick Reports

Kerr, Rec. Kerr on Receivers

Kerr W.& M.Cas. Kerr's Water and Mineral Cases

Kerse Kerse's Manuscript Decisions, Scotch Court of Session

Kersey, Dict. John Kersey's English Dictionary (1708)

Key. Keyes' New York Court of Appeals Reports

Keyes Keyes' New York Court of Appeals Reports

Keyl. Keilwey's English King's Bench Reports

Kh. Khmer

Kilb. Kilburn's Magistrates' Cases (Eng.)

Kilk. Kilkerran's Scotch Court of Session Decisions (1738-52)

Kilkerran Kilkerran's Scotch Court of Session Decisions

King King's Reports, vols. 5, 6 Louisiana Annual

King Cas.temp. Select Cases tempore King, English Chancery (1724-33)

King's Con.Cs. King's Conflicting Cases (Texas)

King's Conf.Ca. King's Conflicting Cases (Texas)

Kinney, Law Dict.& Glos. Kinney's Law Dictionary and Glossary

Kir. Kirby's Reports & Supplement (Connecticut 1785-89)

Kirb. Kirby's Reports & Supplement (Connecticut 1785-89)

Kirby Kirby's Reports & Supplement (Connecticut 1785-89)

Kit. Kitchin's Retourna Brevium, 4 editions (1581-92)

Kitch. Kitchin on Jurisdictions of Courts-Leet, Courts-Baron, etc.

Kitch.Courts Kitchin on Jurisdictions of Courts-Leet, Courts-Baron, etc.

Kitch.Cts. Kitchin on Courts

Kitchen Griqualand West Reports, Cape Colony (S. Africa)

Kluber, Dr.des Gens. Kluber's Droit des Gens

Kn. Knapp's Privy Council Cases (1829-36) (Eng.)

Kn.A.C. Knapp's Appeal Cases (Privy Council (1829-36) (Eng.)

Kn.L.G.R. Knight's Local Government Reports (Eng.)

Kn.N.S.W. Knox's New South Wales Reports

Kn.P.C. Knapp's Privy Council Cases (Eng.)

Kn.& Moo. 3 Knapp's Privy Council Reports (Eng.)

Kn.& O. Knapp & Ombler's English Election Reports (1834-35)

Kn.& Omb. Knapp & Ombler's Election Cases (Eng.)

Knapp. Knapp's Privy Council Reports (Eng.) (12 Eng. Reprint)

Knapp P.C.C.(Eng.) Knapp's Privy Council Reports (Eng.) (12 Eng. Reprint)

Knapp & O. Knapp & Ombler's Election Cases (Eng.)

Knight, Mech.Dict. Knight's American Mechanical Dictionary

Knight's Ind. Knight's Industrial Reports

Knowles Knowles' Reports (3 Rhode Island)

Knox Knox, New South Wales Reports (1877)

Knox & F. Knox & Fitzhardinge (N.S. Wales)

Knox & Fitz. Knox & Fitzhardinge (N. S. Wales)

Koch Koch's Supreme Court Decisions (Ceylon)

Kolze Transvaal Reports by Kolze

Konst.Rat.App. Konstam's Rating Appeals (1904-08)

Konst.& W.Rat.App. Konstam's & Ward Rating Appeals (1909-12)

Korea (DPR) Democratic People's Republic of Korea

Korea (Rep.) Republic of Korea

Kotze Kotze's Transvaal High Court Reports (1857-81)

Kotze & Barber Transvaal Court Reports

Kreider Kreider's Reports (1-23 Washington)

Kress   ●   Kress's Reports (166-194 Pa. State)
         ●   Kress's Reports (2-12 Pa. Superior)

Ks. Kansas Reports

Ks.L.R. Kansas Law Review

Kulp Kulp's Luzerne Legal Register Reports (Pa.)

Ky. Kentucky Supreme Court Reports (1879-1951)

Ky.Acts. Kentucky Acts

Ky.B.J. Kentucky Bar Journal

Ky.Comment'r. Kentucky Commentator

Ky.Dec. Sneed's Kentucky Decisions (2 Ky.)

Ky.L.J. Kentucky Law Journal

Ky.L.R. Kentucky Law Reporter

Ky.L.Rep. Kentucky Law Reporter

Ky.L.Rev. Kentucky Law Review

Ky.Law Rep. Kentucky Law Reporter

Ky.Op. Kentucky Court of Appeals Opinions

Ky.R.C. Kentucky Railroad Commission

Ky.Rev.Stat. Kentucky Revised Statutes (1970)

Ky.Rev.Stat.Ann. Baldwin's Kentucky Revised Statutes Annotated

Ky.Rev.Stat. & Rules Serv. Kentucky Revised Statutes and Rules Service (Baldwin)

Ky.S.B.A. Kentucky State Bar Association

Ky.S.B.J. Kentucky State Bar Journal

Ky.St.B.J. Kentucky State Bar Journal

Ky.St.Law. Morehead and Brown Digest of Statute Laws (Ky.)

Ky.W.C.Dec. Kentucky Workmen's Compensation Board Decisions

Kyd Kyd on Bills of Exchange

Kyd Aw. Kyd on Awards

Kyd Bills Kyd on Bills of Exchange

Kyd Corp. Kyd on Corporations

L

L.
- Laotian
- Lansing, Supreme Court Reports (New York, 7 vols. Law)
- Law
- Lawson, Notes of Decisions, Registration
- Limited
- Refusal to extend decision of cited case beyond precise issues involved (used in Shepard's Citations)

L.A.
- Labor Arbitration Reports
- Lawyers' Reports Annotated
- Los Angeles

L/A Letter of authority

L.A.B. Los Angeles Bar Bulletin

L.A.B.Bull. Los Angeles Bar Bulletin

LABPR Local Advisory Board Procedural Regulation (Office of Rent Stabilization. Economic Stabilization Agency) (U.S.)

L.A.C. Labour Arbitration Cases

LAFTA Latin American Free Trade Association

L.A.R. Labor Arbitration Reports (BNA)

L.Abr. Lilly's Abridgment (Eng.)

L.Alem. Law of the Alemanni

L.All. Leges Allemanni

L.Ap. Louisiana Courts of Appeal Reports

LArbG Landesarbeitsgericht--Provincial Labour Court of Appeal (Germany)

L.B.R. Lower Burma Rulings (India)

L.Bai. Leges Baiarum

L.Baivar. Law of the Bavarians

L.Boior Law of the Bavarians

L.C.
- Labor Cases
- Leading Cases
- Lord Chancellor
- Lower Canada

L.C.A. Leading Cases Annotated

L.C.B. Lord Chief Baron

L.C.C.
- Land Court Cases (New South Wales)
- London County Council

L.C.C.N.S.W. Land Court Cases (New South Wales) (1890-1921)

L.C.Cont. Langdell's Cases on the Law of Contracts

L.C.D. Ohio Lower Court Decisions

L.C.Eq. White & Tudor's Leading Cases in Equity

L.C.G. Lower Courts Gazette (Ontario)

L.C.J.
- Lord Chief Justice
- Lower Canada Jurist, Montreal (1848-91)

L.C.Jur. Lower Canada Jurist

L.C.L.J. Lower Canada Law Journal (1865-68)

L.C.L.Jo. Lower Canada Law Journal

L.C.P. Law and Contemporary Problems

L.C.R. Lower Canada Reports (1850-67)

L.C.Rep.S.Qu. Lower Canada Reports Seignorial Questions

L.C.Sales Langdell's Cases on the Law of Sales

L.C.V. League of Conservation Voters

L.C.Z. Laws of the Canal Zone

L.C.& M.Gaz. Lower Courts & Municipal Gazette (Canada)

L.Comment'y. Law Commentary

L.Ct.,Div. Law Court or Division

L.D.
- Labor Dispute
- Land Office Decisions, United States
- Law Dictionary

L.Dec. Land Office Decisions, United States

L.E. Lawyers' Edition, United States Supreme Court Reports

L.E.2d Lawyers' Edition, United States Supreme Court Reports, Second Series

LEAA Law Enforcement Assistance Administration

LEC Landed Estates Courts Commission (Eng.)

LEICSC Legal Education Institute, United States Civil Service Commission

LETS National Law Enforcement Teletype System

L.Ed. Lawyers' Edition Supreme Court Reports (United States)

L.Ed.2d. Lawyers' Edition Supreme Court Reports, Second Series

L.Ed.(U.S.) Lawyers' Edition Supreme Court Reports (United States)

L.F. ● University of Illinois Law Forum
● Law French

L.Fr. Law French

LG Landgericht--District Court (Germany)

L.G. Law Glossary

L/G Land grant

L.G.B. Local Government Board

L.G.C. Local Government Chronicle (1855)

L.G.R. ● Knight's Local Government Reports (1903)
● Local Government Reports (Eng.)
● Local Government Reports, New South Wales (Australia)

L.G.R.(Eng.) Local Government Reports (Eng.)

L.G.R.(N.S.W.) Local Government Reports (New South Wales)

L.G.R.A. Local Government Reports of Australia

L.Guard. Law Guardian

L/H Leasehold

LHA Lanham Housing Act (U.S.)

L.H.O.B. Longworth House Office Building

L.I. Legal Intelligence (Philadelphia)

L.I.A. International Union of Life Insurance Agents

LICROSS League of Red Cross Societies

L.I.E.E. Law in Eastern Europe

L.I.L. Lincoln's Inn Library

L.I.T. Life Insurance Trust

L.in Trans.Q. Law in Transition Quarterly

L.Inst.J. Law Institute Journal (Aus.)

L.Inst.J.Vict. Law Institute Journal of Victoria

L.J. ● Hall's Law Journal
● House of Lords Journal
● Law Journal
● Law Judge
● Library Journal
● Lord Justice
● New York Law Journal
● Ohio State Law Journal

L.J.Adm. Law Journal, New Series, Admiralty

L.J.Adm.N.S.(Eng.) Law Journal Reports, New Series, Admiralty

L.J.App. Law Journal Reports, New Series, Appeals

L.J.Bank. Law Journal Reports, Bankruptcy

L.J.Bank.N.S. Law Journal Reports, New Series, Bankruptcy

L.J.Bankr. Law Journal Reports, Bankruptcy

L.J.Bankr.N.S.(Eng.) Law Journal Reports, New Series, Bankruptcy

L.J.Bcy. Law Journal Reports, New Series, Bankruptcy

L.J.Bk. Law Journal Reports, Bankruptcy

L.J.C. Law Journal Reports, New Series, Common Pleas (Eng.)

L.J.C.C. Law Journal, County Courts Reporter

L.J.C.C.A. Law Journal Newspaper County Court Appeals

L.J.C.C.R. Law Journal Reports, New Series, Crown Cases Reserved (Eng.)

L.J.C.P. Law Journal Reports, Common Pleas Decisions (Eng.)

L.J.C.P.(Eng.) Law Journal Reports, Common Pleas Decisions (Eng.)

L.J.C.P.(O.S.) Law Journal Common Pleas Old Series (Eng.)

L.J.C.P.D. Law Journal Reports, Common Pleas Decisions (Eng.)

L.J.C.P.N.S.(Eng.) Law Journal Reports, Common Pleas, New Series

L.J.Ch. Law Journal Reports, New Series, Chancery

L.J.Ch.(Eng.) Law Journal Reports, New Series, Chancery

L.J.Ch.(O.S.) Law Journal Reports, Chancery, Old Series (1822-31) (Eng.)

L.J.Ch.N.S.(Eng.) Law Journal Reports, New Series, Chancery

L.J.D.& M. Law Journal Reports, New Series, Divorce & Matrimonial (Eng.)

L.J.Ecc. Law Journal Reports, New Series, Ecclesiastical Cases

L.J.Eccl. Law Journal Reports, New Series, Ecclesiastical Cases

L.J.Ex. Law Journal Reports, New Series, Exchequer Division (Eng.)

L.J.Ex.D. Law Journal Reports, New Series, Exchequer Division (Eng.)

L.J.Ex.Eq. Law Journal, Exchequer in Equity (Eng.)

L.J.Exch. Law Journal Reports, New Series, Exchequer Division (Eng.)

L.J.Exch.(Eng.) Law Journal Reports, New Series, Exchequer Division (Eng.)

L.J.Exch.(O.S.) Law Journal Reports, Exchequer, Old Series

L.J.Exch.in Eq.(Eng.) English Law Journal, Exchequer in Equity

L.J.Exch.N.S.(Eng.) Law Journal Reports, New Series, Exchequer Division (Eng.)

L.J.H.L. Law Journal Reports, New Series, House of Lords (Eng.)

L.JJ. Lord Justices

L.J.K.B. Law Journal Reports, King's Bench

L.J.K.B.(Eng.) Law Journal Reports, King's Bench

L.J.K.B.(N.S.) Law Journal Reports, King's Bench, New Series (1822-1949) (Eng.)

L.J.K.B.N.S.(Eng.) Law Journal Reports, King's Bench, New Series

L.J.K.B.N.S. Law Journal Reports, King's Bench, New Series

L.J.L.C. Law Journal (Lower Canada)

L.J.L.T. Law Journal (Law Tracts) (Eng.)

L.J.M.C. Law Journal Reports, New Series, Magistrates' Cases (Eng.)

L.J.M.C.O.S. Law Journal Reports, Old Series, Magistrates' Cases (Eng.)

L.J.M.Cas. Law Journal Reports, New Series, Magistrates' Cases (Eng.)

L.J.M.P.A. Law Journal Reports, Matrimonial, Probate and Admiralty (Eng.)

L.J.M.& W. Morgan & Williams' Law Journal (1803-04) (London)

L.J.Mag. Law Journal New Series Common Law, Magistrates Cases (discontinued)

L.J.Mag.Cas.(Eng.) Law Journal Reports, Magistrates' Cases

L.J.Mag.Cas.N.S.(Eng.) Law Journal Reports, Magistrates' Cases, New Series

L.J.Mat.(Eng.) Law Journal, Matrimonial (Eng.)

L.J.Mat.Cas. Law Journal, New Series, Divorce and Matrimonial (Eng.)

L.J.N.C. Law Journal, Notes of Cases

L.J.N.C.(Eng.) Law Journal, Notes of Cases (Eng.)

L.J.N.C.C.A. Law Journal Newspaper, County Court Appeals (Eng.)

L.J.N.C.C.R. The Law Journal Newspaper County Court Reports (1934-47) (Eng.)

L.J.N.S. Law Journal, New Series (1832-49) (Eng.)

L.J.News (Eng.) Law Journal Newspaper

L.J.O.S. The Law Journal, Old Series (1822-31) (London)

L.J.O.S.C.P. Law Journal, Old Series, Common Pleas (1822-31)

L.J.O.S.Ch. Law Journal, Old Series, Chancery (1822-23)

L.J.O.S.Ex. Law Journal, Old Series, Exchequer (1830-31)

L.J.O.S.K.B. Law Journal, Old Series, King's Bench (1822-31)

L.M.O.S.M.C. Law Journal, Old Series, Magistrates' Cases (1826-31)

L.J.P. • Law Journal Reports, New Series, Privy Council (Eng.)
        • Law Journal Reports, Probate, Divorce, Admiralty (Eng.)

L.J.P.C. Law Journal Reports, Privy Council (Eng.)

L.J.P.C.(Eng.) Law Journal Reports, Privy Council (Eng.)

L.J.P.C.N.S. Law Journal Reports, New Series, Privy Council (Eng.)

L.J.P.D.& A.(Eng.) Law Journal Reports, New Series, Probate, Divorce, and Admiralty (Eng.)

L.J.P.D.& Adm. Law Journal Reports, New Series, Probate, Divorce, and Admiralty (Eng.)

L.J.P.M.& A. Law Journal Reports, New Series, Probate, Matrimonial, & Admiralty (Eng.)

L.J.P.& M. Law Journal Probate & Matrimonial (Eng.)

L.J.Prob.(Eng.) Law Journal Probate & Matrimonial (Eng.)

L.J.Prob.N.S.(Eng.) Law Journal, Probate, & Matrimonial, New Series (Eng.)

L.J.Prob.& Mat. Law Journal Probate & Matrimonial (Eng.)

L.J.Q.B. Law Journal Reports, New Series, Queen's Bench (Eng.)

L.J.Q.B.(Eng.) Law Journal Reports, New Series, Queen's Bench (Eng.)

L.J.Q.B.D. Law Journal Reports, New Series, Queen's Bench Division (Eng.)

L.J.Q.B.D.N.S. Law Journal Reports, New Series, Queen's Bench Division (Eng.)

L.J.Q.B.N.S.(Eng.) Law Journal Reports, Queen's Bench, New Series

L.J.R. Law Journal Reports (1823-1949)

L.J.R.(Eng.) Law Journal Reports

L.J.Rep. Law Journal Reports

L.J.Rep.N.S. Law Journal Reports, New Series

L.J.Sm. Smith's Law Journal (London)

L.J.U.C. Law Journal of Upper Canada

L.Jo. Law Journal Newspaper (Eng.)

LKartB Landeskartellbehorde--Provincial Cartel Authority (Germany)

L.L. ● Used in citing old collections of statute law, as LL.Hen.I.
● Law Latin
● Law Library (Philadelphia), reprint of English treatises

LL.Aluredi. Laws of Alfred

LL.Athelst. Laws of Athelstan

LL.B Bachelor of Law

LL.Burgund Laws of the Burgundians

LL.C.M. Master of Comparative Laws

LL.Canuti R. Laws of King Canute

LL.D. Doctor of law

LL.Edw.Conf. Laws of Edward the Confessor

LL.Wm.Conq. Laws of William the Conqueror

LL.Hen.I. Laws of Henry I

LL.Inae. Laws of Ina

L.L.J. ● Lahore Law Journal (India)
● Labor Law Journal
● Law Library Journal (U.S.)

LL.L. Licentiate of Laws

LL.Longobard Laws of the Lombards

LL.M. Master of law

LL.Malcom, R.Scott. Laws of Malcolm, King of Scotland

L.L.N.S. Law Library, New Series, Philadelphia Reprint of English Treatises

LL.Neapolit. Laws of Naples

L.L.R. Leader Law Reports (S. Africa)

L.L.T. Lahore Law Times (India)

LL.Wisegotho. Laws of the Visigoths

LL.Wm.Noth. Laws of William the Bastard

L.Lat. Law Latin

L.Lib.J. Law Library Journal

L.M. Law Magazine, London (1828-1915)

L.M.R.A. Labor Management Relations Act

LMSA Labor Management Services Administration

L.M.& L.R. Law Magazine and Law Review (London)

L.M.& P. Lowndes, Maxwell, & Pollock's Rep., Bail Court & Practice (1850-51) (Eng.)

L.Mag. Law Magazine, London (1828-1915)

L.Mag.& L.R. Law Magazine and Law Review (London)

L.Mag.& Rev. Law Magazine & Review (London)

L.N. ● Law Notes, London
● Law Notes, a periodical published by Edward Thompson Company (Northport, Long Island, New York)

- League of Nations
- Legal News (Canada)
- Liber Niger, or the Black Book

L.N.T.S. League of Nations Treaty Series

L.O.
- Legal Observer (1831-56)
- Solicitor's Law Opinion (U. S. Internal Revenue Bureau)

LORAN Long-range navigation

L.Off.Econ.& Man. Law Office Economics & Management

L.P.B. Paper Book of Laurence, J., in Lincoln's Inn Library

L.P.R. Lilly's Practical Register (1745)

L.Q.R. Law Quarterly Review (1885)

L.Q.Rev.
- Law Quarterly Review
- Law Reporter (see List of Anglo-American Legal Periodicals)
- Law Reporter (Law Times Reports, N.S.)
- Law Reports

L.R.
- Law Recorder (1827-38) (Ir.)
- Ohio Law Reporter
- Law Reports (Eng.)
- New Zealand Law Reports
- Alabama Law Review
- Louisiana Reports

L.R.A. Lawyers' Reports Annotated

L.R.A.C. English Law Reports, Appeal Cases

L.R.A.N.S. Lawyers' Reports Annotated, New Series

L.R.A.& E. English Law Reports, Admiralty and Ecclesiastical (1866-75)

L.R.Adm.& Eccl.(Eng.) Law Reports, Admiralty & Ecclesiastical

L.R.App. English Law Reports, Appeal Cases, House of Lords

L.R.App.Cas. English Law Reports, Appeal Cases, House of Lords

L.R.App.Cas.(Eng.) English Law Reports, Appeal Cases, House of Lords

LRB Loyalty Review Board (U.S.)

L.R.B.G.
- Law Reports, British Guiana (1890-1955)
- Reports of Decisions, British Guiana

L.R.Burm. Law Reports (British Burma)

L.R.Burma Law Reports (Burma, 1948)

L.R.C.A. Law Reports, Court of Appeals (New Zealand)

L.R.C.C. English Law Reports, Crown Cases Reserved (1865-75) 2 vols.

L.R.C.C.(Eng.) English Law Reports, Crown Cases Reserved (1865-75) 2 vols.

L.R.C.C.R. Law Reports, Crown Cases Reserved (Eng.)

L.R.C.P. Law Reports, Common Pleas, England (1865-75)

L.R.C.P.(Eng.) Law Reports, Common Pleas (Eng.)

L.R.C.P.D. English Law Reports, Common Pleas Division (Eng.)

L.R.C.P.Div.(Eng.) English Law Reports, Common Pleas Division (Eng.)

L.R.Ch. Law Reports, Chancery Appeal Cases (Eng.)

L.R.Ch.(Eng.) Law Reports, Chancery Appeal Cases (Eng.)

L.R.Ch.App. Chancery Appeal Cases (1865-75)

L.R.Ch.D. English Law Reports, Chancery Division

L.R.Ch.D.(Eng.) Law Reports, Chancery Division, English Supreme Court of Judicature

L.R.Ch.Div.(Eng.) Law Reports, Chancery Division, English Supreme Court of Judicature

L.R.Cr.Cas.Res. Law Reports Crown Cases Reserved (Eng.)

L.R.E.A. Law Reports, East Africa

L.R.E.& I.App. Law Reports, House of Lords (English & Irish Appeals) (1866-75)

L.R.Eq. English Law Reports, Equity (1866-75)

L.R.Eq.(Eng.) English Law Reports, Equity (1866-75)

L.R.Ex. English Law Reports, Exchequer (1866-75)

L.R.Ex.Cas. English Law Reports, Exchequer (1866-75)

L.R.Ex.D. Law Reports, Exchequer Division (1865-75)

L.R.Ex.Div. English Law Reports, Exchequer Division

L.R.Exch. English Law Reports, Exchequer (1866-75)

L.R.Exch.D. English Law Reports, Exchequer Division

L.R.Exch.Div.(Eng.) English Law Reports, Exchequer Division

L.R.Exch.(Eng.) English Law Reports, Exchequer (1866-75)

L.R.H.L. Law Reports, English & Irish Appeals & Peerage Claims, House of Lords (Eng.)

L.R.H.L.(Eng.) Law Reports, English & Irish Appeals & Peerage Claims, House of Lords (Eng.)

L.R.H.L.Sc. English Law Reports, House of Lords, Scotch and Divorce Appeal Cases (1866-75)

L.R.H.L.Sc.App.Cas.(Eng.) English Law Reports, House of Lords, Scotch and Divorce Appeal Cases (1866-75)

L.R.I.A. English Law Reports, Indian Appeals

L.R.Ind.App. English Law Reports, Indian Appeals (1872-1950)

L.R.Ind.App.Supp. English Law Reports, Indian Appeals Supplement

L.R.Indian App. English Law Reports, Indian Appeals

L.R.Indian App.(Eng.) English Law Reports, Indian Appeals

L.R.Ir. Law Reports, Ireland (1877-93)

L.R.K.B. English Law Reports, King's Bench Division

L.R.M. Labor Relations Reference Manual

L.R.Mad. Indian Law Reports, Madras Series

L.R.Misc.D. Law Reports, Miscellaneous Division

L.R.N.S.   ● Irish Law Recorder, New Series

          ● Nova Scotia Law Reports

L.R.N.S.W. Law Reports, New South Wales Supreme Court

L.R.N.Z. Law Reports (New Zealand)

L.R.P. English Law Reports, Probate Division

L.R.P.C. English Law Reports, Privy Council, Appeal Cases (1866-75)

L.R.P.C.(Eng.) English Law Reports, Privy Council, Appeal Cases (1866-75)

L.R.P.Div. English Law Reports, Probate, Divorce, and Admiralty Division

L.R.P.& D. Probate and Divorce Cases (1865-75) (Eng.)

L.R.P.& M. Law Reports, Probate and Matrimonial (1866-75)

L.R.Prob.Div. English Law Reports, ports, Probate, Divorce, and Admiralty Division

L.R.Prob.Div.(Eng.) English Law Reports, Probate, Divorce, and Admiralty Division

L.R.Prob.& M.(Eng.) English Law Reports, Probate, Divorce, and Admiralty Division

L.R.Q.B.   ● English Law Reports, Queen's Bench (1866-75)

          ● Quebec Reports, Queen's Bench (Canada)

L.R.Q.B.D. English Law Reports, Queen's Bench Division (1865-75)

L.R.Q.B.Div. English Law Reports, Queen's Bench Division

L.R.Q.B.Div.(Eng.) English Law Reports, Queen's Bench Division

L.R.Q.B.(Eng.) English Law Reports, Queen's Bench (1866-75)

L.R.R. Labor Relations Reporter (B.N.A.)

L.R.R.M.   ● Labor Relations Reference Manual (BNA)

          ● Labor Relations Reporter: Labor-Management Relations

L.R.R.P.C. Restrictive Practices Cases (Eng.) 1958

L.R.S.A. Law Reports (South Australia)

L.R.S.C. Law Reports, New Zealand Supreme Court

L.R.S.& D.App. Law Reports, Scotch and Divorce Appeals (1866-75)

L.R.Sc.App. Law Reports, Scotch Appeals

L.R.Sc.Div.App. Law Reports, Scotch Appeals

L.R.Sc.& D. English Law Reports, Scotch and Divorce Cases, before the House of Lords

L.R.Sc.& D.App. Scottish and Divorce Cases, before the House of Lords

L.R.Sc.& D.App. Scottish and Divorce Appeals (1866-75)

L.R.Sc.& Div. Scotch and Divorce Appeals (1866-75)

L.R.Sess.Cas. English Law Reports, Sessions Cases

L.R.Stat. English Law Reports, Statutes

L.Rec.O.S. Law Recorder (Ire.) 1st Series, 4 vols.

L.Rep.Mont. Law Reporter (Montreal)

L.Repos. Law Repository

L.Rev. The Law Review (Eng.)

L.Rev.U.Detroit Law Review, University of Detroit

L.Rev.& Quart.J. Law Review and Quarterly Journal (London)

L.Ripuar. Law of the Ripuarians

L.S. Locus sigilli (the place of the seal)

LSA.R.S. West's Louisiana Revised Statutes

L.S.A.T. (U.S.) Law School Admission Test

LSB Louisiana State Bar

L.S.G. Law Society Gazette (Eng.)

L.S.Gaz. Law Society's Gazette (1903)

LSU Institute of Continuing Legal Education, Louisiana State University Law Center

L.Salic. Salic Law

L.Soc.Gaz. Law Society's Gazette

L.Soc.J. Law Society Journal

L.Stu.Mag.N.S. Law Student's Magazine, New Series

L.T. ● Law Times Journal
● Law Times Reports, London
● Law Times, Scranton, Pennsylvania

L.T.B. Law Times Bankruptcy Reports (U.S.)

L.T.(Eng.) Law Times Journal (Eng.)

L.T.J. Law Times Journal (a newspaper)

L.T.Jo.(Eng.) Law Times Journal (a newspaper)

L.T.N.S. ● Law Times, New Series (Pa.)
● Law Times Reports, New Series (Eng.)

L.T.N.S.(Eng.) Law Times, New Series

L.T.O.S. Law Times Reports, Old Series (1843-59) (Eng.)

L.T.R. Law Times Reports (1859-47) (Eng.)

L.T.R.A. Lands Tribunal Rating Appeals (1950)

L.T.R.N.S. Law Times Reports, New Series (1854-1947) (Eng.)

L.T.Rep.N.S. Law Times Reports, New Series (Eng.)

L.T.T. Land title trust

L.Th. La Themis (Lower Canada)

L.Trans.Q. Law in Transition Quarterly

LUSL Loyola University School of Law

L.V.R. Land and Valuation Court Reports (New South Wales)

L.V.Rep. Lehigh Valley Law Reporter (Pa. 1885-87)

L.W. Law Weekly, Madras (India)

L.W.L.R. Land and Water Law Review

L.W.R. Land and Water Law Review

LWV League of Women Voters

L.& A. Leembruggen & Asirvatham's Appeal Court Reports (Ceylon)

L.& B. Leadam & Baldwin's Select Cases before the King's Council (Eng.)

L.& B.Bull. Daily Law & Bank Bulletin (Ohio)

L.& B.Prec. Leake & Bullen's Precedents of Pleading

L.& C. Leigh & Cave, English Crown Cases Reserved (1861-65)

L.& C.C.C. Leigh & Cave, English Crown Cases Reserved

L.& Contemp.Prob. Law and Contemporary Problems

L.& E. English Law and Equity Reports

L.& E.Rep. English Law & Equity Reports (American reprint)

L.& G.t.P.Lloyd & Goold. Selection of Irish Chancery Cases, tempore, Plunkett

L.& G.t.Plunk. Lloyd & Goold's Irish Chancery Reports tempore Plunkett (1834-39)

L.& G.t.S. Lloyd & Goold. Irish Chancery Reports tempore Sugden

L.& G.t.Sug. Lloyd & Goold's Irish Chancery Reports temp. Sugden (1835)

L.& Legis.in G.D.R. Law and Legislation in the German Democratic Republic

L.& M. Lowndes & Maxwell's English Practice Cases (1852-54)

L.& Pol.Int'l.Bus. Law and Policy in International Business

L.& Soc.Order Law & the Social Order

L.& T. Longfield & Townsend, Irish Exchequer Reports (1841-42)

L.& W. Lloyd and Welsby's Commercial and Mercantile Cases (1829-30) (Eng.)

La.   ● Lane, English Exchequer Reports (1605-12)

● Louisiana Reports

● Louisiana Supreme Court Reports

La.A.(Orleans) Louisiana Court of Appeals (Parish of Orleans)

La.Acts State of Louisiana: Acts of the Legislature

La.An. Lawyers' Reports, Annotated

La.Ann. Louisiana Annual Reports

La.App. Louisiana Courts of Appeal Reports

La.App.(Orleans) Court of Appeals, Parish of Orleans Reports

La.B.A. Louisiana Bar Association

La.B.J. Louisiana Bar Journal

La.Civ.Code Ann.(West) West's Louisiana Civil Code Annotated

La.Code Civ.Pro.Ann. West's Louisiana Code of Civil Procedure Annotated

La.Code Crim.Pro.Ann. West's Louisiana Code of Criminal Procedure Annotated

La.L.J.   ● Louisiana Law Journal (New Orleans)

● Louisiana Law Journal (Schmidt's), (New Orleans, 1842)

La.L.R. Louisiana Law Review

La.L.Rev. Louisiana Law Review

La.P.S.C. Louisiana Public Service Commission Reports

La.R.C. Louisiana Railroad Commission

La.Rev.Stat.Ann.(West) West's Louisiana Revised Statutes Annotated

La.Sess.Law Serv. Louisiana Session Law Service

La.T.R. Louisiana Term Reports (3-12 Martin's Louisiana)

La Them.L.C. La Themis (Lower Canada)

Lab.   ● Labatt's District Court Reports (California 1857-58)

● Labor

Lab.Arb.   ● Labor Arbitration

● Labor Arbitration Reports (BNA)

Lab.Arb.Awards Labor Arbitration Awards (CCH)

Lab.Arb.Serv. Labor Arbitration Service

Lab.Arb.& Disp.Settl. Labor Arbitration and Dispute Settlements

Lab.Cas. Labor Cases

Lab.Gaz. Labour Gazette

Lab.L.J. Labor Law Journal

Lab.L.Rep. Labor Law Reporter (CCH)

Lab.Rel.Rep. Labor Relations Reporter (BNA)

Labor C. Labor Code

Labor L.J. Labor Law Journal

Labor Law J. Labor Law Journal

Lac.Jur. Lackawanna Jurist (Pa.)

Lac.R.R.Dig. Lacey, Digest of Railroad Decisions

Lacey Dig. Lacey's Digest Railway Decisions

Lack.Bar. Lackawanna Bar (Pa.)

Lack.Bar.R. Lackawanna Bar Reporter (Pa.)

Lack.Co.(Pa.) Lackawanna County Reports

Lack.Jur. Lackawanna Jurist (Pa.)

Lack.L.N. Lackawanna Legal News (Pa.)

Lack.L.R. Lackawanna Legal Record (Pa.)

Lack.Leg.N. Lackawanna Legal News (Pa.)

Lack.Leg.News (Pa.) Lackawanna Legal News

Lack.Leg.Rec. Lackawanna Legal Record (Pa.)

Ladd. Ladd's Reports (59-64 New Hampshire)

Lah. Indian Law Reports, Lahore (1920-47)

Lah.Cas. Lahore Cases (India)

Lah.L.J. Lahore Law Journal (India)

Lah.L.T. Lahore Law Times (India)

Lalor. Lalor's Supplement to Hill & Denio's New York Reports

Lalor,Pol.Econ. Lalor, Cyclopaedia of Political Science, Political Economy, etc.

Lalor,Supp. Lalor's Supplement to Hill & Denio's Reports (N.Y.)

Lamar. Lamar's Reports (25-40 Florida)

Lamb.
- Lambard's Archainomia, 1568
- Lambard's Eirenarcha; many editions (1581-1619)
- Lamb's Reports (103-105 Wisconsin)

Lamb.Arch. Lambard's Archaionomia

Lamb.Archaion. Lambard's Archaionomia

Lamb.Const. Lambard, Duties of Constables, etc.

Lamb.Eir. Lambard's Eirenarcha

Lamb.Eiren. Lambard's Eirenarcha

Lamb.Explic. Lambard's Explication

Lanc.Bar Lancaster Bar (Pa. 1869-83)

Lanc.L.Rev. Lancaster Law Review

Lanc.Rev. Lancaster Review (Pa.)

Land App.Ct.Cas. Land Appeal Court Cases, N.S.W. (Aus.)

Land Com.Rep. Land Reports, by Roche, Dillon, & Kehoe (1881-82) (Ir.)

Land Dec. Land Decisions, U.S.

Land.Est.C. Landed Estate Court (Eng.)

Land & Water L.Rev. Land & Water Law Review

Lane Lane's Exchequer Reports (Eng.) (1605-12)

Lang. Language

Lang.Ca.Cont. Langdell's Cases on the Law of Contracts

Lang.Ca.Sales. Langdell's Cases on Law of Sales

Lang.Cont.
- Langdell's Cases on Contracts
- Langdell's Summary of the Law of Contracts

Lang.Eq.Pl.
- Langdell's Cases in Equity Pleading
- Langdell's Summary of Equity Pleading

Lang.Sales Langdell's Cases on the Law of Sales

Lang.Sum.Cont. Langdell's Summary of the Law of Contracts

Langd.Cont. Langdell's Cases on Contracts;—Langdell's Summary of the Law of Contracts

Lans. Lansing's Supreme Court Reports (N.Y. 1869-73)

Lans.Ch. Lansing's Select Cases, Chancery (N.Y. 1824, 1826)

Lans.Sel.Cas. Lansing's Select Cases, Chancery (N.Y. 1824, 1826)

Lap.Dec. Laperriere's Speaker's Decisions (Canada)

Las Partidas Las Siete Partidas

Lat. Latch's King's Bench Reports (1625-28) (Eng.)

Latch Latch's King's Bench (1625-28) (Eng.)

Lath. Lathrop's Reports (115-145 Massachusetts)

Lathrop. Lathrop's Reports (115-145 Massachusetts)

Lauder Fountainhall's Session Cases (Scotland) (1678-1712)

Laur.H.C.Ca. Lauren's High Court Cases (S.Africa)

Law.
- Alabama Lawyer
- Law (1st word)
- Lawyer(s)('s)
- The Law, London (periodical)

Law Alm. Law Almanac (New York)

Law Am.Jour. Law Amendment Journal (1855-58)

Law Bk.Rev.Dig. Law Book Review Digest & Current Legal Bibliography

Law Bul. Law Bulletin

Law Bul.Ia. Law Bulletin, State University of Iowa

Law Bul.& Br.   Law Bulletin & Brief

Law Cas.Wm.I.   Law Cases, William I to Richard I (Eng.)

Law Chr.   Law Chronicle (1811-12) and (1854-58)

Law Chr.& Auct.Rec.   Law Chronicle & Auction Record

Law Chr.& Jour.Jur.   Law Chronicle & Journal of Jurisprudence

Law Cl.   Law Clerk (periodical)

Law Coach.   Law Coach (Cambridge) (Eng.)

Law.Con.   Lawson on Contracts

Law Dept.Bull.   Law Department Bulletin, Union Pacific Railroad Co.

Law Dig.   Law Digest, London (periodical)

Law.Ed.   Lawyer's Edition, United States Supreme Court Reports

Law Ex.J.   Law Examination Journal (1869-85)

Law Ex.Rep.   Law Examination Reporter

Law Fr.Dict.   Law French Dictionary

Law Gaz.   Law Gazette

Law.Guild Rev.   Lawyers' Guild Review

Law Inst.J.   Law Institute Journal

Law Int.   Law Intelligencer (U.S.)

Law J.   ● Law Journal (periodical)
        ● Law Journal Reports

Law J.Ch.   Law Journal, New Series, Chancery

Law J.Exch.   Law Journal, New Series, Exchequer

Law J.I.B.   Law Journal, New Series, English Queen's Bench

Law J.P.D.   Law Journal, Probate Division

Law J.Q.B.   Law Journal, New Series, Queen's Bench, England

Law J.R.,Q.B.   Law Journal, New Series, Queen's Bench, England

Law Jour.   Law Journal Reports

Law Jour.(M.& W.)   Morgan & Williams, Law Journal (London)

Law Jour.(Smith's)   J.P. Smith, Law Journal (London)

Law.L.J.   Lawrence Law Journal (Pa.)

Law Lat.Dict.   Law Latin Dictionary

Law Lib.   Law Library (Philadelphia)

Law Lib.J.   Law Library Journal

Law Lib.N.   Law Library News

Law Lib.N.S.   Law Library, New Series (Philadelphia)

Law Libn.   Law Librarian

Law Mag.   Law Magazine (1828-1915)

Law Mag.& R.   Law Magazine and Review

Law Mag.& Rev.   Law Magazine and Review

Law N.   Law Notes (London or Northport, N.Y.)

Law Notes   Law Notes (London or Northport, N.Y.)

Law of Trusts, Tiff.& Bul.   Tiffany and Bullard on Trusts and Trustees

Law Pat.Dig.   Law's Digest of United States Patent Cases

Law Q.Rev.   Law Quarterly Review

Law Quar.Rev.   Law Quarterly Review (London)

Law Quart.Rev.   Law Quarterly Review (London)

Law Rec.   Law Recorder (1827-31) (Ir.)

Law Reg.   ● Law Register, Chicago
        ● American Law Register, Philadelphia

Law Reg.Cas.   Lawson's Registration Cases (Eng.)

Law Rep.   ● Law Reporter (Eng.)
        ● Law Reporter (Ramsey & Morin), Canada
        ● Law Reports (Eng.)
        ● Louisiana Reports
        ● New Zealand Law Reports
        ● Ohio Law Reporter

Law Rep.(Tor.)   Law Reporter (Toronto)

Law Rep.A.& E.   Law Reports, Admiralty and Eccesiastical

Law Rep.App.Cas.   Law Reports, Appeal Cases

Law Rep.C.C.   Law Reports, Crown Cases

Law Rep.C.P.   Law Reports, Common Pleas

Law Rep.C.P.D.   Law Reports, Common Pleas Division

Law Rep.Ch.   Law Reports, Chancery Appeal cases

Law Rep.Ch.D.   Law Reports, Chancery Division

Law Rep.Eq.   Law Reports, Equity Cases

Law Rep.Ex. Law Reports, Exchequer

Law Rep.Ex.D. Law Reports, Exchequer Division

Law Rep.H.L. Law Reports, House of Lords, English and Irish Appeal Cases

Law Rep.H.L.Sc. Law Reports, Scotch and Divorce Appeal Cases, House of Lords

Law Rep.Ind.App. Law Reports, Indian Appeals

Law Rep.Ir. Law Reports, Irish

Law Rep.Misc.D. Law Reports, Miscellaneous Division

Law Rep.N.S. Law Reports, New Series (N.Y.)

Law Rep.P.C. Law Reports, Privy Council, Appeal Cases

Law Rep.P.& D. Law Reports, Probate and Divorce Cases

Law Rep.Q.B. Law Reports, Queen's Bench

Law Rep.Q.B.D. Law Reports, Queen's Bench Division

Law Repos. Carolina Law Repository

Law Rev. Law Review

Law Rev.Comm. Law Revision Commission

Law Rev.Qu. Law Review Quarterly (Albany, N.Y.)

Law Rev.U.Det. Law Review University of Detroit

Law Rev.& Qu.J. Law Review & Quarterly Journal

Law Ser.Mo.Bull. University of Missouri Bulletin, Law Series

Law Soc.Gaz. Law Society's Gazette (London or Regina)

Law Soc.Jo. Law Society of Massachusetts, Journal

Law Soc'y.Gaz. Law Society Gazette

Law Soc'y.J. Law Society Journal (New South Wales)

Law Stu. Law Student

Lw Stu.H. Law Students' Helper

Law Stud. Law Student (American Law Book Co.)

Law Stud.Mag. Law Students' Magazine

Law Stud.Mag.N.S. Law Students' Magazine, New Series

Law T. Law Times Reports

Law T.,N.S. Law Times Reports, New Series

Law T.Rep.N.S. Law Times Reports, New Series

Law T.Rep.O.S. Law Times Reports, Old Series

Law Times (London, Eng.; Scranton, Pa.)

Law Times (N.S.) Law Times, New Series (Lackawanna, Pa.)

Law Times (O.S.) Law Times, Old Series, (Luzerne, Pa.)

Law Tr. Law Tracts

Law W. Law Weekly

Law.Wheat. Lawrence's Edition of Wheaton on International Law

Law.& Bank. ● Lawyer & Banker (New Orleans)
 ● Lawyers' & Bankers' Quarterly (St. Louis)

Law & Banker Lawyer and Banker and Central Law Journal

Law & Bk.Bull. Weekly Law and Bank Bulletin (Ohio)

Law & Comtemp.Prob. Law & Contemporary Problems

Law & Contempt.Problems Law & Contemporary Problems (Duke)

Law & Eq.Rep. Law and Equity Reporter (New York)

Law.& L.N. Lawyer & Law Notes (Eng.)

Law.& Mag. Lawyer and Magistrate, Dublin (1898-99)

Law.& Mag.Mag. The Lawyer's and Magistrate's Magazine (1898-99) (Eng.)

Law & Pol'y.Int'l.Bus. Law and Policy in International Business

Law & Soc. Law and Social Change

Law & Soc.Ord. Law and the Social Order Arizona State Law Journal

Law & Soc'y.Rev. Law and Society Review

Lawes, Pl. Lawes on Pleading

Lawr. Lawrence High Court Reports, Griqualand

Lawrence Lawrence's Reports (20 Ohio)

Lawrence Comp.Dec. Lawrence's First Comptroller's Decisions

Laws Austl.Cap.Terr. Laws of the Australian Capital Territory (1911-1959), in force on 1st January, 1960

Laws.Reg.Cas. Lawson's Registration Cases, Irish (1885-1914)

Lawson,Exp.Ev. Lawson on Expert and Opinion Evidence

Lawson,Pres.Ev. Lawson on Presumptive Evidence

Lawson, Rights, Rem.& Pr. Lawson on Rights, Remedies and Practice

Lawson, Usages & Cust. Lawson on the law of Usages and Customs

Lawy. Lawyer or Lawyers'

Lawy.Mag. Lawyers' Magazine (London)

Lawy.Rev. The Lawyers' Review (Seattle, Wash.)

Lawyer & Banker Lawyer and Banker and Central Law Journal

Lawyers' Med.J. Lawyers' Medical Journal

Lawyers' Rev. The Lawyers' Review, (Seattle, Wash.)

Lay Lay's Chancery Reports (Eng.)

Ld.Birk. Lord Birkenhead's Judgments. House of Lords (Eng.)

Ld.Ken. Lord Kenyon's King's Bench Reports (1753-59) (Eng.)

Ld.Kenyon(Eng.) Lord Kenyon's King's Bench Reports, (Eng.)

Ld.Ray. Lord Raymond's Reports (1694-1732)

Ld.Raym. Lord Raymond's King's Bench & Common Pleas Reports (1694-1732)

Le Mar. Le Marchant's Gardner Peerage Case

Le.& Ca. Leigh & Cave's Crown Cases Reserved (1861-65) (Eng.)

Lea. Lea's Tennessee Reports

Leach. Leach's English Crown Cases (1730-1815)

Leach C.C. Leach's Crown Cases, King's Bench (Eng.)

Leach C.L. Leach, Cases in Crown Law

Leach Cl.Cas. Leach's Club Cases (London)

Leach,Cr.Cas. Leach's English Crown Cases

Lead. Leader Law Reports (Ceylon)

Lead.Cas.Am. American Leading Cases, by Hare & Wallace

Lead.Cas.Eq. Leading Cases in Equity, by White and Tudor

Lead Cas.In.Eq.(Eng.) Leading Cases in Equity, by White and Tudor

Leadam Leadam's Select Cases before King's Council in the Star Chamber (Selden Society Publications, v. 16, 25)

Leadam Req. Select Cases in the Court of Requests. Ed. by I.S. Leadam (Selden Society Publications, vol. 12)

League of Nations O.J. League of Nations Official Journal

League of Nations O.J.,Spec.Supp. League of Nations Official Journal, Special Supplement

League of Nations Off.J. League of Nations Official Journal

Leake ● Leake on Contracts, 8 editions (1861-1931)
     ● Leake's Digest of the Law of Property in Land

Leake, Cont. Leake on Contracts

Leam.& Spic. Leaming and Spicer's Laws, Grants, Concessions and Original Constitutions (N.J.)

Lebanon Lebanon County Legal Journal (Pa.)

Lebanon Co.L.J.(Pa.) Lebanon County Legal Journal (Pa.)

Lec.El.Dr.Civ.Rom. Lecons Elementaries due Droit Civil Romain

Lec.Elm. Lecon's Elementaires du Droit Civile

Lectures L.S.U.C. Special Lectures of the Law Society of Upper Canada

Lee ● Lee's English Ecclesiastical Reports (1752-58)
     ● Lee's Reports (9-12 California)

Lee,Dict. Lee's Dictionary of Practice

Lee Eccl. Lee's Ecclesiastical (Eng.)

Lee G. Sir George Lee's English Ecclesiastical Reports

Lee t.Hard. Lee's Cases tempore Hardwicke (1733-38)

Lee t.Hardw. Lee tempore Hardwicke (1733-38) (Eng.)

Leese Leese's Reports (vol. 26 Nebraska)

Lef.Dec. Lefevre's Parliamentary Decisions, by Bourke (Eng.)

Lef.& Cas. Lefroy and Cassel's Practice Cases (1881-83) (Ontario)

Lefroy Lefroy's Railroad & Canal Cases (Eng.)

Leg. Legislature

Leg.Aid Rev. Legal Aid Review

Leg.Alfred. Leges Alfredi (laws of King Alfred.)

Leg.Bib. Legal Bibliography (Boston)

Leg.Canut. Leges Canuti (laws of King Canute or Knut)

Leg.Chron. Legal Chronicle (Foster's Pa. Reports)

Leg.Chron.Rep. Legal Chronicle Reports (Pottsville, Pa.)

Leg.Edm. Leges Edmundi (laws of King Edmund.)

Leg.Ethel. Leges Ethelredi

Leg.Exam. Legal Examiner (London or N.Y.) (1831-35); (1862-68); (1869-72)

Leg.Exam.N.S. Legal Examiner, New Series (Eng.)

Leg.Exam.W.R. Legal Examiner Weekly Reporter

Leg.Exam.& L.C. Legal Examiner & Law Chronicle (London)

Leg.Exam.& Med.J. Legal Examiner Medical Jurist (London)

Leg.Exch. Legal Exchange (Des Moines, Ia.)

Leg.G. Legal Guide

Leg.Gaz. Legal Gazette

Leg.Gaz.R. Campbell's Legal Gazette Reports (Pennsylvania 1869-71)

Leg.Gaz.Rep. Campbell's Legal Gazette Reports (Pennsylvania 1869-71)

Leg.H.I. Laws of [King] Henry the First

Leg.Inf.Bul. Legal Information Bulletin

Leg.Inq. Legal Inquirer (London)

Leg.Int. Legal Intelligencer (Philadelphia)

Leg.Misc. Legal Miscellany (Ceylon)

Leg.Misc.& Rev. Legal Miscellany & Review (India)

Leg.News Legal News (Montreal; Sunbury, Pa; Toledo, Ohio)

Leg.Notes Legal Notes on Local Government (New York)

Leg.Obs. ● Legal Observer (London)

● Legal Observer & Solicitor's Journal (London)

Leg.Oler. Laws of Oleron

Leg.Op. Legal Opinion (Harrisburg, Pa.)

Leg.Ops.(Pa.) Legal Opinions

Leg.R.(Tenn.) Legal Reporter parallel to Shannon Cas.

Leg.Rec. Legal Record (Detroit, Mich.)

Leg.Rec.Rep. Legal Record Reports (1-2 Schuykill Co. (Pa.) Legal Record Reports)

Leg.Rem. Legal Remembrancer (Calcutta)

Leg.Rep. Legal Reporter (1840-43) (Ir.)

Leg.Rep.(Ir.) Legal Reporter, Irish Courts

Leg.Rev. Legal Review (1812-13) (London)

Leg.T.Cas. Legal Tender Cases

Leg.W. Legal World (India)

Leg.Wisb. Laws of Wisbury

Leg.Y.B. Legal Year Book (London)

Leg.& Ins.Rept. Legal and Insurance Reporter (Philadelphia)

Legal Adv. ● Legal Advertiser (Chicago)

● Legal Adviser (Chicago or Denver)

Legal Gaz.(Pa.) Legal Gazette, Philadelphia

Legg. Leggett, Reports (India)

Legge. ● Legge's Reports (Australia)

● Legge's Supreme Court Cases, New South Wales (1825-62)

Legis. ● Legislation

● Legislative

Legul. The Leguleian (1850-65)

Leh.Co.L.J.(Pa.) Lehigh County Law Journal

Leh.L.J. Lehigh County Law Journal

Leh.V.L.R.(Pa.) Lehigh Valley Law Reporter

Lehigh Co.L.J. Lehigh County Law Journal (Pa.)

Lehigh Val.L.R. Lehigh Valley Law Reporter (Pa.)

Lehigh Val.L.Rep. Lehigh Valley Law Reporter (Pa.)

Lehigh Val.Law Rep. Lehigh Valley Law Reporter (Pa.)

Leigh • Leigh's Virginia Supreme Court Reports (1829-42)
  • Ley's King's Bench Reports (1608-29)

Leigh(Va.) Leigh's Virginia Supreme Court Reports (1829-42)

Leigh & C. Leigh and Cave's Crown Cases (1861-65)

Leigh & C.C.C. Leigh & Cave's Crown Cases (Eng.)

Leo. Leonard's King's Bench Reports (1540-1615) (Eng.)

Leon. Leonard's King's Bench, Common Pleas Exchequer Reports (Eng.)

Lest.P.L. Lester's Decisions in Public Land Cases

Lest.& But. Lester & Butler's Supplement to Lester's Georgia Reports

Lester. Lester's Reports (31-33 Georgia)

Lester Supp. Lester & Butler's Supplement to Lester's Georgia Reports

Lester & B. Lester & Butler's Supplement (Ga.)

Lev. Levinz's King's Bench & Common Pleas Reports (1660-97) (Eng.)

Lev.Ent. Levinz's Entries (Eng.)

Lew. • Lewin's English Crown Cases Reserved (1822-38)
  • Lewis, Missouri
  • Lewis, Nevada

Lew.C.C. Lewin's English Crown Cases

Lew.C.L. Lewis' Criminal Law

Lew.L.Cas. Lewis Leading Cases on Public Land Law

Lewin Lewin on Trusts; 15 editions (1837-1950)

Lewin C.C.(Eng.) Lewin, Crown Cases (168 Eng. Reprint)

Lewin, Cr.Cas. Lewin's English Crown Cases Reserved

Lewis • Lewis' Kentucky Law Reporter
  • Lewis' Reports (29-35 Missouri Appeals)
  • Lewis' Reports (1 Nevada)

Lewis, Em.Dom. Lewis on Eminent Domain

Lewis, Perp. Lewis' Law of Perpetuity

Lex Cust. Lex Custumaria

Lex Man. Lex Maneriorum

Lex Mer.Am. Lex Mercatoria Americana

Lex Merc.Red. Lex Mercatoria Rediviva, by Beawes

Lex Parl. Lex Parliamentaria

Ley • Ley's King's Bench Reports (1608-29) (Eng.)
  • Ley's Court of Wards Reports (Eng.)

Liab. Liability

Lib. • Liberal Party
  • Liberties
  • Library

Lib.Ass. Liber Assisarum (Year Books, Part V)

Lib.Ent. Old Books of Entries

Lib.Feud. Liber Feudorum, at the end of the Corpus Juris Civilis

Lib.Int. Liber Intrationum (Book of Entries) (1510)

Lib.Intr. Liber Intrationum, Old Book of Entries

Lib.L.& Eq. Library of Law and Equity

Lib.Nig. Liber Niger, the Black Book

Lib.Nig.Scacc. Liber Niger Scaccarii; Black Book of the Exchequer

Lib.Pl. Liber Placitandi, Book of Pleading

Lib.Plac. Lilly's Assize Reports (1688-93)

Lib.Rames. Liber Ramesiensis, Book of Ramsey

Lib.Reg. Register Books

Lib.Rub. Liber Rubens, the Red Book

Lib.Rub.Scacc. Liber Ruber Scaccarii; Red Book of the Exchequer

Liberian L. Liberian Law

Lieb.Herm. Lieber's Hermeneutics

Lieber Civ.Lib. Lieber on Civil Liberty and Self Government

Life and Acc.Ins.R. Bigelow's Life and Accident Insurance Reports

Life C. Life Cases, including Health and Accident (Insurance Case Series) (CCH)

Life Cas. Life (Health & Accident) Cases (CCH)

Life Cas.2d Life (Health & Accident) Cases (CCH), Second Series

Life & Acc.Ins.R. Bigelow. Life and Accident Insurance Reports

Lil. Lilly's English Assize Reports (1688-93)

Lil.Abr. Lilly's Abridgment

Lil.Conv. Lilly's Conveyancer

Lil.Reg. Lilly's Practical Register

Lill.Ent. Lilly's Entries (Eng.)

Lilly,Abr. Lilly's Abridgment, or Practical Register

Lilly Assize (Eng.) Lilly's Reports & Pleadings of Cases in Assize (170 Eng. Reprint)

Lincoln L.Rev. Lincoln Law Review (Buffalo)

Lind.Part. Lindley's Laws of Partnership

Lindl.Copartn. Lindley on Partnership

Lindl.Partn. Lindley on Partnerships

Lindley. Lindley's Law of Companies; 6 editions (1860-1950)

Lindley Comp. Lindley on Companies

Lindley P. Lindley on Partnership

Linn Ind. Linn's Index of Pennsylvania Reports

Linn,Laws Prov.Pa. Linn on the Laws of the Province of Pennsylvania

Lit.
- Littell's Reports (11-15 Kentucky)
- Littleton's Common Pleas Reports (1626-32) (Eng.)
- Littleton's Tenures

Lit.Brooke Brooke's New Cases, King's Bench (1515-58) (Eng.)

Lit.Sel.Ca. Littell's Select Kentucky Cases

Lit.& Bl.Dig. Littleton & Blatchley's Insurance Digest

Litt.
- Littell's Kentucky Supreme Court Reports (1822-24)
- Littleton's Common Pleas Reports (Eng.)

Litt.(Ky.) Littell

Litt.Comp.Laws Littell's Statute Law (Ky.)

Litt.Rep. Littleton

Litt.Sel.Cas. Littell's Select Cases (Ky.)

Litt.Ten. Littleton's Tenures.

Litt.& S.St.Law Littell and Swigert's Digest of Statute Law (Ky.)

Littell. Littell's Kentucky Reports

Little Brooke Brooke's New Cases (Eng.)

Littleton. Littleton's English Common Pleas and Exchequer Reports

Liv. Livingston, Mayor's Court Reports (New York)

Liv.Cas. Livingston's Cases in Error (New York)

Liv.Jud.Op.(or Cas.) Livingston, Judicial Opinions (New York)

Liv.L.Mag. Livingston's Law Magazine (New York)

Liv.L.Reg. Livingston's Law Register (New York)

Liverm.Ag. Livermore on Principal and Agent

Livermore, Ag. Livermore on Principal and Agent

Liz.Sc.Exch. Lizar's Exchequer Cases (Sc.)

Lizars Lizar's Scotch Exchequer Cases (1840-50)

Ll.L.Pr.Cas. Lloyd's List Prize Cas. (Eng.)

Ll.L.Rep. Lloyd's List Law Reports (Eng.)

Ll.List.L.R. Lloyd's List Law Reports (Eng.)

Ll.Pr.Cas. Lloyd's List Prize Cases (1914-22; 1940)

Ll.Rep. Lloyd's List Law Reports (1919)

Ll.& G.t.P. Lloyd & Goold's Irish Chancery Reports tempore Plunkett (1834-39)

Ll.& G.t.Pl. Lloyd & Goold's Irish Chancery Reports tempore Plunkett

Ll.& G.t.S. Lloyd & Goold's Irish Chancery Reports tempore Sugden (1835)

Ll.& W. Lloyd & Welsby's English Merchantile Cases (1829-30)

Ll. & Wels. Lloyd & Welsby. C.C.

Lloyd,L.R. Lloyd's Law Reports (Eng.)

Lloyd List Lloyd's List (Eng.)

Lloyd & Goold (t.Plunkett) (Ir.) Lloyd & Goold (tempore Plunkett)

Lloyd & Goold (t.Sugden) (Ir.)   Lloyd & Goold (tempore Sugden)

Lloyd & Goold   (tempore Plunkett)

Lloyd & W.   Lloyd & Welsby's English Mercantile Cases

Lloyd's List.   Lloyd's List (Daily, and weekly) (London)

Lloyd's List L.R.   Lloyd's List Law Reports (Eng.)

Lloyd's Pr.Cas.   Lloyd's Prize Case Reports (Eng.)

Lloyd's Prize Cas.   Lloyd's Prize Cases, (London)

Lloyd's Rep.   Lloyd's List Law Reports (Eng.)

Lo.L.R.   Loyola Law Review

LoN   League of Nations

Lobin.   Lobingier's Extraterritorial Cases, U.S. Court for China

Loc.Acts   Local Acts

Loc.cit.   Loco citato (in the place cited)

Loc.Code   Local Code

Loc.Ct.Gaz.   Local Courts and Municipal Gazette (Toronto, Ontario)

Loc.Gov.   Local Government (Eng.)

Loc.Govt.Chr. & Mag.Rep.   Local Government Chronicle & Magisterial Reporter (London)

Loc.Laws.   Local Laws

Local Fin.   Local Finance

Local Gov't   Local Government and Magisterial Reports (Eng.)

Local Govt.R.Austl.   Local Government Reports of Australia

Locc.de Jur.Mar.   Loccenius de Jure Maritimo

Lock.Rev.Cas.   Lockwood's Reversed Cases (N.Y.)

Locus Standi   Locus Standi Reports (Eng.)

Lofft.   Lofft. English Kings Bench Reports (1772-74)

Lofft,Append.   Lofft's Maxims, Appended to Lofft's Reports

Lofft Max.   Maxims, appended to Lofft's Reports

Lois.Rec.   Lois Recentes du Canada

Lom.C.H.Rep.   Lomas's City Hall Reporter (N.Y.)

Lom.Dig.   Lomax's Digest of Real Property

Lom.Ex.   Lomax on the Law of Executors

Lomax,Ex'rs.   Lomax on Executors

Lond.   London Encyclopedia

Lond.Gaz.   London Gazette

Lond.Jur.   London Jurist Reports (Eng.)

Lond.Jur.N.S.   London Jurist, New Series

Lond.L.M.   London Law Magazine

Long,Irr.   Long on Irrigation

Long.Q.   Long Quinto (Year Books, Part X)

Long & R.   Long & Russell's Election Cases (Mass.)

Long. & T.   Longfield & Townsend's Exchequer Reports (Ireland) (1841-42)

Lor. & Russ.   Loring & Russell's Election Cases (Mass.)

Lords Jour.   Journals, House of Lords (Eng.)

Lorenz   Lorenz's Ceylon Reports (1856-59)

Lorenz.App.R.   Lorenz's Appeal Reports (Ceylon)

Loring & Russell.   Loring & Russell's Massachusetts Election Cases

Los Angeles B.A.B.   Los Angeles Bar

Los Angeles Bd.P.U.   Los Angeles, California, Board of Public Utilities

Los Angeles L.Rev.   Los Angeles Law Review

Loss, Sec.Reg.   Loss' Security Regulations

Loss & Dam.Rev.   Loss & Damage Review

Lou.   Louisiana

Lou.L.Jour.   Louisiana Law Journal

Lou.L.Rev.   Louisiana Law Review

Lou.Leg.N.   Louisiana Legal News

Louisville Law   Louisville Lawyer

Low.   Lowell's District Court Reports (U.S., Mass. District)

Low.C.Seign.   Lower Canada Seignorial Rep.

Low.Can.   Lower Canada Reports

Low.Can.Jur.   Lower Canada Jurist (1848-91)

Low.Can.L.J.   Lower Canada Law Journal

Low.Can.R.   Lower Canada Reports

Low.Can.Rep.   Lower Canada Reports (1850-67)

Low.Can.Rep.S.Q. Lower Canada Reports, Seignorial Questions

Low.Dec.(F) Lowell's Decisions

Lowell Lowell's District Court Reports (U.S., Mass. District)

Lower Can. Lower Canada Reports

Lower Can.Jur. Lower Canada Jurist

Lower Can.S.Q. Lower Canada Reports—Seigniorial Questions

Lower Ct.Dec. Ohio Lower Court Decisions

Lown.Leg. Lowndes on Legacies

Lown.M. & P. Lowndes, Maxwell, & Pollock's English Bail Court Reports (1850-51)

Lown.& M. Lowndes & Maxwell's English Bail Court Reports (1852-54)

Lownd.M. & P. Lowndes, Maxwell, & Pollock's Bail Court Reports (1850-51) (Eng.)

Lownd. & M. Lowndes & Maxwell's Bail Court Reports (1852-54) (Eng.)

Lowndes & M. (Eng.) Lowndes & Maxwell's Bail Court Reports (1852-54) (Eng.)

Loy. Loyola

Loy.Chi.L.J. Loyola University of Chicago Law Journal

Loy.L.A.L.Rev. Loyola University of Los Angeles Law Review

Loy.L.Rev. Loyola Law Review (New Orleans)

Loy.R Loyola Law Review (La.)

Loyola Dig. Loyola Digest

Loyola L.J. Loyola Law Journal

Loyola L.Rev. Loyola Law Review

Loyola U.Chi.L.J. Loyola University of Chicago Law Journal

Loyola U.L.A.L.Rev. Loyola University of Los Angeles Law Review

Loyola U.L.J.(Chicago) Loyola University Law Review

Loyola U.L.Rev.(LA) Loyola University of Los Angeles Law Review

Ltd. Limited

Luc. Lucas' Reports (Modern Reports, Part X) (1710-25)

Lucas. Lucas' Reports (Modern Reports, Part X)

Luck.Ser. Indian Law Reports, Lucknow Series

Lud.E.C. Luder's Election Cases (Eng.)

Lud.El.Cas. Luder's Election Cases (1784-87)

Ludd. Ludden's Reports (vols. 43, 44 Maine)

Ludden. Ludden's Reports (vols. 43, 44 Maine)

Luders Elec.Cas.(Eng) Luders Election Cases

Lum.P.L.C. Lumley's Poor Law Cases (1834-42) (Eng.)

Lumplin Lumpkin's Reports (59-77 Georgia)

Lush. Lushington's English Admiralty Reports (1859-62)

Lush.Adm. Lushington's English Admiralty Reports (1859-62)

Lush Pr. Lush's Common Law Practice

Lush.Pr.L. Lushington on Prize Law

Lut. E. Lutwyche's Entries & Reports, Common Pleas (1682-1704) (Eng.)

Lut.Elec.Cas. Lutwyche's Election Cases (Eng.)

Lut.Ent. Lutwyche's Entries (1704; 1718)

Lut.R.C. Lutwyche's English Registration Appeal Cases (1843-45)

Lut.Reg.Cas. A.J.Lutwyche's Registration Cases (Eng.)

Lutw. A.J.Lutwyche's Registration Cases (Eng.)

Lutw.E. Lutwyche's English Common Pleas Reports

Lutw.Reg.Cas. Lutwyche's Registration Cases (Eng.)

Luz.L.J. Luzerne Law Journal (Pa.)

Luz.L.O. Luzerne Legal Observer (Pa.)

Luz.L.R. Luzerne Legal Register (Pa.)

Luz.L.Reg.Rep. Luzerne Legal Register Reports (Continuation of Kulp) Pa.

Luz.L.T.(N.S.). Luzerne Law Times, New Series (Pa.)

Luz.L.T.(O.S.). Luzerne Law Times, Old Series,(Pa.)

Luz.Law T. Luzerne Law Times, (Pa.)

Luz.Leg.Obs. Luzerne Legal Observer (Pa.)

Luz.Leg.Reg. Luzerne Legal Register (Pa.)

Luz.Leg.Reg.Rep. Luzerne Legal Register Reports (Pa.)

Luzerne L.J.(Pa) Luzerne Law Journal

Luzerne Leg.Obs.(Pa.) Luzerne Legal Observer

Luzerne Leg.Reg.(Pa) Luzerne Legal Register

Luzerne Leg.Reg.R.(Pa) Luzerne Legal Register Reports

Lycoming Lycoming Reporter (Pa.)

Lycoming R.(Pa.) Lycoming Reporter

Lynd. Lyndwood, Provinciale (Eng.)

Lynd.Prov. Lyndwood's Provinciales

Lyndw.Prov. Lyndwode's Provinciale

Lyne Lyne's Chancery Cases (Wallis) (1766-91) (Ir.)

M

m.   Modified; regulation or order modified (used in Shepard's Citations)

M.
- Indian Law Reports, Madras Series
- Macpherson's Session Cases (1862-73) (Sc.)
- Maine; Manitoba; Maryland; Massachusetts; Michigan; Minnesota; Mississippi; Missouri; Montana
- Menzies' Cape Colony Supreme Court Reports
- Miles' Pennsylvania Reports
- Mongolian
- Morison's Dictionary of Sessions (1540-1808) (Sc.)
- New York Miscellaneous Reports
- Ohio Miscellaneous Reports

M.(H.L.)   House of Lords' Appeals, 1862-73, in Macpherson's Court of Sessions Cases, 3d Series

M.A.
- Maritime Administration
- Medicaid
- Missouri Appeals Reports
- Munitions Tribunals Appeals, Great Britain High Court of Justice

MAC   Military Airlift Command

M.A.L.   Modern American Law

M.A.P.   Military Assistance Program

M.A.R.   Municipal Association Reports, New South Wales

M.B.
- Miscellaneous Branch, Internal Revenue Bureau (U.S.)
- Morrell's Bankruptcy Reports (Eng.)
- Munitions Board (U.S.)

M.B.A.   Master of Business Administration

MBACLE   Multnomah Bar Association Committee on Continuing Legal Education

M.B.J.   Michigan State Bar Journal

M.C.
- Magistrates' Cases (1892-1910) (Eng.)
- American Maritime Cases

- Matara Cases (Ceylon)
- Mayor's Court

M.C.C.
- Interstate Commerce Commission Reports, Motor Carrier Cases (U.S.)
- Martin's Mining Cases (British Columbia)
- Mining Commissioner's Cases (Canada)
- Mixed Claims Commission
- Moody's English Crown Cases Reserved (1824-44) (Eng.)
- Motor Carrier Cases (1936-date)
- Municipal Corporation's Chronicle (privately printed)

M.C.Cas.   Municipal Corporation Cases Annotated. 11 vols

M.C.J.   Master of Comparative Jurisprudence

M.C.J.   Michigan Civil Jurisprudence

M.C.L.
- Master of Civil Law
- Master of Comparative Law

M.C.L.A.   Michigan Compiled Laws Annotated

MCLNEL   Massachusetts Continuing Legal Education—New England Law Institute, Inc.

M.C.M.
- Manual for Courts-Martial (U.S.)
- Municipal Court of Montreal

M.C.R.
- Magistrates' Courts Reports (New Zealand)
- Montreal Condensed Reports

M'Cl.   McCleland's Exchequer Reports (Eng.) 148 Eng. Reprint

M'Cl. & Y.   McCleland & Younge's Ex. Reports (Eng.)

M'Cle.   M'Cleland's Exchequer Reports (Eng.) (148 Eng. Reprint)

M'Cle. & Yo. M'Cleland & Younge's Exchequer Reports (Eng.) (148 Eng. Reprint)

M'Clel. (Eng.) McCleland's Exchequer Reports (Eng.) (148 Eng.Reprint)

M'Clel. & Y.(Eng.) M'Cleland & Younge's Exchequer Reports (Eng.) (148 Eng.Reprint)

M'Cord.Eq.(S.C.) M'Cord, South Carolina Equity Reports

M'Cord.L.(S.C.) M'Cord, South Carolina Law Reports

M.Cr.C. Madras Criminal Cases

M.D.
- Application for writ of mandamus dismissed for want of jurisdiction
- Doctor of Medicine
- Master's Decisions (Patents)
- Middle District

M.D. & D. Montagu, Deacon, DeGex's Bankruptcy Reports (Eng.)

M.D. & DeG. Montagu, Deacon, DeGex's Bankruptcy Reports (1840-44) (Eng.)

M.Dict. Morison's Dictionary of Decisions, Scotch Court of Session

MEDLARS Medical literature analysis and retrieval system

MESA Mining Enforcement and Safety Administration

MESBIC Minority Enterprise Small Business Investment Companies

M.F.B.M. 1,000 feet board measure

M'F.R. MacFarlane, Reports, Jury Court (Sc.)

M.G. Motion for mandamus granted

M.G.L.A. Massachusetts General Laws Annotated

M.G.P. Application for mandamus granted in part

M.G. & S. Manning, Granger, & Scott's English Common Pleas Reports (1845-56)

M.H.C. Madras High Court Reports (India)

M.H.C.R. Madras High Court Reports (India)

M.H.L. Scotch Session Cases, House of Lords

M.I. Writ of mandamus will issue

M.I.A. Moore's Indian Appeals (1836-71)

MICLE The Institute of Continuing Legal Education, University of Michigan

MICPEL The Maryland Institute for Continuing Professional Education of Lawyers, Inc.

MIRV Multiple Independently Targetable Reentry Vehicles

MIT Massachusetts Institute of Technology

M.J.S. Master of Juridical Science

ML Military Laws of the United States (Army) annotated

M.L. Master of Laws

MLB Maritime Labor Board (U.S.)

M.L.Dig. & R. Monthly Law Digest & Reporter (Canada)

M.L.E. Maryland Law Encyclopedia

M.L.J.
- Madras Law Journal (India)
- Malayan Law Journal
- Memphis Law Journal

M.L.L. Master of Law Librarianship

M.L.P. Michigan Law and Practice

M.L.Q. Malabar Law Quarterly

M.L.R.
- Maryland Law Record
- Montreal Law Reports
- Modern Law Review

M.L.R.(Q.B.) Montreal Law Report (Queen's Bench)

M.L.R.Q.B. Montreal Law Reports (Queen's Bench)

M.L.R.S.C. Montreal Law Reports, Superior Court (Canada)

M.L.S. Master of Library Science

M.L.T. Madras Law Times (India)

M.L.W. Madras Law Weekly (India)

M'Laur. M'Laurin's Judiciary Cases (1774) (Sc.)

M.M.C. Martin's Reports of Mining Cases (Canada)

M.M.Cas. Martins Reports of Mining Cases (Canada)

M.M.F. Merchant Marine and Fisheries

M.M.R. Mitchell's Maritime Register (Eng.)

M'Mul.Ch.(S.C.). M'Mullan's South Carolina Equity Reports

M'Mul.Ch.S.C. M'Mullan's Equity Reports (South Carolina, 1840-42)

M'Mul.L.S.C. M'Mullan's Law Reports (S.C. 1840-42)

MNCLE Minnesota Continuing Legal Education

MNR Minister of National Revenue

M.O. ● Military Orders issued by the President as Commander in Chief of the Armed Forces

     ● Mineral Order (Defense Minerals Exploration Administration, Department of the Interior) U.S.

     ● Motion for mandamus overruled

MOB The Missouri Bar

MO-JAGA Memorandum Opinions, Judge Advocate General of the Army (U.S.)

M.P.C. Moore's Privy Council Cases (1836-73) (Eng.)

MPI Midwest Practice Institute

M.P.L. Master of Patent Law

M.P.P. Miscellaneous personal property

M.P.R. Maritime Provinces Reports (Canada)

M.Q. Massachusetts Law Quarterly

M.R. ● Application for writ of mandamus refused

     ● Manitoba Law Reports, Canada

     ● Master of the Rolls

     ● Maurititius Decisions

     ● Mauritius Reports

     ● Mining Reports (R.S. Morrison, editor; Chicago, 22 vols.)

     ● Montana Law Review

     ● Roll's Court (Eng.)

M.R.P. Application for writ of mandamus refused in part

M.R.S.A. Maine Revised Statutes Annotated

M.S. Manuscript Reports

M.S.A. ● Minnesota Statutes Annotated

     ● Mutual Security Agency (U.S.)

MSC Military Staff Committee (UN)

MSCLE Mississippi Institute of Continuing Legal Education

Ms.I.T. Manuscript, Inner Temple

Ms.L.I Manuscript, Lincoln's Inn

M.S.L.S. ● Master of Science in Law & Society

     ● Master of Science in Library Service

MS.M.T. Manuscript, Middle Temple

MSSD Model Secondary School for the Deaf

M.S.U.Business Topics. Michigan State University Business Topics

MSUCLE Missouri State University Continuing Legal Education

MT Internal Revenue Bureau (U.S.) Miscellaneous Tax Ruling

MTB Materials Transportation Bureau

MTMTS Military Traffic Management and Terminal Service

M.U.C.C. Michigan Unemployment Compensation Commission

M.U.L.R. Melbourne University Law Review

M.U.R. Montana Utilities Reports

M.V.D. ● Motor Vehicle Department

     ● Secret police of Russia

M.W.N. Madras Weekly Notes (India)

M.W.N.C.C. Madras Weekly Notes, Criminal Cases (India)

M. & A. Montague and Ayrton's Bankruptcy Reports, Eng. (1833-38)

M. & Ayr. Montague & Ayrton's Bankruptcy Reports (Eng.) (1833-38)

M. & B. Montagu and Bligh's Bankruptcy Reports, Eng. (1832-33)

M. & C. ● Montagu and Chitty's Bankruptcy Reports (1838-40)

     ● Mylne and Craig's Chancery Reports, Eng. (1836-40)

M. & C.Partidas. Moreau-Lislet and Carleton's Laws of Las Siete Partidas in force in Louisiana

M. & Cht.Bankr. Montagu & Chitty's English Bankruptcy Reports

M. & G. ● Macnaghten & Gordons Chancery Reports (1848-52) (Eng.)

     ● Maddock & Geldart's Chancery Reports (1815-22) (Eng.)

- Manning & Granger's Common Pleas Reports (1840-44) (Eng.)

M. & Gel. Maddock & Geldart's Chancery Reports (1815-22) (Eng.)

M. & Gord. Macnaghten & Gordon's Chancery Reports (1848-52) (Eng.)

M. & H. Murphy & Hurlstone's Ex. Reports (1836-37) (Eng.)

M. & K. Mylne & Keen's Chancery Reports (1832-35) (Eng.)

M. & M.
- Montagu & Macarthur's Bankruptcy Reports (1828-29) (Eng.)
- Moody & Malkin's Nisi Prius Reports (1826-30) (Eng.)

M. & M'A. Montagu & Macarthur's Bankruptcy Reports (1828-29) (Eng.)

M. & McA. Montague & McArthur's Bankruptcy (Eng.)

M. & P. Moore & Payne's Common Pleas Reports (1827-31) (Eng.)

M. & R.
- Maclean & Robinson's Appeal Cases (1839) (Sc.)
- Manning & Ryland's King's Bench Reports (1827-30) (Eng.)
- Moody & Robinson's Nisi Prius Reports (1830-44) (Eng.)

M. & R.M.C. Manning & Ryland's Magistrates Cases (1827-30) (Eng.)

M. & Rob.
- Maclean & Robinson's Appeal Cases (1839) (Sc.)
- Moody & Robinson's Nisi Prius Reports (1830-44) (Eng.)

M. & S.
- Manning & Scott's Reports (9 Common Bench) (Eng.)
- Maule & Selwyn's King's Bench Reports (1813-17) (Eng.)
- Moore & Scott's Common Pleas Reports (1831-34) (Eng.)

M. & Scott. Moore & Scott's Common Pleas Reports (1831-34) (Eng.)

M. & W. Meeson & Welsby's Exchequer Reports (1836-47) (Eng.)

M. & W.Cas. Mining & Water Cases Annotated (U.S.)

M. & Y. Martin & Yerger's Reports (8 Tenn.)

Ma.
- Malay
- Massachusetts Reports

Ma.A. Massachusetts Appeals Court Reports

Mac.
- Macassey's Reports, New Zealand (1861-72)
- Macnaghten's English Chancery Reports

Mac.C.C. MacGillivray's Copyright Cases (1901-49)

Mac.F. Macfarlane (1838-39)

Mac.G.C.C. MacGillivray's Copyright Cases (Eng.)

Mac.N.Z. Macassey's New Zealand Reports

Mac.P.C. Macrory's Patent Cases (1847-60)

Mac.Pat.Cas. Macrory's Patent Cases (Eng.)

Mac. & G. Macnaghten & Gordon's Chancery Reports (1849-51) (Eng.)

Mac. & ' I. Macrae and Hertslet's Insolvency Cases (1847-52) (Eng.)

Mac. & R. Maclean and Robinson, Appeal Cases (1839) (Sc.)

Mac. & Rob. Maclean & Robinson's Scotch Appeal Cases (1839)

Mac.A.Pat.Cas. MacArthur's Patent Cases (D.C.)

MacAr.
- MacArthur's Patent Cases
- MacArthur's Reports (8-10 District of Columbia)

MacAr.Pat.Cas. MacArthur's Patent Cases (D.C.)

MacAr. & M. MacArthur & Mackey's District of Columbia Supreme Court

MacAr. & Mackey. MacArthur & Mackey's District of Columbia Supreme Court

MacArth.
- MacArthur's Patent Cases
- MacArthur's Reports (8-10 District of Columbia) (1873-79)

MacArth.Pat.Cas. MacArthur's Patent Cases (U.S.)

MacArth. & M.(Dist.Col.) MacArthur & Mackey's District of Columbia Supreme Court (11 D.C.)

MacArthur ● MacArthur's Patent Cases
● MacArthur's Reports (8-10 District of Columbia)

MacArthur, Pat.Cas. MacArthur's Patent Cases (U.S.)

MacArthur & M. MacArthur & Mackey's District of Columbia Supreme Court

MacCarthy MacCarthy's Irish Land Cases (Ir.)

MacDev. MacDevitt's Land Cases (1882-84) (Ir.)

MacFarl. MacFarlane's Reports, Jury Courts (Sc.)

MacS. MacSweeney on Mines, Quarries and Minerals 5 editions (1884-1922)

Macal. McAllister's United States Circuit Court Reports

Macall. McAllister, United States Circuit Court Reports

Macas. Macassey's Reports (New Zealand)

Macaulay, Hist.Eng. Macaulay's History of England

Macc.Cas. Maccala's Breach of Promise Cases

Maccl. Maccala's Reports (Modern Reports, Part X) (1710-25)

Maccl.Tr. Macclesfield's Trial (Impeachment), London (1725)

Macd. Macdevitt's Land Commissioner's Reports (Ir.)

Macd.Jam. Macdougall's Jamaica Reports

Macf. Macfarlane's Reports, Jury Courts (1838-39) (Sc.)

Macfar. Macfarlane's Reports, Jury Courts (1838-39) (Sc.)

Mach. Machine[ry]

Mack.Crim. MacKenzie's Treatise on Criminal Law (Sc.) 4 editions (1678-1758)

Mack.Inst. Mackenzie's Institutes of the Law of Scotland 9 editions (1684-1758)

Mack.Obs. Mackenzie's Observations on Acts of Parliament (1675, etc.) (Sc.)

Mackeld. ● Mackeldey on Modern Civil Law
● Mackeldey on Roman Law

Mackeld.Civil Law Mackeldey on Modern Civil Law

Mackeld.Rom.Law Mackeldey on Roman Law

Mackey ● Mackey's Reports (12-20 D.C.)
● Mackey's District of Columbia Reports (1863-72, 1880-92)

Macl. ● Maclaurin's Scotch Criminal Decisions
● McLean's United States Circuit Court Reports

Macl.Shipp. Maclachlan on Merchant Shipping

Macl. & R. Maclean & Robinson, Scotch Appeal Cases (9 Eng. Reprint)

Macl. & Rob. Maclean & Robinson, Scotch Appeal Cases (9 Eng. Reprint)

Maclean & R.(Sc.) Maclean & Robinson, Scotch Appeal Cases (9 Eng. Reprint)

Macn. ● W.H. Macnaghten's Reports, India
● Macnaghten's Select Cases in Chancery tempore King

Macn.Fr. Francis Macnaghten's Bengal Reports

Macn.N.A.Beng. Macnaghten's Nizamut Adawlut Reports, Bengal (India)

Macn.S.D.A.Beng. (W.H.) Macnaghten's Sadr Diwani Adalat Reports (India)

Macn.Sel.Cas. Select Cases in Chancery tempore King, edited by Macnaghten (1724-33)

Macn. & G. Macnaghten & Gordon's English Chancery Reports (41, 42, Eng. Reprint)

Macn. & G.(Eng.) Macnaghten & Gordon's English Chancery Reports (41, 42 Eng. Reprint)

Macph. ● Macpherson's Court of Session Cases (1862-73) (Sc.)

● Macpherson, Lee & Bell's Session Cases (Sc.)

Macph.Jud.Com. Macpherson, Practice of the Judicial Committee of the Privy Council

Macph.L. & B. Macpherson, Lee & Bell (Sc.)

Macph.Priv.Coun. Macpherson's Privy Council Practice

Macph.S. & L. Macpherson, Shirreff & Lee (Sc.)

Macq. Macqueen's Scotch Appeal Cases (House of Lords) (1851-65)

Macq.D. Macqueen's Debates on Life-Peerage Question

Macq.H.L.Cas. Macqueen's Scotch Appeal Cases (House of Lords)

Macq.Sc.App.Cas. Macqueen Scotch Appeal Cases

Macr. Macrory's Patent Cases (Eng.)

Macr.P.Cas. Macrory's Patent Cases (1847-60)

Macr.Pat.Cas. Macrory's Patent Cases (Eng.)

Macr. & H. Macrae & Hertslet's Insolvency Cases (1847-52) (Eng.)

Mad. ● Indian Law Reports, Madras Series (Eng.)
● Maddock's Chancery Reports (1815-22) (Eng.)
● Maddock's Reports (9-18 Montana)
● Madras High Court Reports (India)

Mad.Exch. Madox's History of the Exchequer

Mad.Form.Angl. Madox' Formulare Anglicanum

Mad.H.C. Madras High Court Reports (India)

Mad.Hist.Exch. Madox' History of the Exchequer

Mad.Jur. Madras Jurist (India)

Mad.L.J. Madras Law Journal (India)

Mad.L.Rep. Madras Law Reporter (India)

Mad.L.T. Madras Law Times (India)

Mad.Law Rep. Madras Law Reporter (India)

Mad.S.D.A.R. Madras Sadr Diwani Adalat Reports (India)

Mad.Sel.Dec. Madras Select Decrees

Mad.Ser. Indian Law Reports, Madras Series

Mad.W.N. Madras Weekly Notes

Mad. & B. Maddox & Bach's Reports (19 Montana)

Mad. & Gel. Maddock & Geldart's English Chancery Reports, vol. 6 Maddock's Reports (1821-22)

Madd. ● Maddock's Chancery Reports (Eng.)
● Maddock's Reports (9-18 Montana)

Madd.Ch.(Eng.) Maddock, Chancery Reports (56 Eng. Reprint)

Madd.Ch.Pr. Maddock's Chancery Practice (Eng.)

Madd. & B. Maddox & Bach's Reports (19 Montana)

Madd. & G. Maddock and Geldart's Reports, Chancery, being volume 6 of Maddock's Reports (Eng.)

Madox ● Madox's Formulare Anglicanum
● Madox's History of the Exchequer

Madras L.J. Madras Law Journal

Mag. ● The Magistrate, London
● Magistrate and Municipal and Parochial Lawyer (London, 5 vols.)
● Magruder's Reports (1, 2 Maryland)

Mag.Cas. ● Magistrates' Cases (Reprinted from Law Journal Reports, 1892-1910)
● Magisterial Cases (Eng.)
● Bittleston, Wise, & Parnell's Magistrates' Cases (Eng.)

Mag.Char. Magna Carta or Charta. See Barrington's Revised Statutes of England, 1870, vol. 1, p. 84, and Coke's Second Institute, vol. 1, first 78 pages

Mag.Ct. Magistrates' Court

Mag.Dig. Magrath's South Carolina Digest

Mag.(Md.) Magruder's Reports (1, 2 Maryland)

Mag.Rot. Magnus Rotulus (the Great Roll of the Exchequer)

Mag. & Con. Magistrate and Constable

Mag.& M.& P.L. Magistrate and Municipal & Parochial Lawyer

Magis.Ct. Magistrate's Court

Magis.& Const.(Pa.) Magistrate & Constable (Pa.)

Magna Cart. Magna Charta (or Carta)

Magna Chart. Magna Charta (or Carta)

Magna Rot.Pip. ● Magnus Rotulus Pipae
     ● Great Roll of the Pipe

Magruder Magruder's Reports (1, 2 Maryland)

Mai. Maine; Maine Reports

Mai.Anc.L. Maine's Ancient Law

Mai.Inst. Maine's History of Institutions

Mai.Vil.Com. Maine's Village Communities

Maine, Anc.Law Maine's Ancient Law

Maine L.Rev. Maine Law Review

Maine P.U.R. Maine Public Utilities Commission Reports

Maine S.B.A. Maine State Bar Association

Maint. Maintenance

Mait. Maitland's Select Pleas of the Crown (1888)

Mait.Gl. Maitland's Pleas of the Crown, County of Gloucester

Maitland ● Maitland's Manuscript Session Cases (Sc.)
     ● Maitland's Pleas of the Crown, 1221 (Eng.)
     ● Maitland's Select Pleas of the Crown (Eng.)

Malcolm, Ethics Malcolm, Legal and Judicial Ethics

Mallory Mallory's Chancery Reports (Ir.)

Malone Editor, vols. 6, 9, and 10, Heiskell's Tennessee Reports

Malynes Malynes, Lex Mercatoria. 3 editions (1622-36)

Man. ● Manhattan
     ● Manitoba
     ● Manitoba Law Reports (1883-date) (Canada)
     ● Manning Reports, Revision Court (1832-35) (Eng.)

● Manning Reports (1 Michigan)

● Manson's Bankruptcy Cases (Eng.)

Man.B.News Manitoba Bar News

Man.Bar News Manitoba Bar News

Man.Cas. Manumission Cases in New Jersey, by Bloomfield

Man.El.Cas. Manning's English Election Cases (Court of Revision)

Man.Exch.Pr. Manning's Exchequer Practice (Eng.)

Man., G.& S. Manning, Granger & Scott, English Common Bench Reports, Old Series (vols. I-VIII)

Man.Gr.& S. Manning, Granger & Scott, English Common Bench Reports, Old Series (vols. I-VIII)

Man.Int.Law Manning, Commentaries on the Law of Nations

Man.L.J. Manitoba Law Journal (Canada)

Man.L.R. Manitoba Law Reports

Man.P.U.C. Manitoba Public Utilities Commission (Canada)

Man.R. Manitoba Law Reports (Canada)

Man.R.t.Wood Manitoba Reports, tempore Wood (Canada)

Man.Rev.Stat. Manitoba Revised Statutes (Canada)

Man.Stat. Manitoba Statutes (Canada)

Man.T.Wood Manitoba Reports, tempore Wood (Canada)

Man.Unrep.Cas. Manning's Unreported Cases (Louisiana)

Man.Unrep.Cas.(La.) Mannings Unreported Cases (La.)

Man.& G. Manning and Granger's C.P. Reports (1840-44) (Eng.)

Man.& R. Manning & Ryland's English Magistrates' Cases

Man.& Ry. Manning & Ryland's English King's Bench Reports (1827-30)

Man.& Ry.Mag.Cas. Manning & Ryland's English Magistrates' Cases (1827-30)

Man.& S. Manning & Scott, English Common Bench Reports (Old Series), Vol. IX

Man.& Sc. Manning & Scott, English Common Bench Reports (Old Series), Vol. IX

Manb.Coke Manby's Abridgment of Coke's Reports

Manitoba ● Armour's Queen's Bench and County Court Reports tempore Wood (Manitoba)
● Manitoba Law Reports

Manitoba L.(Can.) Manitoba Law Reports

Mann. ● Manning, Digest of the Nisi Prius Reports (Eng.)
● Manning, English Court of Revision Reports
● Manning's Reports (Michigan Reports, vol. 1)

Mann.G. & S.(Eng.) Manning, Granger & Scott, English Common Bench Reports, Old Series (vols. I-VIII)

Mann.& G.(Eng.) Manning & Granger English Common Pleas Reports (133-135 Eng. Reprint)

Mann. & R.(Eng.) Manning & Ryland's English King's Bench Reports

Manning ● Manning's Reports (1 Michigan)
● Manning's Unreported Cases (Louisiana)

Mans. ● Mansfield's Reports (49-52 Arkansas)
● Manson's Bankruptcy and Companies' Winding-Up Cases (Eng.)

Mansf.Dig. Mansfield's Digest of Statutes (Ark.)

Manson Manson's Bankruptcy and Winding-Up Cases (1894-1914) (Eng.)

Manson (Eng.) Manson's Bankruptcy (Eng.)

Manson, Bankr.Cas. Manson's Bankruptcy and Winding-Up Cases

Manum.Cas. Bloomfield's Manumission Cases (N.J.)

Manum.Cases Bloomfield's Manumission Cases (N.J.)

Manw. Manwood's Forest Laws

Manw.For.Law Manwood's Forest Law (1592; 1598; 1615)

Manwood Manwood's Forest Laws (1592, 1598, 1615)

Mar. ● Maritime
● March's King's Bench Reports (1639-42) (Eng.)
● Martin Reports (Louisiana 1809-30)
● Martin's Reports (1 N.C.)
● Marshall's Circuit Court Reports (U.S.)
● Marshall's Reports (Bengal)
● Marshall's Reports (Ceylon)
● Marshall's Reports (24-30 Kentucky)
● Marvel's Reports (Del.)

Mar.Br. March's Brooke's New Cases (Eng.)

Mar.Cas. Maritime Cases by Crockford and Cox (1860-71)

Mar.L.C. Maritime Law Cases, by Crockford (1860-71)

Mar.L.C.N.S. Maritime Law Cases, New Series by Aspinall (1870-1940) (Eng.)

Mar.L.J. Maryland Law Journal & Real Estate Record

Mar.L.Rec. Maryland Law Record

Mar.L.Rev. Maryland Law Review

Mar.La. Martin's Louisiana Reports

Mar.N.C. ● March's New Cases, King's Bench (Eng.)
● Martin's Reports (1 North Carolina)

Mar.N.S. Martin's Louisiana Reports, New Series

Mar.N.& Q. Maritime Notes & Queries (1873-1900)

Mar.Prov. Maritime Provinces Reports (Canada)

Mar.R. Maritime Law Reports

Mar.Reg. Mitchell's Maritime Register (1856-83) (London)

March. ● March's Translation of Brooke's New Cases, English King's Bench (82 Eng. Reprint)
● March's King's Bench & Common Pleas Reports (Eng.)

March N.C. ● Translation of Brook's New Cases (1515-58)
● March's New Cases, English King's Bench (1639-42)

Marijuana Rev. The Marijuana Review

Marine Ct.R. Marine Court Reporter (McAdam's) (New York)

Marius Marius, Concerning Bills of Exchange. 4 editions (1651-84)

Marks & Sayre Marks & Sayre's Rep. (108 Ala.)

Marq. Marquette

Marq.L.Rev. Marquette Law Review

Marq.Sc.App.Cas. Macqueen's Scotch Appeal Cases (House of Lords)

Marquette Bus.Rev. Marquette Business Review

Marquette L.Rev. Marquette Law Review

Marr.
- Hay & Marriott's Admiralty Decisions (1776-79) (Eng.)
- Marrack's European Assurance Cases (Eng.)
- Marriage

Marr.Adm. Marriott's Reports, English Admiralty

Mars. Marsden's Select Pleas in the Court of Admiralty (Selden Society Publications, v. 6, 11)

Mars.Adm. Marsden's Admiralty (Eng.)

Marsh.
- Marshall High Court Reports (Bengal)
- Marshall's Circuit Court Decisions (U.S.)
- Marshall's Reports, Ceylon
- Marshall's Common Pleas Reports (1814-16)
- Marshall's Reports (8-10, 24-30 Ky.)
- Marshall's Reports (4 Utah)

Marsh.A.K. A.K. Marshall's Reports (8-10 Ky.)

Marsh.Beng. Marshall's Reports (Bengal)

Marsh.C.P. Marshall's English Common Pleas Reports

Marsh.Calc. Marshall's Reports (Calcutta)

Marsh.Ceylon Marshall's Ceylon Reports

Marsh.Dec.
- Marshall's Circuit Court Decisions, by Brockenbrough (U.S.)
- Marshall on the Federal Constitution

Marsh.(Eng.) Marshall (Common Pleas)

Marsh.Ins. Marshall on Marine Insurance

Marsh.(Ky.) Marshall's Reports (8-10, 24-30 Kentucky)

Marsh.J.J. J.J.Marshall's Reports (24-30 Ky.)

Marsh.Op. Marshall's Constitutional Opinions

Marshall
- Marshall's Reports (Bengal)
- Reports of Cases on Appeal (Calcutta)

Mart.
- Martin (Louisiana Term Reports) (1809-30)
- Martin's North Carolina Reports (1778-98)

Mart.Ark. Martin's Decisions in Equity (Ark.)

Mart.Cond.La. Martin's Condensed Louisiana Reports

Mart.Dec. United States Decisions in Martin's North Carolina Reports

Mart.Ga. Martin's Reports (21-30 Georgia)

Mart.Ind. Martin's Reports (54-70 Indiana)

Mart.La. Martin's Reports (Louisiana, Old and New Series)

Mart.M.C. Martin's Mining Cases (Canada)

Mart.N.C. Martin's Reports (1 N.C.)

Mart.N.S. Martin's Louisiana Reports, New Series (1809-30)

Mart.N.S.(La.) Martin's Louisiana Reports, New Series

Mart.O.S.(La.) Martin's Louisiana Reports, Old Series

Mart.U.S.C.C. Martin's Circuit Court Reports, in 1 North Carolina

Mart.& Y. Martin & Yerger's Tennessee Reports (8 Tennessee) (1825-28)

Mart.& Y.(Tenn.) Martin & Yerger's Tennessee Reports (8 Tennessee) (1825-28)

Mart.& Yer. Martin & Yerger's Tennessee Reports (8 Tennessee) (1825-28)

Mart.& Yerg. Martin & Yerger's Tennessee Reports (8 Tennessee) (1825-28)

Martens Nouveau Recueil Nouveau recueil general des traites

Marth.W.Ca. Martha Washington Cases, see United States v. Cole, 5 McLean, 513, Fed.Cas.No. 14,832

Martin ● Martin's Reports (21-30 Georgia)

       ● Martin's Reports (54-70 Georgia)

       ● Martin's Reports (Louisiana 1809-30)

       ● Martin's Reports (1 North Carolina)

Martin, Dict. Edward Martin's English Dictionary

Martin Index. Martin's Index to Virginia Reports

Marv. Marvel's Reports (15-16 Delaware)

Marv.(Del.) Marvel's Reports (15-16 Delaware)

Marvel Marvel's Reports (15-16 Delaware)

Maryland Maryland Reports

Mas. ● Mason, United States Circuit Court Reports (5 vols.)

       ● Massachusetts Reports

Mascard.de Prob. Mascardus de Probationibus

Mason's Code Mason's United States Code Annotated

Mass. ● Massachusetts

       ● Massachusetts Supreme Judicial Court Reports (1868-date)

Mass.Acts Acts and Resolves of Massachusetts

Mass.Adv.Legis.Serv. Massachusetts Advance Legislative Service (Lawyers Co-op)

Mass.Ann.Laws Annotated Laws of Massachusetts

Mass.App.Ct. Massachusetts Appeals Court Report

Mass.App.Ct.Adv.Sh. Massachusetts Appeals Court Advance Sheets

Mass.App.Dec. Masschusetts Appellate Decisions

Mass.App.Div. Massachusetts Appellate Division Reports

Mass.B.C.& A. Massachusetts Board of Conciliation & Arbitration Reports

Mass.B.T.A. Massachusetts Board of Tax Appeals

Mass.D.I.A. Massachusetts Department of Industrial Accidents Bulletin

Mass.Elec.Ca. Massachusetts Election Cases

Mass.Elec.Cas. Massachusetts Election Cases

Mass.G.& E.L.C. Massachusetts Board of Gas & Electric Light Commissioners

Mass.Gen.Laws Massachusetts General Laws

Mass.Gen.Laws Ann.(West) Massachusetts General Laws Annotated

Mass.High.Com. Massachusetts Highway Commission (Telephone Companies)

Mass.I.A.B. Massachusetts Industrial Accident Board Reports of Cases

Mass.L.Q. Massachusetts Law Quarterly

Mass.L.R. Massachusetts Law Reporter

Mass.L.R.C.Dec. Massachusetts Labor Relations Commission Decisions

Mass.P.S.C. Massachusetts Public Service Commission

Mass.P.U.R. Massachusetts Public Utility Commission Reports

Mass.R.C. Massachusetts Board of Railroad Commissioners

Mass.St.B.C.& A. Massachusetts State Board of Conciliation & Arbitration Reports

Mass.U.C.C.Op. Massachusetts Unemployment Compensation Commission Opinions

Mass.U.C.Dig. Massachusetts Division of Unemployement Compensation Digest of Board of Review Decisions

Mass.U.C.Ops. Massachusetts Division of Unemployment Compensation Opinions

Mass.W.C.C. Massachusetts Workmen's Compensation Cases

Mast. Master's Reports (25-28 Canada Supreme Court)

Mat. Maturity

Mat.Par. Matthew Paris, Historia Minor

Mat.Paris. Matthew Paris, Historia Minor

Math. Mathieu's Quebec Reports

Math.Pres.Ev. Mathews on Presumptive Evidence

Mats. Matsons' Reports (22-24 Connecticut)

Matson Matsons' Reports (22-24 Connecticut)

Matthews ● Matthews' Reports (75 Virginia)

● Matthews' Reports (6-9 West Virginia)

Mau. & Sel. Maule & Selwyn's King's Bench Reports (1813-17) (Eng.)

Maude & P. Maude & Pollock's Law of Merchant Shipping 4 editions (1853-81)

Maude & P.Mer.Shipp. Maude & Pollock's Law of Merchant Shipping

Maude & P.Shipp. Maude & Pollock's Law of Merchant Shipping

Maul. & Sel. Maule & Selwyn's English King's Bench Reports

Maule & S. Maule & Selwyn's English King's Bench Reports

Maur.Dec. Mauritius Decisions

Max.Dig. Maxwell's Nebraska Digest

Maxw.Adv.Gram. W.H.Maxwell's Advanced Lessons in English Grammar

Maxw.Cr.Proc. Maxwell's Treatise on Criminal Procedure

Maxw.Interp.St. Maxwell on the Interpretation of Statutes

Maxwell Maxwell on the Interpretation of Statutes. 10 editions (1875-1953)

May,Ins. May on Insurance

May,L.R. Mayurbhani Law Reporter (India)

May,Parl.Law May's Parliamentary Law

May,Parl.Pr. May's Parliamentary Practice

Mayn. Maynard's Reports, Exchequer Memoranda of Edward I, & Year Books of Edward II (Eng.)

McA.L. & Ten. McAdam on Landlord and Tenant

McAdam, Landl.& T. McAdam on Landlord and Tenant

McAl. McAllister's Circuit Court Reports (U.S.)

McAll. McAllister's Circuit Court Reports (U.S.)

McAr. McArthur's District of Columbia Reports

McArth. & M. MacArthur and Mackey's District of Columbia Reports (1879-80)

McBride McBride's Reports (1 Missouri)

McCah. McCahon's Reports (Kansas 1858-68)

McCahon. McCahon's Reports (Kansas 1858-68)

McCar. McCarter's New Jersey Equity Reports

McCart. ● McCarter's Reports (14, 15 N.J.Equity)

● McCarty's New York Civil Procedure Reports

McCarter McCarter's Chancery (N.J.)

McCartney McCartney's Civil Procedure (N.Y.)

McCarty,Civ.Proc. McCarty's Civil Procedure Reports (N.Y.)

McCl. McCleland's Exchequer Reports (1824) (Eng.)

McCl. & Y. McCleland & Younge's Exchequer Reports (1824-25) (Eng.)

McClain, Cr.Law McClain's Criminal Law

McClain's Code. McClain's Annotated Code and Statutes (Iowa)

McCle. McClelland's Exchequer Reports (1824) (Eng.)

McCle. & Yo. McClelland and Younge's Exchequer Reports (1824-25) (Eng.)

McClel.Dig. McClellan's Digest of Laws (Fla.)

McClell. McClelland's Exchequer (Eng.)

McClell. & Y. McClelland & Younge's Exchequer Reports (1824-25) (Eng.)

McCook McCook's Reports (1 Ohio State)

McCord McCord's Reports (S. C. Law 1821-28)

McCord Ch. McCord's Reports (S. C. Equity 1825-27)

McCord Eq. McCord's South Carolina Chancery Reports (1825-27)

McCorkle McCorkle's Reports (65 North Carolina)

McCr. McCrary's Circuit Court Reports (U.S.)

McCrary,Elect. McCrary's American Law of Elections

McCul.Dict. McCullough's Commercial Dictionary

McCul.Pol.Econ. McCulloch, Political Economy

McDevitt. McDevitt's Land Commissioner's Reports (Ir.)

McDonnell McDonnell's Sierra Leone Reports

McFar. McFarlane's Jury Court Reports (Sc.)

McGill McGill's Manuscript Decisions, Court of Session (Sc.)

McGill L.J. McGill Law Journal

McGl. McGloin's Court of Appeal Reports (1881-84) (La.)

McGloin. McGloin's Court of Appeal Reports (La.)

McGrath McGrath's Mandamus Cases (Michigan)

McKelvey,Ev. McKelvey on Evidence

Mc.L. McLean's Circuit Court Reports (U.S.)

McL. & R. McLean & Robinson's Appeal Cases (1839) (Sc.)

McM.Com.Cas. McMaster's Commercial Cases (U.S.)

McM.Com.Dec. McMaster's Commercial Decisions

McMul. McMullan's Reports (S.C. Law Reports,1840-42)

McMul.Eq. McMullan's Reports (S.C. Equity Reports, 1840-42)

McMull.Eq.(S.C.) McMullan, South Carolina Equity Reports

McMull.L.(S.C.) McMullan, South Carolina Law Reports

McPherson McPherson, Lee, & Bell's Session Cases (Sc.)

McQ. MacQueen's Scotch Appeal (House of Lords) Cases (1851-65)

McQuillinMun.Corp. McQuillin on Municipal Corporations

McWillie McWillie's Reports (73-76 Miss.)

Mch. Michigan Reports

Md. ● Maryland
● Maryland Reports

Md.A. Maryland Appellate Reports

Md.Ann.Code Annotated Code of Maryland

Md.App. Maryland Appellate Reports

Md.B.J. Maryland Bar Journal

Md.Ch. Maryland Chancery Reports, by Johnson, 4 vols.

Md.Code Ann. Annotated Code of Maryland

Md.L.R. Maryland Law Review

Md.L.Rec. Maryland Law Record (Baltimore)

Md.L.Rep. Maryland Law Reporter (Baltimore)

Md.L.Rev. Maryland Law Review

Md.Laws Laws of Maryland

Md.P.S.C. Maryland Public Service Commission

Md.P.U.R. Maryland Public Utility Commission

Md.W.C.C. Maryland Workmen's Compensation Cases

Mdse. Merchandise

Me. ● Maine
● Maine Supreme Judicial Court Reports

Me.Acts Acts, Resolves and Constitutional Resolutions of the State of Maine

Me.L. University of Maine Law Review

Me.Legis.Serv. Maine Legislative Service

Me.P.U.C. Maine Public Utilities Commission

Me.R.C. Maine Railroad Commissioners

Me.Rev.Stat. Maine Revised Statutes

Me.Rev.Stat.Ann. Maine Revised Statutes Annotated

Means. Mean's Kansas Reports

Mechem. ● Mechem on Agency
● Mechem on Partnership

Mechem,Ag.   Mechem on Agency

Mechem,Pub.Off.   Mechem on Public Offices and Officers

Med.
- Mediator
- Medical(cine)
- State Board of Medical Examiners

Med.L.J.   Medico-Legal Journal (New York)

Med.L.N.   Medico Legal News (New York)

Med.L.P.   Medico Legal Papers (New York.)

Med.Leg.Bul.   Medico-Legal Bulletin

Med.Leg.J.   Medico-Legal Journal

Med.Leg.N.   Medico Legal News (New York)

Med.Leg. & Crim.Rev.   Medico-Legal & Criminological Review

Med.Sci. & L.   Medicine, Science & the Law

Med.Tr.T.Q.   Medical Trial Technique Quarterly

Med.Trial Tech.Q.   Medical Trial Technique Quarterly

Medd.   Meddaugh's Reports (13 Michigan)

Meddaugh.   Meddaugh's Reports (13 Michigan)

Mees. & Ros.   Meeson and Roscoe's English Exchequer Reports (1834-36)

Mees. & W.   Meeson and Welsby's English Exchequer Reports (1836-47)

Mees. & Wels.   Meeson and Welsby's English Exchequer Reports (1836-47)

Meg.   Megone's Companies Acts Cases (1888-90) (Eng.)

Megarry   Megarry. The Rent Acts

Megone.   Megone's Company Acts Cases (1888-90)

Meigs   Meigs'Tennessee Supreme Court Reports (1838-39)

Meigs,Dig.   Meigs' Digest of Decisions of the Courts of Tennessee

Melanesian L.J.   Melanesian Law Journal (Papua and New Guinea)

Melb.   Melbourne

Melb.U.L.Rev.   Melbourne University Law Review

Melb.Univ.L.R.   Melbourne University Law Review

Melv.Tr.   Melville's Trial (Impeachment) (London)

Mem.   Memphis

Mem.In Scacc.   Memorandum or memoranda in the Exchequer

Mem.L.J.   Memphis Law Journal (Tenn.)

Memo.   Memorandum (Law Department, Southern Railway)

Memp.L.J.   Memphis Law Journal (Tenn.)

Memphis L.J.   Memphis Law Journal (Tenn.)

Memphis St.U.L.Rev.   Memphis State University Law Review

Men.   Menie's Cape of Good Hope Reports

Menken.   Menken's Reports, vol. 30 New York Civil Procedure Reports

Mental Hyg.   Mental Hygiene

Menz.   Menzie's Cape of Good Hope Reports (1828-49)

Mer.
- Mercer Law Review (Ga.)
- Merivale's English Chancery Reports (1815-17)

Mer.L.J.   Mercantile Law Journal (Madras, India)

Merc.Ad. & Law. & Credit Man   Mercantile Adjuster & Lawyer & Credit Man

Merc.Cas.   Merchantile Cases

Merc.L.J.   Mercantile Law Journal (New York or Madras)

Mercer B.L.Rev.   Mercer Beasley Law Review

Mercer,Beasley L.Rev.   Mercer, Beasley Law Review

Mercer L.Rev.   Mercer Law Review

Mercer Law Rev.   Mercer Law Review

Meredith Lect.   W.C.J. Meredith Memorial Lectures

Meriv.   Merivale's English Chancery Reports (35,36 Eng. Reprint)

Meriv.(Eng.)   Merivale's English Chancery Reports (35,36 Eng. Reprint)

Merl.Quest.   Merlin, Questions de Droit

Merl.Repert.   Merlin, Repertoire de Jurisprudence

Merlin,Quest.de Droit. Merlin's Questions de Droit qui se Presentent le Plus Frequemment Dans les Tribunaux (1819)

Merlin,Repert. Merlin's Repertoire

Mert. Merten's Law of Federal Income Taxation

Met. ● Metcalf's Reports (42-54 Massachusetts) (1840-47)
     ● Metcalf's Reports (3 Rhode Island)
     ● Metcalfe's Reports (58-61 Kentucky) (1858-63)

Metc. ● Metcalf's Reports (42-54 Massachusetts)
     ● Metcalf's Reports (3 Rhode Island)
     ● Metcalfe's Reports (58-61 Kentucky)

Metc.Ky. Metcalfe's Reports (58-61 Kentucky)

Metc.Mass. Metcalf's Reports (42-54 Mass.)

Meth.Ch.Ca. Report of Methodist Church Case

Mews The Reports (1893-95) (Eng.) Mews' Digest of English Case Law

Mex. Mexico

Meyer,des Inst.Judiciares. Meyer, des Institutiones Judiciares

Mfg. Manufacturing

Mfr. ● Manufacturer
     ● Manufacturing

Mgmt. Management

Mi. Michigan; Michigan Reports

Mi.L. ● Michigan Law Review
     ● University of Miami Law Review (Fla.)

Miami L.Q. Miami Law Quarterly

Miami L.Rev. Miami Law Review (Florida)

Mich. ● Michaelmas Term
     ● Michigan
     ● Michigan Supreme Court Reports

Mich.Adv. Michigan Reports Advanced Sheets

Mich.App. Michigan Court of Appeals Reports

Mich.C.C.R. Michigan Circuit Court Reporter Marquette

Mich.Comp.L.Ann. Michigan Compiled Laws Annotated

Mich.Comp.Laws Michigan Compiled Laws

Mich.Comp.Laws Ann. Michigan Compiled Laws Annotated

Mich.Cr.Ct.Rep. Michigan Circuit Court Reporter Marquette

Mich.Jur. Michigan Jurisprudence

Mich.L. Michigan Lawyer

Mich.L.J. Michigan Law Journal

Mich.L.Rev. Michigan Law Review

Mich.Lawyer Michigan Lawyer

Mich.Leg.News Michigan Legal News

Mich.Legis.Serv.(West) Michigan Legislative Service

Mich.N.P. Brown's or Howell's Michigan Nisi Prius Reports or Cases

Mich.P.U.C.Ops. Michigan Public Utilities Commission Orders and Opinions

Mich.Pol.Soc. Michigan Political Science Association

Mich.R.C.Dec. Michigan Railroad Comm. Dec.

Mich.S.B.A.Jo. Michigan State Bar Assn. Journal

Mich.S.B.J. Michigan State Bar Journal

Mich.St.B.J. Michigan State Bar Journal

Mich.Stat.Ann. Michigan Statutes Annotated

Mich.T. Michaelmas Term (Eng.)

Mich.Vac. Michaelmas Vacation

Mich.W.C.C. Michigan Industrial Accident Board, Workmen's Compensation Cases

Michie's Jur. Michie's Jurisprudence of Va. and W. Va.

Middx.Sit. Sittings for Middlesex at Nisi Prius

Mil. ● Miles' Pennsylvania Reports
     ● Military
     ● Miller's Reports (1-5 Louisiana)
     ● Miller's Reports (3-18 Maryland)
     ● Mills' South Carolina Constitutional Reports
     ● Mill's Surrogate's Court Reports (N.Y.)

Mil.Jur.,Cas. & Mat. Military Jurisprudence, Cases,& Materials

Mil.L.Rev. Military Law Review

Mil.Rep. Militia Reporter (Boston)

Mil. & Vet.C. Military and Veterans
Code

Miles Miles' District Court Reports
(Philadelphia 1825-41)

Miles (Pa.) Miles' Pennsylvania Reports

Mill. ● Miles' Pennsylvania Reports
● Miller's Reports (1-5
Louisiana)
● Miller's Reports (3-18 Mary-
land)
● Mills' South Carolina Con-
stitutional Reports (1817-
18)
● Mill's Surrogate's Court Re-
ports (N.Y.)

Mill Const. Mill's South Carolina
Constitutional Reports

Mill, Const.(S.C.) Mill's South Carolina Constitutional Reports

Mill.Dec. ● Miller's Circuit Court
Decisions (Wool-
worths) (U.S.)
● Miller's U.S. Supreme
Court Decisions
(condensed, contin-
uation of Curtis)

Mill.La. Millers Reports (1-5 Louisiana)

Mill,Log. Mill's Logic

Mill.Md. Miller's Reports (3-18 Maryland)

Mill.Op. Miller's Circuit Court Decisions (Woolworth) (U.S.)

Mill,Pos.Ec. Mill's Political Economy

Mill. & V.Code Milliken & Vertrees'
Code (Tenn.)

Miller ● Miller's Reports (1-5
Louisiana)
● Miller's Reports (3-18
Maryland)

Miller,Const. Miller on the Constitution of the United States

Miller's Code. Miller's Revised and
Annotated Code (Iowa)

Mills. Mills' Reports, New York
Surrogate Court

Mills' Ann.St. Mills' Annotated
Statutes (Colo.)

Mills,Em.Dom. Mills on Eminent
Domain

Mills (N.Y.) Mills' Reports, New York
Surrogate Court

Mills'Surr.Ct. Mills' Surrogate Court
Reports (New York)

Milw. Milward's Irish Ecclesiastical
Reports (1819-43)

Milw.B.A.G. Milwaukee Bar Assn.
Gavel

Milw.Ir.Ecc.Rep. Milward's Irish
Ecclesiastical Reports (1819-43)

Mim. United States Internal Revenue
Bureau, Commissioner's Mimeo-
graphed Published Opinions

Min. ● Mineral
● Minnesota Reports
● Minor's Reports (Alabama
1820-26)

Min.Ev. Minutes of Evidence

Min.H.M.D. National Health Insurance (Ministry of Health Decisions)

Min.Inst. Minor's Institutes of
Common and Statute Law

Minn. ● Minnesota
● Minnesota Supreme Court
Reports

Minn.Cont.L.Ed. Minnesota Continuing Legal Education

Minn.Cont.Legal Ed. Minnesota Continuing Legal Education

Minn.Ct.Rep. Minnesota Court
Reporter

Minn.D.L. & I.Comp. Minnesota Department of Labor and Industries.
Compilation of Court Decisions

Minn.Gen.Laws Minnesota General
Laws

Minn.L.J. Minnesota Law Journal
(St. Paul, Minn.)

Minn.L.Rev. Minnesota Law Review

Minn.Law J. Minnesota Law Journal

Minn.Laws Laws of Minnesota

Minn.L.Rev. Minnesota Law Review

Minn.R. & W.C. Minnesota Railroad
and Warehouse Commission

Minn.R & W.C.A.T.Div. Minnesota
Railroad and Warehouse Com-
mission. Auto Transportation Co.
Division. Reports

Minn.S.B.A. Minnesota State Bar
Association

Minn.Sess.Law Serv.(West) Minnesota Session Law Service

Minn.Stat. Minnesota Statutes

Minn.Stat.Ann. Minnesota Statutes Annotated

Minn.Staj.Ann.(West) West's Minnesota Statutes Annotated

Minn.W.C.D. Minnesota Workmen's Compensation Decisions

Minor ● Minor's Institutes
      ● Minor's Alabama Supreme Court Reports (1820-26)

Minor(Ala.) ● Minor's Institutes
      ● Minor's Reports (Alabama 1820-26)

Minor,Inst. Minor's Institutes of Common and Statute Law

Minshew. Minshew (John), "The Guide into the Tongues also the Exposition of the Terms of the Laws of this Land." (Eng.)

Mir. Horne's Mirror of Justices

Mir.Just. Horne's Mirror of Justices

Mir.Pat.Off. Mirror of the Patent Office (Washington, D.C.)

Mirch.D. & S. Mirchall's Doctor and Student

Mirr. Horne's Mirror of Justices

Mis. ● Mississippi
      ● Mississippi Reports

Misc. Miscellaneous Reports (New York)

Misc.2d Miscellaneous Reports, Second Series (New York)

Misc.Dec. Ohio Miscellaneous Decisions (Gottschall 1865-73)

Misc.(N.Y.) Miscellaneous Reports (New York)

Misc.Rep. Miscellaneous Reports (New York)

Miscel. Miscellaneous Reports (New York)

Miss. ● Mississippi
      ● Mississippi Supreme Court Reports
      ● Missouri

Miss.Code Ann. Mississippi Code Annotated

Miss.Dec. Mississippi Decisions

Miss.L.J. Mississippi Law Journal

Miss.Law.Rev. Mississippi Law Review

Miss.Laws General Laws of Mississippi

Miss.R.C. Mississippi Railroad Commission Reports

Miss.S.B.A. Mississippi State Bar Association

Miss.St.Ca. Morris' Mississippi State Cases (1818-72)

Miss.St.Cas. Morris' Mississippi State Cases (1818-72)

Mister Mister's Reports (17-32 Mo. Appeals)

Mit.Ch.Pl. Mitford's Equity Pleading

Mitch.M.R. Mitchell's Maritime Register (1856-83)

Mitch.Mod.Geog. Mitchells Modern Geography

Mitf.Eq.Pl. Mitford on Equity Pleading

Mkt. Market

Mktg Marketing

Mkts. Markets

Mn. Minnesota

Mn.L.R. Minnesota Law Review

Mo. ● Missouri
      ● Missouri Supreme Court Reports (1821-1956)
      ● Modern Reports (Eng.) (1669-1732)
      ● Moore's Privy Council Reports (Eng.) (1836-62)
      ● Moore's Common Pleas Reports (Eng.) (1817-27)
      ● Moore's Indian Appeal Cases (1836-72)
      ● Moore's King's Bench Reports (Eng.) (1512-1621)

Mo.A.R. Missouri Appellate Reporter

Mo.Ann.Stat.(Vernon) Vernon's Annotated Missouri Statutes

Mo.App. Missouri Appeal Reports

Mo.App.Rep. Missouri Appeals Reports

Mo.Bar Missouri Bar

Mo.Bar J. Missouri Bar Journal

Mo.Dec. Missouri Decisions

Mo.(F.). Sir Francis Moore's English King's Bench Reports

Mo.I.A. Moore's Indian Appeals (1836-72)

Mo.J.B. J.B.Moore's Common Pleas Reports (Eng.)

Mo.Jur.   Monthly Jurist

Mo.L.   Missouri Law Review

Mo.L.Mag.   Monthly Law Magazine (1838-47) (London)

Mo.L.Rev.   Missouri Law Review

Mo.Lab.Rev.   Monthly Labor Review

Mo Labor R   Monthly Labor Review

Mo.Law Rep.   Monthly Law Reporter

Mo.Laws   Laws of Missouri

Mo.Leg.Exam.   Monthly Legal Examiner (New York)

Mo.Legis.Serv. (Vernon)   Missouri Legislative Service

Mo.P.C.   Moore's Privy Council Reports (Eng.)

Mo.P.S.C.R.   Missouri Public Service Commission Reports

Mo.P.U.R.   Missouri Public Utility Reports

Mo.R.C.   Missouri Railroad Commissioners

Mo.R. & W.C.   Missouri Railroad & Warehouse Commission

Mo.Rev.Stat.   Missouri Revised Statutes

Mo.St.Ann.   Missouri Statutes Annotated

Mo.W.Jur.   Monthly Western Jurist

Mo. & P.   Moore & Payne's English Common Pleas Reports

Mo. & R.   Moody & Robinson's English Nisi Prius Reports

Mo. & S.   Moore & Scott's English Common Pleas Reports (1831-34)

Mo. & Sc.   Moore and Scott. C.P. Reports (1831-24)

Moak   Moak's English Reports

Moak (Eng.)   Moak's English Reports

Moak Eng.Rep.   Moak's English Reports

Moak Und.   Moak's edition of Underhill on Torts

Moak,Underh.Torts.   Moak's Edition of Underhill on Torts

Moak & Eng.Rep.   Moak's English Reports

Mob.   Mobley, Contested Election Cases, U.S. House of Representatives (1882-89)

Mobl.   Mobley, Contested Election Cases, U.S. House of Representatives (1882-89)

Mod.   ● Modern
● Modern Reports, 1669-1732 (Eng.)
● Modified in
● Modifying
● Style's King's Bench Reports (1646-55) (Eng.)

Mod.Am.Law   Modern American Law

Mod.Ca.per Far.   6 and 7 Modern Reports(1702-45)

Mod.Ca.t.Holt.   7 Modern Reports (1702-45)

Mod.Cas.   Modern Cases (6 Modern Reports) (1702-45)

Mod.Cas.L. & Eq.   Modern Cases at Law and Equity, vols. 8,9 Modern Reports (1721-55)

Mod.Cas.Per.Far.   Modern Cases tempore Holt, by Farresley, vol.7 Modern Reports

Mod.Cas.t.Holt.   Modern Cases tempore Holt, by Farresley, vol.7 Modern Reports

Mod.(Eng.)   English King's Bench Modern Reports (86-88 Eng. Reprint)

Mod.L.Rev.   Modern Law Review

Mod.Pract.Comm.   Modern Practice Commentator

Mod.Rep.   Modern Reports(1669-1732) (Eng.)

Model Bus.Corp.Act.Anno.   Atkins, et al., Model Business Corporation Act, Annotated

Modern L.Rev.   Modern Law Review

Mod'g   Modifying

Modif.   Modified; Modification

Mol.   ● Molloy's Chancery Reports (1827-31) (Ir.)
● Molloy's De Jure Maritimo

Mol.de Jure Mar.   Molloy, De Jure Maritimo et Navali

Moll.   ● Molloy's Chancery Reports (1827-31) (Ir.)
● Molloy's De Jure Maritimo

Moly.   Molyneaux's Reports. English Courts, tempore Car.I.

Mon.   ● Monaghan'a Unreported Cases (Pennsylvania Superior Court)
● T.B. Monroe's Reports (17-23 Kentucky)

- Montana
- Montana Reports
- Montana Territory

Mon.Angl. Monasticon Anglicanum

Mon.B. Monroe's Reports (40-57 Kentucky)

Mon.L.Rev.,Univ.of Detroit Monthly Law Review of University of Detroit

Mon.Law Mag. Monthly Law Magazine (1834-41)

Mon.Law Rep. Monthly Law Reporter

Mon.Leg.R.(Pa.) Monroe Legal Reporter

Mon.T.B. T.B. Monroe's Reports (17-23 Ky.)

Mon.W.J. Monthly Western Jurist

Mona. Monaghan's Reports (147-165 Pennsylvania)

Monag.
- Monaghan's Reports (147-165 Pennsylvania Statutes)
- Monaghan's Reports (Pennsylvania 1888-90)

Monaghan. Monaghan's Reports (147-165 Pennsylvania)

Monaghan (Pa.)
- Monaghan's Reports (147-165 Pennsylvania Statutes)
- Monaghan's Reports (Pennsylvania 1888-90)

Monro. Acta Cancellariae (Eng.)

Monro.A.C. Monro's Acta Cancellariae (1545-1625)

Monroe L.R. Monroe Legal Reporter (Pa.)

Mont.
- Montagu, English Bankruptcy Reports (1829-32)
- Montana
- Montana Supreme Court Reports
- Montriou, Bengal Reports

Mont.B.C. Montagu's English Bankruptcy Reports

Mont.Bank.Rep. Montagu's English Bankruptcy Reports

Mont.Bankr.(Eng.) Montagu's English Bankruptcy Reports

Mont.Cas. Montriou's Cases in Hindoo Law

Mont.Co.L.R. Montgomery County Law Reporter (Pa.)

Mont.Co.L.Rep. Montgomery County Law Reporter (Pa.)

Mont.Cond.Rep. Montreal Condensed Reports (1853-54)

Mont.D.& DeG. Montagu, Deacon, & DeGex, Bankruptcy Reports (1840-44) (Eng.)

Mont.Dig. Montagu's Digest of Pleadings in Equity

Mont.Eq.Pl. Montagu's Digest of Pleadings in Equity

Mont.Ind. Monthly Index to Reporters

Mont.L.R.
- Montreal Law Reports, Queen's Bench
- Montreal Law Reports, Superior Court

Mont.L.R.Q.B. Montreal Law Reports, Queen's Bench

Mont.L.R.S.C. Montreal Law Reports, Superior Court

Mont.L.Rev. Montana Law Review

Mont.Laws Laws of Montana

Mont.Leg.News Montreal Legal News

Mont.R.C. Montana Railroad Commission

Mont.R. & P.S.Co. Railroad and Public Service Commission of Montana

Mont.Rev.Code Ann. Montana Revised Code Annotated

Mont.Rev.Codes Ann. Revised Codes of Montana Annotated

Mont.Sp.L. Montesquieu's Spirit of Laws

Mont.Super. Montreal Law Reports (Superior Court)

Mont. & A. Montagu & Ayrton's English Bankruptcy Reports (1833-38)

Mont. & Ayr. Montagu & Ayrton's English Bankruptcy Reports (1833-38)

Mont. & Ayr.B.L. Montagu & Ayrton on the Bankrupt Laws

Mont. & Ayr.Bankr.(Eng.) Montagu & Ayrton's English Bankruptcy Reports

Mont. & B. Montagu & Bligh's English Bankruptcy Reports

Mont. & B.Bankr.(Eng.) Montagu & Bligh's English Bankruptcy Reports (1832-33)

Mont. & Bl. Montagu & Bligh's English Bankruptcy Reports (1832-33)

Mont. & C. Montagu & Chitty's English Bankruptcy Reports (1838-40)

Mont. & C.Bankr.(Eng.) Montagu & Chitty's English Bankruptcy Reports

Mont. & Ch. Montagu & Chitty's English Bankruptcy Reports

Mont. & Chitt. Montagu & Chitty's English Bankruptcy Reports

Mont. & M. Montagu and Mac-Arthur's English Bankruptcy Reports (1826-30)

Mont. & M.Bankr.(Eng.) Montagu and MacArthur's English Bankruptcy Reports (1826-30)

Mont. & MacA. Montagu and Mac-Arthur's English Bankruptcy Reports (1826-30)

Montana L.Rev. Montana Law Review

Montesq. Montesquieu, Esprit des Lois

Montesq.Esprit des Lois. Montesquieu, Esprit des Lois

Montg. Montgomery County Law Reporter (Pa.)

Montg.Co.L.R. Montgomery County Law Reporter, Pennsylvania

Montg.Co.L.R.(Pa.) Montgomery County Law Reporter (Pa.)

Montg.Co.L.Rep'r. Montgomery County Law Reporter (Pa.)

Montg.Co.Law Rep'r. Montgomery County Law Reporter (Pa.)

Month.J.L. Monthly Journal of Law

Month.Jur. Monthly Jurist (Bloomington, Ill.)

Month.L.Bull.(N.Y.) Monthly Law Bulletin

Month.L.J. Monthly Journal of Law (Wash.)

Month.L.M. Monthly Law Magazine (London)

Month.L.Rep. ● Monthly Law Reporter (Boston)
　　　　　　　● Monthly Law Reports (Canada)

Month.L.Rev. Monthly Law Review

Month.Law Bul. Monthly Law Bulletin (N.Y.)

Month.Law Rep. Law Reporter (Boston)

Month.Leg.Ex. Monthly Legal Examiner

Month.Leg.Exam. Monthly Legal Examiner (N.Y.)

Month.Leg.Exam.(N.Y.) Monthly Legal Examiner (New York)

Month.West.Jur. Monthly Western Jurist

Montr. ● Montriou's Reports, Bengal
　　　　● Montriou's Supplement to Morton's Reports

Montr.Cond.Rep. Montreal Condensed Reports

Montr.Leg.N. Montreal Legal News

Montr.Q.B. Montreal Law Reports Queen's Bench

Montr.Super. Montreal Law Reports, Superior Court

Montreal L.Q.B.(Can.) Montreal Law Reports, Queen's Bench

Montreal L.R.Q.B. Montreal Law Reports, Queen's Bench (Canada)

Montreal L.R.S.C. Montreal Law Reports, Superior Court (Canada)

Montreal L.S.C.(Can.) Montreal Law Reports, Superior Court (Canada)

Moo. ● Moody's English Crown Cases
　　　● Francis Moore's English King's Bench Reports (1512-1621)
　　　● J.M. Moore's English Common Pleas Reports

Moo.A. Moore's Reports (1 Bosanquet & Puller, after page 470) (1796-97)

Moo.C.C. Moody's English Crown Cases Reserved (1824-44)

Moo.C.P. Moore's English Common Pleas Reports

Moo.Cr.C. Moody's English Crown Cases Reserved

Moo.F. F. Moore's King's Bench Reports (1512-1621) (Eng.)

Moo.G.C. Moore: The Gorham Case, English Privy Council

Moo.Ind.App. Moore's Reports, Privy Council, Indian Appeals (1836-72)

Moo.J.B. Moore's English Common Pleas Reports (1817-27)

Moo.K.B. Moore's English King's Bench Reports (1512-1621)

Moo.P.C. Moore's Privy Council Cases, Old and New Series

Moo.P.C.(N.S.) Moore's Privy Council Cases, New Series

Moo.P.C.C. Moore's Privy Council Cases (Eng.)

Moo.P.C.C.N.S. Moore's Privy Council Cases, New Series (Eng.)

Moo.P.C.Cas.N.S. Moore's Privy Council Cases, New Series (Eng.) 9 vols.

Moo.Sep.Rep. Moore, Separate Report of Westerton v. Liddell

Moo.Tr. Moore's Divorce Trials

Moo. & M. Moody and Malkin's Nisi Prius Reports (1826-30)

Moo. & Mal. Moody & Malkin's English Nisi Prius Reports (1826-30)

Moo. & P. Moore & Payne, English Common Pleas Reports, 5 vols. (1828-31)

Moo. & Pay. Moore & Payne, English Common Pleas Reports, 5 vols. (1828-31)

Moo. & R. Moody & Robinson's English Nisi Prius Reports (1830-44)

Moo. & Rob. Moody & Robinson's English Nisi Prius Reports (1830-44)

Moo. & S. Moore & Scott's English Common Pleas Reports (1831-34)

Moo. & Sc. Moore & Scott's English Common Pleas Reports (1831-34)

Mood. Moody's English Crown Cases Reserved (1824-44)

Mood.C.C. Moody's Crown Cases Reserved (Eng.)

Mood. & M. Moody & Malkin's English Nisi Prius Reports

Mood. & Malk. Moody & Malkin's English Nisi Prius Reports

Mood. & R. Moody & Robinson's English Nisi Prius Reports

Mood. & Rob. Moody & Robinson's English Nisi Prius Reports

Moody. Moody's Crown Cases (168, 169 Eng. Reprint)

Moody C.C.(Eng.) Moody's Crown Cases (168, 169 Eng. Reprint)

Moody Cr.C. Moody's Crown Cases (168, 169 Eng. Reprint)

Moody & M. Moody & Mackin's English Nisi Prius Reports (173 Eng. Reprint)

Moody & M.(Eng.) Moody & Mackin's English Nisi Prius Reports

Moody & R. Moody and Robinson's English Nisi Prius Reports (174 Eng. Reprint)

Moody & R.(Eng.) Moody and Robinson's English Nisi Prius Reports (174 Eng. Reprint)

Moon. Moon's Reports (133-144 Indiana and 6-14 Indiana Appeals)

Moore
- Moore's Common Pleas Reports (Eng.)
- Moore's King's Bench Reports (Eng.)
- Moore's Privy Council Reports (Eng.)
- Moore's Reports (67 Alabama)
- Moore's Reports (28-34 Arkansas)
- Moore's Reports (22-24 Texas)

Moore.A. Moore's Reports (1 Bosanquet & Puller, after p. 470) (Eng.)

Moore C.P. Moore's Common Pleas Reports (Eng.)

Moore,Cr.Law. Moore's Criminal Law and Procedure

Moore E.I. Moore's East Indian Appeals

Moore,Fed.Practice Moore's Federal Practice

Moore G.C. Moore, Gorham Case (English Privy Council)

Moore Ind.App. Moore's Indian Appeals Reports

Moore Ind.App.(Eng.) Moore's Indian Appeals (18-20 Eng. Reprint)

Moore Int.L. Moore's Digest of International Law

Moore K.B. Sir F. Moore's English King's Bench Reports

Moore K.B.(Eng.) Sir F. Moore's English King's Bench Reports

Moore P.C. Moore's English Privy Council Reports

Moore P.C.C. Moore's English Privy Council Cases (12-15 Eng. Reprint)

Moore P.C.C.(Eng.) Moore's English Privy Council Cases (12-15 Eng. Reprint)

Moore P.C.C.N.S.(Eng.) Moore's English Privy Council Cases, New Series (15-17 Eng. Reprint)

Moore P.C.N.S. Moore's English Privy Council Reports, New Series

Moore, Presby.Dig. Moore's Presbyterian Digest

Moore Q.B. F. Moore's Queen's Bench Reports (Eng.)

Moore & P. Moore & Payne's English Common Pleas Reports

Moore & P.(Eng.) Moore & Payne's English Common Pleas Reports

Moore & S. Moore & Scott's English Common Pleas Reports

Moore & S.(Eng.) Moore & Scott's English Common Pleas Reports

Moore & W. Moore & Walker's Reports (22-24 Texas)

Moore & Walker. Moore & Walker's Reports (22-24 Texas)

Moot Ct.Bull. University of Illinois Moot Court Bulletin

Mor. Morison's Dictionary of Decisions in the Court of Session, Scotland (1540-1808)

Mor.Corp. Morawetz on Private Corporations

Mor.Dic. Morison, Dictionary of Decisions, Scotch Court of Session

Mor.Dict. Morison, Dictionary of Decisions, Scotch Court of Session

Mor.Ia. Morris' Reports (Iowa 1839-46)

Mor.Min.Rep. Morrison's Mining Reports

Mor.Miss. Morris' Reports (43-48 Miss.)

Mor.Priv.Corp. Morawetz on Private Corporations

Mor.St.Ca. Morris' State Cases (Miss. 1818-72)

Mor.St.Cas. Morris' State Cases (Miss. 1818-72)

Mor.Supp. Morison's Dictionary, Court of Session Decisions, Supplement (1620-1768) (Sc.)

Mor.Syn. Morison's Synopsis, Scotch Session Cases (1808-16)

Mor.Tran. Morrison's Transcript of United States Supreme Court Decisions

Moreau & Carleton's Partidas. Moreau-Lislet and Carleton's Laws of Las Siète Partidas in force in Louisiana

Morey Out.Rom.Law. Morey Outlines of Roman Law

Morg. & W.L.J. Morgan & Williams, Law Journal (London)

Morgan. Morgan's Digest (Ceylon)

Morgan L.M. Morgan's Legal Miscellany (Ceylon)

Morl.Dig. Morley's East Indian Digest

Morr.
- Morrell's Bankruptcy Reports (1884-93) (Eng.)
- Morris' Reports (Iowa 1839-46)
- Morris' Reports (5 California)
- Morris' Reports (Jamaica)
- Morris' Reports (23-26 Oregon)
- Morris' Reports, Bombay (India)

Morr.B.C. Morrell's Bankruptcy Reports (Eng.)

Morr.Bankr.Cas. Morrell's Bankruptcy Cases (Eng.)

Morr.Bomb. Morris' Reports Bombay (India)

Morr.Cal. Morris' Reports (5 California)

Morr.Dig. Morrison, Digest of Mining Decisions

Morr.Jam. Morris' Reports (Jamaica)

Morr.M.R. Morrison's Mining Reports (U.S.)

Morr.Min.R. Morrison's Mining Reports (U.S.)

Morr.Min.Rep. Morrison's Mining Reports

Morr.Mines. Morrison, Digest of Mining Decisions

Morr.Miss. Morris' Reports (43-48 Miss.)

Morr.St.Cas. Morris' State Cases (Miss.)

Morr.Supp. Supplement to Morrison's Dictionary. Scotch Court of Session

Morr.Trans. Morrison's Transcript, United States Supreme Court

Morrell (Eng.) Morrell's English Bankruptcy Cases

Morrell, Bankr.Cas. Morrell's English
Bankruptcy Cases

Morris. ● Morris' Reports (5 California)

  ● Morris Reports (Iowa
1839-46)

  ● Morris' Reports, Bombay
(India)

  ● Morris' Reports Jamaica)

  ● Morris' Reports (23-26
Oregon)

  ● Morrissett's Reports (80,
98 Alabama)

Morris Repl. Morris on Replevin

Morris & Har. Morris & Harrington's
Reports, Bombay (India)

Morse,Banks. Morse on the Law of
Banks and Banking

Morse Exch.Rep. Morse's Exchequer
Reports (Canada)

Morse Tr. Morse's Famous Trials

Morton. Morton's Reports, Calcutta
Superior Court (India)

Mos. Mosely's English Chancery Reports (25 Eng. Reprint)

Mosely (Eng.) Mosely's English Chancery Reports (25 Eng. Reprint)

Moult.Ch. Moulton's Chancery Practice (New York)

Moult.Ch.P. Moulton's Chancery
Practice (New York)

Moyle ● Moyle's Criminal Circulars (India)

  ● Moyle's Entries 1658
(Eng.)

Mozley & W. Mozley & Whitely's Law
Dictionary (Eng.)

Mozley & Whiteley. Mozley & Whiteley's Law Dictionary

Mq.L. Marquette Law Review

Mq.L.R. Marquette Law Review

ms. manuscript

Ms. Mississippi

Ms.D. ● Manuscript Decisions,
Commissioner of Pa-
tents (U.S.)

  ● Manuscript Decisions,
Comptroller General
(U.S.)

Ms.L.J. Mississippi Law Journal

Msc. New York Miscellaneous Reports

Msc2d New York Miscellaneous Reports, Second Series

Mt. ● Montana

  ● Montana Reports

Mt.L.R. Montana Law Review

Mtg. Mortgage

Mthly. Monthly

Mu.Corp.Ca. Municipal Corporation
Cases (U.S.)

Mu.Corp.Cir. Municipal Corporation
Circular (Eng.)

Mu.L.J. Municipal Law Journal

Mulford,Nation. Mulford, The Nation

Mult. Multiple

Mult.Dwell. Multiple Dwelling

Mult.Resid. Multiple Residence

Mum.Jam. Mumford's Jamaica Reports

Mumf. Mumford's Reports (Jamaica)

Mun. ● Munford's Reports (15-20
Eng. Reprint)

  ● Municipal

  ● Municipal Law Reporter

Mun.App. Munitions Appeals Reports (Eng.)

Mun.App.Rep. Munitions Appeals
Reports (Eng.)

Mun.App.Sc. Munitions of War Acts,
Appeal Reports (1916-20) (Sc.)

Mun.Att'y. Municipal Attorney

Mun.Code Municipal Code

Mun.Corp.Cas. Municipal Corporation Cases

Mun.Ct. Municipal Court

Mun.Ct.App.Dist.Col. Municipal
Court of Appeals for the District of
Columbia

Mun.Home Rule Municipal Home
Rule

Mun.L.Ct.Dec. Municipal Law Court
Decisions

Mun.L.J. Municipal Law Journal

Mun.L.R. ● Municipal Law Reporter (Pa.)

  ● Municipal Law Re-
ports (1903-13) (Sc.)

Mun.Ord.Rev. Municipal Ordinance
Review

Mun.Rep. Municipal Reports (Canada)

Mun. & El.Cas. Municipal & Election Cases (India)

Mundy Abstracts of Star Chamber Proceedings (1550-58)

Munf. ● Munford's Reports (15-20 Eng. Reprint)
     ● Munford's Reports (15-20 Virginia) (1810-20)

Munf.(Va.) Munford's Reports (15-20 Virginia)

Munic. Municipal

Munic.L.R.(Pa.) Municipal Law Reporter

Munic. & P.L. Municipal & Parish Law Cases (Eng.)

Municipal Court Rule Rules for the Municipal Courts

Mur. Murphey's North Carolina Reports (1804-19)

Mur. ● Murphey's Reports (5-7 N. C.)
     ● Murray's Reports (Ceylon)
     ● Murray's Reports New South Wales (Aus.)
     ● Murray's Jury Court Cases, (1815-30) (Sc.)

Mur.U.S.Ct. Murray's Proceedings in the United States Courts.

Mur. & H. Murphy & Hurlstone's Exchequer Reports (1836-37)

Mur. & Hurl. Murphy & Hurlstone's English Exchequer Reports (1836-37)

Murat.Antiq.Med.Aevi. Muratori's Antiquitates Medii Aevi

Murd.Epit. Murdoch's Epitome Canada

Murfree, Off.Bonds Murfree on Official Bonds

Murph. Murphey's Reports (5-7 North Carolina)

Murph.(N.C.) Murphey's Reports (5-7 North Carolina)

Murph. & H. Murphy & Hurlstone, English Exchequer Reports

Murph. & H.(Eng.) Murphy & Hurlstone, English Exchequer Reports

Murr. ● Murray's Ceylon Reports
     ● Murray's Laws and Acts of Parliament (Sc.)
     ● Murray's New South Wales Reports

     ● Murray's Jury Court Cases, Sc. (1815-30)

Murr.Over.Cas. Murray's Overruled Cases

Murray Murray's Scotch Jury Court Reports

Murray (Ceylon) Murray's Ceylon Reports

Murray (Scot.) Murray's Scotch Jury Trials

Murray's Eng.Dict. Murray's English Dictionary

Mut. ● Mutual
     ● Mutukisna's Reports (Ceylon)

Mut.Funds Guide Mutual Funds Guide (CCH)

Mutukisna Mutukisna's Ceylon Reports

My. & C. Mylne & Craig's Chancery Reports (Eng.)

My. & Cr. Mylne & Craig's Chancery Reports (Eng.)

My. & K. Mylne & Keen's English Chancery Reports (39, 40 Eng. Reprint)

Myer Dig. Myer's Texas Digest

Myer Fed.Dec. Myer's Federal Decisions

Myl. & C. Mylne & Craig's English Chancery Reports

Myl. & C.(Eng.) Mylne & Craig's English Chancery Reports (40, 41 Egn. Reprint)

Myl. & Cr. Mylne & Craig's English Chancery Reports (40, 41 Eng. Reprint)

Myl. & K. Mylne & Keen's English Chancery Reports (39, 40 Eng. Reprint)

Myl. & K.(Eng.) Mylne & Keen's English Chancery Reports (39, 40 Eng. Reprint)

Mylne & K. Mylne & Keen's English Chancery Reports (39, 40 Eng. Reprint)

Myr. Myrick's California Probate Court Reports (California 1872-79)

Myr.Prob. Myrick's California Probate Court Reports (California 1872-79)

Myrick (Cal.) Myrick's California Probate Court Reports (California 1872-79)

Myrick Prob.(Cal.) Myrick's California Probate Court Reports (California 1872-79)

Mys.Ch.Ct. Mysore Chief Court Reports (India)

Mys.H.C.R. Mysore High Court Reports (India)

Mys.L.J. Mysore Law Journal (India)

Mys.L.R. Mysore Law Reports (India)

Mysore Mysore Law Reports (India)

N

n. footnote

N.
- Nebraska
- Nevada
- North
- Northeastern Reporter
- Northern Ireland Law Reports
- Northwestern Reporter
- Norwegian
- Note
- Novelloe (the Novels of Justinian), north

N.A.
- Nizamut Adalut Reports (India)
- Nonacquiescence

NAA National Academy of Arbitrators

NAACP National Association for the Advancement of Colored People

N.A.B.
- National Alliance of Businessmen
- National Association of Businessmen

N.A.C. Native Appeal Courts (South Africa)

NACA National Advisory Committee for Aeronautics (U.S.)

NACCA National Association of Claimants' Compensation Attorneys

NACCALJ National Association of Claimants' Compensation Attorneys Law Journal

N.A.C. & O. Cape & Orange Free State Native Appeal Court, Selected Decisions

NAE National Academy of Engineering

N.A.I. Netherlands Arbitration Institute

N.A.M.L.Dig. National Association of Manufacturers Law Digest

NARS National Archives and Records Service

NAS National Academy of Science

NASA National Aeronautics and Space Agency

NAS - NRC National Academy of Sciences-National Research Council

N.A.So.Rhod. Southern Rhodesia Native Appeal Court, Reports

NATB National Automobile Theft Bureau

NATO North Atlantic Treaty Organization

N.A.,T. & N. Selected Decisions of the Native Appeal Court (Transvaal and Natal)

N.A. & D.,C. & O. Selection of Cases decided in the Native Appeal and Divorce Court (Cape and Orange Free State)

N.A. & D.T. & N. Transvaal & Natal Native Appeal & Divorce Court Decisions

N.Am.Rev. North American Review

N.Atlantic Reg.Bus.L.Rev. North Atlantic Regional Business Law Review

N.B.
- New Benloe or Bendloe King's Bench Reports
- New Brunswick
- New Brunswick Reports (Canada)

N.B.2d. News Brunswick Reports, 2d Series (Canada)

N.B.Bd.P.U.C. Brunswick Board of Public Utilities Commission, Canada

N.B.Eq. New Brunswick Equity Reports

N.B.Eq.Ca. New Brunswick Equity Cases

N.B.Eq.R. New Brunswick Equity Reports (1894-1912)

N.B.Eq.Rep. New Brunswick Equity Reports (1894-1912)

N.B.J. National Bar Journal

N.B.L.R. North Borneo Law Reports

N.B.N.R. National Bankruptcy News and Reports

N.B.N.Rep. National Bankruptcy News and Reports

N.B.R.
- New Brunswick Reports (1883-1929)
- National Bankruptcy Register Reports (U.S.)

N.B.R.All. Allen's New Brunswick Reports

N.B.R.Ber. Berton's New Brunswick Reports

N.R.B.Carl. Carleton's New Brunswick Reports

N.B.R.Chip. Chipman's New Brunswick Reports

N.B.R.Han. Hannay's New Brunswick Reports

N.B.R.Kerr Kerr's New Brunswick Reports

N.B.R.P. & B. Pugsley & Burbridge's New Brunswick Reports

N.B.R.P. & T. Pugsley & Trueman's New Brunswick Reports

N.B.R.Pug. Pugsley's New Brunswick Reports

N.B.R.Tru. Trueman's New Brunswick Reports

N.B.Rep. New Brunswick Reports

N.B.Rev.Stat. New Brunswick Revised Statutes (Canada)

N.B.S. National Bureau of Standards (U.S.)

N.B.Stat. New Brunswick Statutes (Canada)

N.B.V.Ad. New Brunswick Vice Admiralty Reports

N.Benl. New Benloe's Reports, English King's Bench (1531-1628)

N.Bruns. New Brunswick Reports (1883-1929)

N.C. ● New Cases (Bingham's New Cases) in Common Pleas (1834-40)
   ● Non callable
   ● North Carolina
   ● North Carolina Reports
   ● Notes of Cases (Australian Jurist)
   ● Notes of Cases (Ecclesiastical & Maritime) (1841-50)
   ● Notes of Cases, T. Strange, Madras (India)

N.C. North Carolina Supreme Court Reports

N.C.A. ● No coupons attached
   ● North Carolina Court of Appeals Reports

NCAJ National Center for Administrative Justice

N.C.Adv.Legis.Serv. North Carolina Advance Legislative Service (Michie)

N.C.App. North Carolina Court of Appeals Reports

NCBF North Carolina Bar Foundation

N.C.C. New Chancery Cases (Younge & Collyer) (1841-43) (Eng.)

N.C.C.A. Negligence & Compensation Cases, Annotated

N.C.C.A.3d Negligence & Compensation Cases, Annotated, 3d Series

N.C.C.A.N.S. Negligence & Compensation Cases, Annotated, New Series

N.C.C.C. North Carolina Corporation Commission

NCCD National Council on Crime and Delinquency

NCCDL National College of Criminal Defense Lawyers and Public Defenders

N.C.Cent.L.J. North Carolina Central Law Journal

N.C.Conf. North Carolina Conference Reports

N.C.Conf.Rep.(N.C.) North Carolina Conference Reports

N.C.D. Nemine contra dicente (no one dissenting)

NCDA National College of District Attorneys

N.C.Ecc. Notes of Cases in Ecclesiastical & Maritime Courts (Eng.)

N.C.F.A. National Consumers' Finance Assn. Law Bulletin

N.C.Gen.Stat. General Statutes of North Carolina

NCIC National Crime Information Center

N.C.I.C.Ops. North Carolina Industrial Commission Advance Sheets

NCJCJ National Council of Juvenile Court Judges

NCJJ National College of Juvenile Justice

N.C.J.of L. North Carolina Journal of Law

N.C.L. North Carolina Law Review

NCLE Nebraska Continuing Legal Education, Inc.

N.C.L.J. North Carolina Law Journal

N.C.L.R. North Carolina Law Review

N.C.L.Rep. North Carolina Law Repository

N.C.L.Rev. North Carolina Law Review

N.C.Law Repos. North Carolina Law Repository

N.C.M. Court-Martial Reports, Navy Cases

N.C.R.C. North Carolina Board of Railroad Commissioners

NCSJ National College of the State Judiciary

NCSL National Civil Service League

N.C.Sess.Laws Session Laws of North Carolina

N.C.Str. Strange's Notes of Cases, Madras (1798-1816)

N.C.T.Rep. North Carolina Term Rep. (4 N.C.)

N.C.Term R. North Carolina Term Reports

N.C.Term Rep. North Carolina Term Reports

NCUA National Credit Union Administration

N.C.U.C. North Carolina Utilities Commission Reports

N.C. & B. Naval Courts and Boards (U.S.)

N.Car. North Carolina

N.Cent.School L.Rev. North Central School Law Review

N.Ch.R.　● Nelson's Chancery Reports (Eng.)
　　　　　● H. Finch's Chancery Reports 1673-81 (Eng.)

N.Chip. N. Chipman's Reports (Vermont 1789-91)

N.Chip.(Vt.) N. Chipman's Reports (Vermont 1789-91)

N.Chipm. N. Chipman's Reports (Vermont 1789-91)

N.Cr. New York Criminal Reports

N.D.　● North Dakota
　　　　● North Dakota Supreme Court Reports (1890-1953)
　　　　● Northern District

N.D.A. National Defense Act (U.S.)

NDAA National District Attorneys Association

N.D.B. Navy Department Bulletin (U.S.)

N.D.B.B. North Dakota Bar Brief

N.D.C.of R. North Dakota Commissioners of Railroads

N.D.Cent.Code North Dakota Century Code

N.D.L. Norte Dame Lawyer

N.D.L.R. North Dakota Law Review

N.D.L.Rev. North Dakota Law Review

N.D.P.A. National Democratic Party of Alabama

N.D.R. North Dakota Law Review

N.D.R.C. North Dakota Board of Railroad Commissioners

N.D.Sess.Laws Laws of North Dakota

NDU National Defense University

N.E.　● New edition
　　　　● New England
　　　　● North Eastern Reporter

N.E.2d Northeastern Reporter, Second Series

N.E.C. Notes of Ecclesiastical Cases (Eng.)

N.E.I. Non est inventus (he is not found)

N.E.P.A. National Environmental Policy Act

N.E.R.　● New England Reporter
　　　　● North Eastern Reporter (commonly cited N.E.)

N.E.Rep.　● New England Reporter
　　　　● North Eastern Reporter (commonly cited N.E.)

N.Eng.L.Rev. New England Law Review

N.Eng.Rep. New England Reporter

N.F.　● Newfoundland
　　　　● Newfoundland Reports

NFFE National Federation of Federal Employees

NFLA National Farm Loan Association (U.S.)

NFPA National Fire Protection Association

NFPCA National Fire Protection and Control Administration

NFU National Farmers' Union

NGO Non-Governmental Organization

NGR National Guard Regulation

N.H.　● New Hampshire
　　　　● New Hampshire Supreme Court Reports (1816-date)

N.H.Act National Housing Act

N.H.B.J. New Hampshire Bar Journal

N.H.C. Native High Court Reports (South Africa)

N.H.J. New Hampshire Bar Journal

N.H.L.Rep. New Hampshire Law Reporter

N.H.Laws Laws of the State of New Hampshire

N.H.P.S.C.R. New Hampshire Public Service Commission Reports

N.H.R. New Hampshire Reports

N.H.R.C. New Hampshire Board of Railroad Commissioners

N.H.Rev.Stat.Ann. New Hampshire Revised Statutes Annotated

N.H.T.S.A. National Highway Transportation Safety Administration

N.H. & C. Railway & Canal Cases (1835-55) (Eng.)

N.Hamp.S.B.A. New Hampshire State Bar Assn.

N.I. Northern Ireland Law Reports

NIE National Institute of Education

NIER National Industrial Equipment Reserve

NIH National Institutes of Health

N.I.J. New Irish Jurist

N.I.J.R. New Irish Jurist (1900-05)

N.I.L. Negotiable Instruments Law

NILECJ National Institute of Law Enforcement and Criminal Justice

N.I.L.Q. Northern Ireland Legal Quarterly

N.I.L.R. Northern Ireland Law Reports

N.I.L.Rev. Netherlands International Law Review

NIMH National Institute of Mental Health

N.I.R.C. National Industrial Relations Court--National Labour Tribunal (Eng)

NITA National Institute for Trial Advocacy

N.I.T.M. National Income Tax Magazine

N.Ir. Northern Ireland Law

N.Ir.L.Q. Northern Ireland Legal Quarterly

N.Ir.L.R. Northern Ireland Law Reports

NJ Nederlandse Jurisprudentie (Uitspraken in burgerlijke, straf- en onteigeningszaken) (Holland)

N.J. ● New Jersey
● New Jersey Supreme Court Reports
● Notice of Judgment (official)

NJA Nytt Juridiskt Arkiv (Sweden)

NJ(A) Nederlandse Jurisprudentie (Administratiefrechtelijke Beslissingen) (Holland)

NJB Nederlands Juristenblad (Holland)

NJCLE Institute for Continuing Legal Education (New Jersey)

N.J.Eq. New Jersey Equity Reports (1830-1948)

N.J.F.D. Notices of Judgment, U.S. Food & Drug Administration

N.J.L. New Jersey Law Reports

N.J.L.J. New Jersey Law Journal

N.J.L.Rev. New Jersey Law Review

N.J.Law. New Jersey Law Reports

N.J.Law J. New Jersey Law Journal

N.J.Laws Laws of New Jersey

NJM New Jersey Miscellaneous Reports

N.J.Misc. New Jersey Miscellaneous Reports (1923-49)

N.J.P.U.C. New Jersey Public Utility Commission Reports

N.J.R.C. New Jersey Board of Railroad Commissioners Annual Reports (1907-10)

N.J.Re.Tit.N. New Jersey Realty Title News

N.J.Rev.Stat. New Jersey Revised Statutes

N.J.S. New Jersey Superior Court Reports

N.J.S.S. New Jersey Statutes Annotated

N.J.S.B.A. New Jersey State Bar Association

N.J.S.B.T.A.Ops. New Jersey State Board of Tax Appeals, Opinions

N.J.Sess.Law Serv. New Jersey Session Law Service

N.J.St.B.J. New Jersey State Bar Journal

N.J.Stat.Ann.(West) New Jersey Statutes Annotated

N.J.Super. New Jersey Superior Court Reports

N.L. Nelson's Lutwyche, English Common Pleas Reports

NLADA NLADA Briefcase

NLCPI National Legal Center for the Public Interest

NLF National Law Foundation

N.L.F. National Liberation Front

N.L.G.Q. National Lawyers' Guild Quarterly

N.L.J. Nagpur Law Journal (India)

N.L.L.
- New Library of Law, Harrisburg, Pennsylvania
- New Library of Law and Equity, English

NLM National Library of Medicine

N.L.R.
- Nagpur Law Reports, India
- Natal Law Reports, India
- New Law Reports, Ceylon
- Newfoundland Law Reports

N.L.R.A. National Labor Relations Act

N.L.R.B.
- National Labor Relations Board (U.S.)
- National Labor Relations Board Decisions and Orders

N.L.R.B.Dec. Decisions Comprising Digest of Decisions and Orders (Prentice-Hall)

N.L.Rev. Northeastern Law Review

N.M.
- New Mexico
- New Mexico Supreme Court Reports
- New Mexico Territorial Court

NMB National Mediation Board

NMC Naval Material Command

NMCLE Continuing Legal Education of New Mexico, Inc.

N.M.(J.) New Mexico Reports (Johnson)

N.M.L. New Mexico Law Review

N.N.(G.) New Mexico Reports (Gildersleeve)

N.M.L.R. New Mexico Law Review

N.M.Laws Laws of New Mexico

N.M.S.B.A. New Mexico State Bar Assn.

N.M.S.C.C. New Mexico State Corporation Commission

N.M.St.Bar Assn. New Mexico State Bar Association

N.M.Stat.Ann. New Mexico Statutes Annotated

N.Mag.Ca. New Magistrates' Cases (Eng.)

N.Mex. New Mexico Territorial Courts

N.Mex.L.Rev. New Mexico Law Review

N/O Registered in name of

NOAA National Oceanic and Atmospheric Administration

N.O.I.B.N. Not otherwise indexed by name (used under terms of tariffs, filed with Interstate Commerce Commission

NOLPE School L.J. NOLPE School Law Journal

N.O.V. Non Obstante Veredicto (the judgment notwithstanding)

N.of Cas.
- Notes of Cases at Madras (by Strange)
- Notes of Cases, English Ecclesiastical and Maritime Courts (1841-50)

N.of Cas.Madras. Notes of Cases at Madras (by Strange)

N.P.
- New Practice
- Nisi Prius
- Ohio Nisi Prius Reports
- Notary Public, Nisi Prius (trial of fact before judge)
- Nova Placita

N.P.A. National Production Authority (U.S.)

N.P.C.
- National People's Congress (China)
- National Petroleum Council
- New Practice Cases. Bail Court.(1844-48)
- Nisi Prius Cases, English

N.P.D.
- National Democratic Party (Germany)
- South African Law Reports, Natal Provinces Division

N.P.N.S. Ohio Nisi Prius Rep., New
Series

N.P.Ohio Ohio Nisi Prius Reports

N.P.R. Nisi Prius Reports

N.P. & G.T.Rep. Nisi Prius &
General Term Reports (Ohio)

N.P.N.S. Ohio Nisi Prius Reports,
New Series

N.R. ● Natal Reports (S.Af.)
● Bosanquet & Pullers New
Reports (1804-07) (Eng.)
● The New Reports (1862-
65) (Eng.)

N.R.A. National Recovery Administration (U.S.)

N.R.A.B. ● National Railroad Adjustment Awards
● National Railroad Ad-
justment Board, 1st-
4th Divisions (1934-
date)

N.R.A.B. (1st D.). U.S. National
Railroad Adjustment Board Awards,
First Division

N.R.A.B.(2d D.). U.S. National Railroad Adjustment Board Awards,
Second Division

N.R.A.B.(3d D.). U.S. National Railroad Adjustment Board Awards,
Division

N.R.A.B. (4th D.). U.S. National
Railroad Adjustment Board Awards,
Fourth Division

N.R.B.P. New Reports of Bosanquet
& Puller

NRC ● Nuclear Regulatory Commission
● National Research Council

NRCLS National Resource Center for
Consumers of Legal Services

N.R.L. Revised Laws 1813, N.Y.

NRLI Natural Resources Law Institute

N.R.L.R. Northern Rhodesia Law
Reports

N.R.J. Natural Resources Journal

N.R.N.L.R. Northern Region of
Nigeria Law Reports

N.R.R. & C. Russell & Chesley's
Nova Scotia Reports

N.S. ● new series
● new style
● Nova Scotia
● Nova Scotia Reports, Canada

NSA National Security Agency (U.S.)

NSC National Security Council
(U.S.)

N.S.C. New Session Cases (Sc.)

N.S.Dec. Nova Scotia Decisions (1867-
74)

NSF National Science Foundation

N.S.I. National Security Index of the
American Security Council

N.S.L.R. Nova Scotia Law Reports
(1834-52) (Canada)

N.S.M.C.M. Naval Supplement,
Manual for Courts-Martial (U.S.)

NSOB New Senate Office Building

N.S.R. Nova Scotia Reports (Canada)

N.S.R.B. National Security Resources
Board (U.S.)

N.S.R.Coh. Cohen's Nova Scotia
Reports

N.S.R.2d. Nova Scotia Reports,2d
Series (Canada)

N.S.R.G. & O. Nova Scotia Reports,
Geldert & Oxley

N.S.R.G. & R. Nova Scotia Reports,
Geldert & Russell

N.S.R.J. Nova Scotia Reports (James)

N.S.R.(James) Nova Scotia Reports
(James) (Canada)

N.S.R.Old. Oldright's Nova Scotia
Reports

N.S.R.(Old.). Nova Scotia Reports,
Oldrights (Canada)

N.S.R.R. & G. Russell & Geldert's
Nova Scotia Reports

N.S.R.Thom. Thomson's Nova Scotia
Reports

N.S.R.(Thom.). Nova Scotia Reports
(Thomson) (Canada)

N.S.Rev.Stat. Nova Scotia Revised
Statutes (Canada)

NSSR New School of Social Research

N.S.Stat. Nova Scotia Statutes
(Canada)

N.S.V.P. National Student Volunteer
Program

N.S.W. New South Wales Reports,
Old and New Series (Aus.)

N.S.W.A.R. New South Wales Arbitration Reports

N.S.W.Adm. New South Wales
Reports Admiralty

N.S.W.B. New South Wales Reports, Bankruptcy Cases

N.S.W.Bktcy.Cas. New South Wales Reports, Bankruptcy Cases

N.S.W.C.Eq. New South Wales Reports, Equity

N.S.W.C.R.D. New South Wales Court of Review Decisions

N.S.W.C.R.L. New South Wales Law Reports (Supreme Court)

N.S.W.Eq. New South Wales Equity Reports

N.S.W.Eq.Rep. New South Wales Law Reports Equity

N.S.W.Ind.Arbtn. New South Wales Industrial Arbitration Cases

N.S.W.Ind.Arbtn.Cas. New South Wales Industrial Arbitration Cases

N.S.W.L.R. New South Wales Law Reports (1880-1900) (Aus.)

N.S.W.L.V.R. New South Wales Land Valuation Reports

N.S.W.Land App.Cts. New South Wales Land Appeal Courts

N.S.W.R. New South Wales Reports (Aus.)

N.S.W.Regs., B. & Ords. New South Wales Regulations, By-Laws and Ordinances (Aus.)

N.S.W.S.C.R. New South Wales Supreme Court Reports

N.S.W.S.C.R.N.S. New South Wales Supreme Court Reports, New Series

N.S.W.S.R. New South Wales State Reports

N.S.W.St.R. New South Wales State Reports

N.S.W.W.C.R. New South Wales Workmen's Compensation Reports

N.S.W.W.N. New South Wales Weekly Notes (Aus.)

N.S.Wales New South Wales

N.S.Wales L. New South Wales Law

N.S.Wales L.R.Eq. New South Wales Law Reports Equity

N.Sc.Dec. Nova Scotia Decisions

NTIS National Technical Information Service

N.T.Rep. New Term Reports, Queen's Bench (Eng.)

N.T.Repts. New Term Reports, Queen's Bench

N.T.S.B. National Transportation Safety Board

N.Trans.S.Dec. National Transportation Safety Board Decisions

N.U. Nebraska Unofficial Reports

N.U.L.R. Northwestern University Law Review

N/V No value

N.W.
- North Western Reporter (National Reporter System)
- North-Western Provinces, High Court Reports (India)

N.W.2d. North Western Reporter, Second Series

NWC National War College

N.W.L. Northwestern University Law Review

N.W.L.B. National War Labor Board

N.W.L.Rev. North Western Law Review (Chicago)

N.W.Law Rev. Northwestern Law Review

N.W.P. North-Western Provinces High Court Reports (India)

N.W.P.H.C. Northwest Provinces, High Court Reports (India)

N.W.R. Northwestern Reporter

N.W.Rep. Northwestern Reporter

N.W.Rev.Ord. Northwest Territories Revised Ordinances (Canada)

N.W.T. Northwest Territories Reports (1885-1907) (Canada)

N.W.T.L.R. North West Territories Law Reports

N.W.T.Ord. Northwest Territories Ordinances (Canada)

N.W.T.R. North West Territories Reports, Canada (1885-1907)

N.W.T.Rep. Northwest Territories Reports, Canada

N.W.Terr. Northwest Territories, Supreme Court Reports

N.W.Terr.(Can.) Northwest Territories Reports (1885-1907) (Canada)

NWU Northwestern University School of Law

N.W.U.L.Rev. Northwestern University Law Review

N.Y.
- New York
- New York Court of Appeals Reports

N.Y.2d New York Court of Appeals Reports, Second Series

NYA National Youth Administration

N.Y.Ann.Ca. New York Annotated Cases

N.Y.Ann.Cas. New York Annotated Cases

N.Y.Anno.Cas. New York Annotated Cases

N.Y.Anno.Dig. New York Annotated Digest

N.Y.Annot.Dig. New York Annotated Digest

N.Y.App.Dec.
- New York Court of Appeals Decisions
- New York Appellate Division Decisions

N.Y.App.Div. New York Supreme Court Appellate Division Reports

N.Y.Bank.Law New York Banking Law

NYC Neighborhood Youth Corps

N.Y.C.B.A.Bull. Bulletin of the Association of the Bar of the City of New York

N.Y.C.C.H. New York Advance Digest Service (Commerce Clearing House), cited by year

N.Y.C.R.R. New York Codes, Rules and Regulations

N.Y.Cas.Err. Caines' New York Cases in Error

N.Y.Ch.Sent. New York Chancery Sentinel

N.Y.City Ct. New York City Court

N.Y.City Ct.Rep. New York City Court Reports

N.Y.City Ct.Supp. New York City Court Reports Supplement

N.Y.City Ct.Suppl. New York City Court Reports Supplement

N.Y.City H.Rec. New York City Hall Recorder

N.Y.City Hall Rec. New York City Hall Recorder

N.Y.Civ.Pr.Rep. New York Civil Procedure Reports

N.Y.Civ.Prac.Law & R. New York Civil Practice Law and Rules

N.Y.Civ.Pro. New York Civil Procedure

N.Y.Civ.Pro.R.N.S. New York Civil Procedure, New Series

N.Y.Civ.Proc. New York Civil Procedure

N.Y.Civ.Proc.(N.S.) New York Civil Procedure, New Series

N.Y.Civ.Proc.R. New York Civil Procedure Reports

N.Y.Civ.Proc.R.,N.S. New York Civil Procedure Reports, New Series

N.Y.Cn. New York University Annual Conference on Labor

N.Y.Code R. New York Code Reporter

N.Y.Code R.N.S. New York Code Reports, New Series

N.Y.Code Rep. New York Code Reporter

N.Y.Code Rep.N.S. New York Code Reports, New Series

N.Y.Code Report. New York Code Reporter

N.Y.Code Reports, N.S. New York Code Reports, New Series

N.Y.Code Reptr. New York Code Reporter

N.Y.Code Reptr.N.S. New York Code Reporter, New Series

N.Y.Cond. New York Condensed Reports (1881-82)

N.Y.Cont.L.Ed. New York Continuing Legal Education

N.Y.Cont.Legal Ed. New York Continuing Legal Education

N.Y.County B.Bull. New York County Lawyers Association Bar Bulletin

N.Y.County Law Ass'n.B.Bull. New York County Lawyers Association Bar Bulletin

N.Y.Cr. New York Criminal Reports (1878-1924)

N.Y.Cr.R. New York Criminal Reports

N.Y.Cr.Rep. New York Criminal Reports (1878-1924)

N.Y.Crim. New York Criminal Reports (1878-1924)

N.Y.Ct.App. New York Court of Appeals

N.Y.D.L.W.C.Dec. New York State Department of Labor. Court Decisions and Workmen's Compensation

N.Y.Daily L.Gaz. New York Daily Law Gazette

N.Y.Daily L.Reg. New York Daily Law Register

N.Y.Daily Reg. New York Daily Register

N.Y.Daily Tr. New York Daily Transcript, Old and New Series

N.Y.Dep't R. New York Department Reports

N.Y.E.T.R. New York Estate Tax Reports (P-H)

N.Y.El.Cas. New York Election Cases

N.Y.Elec.Cas. New York Election Cases

N.Y.Elect.Cas. New York Election Cases

N.Y.F. New York Law Forum

N.Y.Jud.Rep. New York Judicial Repository

N.Y.Jur. ● New York Jurisprudence

　　　　　● New York Jurist

N.Y.L. New York University Law Review

N.Y.L.C.Ann. New York Leading Cases Annotated

N.Y.L.Cas. New York Leading Cases

N.Y.L.F. New York Law Forum

N.Y.L.Gaz. New York Law Gazette, N.Y.

N.Y.L.J. New York Law Journal

N.Y.L.R.B. New York State Labor Relations Board and Decisions

N.Y.L.R.B.Dec. New York State Labor Relations Board Decisions and orders

N.Y.L.Rec. New York Law Record

N.Y.L.Rev. New York Law Review

N.Y.L.S.Rev. New York Law School Review

N.Y.L.S.Stud.L.Rev. New York Law School Student Law Review

N.Y. Law (Consol.) New York Consolidated Law Services

N.Y.Law (McKinney) McKinney's Consolidated Laws of New York

N.Y.Law Gaz. New York Law Gazette

N.Y.Law J. New York Law Journal

N.Y.Law Rev. New York Law Review

N.Y.Leg.N. New York Legal News 1880-82

N.Y.Leg.Obs. New York Legal Observer (Owen's).

N.Y.Leg.Reg. New York Legal Register

N.Y.Misc. New York Miscellaneous Reports

N.Y.Misc.2d. New York Miscellaneous Reports, Second Series

N.Y.Mo.L.Bul. New York Monthly Law Bulletin

N.Y.Mo.L.R. New York Monthly Law Reports

N.Y.Mo.L.Rec. New York Monthly Law Record

N.Y.Mo.Law Bul. New York Monthly Law Bulletin (New York City)

N.Y.Month.L.Bul. New York Monthly Law Bulletin

N.Y.Month.L.R. New York Monthly Law Reports

N.Y.Mun.Gaz. New York Municipal Gazette

N.Y.Off.Dept.R. New York Official Department Reports

N.Y.Op.Att.Gen. Sickel's Opinions of the Attorneys-General of New York

N.Y.Ops.Atty.Gen. Sickel's Opinions of the Attorney-General of New York

N.Y.P.R. New York Practice Reports

N.Y.P.S.C.(1st D.) New York Public Service Commission, First District

N.Y.P.S.C.(2d D.). New York Public Service Commission, Second District

N.Y.Pr. New York Practice Reports

N.Y.Pr.Rep. New York Practice Reports

N.Y.R.C. New York Railroad Commission Reports

N.Y.Rec. New York Record

N.Y.Reg. New York Daily Register (1872-89)

N.Y.Rep. New York Court of Appeals Reports

N.Y.Reptr. New York Reporter (Gardenier's) (1820)

N.Y.S. ● New York State
      ● New York State Reporter
      ● New York Supplement

N.Y.S.2d New York Supplement Reporter, Second Series

NYSBA New York State Bar Association

N.Y.S.B.A.Bull. New York State Bar Association Bulletin

N.Y.S.B.J. New York State Bar Journal

N.Y.S.D.R. New York State Department Reports

N.Y.S.E. Guide New York Stock Exchange Guide (CCH)

N.Y.S.R. New York State Reporter

N.Y.Sen.J. New York Senate Journal

N.Y.Spec.Term R. Howard's Practice Reports

N.Y.Spec.Term.Rep. Howard's Practice Reports

N.Y.St. New York State Reporter

N.Y.St.B.J. New York State Bar Journal

N.Y.St.Dept.Rep. New York State Department Reports

N.Y.St.R. New York State Reporter (1886-96)

N.Y.St.Rep. New York State Reporter (1886-96)

N.Y.State Bar J. New York State Bar Journal

N.Y.Sup.Ct. New York Supreme Court Reports (1873-96)

N.Y.Super New York Superior Court Reports

N.Y.Super.Ct. New York Superior Court Reports (various reporters)

N.Y.Supp. New York Supplement

N.Y.Supp.2d New York Supplement, Second Series

N.Y.Supr.Ct. New York Supreme Court Reports

N.Y.Supr.Ct.Repts.(T. & C.). New York Supreme Court Reports by Thompson and Cook

N.Y.Suprm.Ct. New York Supreme Court Reports

N.Y.T.R. New York Term Reports (Caines' Reports)

N.Y.Tax Cas. New York Tax Cases, (CCH)

N.Y.Them. New York Themis (N.Y. City)

N.Y.Trans. New York Transcript (Nos. 1-11, 1861) (New York City)

N.Y.Trans.App. New York Transcript Appeal

N.Y.Trans.N.S. New York Transcript, New Series (New York City)

N.Y.Trans.Rep. New York Transcript Reports

NYU New York University School of Law

N.Y.U.Conf. Charitable New York University Conference on Charitable Foundations Proceedings

N.Y.U.Conf.Charitable Fdn. New York University Conference on Charitable Foundations Proceedings

N.Y.U.Conf.Lab. New York University Conference on Labor

N.Y.U. Inst.Fed.Tax. New York University Institute on Federal Taxation

N.Y.U.Inst.Fed.Taxation New York University Institute of Federal Taxation

N.Y.U.Inst. on Fed.Tax. New York University Institute on Federal Taxation

N.Y.U.Intra.L.Rev. New York Intramural Law Review

N.Y.U.J.Int'l Law & Pol. New York University Journal of International Law and Politics

N.Y.U.L. Center Bull. New York University Law Center Bulletin

N.Y.U.L.Q.Rev. New York University Law Quarterly Review

N.Y.U.L.Qu.Rev. New York University Law Quarterly Review

N.Y.U.L.R. New York University Law Review

N.Y.U.L.Rev. New York University Law Review

NYULT New York University School of Continuing Education, Continuing Education in Law and Taxation

N.Y.U.Rev.Law & Soc.C. New York University Review of Law and Social Change

N.Y.U.T.I. New York University Tax Institute

N.Y.Unconsol.Laws New York Unconsolidated Laws (McKinney)

N.Y.Week.Dig. New York Weekly Digest

N.Y.Wkly.Dig. New York Weekly Digest

N.Z. ● New Zealand
     ● New Zealand Reports

N.Z.App.Rep. New Zealand Appeal Reports

N.Z. Awards. New Zealand Awards, Recommendations, Agreements, etc.

N.Z.Col.L.J. New Zealand Colonial Law Journal

N.Z.Ct.App. New Zealand Court of Appeals

N.Z.Ct.Arb. New Zealand Court of Arbitration

N.Z.G.L.R. New Zealand Gazette Law Reports

N.Z.Gaz.L.R. New Zealand Gazette Law Reports

N.Z.Ind.Arb. New Zealand Industrial Arbitration Awards

N.Z.Jur. New Zealand Jurist (1873-78)

N.Z.Jur.N.S. New Zealand Jurist, New Series

N.Z.Jur. & S. New Zealand Jurist, New Series

N.Z.L.J. New Zealand Law Journal

N.Z.L.J.M.C. New Zealand Law Journal, Magistrates' Court Decisions

N.Z.L.R. New Zealand Law Reports

N.Z.L.R.C.A. New Zealand Law Reports, Court of Appeal

N.Z.P.C.C. New Zealand Privy Council Cases

N.Z.P.C.Cas. New Zealand Privy Council Cases

N.Z.R., Regs. & B. Rules, Regulations and By-Laws under New Zealand Statutes

N.Z.Rep. New Zealand Reports, Court of Appeals

N.Z.S.C. New Zealand Supreme Court

N.Z.T.S. New Zealand Treaty Series

N.Z.U.L.Rev. New Zealand Universities Law Review

N. & H. ● Nott & Hopkins' Reports (8-29 U.S. Court of Claims)
     ● Nott & Huntington's Reports (1-7 U.S. Court of Claims)

N. & M. Nevile & Manning's King's Bench Reports (1831-36) (Eng.)

N. & M.M.C. Nevile and Mannings' Magistrate Cases (1832-36)

N. & M.Mag. Nevile & Manning's English Magistrates' Cases

N. & Macn. Nevile & Macnamara Railway & Canal Cases (Eng.)

N. & Mc. Nott & McCord's South Carolina Reports

N. & McC. Nott & McCords South Carolina Reports

N. & P. Nevile & Perry's English King's Bench Reports (1836-38)

N. & P.M.C. Nevile and Perry's Magistrate Cases (1836-37)

N. & P.Mag. Nevile & Perry's English Magistrates' Cases

N. & S. Nicholls & Stops' Reports (1897-1904) (Tasmania)

Nag.L.J. Nagpur Law Journal (India)

Nag.L.R. Nagpur Law Reports (India)

Nal.St.P. Nalton's Collection of State Papers

Napt. Napton's Reports (4 Missouri)

Napton. Napton's Reports (4 Missouri)

Narcotics Control Dig. Narcotics Control Digest

Narr.Mod. Narrationes Modernae (Style's King's Bench Reports) (1646-55) (Eng.)

Nat. ● National
     ● Natural

Nat.B.C. National Bank Cases (U.S.)

Nat.B.J. National Bar Journal

Nat.B.R. National Bankruptcy Register (U.S.)

Nat.Bar.J. National Bar Journal

Nat.Bankr.Law. National Bankruptcy Law

Nat.Bankr.R. National Bankruptcy Register (U.S.)

Nat.Brev. Natura Brevium

Nat.Corp.Rep. National Corporation Reporter

Nat.Inc.Tax Mag. National Income Tax Magazine

Nat.Ins.Commiss. National Insurance Commissioner

Nat.J.Leg.Ed. National Journal of Legal Education

Nat.L.R. Natal Law Reports

Nat.L.Rec. National Law Record

Nat.L.Rep. National Law Reporter

Nat.L.Rev. National Law Review

Nat.Law Guild Q. National Lawyers' Guild Quarterly

Nat.Mun.Rev. National Municipal Review

Nat.Munic.Rev. National Municipal Review

Nat.Reg. National Register, edited by Mead, 1816

Nat.Rept.Syst. National Reporter System

Nat.Res. Natural Resources

Nat.Rev. National Review (London)

Nat.Tax.J. National Tax Journal

Nat.Tax Mag. National Tax Magazine

Nat.U.L.Rev. National University Law Review

Natl. National

Nat'l Civic Rev. National Civic Review

Nat'l Legal Mag. National Legal Magazine

Nat'l Mun. Rev. National Municipal Review

Natl.Rep.Sys. National Reporter System

Nat'l School L.Rptr. National School Law Reporter

Nat'l Tax J. National Tax Journal

Natural L.F. Natural Law Forum

Natural Resources J. Natural Resources Journal

Nav. Navigation

Nb. Nebraska

Nb.L. Nebraska Law Review

Nb.L.R. Nebraska Law Review

Nd. ● Newfoundland
　　● Newfoundland Reports

Ne. Nepalese

Neb. ● Nebraska
　　● Nebraska Supreme Court Reports

Neb.(Unof). Nebraska Unofficial Reports

Neb.Bd.R.C. Nebraska Board of Railroad Commissioners

Neb.Bd.Trans. Nebraska Board of Transportation

Neb.L.B. Nebraska Law Bulletin

Neb.L.Rev. Nebraska Law Review

Neb.Laws Nebraska Laws

Neb.Leg.N. Nebraska Legal News

Neb.R.C. Nebraska Railway Commission Reports

Neb.Rev.Stat. Revised Statutes of Nebraska

Neb.S.B.J. Nebraska State Bar Journal

Neb.S.R.C. Nebraska State Railway Comm.

Neb.St.B.J. Nebraska State Bar Journal

Neb.Unoff. Nebraska Unofficial Reports (1901-04)

Neb.W.C.C. Nebraska Workmen's Compensation Court Bulletin

Need. Needham's Annual Summary of Tax Cases (Eng.)

Neg.C. Negligence Cases (CCH)

Neg.Cas. Bloomfield's Manumission (or Negro) Cases (N.J.)

Neg.Inst.Law. Negotiable Instrument Law

Negl.Cas. Negligence Cases (CCH)

Negl.Cas.2d Negligence Cases (CCH), Second Series

Negl. & Comp.Cas.Ann. Negligence & Compensation Cases Annotated

Negl. & Comp.Cas.Ann.3d. Negligence & Compensation Cases Annotated, Third Series

Negl. & Comp.Cas.Ann.(N.S.) Negligence & Compensation Cases Annotated, New Series

Negro.Cas. Bloomfield's Manumission (N.J.)

Nel. ● Nelson's Chancery Reports (1625-93) (Eng.)
　　● H. Finch's Chancery Reports (1673-81) (Eng.)

Nel.C.R. Nelson's Chancery Reports (Eng.)

Nell Nell's Reports (1845-55) (Ceylon)

Nels. ● Nelson's Chancery Reports (Eng.)

       ● H. Finch's Chancery Reports (Eng.)

Nels.Arb. Nelson's Abridgment of the Common Law

Nels.Fol.Rep. H. Finch's Chancery Reports, by Nelson (21 Eng. Reprint)

Nelson(Eng.) H. Finch's Chancery Reports, by Nelson (21 Eng. Reprint)

Nelson's Rep. Nelson tempore Finch (1673-81)

Neth. Netherlands

Nev. ● Nevada

      ● Nevada Supreme Court Reports

Nev.P.S.C. Nevada Public Service Commission

Nev.P.S.C.Op. Nevada Public Service Commission Opinions

Nev.R.C. Nevada Railroad Commission

Nev.Rev.Stat. Nevada Revised Statutes

Nev.S.B.J. Nevada State Bar Journal

Nev.St.Bar J. Nevada State Bar Journal

Nev.Stats. Statutes of Nevada

Nev. & M.(Eng.) Nevile & Manning (King's Bench)

Nev. & M.K.B. Nevile & Manning's King's Bench Reports (1832-36) (Eng.)

Nev. & M.M.C. Nevile & Manning's Magistrates' Cases (Eng.)

Nev. & Mac. Neville & Macnamara's Railway Cases (1855-1950) (Eng.)

Nev. & Macn. Neville & Macnamara's English Railway and Canal Cases

Nev. & Man. Nevile & Manning's King's Bench Reports (1831-36) (Eng.)

Nev. & Man.Mag.Cas. Nevile & Manning's Magistrates' Cases (1832-36) (Eng.)

Nev. & McN. Neville & McNamara's Railway Cases (Eng.)

Nev. & P. ● Nevile & Perry's King's Bench Reports (1836-38) (Eng.)

      ● Nevile & Perry's Magistrates' Cases (Eng.)

Nev. & P.Mag.Cas. Nevile & Perry's English Magistrates' Cases (1836-37)

New. Newell, Illinois Appeal Reports

New Ann.Reg. New Annual Register (London)

New B.Eq.Ca. New Brunswick Equity Cases

New B.Eq.Rep. New Brunswick Equity Reports, vol. 1

New Benl. New Benloe's Reports, English King's Bench (1531-1628)

New Br. New Brunswick Reports

New Br.Eq.(Can.) New Brunswick Equity Reports

New Br.Eq.Cas.(Can.) New Brunswick Equity Cases

New Cas. New Cases (Bingham's New Cases)

New Cas.Eq. New Cases in Equity, vols. 8, 9 Modern Reports (1721-55)

New Eng.Hist. New England Historical and Genealogical Register

New English L.Rev. New England Law Review

New Ir.Jur. New Irish Jurist & Local Government Review (1900-05)

New Jersey L.J. New Jersey Law Journal

New Jersey L.Rev. New Jersey Law Review

New Jersey Leg.Rec. New Jersey Legal Record

New Jersey S.B.A.Qu. New Jersey State Bar Association Quarterly

New L.J. New Law Journal

New Mag.Cas. New Magistrates' Cases (Bittleston, Wise & Parnell) (1844-51)

New Mexico L.Rev. New Mexico Law Review

New Nat.Brev. New Natura Brevium

New Pr.Cases. New Practice Cases (1844-48) (Eng.)

New Rep. ● New Reports (1862-65) (Eng.)

      ● Bosanquet & Puller's New Reports (4, 5 Bosanquet & Puller) (1804-07) (Eng.)

New Sess.Cas. New Session Cases (Carrow, Hamerton & Allen) (1844-51)

New So.W.L. New South Wales Law Reports

New So.W.St. New South Wales State Reports

New So.W.W.N. New South Wales Weekly Notes

New Term Rep. ● New Term Reports

● Dowling & Ryland's King's Bench Reports

New York City B.A.Bul. Bulletin of Ass'n. of the Bar of the City of N.Y.

New York Supp. New York Supplement

New Zeal. New Zealand

New Zeal.Jur.R. New Zealand Jurist Reports

New Zeal L. New Zealand Law Reports

New Zeal.L.J. New Zealand Law Journal

New Zeal.L.R. New Zealand Law Reports

Newark L.Rev. University of Newark Law Review

Newb. Newberry's United States District Court, Admiralty Reports

Newb.Adm. Newberry's United States District Court, Admiralty Reports

Newberry Adm.(F.) Newberry's United States District Court, Admiralty Reports

Newbon Newbon's Private Bills Reports (1895-99) (Eng.)

Newbyth Newbyth's Manuscript Decisions, Scotch Session Cases

Newell Newell's Reports, vols. 48-90 Illinois Appeals

Newell,Defam. Newell on Defamation, Slander and Libel

Newell,Eject. Newell's Treatise on the Action of Ejectment

Newell,Mal.Pros. Newell's Treatise on Malicious Prosecution

Newell,Sland. & L. Newell on Slander and Libel

Newf. Newfoundland

Newf.S.Ct. Newfoundland Supreme Court Decisions

Newf.Sel.Cas. Newfoundland Select Cases (1817-28)

Newfld.L.R. Newfoundland Law Reports

Newfoundl.L.R. Newfoundland Law Reports

Newfoundl.R. Newfoundland Reports

Newfoundl.Sel.Cas. Newfoundland Select Cases

Newl.Ch.Pprac. Newland's Chancery Practice

Nfld. ● Newfoundland: Court with jurisdiction in Newfoundland

● Newfoundland Supreme Court Decisions (Canada)

Nfld.L.R. Newfoundland Law Reports

Nfld.R. Newfoundland Reports

Nfld.Rev.Stat. Newfoundland Revised Statutes (Canada)

Nfld.Stat. Newfoundland Statutes (Canada)

Nic.Ha.C. Nicoll, Hare & Carrow, Railway Cases (1835-55)

Nicar. Nicaragua

Nich.H.& C. English Railway and Canal Cases, by Nicoll, etc. vols. 1-2 (1835-55)

Nicholl H. & C. Nicholl, Hare and Carrow (1835-55)

Nichols-Cahill Nichols-Cahill Annotated New York Civil Practice Acts

Nicholson Nicholson, Manuscript Decisions, Scotch Session Cases

Nicolas Proceedings and Ordinances of the Privy Council, edited by Sir Harry Nicolas

Niebh.Hist.Rom. Niebuhr, Roman History

Nient cul. Nient culpable (not guilty)

Nig.L.J. Nigerian Law Journal

Nig.L.R. Nigeria Law Reports

Nigeria L.R. Nigeria Law Reports

Nil.Reg. Niles' Weekly Register

Niles Reg. Niles' Weekly Register

Nisbet Nisbet of Dirleton's Scotch Session Cases (1665-77)

Nisi Prius & Gen.T.Rep. Nisi Prius & General Term Reports (Ohio)

Nix.Dig. Nixon's Digest of Laws (N.J.)

nn. footnotes

no. number

No.Ca.Ecc. & Mar. Notes of Cases (Eng.) Ecclesiastical and Maritime

No.Car.S.B.A. North Carolina State Bar Association

No.Cas.L.J. Notes of Cases, Law Journal

No.East.Rep. Northeastern Reporter (commonly cited N.E.)

No.Ire.L.Q. Northern Ireland Legal Quarterly

No.N. Novae Narrationes, 1516

No.West.Rep. Northwestern Reporter (commonly cited N.W.)

Noble Noble's Current Court Decisions (N.Y.)

Nol. • Nolan's Magistrates' Cases (1791-92) (Eng.)
• Nolan's Settlement Cases (Eng.)

Nol.Mag. Nolan's Magistrates' Cases (1791-92) (Eng.)

nol-pros nolle prosequi

Nolan • Nolan on the Poor Laws. 4 editions (1805-33)
• Nolan's Magistrate's Cases (1791-92) (Eng.)

Non cul. Non culpabilis (not guilty)

Nonacq.(or NA) Nonacquiescence by Commissioner in a Tax Court or Board of Tax Appeals decision (U.S.)

Nor. Norway

Norc. Norcross' Reports (vols. 23-24 Nevada)

Norr. Norris Reports (vols 82-96 Pennsylvania)

Norris Norris Reports (82-96 Pennsylvania)

Norris Seamen Norris' Law of Seamen

Norris & L, Perpetuities Norris & Leach on Rule Against Perpetuities

Nort.L.C. Norton's Leading Cases on Inheritance (India)

North. Reports tempore Northington (1757-67) (Eden. English Chancery Reports)

North.Co. Northampton County Reporter (Pa.)

North.Co.R.(Pa.) Northampton County Reporter

North.Co.Rep. Northampton County Reporter (Pa.)

North U.L.Rev. Northwestern University Law Review (formally Illinois Law Review)

North.W.L.J. Northwestern Law Journal

North & G. North Guthrie's Reports vols. 68-80 Missouri Appeals

Northam. Northampton Law Reporter (Pa.)

Northam.L.Rep. Northampton Law Reporter (Pa.)

Northum. Northumberland County Legal News (Pa.)

Northum Leg.J.(Pa.) Northumberland Legal Journal

Northum.Leg.N.(Pa.) Northumberland County Legal News

Northum.Co.Leg.N. Northumberland County Legal News

Northumb.L.J. Northumberland Legal Journal News (Pa.)

Northumb.L.N. Northumberland Legal Journal (Pa.)

Northumb. Legal J. Northumberland Legal Journal

Northw.L.Rev. Northwestern University Law Review

Northw.Pr. North-west Provinces. India

Northw.Rep. Northwestern Reporter, St. Paul, Minn. (commonly cited N.W.)

nos. numbers

Not.Cas. • Notes of Cases, Ecclesiastical & Maritime (1841-50) (Eng.)
• Notes of Cases at Madras, T. Strange (India)

Not.Cas.Madras. Notes of Cases at Madras (Strange)

Not.Dec. Notes of Decisions (Martin's North Carolina Reports)

Not-For-Profit Corp. Not-for-Profit Corporation

Not.J. Notaries Journal

Not.Op. Wilmot's Notes of Opinions and Judgments

note. footnote in cross-reference

notes. footnotes in cross-reference

Notes of Ca. Notes of Cases (Eng.)

Notes of Cas. Notes of Cases, Ecclesiastical & Maritime (Eng.)

Notes of Cases Notes of Cases, Ecclesiastical & Maritime (Eng.)

Notes on U.S. Notes on United States Reports

Notre Dame Law. Notre Dame Lawyer

Nott & Hop. Nott & Hopkins' Reports (8-15 U.S. Court of Claims)

Nott & Hunt. Nott & Huntington's Reports, vols. 1-7 United States Court of Claims

Nott & M'C.(S.C.) Nott & M'Cord, South Carolina Law Reports

Nott & McC. Nott & McCord's South Carolina Reports (1817-20)

Nov. ● Novellae. The Novels or New Constitutions

     ● Novels (Roman Law)

Nov.Rec. Novissimi Recopilacion de las Leyes de España

Nov.Recop. Novisima Recopilacion

Nov.Sc. Nova Scotia Supreme Court Reports (Canada)

Nov.Sc.Dec. Nova Scotia Decisions

Nov.Sc.L.R. Nova Scotia Law Reports

Nov.Sc.P.U.C. Nova Scotia Board of Commissioners of Public Utilities (Canada)

Noy Noy's King's Bench Reports (1559-1649) (Eng.)

Noy(Eng.) Noy's King's Bench Reports (1559-1649) (Eng.)

Noy,Max. Noy's Maxims

Nts. Notes

Nv. Nevada

Nw. Northwestern

Nw.L. Northwestern University Law Review (Ill.)

Nw.L.S. Northwestern University Law Review, Supplement (Ill.)

Nw.U.L.Rev. Northwestern University Law Review

Ny.L.R. Nyasaland Law Reports (S. Africa)

Nye Nye's Reports (18-21 Utah)

O

o.   ● Order
     ● Overruled; ruling in cited case expressly overruled (Used in Shepard's Citations)

O.   ● Law Opinions
     ● Ohio
     ● Ohio Reports
     ● Oklahoma
     ● Ontario Reports
     ● Oregon
     ● Oregon Reports
     ● Otto, United States Supreme Court Reports (91-107 U.S. Reports)

O.A.   ● Ohio Appellate Reports
       ● Oudh Appeals (India)

O.A.2d Ohio Appellate Reports, Second Series

OAA Old-Age Assistance

OAG Opinions of the Attorneys General of the United States

OAP Office of Alien Property

OAPEC Organization of Arab Petroleum Exporting Countries

O.A.R.   ● Ontario Appeal Reports
       ● Ohio Appellate Reports

OAS Organization of American States (UN)

OASDI Old Age, Survivors, and Disability Benefits

OASI Old Age and Survivors Insurance, Trust Fund

OAU Organization of African Unity

O.App. Ohio Appellate Reports

O.App.2d Ohio Appellate Reports, Second Series

O.B.   ● Official Bulletin, International Commission for Air Navigation
      ● Old Bailey
      ● Old Benloe
      ● Orlando Bridgman

O.B.J. The Journal, Oklahoma Bar Association Journal

O.B.S. Old Bailey's Sessions Papers

O.B.S.P. Old Bailey, Sessions Papers

O.B. & F. Ollivier, Bell, & Fitzgerald's Court of Appeal Reports (1878-80) (New Zealand)

O.B. & F.(C.A.) Ollivier, Bell & Fitzgerald's Reports, Court of Appeal (New Zealand)

O.B. & F.N.Z. Ollivier, Bell & Fitzgerald's New Zealand Reports

O.B. & F.(S.C.) Ollivier, Bell & Fitzgerald's Reports, Supreme Court (New Zealand)

O.Bar Ohio State Bar Assn. Reports

O.Ben. Old Benloe's Reports, English Common Pleas

O.Benl. Old Benloe's Reports, English Common Pleas (1486-1580)

O.Bridg.   ● Carter's Reports tempore Bridgman, Common Pleas Reports (Eng.)
        ● Orlando Bridgman's Common Pleas Reports (Eng.) (124 Eng. Reprint)

O.Bridg.(Eng.)   ● Carter's Reports tempore Bridgman, Common Pleas Reports, England
           ● Orlando Bridgman's Common Pleas Reports, England (124 Eng. Reprint)

O.Bridgm.   ● Carter's Reports tempore Bridgman, Common Pleas Reports (Eng.)
        ● Orlando Bridgman's Common Pleas Reports (Eng.)

O'Brien O'Brien's Upper Canada Reports

O.C.   ● Ope consilio (by aid and counsel, Orphans' Court)
      ● Jersey Ordres du Conseil
      ● Orphans' Court
      ● Oudh Cases, India

O.C.A. Ohio Courts of Appeal Reports (1915-22)

OCAM   Afro-Malagasy and Mauritian Common Organization

O.C.B.   Office of Collective Bargaining (New York City)

O.C.C.   Ohio Circuit Reports or Decisions

O.C.C.N.S.   Ohio Circuit Court Reports, New Series

O.C.D.   • Office of Child Development
             • Ohio Circuit Court Decisions (1901-18)

OCF   Office, Chief of Finance, Army (U.S.)

OCLE   Continuing Legal Education, University of Oklahoma Law Center

O.C.R.   • Department of Interior, Office of Coal Research
             • Organized Crime and Racketeering Section of the Department of Justice

O.C.S.   • Office of Contract Settlement Decisions (U.S.)
             • Outer Continental Shelf

OCSE   Office of Child Support Enforcement

OCT   Overseas Countries and Territories

O'Callaghan, New Neth.   O'Callaghan's History of New Netherland

O.Cr.   Oklahoma Criminal Reports

O.Cr.C.   Oudh Criminal Cases (India)

O.D.   • Office Decision (U.S. Internal Revenue Bureau)
           • Ohio Decisions
           • Overdose of narcotics

ODC   Office of Domestic Commerce (U.S.)

O.D.C.C.   Ohio Decisions, Circuit Court (properly cited Ohio Circuit Decisions)

O.D.E.C.A.   Organization of Central American States

ODM   Office of Denfense Mobilization (U.S.)

O.D.N.P.   Ohio Decisions

O.Dec.Rep.   Ohio Decisions Reprint

O.Dep.Rep.   Ohio Department Reports

OE   Office of Education

OEA   Overseas Education Association

O.E.C.   Ontario Election Decisions

OECD   • Organization for Economic Cooperation and Development
            • Organization for European Cooperation and Development

OEDP   Office of Employment Development Programs

OEEC   Organization of European Economic Cooperation

OEIA   Office of Energy Information and Analysis

OEM   Office for Emergency Management (U.S.)

OEO   Office of Economic Opportunity

OEP   • Office of Emergency Preparedness
           • Office of Energy Research and Development Policy (NSF)

OFCC   Office of Federal Contract Compliance

O.F.D.   Ohio Federal Decisions

OFDI   Office of Foreign Direct Investments

OFR   Office of the Federal Register

O.F.S.   Orange Free State Reports, High Court (1879-83) (South Africa)

OG   Obergericht--Cantonal Court of Appeal (Switzerland)

O.G.   Official Gazette, U.S. Patent Office

OGH   Oberster Gerichtshof--Supreme Court (Austria)

O.G.Pat.Off.   Official Gazette, U.S. Patent Office

OGSM   Office of the General Sales Manager

OHD   Office of Human Development

OHI   Office for Handicapped Individuals

OHMO   Office of Hazardous Materials Operations

OHPA   Ohio Public Defenders Association

OIT   Office of International Trade (U.S.)

O.in C.   Order in council

O.J.Act   Ontario Judicature Act

O.J.T.   On-the-Job Training

O.Jur.   Ohio Jurisprudence

O'Keefe Ord.   O'Keefe's Order in Chancery (Ireland)

O.L.   Ohio Laws

O.L.A.   Ohio Law Abstract

O.L.Abs.   Ohio Law Abstract

O.L.B.   Ohio Law Bulletin

OLCI   Ohio Legal Center Institute

O.L.D.   Ohio Lower Court Decisions

OLG
- Oberlandesgericht (District Court of Appeal)
- Oberlandesgericht--Provincial Court of Appeal (Germ. & Austria)

O.L.J.
- Ohio Law Journal
- Oudh Law Journal (India)

O.L.Jour.
- Ohio Law Journal
- Oudh Law Journal (India)

O.L.N.   Ohio Legal News

O.L.R.
- Ohio Law Reporter
- Ontario Law Reporter
- Ontario Law Reports
- Oregon Law Review
- Oudh Law Reports (India)

O.L.R.B.   Ontario Labour Relations Board Monthly Report

O.L.Rep.   Ohio Law Reporter

O.Legal News   Ohio Legal News

O.Lower D.   Ohio (Lower) Decisions

OMB   Office of Management and Budget

OMBE   Office of Minority Business Enterprise

OMGUS   Office of Military Gov't., U.S. Zone, Germany

OMI   Organization Management, Inc.

O'M. & H.   O'Malley & Hardcastle's Election Cases (Eng.)

O'M. & H.El.Cas.   O'Malley & Hardcastle, Election Cases (Eng.)

O'Mal. & H.   O'Malley and Hardcastel's Election Cases (Eng.)

O.Misc.   Ohio Miscellaneous Reports

ONAP   Office of Native American Programs

O.N.B.   Old Natura Brevium

O.N.P.   Ohio Nisi Prius Reports (1894-1901)

O.N.P.N.S.   Ohio Nisi Prius Reports New Series (1903-13)

O.N.R.   Office of Naval Research

O.O.   Ohio Opinions

O.O.2d   Ohio Opinions, Second Series

OOG   Office of Oil and Gas

OPA   Office of Price Administration (U.S.)

O.P.D.   South African Law Reports, Orange Free State Provincial Division

OPEC   Organization of Petroleum Exporting Countries

OPIC   Overseas Private Investment Corporation

O.P.R.   Ontario Practice Reports

OPS   Office of Price Stabilization (U.S.)

O.P.S.   Official Public Service Reports (N.Y.)

OPSO   Office of Pipeline Safety Operations

O.R.
- Official Reports, South Africa
- Oklahoma Law Review
- Ontario Reports

O.R.C.   Reports of the High Court of the Orange River Colony (South Africa)

ORD   Office of Rural Development

ORS   Office of Rent Stabilization (U.S.)

O.R.S.A.R.   Official Reports, South African Republic

O.S.
- Ohio State Reports
- Old Style; Old Series
- Upper Canada Queen's Bench Reports, Old Series

O.S.2d   Ohio State Reports, Second Series

O.S.A.   Oklahoma Statutes Annotated

OSB   Oregon State Bar

O.S.C.D.   Ohio Supreme Court Decisions, Unreported Cases

OSHA   Occupational Safety and Health Administration

O.S.H.D.   Occupational Safety and Health Decisions

O.S.L.J.   Law Journal of Student Bar Assn., Ohio State University

OSOB   Old Senate Office Building

OSS   Office of Strategic Services (U.S.)

O.S.Supp.   Oklahoma Statutes Supplement

O.S.U. Ohio Supreme Court Decisions, Unreported Cases

O.S. & C.P.Dec. Ohio Superior and Common Pleas Decisions

O.St. Ohio State Reports

O.Su. Ohio Supplement

O.Supp. Ohio Supplement

OT Office of Telecommunications

OTA Office of Technology Assessment

OTB Offtrack betting

OTP Office of Telecommunications Policy

O.U.U.I. Decisions given by the Office of the Umpire (Unemployment Insurance) respecting Claims to Out-of-work Donation (Eng.)

O.U.U.I.B.D. Benefit Decisions of the British Umpire

O.U.U.I.D. Umpire Decisions, Benefit Claims (Eng.)

O.U.U.I.S.D. Benefit & Donation Claims, Selected Decisions of Umpire (Eng.)

OVG Oberverwaltungsgericht--Provincial Administrative Court of Appeal (Germ.)

OWM Office of War Mobilization (U.S.)

O.W.N. ● Ontario Weekly Notes
      ● Oudh Weekly Notes (India)

O.W.R. Ontario Weekly Reporter

OWRT Office of Water Research and Technology

OYD Office of Youth Development

O. & T. Oyer and Terminer

O. & W.Dig. Oldham and White's Digest of Laws, Texas

ObG Obergericht (Court of Appeal)

Occ. Occupation

Occ.N. Occasional Notes, Canada Law Times

Occ. & Prof. Occupations and Professions

Oct.Str. Octavo Strange, Select Cases on Evidence

Odeneal Odeneal's Reports (9-11 Oregon)

Odgers Odgers on Libel and Slander, 6 editions, (1881-1929)

Odg.Lib. Odger on Libel and Slander

Off. ● Office
      ● Official

Off.Br. Officina Brevium, 1679

Off.Brev. Officina Brevium (1679)

Off.Exec. Wentworth's Office of Executors

Off.Gaz. Official Gazette, U.S. Patent Office

Off.Gaz.Pat.Off. Official Gazette, United States Patent Office (Washington, D.C.)

Off.Jl.Pat. Official Journal of Patents (Eng.)

Off.Rep. Official Reports of the High Court of the Transvaal

Officer Officer's Reports (1-9 Minnesota)

Official J.Ind.Comm.Prop. Official Journal of Industrial and Commercial Property (Eire)

Ogd. Odgen's Reports (12-15 Louisiana)

Ogden Ogden's Reports (12-15 Louisiana)

Ogilvie, Dict. Ogilvie's Imperial Dictionary of the English Language

Oh. ● Ohio
      ● Ohio Court of Appeals

Oh.A. Ohio Appellate Reports

Oh.A.2d Ohio Appellate Reports, Second Series

Oh.Cir.Ct. Ohio Circuit Court Reports

Oh.Cir.Ct.N.S. Ohio Circuit Court Reports, New Series

Oh.Cir.Dec. Ohio Circuit Decisions

Oh.Dec. Ohio Decisions

Oh.Dec.(Reprint) Ohio Decisions (Reprint)

Oh.F.Dec. Ohio Federal Decisions

Oh.Jur. Ohio Jurisprudence

Oh.L.Bul. Ohio Law Bulletin

Oh.L.Ct.D. Ohio Lower Court Decisions

Oh.L.J. Ohio Law Journal

Oh.L.Rep. Ohio Law Reporter

Oh.Leg.N. Ohio Legal News

Oh.Misc. Ohio Miscellaneous Reports

Oh.N.P. Ohio Nisi Prius

Oh.N.P.(N.S.) Ohio Nisi Prius Reports New Series

Oh.Prob. Ohio Probate

Oh.S.C.D. Ohio Supreme Court Decisions (Unreported Cases)

Oh.S.L.J. Ohio State Law Journal

Oh.S. & C.P. Ohio Superior & Common Pleas Decisions

Oh.St. Ohio State Reports

Ohio ● Ohio
　　　　● Ohio Supreme Court Reports (1821-51)

Ohio Abs. Ohio Law Abstract

Ohio App. Ohio Appellate Reports

Ohio App.2d Ohio Appellate Reports, Second Series

Ohio B.T.A. Ohio Board of Tax Appeals Reports

Ohio Bar Ohio State Bar Association Report

Ohio C.A. Ohio Courts of Appeals Reports

Ohio C.C. Ohio Circuit Court Reports

Ohio C.C.Dec. Ohio Circuit Court Decisions

Ohio C.C.N.S. Ohio Circuit Court Reports, New Series

Ohio C.C.R. Ohio Circuit Court Reports

Ohio C.C.R.N.S. Ohio Circuit Court Reports, New Series

Ohio C.D. Ohio Circuit Decisions

Ohio C.of R. & T. Ohio Commissioners of Railroads and Telegraphs (1867-1905)

Ohio C.Dec. Ohio Circuit Decisions

Ohio Cir.Ct. Ohio Circuit Court Decisions

Ohio Cir.Ct.(N.S.) Ohio Circuit Court Reports, New Series

Ohio Cir.Ct.R. Ohio Circuit Court Reports

Ohio Cir.Ct.R.N.S. Ohio Circuit Court Reports, New Series

Ohio Cir.Dec. Ohio Circuit Decisions

Ohio Ct.App. Ohio Courts of Appeals Reports

Ohio Dec. Ohio Decisions

Ohio Dec.N.P. Ohio Decisions Nisi Prius

Ohio Dec.Reprint Ohio Decisions, Reprint (1840-93)

Ohio Dep't. Ohio Department Reports

Ohio F.Dec. Ohio Federal Decisions

Ohio Fed.Dec. Ohio Federal Decisions

Ohio Gov't. Ohio Government Reports

Ohio Jur. Ohio Jurisprudence

Ohio Jur.2d Ohio Jurisprudence, Second Series

Ohio L.Abs. Ohio Law Abstract

Ohio L.B. Weekly Law Bulletin (Ohio)

Ohio L.J. Ohio Law Journal

Ohio L.R. Ohio Law Reporter

Ohio L.R. & Wk.Bul. Ohio Law Reporter & Weekly Bulletin

Ohio Law Abst. Ohio Law Abstract

Ohio Law Bull. Weekly Law Bulletin (Ohio)

Ohio Law J. Ohio Law Journal

Ohio Law R. Ohio Law Reporter

Ohio Law Rep. Ohio Law Reporter

Ohio Laws State of Ohio: Legislative Acts Passed and Joint Resolutions Adopted

Ohio Leg.N. Ohio Legal News

Ohio Leg.News Ohio Legal News

Ohio Legal N. Ohio Legal News

Ohio Legis.Bull. Ohio Legislative Bulletin (Anderson)

Ohio Low.Dec. Ohio Lower Court Decisions

Ohio Lower Dec. Ohio Lower Court Decisions

Ohio Misc. Ohio Miscellaneous Reports

Ohio Misc.Dec. Ohio Miscellaneous Decisions

Ohio N.P. Ohio Nisi Prius Reports

Ohio N.P.N.S. Ohio Nisi Prius Reports N.S.

Ohio Op. Ohio Opinions

Ohio Ops. Ohio Opinions

Ohio P.S.C. Ohio Public Service Comm.

Ohio P.U.C. Ohio Public Utilities Comm.

Ohio Prob. Ohio Probate Reports by Goebel

Ohio R.C. Ohio Railroad Commission

Ohio R.Cond. Ohio Reports Condensed

Ohio Rev.Code Ann. Ohio Revised Code Annotated

Ohio Rev.Code Ann.(Anderson) Ohio Revised Code Annotated (Anderson)

Ohio Rev.Code Ann.(Baldwin) Ohio Revised Code Annotated (Baldwin)

Ohio Rev.Code Ann.(Page) Ohio Revised Code Annotated (Page)

Ohio S.B.A. Ohio State Bar Association

Ohio S.L.J. Ohio State Law Journal

Ohio S.U. Ohio Supreme Court Decisions (Unreported Cases)

Ohio S. & C.P.Dec. Ohio Superior and Common Pleas Decisions

Ohio St. Ohio State Reports

Ohio St.L.J. Ohio State Law Journal

Ohio Sup. & C.P.Dec. Ohio Superior Common Pleas Decisions

Ohio Supp. Ohio Supplement

Ohio Unrep. Ohio Supreme Court Unreported Cases, 1 vol.

Ohio Unrep.Jud.Dec. Pollack's Ohio Unreported Judicial Decisions Prior to 1823

Ohio Unrept.Cas. Ohio Supreme Court Decisions (Unreported Cases)

Ohlinger, Fed.Practice Ohlinger's Federal Practice

Oil & Gas Compact Bull. Oil and Gas Compact Bulletin

Oil & Gas Inst. Oil and Gas Institute

Oil & Gas J. Oil and Gas Journal

Oil & Gas Rptr. Oil and Gas Reporter

Oil & Gas Tax Q. Oil and Gas Tax Quarterly

Ok. Oklahoma

Ok.L.R. Oklahoma Law Review

Okl.Cr. Oklahoma Criminal Reports

Okl.St.Ann. Oklahoma Statutes Annotated

Okla. ● Oklahoma
● Oklahoma Supreme Court Reports

Okla.Crim. Oklahoma Criminal Reports

OklaAp.Ct.Rep. Oklahoma Appellate Court Reporter

Okla.B.A.J. The Journal, Oklahoma Bar Assn.

Okla.B.Ass'n.J. Oklahoma Bar Association Journal

Okla.C.C. Oklahoma Corporation Commission

Okla.Cr. Oklahoma Criminal Reports

Okla.Crim. Oklahoma Criminal Reports

Okla.I.C.R. Oklahoma Industrial Commission Reports

Okla.L.J. Oklahoma Law Journal

Okla.L.Rev. Oklahoma Law Review

Okla.S.B.J. Oklahoma State Bar Journal

Okla.Sess.Law Serv. Oklahoma Session Law Service (West)

Okla.Sess.Laws Oklahoma Session Laws

Okla.Stat. Oklahoma Statutes

Okla.Stat.Ann.(West) Oklahoma Statutes Annotated

Olc. Olcott's District Reports (Admiralty) (U.S.)

Olc.Adm. Olcott's District Reports (Admiralty) (U.S.)

Olcott Adm.(F.) Olcott, U.S. District Court (Admiralty)

Old. Oldright's Reports (5, 6 Nova Scotia)

Old Bailey Chr. Old Bailey Chronicle

Old Ben. Benloe in Benloe & Dalison's Common Pleas Reports (Eng.)

Old Benloe Benloe in Benloe and Dalison's Common Pleas Reports, 1486-1580

Old Nat.Brev. Old Natura Brevium

Old S.C. Old Select Cases (Oudh) (India)

Oldb. Oldbright's Reports, Nova Scotia

Oldr. Oldright's Reports, Nova Scotia

Oleck, Corporations Oleck's Modern Corporation Law

Oliv.B. & L. Oliver, Beavan & Lefroy (Eng. Ry. & Canal Cases)

Oll.B. & F. Olliver, Bell & Fitzgerald's Reports (New Zealand)

Olliv.B. & F. Olliver, Bell & Fitzgerald (New Zealand)

Olms. Decisions of the Judicial Committee of the Privy Council re the British North American Act, 1867, and the Canadian Constitution (Canada)

Olwine's L.J.(Pa.) Olwine's Law Journal

Onsl.N.P. Onslow's Nisi Prius

Ont. ● Ontario: Court with Jurisdiction in Ontario
● Ontario Reports (1882-1900) (Canada)

Ont.2d. Ontario Reports, 2d Series (Canada)

Ont.A. Ontario Appeals

Ont.App. Ontario Appeal Reports

Ont.Dig. Digest of Ontario Case Law

Ont.El.Cas. Ontario Election Cases (1884-1900)

Ont.Elec. Ontario Election Cases (1884-1900)

Ont.Elec.C. Ontario Election Cases

Ont.Elect. Ontario Election Cases (1884-1900)

Ont.L. Ontario Law Reports

Ont.L.J.(N.S.) Ontario Law Journal, New Series

Ont.L.R. Ontario Reports (Canada)

Ont.L.Rep. Ontario Law Reports

Ont.P.R. Ontario Practice Reports

Ont.Pr. Ontario Practice

Ont.Pr.Rep. Ontario Practice Reports

Ont.R. Ontario Reports

Ont.R. & W.N. Ontario Reports and Ontario Weekly Notes (Canada)

Ont.Reg. Ontario Regulations (Canada)

Ont.Rev.Stat. Ontario Revised Statutes (Canada)

Ont.Ry. & Mun.Bd. Ontario Railway and Municipal Board (Ontario, Canada)

Ont.Stat. Ontario Statutes (Canada)

Ont.W.N. Ontario Weekly Notes (Canada)

Ont.W.R. Ontario Weekly Reporter

Ont.Week N. Ontario Weekly Notes

Ont.Week R. Ontario Weekly Reporter

Ont.Wkly.Rep. Ontario Weekly Reporter

Ontario Cons.Reg. Ontario Consolidated Regulations (Canada)

Onuphr.de Interp.Voc.Eccles. Onuphrius de Interpretatione Vocum Ecclesiae

Op. Opinion

Op.A.G. Opinion of the Attorney General

Op.Att.Gen. Opinions of the United States Attorneys-General

Op.Att'y.Gen. Opinions of the Attorney General

Op.Attys.Gen. Opinions of the United States Attorneys General

Op.CCCG Opinion, Chief Counsel, U.S. Coast Guard

Op.GCT Opinion, General Counsel, U.S. Treasury Department

Op.JAGAF. Opinion, Judge Advocate General, U.S. Air Force

Op.JAGN. Opinion, Judge Advocate General, U.S. Navy

Op.Let. Opinion letter

Op.N.Y.Atty.Gen. Sickels' Opinions of Attorneys-General of New York

Ops. Operations

Op.Sol.Dept. Opinions of the Solicitor, U.S. Department of Labor

Op.Sol.Dept.Labor Opinions of the Solicitor for the Department of Labor dealing with Workmen's Compensation

Op.Solic.P.O.Dep't. Official Opinions of the Solicitor for the Post Office Department

Ops.A.A.G.,P.O.D. U.S. Post Office Department. Official Opinions of the Solicitor

Ops.A.G. Opinions, Attorney General

Ops.Atty.Gen. Opinions of Attorney General

Ops.J.A.G. Opinions, Judge Advocate General, U.S. Army

Opt.County Gov't. Optional County Government

Or. ● Oregon
● Oregon Supreme Court Reports

Or.A. Oregon Court of Appeals Reports

Or.App. Oregon Reports, Court of Appeal

Or.L.R. Oregon Law Review

Or.Laws Oregon Laws and Resolutions

Or.Laws Adv.Sh. Oregon Laws Advance Sheets

Or.Laws Spec.Sess. Oregon Laws and Resolutions

Or.P.S.C. Oregon Public Service Commission Reports

Or.P.U.C.Ops. Oregon Office of Public Utilities Commissioner. Opinions & Decisions

Or.R.C. Oregon Railroad Commission

Or.Rev.Stat. Oregon Revised Statutes

Or.T.R. Oregon Tax Reporter

Or.T.Rep. Orleans Term Reports (1, 2 Martin, Louisiana)

Ord. ● Order
      ● Ordinance

Ord.Austl.Cap.Terr. Ordinances of the Australian Capital Territory

Ord.Con.Jer. Ordes du Conseil Enregistres a Jersey

Ord. de la Mar. Ordonnance de la Marine de Louis XIV

Ord.Mar. Ordonnance de la Marine

Ords.N.Z. Ordinances of the Legislative Council of New Zealand

Ore. Oregon

Ore.L.Rev. Oregon Law Review

Ore.Rev.Stat. Oregon Revised Statutes

Ore.St.B.Bull. Oregon State Bar Bulletin

Oreg. Oregon

Oreg.L.Rev. Oregon Law Review

org. organization

Orl.Bridg. Orlando Bridgman's English Common Pleas Reports

Orl.Bridgman Orlando Bridgman's English Common Pleas Reports

Orl.T.R. Orleans Term Reports (vols. 1, 2 Martin) (La.)

Orleans App. Orleans Court of Appeals (La.)

Orleans T.R. Orleans Term Reports (vols. 1, 2 Martin) (La.)

Ormond Ormond's Reports (19-107 Alabama)

Orphans' Ct. Orphans' Court

Ort.Hist. Ortolan's History of the Roman Law

Ort.Inst. Ortolan's Institute de Justinian

Osgoode Hall L.J. Osgoode Hall Law Journal

Ot. Otto's United States Supreme Court Reports (91-107 U.S.)

Otago L.Rev. Otago Law Review

Ott. Otto's United States Supreme Court Reports (91-107 U.S.)

Ottawa L.R. Ottawa Law Review

Ottawa L.Rev. Ottawa Law Review

Otto Otto's United States Supreme Court Reports (19-107 U.S.)

Oudh L.R. Oudh Law Reports (India)

Oudh Rev.Sel.Cas. Revised Collection of Selected Cases issued by Chief Commissioner and Financial Commissioner of Oudh

Oudh Wkly.N. Oudh Weekly Notes (India)

Ought. Oughton's Ordo Judiciorum

Out. Outerbridge's Reports (97, 98 Pennsylvania State)

Outer House Outer House of the Court of Session (Sc.)

overr. ● overruled in
      ● overruling

Overt. Overton's Tennessee Supreme Court Reports (1791-1816)

Ow. ● New South Wales Reports, v. 1-3 (Aus.)
      ● Owen's King's Bench Reports (1556-1615) (Eng.)
      ● Owen's Common Pleas Reports (Eng.)

Owen Owen's English King's Bench Reports (1556-1615)

Oxley ● Young's Vice-Admiralty Decisions, ed. Oxley (Nova Scotia)
      ● Oxley's Railway Cases (1897-1903)

P

p. page in cross-references
P. ● Court of Probate (Eng.)
- Law Reports, Probate, Divorce, & Admiralty, since 1890 (Eng.)
- Pacific Reporter
- Pennsylvania
- Persian
- Peter's (26-41 U.S. Reports)
- Pickering (18-41 Massachusetts)
- Private trust (includes testamentary, investment, life insurance, holding title, etc.)

P.2d Pacific Reporter, Second Series
PA ● Paying agent
- Pension agency
- Private agency trust (agency accounts)

P/A Power of attorney
P.A.D. Peters. Admiralty Decisions, United States
PADUD Program of Advanced Professional Development, University of Denver College of Law
PAHO Pan American Health Organization
PANPUB Panel Publishers
P.A.R. Public Administration Review
PASO Pan-American Sanitary Organization
P.A.T. National Patents Appeal Tribunal (Eng.)
PAU Pan-American Union
PBGC Pension Benefit Guaranty Corporation
PBI Pennsylvania Bar Institute
P.B.S. Public Buildings Service (U.S.)
P.C. ● Judicial Committee of the Privy Council
- Parliamentary Cases
- Patent Cases
- Penal Code
- Pleas of the Crown
- Policical Code
- Practice Cases
- Precedents in Chancery
- Price Control Cases
- Prize Court

- Procedure Civile
- Probate Court

P.C.A. Acts of the Privy Council (Eng.)
P.C.App. Law Reports, Privy Council Appeals (Eng.)
P.C.C. ● Peters United States Circuit Court Reports
- Privy Council Cases
- Acts of the Privy Council, Colonial Series

P.C.I. Privy Council Decisions (India)
PCIJ ● Permanent Court of International Justice
- Permanent Court of International Justice Cases

P.C.Int. Pacific Coast International
P.C.Judg. Privy Council Judgments (India)
P.C.L.J. Pacific Coast Law Journal
PCOB Permanent Central Opium Board (U.N.)
P.C.R. ● Parker, Criminal Reports, New York
- Pennsylvania Corporation Reporter
- Pennsylvania County Court Reports

P.C.Rep. English Privy Council Reports
P.Cas. ● Prize Cases 1914-22 (Eng.)
- Prize Cases (Trehearn, Grant) (Eng.)

P.Cl.R. ● Parker's Criminal Reports, New York
- Privy Council Reports

P.Coast L.J. Pacific Coast Law Journal
P.Ct. Probate Court
PD Police Department
P.D. ● Law Reports, Probate Divorce and Admiralty Division (1875-90) (Eng.)
- Pension and Bounty (U.S. Department of Interior)

P.D.A. Probate, Divorce, and Admiralty (Eng.)
PDC Price Decontrol Board (U.S.)

P.D.Div'l Ct. Probate, Divorce, and Admiralty Division and Divisional Court (Eng)

P.Div. Law Reports, Probate Division (Eng.)

PEAL Publishing, Entertainment, Advertising and Allied Fields Law Quarterly

P.E.A.L.Q. Publishing, Entertainment, Advertising & Allied Fields Law Quarterly

P.E.I. Prince Edward Island Reports (Haviland's)

P.E.I.Rep. Prince Edward Island Reports (Haviland's) (1850-1914)

P.E.I.Rev.Atat. Prince Edward Island Revised Statutes (Canada)

P.E.I.Stat. Prince Edward Island Statutes (Canada)

P.E.P. Public Employment Program

PEPUSL Pepperdine University School of Law

P.E.R.B. Public Employment Relations Board (New York State)

PF Peace and Freedom party

P.F.S. P.F.Smith's Reports, vols. 51-81½ Pennsylvania State Reports

P.F.Smith. P.F.Smith's Reports (vols. 51-81½ Pennsylvania State Reports)

P.-H. Prentice-Hall,Inc.

PHA Public Housing Administration (U.S.)

P-HAm.Lab.Arb.Awards American Labor Arbitration Awards (P-H)

P-H Am.Lab.Cas. American Labor Cases (P-H)

P.H.C.C. Punjab High Court Cases (India)

P.-H.Cas. American Federal Tax Reports (P-H)

P-H Corp. Corporation (P-H)

P-H Est.Plan. Estate Planning (P-H)

P-H Fed.Taxes Federal Taxes (P-H)

P-H Fed.Wage & Hour. Federal Wage and Hour (Prentice-Hall)

P-H Ind.Rel.,Lab.Arb. Industrial Relations, American Labor Arbitration (P-H)

P-H Ind.Rel., Union Conts. Industrial Relations, Union Contracts and Collective Bargaining (P-H)

P.-H.N.Y.E.T.R. Prentice-Hall New York Estate Tax Reports

PHS Public Health Service (U.S.)

P-H Soc.Sec. Taxe Social Security Taxes (P-H)

P-H State & Local Taxes State and Local Taxes (P-H)

P-H Tax. Federal Taxes (Prentice-Hall)

P-H Tax Ct.Mem. Tax Court Memorandum Decisions (P-H)

P-H Tax Ct.Rep & Mem.Dec. Tax Court Reported and Memorandum Decisions (P-H)

P.-H.Unrep.Tr.Cas. Prentice-Hall Unreported Trust Cases

P.H.V. Pro hac vice (for this purpose or occasion)

PI Department of Public Instruction

P.I.C.A.O. Provisional International Civil Aviation Organization (UN)

P.I.P.S.C.R. Philippine Islands Public Service Commission Reports

P.I.P.U.C.R. Philippine Islands Public Utility Commission Reports

P.I.Rep. Philippine Islands Reports

P.J. ● Presiding Judge
   ● ICC Practitioners' Journal
   ● Bombay High Court, Printed Judgments

P.J.L.B. Lower Burma, Printed Judgments

P.Jr. & H. Patton, Jr., & Heath's Reports (Virginia Special Court of Appeals)

P.L. Pamphlet Laws; Public Laws

P.L. Boards. Public Law Boards

P.L.E. Encyclopedia of Pennsylvania Law

PLF Pacific Legal Foundation

PLI Practicing Law Institute

P.L.J. ● Pennsylvania Law Journal
   ● Pittsburgh Legal Journal (Pa.)
   ● Punjab Law Reporter (India)

P.L.J.N.S. Pittsburgh Legal Journal New Series (Pa.)

P.L.M. ● Pacific Law Magazine
   ● Poor Law Magazine

P.L.Mag. Poor Law Magazine 1858-1930) (Sc.)

P.L.O. Public Land Order (U.S.)
P.L.R.
- Pacific Law Reporter
- Pennsylvania Law Record, Philadelphia
- University of Pittsburgh Law Review
- Private Legislation Reports (Sc.)
- Punjab Law Reporter (India)

P.L.R.J. & K. Punjab Law Reporter, Jammu & Kashmir Section (India)
P.L.T.
- Patna Law Times (India)
- Punjab Law Times (India)

P.M.
- Postmaster
- Post-meridiem (afternoon)
- Purchase money

PMA Production & Marketing Admin. (U.S.)
PMDS Property Management and Disposal Service
P.N.P. Peake's English Nisi Prius Cases (1790-1812)
P.O.
- Public officer
- Post office

POCS Post Office and Civil Service
P.O.Cas. Perry's Oriental Cases, Bombay (1843-52)
P.O.G. Official Gazette, U.S. Patent Office
P.O.R. Patent Office Reports
P.P. Parliamentary Papers
p.p.a. per power of attorney
P.P.C. Pierce's Perpetual Code (1943)
P.P.I. Policy proof of interest
PPR Price Procedural Regulation (U.S.)
P.Q. United States Patent Quarterly
P.Q.W. Placita de Quo Warranto, Record Commission (Eng.)
P.R.
- Parliamentary Reports (Eng.)
- Pennsylvania Reports (Penrose & Watts)
- Philadelphia Reports (Pennsylvania 1850-51)
- Philippine Island Reports
- Pittsburgh Reports (Pennsylvania 1853-73)
- Press Release (U.S. Government Departments)
- Probate Reports
- Puerto Rico
- Puerto Rico Supreme Court Reports
- Punjab Record (India)
- Pyke's Reports (Canada)

P.R.C. Postal Rate Commission
P.R.C.P. Practical Register in Common Pleas
P.R.Ch. Practical Register in Chancery (Eng.)
P.R.D. Puerto Rico, Decisiones
P.R.F. Puerto Rico Federal Reports
P.R.Fed. Puerto Rico Federal Reports
P.R.I.C.Dec. Puerto Rico Industrial Commission Decisions
P.R. Laws Ann. Laws of Puerto Rico Annotated
PROPRE Property Press
P.R.R. Puerto Rico Supreme Court Reports
P.R.S.C.R. Puerto Rico Supreme Court Reports
P.R.U.C. Practice Reports (1848-1900) (Upper Canada)
P.R. & D. Power, Rodwell and Dew's Election Cases (1847-56)
P.S.
- Pension Trust, Profit-Sharing, Stock Bonus, or Annuity Plan Ruling
- Petty Sessions
- Public Statutes
- Purdon's Pennsylvania Statutes

P.S.C. Public Service Commission
P.S.C.R. Public Service Commission Reports
P.S.C.U.S. Peters' Reports (26-41 US)
P.S.O. Political Science Quarterly
P.S.R. Pennsylvania State Reports
PST Profit-sharing trustee
P.Shaw Patrick Shaw's Justiciary (1819-31) (Sc.)
P.T.
- Pension trustee
- Processing Tax Division, U. S. Internal Revenue Bureau

P.T.B.R. Processing Tax Board of Review Decisions U.S. Internal Revenue Bureau
PTO Patent and Trademark Office

P.Tr. Private trust (includes testamentary, investment, life insurance, holding title, etc.)

P.U.C. Public Utilities Commission

P.U.Fort. Public Utilities Fortnightly

P.U.R. Public Utilities Reports

P.U.R.(N.S.) Public Utilities Reports, New Series

P.W. ● Peere Williams' English Chancery Reports (1695-1736)
● State Department of Public Welfare
● Public Works

PWA Public Works Administration (U.S.)

P.W.N. Patna Weekly Notes (India)

P.W.R. Punjab Weekly Reporter (India)

P.W.T. Public Works and Transportation

P.W.W. Patna Weekly Notes

P.Wms. Peere Williams' English Chancery Reports (1695-1736)

P.Wms.(Eng.) Peere Williams' English Chancery Reports (1695-1736)

P. & A. Page and Adams' Code (1912)

P. & B. Pugsley & Burbridge's Reports (New Brunswick)

P. & C. Prideaux & Cole's Reports, English Courts (New Session Cases, Vol. 4)

P. & C.R. Planning and Compensation Reports

P. & D. Perry and Davison's Queen's Bench Reports (1834-44) (Eng.)

P. & F. ● Pike & Fischer's Administrative Law
● Pike & Fischer's Federal Rules Service
● Pike & Fischer's OPA Price Service

P. & F.Radio Reg. Pike & Fischer's Radio Regulation Reporter

P. & H. Patton (Jr.) & Heath's Reports (Va. Special Court of Appeals)

P. & K. Perry & Knapp's English Election Cases (1833)

P. & L.Dig.Laws Pepper & Lewis' Digest of Laws, Pa.

P. & L.Laws Private and Local Laws

P. & M. ● Law Reports, Probate & Matrimonial Cases (Eng.)
● Pollock & Maitland's History of English Law

P. & M.H.E.L. Pollock & Maitland's History of English Law

P. & R. Pigott and Rodwell, Reports in Common Pleas (1843-45)

P & S Production & Subsistence (U.S.)

P. & T. Pugsley & Trueman's New Brunswick Rep.

P. & W. Penrose & Watts' Reports (Pa. 1829-32)

Pa. ● Paine's Circuit Court Reports (U.S.)
● Pennsylvania Supreme Court Reports (1845-date)

Pa.B.A. Pennsylvania Bar Assn. Reports

Pa.B.A.Q. Pennsylvania Bar Assn. Quarterly

Pa.B.Ass'n.Q. Pennsylvania Bar Association Quarterly

Pa.B.Brief Pennsylvania Bar Brief

Pa. Bar.Asso.Q. Pennsylvania Bar Association Quarterly

Pa.Bk.Cas. Pennsylvania Bank Cases

Pa.C. Pennsylvania Commonwealth Court Reports

Pa.C.C. Pennsylvania County Court Reports

Pa.C.Dec.W.C.C. Pennsylvania Courts, Decisions in Workmen's Compensation Cases

Pa.C.P. Common Pleas Reporter

Pa.C.Pl. Penn. Common Pleas

Pa.Cas. Pennsylvania Supreme Court Cases, Sadler

Pa.Co. Pennsylvania County Court

Pa.Co.Ct. Pennsylvania County Court Reports

Pa.Co.Ct.R. Pennsylvania County Court Reports

Pa.Com.Pl. Pennsylvania Common Pleas Reporter

Pa.Commw.Ct. Pennsylvania Commonwealth Court Reports

Pa.Cons.Stat. Pennsylvania Consolidated Statutes

Pa.Cons.Stat.Ann.(Purdon) Pennsylvania Consolidated Statutes Annotated (Purdon)

Pa.Corp.R. Pennsylvania Corporation Reporter

Pa.Corp.Rep. Pennsylvania Corporation Reporter

Pa.County Ct. Pennsylvania County Court Reports

Pa.D. & C. Pennsylvania District & County Reports

Pa.Dep.L. & I.Dec. Pennsylvania Department of Labor and Industry Decisions

Pa.Dep.Rep. Pennsylvania Department Reports

Pa.Dist. Pennsylvania District Reporter (Pa. 1892-1921)

Pa.Dist.R. Pennsylvania District Reporter (Pa. 1892-1921)

Pa.Dist. & C.Rep. District and County Reports

Pa.Dist. & Co. Pennsylvania District and County

Pa.Fid. Pennsylvania Fiduciary Reporter

Pa.L. University of Pennsylvania Law Review

Pa.L.G. Legal Gazette Reports (Campbells) Pennsylvania

Pa.L.J. ● Pennsylvania Law Journal
   ● Pennsylvania Law Journal Reports (1842-52)

Pa.L.J.R. Clark's Pennsylvania Law Journal Reports

Pa.L.Rec. Pennsylvania Law Record

Pa.L.S. Pennsylvania Law Series

Pa.L.Ser. Pennsylvania Law Series

Pa.Law J. Pennsylvania Law Journal

Pa.Law Jour. Pennsylvania Law Journal (Philadelphia)

Pa.Law. Ser. Pennsylvania Law Series

Pa.Laws Laws of the General Assembly of the Commonwealth of Pennsylvania

Pa.Leg.Gaz. Legal Gazette Reports (Campbell) (Pa.)

Pa.Legis.Serv. Pennsylvania Legislative Service (Purdon)

Pa.Misc. Pennsylvania Miscellaneous Reports

Pa.N.P. Brightly's Nisi Prius Reports (Pa.)

Pa.P.S.C. Pennsylvania Public Service Commission Annual Report

Pa.P.S.C.Dec. Pennsylvania Public Service Comm. Decisions

Pa.Prac. Standard Pennsylvania Practice

Pa.Rec. Pennsylvania Record

Pa.Rep. Pennsylvania Reports

Pa.S. Pennsylvania Superior Court Reports

Pa.S.R.C. Pennsylvania State Railroad Commission

Pa.St. Pennsylvania State Reports

Pa.St.Tr. Pennsylvania State Trials (Hogan)

Pa.Stat.Ann.(Purdon) Pennsylvania Statutes Annotated

Pa.State Penn. State Reports

Pa.Summary Summary of Pennsylvania Jurisprudence

Pa.Super. Pennsylvania Superior Court Reports

Pa.Super.Ct. Pennsylvania Superior Court Reports

Pa.W.C.Bd.(Dep.Rep.Sup.) Workmen's Compensation Supplement to Department Reports of Pennsylvania

Pa.W.C.Bd.Dec. Pennsylvania Workmen's Compensation Board Decisions

Pa.W.C.Bd.Dec.Dig. Digest of Decisions (Workmen's Compensation Board) (Pa.)

Pac. ● Pacific
   ● Pacific Reporter

Pac.Coast L.J. Pacific Coast Law Journal

Pac.Law Mag. Pacific Law Magazine

Pac.Law Reptr. Pacific Law Reporter, San Francisco

Pac.Leg.N. Pacific Legal News

Pac.R. Pacific Reporter (commonly cited as Pac. or P.)

Pac.Rep. Pacific Reporter (commonly Cited as Pac. or P.)

Pacific C.L.J. Pacific Coast Law Journal, San Francisco

Pacific L.J. Pacific Law Journal

Page Page's Three Early Assize Rolls, County of Northumberland (Surtees Society Publications, v. 88)

Page Contr.   Page on Contracts
Page,Wills   Page on Wills
Pai.   ● Paige's New York Chancery
Reports
● Paine's Circuit Court Reports (U.S.)
Pai.Ch.   Paige's New York Chancery
Reports
Paige.   Paige's New York Chancery
Reports
Paige Ch.   Paige's New York Chancery
Reports (1828-45)
Paine.   Paine's United States Circuit
Court Reports
Paine C.C.   Paine's United States Circuit Court Reports
Paine,Elect.   Paine on Elections
Pak.L.R.   Pakistan Law Reports (India)
Pal.   ● Palmer's Assizes at Cambridge (Eng.)
● Palmer's King's Bench Reports (1619-29) (Eng.)
● Palmer's Reports (53-60 Vermont)
Paley, Ag.   Paley on Principal and
Agent, or Agency
Paley,Mor.Ph.   Wm. Paley's Moral
Philosophy (Eng.)
Paley,Print.& Ag.   Paley on Principal
and Agent, or Agency
Palg.Rise, etc.   Palgrave's Rise and
Progress of the English Commonwealth
Palgrave.   ● Palgrave's Proceedings
in Chancery
● Palgrave's Rise and
Progress of the English Commonwealth
Palm.   ● Palmer's Assizes at Cambridge (Eng.)
● Palmer's King's Bench Reports (1619-29) (Eng.)
● Palmer's Reports (53-60
Vermont)
Palmer   ● Palmer's Assizes at Cambridge (Eng.)
● Palmer's King's Bench
Reports (Eng.)
● Palmer's Reports (53-60
Vermont)
Palmer Co.Prec.   Palmer's Company
Precedents. 16 editions (1877-1952)

Pamph.Laws   Pamphlet Laws, Acts
Pamphl.Laws.   Pamphlet Laws, Acts
Pan.   Panama
Pan-Am.T.S.   Pan-American Treaty
Series
Panel   The Panel, Association of
Grand Jurors of New York County
Bar
Papua & N.G.   Papua and New Guinea
Law Reports
Papy   Papy's Reports (5-8 Florida)
Par.   ● Parker's English Exchequer
Reports
● Parker's New York Criminal
Reports
● Parsons' Reports (65-66 New
Hampshire)
● Paragraph
Par.Adm.   Parsons on the Law of
Shipping and Admiralty
Par.Am.Law   Parson's Commentaries
on American Law
Par.Am.Law Comm.   Parson's Commentaries on American Law
Par.Ant.   Parochial Antiquities
Par.Bills & N.   Parsons on Bills and
Notes
Par.Cont.   Parsons on Contracts
Par.Dec.   Parsons' Decisions (from 2-7
Mass.)
Par.Eq.Cas.   Parsons' Select Equity
Cases, Pennsylvania (Pa. 1842-51)
Para.   ● Paragraph
● Paraguay
Park.   ● Parker's Exchequer Reports (1743-67) (Eng.)
● Parker's New York Criminal Cases (1823-68)
● Parker's New Hampshire
Reports
Park.Cr.   Parker's Criminal Reports
(N.Y.)
Park.Cr.Cas.   Parker's New York
Criminal Cases
Park.Crim.(N.Y.)   Parker's Criminal
Cases
Park.Dig.   Parker's California Digest
Park.Exch.   Parker's English Exchequer Reports (1743-67)
Park.Ins.   Parker's Insurance, Eng. 8
editions (1787-1842)
Park.N.H.   Parker's New Hampshire
Reports

Park.Rev.Cas. Parker's English Exchequer Reports (Revenue Cases)

Parker ● Parker, English Exchequer Reports

● Parker, The Laws of Shipping and Insurance (England)

● Parker, New York Criminal Reports, 6 vols.

● Parker, New Hampshire Reports

Parker Cr.Cas. Parker's New York Criminal

Parker,Cr.Cas.(N.Y.) Parker's New York Criminal Reports

Parker,Cr.R. Parker's New York Criminal Reports

Parker,Cr.R.(N.Y.) Parker's New York Criminal Reports

Parks & Rec. Parks & Recreation

Parks & Wild. Parks & Wildlife

Parl. Parliament

Parl.Cas. Parliamentary Cases (House of Lords Reports)

Parl.Deb. Parliamentary Debates (Cobbett, Hansard) 4th Series (1803-1908)

Parl.Eur.Doc. Parlement Europeen Documents de Seance

Parl.Hist.Eng. Parliamentary History of England (pre-1803)

Parl.Reg. Parliamentary Register (Eng.)

Paroch.Ant. Kennett's Parochial Antiquities

Pars. Parsons' Select Equity Cases, Pennsylvania (Pa. 1842-51)

Pars.Ans. Parsons' Answer to the Fifth Part of Coke's Reports

Pars.Bills & N. Parsons on Bills and Notes

Pars.Cont. Parsons on Contracts

Pars.Dec. Parsons' Decisions (from 2-7 Mass.)

Pars.Eq.Cas. Parsons' Select Equity Cases (Pa. 1842-51)

Pars.Mar.Ins. Parsons on Marine Insurance

Pars.Mar.Law Parsons on Maritime Law

Pars.Merc.Law Parsons on Mercantile Law

Pars.Sel.Eq.Cas.(Pa.) Parsons Select Equity Cases

Pars.Shipp. & Adm. Parsons on Shipping and Admiralty

Part. Las Siete Partidas

Partic. ● Participation

● Participating

Partidas. Moreau-Lislet and Carleton's Laws of Las Siete Partidas in force in Louisiana

Pas. (Terminus Paschae) Easter Term

Pas.Belge Pasicrisie Belge (Belgium)

Pas.Lux. Pasicrisie Luxembourgeoise (Luxembourg)

Pasc. ● Paschal or Easter Term

● Paschal's Reports (Supp. to 25; 28-31 Texas)

Pasch. Paschal or Easter Term

Pasch.Dig. Paschal's Texas Digest of Decisions

Paschal. Paschal's Reports, vols. 28-31 Texas and Supplement to vol. 25

Paschal's Ann.Const. Paschal's United States Constitution, Annotated

Pat. ● Patent

● Paterson's Scotch Appeals, House of Lords

● Paton's Scotch Appeals, House of Lords

● Indian Law Reports, Patna Series

Pat.Abr. Paterson's Abridgment of Poor Law Cases (1857-63)

Pat.App. Craigie, Stewart and Paton's House of Lords Appeals from Scotland (1726-1857)

Pat.App.Cas. ● Paterson's Scotch Appeal Cases

● Paton's Scotch Appeal Cases (Craigie, Stewart & Paton)

Pat.Cas. Reports of Patent, Design and Trade Mark Cases (Eng., Sc., Ire.)

Pat.Comp. Paterson's Compendium of English and Scotch Law

Pat.Copyright & T.M.Cas. Patent, Copyright & Trade Mark Cases (Baldwin) (U.S.)

Pat.Dec. Decisions, Commissioner of Patents

Pat.H.L.Sc. Paton's or Paterson's Scotch Appeals

Pat.L.J. Patna Law Journal (India)

Pat.L.R. Patna Law Reports (India)

Pat.L.Reptr. Patna Law Reporter (India)

Pat.L.Rev. Patent Law Review

Pat.L.T. Patna Law Times (India)

Pat.L.W. Patna Law Weekly

Pat.Law Rev. Patent Law Review

Pat.Off.Gaz. Official Gazette, U.S. Patent Office

Pat.Off.Rep. Patent Office Reports

Pat.Ser. Indian Law Reports, Patna Series

Pat.T.M. & Copy.J. Patent, Trademark & Copyright Journal

Pat. & H. Patton, Jr., & Heath's Reports (Va. Special Court of Appeals)

Pat. & Mr. Paterson & Murray's Reports, New South Wales (1870-71)

Pat. & T.M.Rev. Patent and Trade Mark Review

Pat. & Tr.Mk.Rev. Patent and Trade Mark Review

Pater. ● Paterson's New South Wales Reports
　　　　● Paterson's Scotch Appeal Cases

Pater.Ap.Cas. Paterson's Appeal Cases (Sc.)

Pater.App. Paterson's Appeal Cases (Sc.)

Paters.App. Paterson, Cases on Appeal from Scotland (1851-73)

Paters.Comp. Paterson's Compendium of English and Scotch Law

Paterson. ● Paterson's Compendium of English and Scotch Law
　　　　● Paterson's Law and Usages of the Stock Exchange
　　　　● Paterson on the Game Laws
　　　　● Paterson on the Liberty of the Subject
　　　　● Paterson's Scotch Appeal Cases

Paterson Sc.App.Cas. Paterson, Scotch Appeal Cases

Paton. Craigie, Stewart, & Paton's Scotch Appeal Cases

Paton App.Cas. Paton's Appeal Cases (Sc.)

Paton Sc.App.Cas. Paton's Appeal Cases (Sc.)

Patr.Elect.Cas. Patrick's Election Cases (1824-49) (Upper Canada)

Patrick El.Cas. Patrick's Election Cases (Canada)

Patton & H. Patton, Jr., & Heath's Reports (Virginia Special Court of Appeals)

Patton & H.(Va.) Patton, Jr., & Heath's Reports (Virginia Special Court of Appeals)

Paulus. Julius Paulus, Sententiae Receptae

Pe.R. Pennewill's Reports (Delaware)

Pea. Peake's Nisi Prius Reports (1790-1812) (Eng.)

Pea.Add.Cas. Peake's Nisi Prius Reports (v. 2 of Peake)

Peab.L.Rev. Peabody Law Review

Peake Peake Cases (1790-1812)

Peake Add.Cas. Peake, Additional Cases (1795-1812)

Peake Ev. Peake on the Law of Evidence

Peake N.P. Peake's English Nisi Prius Cases (170 Eng. Reprint)

Peake N.P.Add.Cas. Peake, Additional Cases Nisi Prius (Eng.) (170 Eng. Reprint)

Peake N.P.Add.Cas.(Eng.) Peake, Additional Cases Nisi Prius (Eng.) (170 Eng. Reprint)

Peake N.P.Cas.(Eng.) Peake's English Nisi Prius Cases (170 Eng. Reprint)

Pearce C.C. Pearce's Reports in Dearsly's Crown Cases (Eng.)

Pears. Pearson's Reports (Pennsylvania 1850-80)

Pears.(Pa.) Pearson's Reports (Pennsylvania 1850-80)

Pearson Pearson, Common Pleas (Pa.)

Peck. ● Peck's Reports (24-30 Illinois)
　　　　● Peck's Reports (7 Tennessee) (1921-24)
　　　　● Peckwell's Election Cases (1802-06) (Eng.)

Peck (Ill.) Peck's Reports, Illinois Supreme Court Reports (vols. 11-22, 24-30)

Peck (Tenn.) Peck's Tennessee Reports (vol. 7)

Peck.El.Cas. Peckwell's Election Cases (Eng.)

Peck Tr. Peck's Trial (Impeachment)

Peckw. Peckwell's English Election Cases

Peeples. Peeples' Reports (vols. 77-97 Georgia)

Peeples & Stevens Peeples & Stevens Reports (vols. 80-97 Georgia)

Peere Wms. Peere Williams' Chancery & King's Bench Cases (1695-1736) (Eng.)

Pelham. Pelham's South Australia Reports (1865-66) (Aus.)

Pelt. Peltier's Orlean's Appeals (1917-23)

Pemb.Judg. Pemberton, Judgments and Orders

Pen. ● Pennewill Delaware Reports
● Pennington's Reports (2, 3 New Jersey Law)

Pen.C. Penal Code

Pen.Code. Penal Code

Pen.Dec. Pension Decisions, U.S. Interior Department

Pen.Laws. Penal Laws

Pen.N.J. Pennington's Reports (2, 3 New Jersey Law)

Pen.P. Penault's Prerosti de Quebec

Pen. & W. Penrose & Watts' Reports (Pennsylvania 1829-32)

Penal Penal

Penn. ● Pennewill's Delaware Reports
● Pennington's New Jersey Reports
● Pennsylvania
● Pennsylvania State Reports
● Pennypacker's Unreported Pennsylvania Cases

Penn.B.A. Pennsylvania Bar Association

Penn.B.A.Q. Pennsylvania Bar Association Quarterly

Penn.Co.Ct.Rep. Pennsylvania County Court Reports

Penn.Corp.Rep. Pennsylvania Corporation Reporter

Penn.Del. Pennewill's Delaware Reports

Penn.Dist.Rep. Pennsylvania District Reports

Penn.L.G. ● Pennsylvania Legal Gazette
● Pennsylvania Legal Gazette Reports (Campbell)

Penn.L.J. Pennsylvania Law Journal

Penn.L.J.R. Pennsylvania Law Journal Reports (Clark 1842-52)

Penn.L.Rec. Pennsylvania Law Record, Philadelphia

Penn.L.Rev. Pennsylvania Law Review

Penn.Law Jour. Pennsylvania Law Journal

Penn.Rep. ● Pennsylvania State Reports
● Penrose & Watts' Pennsylvania Reports

Penn.St. Pennsylvania State Reports

Penn.St.R. Pennsylvania State Reports

Penna. Pennsylvania

Pennew. Pennewill's Reports (Delaware)

Pennewill. Pennewill's Delaware Supreme Court Reports (1897-1909)

Penning. Pennington's Reports (2, 3 N.J. Law)

Penny. ● Pennypacker's Pennsylvania Colonial Cases
● Pennypacker's Unreported Pennsylvania Cases

Penny.Col.Cas. Pennypacker Colonial Cases (Pa.)

Pennyp. Pennypacker Unreported Pennsylvania Cases

Pennyp.Col.Cas. Pennypacker's Colonial Cases

Pennyp.(Pa.) Pennypacker Unreported Pennsylvania Cases

Penr. & W. Penrose & Watts' Rep. (Pa. 1829-32)

Pens.Plan Guide Pension Plan Guide (CCH)

Peo.L.Adv. People's Legal Advisor, Utica, N.Y.

Pepper & L.Dig. Laws Pepper and Lewis' Digest of Laws (Pa.)

Per. Perera's Select Decisions (Ceylon)

Per.C.S. Perrault's Conseil Superieur (Canada)

Per.Or.Cas. Perry Oriental Cases (Bombay)

Per.P. Perrault's Prévosté de Quebec

Per.Tr. Perry on Trusts

Per. & Dav. Perry & Davison's English King's Bench Reports (1838-41)

Per. & Kn. Perry & Knapp's English Election Reports (1838)

Performing Arts Rev. Performing Arts Review

Perk. ● Perkins on Conveyancing
　　　 ● Perkins on Pleading
　　　 ● Perkins' Profitable Book (Conveyancing)

Perk.Pr.Bk. Perkins' Profitable Book (Conveyancing)

Perm. Permanent

Perp. Perpetual

Perpet. Perpetual

Perrault ● Perrault's Quebec Reports
　　　　 ● Perrault's Conseil Superieur (Canada)
　　　　 ● Perrault's Prévoste de Quebec

Perry. ● Perry's Oriental Cases, Bombay
　　　 ● Sir Erskine Perry's Reports, in Morley's (East) Indian Digest

Perry Ins. Perry's Insolvency Cases-(1831) (Eng.)

Perry O.C. Perry's Oriental Cases (Bombay)

Perry,Trusts, Perry on Trusts

Perry & D. Perry & Davison's English King's Bench Reports

Perry & D.(Eng.) Perry & Davison's English King's Bench Reports

Perry & K. Perry & Knapp's Election Cases (Eng.)

Perry & Kn. Perry & Knapp's English Election Cases

Pers. Personnel Board

Pers.Finance L.Q. Personal Finance Law Quarterly Report

Pers.Inj.Comment'r. Personal Injury Commentator

Pers.Prop. Personal Property

Pershad Privy Council Judgments (1829-69) (India)

Pet. ● Peters
　　 ● Peters' Admiralty Reports, Dist. Ct. (U.S.)
　　 ● Peters' Circuit Court Reports (U.S.)
　　 ● Peters' Supreme Court Reports (26-41 U.S.)
　　 ● Peters' Prince Edward Island Reports (1850-72) (Canada)
　　 ● Petition

Pet.Ab. Petersdorff's Abridgment

Pet.Ad. Peters' United States District Court Reports (Admiralty Decisions)

Pet.Adm. Peters' United States District Court Reports (Admiralty Decisions)

Pet.Br. ● Brooke's New Cases (Petit Brooke) (1515-58)
　　 ● Bellewe's Cases temp. Hen. VIII (Eng.)

Pet.C.C. Peters' United States Circuit Court Reports

Pet.Cond. Peters' Condensed Reports, U.S. Supreme Court

Pet.Dig. ● Peters' United States Digest
　　 ● Peticolas' Texas Digest

Pet.S.C. Peters' Supreme Court Report (26-41 U.S.)

Peter Analysis and Digest of the Decisions of Sir George Jessel by A. P.Peter (Eng.)

Peters Peters' Supreme Court Reports (26-41 U.S.)

Peters Adm. Peters' Admiralty Reports, U.S. District Courts

Peters C.C. Peters' United States Circuit Court Reports

Petersd.Ab. Petersdorff's Abridgment

Petit Br. Petit Brooke, or Brooke's New Cases, English King's Bench (1515-58)

Petn. Petition

Petron.Satyric. Petronius' (Titus) Arbiter, Satyricon, etc.

Pfd.   Preferred

Ph.   ● Phillimore's English Ecclesiastical Reports

      ● Phillips' English Chancery Reports (1841-49)

      ● Phillips' Election Cases (1780-81)

Ph.Ch. Phillips' English Chancery Reports.

Ph.St.Tr. Phillips' State Trials

Phal.C.C. Phalen's Criminal Cases

Phar. Pharmacy Board

Pheney Rep. Pheney's New Term Reports (Eng.)

Phi Delta Delta Phi Delta Delta (periodical)

Phil. ● Philadelphia Reports

      ● Phillimore's English Ecclesiastical Reports

      ● Phillips' Election Cases (1780-81)

      ● Phillips' English Chancery Reports (1841-49)

      ● Phillips' English Election Cases

      ● Phillips' Illinois Reports

      ● Phillips' North Carolina Reports

      ● Phillips' Treatise on Insurance

      ● Philippines

Phil.Civ. & Can.Law. Phillimore's Civil and Canon Law

Phil.Cop. Phillips' Law of Copyright Designs

Phil.Dom. Phillimore's Law of Domicil

Phil.Ecc. ● Phillimore's Ecclesiastical Judgments

      ● Phillimore's Ecclesiastical Law, 2 editions. (1873,1895)

      ● Phillimore's English Ecclesiastical Reports (1809-21)

Phil.Ecc.Law Phillimore's Ecclesiastical law. 2 editions (1873,1895)

Phil.El.Cas. Phillips' English Election Cases

Phil.Eq. Phillips' Equity (North Carolina) (1866-68)

Phil.Ev. Phillips on Evidence

Phil.Ev.Cow. & H. & Edw.Notes. Phillpps' on Evidence, Notes by Cowen, Hill and Edwards

Phil.Fam.Cas. Phillpps' Famous Cases in Circumstantial Evidence

Phil.Ins. Phillips on Insurance

Phil.Int.Law. Phillimore's International Law

Phil.Int.Rom.Law. Phillimore's Introduction to the Roman Law

Phil.Jud. Phillimore's Eccles. Judgments (1867-75) (Eng.)

Phil.Judg. Phillimore's Ecclesiastical Judgments (1867-75)

Phil.L.J. Philippine Law Journal (Manila)

Phil.L.Rev. Philippine Law Review

Phil.Law. Phillips, North Carolina Law Reports (1866-68)

Phil.Mech.Liens. Phillips on Mechanics' Liens

Phil.N.C. Phillips, North Carolina Law Reports

Phil.Pat. Phillips on Patents

Phil.Rom.Law. Phillimore's Private Law among the Romans

Phil.St.Tr. Phillpps' State Trials (Prior to 1688)

Phil. & M. Philip and Mary (as 4 & 5 Phil. & M.)

Phila. Philadelphia Reports (Pennsylvania 1850-91)

Phila.(Pa.) Philadelphia Reports (Pennsylvania 1850-91)

Phila.Law Lib. Philadelphia Law Library

Phila.Leq.Int. Philadelphia Legal Intelligencer, Pa.

Philanthrop. The Philanthropist

Philippine. Philippine Reports

Philippine Co. Philippine Code

Philippine Int'l.L.J. Philippine International Law Journal

Philippine L.J. Philippine Law Journal

Phill. ● Phillips'Chancery Reports (41 Eng.Reprint)

      ● Phillips' Equity, North Carolina

Phill.Ch.(Eng.) Phillips' Chancery Reports (41 Eng. Reprint)

Phill.Ecc.R. Phillimore's Ecclesiastical Reports (1809-21)

Phill.Eccl.Judg. Phillimore Ecclesiastical Judgments. (Eng.)

Phill.Eq.(N.C.) Phillips' Equity, North Carolina

Phill.Ins. Phillips on Insurance

Phill.L.(N.C.) Phillips Law

Phillim. Phillimore, English Ecclesiastical Reports

Phillim.Dom. Phillimore on the Law of Domicil

Phillim.Ecc.Law Phillimore's Ecclesiastical Law

Phillim.Eccl.(Eng.) J.Phillimore Ecclesiastical Reports (161 Eng. Reprint)

Phillim.Int.Law. Phillimore's International law

Phillips. ● Phillips, English Chancery Reports
    ● Phillips, North Carolina Reports: Law or Equity
    ● Phillips' Reports (152-245 Illinois)

Phip. ● Phipson's Digest, Natal Reports (S. Africa)
    ● Phipson's Reports, Natal Supreme Court (S. Africa)

Phipson. Reports of Cases in the Supreme Court of Natal

Pick. Pickering's Massachusetts Supreme Judicial Court Reports (1822-39)

Pick.(Mass.) Pickering's Reports (18-41 Massachusetts)

Pickle Pickle's Reports (85-108 Tenn.)

Pierce,R.R. Pierce on Railroad Law

Pig. Piggott's Common Recoveries. 3 editions (1739-92)

Pig.Rec. Pigott's Recoveries (Eng.)

Pig. & R. Pigott & Rodwell's English Registration Appeal Cases (1843-45)

Pike. Pike's Reports (1-5 Arkansas)

Pike.H.of L. Pike's History of the House of Lords

Pike & F.Adm.Law Pike & Fischer's Administrative Law

Pike & F.Fed.Rules Service Pike & Fischer's Federal Rules Service

Pike & Fischer, Admin.Law Pike & Fischer's Administrative Law

Pin. Pinney's Wisconsin Supreme Court Reports (1839-52)

Ping.Chat.Mortg. Pingrey's Treatise of Chattel Mortgages

Pinn. Pinney's Wisconsin Reports

Pist. Piston's Mauritius Reports

Piston. Piston's Mauritius Reports (1861-62)

Pit.L. University of Pittsburgh Law Review (Pa.)

Pitblado Lect. Isaac Pitblado Lectures on Continuing Legal Education

Pitc. Pitcairn's Criminal Trials (1488-1624) (Sc.)

Pitc.Crim.Tr. Pitcairn's Ancient Criminal Trials, Scotland

Pitc.Tr. Pitcairn, Criminal Trials, 3 vols.(Sc.)

Pitisc.Lex. Pitisci's Lexicon

Pitm.Prin. & Sur. Pitman on Principal and Surety

Pitt. Pittsburgh

Pitt.L.J. Pittsburgh Legal Journal

Pitts. ● Pittsburgh Reports
    ● Pittsburgh, Pa.

Pitts.L.J. Pittsburgh Legal Journal

Pitts.L.Rev. University of Pittsburgh Law Review

Pitts.Leg.J.(N.S.) Pittsburgh Legal Journal, New Series (Pa.)

Pitts.Rep. ● Pittsburg Reports
    ● Pittsburgh, Pa.

Pittsb. ● Pittsburg Reports
    ● Pittsburgh, Pa.

Pittsb.L.Rev. Pittsburgh Law Review

Pittsb.Leg.J. Pittsburgh Legal Journal (Pa.)

Pittsb.Leg.J.(O.S.). Pittsburgh Legal Journal. Old Series

Pittsb.Leg.J.N.S. Pittsburgh Legal Journal New Series (Pa.)

Pittsb.Leg.J.(Pa.) Pittsburgh Legal Journal (Pa.)

Pittsb.Leg.L. Pittsburgh Legal Journal (Pa.)

Pittsb.R.(Pa) Pittsburgh Reporter (Pa.)

Pl. Plowden's Commentaries (1550-80) (Eng.)

Pl.Ang.-Norm. Placita Anglo-Normannica Cases (Bigelow)

Pl.C. Placita Coronae (Pleas of the Crown)

Pl.Com. Plowden's Commentaries (1550-80) (Eng.)

Pl.Par. Placita Parliamentaria

Pl.& Pr.Cas. Pleading & Practice Cas.(1837-38) (Eng.)

Pla.Par. Placita Parliamentaria (Eng.)

Plac.Abbrev. Placitorum Abbreviatio

Plac.Ang.Nor. Bigelow's Placita Anglo-Normanica

Plac.Angl.Nor. Placita Anglo-Normannica (1065-1195)

Plac.Gen. Placita Generalia

Plan. Planning

Plan.Can. Plan Canada

Plan.,Zoning & E.D.Inst. Planning, Zoning & Eminent Domain Institute

Plan & Comp. Planning and Compensation Reports (1949-date) (Eng.)

Platt.
- Platt on Covenants (1829)
- Platt on Leases

Platt,Cov. Platt on the Law of Covenants

Plaxton. Plaxton's Canadian Constitutional Decisions

Plow.
- Plowden's English King's Bench Reports
- Plowden's Commentaries and Reports

Plowd. Plowden's English King's Bench Commentaries or Reports

Plt. Peltier's Orleans Appeals Decisions (La.)

Po Portuguese

Poe,Pl. Poe on Pleading and Practice

Pol.
- Police
- Policy
- Polish
- Political
- Politics
- Pollexfen's English King's Bench Reports (1669-85)
- Poland

Pol.C. Political Code

Pol.Code Political Code

Pol.Cont. Pollock on Contracts

Pol.Dig.Part. Pollock's Digest of the Laws of Partnership

Pol.J. Police Journal (Eng.)

Pol.Sci.Q. Political Science Quarterly

Pol.Sci.Quar. Political Science Quarterly

Polam.L.J. Polamerican Law Journal

Police Police, culture and society

Police J.Ct. Police Justice's Court

Police L.Q. Police Law Quarterly

Poll. Pollexfen's English King's Bench Reports (86 Eng. Reprint)

Poll.C.C.Pr. Pollock's Practice of the County Courts

Pollex. Pollesfen's English King's Bench Reports (86 Eng. Reprint)

Pollexf. Pollexfen's English King's Bench Reports (86 Eng. Reprint)

Pollexfen (Eng.) Pollexfen's English King's Bench Reports (86 Eng. Reprint)

Pollock & Maitl. Pollock and Maitland's History of English Common Law

Pollution Abs. Pollution Abstracts

Pol'y. Policy

Pom.Code Rem. Pomeroy on Code Remedies

Pom.Const.Law Pomeroy's Constitutional Law of the United States

Pom.Eq.Jur. Pomeroy's Equity Jurisprudence

Pom.Rem. Pomeroy on Civil Remedies

Pom.Rem. & Rem.Rights Pomeroy on Civil Remedies & Remedial Rights

Pom.Spec.Perf. Pomeroy on Specific Performance of Contracts

Pomeroy Pomeroy's Reports (vols. 73-128 California)

Pop. Popham's English King's Bench Reports (1592-1627)

Pop.Govt. Popular Government

Pop.Sci.Mo. Popular Science Monthly

Pope, Lun. Pope on Lunacy

Poph. Popham's English King's Bench Reports (1592-1627)

Poph. (2). Cases at the end of Popham's Reports

Popham (Eng.) Popham (King's Bench) (79 Eng. Reprint)

Port.
- Porter's Alabama Supreme Court Reports (1834-39)
- Portugal

Port.(Ala.) Porter's Alabama Reports

Port.Ins. Porter's Laws of Insurance

Port.U.L.Rev. Portland University Law Rev.

Porter • Porter's Alabama Reports
• Porter's Reports (vols. 3-7 Indiana)

Portia L.J. Portia Law Journal

Portland U.L.Rev. Portland University Review

Posey Posey's Unreported Cases (Tex.)

Posey, Unrep.Cas. Posey's Unreported Cases (Tex.)

Post • post (after) Used to refer the reader to a subsequent part of the book
• Post's Reports (vols. 23-26 Michigan)
• Post's Reports (42-64 Missouri)

Post. & Reg. Postage and registration

Poste's Gaius Inst. Poste's Translation of Gaius

Pot.Dwar. Potter's Dwarris on Statutes

Poth.Bail a Rente Pothier, Traité du Conract de Bail à Rente

Poth.Cont. Pothier's Contracts

Poth.Cont.de Change Pothier, Traité du Contract de Change

Poth.Cont.Sale Pothier, Treatise on the Contract of Sale

Poth.Contr.Sale Pothier, Treatise on the Contract of Sale

Poth.Ob. Pothier on the Law of Obligations

Poth.Obl. Pothier on the Law of Obligations

Poth.Oblig. Pothier on the Law of Obligations

Poth.Pand. Pothier's Pandects

Poth.Part. Pothier on Partnership

Pothier, Pand. Pothier, Pandectae Justinianeae, etc.

Pott.Corp. Potter on Corporations

Pott.Dwarris Potter's Edition of Dwarris on Statutes

Potter Potter's Reports (4-7 Wyoming)

Pov.L.Rep. Poverty Law Reporter (CCH)

Pow.App.Proc. Powell's Law of Appellate Proceedings

Pow.Cont. Powell on Contracts

Pow.Dev. Powell, Essay upon the Learning of Devises, etc.

Pow.Mortg. Powell on Mortgages

Pow.R. & D. Power, Rodwell & Drew's English Election Cases (1847-56)

Pow.Surr. Powers' Reports, New York Surrogate Court

Powers Powers' Reports, New York Surrogate Court

Power's Sur. Powers' Reports, New York Surrogate Court

pp. pages in cross-references

Pr. • Practice Reports (various jurisdictions)
• Price's Exchequer Reports (1814-24) (Eng.)
• Prior

PrAB Annual Proceedings of the Section of Labor Relations Law of the American Bar Association

Pr.C.K.B. Practice Cases, King's Bench (Eng.)

Pr.Ca. Great War Prize Cases (Evans) (Eng.)

Pr.Ch. Precedents in Chancery (Finch) (1689-1722) (Eng.)

Pr.Cont. Pratt on Contraband of War (1861)

Pr.Dec. Kentucky Decisions (Sneed, 2 Kentucky)

Pr.Div. Law Reports, Probate Division (Eng.)

Pr.Edw.I. Prince Edward Island Reports (Canada)

Pr.Edw.Isl. Prince Edward Island

Pr.Exch. Price's Exchequer Reports (1814-24) (Eng.)

Pr.Falc. President Falconer's Court of Session Cases (1744-51) (Sc.)

Pr.Min. Printed Minutes of Evidence

Pr.R. • Practice Reports (various jurisdictions)
• Practice Reports (Ontario)
• Practice Reports (Quebec)

Pr.Reg.B.C. Practical Register in the Bail Court

Pr.Reg.C.P. Practical Register in the Common Pleas (1705-42)

Pr.Reg.Ch. Practical Register in Chancery (1 vol.)

Pr.Rep. ● Practice Reports (Eng.)
● Practice Reports (Ontario)

Pr.Rep.B.C. Lowndes, Maxwell, & Pollock's Bail Court Practice Cases (Eng.)

P.R. & D.El.Cas. Power, Rodwell & Dew's Election Cases (Eng.)

Pr.& Div. Law Reports, Probate & Divorce (Eng.)

Pra.Cas. Prater's Cases on Conflict of Laws

Prac. ● Practical
● Practice
● Practitioners'

Prac.Act. Practice Act

Prac.Law. Practical Lawyer

Pract. Practitioner, Baltimore

Pract.Reg. Practical Register of Common Pleas (Eng.)

Pratt ● Pratt's Contraband of War Cases
● Pratt's Supplement to Bott's Poor Laws (1833)

Prax. Brown's Practice (Praxis), or Precedents in Chancery

Pre.Ch. Precedents in Chancery by Finch

Preb.Dig. Preble Digest, Patent Cases

Prec.Ch. Precedents in Chancery (24 Eng. Reprint)

Prec.in Ch.(Eng.) Precedents in (24 Eng. Reprint)

Pref. Preference

Prem. Premium

Prep. Preparation

Prer. Prerogative Court

Prerog.Ct. Prerogative Court, New Jersey

Pres.Falc. President Falconer's Scotch Session Cases (Gilmour & Falconer) (1661-86)

Prest.Conv. Preston on Conveyancing

Prest.Est. Preston on Estates

Prest.Merg. Preston on Merger

Pri. ● Price's Exchequer Reports (1814-24) (Eng.)
● Price's Mining Commissioners' Cases (Eng.)

Price. ● Price's Exchequer Reports (Eng.)

● Price's Mining Commissioners' Cases (Eng.)

Price Min.Cas. Price's Mining Cases

Price Notes P.C. Price's Notes of Practice Cases in Exchequer (Eng.) (1830-31)

Price Notes P.P. Price, Notes of Points of Practice, Exchequer Cases (Eng.)

Price,P.C. Price's Practice Cases (1830-31)

Price Pr.Cas. Price's Practice Cases (Eng.)

Price & St. Price & Stewart's Trade Mark Cases

Prickett Prickett's Reports (1 Idaho)

Prid. & C. Prideaux & Cole's Reports (4 New Sessions Cases) (1850-51)

Prin. Principal

Prin.Dec. Kentucky Decisions (Sneed, 2 Ky.)

Prison L.Rptr. Prison Law Reporter

Pritch.Quar.Sess. Pritchard, Quarter Sessions

Priv.C.App. Privy Council Appeals (Eng.)

Priv.C.D.I. Indian Privy Council Decisions

Priv.Counc.App. Privy Council Appeals (Eng.)

Priv.Counc.D.I. Privy Council Decisions (India)

Priv.Found.Rep. Private Foundations Reporter (CCH)

Priv.Hous.Fin. Private Housing Finance

Priv.Laws Private laws

Priv.St. Private Statutes

Prob. ● English Probate and Admiralty Reports for year cited
● Law Reports, Probate Division
● Probate
● Problems

Prob.(1891) Law Reports, Probate Division (1891)

Prob.C. Probate Code

Prob.Code. Probate Code

Prob.Ct. Probate Court

Prob.Ct.Rep. Probate Court Reporter, Ohio

Prob.Div. Probate Division, English Law Reports

Prob.Pr.Act. Probate Practice Act

Prob.R. Probate Reports

Prob.Rep. Probate Reports

Prob.Rep.Ann. Probate Reports Annotated

Prob. & Adm.Div. Probate and Admiralty Division Law Reports

Prob. & Div. Probate and Divorce, English Law Reports

Prob. & Mat. Probate and Matrimonial Cases

Prob. & Prop. Probate and Property

Proc. ● Procedures
　　　　● Proceedings
　　　　● Proclamation

Proc.Prac. Proctor's Practice

Prod. ● Product
　　　　● Production

Prod.Liab.Rep. Products Liability Reporter (CCH)

prolong. prolonged

Prom. Promissory

Prop. Property

Prop.Law. Property Lawyer (1826-30)

Prop.Law.N.S. Property Lawyer, New Series (Eng.)

Prop. & Comp. Property and Compensation Reports

Prot. Protocol

Proudf.Land Dec. United States Land Decisions (Proudfit)

Prouty. Prouty's Reports (61-68 Vermont)

Prov. Province

Prov.Can.Stat. Statutes of the Province of Canada

Prov.St. Statutes, Laws, of the Province of Massachusetts

Prt.Rep. Practice Reports

Psych. ● Psychiatry
　　　　● Psychology

Psych. & M.L.J. Psychological & Medico-Legal Journal

pt. part

pts. parts

pub. ● public
　　　　● publisher
　　　　● publishing
　　　　● published

Pub.Acts Public Acts

Pub.Acts N.S.W. Public Acts of New South Wales (1824-1957) (Aus.)

Pub.Acts Queensl. Public Acts of Queensland (Reprint) (1828-1936) (Aus.)

Pub.Adm.Rev. Public Administration Review

Pub.Auth. Public Authorities

Pub.Bldgs. Public Buildings

Pub.Contract L.J. Public Contract Law Journal

Pub.Employee Rel.Rep. Public Employee Relations Reports

Pub.Gen.Acts S.Austl. Public General Acts of South Australia (1837-1936)

Pub.Gen.Laws. Public General Laws

Pub.Health U.S. Public Health Service, Court Decisions

Pub.Hous. Public Housing

Pub.L. Public Law

Pub.Lands Public Lands

Pub.Lands Dec. Department of the Interior, Decisions Relating to Public Lands

Pub.Land & Res.L.Dig. Public Land and Resources Law Digest

Pub.Laws. Public Laws

Pub.Manag. Public Management

Pub.No. Public Number. Assigned to laws passed by the U.S. Congress

Pub.Off. Public Officers

Pub.Papers Public Papers of the President

Pub.Res. Public Resources

Pub.Res.C. Public Resources Code

Pub.Res.No. Public Resolution Number (assigned to public resolutions passed by the U.S. Congress)

Pub.Safety Public Safety

Pub.Ser.Comm. Public Service Commission

Pub.Serv. Public Service

Pub.St. Public Statutes

Pub.U.Rep. Public Utilities Reports (PUR)

Pub.Util. Public Utilities

Pub.Util.C. Public Utilities Code

Pub.Util.Comm. Public Utilities Commission

Pub.Util.Fort. Public Utilities Fortnightly

Pub. & Loc.Laws Public and Local Laws

publ. publication

Puerto Rico F. Puerto Rico Federal Reports

Puerto Rico Fed. Puerto Rico Federal Reports

Puffendorf. Puffendorf's Law of Nature

Pug(s). Pugsley's Reports (14-16 New Brunswick)

Pugs. & Bur. Pugsley & Burbidge Reports (17-20 New Brunswick)

Pugs. & Burb. Pugsley & Burbidge Reports (17-20 New Brunswick)

Pugs. & Tru. Pugsley's and Trueman's Reports, New Brunswick (1882-83)

Pull.Accts. Pulling's Law of Mercantile Accounts

Pull.Laws & Cust.Lond. Pulling, Treatise on the Laws, Customs, and Regulations of the City and Port of London

Pull.Port of London. Pulling, Treatise on the Laws, Customs, and Reg-

ulations of the City and Port of London

Pulsifer (Me.) Pulsifer's Reports (35-68 Maine)

Pump Ct. Pump Court (London)

Punj.Rec. Punjab Record (India)

Pur. Purchase

Purd.Dig. Purdon's Digest of Laws, Pennsylvania

Purd.Dig.Laws. Purdon's Digest of Laws (Pa.)

Purple's St. Purple's Statutes, Scates' Compilation

Putnam. Putnam. Proceedings before the Justices of the Peace

Pv. Par value

Pvt. Private

Pwr. Power

Py.R. Pyke, Lower Canada King's Bench Reports (Quebec 1810)

Pyke. Pyke, Lower Canada King's Bench Reports (Quebec 1810)

Pymt. Payment

Q

q. questioned; soundness of decision or reasoning in cited case questioned (used in Shepard's Citations)

Q. ● Quarterly
  ● Quebec
  ● Queensland

Q.B. ● Queen's Bench
  ● Queen's Bench Reports (Adolphus & Ellis, New Series)
  ● Queen's Bench Reports, Quebec
  ● Queen's Bench Reports, Upper Canada
  ● English Law Reports, Queen's Bench (1841-52)

Q.B.D. English Law Reports, Queen's Bench Division, 1876-90

Q.B.Div'l Ct. Queen's Bench Divisional Court (Eng.)

Q.B.(Eng.) Queen's Bench (113-118 Eng. Reprint)

Q.B.L.C. Queen's Bench Reports, Lower Canada

Q.B.R. Queen's Bench Reports, by Adolphus & Ellis (New Series)

Q.B.U.C. Queen's Bench Reports, Upper Canada

Q.C. Queen's Counsel

Q.C.F. Quare clausum fregit (wherefore he broke the close)

Q.C.L.L.R. Crown Lands Law Reports, Queensland (Aus.)

Q.C.R. Queensland Criminal Reports (Aus.)

Q.D. Quasi dicat (as if he should say)

Q.E.N. Quare executionem non (wherefore execution should not be issued)

Q.J.P. Queensland Justice of the Peace Reports

Q.J.P.R. Queensland Justice of the Peace Reports

Q.Japan Com'l.Arb.Ass'n. Quarterly of the Japan Commercial Arbitration Association

Q.L. Quebec Law

Q.L.Beor. Beor's Queensland Law Report (Aus)

Q.L.J. Queen's Law Journal

Q.L.R. ● Quebec Law Reports
  ● Queensland Law Reports

Q.L.R.(Beor). Queensland Law Reports by Beor (Aus.)

Q.O.R. Quebec Official Reports

Q.P.R. Quebec Practice Reports

Q.R. Quebec Official Reports

Q.R.K.B. ● Quebec King's (or Queen's) Bench Reports
  ● Rapports Judiciaires de Quebec, Cour du Banc du Roi

Q.R.S.C. ● Quebec Reports, Superior Court
  ● Rapports Judiciaires de Quebec. Cour Supérieure

Q.S. Quarter Sessions

Q.S.C.R. Queensland Supreme Court Reports (1860-81)

Q.S.R. Queensland State Reports (Aus.)

Q.T. Qui tam (who as well)

Q.U.L.R. Queensland University Law Journal

Q.V. Quod vide (used to refer a reader to the word, chapter, etc., the name of which it immediately follows)

Q.W.N. Queensland Weekly Notes, cited by year

Qd.R. Queensland Reports

Qly.Land R. Fitzgibbon's Irish Land Reports (1895-1920)

Qu.Jour.Int-Amer.Rel. Quarterly Journal of Inter-American Relations

Qu.L.J. Quarterly Law Journal

Qu.L.Rev. Quarterly Law Review

Quart.L.J.(Va.) Quarterly Law Journal

Quart.L.Rev.(Va.) Quarterly Law Review

Que. ● Quebec
  ● Quebec: Court with jurisdiction in Quebec

Que.C.A. Rapports Judiciares Officiels Court du Banc du Roi (de la Reine), Cour d'Appel (1892-date) (Canada)

Que.C.B.R. Rapports Judiciares Officiels, Cour du Blanc du Roi (de la Reine), Cour d'Appel (1892-date) (Canada)

Que.C.S. Rapports Judiciares Officiels, Cour Supérieure (Canada)

Que.K.B. Quebec Official Reports, King's Bench

Que.P.R. Quebec Practice Reports

Que.Q.B. Quebec Official Reports, Queen's Bench

Que.Rev.Stat. Quebec Revised Statutes (Canada)

Que.S.C. Quebec Official Reports, Superior Court

Que.Stat. Quebec Statutes (Canada)

Quebec L.(Can.) Quebec Law Reports

Quebec Pr.(Can.) Quebec Practice

Queen's L.J. Queen's Law Journal

Queensl. ● Queensland
          ● Queensland Reports (Aus.)

Queensl.J.P.(Austr.) Queensland Justice of the Peace

Queensl.L.J.(Austr.) Queensland Law Journal

Queensl.L.J. & R. Queensland Law Journal and Reports (1879-1901) (Aus.)

Queensl.L.J. & St.R. Queensland Law Journal and State Reports (Aus.)

Queensl.L.R. Queensland Law Reports (1876-78) (Aus.)

Queensl.S.C.(Austr.) Queensland Supreme Court Reports

Queensl.S.Ct.R. Queensland Supreme Court Reports (1860-81) (Aus.)

Queensl.St.(Austr.) Queensland State Reports

Queensl.Stat. Queensland Statutes (Aus.)

Queensl.W.N.(Austr.) Queensland Weekly Notes

Quin. Quincy's Massachusetts Reports

Quincy. Quincy's Massachusetts Reports

Quinti,Quinto Year Book 5 Henry V (Eng.)

Quon.Attach. Quoniam Attachiamenta

quot. quoted in, or quoting

R

R.
- Railway
- Range
- Rawle's Reports (Pennsylvania 1828-35)
- Abstracted reappraisement Decisions
- Regina (queen)
- Repealed
- The Reports, Coke's King's Bench (Eng.)
- Kentucky Law Reporter (1880-1908)
- Republican
- Rettie's Court of Session Reports, 4th Series (Scot.)
- Reversed, revoked, or rescinded; existing order abrogated (used in Shepard's Citations) Rex (king)
- Roscoe's Cape of Good Hope
- Reports
- Rule
- Russian

R.A.
- Registration Appeals
- Regulation Appeals
- Rules and Adminstration
- Rules on Appeal

R.A.C. Ramsay's Appeal Cases (Canada)

R.A.P. Rules for Admission to Practice

RB ●· Rechtbank, Arrondissements-rechtbank (District Court) (Belgium)
● Renegotiation Board (U.S.)

R.B.G. British Guiana Reports of Opinions

R. & B. Remington & Ballinger's Code (1910)

R. & B.Supp. Remington & Ballinger's Code (1913 Supplement)

R.C.
- Railway Cases
- Record Commisioners
- Registration Cases
- Remington's Code
- Revised Code
- Revised Statutes 1855, Missouri

- Revue Critique de Legislation et de Jurisprudence de Canada
- Rolls of Court
- Ruling Cases

R.C.D.I.P. Revue Critique de Droit International Privé

R.C.L. Ruling Case Law (an encyclopedia)

R.C.S. Remington's Compiled Statutes (1922)

R.C.S.Supp. Remington's Compiled Statues Supplement

R.C.W.A. Revised Code of Washington Annotated

R.C. & C.R. Revenue, Civil & Criminal Reporter, Calcutta

R.1 Cro. Croke, Elizabeth

R.2 Cro. Croke, James I.

R.3 Cro. Croke, Charles I.

R.D.
- Reappraisement Decisions
- Regio Decreto (Royal Decree)
- Indian Revenue Decisions

R.D.A. Rules for the Discipline of Attorneys

R.D.A.T. Registered Designs Appeal Tribunal

R.D.B. Research & Development Board (U.S.)

R.D.I.P.P. Rivista di Diritto Internazionale Privato e Processuale (Italy)

R.D.S. Rural Development Service

R.D.Sup. Revenue Decisions, Supplement (India)

RdW Rechtspraak van de Week (Holland)

R.de L. Revue de Législation et de Jurisprudence (Canada)

REA Rural Electrification Administration (U.S.)

REAP Rural Environmental Assistance Program

R.E.B. Real Estate Brokers' Board

RECP Rural Environmental Conservation Program

R.E.D. ● New South Wales Reserved Equity Decisions

- Ritchie's Equity Decisions (Russell) (Canada)
- Russell's Equity Decisions (Nova Scotia)

RFC Reconstruction Finance Corporation (U.S.)

RFD Rural Free Delivery

R.F.P. Request for Proposal

R.G. Regula Generalis (general rule or order of court) (Ontario)

R.H. Rotuli Hundredorum, Record Commission (Eng.)

R.H.C. Road Haulage Cases (1950-55) (Eng.)

R.H.L. Rettie, Scotch Sessions Cases, 4th Series (House of Lord's part)

RHOB Rayburn House Office Building

R.I.
- Rhode Island
- Rhode Island Reports
- Rhode Island Supreme Court Reports (1828-date)

R.I.A. Research Institute of America

R.I.A.Tax. Research Institute of America Tax Coordinator

R.I.B.J. Rhode Island Bar Journal

R.I.Bd.R.C. Rhode Island Board of Railroad Commission Reports

R.I.C. University of Richmond Law Review

R.I.Ct.Rec. Rhode Island Court Records

R.I.Dec. Rhode Island Decisions

R.I.Gen.Laws General Laws of Rhode Island

R.I.P.U.C. Rhode Island Public Utilities Commission

R.I.Pub.Laws Public Laws of Rhode Island

R.I.R.C. Rhode Island Railroad Commission

RIS Regulatory Information System

RIW Recht der Internationalen Wirtschaft (Germany)

R.Int'l Arb.Awards United Nations Reports of International Arbitral Awards

R.J. New South Wales, Port Phillip District Judgments (Aus.)

R.(J.) Justiciary Cases in vols. of Session Cases (1873-1898)

R.J.Q. Rapports Judiciaires (Quebec Law Reports)

R.J.R. Mathieu's Quebec Revised Reports

R.J.R.Q. Mathieu's Quebec Revised Reports

RJT La Revue Juridique Thémis

R.J. & P.J. Revenue, Judicial & Police Journal, Calcutta (India)

R.L.
- Revised Laws
- Revue Legale (Canada)
- Roman Law

R.L.B. U.S. Railroad Labor Board Decisions

R.L.B.Dec. Railroad Labor Board Decisions

R.L.N.S. Revue Légale, New Series (Canada)

R.L.O.S. Revue Légale, Old Series (Canada)

R.L.Q.B. Revue Légale Reports, Queen's Bench (Canada)

RLR Rutgers Law Review

R.L.S.C. Revue Legale Reports, Supreme Court (Canada)

R.L.W. Rajasthan Law Weekly (India)

R.L. & S. Ridgeway, Lapp and Schoales' Irish King's Bench Reports (1793-95)

R.L. & W. Robert, Leaming and Wallis' County Court Reports (1849-51)

R.M. Rural Municipality

R.M.C.C. Ryan & Moody's Crown Cases (Eng.)

R.M.C.C.R. Ryan & Moody's Crown Cases (Eng.)

R.M.Ch. P.M.Charlton's Reports (Georgia 1811-37)

R.M.Charlt.(Ga.) P.M. Charlton's Reports (Georgia 1811-37)

R.M.L.R. Rocky Mountain Law Review or University of Colorado Law Review

RMMLF Rocky Mountain Mineral Law Foundation

R.M.M.L.R. Rocky Mountain Mineral Law Review

R.M.R. Rocky Mountain Law Review

R.N.R.E. Application for writ of error refused, no reversible error

ROTC Reserve Officers Training Corps

R.P. ● Rent Regulation (Office of Price Stabilization, Economic Stabilization Agency, U.S.)

● Rotuli Parliamentorum (1278-1533) (Eng.)

R.P.B.S.C. Rules Peculiar to the Business of the Supreme Court

R.P.C. ● Real Property Cases (1843-48) (Eng.)

● Real Property Commissioner's Report (1832) (Eng.)

● Reports of Patent Cases (Eng.)

● Reports of Patent, Design & Trade Mark Cases (Eng.)

● Restrictive Practices Court

R.P.C.Rep. Real Property Commissioners' Report (1832) (Eng.)

R.P.P.P. Rules of Pleading, Practice, and Procedure

RPR Rent Procedural Regulation (Office of Rent Stabilization Economic Stabilization Agency) (U.S.)

R.P.W. Rawle, Penrose & Watts' Reports (Pennsylvania 1828-40)

R.P. & W. Rawle, Penrose, & Watts' Reports (Pennsylvania 1828-40)

R.Pat.Cas. Reports of Patent, Design and Trade Mark Cases

R.R. ● Pike and Fischer's Radio Regulations

● Railroad

● Rent Regulation (Office of Rent Stabilization, Economic Stabilization Agency) U.S.

● Revenue Release

● Revised Reports (Eng.)

● Rural Rehabilitation (U.S.)

R.R.2d Pike and Fischer's Radio Regulations, Second Series

R.R.B. Railroad Retirement Board (U.S.)

R.R.B.L.B. U.S. Railroad Retirement Board Law Bulletin

R.R.Rep. Railroad Reports

R.R.S. Remington's Revised Statutes

R.R. & Can.Cas. Railway & Canal Cases (Eng.)

R.S. ● Revised Statutes (various jurisdictions)

● Rolls Series

R.S.A. ● Rehabilitation Services Administration

● Revised Statutes Annotated

R.S.C. ● Revised Statutes of Canada

● Rules of the Supreme Court (Eng.)

R.S.C.O. Rules of the Supreme Court, 1883 (Great Britain) Order Number. (See Annual Practice 1928 or later Volumes)

R.S.Comp. Statutes of Connecticut, Compilation of 1854

R.S.F.S.R. Russian Soviet Federative Socialist Republic

RSOB Russell Senate Office Building (also known as OSOB)

R.S.S. Revised Statutes of Saskatchewan

R.S.Supp. Supplement to Revised Statutes

RSVP Retired Senior Volunteer Program

RTB Rural Telephone Bank

R.T.D.E. Revue Trimestrielle de Droit Européen (France)

R.t.F. Reports tempore Finch, English Chancery

R.t.H. ● Reports tempore Hardwicke (Eng.)

● Ridgway's Chancery & K.B. Reports, tempore Hardwicke (Eng.)

● Reports of Cases Concerning Settlements, tempore, Holt (Eng.)

R.t.Hardw. Reports tempore Hardwicke, English King's Bench

R.t.Holt. Reports tempore Holt, English King's Bench

R.t.Q.A. Reports tempore Queen Anne (11 Modern) (Eng.)

R.t.W. Manitoba Reports tempore Wood

RW Rechtskundig Weekblad (Belgium)

R. & C. Russell & Chesley's Nova Scotia Reports

R. & C.Ca. Railway & Canal Cases (Eng.)

R. & C.Cas. Railway & Canal Cases (Eng.)

R. & C.N.Sc. Russell & Chesley's Reports (Nova Scotia)

R. & C.Tr.Cas. Railway & Canal Traffic Cases (Neville) (Eng.)

R. & Can.Cas. Railway & Canal Cases (Eng.)

R. & Can.Tr.Cas. Railway & Canal Traffic Cases (Eng.)

R. & D. Research and Development

R. & G. Russell & Geldert's Nova Scotia Reports

R. & G.N.Sc. Russell & Geldert's Reports, Nova Scotia

R. & H.Dig. Robinson & Harrison's Digest (Ontario)

R. & I.T. Rating & Income Tax Reports (Eng.)

R. & J. ● Rabkin & Johnson, Federal, Income, Gift and Estate Taxation
  ● Rafique & Jackson's Privy Council Decisions (India)

R. & J.Dig. Robinson & Joseph's Digest (Ontario)

R. & M. ● Russell & Mylne's English Chancery Reports
  ● Ryan & Moody's English Nisi Prius Reports

R. & M.C.C. Ryan & Moody's Crown Cases Reserved (Eng.)

R. M.Dig. Rapalje & Mack's Digest of Railway Law

R. & M.N.P. Ryan & Moody's Nisi Prius Reports (Eng.)

R. & McG. Income Tax Decisions of Australasia, Ratcliffe and M'Grath (1891-1930)

R. & McG.Ct.of Rev. Court of Review Decisions, Ratcliffe and M'Grath, New South Wales (1913-1927)

R. & My. Russell & Mylne's Chancery Reports (Eng.)

R. & N. Rhodesia and Nyasaland Law Reports (1956)

R. & R. Russell & Ryan Crown Cases (Eng.)

R. & R.C.C. Russell & Ryan's English Crown Cases, Reserved

R. & Ry.C.C. Russell and Ryan's English Crown Cases

Ra.Ca. English Railway and Canal Cases

Rad.Reg. Radio Regulation (P-H)

Rader Rader's Reports (138-163 Missouri)

Rag. Ragland California Superior Court Decisions

Rag.Super.Ct.Dec.(Calif.) Ragland Superior Court Decisions (Calif.)

Rail. & Can.Cas. ● English Railway and Canal Cases
  ● Railway and Canal Traffic Cases

Railw.Cas. Railway Cases

Railw. & Corp.L.J. Railway & Corporation Law Journal

Railway & Corp.Law J. Railway & Corporation Law Journal

Raj. Rajaratam Revised Reports (Ceylon)

Ram. Ramsey's Quebec Appeal Cases Ramanathan's Reports (Ceylon)

Ram Cas.P. & E. Ram's Cases of Pleading and Evidence

Ram F. Ram on Facts

Ram Leg.Judgm.(Towns.Ed.) Ram's Science of Legal Judgment, Notes by Townshend

Ram.S.C. Ramanathon, Reports, Supreme Court, Ceylon

Ram. & Mor. Ramsey & Morin's Montreal Law Reporter

Rams.App. Ramsey's Appeal Cases (1873-86) (Quebec)

Ramsay, App.Cas. Ramsay, Appeal Cases (Canada)

Ramsay App.Cas.(Can.) Ramsay, Appeal Cases (Canada)

Rand. ● Randall's Reports (62-71 Ohio State)
  ● Randolph's Reports (21-56 Kansas)
  ● Randolph's Reports (7-11 Louisiana)
  ● Randolph's Reports (22-27 Virginia) (1821-28)

Rand.Com.Paper Randolph on Commercial Paper

Rand.Em.Dom. Randolph on Eminent Domain

Rand.Perp. Randall on Perpetuities

Raney Raney's Reports (16-20 Florida)

Rang.Cr.L.J. Rangoon Criminal Law Journal

Rang.Dec. Sparks' Rangoon Decisions, British Burmah

Rang.L.R. Rangoon Law Reports (India)

Rap.Contempt. Rapalje on Contempt

Rap.Fed.Ref.Dig. Rapalje's Federal Reference Digest

Rap.Jud.Q.B.R. Rapport's Judiciaries de Quebec Cour du Banc de la Reine

Rap.Jud.Q.C.S. Rapport's Judiciaries de Quebec Cour Supérieure

Rap.Jud.Quebec C.S.(Can.) Rapports Judiciaries de Quebec

Rap.Jud.Quebec K.B.(Can.) Rapports Judiciaries de Quebec

Rap.Jud.Quebec Q.B.(Can.) Rapports Judiciaries de Quebec

Rap.Lar. Rapalje's on Larceny

Rap.N.Y.Dig. Rapalje New York Digest

Rap.Wit. Rapalje's Treatise on Witnesses

Rap. & L. Rapalje & Lawrence, American and English Cases

Rap. & L.Law Dict. Rapalje and Lawrence Law Dictionary

Rap. & Law. Rapalje & Lawrence American and English Cases

Rapal. & L. Rapalje & Lawrence, American and English Cases

Rapalje & L. Rapalje & Lawrence's Law Dictionary

Rapid Trans. Rapid Transit

Rast. Rastoll's Entries & Statutes (Eng.)

Rast.Ent. Rastell, Entries and Statutes

Rat.Sel.Cas. Rattigan, Select Cases in Hindu Law

Rat.Unrep.Cr. Ratanlal's Unreported Criminal Cases (India)

Rate Res. Rate Research published by the National Electric Light Association

Ratt.L.C. Rattigan's Leading Cases on Hindoo Law

Raw. Rawle's Reports, Pennsylvania, 5 vols.

Raw.Eq. Rawle, Equity in Pennsylvania

Rawle Rawle's Pennsylvania Supreme Court Reports (1828-35)

Rawle, Const.U.S. Rawle on the Constitution of the United States

Rawle, Cov. Rawle on Covenants for Title

Rawle Pen. & W. Rawle, Penrose, & Watts' Reports (Pa. 1828-40)

Ray, Med.Jur. Ray's Medical Jurisprudence of Insanity

Raym. Lord Raymond, English King's Bench Reports (3 vols.)

Raym.Ent. Raymond (Lord) Entries

Raym.Ld. Lord Raymond, English King's Bench Reports (3 vols.)

Raym.Sir T. Sir Thomas Raymond, English King's Bench Reports

Raym.T. Sir Thomas Raymond (Eng.)

Raymond Raymond's Reports, vols. 81-89 Iowa

Rayn. Rayner, English Tithe Cases (3 vols.)

Rayn.Ti.Cas. Rayner's Tithe Cases (1575-1782)

Rd. Road

RdW Rechtspraak van de Week (Holland)

Re-af. Re-affirmed

Re.de J. Revue de Jurisprudence (Montreal)

Re.de L. Revue de Jurisprudence et Legislation (Montreal)

Real Est.Comm'n. Real Estate Commission

Real Est.L.Rep. Real Estate Law Report

Real Est.Rec. Real Estate Record, New York

Real Est.Rev. Real Estate Review

Real Estate L.J. Real Estate Law Journal

Real Pr.Cas. Real Property Cases (Eng.)

Real Prop. Real Property

Real Prop.Acts Real Property Actions and Proceedings

Real Prop.Prob. & Tr.J. Real Property, Probate & Trust Journal

Real Prop.Tax   Real Property Tax
Reapp.Dec.   Reappraisement Decisions, U.S. Treasury
Rec.   ● Receipt
        ● American Law Record
        ● Recorder
        ● Records
Rec.Ass'n.Bar City of N.Y.   Record of the Association of the Bar of the City of New York
Rec.Comm.   Record Commission (Eng.)
Rec.Dec.   Vaux' Recorders Dec. (Pa. 1841-45)
Rec.Laws   Recent Laws in Canada
Recd.   Received
Record   Record, Association of the Bar, City of New York
Record of N.Y.C.B.A.   Record of the Association of the Bar of the City of New York
Red.   ● Redfield's New York Surrogates' Reports
        ● Redington's Reports (31-35 Maine)
Red.Am.R.R.Cas.   Redfield's Leading American Railway Cases
Red.Cas.R.R.   Redfield's Leading American Railway Cases
Red.Cas.Wills   Redfield's Leading Cases on Wills
Red.R.R.Cas.   Redfield's Leading American Railway Cases
Red.Wills   Redfield on the Law of Wills
Red. & Big.Cas.B. & N.   Redfield & Bigelow's Leading Cases on Bills and Notes
Redem.   Redemption
Redf.   Redfield's New York Surrogate Reports
Redf.(N.Y.)   Redfield's New York Surrogate Reports
Redf.Am.Railw.Cas.   Redfield's American Railway Cases
Redf.Carr.   Redfield on Carriers and Bailments
Redf.R.Cas.   Redfield's Railway Cases, Eng.
Redf.Railways   Redfield on Railways
Redf.Sur.(N.Y.)   Redfield's New York Surrogate Court Reports

Redf.Surr.   Redfield's New York Surrogate Reports
Redf.Surr.(N.Y.)   Redfield's New York Surrogate Court Reports (5 vols.)
Redf.Wills   Redfield's Leading Cases on Wills
Redf. & B.   Redfield & Bigelow's Leading Cases, Eng.
Redington   Redington's Reports (vols. 31-35 Maine)
Redman   Redman on Landlord and Tenant
Reed   Reed on Bills of Sale
Reed Fraud.   Reed's Leading Cases on Statute of Frauds
Rees' Cyclopaedia   Abraham Rees' English Cyclopaedia
Reese   Reporter, vols. 5, 11 Heiskell's Tennessee Reports
Reeve, Eng.Law   Reeve's History of the English Law
Reeve, Hist.Eng.Law   Reeve's History of the English Law
Reeves H.E.L.   Reeves' History of English Law
Ref.   ● Referee
        ● Referee's
        ● Refining
        ● Reform
        ● Refunding
Ref.Dec.   Referee's Decision
Ref.J.   Referees' Journal (Journal of National Association of Referees in Bankruptcy) (Eng.)
Ref.n.r.e.   Refused, not reversible error
Ref.Trib.   Referee Tribunal
Ref.w.m.   Refused, want of merit
Reg.   ● Register
        ● The Daily Register, New York City
        ● Registered
        ● Registrar
        ● Regulation
        ● Regulations
Reg.App.   Registration Appeals (Eng.)
Reg.Brev.   Register of Writs
Reg.Cas.   Registration Cases (Eng.)
Reg.Deb.   Gales & Seaton's Register of Debates in Congress (1824-37)
Reg.Deb.(G. & S.)   Gales & Seaton's Register of Debates in Congress (1824-37)

Reg.Deb.(Gales) Register of Debates in Congress (1789-91) (Gales)

Reg.Lib. ● Register Book
● Registrar's Book, Chancery

Reg.Maj. Books of Regiam Majestatem (Sc.)

Reg.Om.Brev. Registrum Omnium Brevium

Reg.Orig. Registrum Originale

Reg.Plac. Regula Plactiandi

Reg.Writ. Register of Writs

Reh.allowed Rehearing allowed (used in Shepard's Citations)

Reh.den. Rehearing denied (used in Shepard's Citations)

Reh.dis. Rehearing dismissed (used in Shepard's Citations)

Reh'g. Rehearing

Reilly Reilly's English Arbitration Cases

Reilly, E.A. Reilly, European Arbitration. Lord Westbury's Decisions

Rein. reinstated; regulation or order reinstated (used in Shepard's Citations)

Rel. Relations

Rel. & Pub.Order Religion and the Public Order

Relig.Corp. Religious Corporations

Rem.Cr.Tr. Remarkable Criminal Trials

Rem.Tr. Cummins & Durphy, Remarkable Trials

Rem.Tr.No.Ch. Benson's Remarkable Trials and Notorious Characters

Rem'd. Remanded

Rem'g. Remanding

Remington, Bankruptcy Remington on Bankruptcy

Remitt. Remittance

Remy Remys' Reports (145-162 Indiana; 15-33 Indiana Appellate)

Ren. Renner's Reports, Gold Coast Colony

Reorg. Reorganizations

Rep. ● Repealed
● Repertoire
● Report
● Reporter
● Reports
● The Reporter, Boston, Mass.

● The Reporter, Washington & New York
● Wallace's "The Reporters"
● Coke's English King's Bench Reports
● Knapp's Privy Council Reports (Eng.)

Rep.Ass.Y. Clayton's Reports of Assizes at Yorke

Rep.Atty.Gen. Attorneys General's Reports (U.S.)

Rep.Att'y.Genl. Reports of Attorney General, United States

Rep.Cas.Eq. Gilbert's Chancery Reports (Eng.)

Rep.Cas.Inc.Tax Reports of Cases relating to Income Tax (1875)

Rep.Cas.Madr. Reports of Cases, Dewanny Adawlut, Madras

Rep.Cas.Pr. Cooke's Practice Cases (1706-47)

Rep.Ch. Reports in Chancery (1615-1710) (Eng.)

Rep.Ch.Pr. Reports on Chancery Practice (Eng.)

Rep.Com.Cas. Report of Commercial Cases (1895-1941)

Rep.Const.Ct. South Carolina Constitutional Court Reports

Rep.Cr.L.Com. Reports of Criminal Law Commissioners (Eng.)

Rep.Eq. Gilbert's Reports in Equity (Eng.)

Rep.Fam.L. Reports of Family Law

Rep.in C.of A. Reports, Courts of Appeal (New Zealand)

Rep.in Can. Reports in Chancery (Eng.)

Rep.in Ch. Reports in Chancery (21 Eng. Reprint)

Rep.in Ch.(Eng.) Reports in Chancery (21 Eng. Reprint)

Rep.in Cha. Bittleston's Chamber Cases (1883-84)

Rep.Jur. Repertorium Juridicum (Eng.)

Rep.M.C. Reports of Municipal Corporations

Rep.of Sel.Cas.in Ch. Kelynge's Select Cases in Chancery (1730-32)

Rep.Pat.Cas. Reports of Patents, Designs and Trade-Mark Cases (Eng.)

Rep.Pat.Des. & Tr.Cas. Reports of Patents, Designs & Trademark Cases

Rep.Q.A. Reports temp. Queen Anne (11 Modern Reports)

Rep.Sel.Cas.Ch. Kelynge's (W.) Reports, English Chancery

Rep.t.F. Reports, Court of Chancery tempore Finch (1673-81)

Rep.t.Finch Reports, Court of Chancery tempore Finch (1673-81)

Rep.t.Finch (Eng.) Reports, Court of Chancery tempore Finch, (1673-81)

Rep.t.Hard. Lee's Reports tempore Hardwicke, King's Bench (1733-38)

Rep.t.Hardw. Lee's Reports tempore Hardwicke, King's Bench (1733-38)

Rep.t.Holt Reports tempore Holt (English Cases of Settlement)

Rep.t.O.Br. Carter's English Common Pleas Reports tempore O. Bridgman

Rep.t.Q.A. Reports tempore Queen Anne, vol. 11 Modern Reports

Rep.t.Talb. Reports tempore Talbot, English Chancery

Rep.t.Wood Manitoba Reports temp. Wood

Rep.York Ass. Clayton's Pleas of Assize at York (Eng.)

repl. replacement

Repr. Representing

Repr.Acts W.Austl. Reprinted Acts of Western Australia

Repr.Stat.N.Z. Reprint of the Statutes of New Zealand

Reprint English Reports, Full Reprint

Rept.t.Finch Cases temp. Finch (Chancery) (Eng.)

Rept.t.Holt Cases temp. Holt (King's Bench) (Eng.)

Reptr. The Reporter (Boston, Los Angeles, New York, Washington)

Res. ● Reserve
     ● Resolution of a legislative body
     ● Resources

Res.Cas. Reserved Cases (Ir.)

Res.Gamma Eta Gamma Rescript of Gamma Eta Gamma

Res Ipsa Res Ipsa Loquitur

Res.Jud. Res Judicatae (periodical) (Aus.)

Res. & Eq.Jud. Reserved and Equity Judgments, New South Wales (1845)

Reserv.Cas. Reserved Cases (1860-64) (Ir.)

Restric.Prac. Reports of Restrictive Practices Cases

Ret. Wisconsin Retirement Fund

RETIRE. & Soc.Sec. Retirement & Social Security

Rett. Rettie's Court of Session Cases, 4th Series (Sc.)

Rettie Rettie's Court of Session Cases, 4th Series (Sc.)

Rev. ● Cour de Revision (Monaco)
     ● Reversed in, or reversing (used in Shepard's Citations)
     ● Review
     ● revised, revision
     ● Revision of the Statutes

Rev.Bar. Revue du Barreau

Rev.Bd. Review Board

Rev.C.Abo.Pr. Revista de Derecho del Colegio de Abogados de Puerto Rico

Rev.C. & C.Rep. Revenue, Civil, & Criminal Reporter, Calcutta (India)

Rev.Cas. Revenue Cases

Rev.Civ.Code Revised Civil Code

Rev.Civ.St. Revised Civil Statutes

Rev.Code Revised Code

Rev.Code Civ.Proc. Revised Code Civil Procedure

Rev.Code Cr.Proc. Revised Code of Criminal Procedure

Rev.Cr.Code Revised Criminal Code

Rev.Crit. Revue Critique, Montreal

Rev.Crit.de Légis.et.Jur. Revue Critique de Législation et de Jurisprudence (Montreal)

Rev.D.P.R. Revista de Derecho Puertorriqueno

Rev.de Jur. Revue de Jurisprudence (Quebec)

Rev.de Leg. Revue de Législation et de Jurisprudence (Montreal)

Rev.de Legis. Revue de Législation (Canada)

Rev.du B. Revue du Barreau de la Province de Quebec

Rev.du Dr. Revue du Droit, Quebec

Rev.du Not. Revue du Notariat (Quebec)

Rev.ed. revised edition

Rev.Gen.Reg. Revised General Regulation, General Accounting Office (U.S.)

Rev.J. & P.J. Revenue, Judicial, & Police Journal (Bengal)

Rev.Jur.U.P.R. Revista Jurídica, Universidad de Puerto Rico

Rev.Laws Revised Laws

Rev.Leg. Revue Legale (Canada)

Rev.Leg.(O.S.) Revue Legale, Old Series

Rev.Leg.N.S. Revue Legale New Series (Canada)

Rev.Legale Revue Legale

Rev.Mun.Code Revised Municipal Code

Rev.Not. Revue de Notariat

Rev.Ord. Revised Ordinances

Rev.Ord.N.W.T. Revised Ordinances, Northwest Territories (Canada) (1888)

Rev.P.R. Revista de Derecho Puertorrinqueno

Rev.Proc. Revenue Procedure (U.S. Internal Revenue Service)

Rev.R. Revised Reports (1759-1866) (Eng.)

Rev.reh. Reversed on rehearing, or reversing on rehearing (used in Shepard's Citations)

Rev.Rep. Revised Reports (Eng.)

Rev.Rul. Revenue Ruling

Rev.Sec.Reg. Review of Securities Regulation, The

Rev.Sel.Code Leg. Review of Selected Code Legislation

Rev.St. Revised Statutes

Rev.Stat. Revised Statutes (various jurisdictions)

Rev. & T.C. Revenue and Taxation Code

Rev. & Tax Revenue and Taxation

Rev'd. Reversed

rev'g. Reversing

Revised R.(Eng.) Revised Reports

Reyn. Reynolds, Reports (40-42 Missisippi)

Reynolds Reynolds, Reports (40-42 Mississippi)

Reynolds' Land Laws Reynold's Spanish and Mexican Land Laws

Rice Rice's South Carolina Law Reports (1838-39)

Rice Ch. Rice's South Carolina Equity Reports

Rice's Code Rice's Code of Practice (Colo.)

Rice Dig. Rice, Digest of Patent Office Decisions

Rice Eq. Rice's South Carolina Equity Reports (1838-39)

Rice, Ev. Rice's Law of Evidence

Rice L.(S.C.) Rice, South Carolina Law Reports

Rich. ● Richardson's South Carolina Law Reports
      ● Richardson's Reports (vols. 2-5 New Hampshire)

Rich.C.P. Richardson's Practice Common Pleas (Eng.)

Rich.Cas. Richardson's South Carolina Cases (1831-32)

Rich.Cas.(S.C.) Richardson, South Carolina Equity Cases

Rich.Ch. Richardson's South Carolina Equity Reports

Rich.Ct.Cl. Richardson's Court of Claims Reports

Rich.Dict. Richardson's New Dictionary of the English Language

Rich.Eq. Richardson's South Carolina Equity Reports (1844-46, 1850-68)

Rich.Eq.Cas. Richardson's South Carolina Equity Reports

Rich.Eq.Ch. Richardson's South Carolina Equity Reports

Rich.L.(S.C.) Richardson, South Carolina Law Reports

Rich.Law (S.C.) Richardson's South Carolina Law Reports

Rich.N.H. Richardson's Reports (3-5 N.H.)

Rich.N.S. Richardson's South Carolina Reports, New Series

Rich.P.R.C.P. Richardson's Practical Register of Common Pleas (Eng.)

Rich.Pr.Reg. Richardson's Practical Register, English Common Pleas

Rich.Wills Richardson's Law of Testaments and Last Wills

Rich. & H. Richardson & Hook's Street Railway Decisions

Rich. & S. Richardson & Sayles' Select Cases of Procedure without Writ (Selden Soc. Pub. 60)

Rich. & W.   Richardson & Woodbury's Reports (2 New Hampshire)

Richardson, Law Practice   Richardson's Establishing a Law Practice

Rick. & M.   Rickards & Michael's Locus Standi Reports (Eng.)

Rick. & S.   Rickards & Saunders' Locus Standi Reports (Eng.)

Riddle's Lex.   Riddle's Lexicon

Ridg.   Ridgeway's Reports temp. Hardwicke, Chancery & King's Bench (Eng.)

Ridg.Ap.   Ridgeway's Appeal Cases (Ir.)

Ridg.Cas.   Ridgeway's Reports temp. Hardwicke, Chancery & King's Bench (Eng.)

Ridg.L. & S.   Ridgeway, Lapp, & Schoales' Irish Term Reports

Ridg.P.C.   Ridgeway's Appeal Cases (Ir.)

Ridg.Pr.Rep.   Ridgeway's Appeal (or Parliamentary) Cases (Ir.)

Ridg.Rep.   Ridgeway's (Individual) Reports of State Trials in Ireland

Ridg.St.Tr.   Ridgeway's (Individual) Reports of State Trials in Ireland

Ridg.t.Hard.   Ridgeway's Reports tempore Hardwicke, Chancery and King's Bench (27 Eng. Reprint)

Ridg.t.Hardw.   Ridgeway's Reports tempore Hardwicke, Chancery and King's Bench (27 Eng. Reprint)

Ridgew.   Ridgeway's Reports tempore Hardwicke, Chancery & King's Bench (Eng.)

Ridgew.L. & S.(Ir.)   Ridgeway, Lapp & Schoales Irish Term Reports

Ridgew.t.Hardw.(Eng.)   Ridgeway tempore Hardwicke (27 Eng. Reprint)

Ridgw.Ir.P.C.   Ridgeway Irish Appeal or Parliamentary Cases

Ridley, Civil & Ecc.Law   Ridley's Civil and Ecclesiastical Law

Ried.   Riedell's Reports (68, 69 N.H.)

Rigg   Select Pleas, Starrs, and other Records from the Rolls of the Exchequer of the Jews, ed. J.M. Riggs (Selden Society Publication, v. 15)

Ril.   ● Riley, South Carolina Equity Reports

● Riley's South Carolina Chancery Reports (1836-37)

Ril(ey)   ● Riley's Reports (Law & Equity)

● Riley's Reports (37-42 West Virginia)

Ril.Harp.   Riley's edition of Harper's South Carolina Reports

Riley   ● Riley's South Carolina Chancery Reports

● Riley's South Carolina Law Reports

● Riley's Reports (37-42 West Virginia)

Riley Ch.   Riley, South Carolina Equity Reports

Riley Eq.   Riley, South Carolina Equity Reports

Riley Eq.(S.C.)   Riley, South Carolina Equity Reports

Riley L.(S.C.)   Riley's South Carolina Law Reports

Rin.   Riner's Reports (2 Wyoming)

Riner   Riner's Reports (2 Wyoming)

Ritch.   ● Ritchie, Cases decided by Francis Bacon (1617-21)

● Ritchie's Equity Reports, Nova Scotia (1872-82)

Ritch.Eq.Dec.   Ritchie's Equity Decisions (Nova Scotia)

Ritch.Eq.Rep.   Ritchie's Equity Reports (Nova Scotia)

Ritchie   Ritchie's Equity (Canada)

Riv.Ann.Reg.   Rivington's Annual Register

Rmdr.   Remainder

Rn.   Renumbered; existing article renumbered (used in Shepard's Citations)

Ro.   ● Rolle's Abridgment

● Romanian

Ro.Rep.   ● Rolle's King's Bench Reports (Eng.)

● Robards' Conscript Cases (Texas 1862-65)

Rob.   ● Robard's Reports (12, 13 Missouri)

● Robards' Conscript Cases, (Texas)

● Roberts' Reports (29-31 Louisiana Annual)

- Robertson's Ecclesiastical Reports (Eng.)
- Robertson's Reports (1 Hawaii)
- Robertson's Scotch Appeal Cases (1707-27)
- Robinson's English Admiralty Reports (1799-1809, 1838-1852)
- Robinson's English Ecclesiastical Reports (1844-53)
- Robinson's Louisiana Reports (1-4 Louisiana Annual; Supreme Court Louisiana 1841-46)
- Robinson's Reports (38 California)
- Robinson's Reports (2-9, 17-23 Colorado Appeals)
- Robinson's Reports (1 Nevada)
- Robinson's Reports (1-8 Ontario)
- Robinson's Reports (40, 41 Virginia)
- Robinson's Scotch Appeal Cases 1840-41)
- Chr.Robinson's Upper Canada Reports
- J.L. Robinson's Upper Canada Reports

Rob.(La.Ann.) Robinson's Reports, (Louisiana Annual, vols. 1-4)

Rob.(Mo.) Robard's Missouri Reports

Rob.(N.Y.) Robertson's Reports (New York City Superior Court Reports, vols. 24-30)

Rob.(Nev.) Robinson's Reports (Nevada Reports, vol. 1)

Rob.A. C. Robinson's Admiralty Reports (1799-1809)

Rob.Adm.
- C. Robinson's Admiralty Reports (Eng.)
- W. Robinson's Admiralty Reports (Eng.)

Rob.Adm. & Pr. Roberts on Admiralty and Prize

Rob.App. Robinson's Scotch Appeal Cases (1840-41)

Rob.Cal. Robinson's Reports (38 California)

Rob.Car.V. Robertson's History of the Reign of the Emperor Charles V.

Rob.Cas. Robinson's Scotch Appeal Cases (1840-41)

Rob.Chr. Chr.Robinson, English Admiralty Reports, 6 vols. (1798-08)

Rob.Colo. Robinson's Reports (2-9, 17-23 Colorado App.)

Rob.Cons.Cas.(Tex.) Robards' Conscript Cases

Rob.Consc.Cas. Robards' Texas Conscript Cases

Rob.E. Robertson, English Ecclesiastical Reports (2 vols.) (1844-53)

Rob.Ecc. Robertson, English Ecclesiastical Reports (2 vols.) (1844-53)

Rob.Eccl. Robertson, English Ecclesiastical Reports (2 vols.) (1844-53)

Rob.Eq. Roberts' Principles of Equity

Rob.Hawaii Robinson's Reports (1 Hawaii)

Rob.Jun. William Robinson's Admiralty Reports (Eng.) 1838-1852

Rob.L. & W. Roberts, Leaming, & Wallis' County Court Reports (1849-51)

Rob.La. Robinson's Reports (1-4 La. Annual; La.Supreme Court 1841-46)

Rob.Mar.(N.Y.) Robertson & Jacob's New York Marine Court Reports

Rob.Mo. Robards' Reports (12, 13 Missouri)

Rob.N.Y. Robertson's Reports (24-30 N.Y. Superior Court)

Rob.Nev. Robinson's Reports (1 Nevada)

Rob.Ont. Robinson's Reports (1-8 Ontario)

Rob.Pat. Robinson on Patents

Rob.S.I. Robertson's Sandwich Island Reports (1 Hawaii)

Rob.Sc.App. Robinson's Scotch Appeal Cases

Rob.Sr.Ct. Robertson, New York Superior Court Reports, vols. 24-30

Rob.Super.Ct. Robertson's Reports (24-30 New York Superior Court)

Rob.U.C. Robinson's Reports (Upper Canada)

Rob.Va. Robinson's Reports (40, 41 Va.)

Rob.Wm.Adm. Wm. Robinson, English Admiralty Reports (3 vols.) (1838-50)

Rob. & J. Robards' & Jackson's Reports (26, 27 Texas)

Robards ● Robards' Reports (12, 13 Missouri)

● Robards' Conscript Cases (Texas 1862-65)

Robards & Jackson Robards & Jackson's Reports (vols. 26-27 Texas)

Robb. ● Robbins' Reports (67-70 N.J. Equity)

● Robb's United States Patent Cases

Robb.(N.J.) Robbins' New Jersey Equity Reports

Robb Pat.Cas. Robb's United States Patent Cases

Robert.App. Robertson's House of Lords Appeals (Sc.)

Robert.App.Cas. Robertson's House of Lords Appeals (Sc.)

Roberts Roberts' Reports (vols. 29-31 Louisiana Annual)

Roberts Emp.Liab. Roberts on Federal Liabilities of Carriers

Robertson ● Robertson's Ecclesiastical Reports (Eng.)

● Robertson's Reports (1 Hawaii)

● Robertson's Reports New York Marine Court)

● Robertson's Reports (24-30 New York Superior)

● Robertson's Scotch Appeal Cases (1707-27)

Robin.App. Robinson's House of Lords Appeals (Sc.)

Robin.Sc.App. Robinson's Scotch Appeal Cases (1840-41)

Robinson. ● Chr. Robinson's English Admiralty reports

● W. Robinson's English Admiralty Reports

● Robinson's English Ecclesiastical Reports (1844-53)

● Robinson's Reports (38 California)

● Robinson's Reports (17-23 Colorado)

● Robinson's Reports (Louisiana 1841-46)

● Robinson's Reports (1 Nevada)

● Robinson's Reports (Ontario)

● J.L. Robinson's Upper Canada Reports

● Robinson's House of Lords Appeals (Sc.)

● Robinson's Reports (40-41 Virginia)

Robinson Sc.App.Cas. Robinson's Scotch Appeal Cases (1840-41)

Robs.Bankr. Robertson's Handbook of Bankers' Law

Robson. Robson on Bankruptcy, 7 editions (1870-94)

Robt.(N.Y.). Robertson's Reports, New York City Superior Court Reports, vols. 24-30

Robt.Eccl.(Eng.) Robertson's English Ecclesiastical (163 Eng. Reprint)

Robt.Sc.App.Cas. Robertson's Scotch Appeal Cases

Rocc.de Nav.et Nau. Roccus de Navibus et Naulo

Roccus.Ins. Roccus on Insurance

Roche D. & K. Roche, Dillon, Kehoe, Land Reports (1881-82) (Ir.)

Rocky Mt.L.Rev. Rocky Mountain Law Review

Rocky.Mt.M.L.Inst. Rocky Mountain Mineral Law Institute

Rocky Mt.Miner.L.Rev. Rocky Mountain Mineral Law Review

Rocky Mtn. Rocky Mountain

Rodm. Rodman's Reports (78-82 Kentucky)

Rodman. Rodman's Reports (78 Kentucky)

Rog.C.H.R. Rogers' City Hall Recorder (New York 1816-22)

Rog.Ecc.Law Rogers' Ecclesiastical Law

Rog.Hov. Roger de Hovenden, Chronica

Rog.Rec. Rogers' New City Hall Recorder

Rogers. ● Rogers on Elections (2 editions) (1812, 1818-19)

● Rogers' Reports (47-51 Louisiana Annual)

Rol. ● Rolle, Abridgment (2 vols.)

● Rolle, English King's Bench Reports (2 vols.)

Rol.Ab. Rolle's Abridgment

Roll. ● Roll of the Term

● Rolle, Abridgment (2 vols.)

● Rolle, English King's Bench Reports (2 vols.)

Roll.Abr. Rolle's Abridgment

Roll.Rep. Rolle's English King's Bench Reports (2 vols.) (1614-25)

Rolle. ● Rolle, Abridgment

● Rolle, English King's Bench Reports (2 vols.) (1614-25)

Rolle,Abr. Rolle's Abridgement of the Common Law

Rolle R. Rolle's English King's Bench Reports (2 vols.) (1614-25)

Rolls Ct.Rep. Rolls' Court Reports

Rom. ● Romania

● Romilly's Notes of Chancery Cases (1767-87) (Eng.)

Rom.Cas. Romilly's Notes of Chancery Cases (1767-87) (Eng.)

Rom.Law. Mackeldy's Handbook of the Roman Law

Romilly N.C.(Eng.) Romilly's Notes of Cases

Root. ● Root's Connecticut Supreme Court Reports (1789-98)

● Root's Reports (Connecticut 1774-89)

Rop. Roper on Legacies (4 editions) (1799-1847)

Rop.Husb. & Wife Roper on Husband and Wife

Rop.Leg. Roper on Legacies

Rorer,Jud.Sales. Rorer on Void Judicial Sales

Rorer,R.R. Rorer on Railways

Rosc.Adm. Roscoe's Admiralty Jurisdiction and Practice

Rosc.Cr. Roscoe's Law of Evidence in Criminal Cases, 16 Editions (1835-1952)

Rosc.Crim.Ev. Roscoe's Law of Evidence in Criminal Cases, 16 editions (1835-1952)

Rosc.Jur. Roscoe's Jurist (Eng.)

Rosc.N.P. Roscoe's Law of Evidence at Nisi Prius, 20 editions (1827-1934)

Rosc.P.C. Roscoe's Prize Cases (1745-1859)

Roscoe. Roscoe's Reports of Supreme Court of Cape of Good Hope (S. Africa)

Roscoe,Bldg.Cas. Roscoe, Digest of Building Cases (Eng.)

Roscoe,Cr.Ev. Roscoe's Law of Evidence in Criminal Cases, 16 Editions (1835-1952)

Roscoe's B.C. Roscoe's Digest of Building Cases (Eng.)

Rose. Rose's Reports, English Bankruptcy

Rose B.C. Rose's Reports, English Bankruptcy

Rose Bankr.(Eng.) Rose's Reports, English Bankruptcy

Rose Notes. Rose's Notes on United States Reports

Rose W.C. Rose Will Case, New York

Rosenberger Street Railway Law (U.S.)

Rosenberger Pock.L.J. Rosenberger's Pocket Law Journal

Ross,Cont. Ross on Contracts

Ross,Conv. Ross' Lectures on Conveyancing, etc. (Sc.)

Ross L.C. Ross's Leading Cases in Commercial Law (Eng.)

Ross Ldg.Cas. Ross's Leading Cases on Commercial Law

Ross Lead.Cas. Ross' Leading Cases (Eng.)

Rot.Chart. Rotulus Chartarum (The Charter Roll)

Rot.Claus. Rotuli Clause (The Close Roll)

Rot.Cur.Reg. Rotuli Curiae Regis 1194-99

Rot.Flor. Rotae Florentine Reports of the Supreme Court, or Rota, of Florence)

Rot.Parl. Rotulae Parliamentariae

Rot.Pat. Rotuli Patenes

Rot.Plac Rotuli Placitorum

Rotuli Curiae Reg. Rotuli Curiae Regis (Eng.)

Rowe. Rowe's Interesting Parliamentary and Military Cases

Rowe Rep. Rowe's Reports (Irish)

Rowell. Rowell's Reports (vols.45-52 Vermont)

Rowell, El.Cas. Rowell's Contested Election Cases, U.S. House of Representatives

Roy.Dig. Royall's Digest Virginia Reports

Rp. Revoked or rescinded in part; existing regulation or order abrogated in part (used in Shepard's Citations)

Rt(s). Right (s)

Rt.Law Rep. Rent Law Reports (India)

Rucker Rucker's Reports (43-46 West Va.)

Ruff. ● Statutes at Large, Ruffhead's Edition (Eng.)
● Ruffin & Hawks' Reports (8 North Carolina)

Ruff. & H. Ruffin & Hawks' Reports (8 North Carolina)

Rul.Cas. Campbell's Ruling Cases (Eng.)

Rules Sup.Ct. Rules of the Supreme Court

Runn. ● Runnell's Reports (38-56 Iowa)
● Statutes at Large, Runnington Ed. (Eng.)

Runnell. Runnell's Reports (38-56 Iowa)

Rural Elec.Coop. Rural Electric Cooperative

Rus. Russell's English Chancery Reports

Rus.E.C. Russell's Election Reports (Ir.)

Rus.Eq.Rep. Russell's Equity Decisions (Nova Scotia)

Rus. & C.Eq. Cas. Russell & Chesley's Equity Cases (N.S.)

Rushw. Rushworth's Historical Collections

Russ. Russell's English Chancery Reports

Russ.Arb. Russell on Arbitrators

Russ.Ch. Russell's English Chancery Reports

Russ.Con.El.(Mass.) Russell's Contested Elections, Massachusetts

Russ.Cr. Russell on Crimes and Misdemeanors

Russ.Crimes. Russell on Crimes and Misdemeanors

Russ.Elect.Cas. ● Russell's Election Cases, Massachusetts
● Russell's Election Cases (Nova Scotia)

Russ.Eq. Russell's Equity Cases (Nova Scotia)

Russ.Eq.Cas. Russell's Equity Cases (Nova Scotia)

Russ.Eq.Rep. Russell's Equity Decisions (Nova Scotia)

Russ.Fact. Russell on Factors and Brokers

Russ.Merc.Ag. Russell on Mercantile Agency

Russ.N.Sc. Russell's Equity Cases (Nova Scotia)

Russ.t.Fld. Russell's English Chancery Reports *tempore* Elden

Russ. & C.Eq.Cas. Russell's & Chesley's Equity Cases (Nova Scotia)

Russ. & Ches. Russell & Chesley's Reports (Nova Scotia)

Russ.& Ches.Eq. Russell & Chesley's Equity Reports (Nova Scotia)

Russ. & Eq. Russell & Chesley, Equity Reports (Nova Scotia)

Russ. & Geld. Russell & Geldert's Reports (Nova Scotia)

Russ. & Jap.P.C. Russian and Japanese Prize Cases (London)

Russ. & M. Russell & Mylne Chancery (1829-33) (Eng.)

Russ. & My. Russell & Mylne Chancery (1829-33) (Eng.)

Russ. & R. Russell and Ryan's Crown Cases Reserved (1799-1823) (Eng.)

Russ.& R.C.C.(Eng.) Russell and Ryan's Crown Cases Reserved (1799-1823) (Eng.)

Russ. & R.Cr.Cas.   Russell and Ryan's English Crown Cases Reserved

Russ. & Ry.   Russell & Ryan's English Crown Cases Reserved

Russell.   Russell's Equity Decisions (Nova Scotia)

Russell N.S.   Russell's Nova Scotia Equity Decisions

Russian Rev.   Russian Review

Rut.-Cam.   Rutgers-Camden

Rutg.Cas.   Rutger-Waddington Case, New York City, 1784

Rutg.L.Rev.   Rutgers Law Review

Rutgers-Camden L.J.   Rutgers-Camden Law Journal

Rutgers J.Computers & Law   Rutgers Journal of Computers and the Law

Rutgers L.Rev.   Rutgers Law Review

Rutgers U.L.Rev.   Rutgers University Law Review

Ruth.Inst.   Rutherford's Institutes of Natural Law

Rv.   Revised; regulation or order revised (used in Shepard's Citations)

Ry.   Railway

Ry.Cas.   Reports of Railway Cases (Eng.)

Ry.Corp.Law Jour.   Railway & Corporation Law Journal

Ry.F.   Rymer's Foedera, 20 vols. (1704-35)

Ry.M.C.C.   Ryan & Moody Crown Cases (Eng.)

Ry.Med.Jur.   Ryan's Medical Jurisprudence

Ry. & C.Cas.(Eng.)   Railway & Canal Cases

Ry. & C.Traffic Cas.(Eng.)   Railway and Canal Traffic Cases (Eng.)

Ry. & Can.Cas.   Railway and Canal Cases (Eng.)

Ry. & Can.Tr.Cas.   Reports of Railway and Canal Traffic Cases (1855-1950)

Ry. & Can.Traf.Ca.   Railway and Canal Traffic Cases

Ry. & Can.Traffic Cas.   Railway and Canal Traffic Cases (Eng.)

Ry. & Corp.Law J.   Railway and Corporation Law Journal

Ry. & Corp.Law.Jour.   Railway and Corporation Law Journal

Ry. & M.   Ryan & Moody's Nisi Prius Reports (Eng.)

Ry. & M.C.C.   Ryan and Moody's Crown Cases Reserved (Eng.)

Ry. & M.N.P.   Ryan & Moody's Nisi Prius Reports (Eng.)

Ry. & Moo.   Ryan & Moody (1823-26)

Ryan. & M.   Ryan and Moody's English Nisi Prius Reports (171 Eng. Reprint)

Ryan. & M.(Eng.)   Ryan and Moody's English Nisi Prius Reports (171 Eng. Reprint)

Ryde.   Ryde's Rating Appeals (1871-1904)

Ryde Rat.App.   Ryde's Rating Appeals (1871-1904)

Ryde & K.Rat.App.   Ryde and Konstam's Reports of Rating Appeals (1894-1904)

Ryl.Plac.Parl.   Ryley's Placita Parliamentaria (1290-1307) (Eng.)

S

S.
- Scotland
- Searle's Cape of Good Hope Reports (S. Africa)
- Section
- Senate Bill
- Shaw, Dunlop, & Bell's Scotch Court of Session Reports (1st Series)
- Shaw's Court of Session Cases (Sc.)
- Shaw's Scotch House of Lords Appeal Cases
- Solicitor's Opinion
- South(ern)
- Southeastern Reporter (properly cited S.E.)
- Southern Reporter
- Southwestern Reporter (properly cited S.W.)
- Spanish
- Statute
- Superseded; new regulation or order substituted for an existing one (used in Shepard's Citations)
- New York Supplement
- Supreme Court Reporter

s.
- Same case; same case as case cited (used in Shepard's Citations)
- sec
- Scilicet (to wit)
- Section (of Act of Parliament)

S. New York Supplement

S.2d New York Supplement, second series

S/A Survivorship agreement

S.A.C. Strategic Air Command

S.A.I.R. South Australian Industrial Reports

S.A.L.R.
- South African Law Reports
- South Australian Law Reports

S.A.L.R.,S.W.A. South African Law Reports, South West African Reports

S.A.L.T.
- South African Law Times
- Strategic Arms Limitation Talks

SAO Smithsonian Astrophysical Observatory

S.A.R.
- South African Republic High Court Reports
- South Australian Reports

S.A.S.R. South Australian State Reports, cited by year. Continuation of South Australian Law Reports beginning with 1921 title changed as noted

S.A.Tax Cas. South African Tax Cases

S.Afr.L.J. South African Law Journal

S.Afr.L.R. South African Law Reports

S.Afr.L.R.App. South African Law Reports Appellate

S.Afr.Tax Cas. South African Tax Cases

S/Ag. Supervised Agency

S.App. Shaw's Scottish House of Lords Cases (1821-24)

S.Aust.L. South Australia Law

S.Aust.L.R. South Australian Law Reports

S.Austl. South Australia State Reports

S.Austl.L.R. South Australian Law Reports (1866-1920)

S.Austl.St.R. South Australia State Reports (1921-date)

S.Austr. South Australia

S.Austr.L. South Australia Law

S.B.
- Senate Bill (in state legislation)
- Small Business
- Special Bulletin, N.Y. Dept. of Labor
- Supreme Bench

SBA Small Business Administration

SBA State Bar of Arizona

SBIC Small Business Investment Companies

SBLI Southeastern Bankruptcy Law Institute

SBM State Bar of Montana

SBT Professional Development Program, State Bar of Texas

S.Bar J. State Bar Journal of California

SC Security Council (UN)

S.C. ● Cape of Good Hope Reports (S.Af.)
- Court of Session Cases (Sc.)
- Same Case
- Select Cases, Oudh (India)
- South Carolina
- South Carolina Reports
- Superior Court
- Supreme Court
- Supreme Court Reporter (National Reporter System)
- United Nations Security Council

S.C.(Scot.) Scottish Court of Session Cases, New Series

SCA ● Subsequent coupons attached
- Supreme and Exchequer Courts Act (Canada)

SCAP Supreme Commander, Allied Powers

S.C.Acts Acts and Joint Resolutions of South Carolina

SCB South Carolina Bar

S.C.Bar Assn. South Carolina Bar Association

S.C.C. ● Select Cases in Chancery *tempore* King, ed. by Macnaghten (Eng.)
- Small Cause Court (India)
- Cameron's Supreme Court Cases (Canada)
- Supreme Court of Canada

S.C.Cas. Supreme Court Cases

S.C.Code Code of Laws of South Carolina

S.C.D.C. Supreme Court Reports, District of Columbia

S.C.D.C.N.S. Supreme Court Reports, District of Columbia, New Series

S.C.Dig. Cassell's Supreme Court Digest (Canada)

S.C.E. Select Cases Relating to Evidence, Strange

S.C.Eq. South Carolina Equity Reports

S.C.H.L. Court of Session Cases, House of Lords (Sc.)

S.C.,J. Court of Justiciary Cases (Sc.)

S.C.J.B. Jamaica Supreme Court Judgment Books

S.C.L. ● Santa Clara Lawyer
- South Carolina Law Reports (pre-1868)
- Stock Corporation Law

S.C.L.J. South Carolina Law Journal

S.C.L.Q. South Carolina Law Quarterly

S.C.L.R. South Carolina Law Review

S.C.L.Rev. South Carolina Law Review

SCORE Service Corps of Retired Executives

S.C.Oudh. Oudh Select Cases (India)

S.C.P.S.C. South Carolina Public Service Commission Reports

S.C.R. ● Canada Supreme Court Reports
- Canada Law Reports, Supreme Court
- Cape Colony Supreme Court Reports
- South Carolina Reports

SCRIBE Scribes, The American Society of Writers on Legal Subjects

S.C.R.N.S.W. New South Wales Supreme Court Reports

S.C.Res. Senate Concurrent Resolution

S.C.S. Soil Conservation Service

S.C.T.I. University of Southern California Tax Institute

S.C.U.C.C.Dec. South Carolina Unemployment Compensation Commission Decisions

S.C.U.C.C.R. South Carolina Unemployment Compensation Commission Reports of Hearings

S.Ca.L.R. Southern California Law Review

S.Cal.L.Rev. Southern California Law Review

S.Calif.Law Rev. Southern California Law Review

S.Car. ● South Carolina
- South Carolina Reports

S.Con.Res. Senate Concurrent Resolution

S.Ct. ● Supreme Court
- Supreme Court Reporter

S.Ct.Rev. Supreme Court Review

S.Ct.Vict. Reports of Cases--Supreme Court of Victoria (1861-69) (Aus.)

S.D. ● Sadr Diwani Adalat Court, Bengal (India)
● South Dakota
● South Dakota Compiled Laws Annotated
● South Dakota Reports
● Southern District

S/D School district

S.D.A. ● Special Disbursing Agent, Bureau of Indian Affairs (U.S.)
● Sudder Dewanny Adawlut Reports, India

SDB State Bar of South Dakota

S.D.B.Jo. South Dakota Bar Journal

S.D.C. Supreme Court, District of Columbia Reports, New Series

S.D.Compiled Laws Ann. South Dakota Compiled Laws Annotated

S.D.K. Si De Ka Quarterly (Ann Arbor, Mich.)

S.D.L.Rev. South Dakota Law Review

S.D.P.A. Small Defense Plants Administration (U.S.)

S.D.R. New York State Department Reports

S.D.R.C. South Dakota Railroad Commission

S.D.R.C.Ops. South Dakota Board of Railroad Commissioners Opinions

S.D.Sess.Laws South Dakota State Bar Journal

S.D.St.B.J. South Dakota State Bar Journal

S.D.Uniform Prob.Code South Dakota Uniform Probate Code

S.D. & B. Shaw, Dunlop, & Bell's Session Reports (1821-38) (Sc.)

S.D. & B.Sup. Shaw, Dunlop, & Bell's Supplement, containing House of Lords Decisions

S.Dak. ● South Dakota
● South Dakota Reports

S.Doc. Senate Document

S.E. Southeastern Reporter, National Reporter System

S.E.2d. Southeastern Reporter, Second Series

SEATO Southeast Asia Treaty Organization

S.E.C. Securities and Exchange Commission Decisions and Reports

S.E.C.Jud.Dec. Securities & Exchange Commission Judicial Decisions

S.E.I.U. Service Employees' International Union (AFL-CIO)

SELA Latin American Economic System

SESA Social and Economic Statistics. Administration

S.E.W. Sociaal-Economische Wetgeving (Holland)

S.F. ● San Francisco
● Sinking Fund
● Standard Form
● Used by the West Publishing Company to locate place where decision is from, as, "S.F. 59," San Francisco Case No. 59 on Docket

S.F.A. Sudder Foujdaree Adawlut Reports (India)

S.F.L.J. San Francisco Law Journal

SFLR University of San Francisco Law Review

SFO Defense Solid Fuels Order (U.S.)

S.F.S. Sine fraude sua (without fraud on his part)

S.H.A. Smith-Hund Illinois Annotated Statutes

SHAPE Supreme Headquarters, Allied Powers in Europe

S.H.J.R. Senate-House Joint Reports

S.I. Statutory Instruments

S.I.T.C. Standard International Tariff Classification

S.I.T.E.S. Smithsonian Institution Traveling Exhibition Service

S.J. Scottish Jurist (1829-73) Solicitors' Journal

S.J.D. ● Doctor of the Science of Law
● Doctor of Juristic Science

S.J.L.B. Selected Judgments, Lower Burma

S.J.L.R. St. John's Law Review

S.J.Res. Senate Joint Resolution

SJZ Schweizerische Juristen-Zeitung (Switzerland)

S.Jur. Sirey, Jurisprudence (France)

S.Jur.I Sirey, Jurisprudence, Cour de Cassation (France)

S.Jur.II Sirey, Jurisprudence, Other Courts (France)

S.Jur.III Sirey, Jurisprudence, Jurisprudence administrative (France)

S.Just. Shaw's Justiciary Cases (Sc.)

S.L. Session laws

S.L.C.
- .Scottish Land Court Reports
- Smith's Leading Cases
- Stuart's Appeals, Lower Canada (1810-35)

S.L.C.App. Stuart's Lower Canada Appeal Cases

S.L.C.R. Scottish Land Court Reports

S.L.Co. Appendices of Proceedings of the Scottish Land Court

S.L.Co.R. Appendices of Proceedings of the Scottish Land Court

SLF The Southwestern Legal Foundation

S.L.F.C. Sierra Leone Full Court Reports

S.L.G. Scottish Law Gazette

S.L.J.
- Scottish Law Journal, Edinburgh
- Southwestern Law Journal

S.L.L.R. Sierra Leone Law Recorder

S.L.R.
- Saskatchewan Law Reports
- Scottish Law Reporter, (Edinburgh)
- Sind Law Reporter, (India)
- Southern Law Review (St. Louis, Mo.)
- Stanford Law Review

S.L.R.B. State Labor Relations Board

S.L.Rev. Scottish Law Review & Sheriff Court Reports

SLS Saint Lawrence Seaway Development Corporation

S.L.T.
- Scots Law Times (Scotland)
- Scots Law Times Reports

S.L.T.(Lyon Ct.) Scots Law Times Lyon Court Reports

S.L.T.(notes) Scots Law Times Notes of Recent Decisions

S.L.T.(Sh.Ct.) Scots Law Times Sheriff Court Reports

S.L.U.L.J. Saint Louis University Law Journal

S.M. Solicitor's Memorandum, U.S. Internation Revenue Bureau

S.M.H. Sydney Morning Herald (New South Wales)

S.M.L.J. St. Mary's Law Journal

SMSA Standard Metropolitan Statistical Area

SMU Southern Methodist University

S.N. Session Notes, Scotland

S.N.A. Sudder Nizamat Adawlut Reports (India)

SNCC The Student Nonviolent Coordinating Committee

SNCLAR University of Santa Clara School of Law

S.O. Solicitor's Opinion

S.O.C. Standards of Official Conduct

S.O.L.Rev. School of Law Review (Canada)

S.P. Sine prole (without issue); same principle; same point

SPA State Planning Agency

SPARS Women's Coast Guard Reserves (from Coast Guard motto "Semper Paratus--Always Ready")

SPC South Pacific Commission (UN)

SPCA Society for the Prevention of Cruelty to Animals

S.P.R.
- Porto Rico Reports, Spanish edition
- Statement of Procedural Rules

S.Q.R. State Reports (Queensland)

S.Q.T. Queensland State Reports (Aus.)

S.R.
- Solicitor's Recommendation, U.S. Internal Revenue Bureau
- Special Regulation, U.S. Army
- New South Wales State Reports
- New York State Reporter
- Supreme Court of Quebec, Reports
- Southern Rhodesia High Court Reports

SRA Service & Regulatory Announcement, Dept. of Agric. (U.S.)

S.R.C. Stuart's Lower Canada Reports

S.R.,H.C.R. Southern Rhodesia High Court Reports (1911-55)

SRM Ship Repairs Maintenance Order, Nat'l. Shipping Authority Maritime Adm. (U.S.)

S.R.N.S.W. New South Wales State Reports

S.R.Q. State Reports (Queensland)

S.R.R. Scots Revised Reports

SRS Statistical Reporting Service Social and Rehabilitation Service

S.R. & O. Statutory Rules & Orders (Eng.)

S.Rept. U.S. Senate Committee Report

S.Res. U.S. Senate Resolution

S.S. ● Selden Society
● Silvernail's New York Supreme Court Reports
● Social Security
● Steamship
● Synopsis Series of United States Treasury Decisions

S.S.A. ● Social Security Act
● Social Security Administration (U.S.)

S.S.A.A. Social Security Acts Amendments

SSB ● Salary Stabilization Board (U.S.)
● Social Security Board ruling
● Social Security Board

S.S.C. ● Sanford's Superior Court Reports, New York City
● Sarawak Supreme Court Reports
● Scotch Session Cases

S.S.C.R. Sind Sudder Court Reports (India)

SSIE Smithsonian Science Information Exchange, Inc.

S.S.L.R. Straits Settlements Law Reports

S.S.R. Soviet Socialist Republic

SSR Social Security Ruling on old-age, survivors, and disability insurance benefits (U.S. Internal Revenue Bureau)

SSS Selective Service System (U.S.)

S.S.T. ● Social Security Tax Ruling (I.R. Bull.)
● Supersonic Transport

S.T. ● Sales Tax Branch, U.S. Internal Revenue Bureau
● Sales Tax Rulings, U.S. Internal Revenue Bureau
● Science and Technology

● State Trials

S.T.C. State Tax Cases (CCH)

S.T.D. Synopsis Decisions, U.S. Treasury

S.T.L.J. South Texas Law Journal

S.Teind. Shaw's Teind Cases (Sc.)

S.Tex.L.J. South Texas Law Journal

SUCL Stetson University College of Law

S.V.A.R. Stuart's Vice-Admiralty Reports (1836-74) (Quebec)

S.W. South Western Reporter (Nat. Reporter System)

S.W.2d South Western Reporter Second Series

S.W.L.J. Southwestern Law Journal & Reporter

S.W.L.Rev. Southwestern Law Review

S.W.Law J. Southwestern Law Journal and Reporter (Nashville, Tenn.)

S.W.Pol.Sci.Q. Southwestern Political Science Quarterly

S.W.Rep. South Western Reporter (commonly cited S.W.)

SWUSL Southwestern University School of Law

SYRUCL Syracuse University College of Law

S. & B. ● Saunders and Bidder's Locus Standi Reports (1905-19)
● Smith and Batty's Irish King's Bench Reports (1824-25)

S. & C. ● Saunders & Cole's English Bail Court Reports
● Swan & Critchfield, Revised Statutes (Ohio)

S. & C.Rev.St. Swan and Critchfield's Revised Statutes, Ohio

S. & D. Shaw, Dunlop, & Bell's Scotch Court of Session Reports (1st series) (1821-38)

S. & G. ● Smale & Giffard's Vice-Chancery Reports (Eng.)
● Stone & Graham's Court of Referees Reports (Eng.)
● Stone & Graham's Private Bills Reports (Eng.)

S. & L. Schoales & Lefroy's Irish Chancery Reports (1802-06)

S. & M. ● Shaw & Maclean's House of Lords Cases

     ● Smedes & Marshall's Reports (9-22 Miss.) (1843-50)

     ● Smedes & Marshall's Chancery Reports

S. & M.Ch. Smedes & Marshall's Mississippi Chancery Reports

S. & M.Chy. Smedes & Marshall's Mississippi Chancery Reports

S. & Mar. Smedes & Marshall's Reports (9-22 Miss.)

S. & R. Sergeant & Rawles' Reports (Pa. 1824-28)

S. & R.Neg. Shearman & Redfield on the Law of Negligence

S. & R.on Neg. Shearman and Redfield on Negligence

S. & S. ● Sausse and Scully's Irish Rolls Court Reports (1837-40)

     ● Simons and Stuart's Vice-Chancellors' Reports (1822-26)

     ● Swan and Sayler, Revised Statutes of Ohio

S. & Sc. Sausse & Scully's Rolls Court (Ir.)

S. & Sm. Searle & Smith's Probate & Divorce Reports (Eng.)

S. & T. Swabey and Tristram's Probate and Divorce Reports (1858-65)

Sachse N.M. Sachse's Minutes, Norwich Mayoralty Court

Sad.Pa.Cas. Sadley's Cases (Pennsylvania 1885-88)

Sad.Pa.Cs. Sadley's Cases (Pennsylvania 1885-88)

Sadler (Pa.) Sadler's Cases

Saint. Saint's Digest of Registration Cases (Eng.)

Sal. Salinger's Reports (88-117 Iowa)

Salk. Salkeld's King's Bench Reports (91 Eng. Reprint)

Salk.(Eng.) Salkeld's King's Bench Reports (91 Eng. Reprint)

Salm.Abr. Salmon's Abridgment of State Trials

Salm.St.R. Salmon's Edition of the State Trials

San.D.L.R. San Diego Law Review

San. Diego L.Rev. San Diego Law Review

San.F.L.J. San Francisco Law Journal

San Fern.V. San Fernando Valley

San Fr.L.B. San Francisco Law Bulletin

San Fr.L.J. San Francisco Law Journal

San Fran.L.B. San Francisco Law Bulletin

San Fran.L.J. San Francisco Law Journal

San Fran.Law Bull. San Francisco Law Bulletin

Sanb. & B.Ann.St. Sanborn and Berryman's Annotated Statutes (Wis.)

Sand. Sandford, New York Superior Court Reports, vols. 3-7

Sand.Ch. Sandford's Reports (N.Y. Chancery 1843-47)

Sand.Chy. Sandford, New York Chancery Reports, 4 vols

Sand.I.Rep. Sandwich Islands (Hawaiian) Reports

Sand.Inst.Just.Introd. Sandars' Edition of Justinian's Institutes

Sand.Uses and Trusts. Sanders on Uses and Trusts

Sand. & H.Dig. Sandels and Hill's Digest of Statutes, Ark.

Sandars, Just.Inst. Sandars' Edition of Justinian's Institutes

Sandf. Sandford's Reports (3-7 New York Superior)

Sandf.Ch. Sandford's New York Chancery Reports

Sandf.Ch.(N.Y.) Sandford's Reports (3-7 New York Superior)

Sanf.(N.Y.) Sanford's Reports (3-7 New York Superior)

Sandl.St.Pap. Sandler's State Papers

Sanf. Sanford's Reports, vol. 59 Alabama

Santa Clara Law. Santa Clara Lawyer

Santerna de Ass. Santerna de Assecurationibus et Sponsionibus Mercatorum

Sar. Sarswati's P.C. Judgments (India)

Sar.Ch.Sen. Saratoga Chancery Sentinel (N.Y.)

Sarat.Ch.Sent. Saratoga Chancery Sentinel (New York) (1841-47)

Sarbah Sarbah, Fantti Law Reports (Gold Coast)

Sarbah F.C. Sarbah, Fantti Customary Laws (Gold Coast)

Sask. ● Saskatchewan
       ● Saskatchewan Law Reports (1907-31) (Canada)

Sask.B.Rev. Saskatchewan Bar Review

Sask.Gaz. Saskatchewan Gazette

Sask.L. Saskatchewan Law

Sask.L.R. Saskatchewan Law Reports (Canada)

Sask.L.Rev. Saskatchewan Law Review

Sask.Rev.Stat. Saskatchewan Revised Statutes (Canada)

Sask.Stat. Saskatchewan Statutes (Canada)

Sau.L.R. Saurastra Law Reports (India)

Sau.& Sc. Sausee & Scully, Rolls Court (1837-40) (Ir.)

Sauls. Reports time of Saulsbury (5-6 Delaware)

Saund. Saunders' King's Bench Reports (1666-73)

Saund.Pl. & Ev. Saunders Pleading and Evidence

Saund. & A. Saunders and Austin's Locus Standi Reports (1895-1904)

Saund. & Aust. Saunders & Austin, Locus Standi Reports (2 vols.)

Saund. & B. Saunders & Bidder's Locus Standi Reports (Eng.)

Saund. & B.C. Saunders and Cole's Bail Court Reports (1846-48)

Saund. & C. Saunders and Cole's Bail Court Reports (1846-48)

Saund. & M. Saunders & Macrae's County Courts & Insolvency Cases (County Courts Cases & Appeals, v. II-III) (Eng.)

Saund. & Mac. Saunders & Macrae's English County Court Cases

Sausse & Sc. Sausse & Scully's Irish Rolls Court Reports (1837-40)

Sav. ● Savile's English Common Pleas Reports
       ● Savings

Sav.Dr.Rom. Savigny Droit Romaine

Sav.Priv. Trial of the Savannah Privateers

Sav.Syst. Savigny, System des Heutigen Römischen Richts

Savigny,Hist.Rom.Law. Savigny's History of the Roman Law

Savigny,System. Savigny's System des Leutigen Romischen Rechts

Savile(Eng.) Savile's English Common Pleas Reports (123 Eng. Reprint)

Saw. Sawyer's Circuit Court Reports (U.S.)

Sax. Saxton's New Jersey Chancery Reports

Saxt. Saxton's New Jersey Chancery Reports

Saxt.Ch. Saxton's Chancery (N.J.)

Say. Sayer's English King's Bench Reports (96 Eng. Reprint)

Sayer(Eng.) Sayer's English King's Bench Reports (96 Eng. Reprint)

Sayles' Ann.Civ.St. Sayles' Annotated Civil Statutes (Tex.)

Sayles' Civ.St. Sayles' Revised Civil Statutes (Tex.)

Sayles' Rev.Civ.St. Sayles' Revised Civil Statutes (Tex.)

Sayles' St. Sayles' Revised Civil Statutes (Tex.)

Sayles' Supp. Supplement to Sayles' Annotated Civil Statutes (Tex.)

Sayre, Adm.Cas. Sayre's Cases on Admiralty

Sc. ● Scammon, Illinois Reports, vols. 2-5
       ● Scotch or Scotland
       ● Scott's Reports, English Common Pleas

Sc.Jur. Scottish Jurist, 46 vols.

Sc.L.J. Scottish Law Journal and Sheriff Court Record

Sc.L.M. Scottish Law Magazine and Sheriff Court Reporter

Sc.L.R. ● Scottish Law Reporter
       ● Scottish Law Review Sheriff Court Reports

Sc.L.Rep. Scottish Law Reporter, Edinburgh

Sc.L.T. Scots Law Times

Sc.La.R. Scottish Land Court Reports, being supplementary to the Scottish Law Review

Sc.La.Rep. Report by the Scottish Land Court

Sc.La.Rep.Ap. Appendices to the Report by the Scottish Land Court

Sc.Mun.App.Rep. Scotch Munitions Appeals Reports (Edinburgh and Glasgow)

Sc.N.R. Scott's New Reports (Eng.)

Sc.R.R. Scotch Revised Reports

Sc.Sess.Cas. Scotch Court of Session Cases

Sc. & Div. Law Reports, Scotch and Divorce Appeals

Sc. & Div.App. Scotch and Divorce Appeals (English Law Reports)

Sc.Rev.Rept. Scots Revised Reports

Scac. Scaccaria Curia (Court of Exchequer)

Scam. Scammon's Reports (vols. 2-5 Illinois)

Scates' Comp.St. Treat, Scates & Blackwell Compiled Statutes (Ill.)

Sch. School

Sch.Bailm. Schouler on Bailment

Sch.Dom.Rel. Schouler on Domestic Relations

Sch.H. & W. Schouler on Husband and Wife

Sch.L.R. Schuylkill Legal Record (Pa.)

Sch.Per.Prop. Schouler on the Law of Personal Property

Sch.Reg. Schuylkill Register (Pa.)

Sch. & Lef. Schoales & Lefroy's Irish Chancery Reports

Schalk Schalk's Jamaica Reports

Scher. Scherer, New York Miscellaneous Reports, vols. 22-47

Schm.Civil Law Schmidt's Civil Law of Spain and Mexico

Schm.L.J. Schmidt, Law Journal (New Orleans)

Schmidt, Civ.Law Schmidt's Civil Law of Spain and Mexico

Schoales & L. Schoales and Lefroy's Irish Chancery Reports

Schomberg, Mar.Laws Rhodes Schomberg, Treatise on the Maritime Laws of Rhodes

School C. School Code

School of Advanced Studies Rev. School of Advanced International Studies Review

Schouler, Bailm. Schouler on Bailments

Schouler, Dom.Rel. Schouler on Domestic Relations

Schouler, Pers.Prop. Schouler on Personal Property

Schouler, U.S.Hist. Schouler's History of the United States under the Constitution

Schouler, Wills Schouler on Wills

Schuy.Leg.Rec.(Pa.) Schuylkill Legal Record

Schuy.Reg.(Pa.) Schuylkill Register

Schuyl.Leg.Rec. Schuylkill Legal Record (Pa.)

Schuyl.Leg.Reg. Schuylkill Legal Register (Pottsville, Pa.)

Sci. Science(s)

Sci.Fa. Scire facias (revival of judgment)

Sci.fa.ad dis.deb. Scire facias ad disprobandum debitum

Sco. Scott's Common Pleas Reports (Eng.)

Sco.N.R. Scott's New Reports, Com. Pleas (Eng.)

Scot. Scotland; Scots; Scottish

Scot.App.Rep. Scottish Appeal Reports

Scot.Jur. Scottish Jurist

Scot.L.J. Scottish Law Journal & Sheriff Court Record

Scot.L.M. Scottish Law Magazine & Sheriff Court Reporter

Scot.L.R. ● Scottish Law Reporter
         ● Scottish Law Review

Scot.L.Rep. Scottish Law Reporter

Scot.L.Rev. Scottish Law Review and Sheriff Court Reports

Scot.L.T. Scots Law Times

Scot.Law J. Scottish Law Journal (Glasgow)

Scots L.T. Scots Law Times

Scots L.T.R. Scots Law Times Reports

Scots R.R. Scots Revised (1707-1873)

Scott ● Scott's Common Pleas Reports (Eng.)
     ● Scott's Reports (25, 26 N.Y. Civil Procedure)

Scott (Eng.) Scott's Reports

Scott J. Reporter, English Common Bench Reports

Scott N.R. Scott's New Common Pleas Reports (Eng.)

Scr.L.T. Scranton (Pa.) Law Times

Scrib.Dow. Scribner on the Law of Dower

Scriven Scriven, Law of Copyholds

Scrutton Scrutton on Charter-parties. 16 editions (1886-1955)

Sd. Suspended; regulation or order suspended (used in Shepard's Citations)

Sdp. Suspended in part; regulation or order suspended in part

Sea. & Sm. Searle & Smith's Probate & Divorce Reports (Eng.)

Searle Searle's Supreme Court Reports, Cape Colony (1850-67)

Searle Sm. Searle & Smith's English Probate and Divorce Reports

Seb.Trade-marks Sebastisan on Trade-marks

Sec. Securities

Sec.Bk.Judg. Second Book of Judgments (Huxley) (Eng.)

Sec.Int. Secretary of the Interior (U.S.)

Sec.L.Rev. Securities Law Review

Sec.leg. Secundum legum (according to law)

Sec.of State Secretary of State

Sec.reg. Secundum regulam (according to rule)

Sec.Reg.Guide Securities Regulation Guide (P-H)

Sec.Reg. & L.Rep. Securities Regulation & Law Reports (BNA)

Sec.Reg. & Trans. Securities Regulations and Transfer Report

Sec. & Ex.C. Securities & Exchange Commission

Secd.pt.Edw.III Year Books, Part III (Eng.)

Secd.pt.H.VI Year Books, Part VIII (Eng.)

Sedg.Dam. Sedgwick on the Measure of Damage

Sedg.L.Cas.
- Sedgwick's Leadin' Cases on Damages
- Sedgwick's Leading Cases on Real Property

Sedg.St. & Const.Law Sedgwick on Statutory and Constitutional Law

Sedg. & W.Tr.Title Land Sedgwick and Wait on the Trial of Title to Land

Seign.Rep. Lower Canada Seigniorial Reports

Sel.Cas. Select Cases Central Provinces (India)

Sel.Cas.Ch. Select Cases in Chancery (Eng.)

Sel.Cas.D.A. Select Cases Sadr Diwani Adalat (India)

Sel.Cas.Ev. Select Cases in Evidence (Strange) (Eng.)

Sel.Cas.K.B.Edw.I. Select Cases in K.B. under Edward I (Sayles) (Eng.)

Sel.Cas.N.F. Select Cases, Newfoundland

Sel.Cas.N.W.P. Select Cases, Northwest Provinces (India)

Sel.Cas.N.Y. Yates' Select Cases (N.Y. 1809)

Sel.Cas.S.D.A. Select Cases Sadr Diwani Adalat (Bengal, Bombay) (India)

Sel.Cas.t.Br. Cooper's Select Cases tempore Brougham

Sel.Cas.t.King Select Cases in Chancery tempore King (Eng.)

Sel.Cas.t.Nap. Select Cases tempore Napier (Ir.)

Sel.Cas.with Opin. Select Cases with Opinions, by a Solicitor

Sel.Ch.Cas. Select Cases in Chancery tempore King, ed. Macnaghten (Eng.)

Sel.Col.Cas. Select Collection of Cases (Eng.)

Sel.Com. Select Committee

Sel.Dec.Bomb. Select Cases Sadr Diwani Adalat, Bombay (India)

Sel.Dec.Madr. Select Decrees, Sadr Adalat, Madras (India)

Sel.L.Cas. Select Law Cases (Eng.)

Sel.N.P. Selwyn's Law of Nisi Prius

Sel.Pr. Sellon's Practice

Sel.Serv.L.Rep. Selective Service Law Reporter

Sel.Serv.L.Rptr. Selective Service Law Reporter

Seld. Selden's Reports (5-10 N.Y.)

Seld.Mare Claus. Selden's Mare Clausum

Seld.Notes   Selden's Notes, N.Y. Court of Appeals

Seld.Soc.   Selden Society

Seld.Soc.Yrbk.   Selden Society Yearbook (U.S.)

Seld.Tit.Hon.   Selden's Titles of Honor

Sell.Pr.   Sellon's Practice in the King's Bench

Sell.Prac.   Sellon's Practice in the King's Bench

Selw.N.P.   Selwyn Law of Nisi Prius (Eng.)

Selw. & Barn.   Barnewall & Alderson's K.B. Reports, 1st part (Eng.)

Seminar   (Annual extraordinary number of the Jurist, Catholic University of America)

Sen.Doc.   Senate Document

Sen.J.   Senate Journal

Sen.Jo.   Senate Journal

Sen.Rep.
- Senate Report
- United States Senate Committee Report

Ser.   Series

Serg.Land Laws Pa.   Sergeant on the Land Laws of Pennsylvania

Serg. & Lowb.   English Common Law Reports, ed. Sergeant & Lowber

Serg. & Lowb.Rep.   English Common Law Reports, American reprints edited by Sergeant & Lowber

Serg.& R.   Sergeant & Rawle's Pennsylvania Reports

Serg. & Raw.   Sergeant & Rawle's Pennsylvania Reports

Serg. & Rawl.   Sergeant and Rawle's Pennsylvania Supreme Court Reports (1814-28)

Serv.   Service

Sess.   Session

Sess.Acts   Session Acts

Sess.Ca.   Scotch Court of Session Cases

Sess.Cas.
- Scotch Court of Session Cases
- Session Cases, High Court of Justiciary Section (1906-16) (Sc.)
- Sessions Cases, King's Bench (Eng.)
- Sessions Settlement Cases, K.B. (Eng.)

Sess.Cas.K.B.   Sessions Settlement Cases, King's Bench (Eng.)

Sess.Cas.Sc.   Scotch Court of Session Cases

Sess.Laws   Session Laws

Sess.N.   Session Notes (Sc.)

Sess.Pap.C.C.C.   Central Criminal Court Session Papers (Eng.)

Sess.Pap.O.B.   Old Bailey Session Papers

Set.   English Settlement and Removal Cases (Burrow's Settlement Cases)

Seton   Seton on Decrees, 7 editions (1830-1912)

Seton Hall L.Rev.   Seton Hall Law Review

Sett.Cas.
- Settlements & Removals, Cases in Kings Bench (Eng.)
- Burrow's Settlement Cases (Eng.)

Sett. & Rem.   Settlement & Removals, Cases in Kings Bench (Eng.)

Sev.H.C.   Sevestre's Bengal High Court Reports (India)

Sev.S.D.A.   Sevestre's Sadr Diwani Adalat Reports, Bengal (India)

Sevestre   Calcutta Reports of Cases in Appeal

Sewell, Sheriffs   Sewell on the Law of Sheriffs

Sex Prob.Ct.Dig.   Sex Problems Court Digest

Seych.L.R.   Seychelles Law Reports

Sg.   Supplementing; new matter added to an existing regulation or order (used in Shepard's Citations)

Sh.
- Shadforth's Reserved Judgments (Aus.)
- Shand's Reports (11-41 South Carolina)
- Shaw's Appeal Cases (Sc.)
- Shaw's Session Cases (Sc.)
- Shaw's Scotch Justiciary Cases
- Shaw's Teind Court Reports (Sc.)
- G.B. Shaw's Reports (10, 11 Vermont)
- W.G. Shaw's Reports (30-35 Vermont)
- Sheil's Cape Times Law Reports (S. Africa)

- Sheldon's Reports (Buffalo, N.Y. Superior Court)
- Shepherd's Alabama Reports
- Shepley's Reports (13-18, 21-30 Maine)
- Shipp's Reports (66, 67 North Carolina)
- Shirley's Reports (49-55 New Hampshire)
- Shower's King's Bench Reports (Eng.)
- Shower's Parliamentary Cases (Eng.)

Sh.App. Shaw's House of Lords Appeal Cases (Sc.)

Sh.C. Sheriff's Court

Sh.Crim.Cas. Shaw's Justiciary Court, Criminal Cases (Sc.)

Sh.Ct. Sheriff Court--District Court (Sc.)

Sh.Ct.of Sess. Shaw's Court of Session Cases (Sc.)

Sh.Ct.Rep. Sheriff Court Reports (Sc.)

Sh.Dig. Shaw's Digest of Decisions (Sc.)

Sh.Jus. Shaw's Justiciary Cases (Sc.)

Sh.Just. P. Shaw's Justiciary Decisions (Sc.)

Sh.Sc.App. Shaw's Scotch Appeals, House of Lords

Sh.Teind Ct. Shaw's Teind Court Decisions (Sc.)

Sh.W. & C. Shaw, Wilson & Courtenay's Scotch Appeals Reports (Wilson & Shaw's Reports)

Sh. & Dunl. Shaw & Dunlop's Scotch Court of Session Reports (1st Series)

Sh. & Macl. Shaw & Maclean's Scotch Appeal Cases

Shad. Shadforth's Reports (Aus.)

Shale Decrees & Judgments in Federal Anti-Trust Cases (U.S.)

Shan. Shannon's Unreported Cases (Tenn.)

Shan.Cas. Shannon's Tennessee Cases

Shand Pr. Shand, Practice, Court of Sessions (Sc.)

Shankland's St. Shankland's Public Statutes (Tenn.)

Shannon Cas.(Tenn.) Shannon's Unreported Tennessee Cases

Shannon's Code Shannon's Annotated Code (Tenn.)

Sharpe Calendar of Coroners Rolls of the City of London

Shars.Bl.Comm. Sharswood's Blackstone's Commentaries

Shars.Comm.L. Sharswood's Commercial Law

Shars.Law Lec. Sharswood's Lectures on the Profession of the Law

Shars.Leg.Eth. Sharswood's Legal Ethics

Shars.Tab.Ca. Sharswood's Table of Cases, Connecticut

Shars. & B.Lead.Cas.Real Prop. Sharswood and Budd's Leading Cases of Real Property

Shaw
- Shaw's Scotch Appeal Cases
- Shaw's Court of Session Cases, 1st Series
- Shaw's Justiciary Cases (Sc.)
- Shaw's Teind Court Reports (Sc.)
- G.B. Shaw's Reports (10, 11 Vermont)
- W.G. Shaw's Reports (30-35 Vermont)

Shaw (G.B.) G.B. Shaw's Reports (10, 11 Vermont)

Shaw (Vt.)
- G.B. Shaw's Reports (10, 11 Vermont)
- W.G. Shaw's Reports (30-35 Vermont)

Shaw (W.G.) W.G. Shaw's Reports (30-35 Vermont)

Shaw App. Shaw's Appeal Cases, English House of Lords, Appeals from Scotland

Shaw Crim.Cas. Shaw's Criminal Cases, Justiciary Court (Sc.)

Shaw, D. & B.
- Shaw, Dunlop & Bell's Court of Sessions (1st Series) (Sc.)
- Shaw, Dunlop & Bell's Session Cases (Sc.)

Shaw, D. & B. Supp. Shaw, Dunlop, & Bell's Supplement, House of Lords Decisions (Sc.)

Shaw Dec. Shaw's Decisions in Scotch Court of Sessions (1st Series)

Shaw Dig. Shaw's Digest of Decisions (Sc.)

Shaw, Dunl. & B. Shaw, Dunlop and Bell, Session Cases (1821-38) (Sc.)

Shaw, H.L. Shaw's Scotch Appeal Cases, House of Lords (1821-24)

Shaw, J. John Shaw's Justiciary Cases (1848-52) (Sc.)

Shaw Jus. John Shaw's Justiciary Cases (1848-52) (Sc.)

Shaw, P. Patrick Shaw, Justiciary Cases (1819-31) (Sc.)

Shaw P.L. Shaw's Parish Law

Shaw Sc.App.Cas.(Scot.) Shaw's Scotch Appeal Cases, House of Lords

Shaw T.C. Shaw, Teind Cases (1821-31) (Sc.)

Shaw T.Cas. Shaw's Scotch Teind Court Reports

Shaw, W. & C. Shaw, Wilson & Courtenay's Scotch Appeals Reports, House of Lords

Shaw & D. Shaw & Dunlop's Court of Session Reports, 1st Series (Sc.)

Shaw & Dunl. Shaw & Dunlop's Court of Session Reports, 1st Series (Sc.)

Shaw & M. Shaw & Maclean's Scotch Appeal Cases

Shaw & M.Sc.App.Cas.(Scot.) Shaw & Maclean's Scotch Appeal Cases

Shaw & Macl. Shaw & Maclean's Scotch Appeal Cases

Shear. & R.Neg. Shearman and Redfield on Negligence

Shearm. & Red.Neg. Shearman & Redfield on Negligence

Sheil. Cape Times Law Reports, edited by Sheil

Shel.Ca. Shelley's Cases in vol. 1 Coke's Reports

Sheld. Sheldon's Reports, Superior Court of Buffalo, New York

Sheld.Subr. Sheldon on Subrogation

Sheldon Sheldon's Reports, Superior Court of Buffalo, New York

Shelf.Lun. Shelford on Lunacy

Shelf.Mar. & Div. Shelford on Marriage and Divorce

Shep. ● Shepherd's Reports, Alabama

● Select Cases (in 37-39 Ala.)

● Shelpley's Reports (13-18, 21-30 Maine)

Shep.Abr. Sheppard's Abridgment

Shep.Touch. Sheppard's Touchstone of Common Assurances

Sheph.Sel.Cas. Shepherd's Select Cases (Ala.)

Shepherd Shepherd. Reports (19-21, 24-41, 60, 63, 64 Alabama)

Shepley Shepley, Reports (13-18 and 21-30 Maine)

Sher.Ct.Rep. ● Sheriff Court Reporter

● Sheriff Court Reports (Sc.)

Shiel. Shiel's Reports (Cape Colony)

Shill.W.C. Shillman's Workmen's Compensation Cases (Ir.)

Shingle The Shingle, Phila.. Bar Association

Shinn, Repl. Shinn's Treatise on American Law of Replevin

Ship.Gaz. Shipping Gazette, London

Shipp Shipp. Reports (66-67 North Carolina)

Shirl. Shirley's Reports (49-55 New Hampshire)

Shirl.L.C. Shirley's Leading Crown Cases (Eng.)

Shirley Shirley, Reports (49-55 New Hampshire)

Shome L.R. Shome's Law Reporter (India)

Shortt, Inform. Shortt on Informations, Criminal, Quo Warranto, Mandamus, and Prohibition

Show. ● Shower's King's Bench Reports (Eng.)

● Shower's Parliamentary Cases

Show.K.B. Shower's King's Bench Reports (Eng.)

Show.P.C. Shower's Parliamentary Cases (1 Eng. Reprint)

Show.Parl.Cas. Shower's Parliamentary Cases (1 Eng. Reprint)

Shower K.B. (Eng.) Shower's King's Bench Reports (89 Eng. Reprint)

Shower P.C.(Eng.) Shower's Parliamentary Cases (1 Eng. Reprint)

Sick. Sickels' Reports (46-85 N.Y.)

Sick.Min.Dec. Sickels' U.S. Mining Laws & Decisions

Sick.Op. Sickels' Opinions of the New York Attorneys-General

Sid. Siderfin's King's Bench Reports (82 Eng. Reprint)

Sid.(Eng.) Siderfin's King's Bench Reports (82 Eng. Reprint)

Sil. Silver Tax Division (I.R. Bull.)

Silv.
- Silvernails Reports (N.Y. 1886-92)
- Silvernail's Reports (9-14 N.Y. Criminal Reports)
- Silvernail's Supreme (1889-90)

Silv.A. Silvernail's Court of Appeals Reports

Silv.App. Silvernail's Court of Appeals Reports

Silv.Cit. Silvernail's New York Citations

Silv.Ct.App.(N.Y.) Silvernail's Court of Appeals Reports

Silv.Sup. Silvernail's Supreme Court (N.Y.)

Silv.Unrep. Silvernail's Unreported Cases (N.Y.)

Sim.Dig.Pat.Dec. Simonds, Digest of Patent Office Decisions (U.S.)

Sim.(Eng.)
- Simons' Reports, vols. 95-97, 99 Wisconsin
- Simons' Vice-Chancery Reports (57-60 Eng. Reprint)

Sim.N.S. Simons' English Vice-Chancery Reports, New Series (61 Eng. Reprint)

Sim.N.S.(Eng.) Simons' English Vice-Chancery Reports, New Series (61 Eng. Reprint)

Sim. & C. Simmons & Conover's Reports (99-100 Wis.)

Sim. & S. Simons & Stuart's Vice-Chancery Reports (57 Eng. Reprint)

Sim. & St. Simons & Stuart's Vice-Chancery Reports (57 Eng. Reprint)

Sim. & Stu. Simon's & Stuart's Vice-Chancery Reports (57 Eng. Reprint)

Sim. & Stu.(Eng.) Simons & Stuart's Vice-Chancery Reports (57 Eng. Reprint)

Simes & S.,Future Interests Simes & Smith on the Law of Future Interests

Sinclair Sinclair's Manuscript Decisions, Scotch Session Cases

Singer Prob.Cas.(Pa.) Singer's Probate Cases

Singers Singers Probate Court (Pa.)

Sir J.S. Sir John Strange's Reports (Eng.)

Sir L.Jenk. Wynne's Life of Sir Leoline Jenkins (1724)

Sir T.J. Sir Thomas Jones' Reports, King's Bench & Common Pleas (Eng.)

Sir T.Ray. T. Raymond's King's Bench Reports (Eng.)

Skene Sir John Skene's De verborum significatione, 7 editions (1597-1683)

Skene de Verb.Sign. Skene de Verborum Significatione

Skill.Pol.Rep. Skillman's N.Y. Police Reports

Skin. Skinner's King's Bench Reports (Eng.)

Skinker Skinker's Reports (65-79 Missouri)

Skinner (Eng.) Skinner's King's Bench Reports (90 Eng. Reprint)

Sl Slovene

Slade Slade's Reports (15 Vermont)

Sloan Leg.Reg. Sloan's Legal Register (N.Y.)

Sm. Smith

Sm.C.C.M. Smith's Circuit Courts-Martial Reports, Maine

Sm.Cond.Ala. Smith's Condensed Alabama Reports

Sm.E.D. E.D. Smith's Common Pleas Reports (N.Y.)

Sm.Eng. Smith's King's Bench Reports (Eng.)

Sm.Eq.
- Smith's (J.W.) Manual of Equity
- Smith's Principles of Equity

Sm.Ind. Smith's Reports (In 1-4 Indiana)

Sm.K.B. Smith's King's Bench Reports (Eng.)

Sm.L.C. Smith's Leading Cases

Sm.L.Cas.Com.L. Smith's Leading Cases on Commercial Law

Sm.L.J. Law Journal (Smith) (Eng.)

Sm.Me. Smith's Reports (61-84 Maine)

Sm.Pl. Somersetshire Pleas Civil & Criminal, ed. Chadwyck-Healey and Landon (Somerset Record Society Publications, v. 11, 36, 41, 44)

Sm. & B.R.R.Cas. Smith & Bates' American Railway Cases

Sm. & Bat. Smith & Batty's K.B. Reports (Ir.)

Sm. & G.
- Smale & Giffard's Chancery Reports (Eng.)
- Smith & Guthrie's Reports (81-101 Mo. App.)

Sm.& M. Smedes & Marshall's Reports (9-22 Miss.)

Sm.& M.Ch. Smedes & Marshall's Reports (9-22 Miss.)

Sm. & M.Ch. Same as above

Sm. & S. Smith & Sager's Drainage Cases (Can.)

Sma. & Giff. Smale & Giffard's English Vice-Chancellors' Reports

Smale & G. Smale & Giffard's English Vice-Chancellors' Reports

Smed. & M. Smedes & Marshall's Mississippi Reports

Smed. & M.Ch. Smedes & Marshall's Mississippi Chancery Reports

Smedes & M.(Miss.) Smedes & Marshall's Mississippi Reports

Smedes & M.Ch. Smedes & Marshall's Chancery Reports (Miss.)

Smee. Collection of Abstracts of Acts of Parliament

Smeth.L.S. Smethurst on Locus Standi, 1867

Smi. & Bat. Smith and Batty, Irish King's Bench Reports

Smith
- E.B. Smith's Reports (21-47 Illinois Appeals)
- E.D. Smith's New York Common Pleas Reports
- E.H. Smith's Reports (147-162 New York Court of Appeals)
- E.P. Smith's Reports (15-27 New York Court of Appeals)
- J.P. Smith's English King's Bench Reports

- P.F. Smith's Pennsylvania State Reports
- Smith, English Registration
- Smith, Reporter (7, 12 Heiskell's Tennessee Reports)
- Smith's Indiana Reports
- Smith's New Hampshire Reports
- Smith's Reports (54-62 California)
- Smith's Reports, (2-4 Dakota)
- Smith's Reports, (61-64 Maine)
- Smith's Reports (81-83 Missouri Appeals)
- Smith's Reports (1-11 Wisconsin)

Smith, Act. Smith's Actions at Law

Smith, C.C.M. Smith's Circuit Courts-Martial Reports (Me.)

Smith C.P. E.D. Smith's Common Pleas Reports, New York

Smith, Ch.Pr. Smith's Chancery Practice

Smith, Com.Law Smith's Manual of Common Law

Smith Cond.Rep. Smith's Condensed Reports (Ala.)

Smith, Cont. Smith on Contracts

Smith Ct.App. E.P. Smith's Reports, vols. 15-27 New York Court of Appeals

Smith de Rep.Angl. Smith (Sir Thomas), De Republica Anglica (The Commonwealth of England and the Manner of Government Thereof. 1621)

Smith, Dict.Antiq. Smith's Dictionary of Greek and Roman Antiquities

Smith E.H. Smith's (E.H.) Reports (147-162 New York Court of Appeals)

Smith E.P. E.P. Smith's Reports (15-27 New York Court of Appeals)

Smith, Ex.Int. Smith on Executory Interest

Smith-Hurd Ann.St. Smith-Hurd Illinois Annotated Statutes

Smith Ind. Smith's Indiana Reports

Smith J.P. J.P. Smith's English King's Bench Reports

Smith K.B. Smith's King's Bench (Eng.)

Smith L.C. Smith's Leading Cases

Smith, L.J. Smith's Law Journal

Smith, Laws Pa. Smith's Laws of Pennsylvania

Smith, Lead.Cas. Smith's Leading Cases

Smith, Man.Eq.Jur. Smith's Manual of Equity Jurisprudence

Smith Me. Smith's Reports (vols. 61-64 Maine)

Smith, Merc.Law Smith on Mercantile Law

Smith N.H. Smith's New Hampshire Reports

Smith N.Y. Smith's Reports (vols 15-27 and 147-162 New York Court of Appeals)

Smith P.F. P.F. Smith's Pennsylvania State Reports

Smith Pa. P.F. Smith's Pennsylvania State Reports

Smith Reg. C.L. Smith's Registration Cases (Eng.)

Smith Reg.Cas. C.L. Smith's Registration Cases (Eng.)

Smith, Wealth Nat. Smith, Inquiry into the Nature and Causes of the Wealth of Nations

Smith Wis. Smith's Reports (1-11 Wisconsin)

Smith & B. ● Smith & Batty's Irish King's Bench Reports
 ● Smith & Bates' American Railway Cases

Smith & B.R.R.C. Smith & Bates' American Railway Cases

Smith & Bat. Smith & Batty, Irish King's Bench Reports

Smith & G. Smith & Guthrie's Missouri Appeal Reports, vols. 81-101

Smith & H. Smith & Heiskell (Tenn.)

Smith's Laws Smith's Laws (Pa.)

Smith's Lead.Cas. Smith's Leading Cases

Smoult Notes of Cases in Smoult's Collection of Orders, Calcutta (India)

Smy. Smythe's Irish Common Pleas Reports (1839-40)

Smy. & B. Smythe and Bourke's Irish Marriage Cases (1842)

Smythe Smythe's Irish Common Pleas Reports (1839-40)

Sneed ● Sneed's Kentucky Decisions (2 Ky.)
 ● Sneed's Reports (33-37 Tennessee)

Sneed Dec. Sneed's Kentucky Decisions (2 Ky.)

Snell, Eq. Snell's Principles in Equity

Snow Snow's Reports (3 Utah)

Snyder, Mines Snyder on Mines and Mining

So. ● Southern
 ● Southern Reporter, National Reporter System

So.Afr.L.J. South Africa Law Journal

So.Afr.L.R. South African Law Reports

So.Afr.L.T. South African Law Times

So.Afr.Prize Cas. South African Prize Cases (Juta)

So.African L. South African Law Reports

So.African L.J. South African Law Journal

So.Aust.L.R. South Australian Law Reports

So.Austr.L. South Australian Law Reports

So.Austr.St. South Australian State Reports

So.C. South Carolina Reports

So.Calif.L.Rev. Southern California Law Review

So.Calif.Tax Inst. University of Southern California School of Law Tax Institute

So.Car. ● South Carolina
 ● South Carolina Reports

So.Car.Const. South Carolina Constitutional Reports (by Treadway, by Mill, or by Harper)

So.Car.L.J. South Carolina Law Journal, Columbia

So.Dak.B.Jo. South Dakota Bar Journal

So.East.Rep. Southeastern Reporter, commonly cited S.E.

So. Jersey L.S.Dictum. South Jersey Law School Dictum

So.L.J. Southern Law Journal & Reporter

So.L.Q. Southern Law Quarterly

So.L.R. Southern Law Review (Nashville, Tenn.)

So.L.R.N.S. Southern Law Review, New Series (St. Louis, Mo.)

So.L.Rev. ● Southern Law Review (Nashville, Tn.)
● Southern Law Review (St. Louis)

So.L.Rev.N.S. Southern Law Review New Series (St. Louis, Mo.)

So.L.T. Southern Law Times

So.Law Southern Lawyer

So.Rep. Southern Reporter (commonly cited South, or So.)

So.Tex.L.J. South Texas Law Journal

So.West.L.J. Southwestern Law Journal

So.West.Rep. Southwestern Reporter (commonly cited S.W.)

Soc. Social, Sociological, Sociology

Soc.Econ. Social Economist

Soc.Sec. Social Security

Soc.Sec.Bull. Social Security Bulletin

Soc.Ser. Social Services

Soc.Serv. Social Services

Soc'y Society

Soil & Water Conserv.Dist. Soil and Water Conservation Districts

Sol. ● The Solicitor
● Soloman's Court of Request Appeals (Ceylon)

Sol.J. Solicitor's Journal (1856-date) (Eng.)

Sol.J. & R. Solicitors' Journal & Reporter

Sol.Jo.(Eng.) Solicitors' Journal

Sol.Op. Solicitors' Opinion (especially of Internal Revenue Bureau) (U.S.)

Som. Somerset Legal Journal (Pa.)

Som.L.J. Somerset Legal Journal (Pa.)

Som.Leg.J.(Pa.) Somerset Legal Journal (Pa.)

Som.Pl. Somersetshire Pleas (Civil and Criminal) edited by Chadwyck-Healey and Landon. (Somerset Record Society Pulications, vols. 11, 36, 41, 44)

Somerset L.J. Somerset Legal Journal

Sou.Aus.L.R. South Australian Law Reports

Soule, Syn. Soule's Dictionary of English Synonymes

South. Southern Reporter (National Reporter System)

South Aus.L.R. South Australian Law Reports

South Car. ● South Carolina
● South Carolina Reports

South.L.J. Southern Law Journal

South.L.J. & Rep. Southern Law Journal & Reporter

South.L.Rev. Southern Law Review

South.L.Rev.N.S. Southern Law Review, New Series

South.Law J. Southern Law Journal (Tuscaloosa, Ala.)

South.Law J. & Rep. Southern Law Journal and Reporter

South.Law Rev. Southern Law Review

South.Law Rev.N.S. Southern Law Review, New Series

Southard Southard, New Jersey Law Reports, vols. 4-5

Southw.L.J. Southwestern Law Journal & Reporter

Southwestern L.J. Southwestern Law Journal

Sov. & E.Eur.For.Tr. American Review of Soviet and Eastern European Foreign Trade

Soviet L. & Govt. Soviet Law and Government

sp. superseded in part; new matter substituted for part of an existing regulation or order (used in Shepard's Citations)

Sp. ● Spear's Reports (S.C. Law 1842-44)
● Spinks' Ecclesiastical & Admiralty Reports (Eng.)

Sp.Acts Special Acts

Sp.C. Special Commissioner

Sp.CM Special Court-Martial (U.S. Navy)

Sp.Ch. Spears' (or Speers') South Carolina Chancery Reports

Sp.Com. Special Committee

Sp.Eq. Spears' (or Speers') South Carolina Equity Reports

Sp.Glos. Spelman's Glossary

Sp.Laws Spirit of the Laws, Montesquieu

Sp.Pr.Cas. Spinks' Prize Cases (1854-56) (Eng.)

Sp.Sess. Special Session

Sp.St. Private and Special Laws

Sp.Tax.Rul. Special Tax Ruling (U.S. Internal Revenue Service

Sp. & Sel.Cas. Special and Selected Law Cases (1648) (Eng.)

Sparks. Sparks' Reports, British Burmah.

Spaulding. Spaulding's Reports (71-73 Maine)

Spear Ch. Spears' (or Speers') South Carolina Chancery Reports

Spear Eq. Spears' (or Speers') South Carolina Equity Reports

Spears Spears' Reports (S. C. Law or Equity)

Spears Eq. Spears' (or Speers') South Carolina Equity Reports

spec. special

Speers. Spears' (or Speers') South Carolina Law Reports

Speers Eq. Spears' (or Speers') South Carolina Equity Reports

Speers Eq.(S.C.) Speers' (or Spears') South Carolina Equity Reports

Speers L.(S.C.) Speers' (or Spears'), South Carolina Law Reports

Spel.Feuds. Spelman on Feuds

Spel.Gl. Spelman's Glossary

Spel.L.T. Spelman's Law Tracts

Spel.Rep. Spelman's Reports, Manuscript, English King's Bench

Spell.Extr.Rel. Spelling on Extraordinary Relief in Equity and in Law

Spell.Extr.Rem. Spelling's Treatise on Injunctions and Other Extraordinary Remedies

Spelm. Spelman's Glossarium Archailogicum. 3 editions (1626-87)

Spelman. Spelman's Glossarium Archailogicum. 3 editions (1626-87)

Spen.(N.J.) Spencer's Reports (20 New Jersey Law)

Spenc. ● Spencer's Reports (10-20 Minn.)

● Spencer's Reports (20 New Jersey Law)

Spence,Ch. Spence's Equitable Jurisdiction of the Court of Chancery

Spence,Eq.Jur. Spence's Equitable Jurisdiction of the Court of Chancery

Spencer ● Spencer's Reports (10-20 Minn.)

● Spencer's Reports (20 New Jersey Law)

Spens Sel.Cas. Spens' Select Cases, Bombay (India)

Spinks Spinks' English Ecclesiastical and Admiralty Reports (164 Eng. Reprint)

Spinks Eccl. & Adm.(Eng.) Spinks' English Ecclesiastical and Admiralty Reports (164 Eng. Reprint)

Spinks,P.C. Spinks' English Prize Cases

Spinks,Prize Cas. Spinks' Admiralty Prize Cases (164 Eng. Reprint)

Spinks Prize Cas.(Eng.) Spinks' Admiralty Cases (164 Eng. Reprint)

Spoon. Spooner's Reports (12-15 Wisconsin)

Spooner. Spooner's Reports (12-15 Wisconsin)

Spott.Eq.Rep. Spottiswoode's English Equity Reports

Spottis. R. Spottiswoode's Court of Session Reports (Sc.)

Spottis.C.L. & Eq.Rep. Common Law and Equity Reports, published by Spottiswoode

Spottis.Eq. Spottiswoode's Equity (Sc.)

Spottisw. Spottiswoode's Equity (Sc.)

Spottisw.Eq. Spottiswoode's Equity (Sc.)

Spr. Sprague's United States District Court (Admiralty) Decisions

Sprague. Sprague's United States District Court (Admiralty) Decisions

ss. scilicet (to wit)

St. ● Laws or Acts, in some states

● Stair's Decisions, Court of Session (Sc.)

● State

● Statutes

- Story's Circuit Court Reports (U.S.)
- Street
- Stuart, Milne, & Peddie's Session Cases (Sc.)
- United States Statutes at Large

St.Ab. Statham's Abridgment

St.Adm.N.S. Stuart's Lower Canada Vice-Admiralty Reports, New Series

St.at Large. Statutes at Large

St.Brown. Stewart-Brown Cases in the Court of the Star Chamber (1455-1547)

St.Cas. Stillingfleet, Ecclesiastical Cases (Eng.)

St.Ch.Cas. Star Chamber Cases (Eng.)

St.Clem. St. Clement's Church Case (Philadelphia, Pa.)

St.Dept. State Department Reports

St.Eccl.Cas. Stillingfleet, Ecclesiastical Cases

St.Gloc. Statute of Glocester

St.Inst. Statutory Instruments (Eng.)

St.J.Mo.P.U.C. St.Joseph, Missouri, Public Utilities Commission Reports

St.John's L.Rev. St. John's Law Review (Brooklyn, N.Y.)

St.L.U.Intra.L.Rev. St. Louis University Intramural Law Review

St.Law. Loughborough's Digest of Statute Law (Ky.)

St.Lim. Statute of Limitations

St.Louis L.Rev. St.Louis Law Review

St.Louis U.L.J. Saint Louis University Law Journal

St.M. & P. Stuart, Milne & Peddie, Scotch

St.Mark. St. Mark's Church Case, Philadelphia

St.Marlb. Statute of Marlbridge

St.Mary's L.J. St. Mary's Law Journal

St.Mert. Statute of Merton

St.Mod.Lev.Fin. Statute Modus Levandi Fines

St.P. State Papers

St.Pl.Cr. Staundford's Pleas of Crown (Eng.)

St.Pr.Reg. Style's Practical Register (Eng.)

St.R.Q. Queensland State Reports (Aus.)

St.R.Qd. Queensland State Reports (Aus.)

St.R.Queensl. State Reports, Queensland (1908-58) (Aus.)

St.Rep.
- State Reports
- State Reporter

St.Rep.N.S.W. State Reports (New South Wales)

St.Rep.Queensl.(Austr.) Queensland State Reports

St.Ry.Rep. Street Railway Reports (U.S.)

St.Tr. Howell's State Trials (1163-1820)

St.Tr.N.S. Macdonell's State Trials (1820-58)

St.Tri. State Trials

St.Westm. Statute of Westminster

Stab. Stabilization

Stafford. Stafford's Reports (69-71 Vermont)

Stair. Stair's Decisions of the Lords of Council and Session (1661-81) (Sc.)

Stair I. Stair's Institutes, 5 editions (1681-1832)

Stair,Inst. Stair's Institutes, 5 editions (1681-1832)

Stan. Stanford

Stan.J.Int'l.Stud. Stanford Journal of International Studies

Stan.L.R. Stanford Law Review

Stan.L.Rev. Stanford Law Review

Stan.Pa.Prac. Standard Pennsylvania Practice

Stand.Dict. Standard Dictionary

Stand.Ex.Prof.Tax.Rep. Standard Excess Profits Tax Reporter (CCH)

Stand.Fed.Tax Rep. Standard Federal Tax Reporter (CCH)

Stand.Ga.Prac. Standard Georgia Practice

Stand.Pa.Prac. Standard Pennsylvania Practice

Stanford Staundford's Pleas of the Crown (Eng.)

Stanford L.Rev. Stanford Law Review

Stanton. Stanton's Reports (11-13 Ohio)

Stanton's Rev.St. Stanton's Revised Statutes (Ky.)

Star. Starkie's English Nisi Prius Reports

Star Ch.Ca. Star Chamber Cases (1477-1648) (Eng.)

Star Ch.Cas. Star Chamber Cases (1477-1648) (Eng.)

Star.S.C. Star Session Cases (1824-25)

Stark. Starkie's Nisi Prius Reports (1815-22) (Eng.)

Stark.C.L. Starkie's Criminal Law

Stark.Cr.Pl. Starkie's Criminal Pleading

Stark.Ev. Starkie on Evidence

Stark.Jury Tr. Starkie on Trial by Jury

Stark.Lib. Starkie on Libel

Stark.N.P. Starkie's English Nisi Prius Reports

Stark.Sl. & L. Starkie on Slander & Libel

Starkie. Starkie's English Nisi Prius Reports

Starkie (Eng.) Starkie's English Nisi Prius Reports (171 Eng. Reprint)

Starkie, Ev. Starkie on Evidence

Starkie, Stand. & L. Starkie, on Slander and Libel

Starkie's English Nisi Prius Reports (171 Eng. Reprint)

Starr & C.Ann.St. Starr and Curtis' Annotated Statutes (Ill.)

Stat. ● Statutes
　　　● Statutes Revised
　　　● U.S. Statutes at Large (Official)

Stat.at L. U.S. Statutes at Large

Stat.Def. Statutory Definition(s)

Stat.Glo. Statute of Gloucester

Stat.Inst. Statutory Instruments

Stat.Local Gov'ts Statute of Local Governments

Stat.Marl. Statute of Marlbridge

Stat.Merl. Statute of Merton

Stat.Mod.Lev.Fin. Statute Modus Levandi Fines

Stat.N.S.W. Statutes of New South Wales (Aus.)

Stat.N.Z. Statutes of New Zealand

Stat.O. & R. Statutory Orders and Regulations (Canada)

Stat.R. & O. Statutory Rules and Orders (1890-1947) (Eng.)

Stat.R. & O.N.I. Statutory Rules and Orders of Northern Ireland

Stat.R. & O. & Stat.Inst.Rev. Statutory Instruments Revised, to December 31, 1948 (Eng.)

Stat.Realm Statutes of the Realm (Eng.)

Stat.Reg.N.Z. Statutory Regulations (New Zealand)

Stat.Westm. Statute of Westminster

Stat.Winch. Statute of Winchester

State Fin. State Finance

State Gov't State Government

State Mot.Carr.Guide State Motor Carrier Guide (CCH)

State Print. State Printing

State Tax Cas. State Tax Cases (CCH)

State Tax Cas.Rep. State Tax Cases Reporter (CCH)

State Tr. State Trials (Howell) (Eng.)

State Tr.N.S. State Trials, New Series, edited by Macdonell (Eng.)

State & Loc.Taxes State and Local Taxes (BNA)

Stath.Abr. Statham's Abridgment

Staund.Pl Staundford's Pleas of Crown (1557) (Eng.)

Staundef. Staundeforde, Exposition of the King's Prerogative

Staundef.P.C. Staundeforde, Les Plees del Coron

Staundf.Pl.Cor. Staundford's Placita Coronae

Staundf.Prerog. Staundford's Exposition of the King's Prerogative

Stearns,Real Act. Stearn's Real Actions

Stecher, Agency & Partnership Stecher's Cases on Agency and Partnership

Stenton Stenton, Rolls of the Justices in Eyre for Lincolnshire & Worcestershire (Selden Society Publication, v. 53)

Stenton G. Stenton, Rolls of the Justices in Eyre for Gloucestershire & Staffordshire (Selden Society Publication, v.59)

Stenton Y. Stenton, Rolls of the Justices in Eyre for Yorkshire (Selden Society Publication, v. 56)

Steph.Com Stephen's Commentaries on the Laws of England

Steph.Comm. Stephens Commentaries on the Laws of England

Steph.Const. Stephens on the English Constitution

Steph.Cr. Stephen's Digest of the Criminal Law

Steph.Cr.L. Stephen's General View of the Criminal Law. 9 editions (1877-1950)

Steph.Cr.Law. Stephen's General View of the Criminal Law

Steph.Crim.Dig. Stephen's Digest of the Criminal Law

Steph.Dig. Stephen's Digest, New Brunswick Reports

Steph.Dig.Cr.L. Stephens Digest of the Criminal Law

Steph.Dig.Ev. Stephen's Digest of the Law of Evidence

Steph.Ev. Stephens Digest of the Law of Evidence

Steph.Lect. Stephen, Lectures on History of France

Steph.N.P. Stephen's Law of Nisi Prius

Steph.Pl. Stephen on Pleading

Stephen,H.C.L. Stephen's History of Criminal Law

Stephens. Supreme Court Decisions, by J.E.R. Stephens

Stev.Dig. Stevens' New Brunswick Digest

Stevens & G. Stevens & Graham's Reports (98-139 Georgia)

Stew. ● Stewart's Reports (Alabama 1827-31)
    ● Stewart's Reports (28-45 New Jersey Equity)
    ● Stewart's Nova Scotia Admiralty Reports
    ● Stewart's Reports (1-10 South Dakota)

Stew.Adm. Stewart's Vice-Admiralty Reports (1803-13) (Nova Scotia)

Stew.Admr. Stewart's Nova Scotia Admiralty Reports

Stew.Ans. Stewart's Answers to Dirleton's Doubts (Sc.) 2 editions (1715,1762)

Stew.Dig. Stewart's Digest of Decisions of Law and Equity (N.J.)

Stew.Eq. Stewart's Reports (28-45 N.J. Eq.)

Stew.N.Sc. Stewart's Nova Scotia Admiralty Reports

Stew.V.A. Stewart's Vice-Admiralty Reports (Nova Scotia)

Stew. & P. Stewart and Porter's Alabama Supreme Court Reports (1831-1834)

Stewart. ● Stewart's Reports (Alabama 1827-31)
    ● Stewart's Reports (28-45 New Jersey Equity)
    ● Stewart's Nova Scotia Admiralty Reports
    ● Stewart's Reports (1-10 South Dakota)

Stewart-Brown. Stewart-Brown's Lancashire and Cheshire Cases in the Court of Star Chamber

Stewart Vice-Adm.(Nov.Sc.) Stewart's Nova Scotia Vice-Admiralty Reports

Sth.Afr.Rep. South African Reports, High Court

Stil. Stillingfleet's Ecclesiastical Cases (1702-1704)

Stiles. Stiles' Reports (22-29 Iowa)

Stiles (Ia.) Stiles' Reports (22-29 Iowa)

Still.Eccl.Cas Stillingfleet's Ecclesiastical Cases

Stim.Gloss. Stimson's Law Glossary

Stim.Law Gloss. Stimson's Law Glossary

Stimson. Stimson's Law Glossary

Stiness. Stiness' Reports (vols. 20-34 Rhode Island)

Stk. Stock

Stmt. Statement

Stn.L. Stanford Law Review

Sto. ● Storey's Reports (Del.)
    ● Story's United States Circuit Court Reports (3 vols.)

Sto.Ag. Story on Agency

Sto.Bailm. Story on Bailment

Sto.Bills. Story on Bills

Sto.C.C. Story's United States Circuit Court Reports

Sto.Comm. Story's Commentaries

Sto.Con. Story on Contracts

Sto.Conf.Law. Story on Conflict of Laws

Sto.Const. Story's Commentaries on the Constitution of the United States

Sto.Const.Cl.B. Story's Constitutional Class Book

Sto.Cont. Story on Contracts

Sto.Eq.Jur. Story on Equity Jurisprudence

Sto.Eq.Pl. Story on Equity Pleadings

Sto.Part. Story on Partnership

Sto.Pl. Story's Civil Pleading

Sto.Sales. Story on Sales of Personal Property

Sto. & G. Stone and Graham's Private Bills Decisions (1865)

Stock. ● Stockton's New Jersey Equity Reports
　　　　● Stockton's Vice-Admiralty Reports, New Brunswick (1879-91)

Stock.Adm. Stockton's Admiralty Repts. (New Brunswick)

Stockett. Stockett's Reports (27-53 Maryland)

Stockt. Stockton's Reports (9-11 N.J. Equity)

Stockt.Ch. Stockton's Reports (9-11 N.J. Equity)

Stockt.Vice-Adm. Stockton's Vice-Admiralty (New Brunswick)

Stockton. Stockton's Vice-Admiralty Reports (New Brunswick)

Stockton Adm.(New Br.) Stockton, Vice-Admiralty Reports, New Brunswick

Stone. Stone's Justices' Manual (Annual)

Stor.Dict. Stormouth's Dictionary of the English Language

Story. ● Story on Equitable Jurisprudence, U.S.A. (1836-1920)
　　　　● Story's United States Circuit Court Reports

Story,Ag. Story on Agency

Story,Bailm. Story on Bailments

Story,Bills. Story on Bills

Story,Comm.Const. Story's Commentaries on the Constitution of the United States

Story,Confl.Laws Story on Conflict of Laws

Story,Const. Story's Commentaries on the Constitution of the United States

Story,Cont. Story on Contracts

Story Eq.Jur. Story on Equity Jurisprudence

Story,Eq.Pl. Story's Equity Planning

Story,Laws. Story's Laws of the United States

Story,Merchants Abbott's Merchant Ships and Seamen by Story

Story,Partn. Story on Partnership

Story,Prom.Notes Story on Promissory Notes

Story,Sales Story on Sales of Personal Property

Story,U.S.Laws. Story's Laws of the United States

Story's Laws Story's United States Laws

Str. ● Strange's Cases of Evidence (1698-1732) (Eng.)
　　　　● Strange's King's Bench Reports (1716-1749) (Eng.)

Str.Cas.Ev. Strange's Cases of Evidence ("Octavo Strange")

Str.N.C. Sir T. Strange's Notes of Cases, Madras

Str. & H.C. Streets and Highways Code

Stra. Strange

Strahan Strahan's Reports (vol. 19 Oregon)

Stran. Strange

Strange. Strange's Reports, English Courts

Strange (Eng.) Strange's Reports, English Courts (93 Eng. Reprint)

Strange,Madras. Strange's Notes of Cases, Madras

Stratton. Stratton's Reports (vols. 12-14 Oregon)

Street Ry.Rep. Street Railway Reports

Stringf. Stringfellow's Reports (9-11 Missouri)

Stringfellow. Stringfellow's Reports (9-11 Missouri)

Strob. Strobhart's South Carolina Law Reports (1846-50)

Strob.Ch. Strobhart's South Carolina Equity Reports

Strob.Eq. Strobhart's South Carolina Equity Reports (1846-50)

Strobh.Eq.(S.C.) Strobhart, South Carolina Equity

Strobh.L.(S.C.) Strobhart, South Carolina Law

Struve Struve's Reports (Washington Territory 1854-88)

Sts. & Hy. Streets & Highways

Stu.Adm. Stuart's Lower Canada Vice-Admiralty Reports

Stu.Adm.V.A. Stuart's Lower Canada Vice-Admiralty Reports

Stu.Ap. Stuart's Lower Canada King's Bench Reports, Appeal Cases

Stu.K.B. Stuart's Lower Canada King's Bench Reports (1810-35)

Stu.L.C. Stuart's Lower Canada King's Bench Reports (1810-35)

Stu.M. & P. Stuart, Milne, & Peddie's Scotch Court of Sessions Reports

Stu.Mil. & Ped. Stuart, Milne & Peddie's Scotch Court of Sessions Reports

Stuart. ●   Stuart, Milne & Peddie's Scotch Session Cases
     ●   Stuart's Lower Canada Reports
     ●   Stuart's Vice-Admiralty Reports

Stuart,Adm.N.S. Stuart's Vice-Admiralty (Lower Canada Cases)

Stuart K.B. Stuart's Kings Bench Reports (Quebec, 1810-25) 1 vol.

Stuart K.B.(Quebec) Stuart, Lower Canada King's Bench Reports

Stuart L.C.K.B. Stuart's Lower Canada King's Bench Reports

Stuart L.C.V.A. Stuart's Lower Canada Vice-Admiralty Reports

Stuart M. & P. Stuart, Milne and Peddie, Court of Session Cases (1851-53) (Sc.)

Stuart Vice-Adm. Stuart's Vice-Admiralty (Lower Canada)

Stuart's Adm. Stuart's Vice-Admiralty Reports (1836-74) (2 vols.) (Quebec)

Stubbs,C.H. Stubb's Constitutional History

Stubbs Sel.Ch. Stubb's Select Charters

Stud. Studies

Stud.Hist. Studies in History, Economics and Public Law

Student Law. Student Lawyer

Student Law.J. Student Lawyer Journal

Studies Crim.L. Studies in Criminal Law and Procedure

Sty. Style's King's Bench Reports (1646-1655)

Sty.Pr.Reg. Style's Practical Register (1657-1710)

Style. Style's English King's Bench Reports

Style,Pr.Reg. Style's Practical Register

Su. Superior Court

Su.Ct.Cir. Supreme Court (Ceylon)

Su.L.R. Suffolk University Law Review

Sub. ●   Subcommittee
     ●   Subordinated

sub.nom. under the name

Subd. Subdivision

Subpar. Subparagraph

Subs.Leg.Austl.Cap.Terr. Subsidiary Legislation of the Australian Capital Territory

Subsc. Subscription

Subsec. Subsection

Suc. Successor

Sud.Dew.Ad. Sudder Dewanny Adawlut Reports (India)

Sud.Dew.Rep. Sudder Dewanny Reports, N.W. Province (India)

Suffolk U.L.Rev. Suffolk University Law Review

Sug.Est. Sugden on the Law of Estates.

Sug.Hd.Bk. Sugden's Hand-Book of Property Law

Sug.Pow. Sugden on Powers, 8 editions (1808-61)

Sug.Pr. Sugden on the Law of Property

Sug.Pr.St. Sugden on Property Statutes

Sug.Prop. Sugden on the Law of Property as administered by the House of Lords

Sug.V. & P. Sugden on Vendors and Purchasers. 14 editions (1805-62)

Sug.Vend. Sugden on Vendors and Purchasers

Sugd.Powers. Sugden on Powers

Sugd.Vend. Sugden on Vendors and Purchasers

Sull.Lect. Sullivan's Lectures on Constitution and Laws of England

Sum. Sumner's Circuit Court Reports (U.S.)

Sum. • Sumner's Circuit Court Reports (U.S.)
       • Hale's Summary of Pleas of the Crown (Eng.)

Sum.Dec. Summary Decisions, Bengal (India)

Sum.Ves. Sumner's Edition of Vesey's Reports

Summerfield Summerfield's Reports (21 Nevada)

Summerfield,S. Summerfield's (S.) Reports (21 Nevada)

Summers,Oil & Gas Summers on Oil and Gas

Sumn. Sumner's United States Circuit Court Reports

Sumn.Ves. Sumner's Edition of Vesey's Reports

Sumner. Sumner's United States Circuit Court Reports

Sup. Supreme

Sup.Ct. • Supreme Court
       • Supreme Court Reporter (National Reporter System)

Sup.Ct.Pr. Supreme Court Practice

Sup.Ct.Rep. Supreme Court Reporter

Sup.Ct.Rev. Supreme Court Review

Sup.Jud.Ct. Supreme Judicial Court, Massachusetts

Sup.Trib. Supremo Tribunal (Supreme Court of Appeal)

Super. • Superior Court
       • Superior Court Reports

Super.Ct. Superior Court

Super.Ct.(R.I.) Rhode Island Superior Court

Super.Ct.App.Div. Superior Court Appellate Division (New Jersey)

Super.Ct.Ch.Div. Superior Court Chancery Division (New Jersey)

Super.Ct.Law Div. Superior Court Law Division (New Jersey)

Super.Ct.Rep. Superior Court Reports (New York, Pennsylvania, etc.)

Supp. • New York Supplement Reports
       • Supplement

Supp.Code. Supplement to Code

Supp.Gen.St. Supplement to the General Statutes

Supp.Rev. Supplement to the Revision

Supp.Rev.Code. Supplement to the Revised Code

Supp.Rev.St. Supplement to the Revised Statutes

Supp.Ves.Jun. Supplement to Vesey, Jr.'s, Reports

suppl. Supplement; supplemented

Supr. Superior Court Reports Supreme

Supr.Ct.Rep. Supreme Court Reporter

supra. above (in same article or treatise)

Sur. Surety

Sur.Ct. Surrogate's Court

Surr. Surrogate

Surr.Ct. Surrogate's Court

Surr.Ct.Proc.Act Surrogate's Court Procedure Act

Sus.Leg.Chron. Susquehanna Legal Chronical (Pa.)

susp. suspended

Susq.L.C. Susquehanna Leading Chronicle (Pa.)

Susq.L.Chron. Susquehanna Legal Chronicle, Pennsylvania

Susq.Leg.Chron. Susquehanna Legal Chronicle, (Pa.)

Susquehanna Leg.Chron.(Pa.) Susquehanna Legal Chronicle (Pa.)

Suth. Sutherland's Calcutta Reports (India)

Suth.Bengal Sutherland's Bengal High Court Reports (India)

Suth.Dam. Sutherland on the Law of Damages

Suth.F.B.R. Sutherland's Bengal Full Bench Reports (India)

Suth.Mis. India Weekly Reporter, Miscellaneous Appeals

Suth.P.C.A. Sutherland Privy Council Appeals

Suth.P.C.J. Sutherland Privy Council Judgments (same as above)

Suth.Sp.N. • Full Bench Rulings (Calcutta)

- Sutherland Special Number of Weekly Reporter

Suth.St.Const. Sutherland on Statutes and Statutory Construction

Suth.Stat.Const. Sutherland's Statutory Construction

Suth.W.R. Sutherland's Weekly Reporter, Calcutta (1864-76)

Sutton. Sutton on Personal Actions at Common Law

SvJT Svensk Juristtidning (Sweden)

Sw.
- Southwest(ern)
- Swabey's Admiralty Reports (Eng.)
- Swan's Reports (31, 32 Tennessee)
- Swanston's Chancery Reports (Eng.)
- Swedish
- Sweeney's N.Y. Superior Court Reports
- Swinton's Scotch Justiciary Cases

Sw.L.J. Southwestern Law Journal

Sw.U.L.Rev. Southwestern University Law Review

Sw. & Tr. Swabey and Tristram's Probate and Divorce Reports (164 Eng. Reprint)

Swab.Admr. Swabey's English Admiralty Reports (166 Eng. Reprint)

Swab. & T. Swabey and Tristram's Probate and Divorce Reports (164 Eng. Reprint)

Swab. & Tr. Swabey and Tristram's Probate and Divorce Reports (164 Eng. Reprint)

Swabey Adm.(Eng.) Swabey's Admiralty (166 Eng. Reprint)

Swabey & T.(Eng.) Swabey & Tristram (164 Eng. Reprint)

Swan
- Swan's Tennessee Supreme Court Reports (1851-53)
- Swanston's Chancery Reports (Eng.)

Swan.Ch. Swanston's English Chancery Reports

Swan Tr. Swan's Treatise (Ohio)

Swan & C.R.St. Swan and Critchfield's Revised Statutes (Ohio)

Swan & S.St. Swan and Sayler's Supplement to the Revised Statutes (Ohio)

Swans. Swanston's English Chancery Reports

Swan's St. Swan's Statutes (Ohio)

Swanst. Swanston's English Chancery Reports (36 Eng. Reprint)

Swanst.(Eng.) Swanston's English Chancery Reports (36 Eng. Reprint)

Swed. Sweden

Sweeney (N.Y.) Sweeney, New York Superior Court Reports, vols. 31-32)

Sweeny. Sweeney, New York Superior Court Reports, vols. 31-32

Sweet.
- Sweet on the Limited Liability Act
- Sweet on Wills
- Sweet's Law Dictionary
- Sweet's Marriage Settlement Cases
- Sweet's Precedents in Conveyancing

Sweet M.Sett.Cas. Sweet's Marriage Settlement Cases (Eng.)

Swen. Sweeney, New York Superior Court Reports, vols. 31-32

Swift,Dig. Swift's Digest, Connecticut

Swin.
- Swinburne on Wills. 10 editions (1590-1803)
- Swinton's Justiciary Reports (1835-41)

Swin.Jus.Cas. Swinton's Scotch Justiciary Cases

Swin.Reg.App. Swinton's Scots Registration Appeal Cases (1835-41)

Swinb.Wills Swinburne on Wills

Swint. Swinton's Justiciary Cases (Sc.)

Switz. Switzerland

Sy.L.R. Syracuse Law Review

Syd.App. Sydney Appeals (Aus.)

Syd.L.R. Sydney Law Review

Sydney L.Rev. Sydney Law Review

Syl. The Syllabi

Syme. Syme's Justiciary Reports (1826-30)

Symp. Symposium

Symposum Jun.Bar Symposium l'Association de jeune Barreau de Montréal

Syn.Ser. Synopsis Series of the United States Treasury Decisions

Synop. Synopsis

Syracuse J.Int'l. L. & Com. Syracuse Journal of International Law and Commerce

Syracuse L.Rev. Syracuse Law Review

Sys. System

T

T. ●   Tappan's Common Pleas Reports (Ohio)
   ●   Taxes
   ●   Tempore (in the time of)
   ●   Term
   ●   Territory
   ●   Title
   ●   Tobacco Tax Ruling, Internal Revenue Bureau (U.S.)
   ●   Trinity
   ●   Turkish

T.A. ●   Board of Tax Appeals
   ●   trading as
   ●   Trustee under agreement

TAB   Technical Assistance Board (UN)

T.Ad.   The Tax Advisor

TBA   Tennessee Bar Association

T.B.M.   Tax Board Memorandum (Internal Revenue Bulletin) (U.S.)

T.B.Mon.   T.B.Monroe's Kentucky Supreme Court Reports (1824-28) (17-23 Kentucky)

T.B.Mon:(Ky.)   T.B. Monroe's Reports (17-23 Kentucky)

T.B.R.   Advisory Tax Board Recommendation (Internal Revenue Bureau) (U.S.)

T.B. & M.   Tracewell, Bowers, & Mitchell's U.S. Comptroller's Decisions

TC   Trusteeship Council (UN)

T.C. ●   Tax Court of the United States
   ●   Reports of Tax Cases (Eng.)
   ●   Trade Cases (CCH)

TCM ●   Tax Court Memorandum Decisions (CCH)
   ●   Tax Court Memorandum Decisions (P-H)

T.C.Memo.   Tax Court Memorandum Decisions (P-H)

T.C.Q.   Tax Counselor's Quarterly

T.C.R.   Transit Commission Reports (N.Y.)

T.Ct.   Tax Court of the United States Reports

T.Ct.Mem.   Tax Court of U.S. Memorandum

T.Cv.   Tax Convention

T.D.   Treasury Decisions (U.S. Treasury Dept.)

TDB   Trade and Development Board (UN)

TDC   Treasury Department Circular

TDO   Treasury Department Order

T.E.A.   Trade Expansion Act of 1962 (U.S.)

TEI   Thorne Ecological Institute

T.H.   Reports of the Witwatersrand High Court (Transvaal Colony) (South Africa)

TIAS   United States Treaties and Other International Acts Series

TIC   Trust Investment Committee

TICER   Temporary International Council for Educational Reconstruction

T.I.C.M.   Trust Investment Committee Memorandum

T.I.R.   Technical Information Release, Internal Revenue Service

T.I.S.   Tea Inspection Service (U.S.)

T.Jo.   T.Jones' English King's Bench Reports (84 Eng. Reprint)

T.Jones.   T. Jones English King's Bench Reports (84 Eng. Reprint)

T.Jones (Eng.)   T. Jones' English King's Bench Reports (84 Eng. Reprint)

T.L. ●   Reports of the Witwatersrand High Court, Transvaal (S.Af.)
   ●   Termes de la Ley

T.L.J.   Travancore Law Journal (India)

T.L.Q.   Temple Law Quarterly

T.L.R. ●   Tasmanian Law Journal Reports (Aus.)
   ●   Tax Law Review
   ●   Times Law Reports (1884-1952) (Eng.)
   ●   Travancore Law Reports (India)

T.L.T.   Travancore Law Times (India)

T.Lwyr.   The Tax Lawyer

T.M. ●   National Income Tax Magazine

- Tax Magazine
- Tax Management
- Technical Manual, U.S. Army
- Trademark

T.M.Bull. Trade Mark Bulletin, New Series

T.M.M. Tax Management Memorandum (Bna)

T.M.R. Trade Mark Reporter

T.M.Rep. Trade Mark Reporter

T.N.E.C. Temporary National Economic Committee

T.O.C.M. Trust Officers Committee Minutes

T.P.
- Tax Planning
- Transvaal Supreme Court Reports (S. Africa)

T.P.D. South African Law Reports, Transvaal Provincial Division (S. Africa)

T.P.I. Tax Planning Ideas

TR State Teachers Retirement Board

T.R.
- Taxation Reports (Eng.)
- Term Reports (Durnford & East) (Eng.)
- Caine's Term Reports (N.Y.)

T.R.(Eng.) Term Reports (99-101 Eng. Reprint)

T.R.E. Tempore Regis Edwardi (in the time of King Edward)

T.R.N.S. Term Reports, New Series (East's Reports) 1801-1812

T.R.(N.Y.) Caines'(Term) Reports (New York)

T.R.R. Trade Regulation Reporter

T.Raym. Sir T. Raymond's King's Bench Reports (83 Eng. Reprint)

T.Raym.(Eng.) Sir T. Raymond's King's Bench Reports (83 Eng. Reprint)

T.S. Transvaal Supreme Court Reports, South Africa, cited by year

TS United States Treaty Series

T.T. Tobacco Tax Ruling Trinity Term

T.T.I. Tulane Tax Institute

TTPI Trust Territory of the Pacific Islands

T.T.R. Tarl Town Reports (New South Wales)

T/U/Ag Trustee under agreement

T.U.C. Temporary Unemployment Compensation

T.U.P.Charlt. T.U.P. Charlton's Reports (Ga.)

T.U.W. Trustee Under Will

T.V.A. Tennessee Valley Authority (U.S.)

T.W. Trustee Under Will

T. & B. Taylor & Bell's Calcutta Supreme Court Reports (India)

T. & C. Thompson & Cook's New York Supreme Court Reports

T. & G. Tyrwhitt & Granger, English Exchequer Reports (1835-36)

T. & H.Prac. Troubat and Haly's Pennsylvania Practice

T. & M.
- Temple & Mew's Criminal Appeal Cases (Eng.)
- Temple & Mew's Crown Cases (1848-51) (Eng.)

T. & P. Turner & Phillips' Reports, English Chancery

T. & R. Turner & Russell, English Chancery Reports (1822-25)

T. & T.Supp. Trinidad & Tobago Supreme Court Judgments

Tait.
- Tait's Index to Morison's Dictionary (Sc.)
- Tait's Index to Scottish Session Cases (1823)
- Tait's Manuscript Decisions, Scotch Session Cases

Tal.
- Cases tempore Talbot, English Chancery
- Talbot's Cases in Equity (1734-38)

Talb.
- Cases tempore Talbot, English Chancery
- Talbot's Cases in Equity (1734-38)

Tam. Tamlyn's English Rolls Court Reports (48 Eng. Reprint)

Tamb. Tambyah's Reports (Ceylon)

Taml. Tamlyn's English Rolls Court Reports (48 Eng. Reprint)

Tamlyn. Tamlyn's English Rolls Court Reports (48 Eng. Reprint)

Tamlyn (Eng.) Tamlyn's English Rolls Court Reports (48 Eng. Reprint)

Tamlyn Ch. Tamlyn's English Rolls Court Reports (48 Eng. Reprint)

Tan. Taney's United States Circuit Reports

Tan.L.R. Tanganyika Territory Law Reports

Taney. Taney's United States Circuit Court Reports

Tann. Tanner's Reports (8-14 Indiana)

Tanner ● Tanner's Reports (8-14 Indiana)

         ● Tanner's Reports (13-17 Utah)

Tap. Tappan's Ohio Common Pleas Reports

Tapp. Tappan's Ohio Common Pleas Reports

Tappan. Tappan's Ohio Common Pleas Reports

Tappan (Ohio) Tappan's Ohio Common Pleas Reports

Tapping. Tapping on the Writ of Mandamus

Tariff Ind.,New. New's Tariff Index

Tarl. Tarleton Term Reports (1881-83) (New South Wales)

Tarl.Term R. Tarleton's Term Reports (New South Wales)

Tas.L.R. Tasmanian Law Reports (Aus.)

Tas.S.R. Tasmanian State Reports

Tasm. Tasmanian State Reports

Tasm.L.R. Tasmania Law Reports (Aus.)

Tasm.St.R. Tasmania State Reports (Aus.)

Tasm.Stat. Tasmanian Statutes (Aus.)

Tasm.Stat.R. Tasmanian Statutory Rules, with Tables (Aus.)

Tasm.U.L.Rev. Tasmania University Law Review

Tasmania U.L.Rev. Tasmania University Law Review

Tate's Dig. Tate's Digest of Laws (Va.)

Taun. Taunton's English Common Pleas Reports

Taunt. Taunton's English Common Pleas Reports

Taunt.(Eng.) Taunton's English Common Pleas Reports (127,129 Eng. Reprint)

Tax ● Department of Taxation

      ● Taxation

Tax A.B.C. Canada Tax Appeal Board Cases

Tax Adm'rs. News Tax Administrators News

Tax Cas. Tax Cases (1875-date) (Eng.)

Tax.Coun.Q. Tax Counselor's Quarterly

Tax Counselor's Q. Tax Counselor's Quarterly

Tax Ct.Mem.Dec. Tax Court Memorandum Decisions (CCH)

Tax Ct.Rep. Tax Court Reporter (CCH)

Tax Ct.Rep.Dec. Tax Court Reported Decisions (P-H)

Tax-Exempt Orgs. Tax-Exempt Organizations (CCH)

Tax.L.R. Tax Law Reporter

Tax L.Rep Tax Law Reporter

Tax L.Rev. Tax Law Review

Tax Law. The Tax Lawyer

Tax Law Rep. Tax Law Reporter

Tax Management Int'l. Tax Management International Journal

Tax Mag. Tax Magazine

Tax Mngm't. Tax Management (BNA)

Tax.R. Taxation Reports (1939-date) (Eng.)

Tax Rev. Tax Review

Tax. & Rev. Taxation and Revenue

Taxes ● Taxes

       ● The Tax Magazine

Tay. ● Taylor

      ● Taylor's King's Bench Reports, Ontario (1823-1827)

      ● Taylor's Reports (1 North Carolina) (1798-1802)

Tay.J.L. J. L. Taylor's Reports (1 N.C.)

Tay.L. & T. Taylor's Landlord and Tenant

Tay.N.C. Taylor's Reports (1 North Carolina)

Tay.U.C. Taylor, Upper Canada Reports (K. B. 1823-27) 1 vol.

Tay. & B. Taylor & Bell's Bengal Reports (India)

Tayl.Civil Law Taylor on Civil Law

Tayl.Corp. Taylor on Private Corporations

Tayl.Ev. Taylor on Evidence

Tayl.Gloss. Taylor's Law Glossary

Tayl.Hist.Gav. Taylor (Silas), History of Gavelkind

Tayl.Landl. & Ten. Taylor's Landlord and Tenant

Tayl.Med.Jur. Taylor's Medical Jurisprudence

Tayl.N.C. Taylor's Reports (1 N.C.)

Tayl.Priv.Corp. Taylor on Private Corporations

Tayl.St. Taylor's Revised Statutes (Wis.)

Taylor.
- Taylor's King's Bench Reports (Canada)
- Taylor's Reports, Bengal (India)
- Taylor's Reports (1 North Carolina)
- Taylor's Term Reports (4 North Carolina)

Taylor K.B.(Can.) Taylor, Upper Canada King's Bench Reports

Taylor U.C. Taylor's King's Bench Reports, Ontario

Tchrs. Teachers

Tech.
- Technical
- Technique
- Technology

Techn.Dict. Crabb's Technological Dictionary

Teiss. Teisser's Court of Appeal, Parish of Orleans Reports (1903-1917)

Tel.
- Telephone
- Telegraph

Tem. The Templar (1788-79) (London)

Tem.
- Temple
- Temporary
- Tempore (in the time of)

Temp.Geo.II. Cases in Chancery tempore George II. (Eng.)

Temp.L.Q. Temple Law Quarterly

Temp.Wood. Manitoba Reports tempore Wood (Canada)

Temp. & M. Temple and Mew's Crown Cases (1848-51)

Temple L.Q. Temple Law Quarterly

Temple & M. Temple & Mew Crown Cases (Eng.)

Temple & M.(Eng.) Temple & Mew Crown Cases (Eng.)

Ten.
- Tennessee
- Tennessee Reports

Ten.Cas.
- Shannon's Cases, Tennessee
- Thompson's Unreported Cases, Tennessee

Tenn.
- Tennessee
- Tennessee Supreme Court Reports

Tenn.App. Tennessee Civil Appeals Reports

Tenn.App.Bull. Tennessee Appellate Bulletin

Tenn.B.A. Tennessee Bar Association

Tenn.C.C.A. Tennessee Court of Civil Appeals

Tenn.Cas. Shannon's Unreported Cases (Tenn.1847-1894)

Tenn.Ch. Cooper's Tennessee Chancery Reports (1878)

Tenn.Ch.A. Tennessee Chancery Appeals

Tenn.Ch.App. Tennessee Chancery Appeals (Wright)

Tenn.Civ.A. Tennessee Civil Appeals

Tenn.Civ.App. Tennessee Civil Appeals

Tenn.Code Ann. Tennessee Code Annotated

Tenn.L.Rev. Tennessee Law Review

Tenn.Leg.Rep. Tennessee Legal Reporter

Tenn.Pub.Acts Public Acts of the State of Tennessee

Tenn.R.C. Tennessee Railroad Commission

Tenn.R. & P.U.C. Tennessee Railroad & Public Utilities Commission Board

Ter. Terry's Reports (Delaware)

Ter.Laws. Territorial Laws

Term
- Term Reports (North Carolina) (1816-18)
- Term Reports, English King's Bench (Durnford & East's Reports)

Term.de la L. Les Termes de la Ley

Term.N.C. Term Reports (Taylor, 4 N.C.)

Term R.   Term Reports, English King's Bench (Durnford & East's Reports)

Term.Rep.   Term Reports (Durnford & East) (Eng.)

Term.Rep.(N.C.)   Taylor's Term Reports (4 North Carolina)

Termes de la Ley.   Terms of the Common Laws and Statutes Expounded and Explained by John Rastell (1685)

Terr.   ●   Terrell's Reports (38-71 Texas)
        ●   Territory

Terr.L.   Territories Law (Northwest Territories)

Terr.L.(Can.)   Territories Law Reports (1885-1907) (Canada)

Terr.L.R.   Territories Law Reports (1885-1907) (Canada)

Terr. & Walk.   Terrell & Walker's Reports, vols. 38-51 Texas

Test.   Testamentary

Tex.   ●   Texas
        ●   Texas Supreme Court Reports

Tex.A.   Texas Court of Appeals

Tex.A.Civ.   White & Wilson's Texas Civil Appeal Cases

Tex.A.Civ.Cas.   White & Wilson's Texas Civil Appeal Cases

Tex.A.Civ.Cas.(Wilson).   Texas Court of Appeal Civil Cases

Tex.App.   ●   Texas Civil Appeals Cases
        ●   Texas Court of Appeals Reports (Criminal Cases)

Tex.App.Civ.Cas.(Willson)   White & Wilson's Texas Civil Appeal Cases

Tex.B.J.   Texas Bar Journal

Tex.Bus.Corp.Act Ann.   Texas Business Corporation Act Annotated

Tex.Civ.App.   Texas Civil Appeals Reports

Tex.Civ.Cas.   Texas Court of Appeals Decisions, Civil Cases (White & Willson) (1876-92)

Tex.Civ.Rep.   Texas Civil Appeals Reports

Tex.Code Ann.   Texas Codes Annotated

Tex.(subject)Code Ann.   (Vernon) Texas Codes Annotated

Tex.Code Crim.Proc.Ann.   Texas Code of Criminal Procedure Annotated

Tex.Com.App.   Texas Commission of Appeals

Tex.Cr.App.   Texas Criminal Appeals Reports

Tex.Cr.R.   Texas Criminal Appeals Reports

Tex.Crim.   Texas Criminal Reports (Texas Court of Appeals Reports)

Tex.Crim.Rep.   Texas Criminal Reports

Tex.Ct.App.Dec.Civ.   Texas Court of Appeals Decisions, Civil Cases

Tex.Ct.App.R.   Texas Court of Appeals Reports

Tex.Ct.Rep.   Texas Court Reporter

Tex.Dec.   Texas Decisions

Tex.Elec.Code Ann.   Texas Election Code Annotated

Tex.Gen.Laws   General and Special Laws of the State of Texas

Tex.Ins.Code Ann.   Texas Insurance Code Annotated

Tex.Int.L.Forum   Texas International Law Forum

Tex.Int.L.J.   Texas International Law Journal

Tex.Jur.   Texas Jurisprudence

Tex.Jur.2d   Texas Jurisprudence, 2d Edition

Tex.L.J.   Texas Law Journal, Tyler

Tex.L.Rev.   Texas Law Review

Tex.Law & Leg.   Texas Law and Legislation

Tex.Prob.Code Ann.   Texas Probate Court Annotated

Tex.R.C.   Texas Railroad Commission

Tex.Rev.Civ.Stat.Ann.(Vernon)   Texas Revised Civil Statutes Annotated

Tex.S.   Texas Supreme Court Reports, Supplement

Tex.S.Ct.   Texas Supreme Court Reporter

Tex.Sess.Law Serv.   Texas Session Law Service (Vernon)

Tex.So.Intra.L.Rev.   Texas Southern Intramural Law Review

Tex.So.U.L.Rev. Texas Southern University Law Review

Tex.Stat.Ann. Texas Statutes Annotated

Tex.Supp. Texas Supplement

Tex.Tax-Gen.Ann. Texas Tax-General Annotated

Tex.Tech L.Rev. Texas Tech Law Review

Tex.Unrep.Cas. Posey's Unreported Cases (Texas)

Texas Bus.Rev. Texas Business Review

Texas Int'l.L.J. Texas International Law Journal

Texas L.Rev. Texas Law Review

Th Thai

Th.br. Thesaurus Brevium. 2 editions (1661,1687)

Th.C.C. Thacher's Criminal Cases (Mass. 1823-42)

Th.C.Const.Law. Thomas' Leading Cases in Constitutional Law

Th. & C. Thompson & Cook's Reports (N.Y. Supreme 1873-75)

Thac.Cr.Cas. Thacher's Criminal Cases (Mass. 1823-42)

Thach.Cr. Thacher's Criminal Cases (Mass.)

Thacher,Cr.Cas. Thacher's Criminal Cases (Mass.)

Thacher Crim.Cas.(Mass) Thacher Criminal Cases (Mass.)

Thatcher Cr. Thatcher's Criminal Cases (Mass.)

Thayer Thayer's Reports (18 Oregon)

Thayer,Prelim.Treatise Ev. Thayer's Preliminary Treatise on Evidence

The Rep. ● The Reporter, Phi Alpha Delta

● The Reports, Coke's Reports (Eng.)

Thel. Theloall, Le digest des Briefs. 2 editions (1579,1687)

Them. ● American Themis (N.Y.)

● La Themis, Montreal, Quebec

Themis La Revue Juridique Themis

Theobald. Theobald on Wills, 11 editions (1876-1954)

Thes.Brev. Thesaurus Brevium

Thom. ● Thomas' Reports (vol. 1 Wyoming)

● Thomson, Reports (Nova Scotia)

Thom.Co.Litt. Thomas' Edition of Coke upon Littleton

Thom.Const.L. Thomas' Leading Cases on Constitutional Law

Thom.Dec. 1 Thomson, Nova Scotia Reports, vol.1.(1834-52)

Thom.L.C. Thomas' Leading Cases on Constitutional Law

Thom.Rep. Thomson, Nova Scotia Reports

Thom.Sel.Dec. Thomson, Select Decisions (Nova Scotia)

Thom. & Fr. Thomas & Franklin Reports (1 Maryland Chancery)

Thomas Thomas' Reports (1 Wyoming)

Thomas,Mortg. Thomas on Mortgages

Thomas,Negl. Thomas on Negligence

Thomp.Cal. Thompson's Reports (39, 40 California)

Thomp.Cit. Thompson's Citations (Ohio)

Thomp.Corp. Thompson's Commentaries on Law of Private Corporations

Thomp.Dig. Thompson's Digest of Laws (Fla.)

Thomp.Liab.Stockh. Thompson on Liability of Stockholders

Thomp.N.B.Cas. Thompson's National Bank Cases

Thomp.Neg. Thompson's Cases on Negligence

Thomp.Tenn.Cas. Thompson's Unreported Tennessee Cases

Thomp.Trials. Thompson on Trials

Thomp. & C. Thompson & Cook's New York Supreme Court Reports

Thomp. & St.Code. Thompson and Steger's Code (Tenn.)

Thomps.Cas. Thompson's Cases (Tenn.)

Thompson. ● Thompson's Nova Scotia Reports

● Thompson's Reports (39,40 California)

Thompson Unrep.(Pa.) Thompson's Unreported Cases

Thompson's Fla.Dig. Thompson's Digest of Laws, Florida

Thor. Thorington's Reports (107 Alabama)

Thorn. Thornton, Notes of Ecclesiastical and Maritime Cases (1841-50)

Thornt. & Bl.Bldg. & Loan Ass'ns. Thornton and Blackledge's Law Relating to Building and Loan Associations

Thornton,Gifts. Thornton on Gifts and Advancements

Thorpe. Thorpe's Reports (52 Louisiana Annual)

Throop,Pub.Off. Throop's Treatise on Public Officers

Tichb.Tr. Report of the Tichborne Trial (London)

Tidd. ● Tidd's Costs
      ● Tidd's Practice

Tidd App. Appendix to Tidd's Practice

Tidd Pr. Tidd's Practice

Tidd,Prac. Tidd's Practice

Tied.Lim.Police Power. Tiedeman's Treatise on the Limitations of Police Power in the United States

Tied.Mun.Corp. Tiedeman's Treatise on Municipal Corporations

Tiedeman,Real.Prop. Tiedeman on Real Property

Tiff. Tiffany's Reports (28-39 New York Court of Appeals)

Tiffany. Tiffany's Reports (28-39 New York Court of Appeals)

Tiffany Landl. & T. Tiffany on Landlord and Tenant

Tiffany,Landlord & Ten. Tiffany on Landlord & Tenant

Tiffany Real Prop. Tiffany on Real Property

Till. & Yates App. Tillinghast & Yates on Appeals

Tillman. Tillman's Reports (vols. 68, 69,71,73,75 Alabama)

Times L.(Eng.) Times Law Reports

Times L.R. ● Times Law Reports (Ceylon)
      ● Times Law Reports (Eng.)

Times L.Rep. ● Times Law Reports (Ceylon)
      ● Times Law Reports (Eng.)

Tinw. Tinwald's Reports, Court of Session (Sc.)

Tn. ● Tennessee
   ● Tennessee Reports

Tn.A. Tennessee Appeals Reports

Tn.Cr. Tennessee Criminal Appeals Reports

Tn.L. Tennessee Law Review

Tn.L.R. Tennessee Law Review

To.Jo. Sir Thomas Jones' English King's Bench Reports (1667-84)

To.L.R. University of Toledo Law Review

Tob. Tobacco Branch, U.S. Internal Revenue Bureau

Tobey Tobey's Reports (9,10 Rhode Island)

Tol. Toledo

Toller. Toller on Executors

Tomkins & J.Mod.Rom.Law. Tomkins & Jencken, Compendium of the Modern Roman Law

Toml. Tomlins' Election Cases (1689-1795)

Toml.Cas. Tomlins' Election Cases (1689-1795)

Toml.Law Dict. Tomlins' Law Dictionary

Toml.Supp.Br. Tomlins' Supplement to Brown's Parliamentary Cases

Tomlins. Tomlins' Law Dictionary

Tot. ● Tothill's English Chancery Reports
    ● Tothills Transactions in Chancery (21 Eng. Reprint)

Toth. ● Tothills English Chancery Reports
     ● Tothill's Transactions in Chancery (21 Eng. Reprint)

Tothill (Eng.) ● Tothills English Chancery Reports
      ● Tothill's Transactions in Chancery (21 Eng. Reprint)

Touch. Sheppard's Touchstone

Toull. Toullier's Droit Civil Francais

Town.Sl. & Lib. Townshend on Slander and Libel

Town.St.Tr. Townsend Modern State Trials (1850)

Townsh.Pl. Townshend's Pleading

Townsh.Sland. & L. Townshend on Slander and Libel

Tr. ● Tristram's Consistory Judgments (Eng.)
● Trust
● Trustee

Tr.App. Transcript Appeals (N.Y. 1867-68)

Tr.Ch. Transactions of the High Court of Chancery (Tothill's Reports)

Tr.Consist.J. Tristram's Consistory Judgments (1872-90) (Eng.)

Tr.L.R. Trinidad Law Reports

Tr.Law Guide Trial Lawyer's Guide

Tr.Law Q. Trial Lawyer's Quarterly

Tr.& Est. Trusts & Estates

Tr. & H.Pr. Troubat & Haly's Practice (Pa.)

Trace. & M. Tracewell and Mitchell, United States Comptroller's Decisions

Tracey,Evidence Tracey's Cases on Evidence

Trade Cas. Trade Cases (CCH)

Trade Mark R. Trade Mark Reporter

Trade Reg.Rep. Trade Regulation Reporter (CCH)

Trade Reg.Rev. Trade Regulation Review

Trademark Trademark

Trademark Bull. Bulletin of United States Trademark Association Series

Trademark Bull.(N.S.) Trademark Bulletin (Bulletin of United States Trademark Association), New Series

Trademark Rep. Trademark Reporter

Trademark Rptr. Trademark Reporter

Traff.Cas. Railway, Canal and Road Traffic Cases

Traite du Mar. Pothier, Traite du Contrat de Mariage

trans. ● translation
● translator

Trans.Ap. Transcript Appeals (N.Y. 1867-68)

Trans.App. Transcript Appeals, New York (7 vols.)

Trans. & Wit. Transvaal & Witswatersrand Reports

Transc.A. Transcript Appeals (N.Y.)

Transcr.A. Transcript Appeals (N.Y.)

transf. ● transferred from
● transferred to

Transnat'l. Transnational

Transnat'l.Rep. Transnational Reporter

Transp. Transportation

Transp.Corp. Transportation Corporations

Transp.L.J. Transportation Law Journal

Trav.L.J. Travancore Law Journal (India)

Trav.L.R. Travancore Law Reports (India)

Trav.L.T. Travancore Law Times (India)

Tray.Lat.Max. Trayner, Latin Maxims and Phrases, etc.

Tray.Leg.Max. Trayner, Latin Maxims and Phrases, etc.

Tread. ● Treadway's South Carolina Constitutional Reports
● Treadway's South Carolina Law Reports (1812-16)

Tread.Const. Treadway's South Carolina Constitutional Reports

Treadway Const.(S.C.) Treadway's South Carolina Constitutional Reports

Treas. ● Treasurer
● Treasury

Treas.Dec. Treasury Decisions Under Customs and Other Laws (U.S.)

Treas.Dec.Int.Rev. Treasury Decisions Under Internal Revenue Laws

Treas.Dept. Treasury Department

Treas.Regs. United States Treasury Regulations

Tred. Tredgold's Cape Colony Reports

Trehern British & Colonial Prize Cases, vol. 1

Trem. Tremaine's Pleas of the Crown (Eng.)

Trem.P.C. Tremaine's Pleas of the Crown (Eng.)

Trf. Transfer

Tri.Bish. Trial of the Seven Bishops

Tri.E.of Cov. Trial of the Earl of Coventry

Trial Law.Guide Trial Lawyer's Guide

Trial Law.Q.   Trial Lawyers' Quarterly
Trib.   ● Tribunale, ordinary court
            of first instatnce (Italy)
        ● Tribunal
Trib.admin.   Tribunaux administratifs
(France)
Trib.Arb.Mixtes   Tribunaux Arbitraux
Mixtes
Trib.Con.   Tribunal des conflits
(France)
Trin.   Trinity Term
Trint.T.   Trinity Term (Eng.)
Tripp   Tripp's Reports (5, 6 Dakota)
Trist.   ● Tristram's Consistory Judg-
            ments (Eng.)
        ● Supplement to 4 Swabey &
            Tristram's Probate &
            Divorce Reports (Eng.)
Tristram   Tristram's Supplement to 4
Swabey & Tristram
Troub.Lim.Partn.   Troubat on Limited
Partnership
Troub. & H.Prac.   Troubat & Haly's
Practice (Pa.)
Tru.   Trueman's Equity Cases (1876-
93) (New Brunswick)
Tru.Railw.Rep.   Truman's American
Railway Rep.
True.   Trueman's New Brunswick
Reports
Truem.Eq.Cas.   Trueman's Equity
Cases (New Brunswick)
Trueman Eq. Cas.   Trueman's Equity
Cases (New Brunswick)
Trust Bull.   Trust Bulletin, American
Bankers Association
Trust Terr.   Trust Territory Reports
Trusts & Es.   Trusts & Estates
Tyre, Jus Filiz.   Trye's Jus Filizarii
Ts.L.J.   Tulsa Law Journal
Tu.L.   Tulane Law Review (La.)
Tu.L.R.   Tulane Law Review
Tuck.   ● Tucker's Reports (District
            of Columbia)
        ● Tucker's Reports (156-175
            Massachusetts)
        ● Tucker's N.Y. Surrogate
            Reports
        ● Tucker's Select Cases
            (Newfoundland)
Tuck.Sel.Cas.   Tucker's Select Cases,
Newfoundland (1817-28)

Tuck.Sur.   Tucker's Surrogate, Re-
ports (City of New York)
Tuck.Surr.   Tucker's Surrogate, Re-
ports, City of New York
Tuck. & C.   Tucker & Clephane's Re-
ports (21 D.C.)
Tuck. & Cl.   Tucker and Clephane's
District of Columbia Reports (1892-
93) (21 D.C.)
Tucker (N.Y.)   Tucker's New York
Surrogate Reports
Tucker's Blackstone   Tucker's Black-
stone's Commentaries
Tud.Cas.Merc.Law   Tudor's Leading
Cases on Mercantile Law 3 editions
(1860-84)
Tud.Cas.R.P.   Tudor's Leading Cases
on Real Property 4 editions (1856-
1898)
Tud.Char.Trusts   Tudor's Charitable
Trusts 2d edition (1871)
Tudor, Lead.Cas.Real Prop.   Tudor's
Leading Cases on Real Property
Tudor's L.C.M.L.   Tudor's Leading
Cases on Mercantile Law
Tudor's L.C.R.P.   Tudor's Leading
Cases on Real Property
Tul.   Tulane
Tul.L.Rev.   Tulane Law Review
Tul.Tax Inst.   Tulane Tax Institute
Tulane L.Rev.   Tulane Law Review
(formerly Southern Law Quarterly)
Tulsa L.J.   Tulsa Law Journal
Tup.App.   Tupper's Appeal Reports
(Ontario)
Tupp.   ● Tupper's Reports, Ontario
            Appeals
        ● Tupper's Upper Canada
            Practice Reports
Tupper   ● Tupper's Reports, On-
            tario Appeals
        ● Tupper's Upper Canada
            Practice Reports
Tur.   ● Turkey
        ● Turner's Reports (35-48
            Arkansas)
        ● Turner's Reports (99-101
            Kentucky)
        ● Turner Select Pleas of the
            Forest (Selden Society.
            Publication, v. 13)

Turn.   ● Turner's Reports (35-48 Arkansas)
      ● Turner's Reports (99-101 Kentucky)
      ● Turner Select Pleas of the Forest (Selden Society Publication, v. 13)

Turn.Anglo.Sax. Turner, History of the Anglo Saxon

Turn. & P. Turner & Phillips' Reports, English Chancery

Turn. & Ph. Turner & Phillips' Reports, English Chancery

Turn. & R. Turner and Russell's Chancery Reports (37 Eng. Reprint)

Turn. & R.(Eng.) Turner and Russell's Chancery Reports (37 Eng. Reprint)

Turn. & Rus. Turner & Russell's English Chancery Reports (37 Eng. Reprint)

Turn. & Russ. Turner & Russell's English Chancery Reports (37 Eng. Reprint)

Tutt. & C. Tuttle & Carpenter's Reports (52 California)

Tutt. & Carp. Tuttle & Carpenter's Reports (52 California)

Tuttle Tuttle & Carpenter's Reports (52 California)

Tuttle & Carpenter Tuttle & Carpenter's Reports (52 California)

Twp. Township

Tx.   ● Texas
      ● Texas Reports

Tx.Ci. Texas Civil Appeals Reports

Tx.Cr. Texas Criminal Appeals Reports

Tx.L. Texas Law Review

Tx.L.R. Texas Law Review

Tyl. Tyler's Vermont Supreme Court Reports (1800-03)

Tyler Tyler's Reports (Vermont, 1800-03)

Tyler, Ej. Tyler on Ejectment and Adverse Enjoyment

Tyler, Steph.Pl. Tyler's Edition of Stephen on Principles of Pleading

Tyng Tyng's Reports (2-17 Massachusetts)

Tyr. Tyrwhitt & Granger's English Exchequer Reports (1830-35)

Tyr. & Gr. Tyrwhitt and Granger's Exchequer Reports (1835-36)

Tyrw. Tyrwhitt & Granger's English Exchequer Reports (1830-35)

Tyrw. & G. Tyrwhitt and Granger's Exchequer Reports (1835-36)

Tyrw. & G.(Eng.) Tyrwhitt and Granger's Exchequer Reports (1835-36)

Tytler, Mil.Law Tytler on Military Law and Courts-Martial

U

U.   • University
      • Utah
      • Utah Reports

U.2d   Utah Reports, Second Series

U/A   Under agreement

UAW   United Auto Workers

U.B.   Upper Bench

U.B.C.L.Rev.   University of British Columbia Law Review

U.B.C.Legal N.   University of British Columbia Legal Notes

U.B.Pr.   Upper Bench Precedents tempore Car. I

U.B.R.   Upper Burma Rulings (India)

U.Brit.Col.L.Rev.   University of British Columbia Law Review

U.C.   Upper Canada

UCA   Unemployment Compensation Agency

U.C.App.   Upper Canada Appeal Reports

U.C.App.(Can.)   Upper Canada Appeal Reports

U.C.App.Rep.   Upper Canada Appeal Reports

UCB   • Bureau of Unemployment Compensation
      • Unemployment Compensation Board
      • Unemployment Compensation Bureau

UCC   Unemployment Compensation Commission

U.C.C.   Uniform Commercial Code

U.C.C.Law Letter   Uniform Commercial Code Law Letter

U.C.C.P.   Upper Canada Common Pleas Reports

U.C.C.P.(Can.)   Upper Canada Common Pleas Reports

U.C.C.P.D.   Upper Canada Common Pleas Division Reports (Ontario)

U.C.C.R.   Upper Canada Court Records (Report of Ontario Bureau of Archives)

U.C.C.Rep.Serv.   Uniform Commercial Code Reporting Service

U.C.Ch.   Upper Canada Chancery Reports (1849-82)

U.C.Ch.(Can.)   Upper Canada Chancery Reports

U.C.Cham.   Upper Canada Chambers Reports

U.C.Cham.(Can.)   Upper Canada Chambers Reports (1846-52)

U.C.Chamb.   Upper Canada Chambers Reports (1846-52)

U.C.Chan.   Upper Canada Chancery Reports

UCD   Unemployment· Compensation Division

U.C.D.L.Rev.   University of California at Davis Law Review

U.C.E. & A.   Upper Canada Error and Appeal Reports (1846-66)

U.C.Err. & App.   Upper Canada Error and Appeal Reports (1846-66)

U.C.Err. & App.(Can.)   Upper Canada Error and Appeal Reports (1846-66)

UCHILS   The University of Chicago Law School

UCIS Ben.Ser.   Unemployment Compensation Interpretation Service

U.C.Jur.   Upper Canada Jurist

U.C.Jur.(Can.)   Upper Canada Jurist

U.C.K.B.   Upper Canada King's Bench Reports, Old Series (1831-44)

U.C.K.B.(Can.)   Upper Canada King's Bench Reports, Old Series (1831-44)

U.C.L.A.-Alaska L.Rev.   U.C.L.A.-Alaska Law Review

U.C.L.A.Intra.L.Rev.   U.C.L.A.Intramural Law Review

U.C.L.A. L.Rev.   U.C.L.A. Law Review

U.C.L.A.Law Rev.   University of California at Los Angeles Law Review

U.C.L.J.   Upper Canada Law Journal (1855-1922)

U.C.L.J.(Can.)   Upper Canada Law Journal

U.C.L.J.N.S.   Upper Canada Law Journal, New Series

U.C.L.J.N.S.(Can.)   Upper Canada Law Journal, New Series

U.C.L.J.O.S.   Canada Law Journal, Old Series (10 vols.)

UCMJ Uniform Code of Military Justice (U.S.)

U.C.O.S. Upper Canada King's Bench Reports, Old Series (1831-44)

UCOSL University of Colorado School of Law

UCPD Unemployment Compensation and Placement Division

U.C.P.R. Upper Canada Practice Reports

U.C.Pr. Upper Canada Practice Reports

U.C.Pr.(Can.) Upper Canada Practice Reports

U.C.Pr.R. Upper Canada Practice Reports

U.C.Q.B. Upper Canada Queen's Bench Reports

U.C.Q.B.O.S. Upper Canada Queen's (King's) Bench Reports, Old Series

U.C.Q.B.O.S.(Can.) Upper Canada Queen's (King's) Bench Reports, Old Series

U.C.R. ● University of Cincinnati Law Review (Ohio)
　　　　● Upper Canada Reports

U.C.Rep. Upper Canada Reports

U.Chi.L.Rec. University of Chicago Law School Record

U.Chi.L.Rev. University of Chicago Law Review

U.Chi.L.S.Rec. University of Chicago Law School Record

U.Chicago L.Rev. University of Chicago Law Review

U.Cin.L.Rev. University of Cincinnati Law Review

U.Colo.L.Rev. University of Colorado Law Review

U.Com. Uniform Commercial

UDEAC Economic and Customs Union of Central Africa

U.Det.L.J. University of Detroit Law Journal

U.Detroit L.J. University of Detroit Law Journal

UEAC Union of Central African States

U.Fla.L.Rev. University of Florida Law Review

UIC Unemployment Insurance Commission

U.I.D. Selected Decisions by Umpire for Northern Ireland, respecting Claims to Benefit

UID ● Unemployment Insurance Division
　　　● Division of Placement and Unemployment Insurance

UIS Unemployment Insurance Service

U.Ill.L.F. University of Illinois Law Forum

U.Ill.L.Forum University of Illinois Law Forum

U.Iowa L.Rev. University of Iowa Law Review

U.K. United Kingdom

UKADR United Kingdom NATO Air Defense Region

U.Kan.City L.Rev. University of Kansas City Law Review

U.L.A. Uniform Laws Annotated

ULR ● Uganda Law Reports
　　　● Utah Law Review
　　　● Utilities Law Reporter

U.L.R. Uniform Law Review

UMKCLR University of Missouri at Kansas City Law Review

UMKCL Rev. University of Missouri at Kansas City Law Review

UMLC Institute of Estate Planning, University of Miami Law Center

U.M.L.R. University of Miami Law Review

UMTA Urban Mass Transportation Administration

U.Miami L.Rev. University of Miami Law Review

U.Mich.J.Law Reform University of Michigan Journal of Law Reform

U.Missouri at K.C.L.Rev. University of Missouri at Kansas City Law Review

U.Mo.B., Law Ser. University of Missouri Bulletin, Law Series

U.Mo.Bull.L.Ser. University of Missouri Bulletin Law Series

U.Mo.K.C.L.Rev. University of Missouri at Kansas City Law Review

U.Mo.L.Bull. University of Missouri Law Bulletin

UN United Nations

UNAC United Nations Appeal for Children

UNAIS United Nations Association International Service (British)

UNBCL University of Nebraska College of Law

U.N.B.L.J. University of New Brunswick Law Journal

UNCDF United Nations Capital Development Fund

UNCHR United Nations High Commissioner for Refugees

UNCIO United Nations Conference on International Organization

UNCIO Doc. United Nations Conference on International Organization Documents

UNCIP United Nations Commission for India and Pakistan

UNCITRAL United Nations Commission on International Trade Law

UNCLOS United Nations Conference on the Law of the Sea

UNCOK United Nations Commission on Korea

UNCOPUOS United Nations Committee on the Peaceful Use of Outer Space

UNCTAD United Nations Conference on Trade and Development

UNCURK United Nations Commission for Relief & Rehabilitation of Korea

UNDAT United Nations Development Advisory Team

UNDCC United Nations Development Cooperation Cycle

UNDP United Nations Development Program

UNDRO United Nations Disaster Relief Office

UNDoc. United Nations Documents

UNECA United Nations Economic Commission for Africa

UNEF United Nations Emergency Force

UNEP United Nations Environment Programme

UNESCO United Nations Educational, Scientific and Cultural Organization

UNESCOR United Nations Economic and Social Council Official Record

UNESOB United Nations Economic and Social Office at Beirut (Lebanon)

UNFICYP United Nations Force in Cyprus

UNFPA United Nations Fund for Population Activities

UNGAOR United Nations General Assembly Official Record

UNHCR United Nations High Commissioner for Refugees

UNICEF United Nations Children's Fund

UNIDO United Nations Industrial Development Organization

UNIDROIT International Institute for the Unification of Private Law

UNITAR United Nations Institute for Training and Research

U.N.Juridical Y.B. United Nations Juridical Year Book

UNKRA United Nations Korean Reconstruction Agency

UNLOS United Nations Law of the Sea (Conference)

UNMOGIP United Nations Military Observer Group for India and Pakistan

UN Mo.Chron. UN Monthly Chronicle

UNRIAA United Nations Reports of International Arbitral Awards

UNROD United Nations Relief Operation in Dacca

UNRPR United Nations Relief for Palestine Refugees

UNRRA United Relief and Rehabilitation Administration

UNRWA United Nations Relief and Works Agency

UNRWAPR United Nations Relief & Works Agency for Palestine Refugees in the Near East

UNRWAPRNE United Nations Relief and Works Agency for Palestine Refugees in the Near East

UNSCCUR United Nations Scientific Conference on the Conservation & Utilization of Resources

UNSCOB United Nations Special Committee on the Balkans

UNSCOP United Nations Special Committee on Palestine

UNSDD United Nations Social Development Division

UNTCOK United Nations Temporary Commission on Korea

UNTCOR United Nations Trusteeship Council Official Record

UNTEA United Nations Temporary Executive Authority

UNTFDPP United Nations Trust for Development Planning and Projections

UNTFDS United Nations Trust Fund for Social Development

UNTS United Nations Treaty Series

UNTSO United Nations Truce Supervision Organization

U.N.Y.B. United Nations Year Book

U.Newark L.Rev. University of Newark Law Review

U.of M.L.B. University of Missouri Law Bulletin

U.of Omaha Bull. Night Law School Bulletin, University of Omaha

U.of P.L.R. University of Pennsylvania Law Review

U.of P.L.Rev. University of Pennsylvania Law Review

UPEB Union of Banana Exporting Countries

U.P.News Unauthorized Practice News

UPSSL University of Puget Sound School of Law

U.P.U. Universal Postal Union

U.Pa.L.Rev. University of Pennsylvania Law Review

U.Pitt.L.Rev. University of Pittsburgh Law Review

U.Queens.L.J. University of Queensland Law Journal

U.R. Uti rogas (be it as you desire) (a ballot)

URC Unemployment Reserves Commission

URG Urheberrechtsgesetz (German Copyright Act)

U.Rich.L.Rev. University of Richmond Law Review

U.Richmond L.Rev. University of Richmond Law Review

U.S. United States Supreme Court Reports

USA ● United States Army
      ● United States of America

USAA United States Arbitration Act

USAAF United States Army Air Force

USAF United States Air Force

USAFR United States Air Force Reserve

U.S.Ap. United States Appeals Reports

U.S.App. United States Appeals Reserves

U.S.App.D.C. U.S. Court of Appeals for District of Columbia

U.S.Av. United States Aviation Reports

U.S.Av.R. United States Aviation Reports

U.S.Aviation Rep. United States Aviation Reports

U.S.C. United States Code

U.S.C.A. United States Code Annotated

USCAPP Advanced Professional Programs, University of Southern California Law Center

U.S.C.App. United States Code Appendix

U.S.C.C. ● United States Circuit Court
       ● United States Court of Claims

U.S.C.C.A. United States Circuit Court of Appeals Reports

USCG United States Coast Guard

U.S.C.Govt'l.Rev. University of South Carolina Governmental Review

USCMA Official Reports, United States Court of Military Appeals

U.S.C.M.A.,Adv.Op. United States Court of Military Appeals, Advance Opinions

U.S.C.S. United States Code Service

U.S.C.Supp. United States Code Supplement

U.S.cert.den. Certiorari denied by U.S. Supreme Court

U.S.cert.dis. Certiorari dismissed by U.S. Supreme Court

U.S.Code Cong. & Ad.News United States Code Congressional & Administrative News

U.S.Comp.St. United States Compiled Statutes

U.S.Comp.St.Supp. United States Compiled Statutes Supplement

U.S.Cong. & Adm.Serv. U.S. Congressional and Administrative Service

U.S.Ct.Cl. United States Court of Claims

USDA United States Department of Agriculture

U.S.D.C. ● United States District Court
● United States District of Columbia

U.S.Daily United States Daily, Washington, D.C.

U.S.Dept.Int. United States Department of Interior

U.S.Dig. United States Digest

U.S.Dig.(L.ed.) Anno. United States Supreme Court Digest Annotated

U.S.Dist.Ct.Haw. United States District Court for Hawaii

U.S.E. Encyclopedia of United States Reports

USES United States Employment Service

U.S.F.V.L.Rev. University of San Fernando Valley Law Review

USHA United States Housing Authority

USIA United States Information Agency

U.S.I.C.C.V.R. U.S. Interstate Commerce Commission Valuation Reports

USIS U.S. Indian Serivce

U.S.Jur. United States Jurist

U.S.L.Ed. Lawyers' Edition, United States Supreme Court Reports

U.S.L.Ed.2d Lawyers' Edition United States Supreme Court Reports, Second Series

U.S.L.J. United States Law Journal (New Haven and New York)

U.S.L.Mag. United States Law Magazine

U.S.L.Rev. United States Law Review

U.S.L.W. United States Law Week (BNA)

U.S.Law.Ed. United States Supreme Court Reports, Lawyers' Edition

U.S.Law Int. United States Law Intelligencer and Review (Providence and Philadelphia)

U.S.Law Jour. United States Law Journal

U.S.Law Mag. United States Law Magazine

USMC ● United States Marine Corps
● United States Maritime Commission

USMCR United States Marine Corps Reserve

U.S.Month.Law Mag. United States Monthly Law Magazine

USN United States Navy

U.S.P.Q. United States Patents Quarterly (BNA)

USPS United States Postal Service

U.S.Pat.Q. U.S.Patent Quarterly

U.S.Pat.Quar. United States Patent Quarterly

U.S.Pat.Quart. United States Patent Quarterly

U.S.R. United States Supreme Court Reports

U.S.R.R.Lab.Bd. United States Railroad Labor Board

U.S.R.R.Lab.Bd.Dec. Decisions of the United States Railroad Labor Board

U.S.R.S. United States Revised Statutes

U.S.Reg. United States Register (Philadelphia)

U.S.reh.den. Rehearing denied by U.S. Supreme Court

U.S.reh.dis. Rehearing dismissed by U.S. Supreme Court

U.S.Rep. United States Reports

U.S.Rep.(L.Ed.) United States Reports, Lawyers' Edition

U.S.Rev.St. United States Revised Statutes

U.S.S.B. United States Shipping Board Decisions

U.S.S.B.B. United States Shipping Board Bureau Decisions

U.S.S.C.Rep. United States Supreme Court Reports

U.S.S.R. United Soviet Socialist Republic

U.S.St.at L. United States Statutes at Large

U.S.St.Tr. United States Trials (Wharton)

U.S.Stat. United States Statutes at Large

U.S.Sup.Ct. United States Supreme Court Reporter

U.S.Sup.Ct.(L.Ed.) United States Reports, Lawyers' Edition

U.S.Sup.Ct.Rep. United States Supreme Court Reporter

UST United States Treaties & Other International Agreements

U.S.T.C. United States Tax Cases (CCH)

U.S.T.D. United States Treaty Development

U.S.Tax Cas. United States Tax Cases (CCH)

U.S.Treas.Dept. United States Treasury Department

U.S.Treas.Reg. United States Treasury Regulations

U.S.Treaty Ser. United States Treaty Series

U.S.V.A.A.D. U.S. Veterans Administration Administrator's Decisions

U.S.V.B.D.D. U.S. Veterans Bureau Directors Decisions

U.S. & Can.Av. United States and Canadian Aviation Reports

U.San Fernando V.L.Rev. University of San Fernando Valley Law Review

U.San.Fran.L.Rev. University of San Francisco Law Review

U.San.Francisco L.Rev. University of San Francisco Law Review

U.So.Cal.Tax Inst. University of Southern California Tax Institute

UStG Umsatzsteuergesetz (German Turnover Tax Act)

U/T Under trust

U.T.Faculty L.R. Faculty of Law Review, University of Toronto

UTLC University of Tennessee College of Law

UTOLCL University of Toledo College of Law

U.Tasm.L,Rev. University of Tasmania Law Review (or Tasmania University Law Review)

U.Toledo L.Rev. University of Toledo Law Review

U.Tor.L.Rev. University of Toronto School of Law Review

U.Toronto L.J. University of Toronto Law Journal

UTSL University of Texas School of Law

U/W Under will

U.W.Austl.L.Rev. University of Western Australia Law Review

UWCLA Center for Latin America, University of Wisconsin-Milwaukee

UWG Gesetz gegen den unlauteren Wettbewerb (German Law against Unfair Competition)

U.W.L.A.L.,Rev. University of West Los Angeles School of Law, Law Review

U.W.L.A.Rev. University of West Los Angeles School of Law, Law Review

U.Wash.L.Rev. University of Washington Law Review

U.West.Aust.Ann.L.Rev. University of Western Australia Annual Law Review

U.Western Aust.L.Rev. University of Western Australia Law Review

U.Windsor L.Rev. University of Windsor Law Review

U/wrs Underwriters

U.Y.A. University Year for Action

UDAL Udal's Fiji Law Reports

UfR Ugeskrift for Retsvoesen (Denmark)

Ug.L.R. Uganda Law Reports (Africa)

Ug.Pr.L.R. Uganda Protectorate Law Reports (Africa)

Ulm.L.Rec. Ulman's Law Record (New York)

Ulp. Ulpiani Fragmenta

Un.Ins.Co. Unemployment Insurance Code

Un.Prac.News. Unauthorized Practice News

Un.Trav.Dec. Unreported Travancore Decisions

Unauth.   Unauthorized
Unconsol.Laws   Unconsolidated Laws
Und.   Undivided
Und.Torts   Underhill on Torts
Und.Tr.   Underhill on Trusts and Trustees
Underhill,Ev.   Underhill on Evidence
Unemp.Ins.   Unemployment Insurance
Unempl.Ins.Rep.   Unemployment Insurance Reporter (CCH)
Unempl.Ins.Rep.(CCH)   Unemployment Insurance Reports (CCH)
Unif.   ● Unified
● Uniform
Uniform City Ct.Act.   Uniform City Court Act
Uniform Dist.Ct.Act   Uniform District Court Act
Union Pac.L.D.B.   Union Pacific Law Department Bulletin
Univ.   University
Unof.   Unofficial Reports
Unrep.N.Y.Est.T.C.   Unreported New York Estate Tax Cases (P-H)
Unrep.Wills Cas.   Unreported Wills Cases (P-H)
Up.Ben.Pr.   Upper Bench Precedents temp. Car. I (Eng.)
Up.Ben.Pre.   Upper Bench Precedents, tempore Car. I.

Up.Can.   Upper Canada
Ur   Urdu
Urb.   Urban
Urb.Aff.Rep.   Urban Affairs Reporter (CCH)
Urban L.Ann.   Urban Law Annual
Urban Law.   The Urban Lawyer
Uban Law Ann.   Urban Law Annual
Uru.   Uruguay
Ut.   ● Utah
● Utah Reports
Ut.L.R.   Utah Law Review
Utah   ● Utah
● Utah Supreme Court Reports
Utah 2d   Utah Reports Second Series
Utah B.Bull.   Utah Bar Bulletin
Utah Code Ann.   Utah Code Annotated
Utah I.C.Bull.   Utah Industrial Commission Bulletin
Utah L.Rev.   Utah Law Review
Utah Laws   Laws of Utah
Utah P.U.C.   Utah Public Utilities Commission Report
Utah S.B.A.   Utah State Bar Association
Util.   Utility; Utilities
Util.L.Rep.   Utilities Law Reporter (CCH)

V

v.   versus
V.   ● Abstracted Valuation Decisions
     ● Vacated; same case vacated (used in Shepard's Citations)
     ● Verb
     ● Vermont
     ● Vermont Reports
     ● Victoria
     ● Vide (see)
     ● Vietnamese
     ● Virginia
     ● Virginia Reports
     ● Voce (word)
     ● Void; decision or finding held invalid for reasons given (used in Shepard's Citations)
     ● Volume
VA ● Veterans Administration
     ● Veterans' Affairs
VACLE   Joint Committee on Continuing Legal Education of the Virginia State Bar and The Virginia Bar Association
V.A.D.   Veterans' Affairs Decisions, Appealed Pension & Civil Service Retirement Cases (U.S.)
V.A.M.S.   Vernon's Annotated Missouri Statutes
VANUSL   Vanderbilt University School of Law
V.A.S.C.A.R.   Visual Average Speed Computer and Recorder
V.A.T.S.   Vernon's Annotated Texas Statutes
V.B.   Veterans' Bureau (U.S.)
V.C.   ● Vice-Chancellor
     ● Vice-Chancellor's Courts (Eng.)
V.C.Adm.   Victoria Reports, Admiralty
V.C.C.   Vice-Chancellor's Court
V.C.Eq.   Victoria Reports, Equity
V.C.Rep.   Vice-Chancellor's Reports (English; Canadian)
V.D.   Valuation Decisions

V.E.   Venditioni exponas (you expose to sale)
V.G.   Verbi gratia (for the sake of example)
VGH   Verwaltungsgerichtshof--District Administrative Court of Appeal (Germ. & Austria)
V.I.   ● Virgin Islands
     ● Virgin Island Reports
V.I.B.J.   Virgin Islands Bar Journal
V.I.Code Ann.   Virgin Islands Code Annotated
VISTA   Volunteers in Service to America
VITA   Volunteers in Technical Assistance
V.L.   Vestre Landsret--Western Court of Appeal (Denmark)
V.L.R.   ● Vanderbilt Law Review (Tenn.)
     ● Victorian Law Reports, (Australia)
V.L.T.   Victorian Law Times (1856-57)
V.N.   Van Ness' Prize Cases (U.S.)
V.O.A.   Voice of America (U.S.)
v.p.   vice president
V.R.   ● Valuation Reports, Interstate Commerce Commission (U.S.)
     ● Vermont Reports
     ● Victorian Reports, Australia (1870-72)
     ● Villanova Law Review (Pa.)
V.R.Adm.   Victorian Reports, Admiralty (Aus.)
V.R.(Eq.)   Victorian Reports (Equity) (Aus.)
V.R.L.   Victorian Law Reports (Aus.)
V.R.(law)   Victorian Law Reports (Aus.)
V.S.   Vermont Statutes
VTC   Voting trust certificate
VTCLE   Vermont Bar Association Committee on Continuing Legal Education
V.U.L.R.   Valparaiso University Law Review

V.U.W.L.Rev. Victoria University of Wellington Law Review

V. & B. Vesey & Beames' English Chancery Reports (1812-14)

V. & S. Vernon & Scriven's Irish King's Bench Reports (1786-88)

Va. ● Gilmer, Virginia Reports
   ● Valid;· decision or finding held valid for reasons given (used in Shepard's Citations)
   ● Virginia
   ● Virginia Reports
   ● Virginia Supreme Court Reports

Va.Acts Acts of the General Assembly of the Commonwealth of Virginia

Va.B.A. Virginia State Bar Association

Va.Bar Assn. Virginia State Bar Association

Va.Bar News Virginia Bar News

Va.Cas. ● Virginia Cases (by Brockenbrough & Holmes)
   ● Virginia Criminal Cases, Virginia Reports, vols. 3-4 (1789-1826)

Va.Ch.Dec. Wythe's Chancery (1789-99) (Va.)

Va.Code Code of Virginia

Va.Col.Dec. Virginia Colonial Decisions (Randolph & Barradall)

Va.Dec. Virginia Decisions

Va.I.C.Ops. Virginia Industrial Commission Opinions

Va.J.Int'l.L. Virginia Journal of International Law

Va.L. Virginia Law Review

Va.L.Dig. Virginia Law Digest

Va.L.J. Virginia Law Journal

Va.L.Reg. Virginia Law Register

Va.L.Reg.N.S. Virginia Law Register, New Series

Va.L.Rev. Virginia Law Review

Va.L.Wk.Dicta Comp. Virginia Law Weekly Dicta Compilation

Va.Law J. Virginia Law Journal (Richmond)

Va.R. Gilmer's Virginia Reports

Va.S.C.C. Virginia State Corporation Commission

Val. Valparaiso

Val.Com. Valen's Commentaries

Val.Rep. Valuation Reports, Interstate Commerce Commission

Val.Rep.I.C.C. Valuation Reports, Interstate Commerce Commission

Val.U.L.Rev. Valparaiso University Law Review

Vaizey Vaizey's Law of Settlements (1887)

Van Fleet, Coll.Attack Van Fleet on Collateral Attack

Van K. Van Koughnet's Reports, vols. 15-21 Upper Canada Common Pleas (1864-71)

Van.L. Vander Linden's Practice (Cape Colony)

Van N. Van Ness' Prize Cases, U.S. District Court, District of New York

Van Ness, Prize Cas. Van Ness' Prize Cases, U.S. District Court, District of New York

Vand. Vanderbilt

Vand.Int. The Vanderbilt International

Vand.J.Transnat'l.L. Vanderbilt Journal of Transnational Law

Vand.L.Rev. Vanderbilt Law Review

Vanderstr. Vanderstraaten's Reports (1869-71) (Ceylon)

Vatt. Vattel's Law of Nations

Vattel Vattel's Law of Nations

Vattel, Law Nat. Vattel's Law of Nations

Vaug. Vaughan's English Common Pleas Reports (124 Eng. Reprint)

Vaugh. Vaughan's English Common Pleas Reports (124 Eng. Reprint)

Vaughan Vaughan's English Common Pleas Reports (124 Eng. Reprint)

Vaughan (Eng.) Vaughan's English Common Pleas Reports (124 Eng. Reprint)

Vaux Vaux's Recorder's Decisions, Philadelphia, Pa. (Pa. 1841-45)

Vaux (Pa.) Vaux's Recorder's Decisions, Philadelphia, Pa. (Pa. 1841-45)

Vaux Rec.Dec. Vaux's Recorder's Decisions, Philadelphia, Pa. (Pa. 1841-45)

Ve. Vroom's Reports (30-85 New Jersey Law)

Ve. & B.   Vesey & Beames' English Chancery Reports

Vea. & B.   Vesey & Beames' English Chancery Reports

Veazey   Veazey's Reports (36-44 Vermont)

Veh.   Vehicles

Veh.C.   Vehicle Code

Veh. & Traf.   Vehicle and Traffic

Venez.   Venezuela

Vent.   ●   Ventris' English Common Pleas Reports (86 Eng. Reprint)
     ●   Ventris' English King's Bench Reports

Vent.(Eng.)   ●   Ventris' English Common Pleas Reports (86 Eng. Reprint)
     ●   Ventris' English King's Bench Reports

Ventr.   Ventris' English Common Pleas Reports (86 Eng. Reprint)

Ver.   Vermont Reports

VerfGH   Verfassungsgerichtshof--Provincial Constitutional Court (Ger.)

Verm.   Vermont Reports

Vern.   Vernon's English Chancery Reports (23 Eng. Reprint)

Vern.(Eng.)   Vernon's English Chancery Reports (23 Eng. Reprint)

Vern. & S.   Vernon and Scriven's Irish King's Bench Reports (1786-88)

Vern. & S.(Ir.)   Vernon and Scriven's Irish King's Bench Reports (1786-88)

Vern. & Scr.   Vernon and Scriven's Irish King's Bench Reports (1786-88)

Vern. & Scriv.   Vernon and Scriven's Irish King's Bench Reports (1786-88)

Vernon's Ann.C.C.P.   Vernon's Annotated Texas Code of Criminal Procedure

Vernon's Ann.Civ.St.   Vernon's Annotated Texas Civil Statutes

Vernon's Ann.P.C.   Vernon's Annotated Texas Penal Code

VerwGH   Verwaltungsgerichtshof (Administrative Court of Appeal) (Ger.)

Ves.   Vesey, Senior's, English Chancery Reports

Ves.Jr.   Vesey, Junior's, English Chancery Reports (30-34 Eng. Reprint)

Ves.Jr.(Eng.)   Vesey, Junior's English Chancery Reports (30-34 Eng. Reprint)

Ves.Jr.Suppl.   Supplement to Vesey, Junior's, English Chancery Reports (34 Eng. Reprint)

Ves.Jun.   Vesey, Junior's, English Chancery Reports (30-34 Eng. Reprint)

Ves.Jun.Supp.   Supplement to Vesey, Junior's, English Chancery Reports, (34 Eng. Reprint)

Ves.Jun.Supp.(Eng.)   Supplement to Vesey, Junior's, English Chancery Reports (34 Eng. Reprint)

Ves.Sen.   Vesey, Senior's, English Chancery Reports (27, 28 Eng. Reprint)

Ves.Sen.Supp.   Supplement to Vesey, Senior's, English Chancery Reports (28 Eng. Reprint)

Ves.Sr.   Vesey, Senior's, English Chancery Reports (27, 28 Eng. Reprint)

Ves.Sr.(Eng.)   Vesey, Senior's, English Chancery Reports (27, 28 Eng. Reprint)

Ves.Sr.Supp.(Eng.)   Supplement to Vesey, Senior's, English Chancery Reports (28 Eng. Reprint)

Ves. & B.   Vesey & Beames' English Chancery Reports (35 Eng. Reprint)

Ves. & B.(Eng.)   Vesey & Beames' English Chancery Reports (35 Eng. Reprint)

Ves. & Bea.   Vesey & Beames' English Chancery Reports (35 Eng. Reprint)

Ves. & Beam.   Vesey & Beames' English Chancery Reports (35 Eng. Reprint)

Vet.Na.B.   Old Natura Brevium

Vez.   Vezey's (Vesey's) English Chancery Reports

Vicat   Vicat's Vocabularium Juris Utriusque ex Variis Ante Editis

Vicat Voc.Jur.   Vicat's Vocabularium Juris Utriusque ex Variis Ante Editis

vice pres.   vice president

Vict.   ●   Victoria
     ●   Victorian Reports (Aus.)

Vict.Admr.   Victorian Admiralty

Vict.Eq. Victorian Equity

Vict.L. Victorian Law

Vict.L.(Austr.) Victorian Law Reports (Aus.)

Vict.L.J. Victorian Law Journal (Aus.)

Vict.L.R. Victorian Law Reports (Aus.)

Vict.L.R.Min. Victorian Mining Law Reports (Aus.)

Vict.L.T. Victorian Law Times (Melbourne) (Aus.)

Vict.Rep. Victorian Reports (Aus.)

Vict.Rep.(Adm.) Victorian Reports (Admiralty) (Aus.)

Vict.Rep.(Austr.) Victorian Reports (Aus.)

Vict.Rep.(Eq.) Victorian Reports (Equity) (Australia)

Vict.Rep.(Law) Victorian Reports (Law) (Aus.)

Vict.Rev. Victorian Review

Vict.St.Tr. Victorian State Trials (Aus.)

Vict.Stat. Victorian Statutes: the General Public Acts (Aus.)

Vict.Stat.R.,Regs. & B. Victorian Statutory Rules, Regulations and By-Laws (Aus.)

Vict.U.L.Rev. Victoria University Law Review

Vict.U.Well.L.Rev. Victoria University of Wellington Law Review

Vid. Vidian's Exact Pleader (1684)

Viet-Nam (DR) Democratic Republic of Viet-Nam

Viet-Nam (Rep.) Republic of Viet-Nam

Vil. & Br. Vilas & Bryant's Edition of the Wisconsin Reports

Vilas Vilas' Reports (1-5 N.Y. Criminal Reports

Vill. Villanova

Vill.L.Rev. Villanova Law Review

Vin.Abr. Supplement to Viner's Abridgment of Law and Equity (Eng.)

Vin.Abr.(Eng.) Viner's Abridgment of Law & Equity (1741-53) (Eng.)

Vin.Supp. Supplement to Viner's Abridgment of Law and Equity

Viner, Abr. Viner's Abridgment of Law & Equity (1741-53)

Vinn.ad Inst. Vinnius' commentary on the Institutes of Justinian

Vir. ● Virginia
   ● Virginia Cases (Brockenbrough & Holmes)
   ● Virgin's Reports (52-60 Maine)

Vir.L.J. Virginia Law Journal

Virg. ● Virginia
   ● Virginia Cases (by Brockenbrough & Holmes)
   ● Virgin's Reports (52-60 Maine)

Virg.Cas. Virginia Cases (by Brockenbrough & Holmes)

Virg.L.J. Virginia Law Journal (Richmond)

Virgin Virgin's Reports (52-60 Maine)

Viz. Videlicet (that is to say) or (namely)

Vo.L.R. Villanova Law Review

Vo. Verbo

vocat. vocational

Voet, Com.ad Pand. Voet, Commentarius ad Pandectas

vol. ● volume
   ● volunteer

Vol.Fire Ben. Volunteer Firemen's Benefit

Von H.Const.Hist. Von Holst's Constitutional History of the United States

Von Ihr.Str.for L. Von Ihring's Struggle for Law

Vp. Void in part; decision or finding held invalid in part for reasons given (used in Shepard's Citations)

Vroom Vroom's Reports (30-85 New Jersey Law Reports)

Vroom (G.D.W.) G.D.W. Vroom's Reports (36-63 New Jersey Law Reports)

Vroom (N.J.) Vroom's Reports (30-85 New Jersey Law Reports)

Vroom (P.D.) P.D. Vroom's Reports (30-35 New Jersey Law Reports)

Vt. ● Vermont
   ● Vermont Reports

Vt.Acts Laws of Vermont

Vt.P.S.C. Vermont Public Service Commission

Vt.R.C. Vermont Railroad Commission

Vt.Stat.Ann. Vermont Statutes Annotated

W

W.   ● Watermayer's Reports, Supreme Court (Cape of Good Hope)
     ● Watt's Pennsylvania Reports
     ● Wendell's Reports (New York 1826-41)
     ● West
     ● Western
     ● Westminster
     ● Wheaton's Reports (14-25 United States)
     ● William (King of England)
     ● Willson's Reports (Texas Civil Cases, Court of Appeals)
     ● Wisconsin Reports
     ● Wright's Ohio Reports (1831-34)
     ● Wyoming Reports
W.2d Washington State Reports, Second Series
W.A.   ● Western Australia
           ● Withholding agent
W.A.A. War Assets Adminstration (U.S.)
W.A.A.R. Western Australian Arbitration Reports
W.A'B. & W. Webb, A'Beckett & Williams Reports (1870-72) (Aus.)
W.A.C.A. West African Court of Appeal, Selected Judgments
W.A.F. Women's Air Force
W.A.L.R. Western Australian Law Reports
W.A.R. Western Australian Reports
WATS State Bar of Wisconsin Advanced Training Seminars
WAVES Women Accepted for Volunteer Emergency Service
W.Afr.App. West African Court of Appeal Reports
W.Ap. Washington Appellate Reports
W.Austl. Western Australia Reports
W.Austl.Acts Western Australian Acts
W.Austl.Ind.Gaz. Western Australia Industrial Gazette

W.Austl.J.P. Western Australia Justice of the Peace
W.Austl.L.R. Western Australia Law Reports
w.b.a. weekly benefit amount
W.Bl.(Eng.) Sir William Blackstone's English King's Bench Reports (96 Eng. Reprint)
W.Bla. Sir William Blackstone's English King's Bench Reports (96 Eng. Reprint)
W.C.A. Workmen's Compensation Act
W.C.B. Workmen's Compensation Bureau
W.C.C.   ● Washington's Circuit Court Reports (U.S.)
             ● Wisconsin Conservation Commission
             ● Workmen's Compensation Cases (Minton-Senhouse)
W.C.Ins.Rep. Workmen's Compensation & Insurance Reports
W.C.L.J. Workmen's Compensation Law Journal
W.C.Ops. Workmen's Compensation Opinions, U.S. Department of Commerce
W.C.R.N.S.W. Workers' Compensation Commission Reports of Cases, New South Wales (Aus.)
W.C.Rep. Workmen's Compensation Reports
W.C. & I.Rep. Workmen's Compensation Insurance Reports (Eng.)
W.C. & Ins.(Eng.) Workmen's Compensation and Insurance Reports (Eng.)
W.C. & Ins.Rep. Workmen's Compensation and Insurance Reports (Eng.)
W.Coast Rep. West Coast Reporter
W.Ct.S.A. Union of South Africa Water Courts Decisions
W.D. Western District
W/D Withdrawal
W.E.U. Western European Union

W.Ent. Winch's Book of Entries

WFC World Food Council

WFO War Food Order (U.S.)

W.F.T.U. World Federation of Trade Unions

WGLI Warren, Gorham & Lamont Inc.

W.Ger. West Germany

W.H. ● Wage & Hour Cases (BNA)
● Withholding

W.H.C. South African Law Reports, Witwatersrand High Court

W.H.Cas. Wage & Hour Cases (BNA)

W.H.Chron. Westminster Hall Chronicle and Legal Examiner (1835-36)

W.H.Man. Wages & Hours Manual (BNA)

WHO World Health Organization (UN)

W.H.R. Wage & Hour Reporter (BNA)

W.H.R.Man. Wage & Hour Reference Manual (BNA)

WHSUPA Wharton School, University of Pennsylvania

W.H. & G. Welsby, Hurlstone and Gordon's Exchequer Reports (1848-56)

W.I. West Indies

WILUCL Willamette University College of Law

WIP Work Incentive Program

WIPO World Intellectual Property Organization

W.I.S.A.Law Rep. West India States Agency Law Reports

W.I.S.A.Law Reports Western India States Agency Law Reports

W.J. Western Jurist (U.S.)

W.Jo. Sir William Jones' King's Bench Reports (82 Eng. Reprint)

W.Jones (Eng.) Sir William Jones' King's Bench Reports (82 Eng. Reprint)

W.Kel. William Kelynge's Chancery Reports (25 Eng. Reprint)

W.Kelynge (Eng.) William Kelynge's Chancery Reports (25 Eng. Reprint)

W.L.B. Weekly Law Bulletin, Ohio

W.L.Bull.(Ohio) Weekly Law Bulletin, Ohio

W.L.D. South African Law Reports, Witwatersrand Local Division

W.L.G. Weekly Law Gazette, Ohio

W.L.Gaz.(Ohio) Weekly Law Gazette, Ohio

W.L.J. ● Washburn Law Journal
● Western Law Journal
● Wyoming Law Journal

W.L.Jour. ● Washburn Law Journal
● Western Law Journal
● Wyoming Law Journal

W.L.L.R. Washington & Lee Law Review

W.L.M. Western Law Monthly, Cleveland, Ohio

W.L.Q. Washington University Law Quarterly (Missouri)

W.L.R. ● Washington Law Reporter (D.C.)
● Weekly Law Reports (Eng.)
● Western Law Reporter (Canada)
● Wisconsin Law Review

W.L.T. Western Law Times (1890-95) (Canada)

W.M. Ways and Means

W.M.L. Willamette Law Journal (Or.)

W.M.L.R. William & Mary Law Review

W.M.O. World Meteorological Organization (UN)

W.M.R. William and Mary Review of Virginia Law (Va.)

W.N. ● Calcutta Weekly Notes
● Weekly Notes of English Law Reports

W.N.(Calc.) Calcutta Weekly Notes

W.N.(Eng.) Weekly Notes of English Law Reports

W.N.C. Weekly Notes of Cases (Pa. 1874-99)

W.N.C.(Pa.) Weekly Notes of Cases (Pa. 1874-99)

W.N.Cas. Weekly Notes of Cases (Pa. 1874-99)

W.N.Misc. Weekly Notes, Miscellaneous

W.N.N.S.W. Weekly Notes, New South Wales

WOAR Women Organized Against Rape

W.Ont.L.Rev. Western Ontario Law Review

W.P. Water Pollution Committee

W.P.A. Works Progress Administration (later known as the Projects Administration)

WPC World Peace Council

W.P.C. ● Webster's Patent Cases (1601-1855)
     ● Wollaston's English Bail Court Practice Cases

W.P.Cas. ● Webster's Patent Cases (1601-1855)
     ● Wollaston's English Bail Court Practice Cases

W.P.R. Webster's Patent Reports (Eng.)

WPTLC World Peace Through Law Center

W.R. ● Sutherland's Weekly Reporter (India)
     ● War Risk Insurance Deccisions (U.S.)
     ● Weekly Reporter, Bengal (India)
     ● Weekly Reporter (Eng.)
     ● Weekly Reporter, Cape Provincial Division (S. Africa)
     ● Wendell's Reports (N.Y. 1826-41)
     ● West's Chancery Reports (1736-39) (Eng.)
     ● Wisconsin Reports

W.R.C.R. Wisconsin Railroad Commission Reports

W.R.Calc. Sutherland's Weekly Reporter (India)

W.R.L. Western Reserve Law Review (Ohio)

W.R.N.L.R. Western Region of Nigeria Law Reports

W.Rep. West's Reports *tempore* Hardwicke, English Chancery (1736-39)

W.Res.L.Rev. Western Reserve Law Review

W.Rob. W. Robinson's English Admiralty Reports (166 Eng. Reprint)

W.Rob.Adm. W. Robinson's English Admiralty Reports (166 Eng. Reprint)

W.Rob.Adm.(Eng.) W. Robinson's English Admiralty Reports (166 Eng. Reprint)

W.S. Wagner's Statutes (Mo.)

W.S.A. Wisconsin Statutes Annotated

WSB Wage Stabilization Board

WSBA Washington State Bar Association

WSG International Wool Study Group

W.T. Washington Territory Reports

W.T.B.R. War Trade Board Rulings (U.S.)

WTI The World Trade Institute

WTO Warsaw Treaty Organization

W.T.R. Weekly Transcript Reports (N.Y.)

W.Ty.R. Washington Territory Reports (1854-88)

WUTSL Washburn University School of Law

W.V. West Virginia Reports

W.V.L. West Virginia Law Review

W.V.L.R. West Virginia Law Review

W.Va. ● West Virginia
     ● West Virginia Supreme Court Reports

W.Va.Acts Acts of the Legislature of West Virginia

W.Va.Code West Virginia Code

W.Va.L.Q. West Virginia Law Quarterly

W.Va.L.Rev. West Virginia Law Review

W.Va.P.S.C. West Virginia Public Service Commission Decisions

W.Va.P.S.C.R. West Virginia Public service Commission Reports

W.Va.P.U.R. West Virginia Public Utility Commission Reports

W.W. With warrants

W.W.H. W.W. Harrington's Reports (31-39 Delaware)

W.W.Harr. W.W. Harrington's Reports (31-39 Delaware)

W.W.Harr.Del. W.W. Harrington's Reports (31-39 Delaware)

W.W.R. Western Weekly Reports (Canada)

W.W.R.(N.S.) Western Weekly Reports New Series (Canada)

W.W. & A'B. Wyatt, Webb & A'Beckett's Reports, Victoria (1864-69)

W.W. & D. Willmore, Wollaston and Davison's Queen's Bench Reports (1837)

W.W. & H. Willmore, Wollaston and Hodges' Queen's Bench Reports (1838-39)

W.W. & H.(Eng.) Willmore, Wollaston and Hodges' Queen's Bench Reports (1838-39)

W. & B. Wolferstan and Bristowe, Election Cases (1859-65)

W. & B.Dig. Walker & Bates' Digest (Ohio)

W. & C. Wilson & Courtenay's Scotch Appeal Cases

W. & D. Wolferstan and Dew, Election Cases (1856-58)

W. & H. Wage and Hour Division, U.S. Department of Labor

W. & L. Washington and Lee Law Review (Va.)

W. & L.Dig. Wood & Long's Digest (Illinois)

W. & M. ● William & Mary Law Review
      ● Woodbury & Minot, United States Circuit Court Reports, 3 vols.

W. & S. ● Watts & Sergeant's Reports (Pa. 1841-1845)
      ● Wilson & Shaw's Scotch Appeal Cases, English House of Lords

W. & S.App. Wilson & Shaw's Scotch Appeals Cases, English House of Lords

W. & T.Eq.Ca. White and Tudor's Leading Cases in Equity. 9 editions (1849-1928)

W. & T.L.C. White and Tudor's Leading Cases in Equity. 9 editions (1849-1928)

W. & W. ● de Witt & Weeresinghe's Appeal Court Reports (Ceylon)
      ● White & Wilson's Texas Civil Cases, Court of Appeals
      ● Wyatt & Webb's Victorian Reports (1864-69) (Aus.)

W. & W.Vict. Wyatt & Webb's Victorian Reports (1864-69) (Aus.)

Wa. ● Washington
      ● Watts' Reports (Pa. 1832-40)

Wa.2d Washington State Reports, Second Series

Wa.A. Washington Appellate Reports

Wa.L.R. Washington Law Review

Wade, Am.Mining Law Wade on American Mining Law

Wade,Attachm. Wade on Attachment and Garnishment

Wag.St. Wagner's Statutes (Mo.)

Wage and Hour Cas. Wage and Hour cases (BNA)

Wait Act. & Def. Wait's Actions and Defences

Wait Dig. Wait's Digest (New York)

Wait St.Pap. Wait's State Papers of the United States

Wait's Prac. Wait's New York Practice

Wake For.L.Rev. Wake Forest Law Review

Wake Forest Intra.L.Rev. Wake Forest Intramural Law Review

Wal. Wallace (usually abbreviated as Wall)

Wal.by L. Wallis' Irish Reports, by Lyne (1766-91)

Wal.Jr. J.W. Wallace's United States Circuit Court Reports

Wal.Sr. J.B. Wallace's United States Circuit Court Reports

Walk. ● Walker's Michigan Chancery Reports
      ● Walker's Reports (96, 109 Alabama)
      ● Walker's Reports (1 Mississippi)
      ● Walker's Reports (Pa. 1855-1885)
      ● Walker's Reports (22-25, 38-51, 72-88 Texas; 1-10 Civil Appeals Texas)

Walk.Am.Law Walker's American Law

Walk.Ch. Walker's Michigan Chancery Reports

Walk.Ch.Cas. Walker's Michigan Chancery Reports

Walk.Ch.Mich. Walker's Michigan Chancery Reports

Walk.Miss. Walker's Reports (1 Mississippi)

Walk.Pa. Walker's Reports (Pa. 1855-85)

Walk.Pat. Walker on Patents

Walk.Tex. Walker's Reports (22-25, 38-51, 72-88 Texas; 1-10 Civil Appeals Texas)

Walker • Walker's Michigan Chancery Reports
- Walker's Reports (96, 109 Alabama)
- Walker's Reports (1 Mississippi)
- Walker's Reports (Pa. 1855-1885)
- Walker's Reports (22-25, 38-51, 72-88 Texas; 1-10 Civil Appeals Texas)

Wall. • Wallace
- Wallace's Reports (68-90 U.S.)
- Wallace's Circuit Court Reports (U.S.)
- Wallis
- Wallis' Irish Chancery Reports
- Wallis Philadelphia Reports (Pa. 1855-85)

Wall.C.C. Wallace's Circuit Court Reports (U.S.)

Wall.Jr. J.W. Wallace's Circuit Court Reports (U.S.)

Wall.Jr.C.C. J.W. Wallace's Circuit Court Reports (U.S.)

Wall.Lyn. Wallis' Irish Chancery Reports by Lyne (1776-91)

Wall.Rep. • Wallace, The Reporters (treatise)
- Wallace's Reports (68-90 U.S.)

Wall.S.C. Wallace's Reports (68-90 U.S.)

Wall.Sen. J.B. Wallace's United States Circuit Court Reports

Wallis. Wallis' Irish Chancery Reports

Wallis by L. Wallis' Irish Chancery Reports by Lyne (1776-91)

Wallis(Ir.) Wallis' Irish Chancery Reports

Walp.Rub. Walpole's Rubric of Common Law

Walsh. Walsh, Registry Cases (Ir.)

Walter. Walter's Reports (14-16 New Mexico)

War. Warrants

War Dept.B.C.A. U.S. War Department, Decisions of Board of Contract Adjustment

War.Op. Warwick's Opinions (City Solicitor of Philadelphia, Pa.)

War Trade Reg. War Trade Regulations (U.S.)

Ward. Warden's Reports (2, 4 Ohio State)

Ward,Leg. Ward on Legacies

Ward. & Sm. Warden & Smith's Reports (3 Ohio State Reports)

Warden Warden's Reports (2, 4 Ohio State Reports)

Warden & Smith Warden & Smith's Reports (3 Ohio State)

Warden's Law & Bk.Bull. Weekly Law & Bank Bulletin (Ohio)

Ware. Ware's United States District Court Reports

Warth Code. West Virginia Code (1899)

Warv.Abst. Warvelle on Abstracts of Title

Warv. El.R.P. Warvelle's Elements of Real Property

Warv.V. & P. Warvelle's Vendors and Purchasers of Real Property

Warwick's Op. Warwick's Opinions (City Solicitor of Philadelphia, Pa.)

Wash. • Washburn
- Washington
- Washington Territory or State Reports
- Washington's Circuit Court Reports (U.S.)
- Washington's Reports (16-23 Vermont)
- Washington's Reports (1, 2 Virginia)

Wash.2d Washington Reports, Second Series

Wash.App. Washington Appellate Reports

Wash.C.C. Washington's United States Circuit Court Reports

Wash.Co. Washington County Reports, Pennsylvania

Wash.Co.(Pa.) Washington County Reports, Pennsylvania

Wash.Cr.L. Washburn on Criminal Law

Wash.D.P.W. Washington Department of Public Works

Wash.Dec. Washington Decisions

Wash.Jur. Washington Jurist

Wash. L.R.(Dist Col) Washington Law Reporter (D.C.)

Wash.L.Rep. Washington Law Reporter (D.C.)

Wash.L.Rev. Washington Law Review

Wash.Law Rep. Washington Law Reporter (D.C.)

Wash.Laws Laws of Washington

Wash.Legis.Serv. Washington Legislative Service (West)

Wash.P.S.C. Washington Public Service Commission

Wash.P.U.R. Washington Public Utility Commission Reports

Wash.R.P. Washburn on Real Property

Wash.Rev. Code Revised Code of Washington

Wash.Rev.Code Ann. Washington Revised Code Annotated

Wash.St. Washington State Reports

Wash.T. ● Washington Territory Opinions (1854-64)
● Washington Territory Reports (1854-88)

Wash.Ter. ● Washington Territory Opinions (1854-64)
● Washington Territory Reports (1854-88)

Wash.Ter.N.S. Allen's Washington Territory Reports, New Series

Wash.Terr. ● Washington Territory Opinions (1854-64)
● Washington Territory Reports (1854-88)

Wash.Ty. ● Washington Territory Opinions (1854-64)
● Washington Territory Reports (1854-88)

Wash.U.L.Q. Washington University Law Quarterly

Wash.U.L.Rev. Washington University Law Review

Wash.Va. Washington's Reports (1,2 Va.)

Wash. & Haz.P.E.I. Washburton & Hazard's Reports (Prince Edward Island, Canada)

Wash. & Lee L.Rev. Washington & Lee Law Review

Washb.Easem. Washburn on Easements and Servitudes

Washb.Real Prop. Washburn on Real Property

Washburn Washburn's Reports (18-23 Vermont)

Washburn L.J. Washburn Law Journal

Wat.C.G.H. Watermeyer's Cape of Good Hope Reports (S. Africa)

Wat.Cr.Dig. Waterman's Criminal Digest (United States)

Wat.Set-Off. Waterman on Set-Off

Watch. Board of Examiners in Watchmaking

Water C. Water Code

Watermeyer. Watermeyer's Cape of Good Hope Reports (S. Africa)

Watk.Con. Watkins on Conveyancing

Watk.Conv. Watkins' Conveyancing

Watk.Cop. Watkins on Copyholds

Watk.Copyh. Watkins' Copyholds

Watk.Des. Watkins on Descents

Wats.Arb. Watson on Arbitration

Wats.Cler.Law. Watson's Clergyman's Law

Wats.Comp.Eq. Watson's Compendium of Equity

Watson. Watson's Compendium of Equity. 2 Editions (1873, 1888)

Watson Eq. Watson's Practical Compendium of Equity

Watts. ● Watts' Reports (Pa. 1832-40)
● Watts' Reports (16-24 West Virginia)

Watts(Pa.) Watts' Reports (Pa. 1832-40)

Watts & S. Watts & Sergeant's Reports (Pennsylvania 1841-45)

Watts. & S.(Pa.) Watts & Sergeant's Reports (Pennsylvania 1841-45)

Watts & Serg. Watts & Sergeant's Reports (Pennsylvania 1841-45)

Wayne L.Rev. Wayne Law Review

We.
- West's Chancery Reports (Eng.)
- West's Reports, House of Lords (Eng.)
- Western Tithe Cases (Eng.)

Web.P.C. Webster's Patent Cases (1601-1855)

Web.Tr. The Trial of Professor Webster for Murder

Webb.
- Webb's Reports (Vols. 6-20 Kansas)
- Webb's Reports (Vols. 11-20 Texas Civil Appeals)

Webb,A'B. & W.Eq. Webb, A'Beckett, & Williams' Victorian Equity Reports (Aus.)

Webb,A'B. & W.I.P. & M. Webb, A'Beckett, & Williams' Insolvency, Probate & Matrimonial Reports, (Aus.)

Webb,A'B. & W.Min. Webb, A'Beckett, & Williams Mining Cases (Aus.)

Webb. & D. Webb & Duval's Reports (vols. 1-3 Texas)

Webb & Duval Webb & Duval's Reports (vols. 1-3 Texas)

Webs. Webster's Patent Cases (Eng.)

Webs.Pat.Cas. Webster's Patent Cases (Eng.)

Webst.Dict. Webster's Dictionary

Webst.Dict.Unab. Webster's Unabridged Dictionary

Webst.Int.Dict. Webster's International Dictionary

Webst. New Int.D. Webster's New International Dictionary

Webster Dict. Webster's Dictionary

Webster In Sen.Doc. Webster in Senate Documents

Webster Pat.Cas.(Eng.) Webster Patent Cases

Wedgw.Dict.Eng.Etymology Wedgwood's Dictionary of English Etymology

Week.Cin.L.B. Weekly Cincinnati Law Bulletin

Week.Dig. New York Weekly Digest (1876-88)

Week.Dig.(N.Y.) New York Weekly Digest (1876-88)

Week.Jur. Weekly Jurist (Bloomington, Ill.)

Week.L.Gaz. Weekly Law Gazette

Week L.R.(Eng.) Weekly Law Reports (Eng.)

Week.L.Rec. Weekly Law Record

Week.L.Record. Weekly Law Record

Week.L.Rev. Weekly Law Review (San Francisco)

Week.Law Bull. Weekly Law Bulletin and Ohio Law Journal

Week.Law Gaz. Weekly Law Gazette (Ohio)

Week.Law & Bk.Bull. Weekly Law & Bank Bulletin

Week.No.
- Weekly Notes of Cases (Law Reports) (England)
- Weekly Notes of Cases (Pennsylvania 1874-99)

Week.No.Cas.
- Weekly Notes of Cases (Law Reports) England
- Weekly Notes of Cases (Pennsylvania 1874-99)

Week.R.(Eng.) Weekly Reporter (Eng.)

Week.Rep. Weekly Reporter (Eng.)

Week.Reptr.
- Weekly Reporter, London
- Weekly Reporter, Bengal

Week.Trans.Rep. Weekly Transcript Reports (N.Y.)

Week.Trans.Repts. Weekly Transcript Reports (N.Y.)

Weekly Comp.of Pres.Doc. Weekly Compilation of Presidential Documents

Weekly L.R. Weekly Law Reports (Eng.)

Weekly Notes Weekly Notes (of Law Reports) (Eng.)

Weer. Weerakoon's Appeal Court Reports (Ceylon)

Weight.Med.Leg.Gaz. Weightman's Medico-Legal Gazette

Wel. Welsh's Irish Registry Cases

Welf. Welfare

Welf. & Inst. Welfare & Institutions

Welf. & Inst.C. Welfare and Institutions Code

Welfare L.Bull. Welfare Law Bulletin

Welfare L.News Welfare Law News

Wells,Repl. Wells on Replevin

Wells Res.Ad. Wells' Res Adjudicata and Stare Decisis

Welsb.H. & G. Welsby, Hurlstone and Gordon's English Exchequer Reports (1848-56)

Welsb.,Hurl. & G. Welsby, Hurlstone and Gordon's English Exchequer Reports (1848-56)

Welsby H. & G.(Eng.) Welsby, Hurlstone and Gordon's English Exchequer Reports (1848-56)

Welsh.
- Welsh's Irish Case of James Feighny, 1838
- Welsh's Irish Case at Sligo (1838)
- Welsh's Registry Cases (Ireland)

Welsh Reg.Cas. Welsh's Irish Registry Cases

Wend. Wendell's Reports (N.Y. 1826-1841)

Wend.(N.Y.) Wendell's Reports (N.Y. 1826-1841)

Wendell. Wendell's Reports (N.Y. 1826-1841)

Wendt. Wendt, Reports of Cases, Ceylon

Wenz. Wenzell's Reports (60 Minnesota)

Wes.C.L.J. Westmoreland County Law Journal

Wes.Res.Law Jo. Western Reserve Law Journal

Wes.Res.Law Jrl. Western Reserve Law Journal, Ohio

Wesk.Ins. Weskett's Complete Digest of the Theory, Laws and Practice of Insurance

Weskett,Ins. Weskett's Complete Digest of the Theory, Laws and Practice of Insurance

West.
- Westbury, European Arbitration (Reilly)
- Western's London Tithe Cases (Eng.)
- Westmoreland County Law Journal (Pa.)

- Weston's Reports (11-14 Vermont)
- West's Chancery Reports (Eng.)
- West's Reports, House of Lords (Eng.)

West A.U.L.R. West Australia University Law Review

West.Aus. Western Australia

West.Austl. Western Australian Reports

West Austr.L. West Australian Law Reports

West Ch. West's English Chancery Cases (25 Eng. Reprint)

West Ch.(Eng.) West's English Chancery Cases (25 Eng. Reprint)

West.Chy. West's English Chancery Cases (25 Eng. Reprint)

West Co.Rep. West Coast Reporter

West Coast Rep. West Coast Reporter

West H.L. West's Reports, English House of Lords

West.Jur. Western Jurist (Des Moines, Iowa)

West.L.Gaz. Western Law Gazette, Cincinnati (Ohio)

West.L.J. Western Law Journal (Ohio)

West.L.J.(Ohio) Western Law Journal (Ohio)

West.L.M. Western Law Monthly (Ohio)

West.L.Mo. Western Law Monthly (Ohio)

West.L.Month. Western Law Monthly (Ohio)

West.L.R. Western Law Reporter (Canada)

West L.R.(Can.) Western Law Reporter (Canada)

West.L.Rev. Western Law Review

West.L.T. Western Law Times (Canada)

West.Law J. Western Law Journal (Cincinnati, Ohio)

West.Law M. Western Law Monthly (Ohio)

West.Law Month. Western Law Monthly (Ohio)

West.Leg.Obs. Western Legal Observer

West.R. Western Reporter
West.Rep. Western Reporter
West.Res.Law Rev. Western Reserve Law Review
West.School L.Rev. Western School Law Review
West,Symb. West's Symboleography
West t.H. West's Chancery Reports tempore Hardwicke (1736-39)
West.t.Hard. West's Chancery Reports tempore Hardwicke (1736-39)
West t.Hardw. West's Chancery Reports tempore Hardwicke (1736-39)
West.Tithe Cas. Western's London Tithe Cases (Eng.)
West Va. ● West Virginia
  ● West Virginia Reports
West Va.B.A. West Virginia Bar Association
West Week(Can.) Western Weekly Notes (Canada)
West.Week.N. Western Weekly Notes (Canada)
West Week N.(Can.) Western Weekly Notes (Canada)
West Week N.S.(Can.) Western Weekly New Series (Canada)
West.Week.Rep. Western Weekly Reports (Canada)
West.Wkly. Western Weekly (Canada)
Western Ont.L.Rev. Western Ontario Law Review
Western Res.L.Rev. Western Reserve Law Review
Western Reserve L.N. Western Reserve Law Notes
Westl.Priv.Int.Law. Westlake's Private International Law
Westlake Int.Private Law. Westlake's Private International Law
Westm. State of Westminster Westmoreland County Law Journal (Pennsylvania)
Westm.L.J. Westmoreland County Law Journal (Pa.)
Westm.Rev. Westminster Review
Westmore Co.L.J.(Pa.) Westmoreland County Law Journal (Pa.)
Westmoreland Co.L.J. Westmoreland County Law Journal (Pa.)
Weston Weston's Reports (11-14 Vermont)

West's Op. West's Opinions (City Solicitor of Philadelphia, Pa.)
West's Symb. West's Symboleography. Many editions (1590-1641)
Weth. Wethey's Reports (Canada)
Weth.U.C. Wethey's Reports, Upper Canada Queen's Bench
Wethey. Wethey's Reports, Upper Canada Queen's Bench
Wh. ● Warton's Reports (Pa. 1835-41)
  ● Wheaton's International Law
  ● Wheaton's Reports (14-25 U.S.)
  ● Wheeler, New York Criminal Reports, 3 vols.
Wh.Cr.Cas. Wheeler, New York Criminal Cases, 3 vols.
Wh. & T.L.C. White and Tudor's Leading Cases in Equity. 9 editions (1849-1928)
Whar. Wharton's Reports (Pa. 1835-41)
Whar.Ag. Wharton on Agency
Whar.Am.Cr.L. Wharton's American Criminal Law
Whar.Con.Law. Wharton's Conflict of Laws
Whar.Cr.Ev. Wharton on Criminal Evidence
Whar.Cr.Law. Wharton's American Criminal Law
Whar.Cri.Pl. Wharton's Criminal Pleading and Practice
Whar.Dig. Wharton's Digest (Pennsylvania)
Whar.Hom. Wharton's Law of Homicide
Whar.Neg. Wharton's Law of Negligence
Whar.St.Tr. Wharton's U.S. State Trials
Whar. & St.Med.Jur. Wharton & Stille's Medical Jurisprudence
Whart. Wharton's Pennsylvania Supreme Court Reports (1835-41)
Whart.Ag. Wharton on Agency
Whart.Am.Cr.Law. Wharton's American Criminal Law
Whart.Confl.Laws. Wharton's Conflict of Laws
Whart.Cr.Ev. Wharton on Criminal Evidence

Whart.Cr.Law. Wharton's American Criminal Law

Whart.Cr.Pl. & Prac. Wharton's Criminal Pleading & Practice

Whart.Crim.Law. Wharton's American Criminal Law

Whart.Ev. Wharton on Evidence in Civil Issues

Whart.Hom. Wharton's Law of Homicide

Whart.Homicide Wharton's Law of Homicide

Whart.Law Dict. Wharton's Law Dictionary, or Law Lexicon

Whart.Law Lexicon Wharton's Law Dictionary (or Law Lexicon)

Whart.Lex. Wharton's Law Lexicon

Whart.Neg. Wharton on Negligence

Whart.Pa. Wharton's Reports (Pa. (1835-41) (Pa.)

Whart.St.Tr. Wharton's State Trials, U.S.

Whart.State Tr. Wharton's State Trials, U.S.

Whart. & S.Med.Jur. Wharton & Stille's Medical Jurisprudence

Wharton. • Wharton's American Criminal Law
- Wharton's Law Lexicon
- Wharton's Reports 1835-41) (Pa.)

Wharton,Crim.Evidence. Wharton's Criminal Evidence

Wharton,Crim.Proc. Wharton's Criminal Law & Procedure

Wheat. Wheaton's Reports (14-25 U.S.)

Wheat.El.Int.Law. Wheaton's Elements of International Law

Wheat.Hist.Law Nat. Wheaton's History of the Law of Nations

Wheat.Int.Law. Wheaton's International Law

Wheaton. Wheaton's Reports (14-25 U.S.)

Wheel. • Wheelock's Reports (32-37 Texas)
- Wheeler's Criminal Cases (N.Y.)

Wheel.(Tex.) Wheelock's Reports (32-37 Texas)

Wheel.Br.Cas. Wheeling Bridge Case

Wheel.Cr.Cas. Wheeler's Criminal Cases (N.Y.)

Wheel.Cr.Rec. Wheeler's Criminal Recorder (1 Wheeler's Criminal Cases) (N.Y.)

Wheeler, Am.Cr.Law Wheeler's Abridgment of American Common Law Cases

Wheeler Abr. Wheeler's Abridgment

Wheeler C.C. Wheeler's Criminal Cases (N.Y.)

Wheeler,Cr.Cas. Wheeler's Criminal Cases (N.Y.)

Whishaw. Whishaw's Law Dictionary

Whit.Pat.Cas. Whitman's Patent Cases (U.S.)

Whitak.Liens Whitaker on Liens

White. • White, Justiciary Court Reports (Scotland), 3 vols.
- White, Reports (10-15 West Virginia)
- White's Reports (31-44 Texas Court of Appeals)

White,Coll. White's New Collection of the Laws, etc., of Great Britain, France or Spain

White,Recop. White, New Recopilacion. A New Collection of Laws and Local Ordinances of Great Britain, France, and Spain, Relating to the Concessions of Land in Their Respective Colonies, with the Laws of Mexico and Texas on the Same Subject

White & Civ.Cas.Ct.App. White & Willson's Civil Cases Ct. of Appeals (Texas)

White & T.L.Cas. White & Tudor's Leading Cases in Equity

White & T.Lead Cas.Eq. White & Tudor's Leading Cases in Equity (Eng.)

White & T.Lead Cas.in Eq.(Eng.) White & Tudor, Leading Cases in Equity

White & Tudor. White & Tudor's Leading Cases in Equity

White & W. White & Willson's Reports (Texas Civil Cases of Court of Appeals)

White & W.(Tex.) White & Willson's Reports (Texas Civil Cases of Court of Appeals)

White & W.Civ.Cas.Ct.App. White & Willson's Civil Cases Court of Appeals (Tex.)

White's Ann.Pen.Code White's Annotated Penal Code, Tex.

White's Rep. ● White's Reports (31-44 Texas Appeals)
● White's Reports (10-15 West Virginia)

Whitm.Lib.Cas. Whitman's Massachusetts Libel Cases

Whitm.Pat.Cas. Whitman's Patent Cases (U.S.)

Whitm.Pat.Law Rev. Whitman, Patent Law Review Washington, D.C.

Whitman Pat.Cas.(U.S.) Whitman Patent Cases

Whitney Whitney's Land Laws (Tennessee)

Whitt. Whittlesey's Reports (32-41 Mo.)

Whittlesey Whittlesey's Reports (32-41 Mo.)

Wi. Wisconsin

Wi.L.R. Wisconsin Law Review

Wig.Wills Wigmore on Wills

Wight. Wightwick's Exchequer Reports (Eng.) (145 Eng. Reprint)

Wight El.Cas. Wight, Scottish Election Cases (1784-96)

Wightw. Wightwick's Exchequer Reports (Eng.) (145 Eng. Reprint)

Wightw.(Eng.) Wightwick's Exchequer Reports (Eng.) (145 Eng. Reprint)

Wigm.Ev. Wigmore on Evidence

Wigmore, Evidence Wigmore on Evidence

Wilberforce Wilberforce on Statute Law

Wilc.Cond. Wilcox Condensed Ohio Reports (1-7 Ohio, Reprint)

Wilc.Cond.Rep. Wilcox's Condensed Ohio Reports (1-7 Ohio, Reprint)

Wilcox ● Wilcox's Reports (10 Ohio)
● Wilcox's Lackawanna Reports (Pa.)

Wildm.Int.Law Wildman's International Law

Wilk. ● Wilkinson, Owen, Paterson & Murray's New South Wales Reports (1862-65)
● Wilkinson's Texas Court of Appeals and Civil Appeals

Wilk.P. & M. Wilkinson, Paterson, & Murray's Reports, New South Wales Reports (1862-65)

Wilk. & Mur. Wilkinson, Owen, Paterson & Murray's New South Wales Reports (1862-65)

Wilk. & Ow. Wilkinson, Owen, Paterson & Murray's New South Wales Reports (1862-65)

Wilk. & Pat. Wilkinson, Owen, Paterson & Murray's New South Wales Reports (1862-65)

Will. ● Willes' English Common Pleas Reports
● William, as 1 Will. IV
● Willson's Reports, vols. 29-30 Texas Appeals, also vols. 1, 2, Texas Civil Appeals

Will.Ann.Reg. Williams, Annual Register, New York

Will.-Bund St.Tr. Willis-Bund's Cases from State Trials

Will.Eq.Jur. Willard's Equity Jurisprudence

Will.L.J. Willamette Law Journal

Will.Mass. Williams' Reports (1 Massachusetts)

Will.P. Peere-Williams' English Chancery Reports

Will.Saund. Williams' Notes to Saunders' Reports (1666-73)

Will.Vt. Williams Reports (27-29 Vermont)

Will.Woll. & D. Willmore, Wollaston, Davison's Queen's Bench Reports, 1837 (Eng.)

Will.,Woll. & Dav. Willmore, Wollaston, Davison's Queen's Bench Reports, 1837 (Eng.)

Will.Woll. & H. Willmore, Wollaston and Hodges' Queen's Bench Reports (1838)

Will.Woll. & Hodg. Willmore, Wollaston and Hodges' Queen's Bench Reports (1838)

Willamette L.J. Willamette Law Journal

Willc.Const. Willcock, The Office of Constable

Willcock, Mun.Corp. Willcock's Municipal Corporation

Willes Willes English Common Pleas Reports (125 Eng. Reprint)

Willes (Eng.) Willes English Common Pleas Reports (125 Eng. Reprint)

Williams ● Peere Williams' Chancery Reports (Eng.)
● Williams' Reports (1 Massachusetts)
● Williams' Reports (10-12 Utah)
● Williams' Reports (27-29 Vermont)

Williams B.Pr. Williams' Bankruptcy Practice. 17 editions (1870-1958)

Williams, Common Williams on Rights of Common

Williams, Ex'rs. Williams on Executors

Williams, Ex'rs.,R. & T.Ed. Williams on Executors, Randolph and Talcott Edition

Williams P. Peere Williams' English Chancery Reports (1695-1736)

Williams, Pers.Prop. Williams on Personal Property

Williams, Real Prop. Williams on Real Property

Williams, Saund. Williams' Notes to Saunders' Reports

Williams, Seis. Williams on Seisin

Williams & B.Adm.Jur. Williams and Bruce's Admiralty Practice, 3 editions (1869-1902)

Williams & Bruce Ad.Pr. Williams and Bruce's Admiralty Practice, 3 editions (1869-1902)

Willis, Trustees Willis on Trustees

Williston ● Williston on Contracts
● Williston on Sales

Williston, Contracts Williston on Contracts

Willm.W. & D. Willmore, Wollaston, Davison's Queen's Bench Reports (Eng.)

Wills, Circ.Ev. Wills on Circumstantial Evidence

Wills, Civ.Ev. Wills on Circumstantial Evidence

Wills, Est.,Tr. Wills, Estates, Trusts (P-H)

Willson Willson's Reports, vols. 29-30 Texas Appeals, also vols. 1, 2 Texas Court of Appeals, Civil Cases

Willson Civ.Cas.Ct.App. White & Willson's Civil Cases of Texas Court of Appeals

Willson, Tex.Cr.Law Willson's Revised Penal Code, Code of Criminal Procedure, and Penal Laws of Texas

Wilm. Wilmot's Notes and Opinions, King's Bench (97 Eng. Reprint)

Wilm.Judg. Wilmot's Notes and Opinions, King's Bench (97 Eng. Reprint)

Wilm.Op. Wilmot's Notes and Opinions, King's Bench (97 Eng. Reprint)

Wilm.W. & D. Willmore, Wollaston & Davison, English Queen's Bench Reports

Wilmington, Del.P.U.C. Wilmington, Delaware, Board of Public Utility Commission

Wilmot's Notes (Eng.) Wilmot's Notes and Opinions, King's Bench (97 Eng. Reprint)

Wils. Wilson, English Common Pleas Reports, 3 vols. (95 Eng. Reprint)

Wils.Ch. Wilson's English Chancery Reports (37 Eng. Reprint)

Wils.Ch.(Eng.) Wilson's English Chancery Reports (37 Eng. Reprint)

Wils.(Eng.) Wilson, English Common Pleas Reports, 3 vols. (95 Eng. Reprint)

Wils.Ent. Wilson's Entries & Pleading (3 Lord Raymond's King's Bench & Common Pleas Reports) (Eng.)

Wils.Exch. Wilson's English Exchequer Reports (159 Eng. Reprint)

Wils.Exch.(Eng.) Wilson's English Exchequer Reports (159 Eng. Reprint)

Wils.Ind. Wilson's Reports, Indiana Superior Court

Wils.Ind.Gloss. Wilson, Glossary of Indian Terms

Wils.K.B. Sergeant Wilson's English King's Bench Reports (1724-74)

Wils.Minn. Wilson's Reports (48-59 Minn.)

Wils.Oreg. Wilson's Reports (1-3 Oregon)

Wils.P.C. Wilson's English Privy Council Reports

Wils.Super.(Ind.) Wilson's Reports, Indiana Superior Court

Wils. & Court. Wilson & Courtenay's Scotch Appeals Cases (see Wilson & Shaw)

Wils. & S. Wilson and Shaw's Scottish Appeal Cases (1825-35)

Wils. & S.(Scot.) Wilson and Shaw's Scottish Appeal Cases (1825-35)

Wils. & Sh. Wilson and Shaw's Scottish Appeal Cases (1825-35)

Wilson ● Wilson's Chancery Reports (Eng.)

● Wilson's King's Bench & Common Pleas Reports (Eng.)

● Wilson's Exchequer in Equity Reports (Eng.)

● Wilson's Reports, Indiana Superior Court

● Wilson's Reports (48-59 Minnesota)

● Wilson's Reports (1-3 Oregon)

Wilson & Shaw Wilson and Shaw's Scottish Appeals

Wilson's Rev. & Ann.St. Wilson's Revised and Annotated Statutes, Oklahoma

Win. ● Winch's Common Pleas Reports, England (124 Eng. Reprint)

● Winer's Unreported Opinions (N.Y. Supreme Court, Erie County)

● Winston's North Carolina Reports (1863-64)

Win.Eq. Winston's Equity Reports, North Carolina

Winch Winch's Common Pleas Reports (124 Eng. Reprint)

Winch (Eng.) Winch's Common Pleas Reports (124 Eng. Reprint)

Winfield, Words & Phrases Winfield's Adjudged Words and Phrases, with Notes

Wing. Wingate's Maxims

Wing.Max. Wingate's Maxims

Winst. Winston's Law or Equity Reports, North Carolina

Winst.Eq. Winston's Law or Equity Reports, North Carolina

Winst.Eq.(N.C.) Winston's North Carolina Equity Reports

Winst.L.(N.C.) Winston's North Carolina Law Reports

Wis. ● Wisconsin
● Wisconsin Reports

Wis.2d Wisconsin Reports, Second Series

Wis.B.A.Bull. Wisconsin State Bar Association Bulletin

Wis.B.Bull. Wisconsin Bar Bulletin

Wis.Bar Assn. Wisconsin State Bar Association

Wis.Bar Bull. Wisconsin State Bar Association Bulletin

Wis.I.C. Wisconsin Industrial Commission (Workmen's Compensation Reports)

Wils.K.B. Wilson's King's Bench (Eng.)

Wis.L.N. Wisconsin Legal News, Milwaukee

Wis.L.R.Bd.Dec. Wisconsin Labor Relations Board Decisions

Wis.L.Rev. Wisconsin Law Review

Wis.Laws Laws of Wisconsin

Wis.Leg.N. Wisconsin Legal News, Milwaukee

Wis.Legis.Serv. Wisconsin Legislative Service (West)

Wis.P.S.C. Wisconsin Public Service Commission Reports

Wis.P.S.C.Ops. Wisconsin Public Service Commission Opinions & Decisions

Wis.R.C.Ops. Wisconsin Railroad Commission Opinions and Decisions

Wis.R.C.R. Wisconsin Railroad Commission Reports

Wis.S.B.A. Wisconsin State Bar Association

Wis.S.B.A.Bull. Wisconsin State Bar Association Bulletin

Wis.Stat. Wisconsin Statutes

Wis.Stat.Ann.(West) West's Wisconsin Statutes Annotated

Wisb. Laws of Wisbuy

Wisc.Stud.B.J. Wisconsin Student Bar Journal

With.Corp.Cas. Withrow, American Corporation Cases

Withrow ● Withrow's American Corporation Cases

● Withrow's Reports (9-21 Iowa)

Witkin, Cal.Summary Witkin's Summary of California Law

Witthaus & Becker's Med.Jur. Witthaus and Becker's Medical Jurisprudence

Wkly.Dig. New York Weekly Digest

Wkly.L.Bul. Weekly Law Bulletin (Ohio)

Wkly.L.Gaz. Weekly Law Gazette (Ohio)

Wkly.Law Bul. Weekly Law Bulletin, (Ohio)

Wkly.Law Gaz. Weekly Law Gazette, (Ohio)

Wkly.N.C. Weekly Notes of Cases (Pa.)

Wkly.Notes Cas. Weekly Notes Cases (Pa.)

Wkly.Rep. Weekly Reporter, London, Eng.

Wm. William, as 9 Wm. III

Wm.Bl. William Blackstone's English King's Bench Reports (1746-80)

Wm.L.J. Willamette Law Journal

Wm.Rob. William Robinson's English Admiralty Reports (1838-52)

Wm.Rob.Adm. William Robinson's English Admiralty Reports (1838-52)

Wm. & Mary William and Mary

Wm. & Mary L.Rev. William & Mary Law Review

Wms.Ann.Reg. Williams' Annual Register, New York

Wms.Bank. Williams (R.V.) on Bankruptcy. 17 editions (1870-1958)

Wms.Exors. Williams (E.V.) on Executors. 13 editions (1832-1953)

Wms.Ex'rs. Williams (E.V.) on Executors. 13 editions (1832-1953)

Wms.Exs. Williams (E.V.) on Executors. 13 editions (1832-1953)

Wms.Mass. Williams' Reports (1 Mass.)

Wms.Notes Williams' Notes to Saunders' Reports (Eng.)

Wms.P. Peere Williams' Chancery Reports (1695-1736)

Wms.P.P. Williams (J.) on Personal Property. 18 editions (1848-1926)

Wms.Peere Peere Williams' Chancery Reports (Eng.)

Wms.R.P. Williams (J.) on Real Property 24 editions (1824-1926)

Wms.Saund. Saunders (Sir Edmund Reports, edited by Williams) (85 Eng. Reprint)

Wms.Saund.(Eng.) Saunders (Sir Edmund) Reports, edited by Williams (85 Eng. Reprint)

Wms.Vt. Williams' Reports (27-29 Vermont)

Wms. & Bruce Williams (R.G.) and Bruce (Sir G.), Admiralty Practice. 3 editions (1869-1902)

Wn. Washington Reports

Wn.2d Washington Reports, Second Series

Wn.L. Wayne Law Review (Mich.)

Wn.L.R. ● Washington Law Review

● Wayne Law Review

Wn.T. Washington Territory Reports

Woerner, Adm'n. Woerner's Treatise on the American Law of Administration

Wol. ● Wolcott's Reports (7 Delaware Chancery)

● Wollaston's Bail Court Reports (Eng.)

Wolf. & B. Wolferstan and Bristow's Election Cases, England (1859-65)

Wolf. & D. Wolferstan and Dew's Election Cases, England (1856-58)

Wolff.Dr.de la Nat. Wolffius, Droit de la Nature

Wolff.Inst. Wolffius, Institutiones Juris Naturae et Gentium

Wolff.Inst.Nat. Wolffius, Institutiones Juris Naturae et Gentium

Wolffius Wolffius, Institutiones Juris Naturae et Gentium

Wolffius, Inst. Wolffius, Institutiones Juris Naturae et Gentium

Woll. Wollaston's English Bail Court Reports, Practice Cases (1840-41)

Women L.Jour. Women's Law Journal

Women Law J. Women Lawyers Journal

Women Lawyer's J. Women Lawyers Journal

Women's Rights L.Rptr. Women's Rights Law Reporter

Wood ● Wood, English Tithe Cases, Exchequer, 4 vols.
- ● Wood on Mercantile Agreements
- ● Woods, United States Circuit Court Reports

Wood Conv. Wood on Conveyancing

Wood Decr. Wood's Tithe Cases (Eng.)

Wood H. Hutton Wood's Decrees in Tithe Cases (Eng.)

Wood, Inst. Wood's Institutes of English Law

Wood, Inst.Com.Law Wood's Institutes of the Common Law

Wood Land. & T. Wood on Landlord and Tenant

Wood, Landl. & Ten. Wood on Landlord and Tenant

Wood.Lect. Wooddeson's Lectures on Laws of England

Wood, Lim. Wood on Limitation of Actions

Wood, Mast. & Serv. Wood on Master and Servant

Wood, Nuis. Wood on Nuisances

Wood, Ry.Law Wood's Law of Railroads

Wood Ti.Cas. Wood's Tithe Cases (1650-1798)

Wood. & M. Woodbury & Minot's United States Circuit Court Reports

Woodb. & M. Woodbury & Minot's United States Circuit Court Reports

Woodd.Lect. Wooddeson's Lectures on the Laws of England

Wooddesson, Lect. Wooddesson's Lecture

Woodf. Woodfall on Landlord and Tenant. 25 editions (1802-1958)

Woodf.Cel.Tr. Woodfall's Celebrated Trials

Woodf.Landl. & T. Woodfall on Landlord and Tenant. 25 Editions (1802-1958)

Woodf.Landl. & Ten. Woodfall on Landlord and Tenant. 25 editions (1802-1958)

Woodman Cr.Cas. Woodman's Reports of Thacher's Criminal Cases (Mass.)

Woods Woods' United States Circuit Court Reports

Woods C.C. Woods' United States Circuit Court Reports

Wood's Civ.Law Wood's Institutes of the Civil Law of England

Wood's Dig. Wood's Digest of Laws, Cal.

Woods, Ins. ● Wood on Fire Insurance
- ● Wood's Institutes of English Law

Wood's R. Wood's Manitoba Reports (1875-83)

Woods, St.Frauds Wood's Treatise on the Statutes of Frauds

Woodw.Dec. Woodward's Decisions (Pa. 1862-74)

Woodw.Dec.Pa. Woodward's Decisions (Pa. 1861-74)

Wool. Woolworth's Circuit Court Reports (U.S.)

Wool.C.C. Woolworth's Reports, United States Circuit Court (Miller's Decisions)

Woolr.Waters Woolrych's Law of Waters

Wools.Pol.Science Woolsey's Political Science

Woolsack Woolsack (a periodical) (Eng.)

Woolsey, Polit.Science Woolsey's Political Science

Woolw. ● Woolworth's Reports (1 Nebraska)
- ● Woolworth's United States Circuit Court Reports

Woolw.Rep. ● Woolworth's Reports (1 Nebraska)
- ● Woolworth's United States Circuit Court Reports

Wor.Dict. Worcester's Dictionary

Worcest.Dict. Worcester's Dictionary

Worcester Worcester, Dictionary of the English Language

Words.Elect.Cas. Wordsworth's Election Cases (Eng.)

Work.Comp. Workmen's Compensation Law of Pennsylvania

Workmen's Comp.Div. Workmen's Compensation Division

Workmen's Comp.L.Rep. Workmen's Compensation Law Reporter (CCH)

Works, Courts Works on Courts and Their Jurisdiction

Works, Pr. Works' Practice, Pleading, and Forms

World Today The World Today

Wr. ● Wright
　　 ● Wright's Reports (vols. 37-50 Pennsylvania State Reports)

Wr.Ch. Wright's Reports, Ohio

Wr.Ohio Wright's Reports, Ohio

Wr.Pa. Wright's Reports (37-50 Pennsylvania State Reports)

Wright ● Wright's Reports (Ohio 1831-34)
　　　 ● Wright's Reports (37-50 Pa. State)

Wright Ch. Wright's Reports (Ohio 1831-34)

Wright N.P. Wright's Nisi Prius Reports (Ohio)

Wright, Ten. Wright on Tenures

Writ of error den. Writ of error denied

Ws.L. Washington Law Review and State Bar Journal, Washington Law Review (Washington)

Wsb. Washburn Law Journal (Kansas)

Wsh. Washington State Reports

WuW Wirtschaft und Wettbewerb (Germany)

Wy. ● Wyoming
　　 ● Wyoming Reports
　　 ● Wythe's Chancery Reports (Va. 1788-99)

Wy.Dic. Wyatt's Dickens' Chancery Reports

Wy.Dick. Dickens' Chancery Reports, by Wyatt (Eng.)

Wy.L.J. Wyoming Law Journal

Wy.Pr.R. Wyatt's Practical Register in Chancery (Eng.)

Wy.W. & A'Beck. Wyatt, Webb & A'Beckett (Vict.)

Wy. & W. Wyatt & Webb's Victorian Equity Reports (Aus.)

Wyat. & W.Eq. Wyatt & Webb's Victorian Equity Reports (Aus.)

Wyatt Pr.R. Wyatt's Practical Register in Chancery (1800)

Wyatt, Prac.Reg. Wyatt's Practical Register in Chancery (1800)

Wyatt, W. & A'B. Wyatt, Webb & A'Beckett's Reports, Victoria

Wyatt, W. & A B.Eq. Wyatt, Webb & A'Beckett's Equity Reports (Aus.)

Wyatt, W. & A'B.Ew. Wyatt, Webb & A'Beckett's Equity Reports, Victoria

Wyatt, W. & A'B.I.P. & M. Wyatt, Webb, & A'Beckett's Victorian Insolvency, Probate, & Matrimonial Reports (Aus.)

Wyatt, W. & A'B.Min. Wyatt, Webb, & A'Beckett's Victorian Mining Cases (Aus.)

Wyatt & W.Eq. Wyatt & Webb, Equity Reports, Victoria

Wyatt & W.I.P. & M. Wyatt & Webb's Insolvency, Probate, & Matrimonial Reports, Victoria (Aus.)

Wyatt & W.Min. Wyatt & Webb's Victorian Mining Cases (Aus.)

Wyatt & Webb Wyatt & Webb's Reports, Victoria (Aus.)

Wyman Wyman's Reports, India

Wynne Bov. Wynne, Bovill's Patent Cases

Wyo. ● Wyoming
　　　 ● Wyoming Reports

Wyo.B.A. Wyoming Bar Association

Wyo.L.J. Wyoming Law Journal

Wyo.P.S.C. Wyoming Public Service Commission Reports

Wyo.Sess.Laws Session Laws of Wyoming

Wyo.Stat. Wyoming Statutes

Wyo.T. Wyoming Territory

Wythe Wythe's Chancery Reports (Va. 1788-1799)

Wythe Ch.(Va.) Wythe's Chancery Reports (Virginia 1788-1799)

Wythe (Va.) Wythe's Chancery Reports (Virginia 1788-99)

X-Y-Z

X.W. ● Ex warrants
    ● Without warrants

Y. Yeates Reports (Pa. 1791-1808)

Y.A.D. Young's Admiralty Decisions (Nova Scotia)

Y.B. Year Book

Y.B. Air & Space L. Yearbook of Air and Space Law

Y.B.Ames Year Books, Ames Foundation

Y.B.Ed.I. Year Books of Edward I

Y.B.Eur.Conv.On Human Rights Year Book of the European Convention on Human Rights

Y.B.Int'l.L.,Comm'n. Yearbook of the International Law Commission

Y.B.Int'l.Org. Yearbook of International Organizations

Y.B.P.1,Edw.II. Year Books, Part 1, Edward II

Y.B.Rich.II Bellewe's Les Ans du Roy Richard le Second (1378-1400)

Y.B.(Rolls Ser.) Year Books, Rolls Series (1292-1546)

Y.B.(R.S.) Year Books, Rolls Series (1292-1546)

Y.B.S.C. Year Books, Selected Cases

Y.B.(S.S.) Year Books, Selden Society (1307-19)

Y.C.P. Youth Challenge Program

Y. & C. ● Younge and Collyer's Chancery Reports, England (1841-43)
    ● Younge and Collyer's Exchequer Equity Reports, England (1834-42)

Y. & C.Ch. Younge and Collyer's Chancery Reports, England (1841-43)

Y. & C.Ex. Younge and Collyer's Exchequer Equity Reports, England (1834-42)

Y. & C.Exch. Younge and Collyer's Exchequer Equity Reports, England (1834-42)

Y. & Coll. ● Younge and Collyer's Chancery Reports, England (1841-43)
    ● Younge and Collyer's Exchequer Equity Reports, England (1834-42)

Y.L.J. Yale Law Journal

Y.L.R. York Legal Record (Pa.)

Y.T. Yukon Territory: Court with jurisdiction in Yukon Territory

Y.U.N. Yearbook of the United Nations

Y. & J. Younge & Jervis' English Exchequer Reports (1826-30)

Yale L.J. Yale Law Journal

Yale Rev.Law & Soc.Act'n. Yale Review of Law and Social Action

Yates Sel.Cas. Yates' Select Cases (N.Y. 1809)

Yates Sel.Cas.(N.Y.) Yates' Select Cases (New York 1809)

Yates-Lee. Yates-Lee on Bankruptcy. 3 editions (1871-91)

Yea. Yeates' Reports (Pa.1791-1808)

Yearb. Year Book, English King's Bench, etc.

Yearb.P.7,Hen.VI. Year Books, Part 7, Henry VI

Yeates. Yeates' Reports (Pa.1791-1808)

Yeates(Pa.) Yeates' Reports (Pennsylvania 1791-1808)

Yel. Yelverton's King's Bench Reports 1603-13) (Eng.)

Yelv. Yelverton's King's Bench Reports (1603-13) (Eng.)

Yelv.(Eng.) Yelverton's King's Bench Reports (1603-13) (Eng.)

Yer. Yerger's Tennessee Supreme Court Reports (1828-37)

Yerg. Yerger's Reports (9-18 Tennessee)

Yerg.(Tenn.) Yerger's Reports (9-18 Tennessee)

Yo. Younge's Exchequer Equity Reports (Eng.)

York York Legal Record (Pa.)

York Ass. Clayton's Reports (York Assizes)

York Leg.Rec. York Legal Record (Pa.)

York Leg.Rec.(Pa.) York Legal Record (Pa.)

Yorke Ass. Clayton's Reports, Yorke Assizes

You. Younge's Exchequer Equity Reports (1830-32) (Eng.)

You. & Coll.Ch. Younge and Collyer's Chancery Reports (1841-43) (Eng.)

You. & Coll.Ex. Younge and Collyer's Exchequer Equity Reports (1834-42) (Eng.)

You. & Jerv. Younge & Jervis' Exchequer Reports (Eng.)

Young Young's Reports (21-47 Minnesota)

Young Adm. Young's Nova Scotia Admiralty Cases

Young Adm.Dec. Young's Nova Scotia Vice-Admiralty Decisions

Young Adm.Dec.(Nov.Sc.) Young's Nova Scotia Vice-Admiralty Decisions

Young M.L.Cas. Young's Maritime Law Cases (Eng.)

Young,Naut.Dict. Young, Nautical Dictionary

Young V.A.Dec. Young's Nova Scotia Vice-Admiralty Decisions

Younge. Younge's English Exchequer Equity Reports (159 Eng. Reprint)

Younge Exch.(Eng.) Younge's English Exchequer Equity Reports (159 Eng. Reprint)

Younge M.L.Cas. Younge Maritime Law Cases (Eng.)

Younge & C.Ch. Younge & Collyer's English Chancery Reports (62, 63 Eng. Reprint)

Younge & C.Ch.Cas.(Eng.) Younge & Collyer's English Chancery Reports (62, 63 Eng. Reprint)

Younge & C.Exch. Younge & Collyer's English Exchequer Equity Reports (160 Eng. Reprint)

Younge & C.Exch.(Eng.) Younge & Collyer's English Exchequer Equity Reports (160 Eng. Reprint)

Younge & Coll.Ch. Younge & Collyer's English Chancery Reports (62, 63 Eng. Reprint)

Younge & Coll.Ex. Younge & Collyer's English Exchequer Equity Reports (160 Eng. Reprint)

Younge & J. Younge & Jervis' English Exchequer Reports (148 Eng. Reprint)

Younge & J.(Eng.) Younge & Jervis English Exchequer Reports (148 Eng. Reprint)

Younge & Je. Younge & Jervis' English Exchequer Reports (148 Eng. Reprint)

Younge & Jerv. Younge & Jervis' English Exchequer Reports (148 Eng. Reprint)

Youth Ct. Youth Court

Yugo. Yugoslavia

Yuk. Yukon Territory

Yuk.Ord. Yukon Ordinances (Canada)

Yuk.Rev.Ord. Yukon Revised Ordinances (Canada)

Yukon Terr. Yukon Territory

ZPO Zivilprozessordnung (German Code of Civil Procedure)

Za. Zabriskie's Reports (21-24 New Jersey)

Zab.(N.J.) Zabriskie's Reports (21-24 New Jersey)

ZFL Zeitschrift fur Lufrecht und Weltraumrechtsfragen (Germany)

Zivilgericht Cantonal District Court (Switzerland)

Zane. Zane's Reports (4-9 Utah)

Zanzib.Prot.L.R. Zanzibar Protectorate Law Reports (Africa)

Zilla C.D. Zilla Court Decisions (Bengal, Madras, North West Provinces) (India)

Zinn Ca.Tr. Zinn's Select Cases in the Law of Trusts

Zululand Zululand Commissioner's Court Cases

UNITED STATES COURTS OF APPEALS

1st Cir.	U.S. Court of Appeals, First Judicial Circuit
2d Cir.	U.S. Court of Appeals, Second Judicial Circuit
3d Cir.	U.S. Court of Appeals, Third Judicial Circuit
4th Cir.	U.S. Court of Appeals, Fourth Judicial Circuit
5th Cir.	U.S. Court of Appeals, Fifth Judicial Circuit
6th Cir.	U.S. Court of Appeals, Sixth Judicial Circuit
7th Cir.	U.S. Court of Appeals, Seventh Judicial Circuit
8th Cir.	U.S. Court of Appeals, Eighth Judicial Circuit
9th Cir.	U.S. Court of Appeals, Ninth Judicial Circuit
10th Cir.	U.S. Court of Appeals, Tenth Judicial Circuit
D.C. Cir.	U.S. Court of Appeals, District of Columbia Circuit

UNITED STATES DISTRICT COURTS

Alabama

M.D.Ala.	U.S. District Court for the Middle District of Alabama
N.D.Ala.	U.S. District Court for the Northern District of Alabama
S.D.Ala.	U.S. District Court for the Southern District of Alabama

Alaska

D.Alas.	U.S. District Court for the District of Alaska

Arizona

D.Ariz.	U.S. District Court for the District of Arizona

Arkansas

E. & W.D.Ark.	U.S. District Court for the Eastern and Western Districts of Arkansas

California

C.D.Cal.	U.S. District Court for the Central District of California
E.D.Cal.	U.S. District Court for the Eastern District of California
N.D.Cal.	U.S. District Court for the Northern District of California
S.D.Cal.	U.S. District Court for the Southern District of California

Colorado

D.Colo.	U.S. District Court for the District of Colorado

Connecticut

D.Conn.	U.S. District Court for the District of Connecticut

Delaware

D.Del.	U.S. District Court for the District of Delaware

District of Columbia

D.D.C.	U.S District Court for the District of Columbia

Florida

M.D.Fla.	U.S. District Court for the Middle District of Florida
N.D.Fla.	U.S. District Court for the Northern District of Florida
S.D.Fla.	U.S. District Court for the Southern District of Florida

UNITED STATES DISTRICT COURTS

Georgia

M.D.Ga.	U.S. District for the Middle District of Georgia
N.D.Ga.	U.S. District for the Northern District of Georgia
S.D.Ga.	U.S. District for the Southern District of Georgia

Guam

D.Guam	U.S. District Court for the District of Guam

Hawaii

D.Hawaii	U.S. District Court for the District of Hawaii

Idaho

D.Idaho	U.S. District Court for the District of Idaho

Illinois

E.D.Ill.	U.S. District Court for the Eastern District of Illinois
N.D.Ill.	U.S. District Court for the Northern District of Illinois
S.D.Ill.	U.S. District Court for the Southern District of Illinois

Indiana

N.D.Ind.	U.S. District Court for the Northern District of Indiana
S.D.Ind.	U.S. District Court for the Southern District of Indiana

Iowa

N.D.Iowa	U.S. District Court for the Northern District of Iowa
S.D.Iowa	U.S. District Court for the Southern District of Iowa

Kansas

D.Kan.	U.S. District Court for the District of Kansas

Kentucky

E.D.Ky.	U.S. District Court for the Eastern District of Kentucky
W.D.Ky.	U.S. District Court for the Western District of Kentucky

Louisiana

E.D.La.	U.S. District Court for the Eastern District of Louisiana
M.D.La.	U.S. District Court for the Middle District of Louisiana
W.D.La.	U.S. District Court for the Western District of Louisiana

UNITED STATES DISTRICT COURTS

Maine

    D.Me.   U.S. District Court for the District of Maine

Maryland

    D.Md.   U.S. District Court for the District of Maryland

Massachusetts

    D.Mass.   U.S. District Court for the District of Massachusetts

Michigan

    E.D.Mich.   U.S. District Court for the Eastern District of Michigan
    W.D.Mich.   U.S. District Court for the Western District of Michigan

Minnesota

    D.Minn.   U.S. District Court for the District of Minnesota

Mississippi

    N.D.Miss.   U.S. District Court for the Northern District of Mississippi
    S.D.Miss.   U.S. District Court for the Southern District of Mississippi

Missouri

    E.D.Mo.   U.S. District Court for the Eastern District of Missouri
    W.D.Mo.   U.S. District Court for the Western District of Missouri

Montana

    D.Mont.   U.S. District Court for the District of Montana

Nebraska

    D.Neb.   U.S. District Court for the District of Nebraska

Nevada

    D.Nev.   U.S. District Court for the District of Nevada

New Hampshire

    D.N.H.   U.S. District Court for the District of New Hampshire

UNITED STATES DISTRICT COURTS

New Jersey

    D.N.J.   U.S. District Court for the District of New Jersey

New Mexico

    D.N.M.   U.S. District Court for the District of New Mexico

New York

    E.D.N.Y.   U.S. District Court for the Eastern District of New York
    N.D.N.Y.   U.S. District Court for the Northern District of New York
    S.D.N.Y.   U.S. District Court for the Southern District of New York
    W.D.N.Y.   U.S. District Court for the Western District of New York

North Carolina

    E.D.N.C.   U.S. District Court for the Eastern District of North Carolina
    M.D.N.C.   U.S. District Court for the Middle District of North Carolina
    W.D.N.C.   U.S. District Court for the Western District of North Carolina

North Dakota

    D.N.D.   U.S. District Court for the District of North Dakota

Ohio

    N.D.O.   U.S. District Court for the Northern District of Ohio
    S.D.O.   U.S. District Court for the Southern District of Ohio

Oklahoma

    E.D.Okl.   U.S. District Court for the Eastern District of Oklahoma
    N.D.Okl.   U.S. District Court for the Northern District of Oklahoma
    W.D.Okl.   U.S. District Court for the Western District of Oklahoma

Oregon

    D.Or.   U.S. District Court for the District of Oregon

Pennsylvania

    E.D.Pa.   U.S. District Court for the Eastern District of Pennsylvania
    M.D.Pa.   U.S. District Court for the Middle District of Pennsylvania
    W.D.Pa.   U.S. District Court for the Western District of Pennsylvania

UNITED STATES DISTRICT COURTS

Puerto Rico

    D.P.R.   U.S. District Court for the District Court of Puerto Rico

Rhode Island

    D.R.I.   U.S. District Court for the District of Rhode Island

South Carolina

    D.S.C.   U.S. District Court for the District of South Carolina

South Dakota

    D.S.D.   U.S. District Court for the District of South Dakota

Tennessee

    E.D.Tenn.   U.S. District Court for the Eastern District of Tennessee
    M.D.Tenn.   U.S. District Court for the Middle District of Tennessee
    W.D.Tenn.   U.S. District Court for the Western District of Tennessee

Texas

    E.D.Tex.   U.S. District Court for the Eastern District of Texas
    N.D.Tex.   U.S. District Court for the Northern District of Texas
    S.D.Tex.   U.S. District Court for the Southern District of Texas
    W.D.Tex.   U.S. District Court for the Western District of Texas

Utah

    D.Ut.   U.S. District Court for the District of Utah

Vermont

    D.Vt.   U.S. District Court for the District of Vermont

Virgin Islands

    D.V.I.   U.S. District Court for the District of the Virgin Islands

Virginia

    E.D.Va.   U.S. District Court for the Eastern District of Virginia
    W.D.Va.   U.S. District Court for the Western District of Virginia

UNITED STATES DISTRICT COURTS

Washington

E.D.Wash.   U.S. District Court for the Eastern District of Washington

W.D.Wash.   U.S. District Court for the Western District of Washington

West Virginia

N.D.W.Va.   U.S. District Court for the Northern District of West Virginia

S.D.W.Va.   U.S. District Court for the Southern District of West Virginia

Wisconsin

E.D.Wis.   U.S. District Court for the Eastern District of Wisconsin

W.D.Wis.   U.S. District Court for the Western District of Wisconsin

Wyoming

D.Wyo.   U.S. District Court for the District of Wyoming